Edward Rice

NTSU

February 1980

Gracchus Babeuf

R. B. ROSE

Gracchus Babeuf
The First Revolutionary Communist

Stanford University Press

Stanford, California

1978

Stanford University Press, Stanford, California
© 1978 by the Board of Trustees of the
Leland Stanford Junior University
Printed in the United States of America
ISBN 0-8047-0949-1
LC 76-54099

Prefatory Note

I began work on a biography of Babeuf in 1966, immediately after the publication of my study *The Enragés: Socialists of the French Revolution?* The biography was intended as a further, deeper essay in "history from below," history as seen from the perspective of the poor and the politically disfranchised. The themes that interest me most as a historian are those concerned with the development of the democratic ideas and organizational traditions that have led to the achievement of greater political freedom and social equality in the modern world. On all counts, and particularly for a student of the French and Russian revolutionary movements, Babeuf seemed to demand a new evaluation.

I began in a skeptical mood. The Enragés had proved to be less important and more limited figures than I had anticipated. Perhaps Babeuf too would diminish on closer acquaintance. This did not happen: with all his defects, Babeuf emerged, after a decade of research, as a democrat and revolutionary of considerable stature and some personal nobility.

Acknowledgments are due to many persons and institutions for their help in the preparation of this work: to Sydney University for granting sabbatical leave in 1966 and 1970; to the trustees of the Simon Fellowships for financing a productive term at Manchester University in 1970; to Dr. Noel Higham, who for the pure love of scholarship alone offered to translate Professor Dalin's biography from the Russian, and again to Sydney University for agreeing to pay him nevertheless; finally to the University of Tasmania for practical assistance in preparing the text for publication, and to Peter Chapman for reading the text and making many useful suggestions.

Chapter 5 is a revised version of my article "Tax Revolt and Popular Organisation in Picardy, 1789-1791," which first appeared in *Past & Present: A Journal of Historical Studies,* no. 43 (May 1969), pp. 92-108 (World Copyright: The Past and Present Society, Corpus Christi College, Oxford, England).

Quotations from the French in the text have been translated, with the original supplied in parentheses where there is no reasonably close English equivalent. Similarly, all dates in the text that refer to events occurring after the adoption of the French revolutionary calendar in September 1793 have been transcribed as their Gregorian equivalents to maintain continuity. In the notes I have preferred short titles to *op. cit.,* and short titles of journal articles to abbreviated location indications.

R.B.R.

Contents

Illustration Credits

Frontispiece. Babeuf c. 1790, from a contemporary engraving. Original in the Cabinet des Estampes of the Bibliothèque Nationale, Paris.

Burning of La Conférence excise barrier (p. 60). Drawing by Prieur, engraved by Berthault. Original in the Cabinet des Estampes of the Bibliothèque Nationale, Paris.

Journal de la confédération (p. 76). Original in the John Rylands Library of the University of Manchester, Manchester, England.

Babeuf c. 1794 (p. 159). From a drawing and engraving by Bonneville. Original in the Cabinet des Estampes of the Bibliothèque Nationale, Paris.

Tribun du peuple (p. 212). Original in the John Rylands Library of the University of Manchester, Manchester, England.

Act of Insurrection (p. 236). Original in the Department of Printed Books, British Museum, London.

Skirmish at Grenelle (p. 284). Engraving by Bourdon and Keilhauer. From Armand Dayot, *La Révolution française d'après des peintures* (Paris: Flammarion, 1896), p. 324.

Abbaye de la Trinité (p. 293). After a plan of 1677 in the Municipal Library of Vendôme.

Anti-Babouvist satire (p. 310). Anonymous original in the Cabinet des Estampes of the Bibliothèque Nationale, Paris.

Gracchus Babeuf

Introduction

"Babouvism is like a little red flower which thrusts its head above the vast mass of the French Revolution," a French socialist historian wrote in the 1930s, "but the scarlet petals, blown along by the winds of history, have been scattered all along the route subsequently trodden by the great revolutionaries."

As the first revolutionary communist of modern times Gracchus Babeuf has been for many years a figure of considerable veneration for Marxists. In 1845 Marx and Engels paid their own tribute in *The Holy Family* to the rôle of Babeuf and of the Conspiracy of the Equals of 1796 in passing on the idea of communism from the utopians of the Enlightenment, through the mediation of Buonarroti, to the nineteenth century; in the *Communist Manifesto* Babeuf was recognized as the spokesman of the proletariat in the French Revolution.[1]

In 1919, on the morrow of the Bolshevik Revolution, Leon Trotsky proclaimed Babeuf the first of a long line of revolutionary heroes and martyrs whose struggle had prepared the way for the Communist International and the world proletarian revolution.

During the years that followed Babeuf was incorporated even more directly into the official Soviet canon. The main collection of Babeuf's private papers, purchased by Riazanov in the 1920s, was placed in the Archive of the Central Committee of the Communist Party of the Soviet Union, in the Marxist-Leninist Institute in Moscow. The most recent Soviet biography has discovered in Babeuf's writings "gleams of a dialectic and materialist understanding of the development of nature and society," and depicts him as the spokesman of the French proletariat in their struggle against rising capitalism, as the first leader of the people to recognize that the road to achievement of communism lay through a revolutionary dictatorship, and even as the earliest protagonist of collective farms.[2]

Long before Trotsky's 1919 proclamation, French socialists had already claimed Babeuf as their own. In 1877 Jules Guesde stressed the direct affiliations of his newly founded Parti des Travailleurs with Babeuf's Conspiracy of the Equals of 1796. In the "declaration of principles" endorsed by the Fourth Congress of the French Socialist Party at Tours in 1902, Jean Jaurès similarly affirmed the debt owed by the modern French socialist movement to "*notre grand Babeuf.*" In 1911 the Eighth Socialist Party Congress met at Babeuf's birthplace, Saint-Quentin, with all appropriate solemnities.[3]

By contrast Babeuf has received only marginal recognition within the English democratic and socialist tradition. In 1836 Bronterre O'Brien, the Chartist leader, published his English translation of Philippe Buonarroti's *Conspiration pour l'égalité*, but thereafter the Babouvist tradition was virtually forgotten until the appearance, in 1911, of Belfort-Bax's *Last Episode of the French Revolution*, the work of an English Marxist. Nor have academic historians found the subject more attractive. Belfort-Bax's study remained the most substantial account in English until David Thomson's less than sympathetic exposition of *The Babeuf Plot* in 1947.[4] Thus there is no full English-language biography of Babeuf, and the most substantial treatment of the topic appeared over a quarter of a century ago.

A great deal more is known about Babeuf in 1977 than was known in 1947. Indeed none of the leaders of the French Revolution has received as much attention from historians in recent years. At the International Congress of Historians at Stockholm in 1960, which coincided with the Babeuf bicentenary, it proved necessary to hold a special subconference on Babeuf and the Equals, at which papers were presented by French, Italian, Norwegian, American, East German and Russian historians. Since then there have been biographies of Babeuf in three languages: one in French by Claude Mazauric (1962), one by the Soviet historian Viktor Dalin (1963), and another by a West German writer, Karl Hans Bergmann (1965). In 1970 Maurice Dommanget, whose first study of Babeuf appeared in 1922, published an important collection of essays containing much biographical material. A recent bibliography of Babeuf studies lists 32 articles, *glanes* and colloquia which appeared in the pages of the *Annales historiques de la Révolution française* (the leading international journal of French Revolution studies) between 1955 and 1966, together with an equal number of items in other learned journals. There have even been studies on such unlikely topics as Napoleon and the Babouvists, and the influence of Babouvist ideas on Fichte.[5]

The need for an English biography which will take account of these and other recent researches is plain. There are, however, other and stronger justifications for a new study of Babeuf than the propriety of filling an evident gap in historical scholarship. In the aftermath of the Russian and Chinese revolutions, in an age in which, for many, revolution and violent change are regarded as the norm, and gradual development and continuity the exception, a purely arbitrary and personal curiosity about the mechanism of revolution and the psychology of revolutionaries may be defended on the grounds of relevance. On both counts the career of Babeuf has a particular significance. Babeuf and his fellow conspirators were among the first to face the contradictions between mass democracy and élitist revolutionary goals, between utopian aspirations and the pragmatic demands posed by the necessary conquest of power. They were among the first to begin to conceive of revolutionary struggle in terms of class war rather than of a conflict of rights or opinions. The solutions they adopted, and the positions they took up, influenced succeeding generations of French and Russian revolutionaries, down to the Bolshevik Revolution itself, and continue to influence revolutionaries of the present-day New Left, as the revolutionary tradition turns increasingly towards a new utopianism and the reaffirmation of revolution as an act of will.[6]

The nature of the revolutionary personality is equally a subject of continued lively interest for historians and political scientists. Crane Brinton had Robespierre and Saint-Just chiefly in mind when he described "orthodox and successful extremists" as "crusaders, fanatics, ascetics, men who seek to bring heaven to earth." The Russian novelist Boris Pasternak was perhaps thinking chiefly of Lenin and Trotsky when he wrote that "revolutions are made by fanatical men of action with one-track minds, men who are narrowminded to the point of genius." Yet both writers, from their different perspectives, had no difficulty in recognizing and delineating a commonly recurring type, the revolutionary extremist personality. In *The Origins of Totalitarian Democracy*, which was based on a study of the Jacobins and the Babouvists, J.L. Talmon defined the essence of revolutionary extremism as "totalitarian messianism": "a state of mind, a way of feeling, a pattern of mental, emotional and behavioristic elements best compared to a set of attitudes engendered by a religion."[7]

If the "revolutionary extremist" exists at all as an identifiable type, he exists in purest incarnation as Gracchus Babeuf. No revolutionary better fits the description "narrowminded to the point of genius"; few have defined their heaven more clearly or crusaded so fanatically, ascetically, so *religiously* to bring it to earth. A Babeuf biography might find its sole and ample justification therefore in tracing the development of so perfect an example of the extremist personality.

The sources for such a biography are plentiful, and indeed sometimes embarrassingly so. This is particularly true for the period of the Conspiracy of the Equals of 1796 and the subsequent state trial before the high court of Vendôme. Buonarroti's two-volume account, compiled by an actual participant in the conspiracy, is a basic source. In the course of preparing their case at Vendôme the prosecution accumulated forty-eight cartons of papers, and much of this material has been preserved in the Archives Nationales in Paris, together with the reports of prison concierges and other administrative records. More than twenty volumes of indictment, evidence and trial proceedings were published on the initiative of the Directory. No fewer than three independent journals were founded specifically to provide an account of the trial and its antecedents. Much of the printed propaganda of the conspiracy survives in contemporary journals and tracts, as well as in publications by the defendants and their sympathizers during the course of the trial.[8] The present biography makes use of all this material, including a number of previously undiscovered items in the F and FR tracts in the British Museum, which contain more than 140 items relating to the Babeuf conspiracy.

Despite, or perhaps because of, this wealth of evidence, many aspects of the conspiracy remain obscure. While it was the prosecution's business at Vendôme to make the most of the evidence for a violent communist conspiracy, the defense strategy was to deny everything, and to impugn the validity of documentary evidence and the reliability of witnesses. To confound confusion still further, in 1828 Buonarroti openly avowed the communist conspiracy, but he did so in an account written over thirty years after the event, in which many of the details were based admittedly on an old man's fallible memory,[9] and arguably influenced by a distinct personal *parti pris*. Faced by such conflicting evidence the historian may only attempt to steer a course along the inadequately charted channels of probability.

The narrative of Babeuf's early life was long bedeviled by old wives' tales derived from his son Robert's deliberate mystifications

and from the inaccuracies retailed by nineteenth-century an-
tiquarians and myth-makers, too often taken at their face value by
serious historians. During the last few years the investigations of
French historians like Robert Legrand and Antoine Pelletier, using
the archives of the Somme Département and the Archives
Nationales, have provided a basis for a fuller documentation and for
accurate revisions. The most comprehensive single source for
Babeuf's career down to 1794 remains the collection of papers
preserved in the Marxist-Leninist Institute, a collection which includes more than five hundred drafts of Babeuf's own correspondence and three hundred letters received by him, together with
numerous notes and manuscript drafts of publications. The present
writer was not permitted access to this collection, which appears to
be reserved for selected Communists in good political standing.[10]

Two factors made this problem of access to such an important
source less significant than it might otherwise have been. The first is
the availability of Viktor Dalin's Russian-language biography,
whose quarter of a million words are based extensively on a detailed
exposition of the Babeuf papers in the Marxist-Leninist Institute.
The second factor is a product of the complicated history of the
papers themselves. For some years before and after 1882, when the
collection was in the possession of a French antiquarian, the contents
were accessible to French scholars. They were explored, for example,
by Victor Advielle in compiling his two-volume pioneer *Histoire de
Babeuf et du Babouvisme*, published in 1884-5, a study which included numerous reproductions of original documents. Copies made of
the contents of the collection were also used by Maurice Dommanget
when he edited his selection of *Pages choisies de Babeuf* in 1935. A
quite different series of copies was acquired, together with some
original items, by the Archives of the Somme Département at some
time between 1927 and 1931. In 1960 the Abbé Berthe discovered
fifty-nine original letters written by Babeuf in the 1780s among the
papers of the Arras Academy, and there are also important Babeuf
manuscripts in the Institute of Social History, Amsterdam.[11] By
making use of these and other sources and comparing them with
Dalin's work it is possible for most practical purposes to bridge the
gap created by the uncooperative policies of the Marxist-Leninist
Institute, at the same time correcting inaccuracies and supplemen-
ting inadequacies in the available West European sources and
critically evaluating the interpretations placed upon the Moscow
collection by their Soviet commentator.

Apart from the archival sources, Babeuf's journals and occasional pamphlets provide the main source for the development of his political ideas and outlook. To obtain the most complete coverage possible, the resources of the John Rylands Library of Manchester University and the British Museum, together with the Bibliothèque Nationale, have been supplemented, where rare items were concerned, by those of the municipal library of Amiens and Cornell University Library, and by the dossiers of the Archives Nationales, which occasionally include printed materials.

Thanks largely to his habit of hoarding notes and making copies of his correspondence, and his indefatigable energy as a publicist, Babeuf's life and opinions are better documented than those of most of his French revolutionary contemporaries. Yet important gaps remain. A biographer would like to know more of the domestic details of Babeuf's intimate personal life, of those sectors of his experience which lay outside politics, even though during his later, revolutionary years, politics seem to have dominated Babeuf's existence almost exclusively.

The uniform impression given by the documents even for the earlier years is of a man sternly disciplined and indeed constricted by his own hypertrophied rationality. There is little data here to support speculation about the psychopathology of extremism. Some hints may, perhaps, be caught of the pervading influence of drives rooted in an insecure and father-dominated childhood. Yet in the absence of adequate evidence only a "political biography" of Babeuf is possible.

Such an enterprise is itself no minor undertaking. It is my belief that history may be best understood as a dialectic between human ideas and aspirations and material circumstances, and that this dialectic may be best discerned through an observation and narrative of the changes which take place in human beings, whether as individuals, as groups or as classes. Thus a biographer must consider the "material circumstances" in their widest interpretation: the economic and social setting, the historically significant conflicts and movements within which the life of his subject is lived out. A biography of Babeuf, for example, is inevitably also, to an extent, a history of the peasants and artisans of Picardy, and of the *sans-culottes* of the Paris faubourgs. By placing Babeuf firmly within his historical context I hope, if possible, to avoid the opposing but strangely complementary distortions of those who see him as the mouthpiece of the rising proletariat and those who regard him as the harbinger of "totalitarian democracy."

One

The Formative Years

In 1783 the mayor and aldermen of the little Picard town of Saint-Quentin wrote to complain to Louis XVI's Conseil d'Etat about the stubborn resistance of the inhabitants to their attempts to clean up the town. Within the seventeenth-century walls and in the faubourgs beyond many of the ten thousand inhabitants lived in streets noisome with mud and domestic filth. Saint-Quentin was nevertheless a place of some importance. Capital of the ancient Comté de Vermandois and the chief town of Haute Picardie, it was the seat of *prévôté royal* and bailliage courts and of the administration of the taille and the salt tax.

The administrators and legal officials of these institutions provided the social aristocracy of the town: the *prévôt royal* and the *procureur du roi,* the civil and criminal lieutenants of the bailliage, the president of the *grenier à sel* and his subordinates, together with a host of lesser officers, counsellors, advocates and attorneys clustered around the courts. The dean and the chapter of the collegiate church were the leaders of another important social element, the clergy, sustained by thirteen parishes, two monasteries and half a dozen more religious foundations of nuns and friars.

In their own distinct quarter of the town lived the score or so families of merchants, many of them Protestants, who had grown rich from the linen trade for which Saint-Quentin was famous. Some were already branching out into the cotton manufacture which, having begun in the middle of the eighteenth century, would soon displace linen as the staple product of the textile region of which Saint-Quentin was the center.[1]

Born in the Faubourg Saint-Martin on 23 November 1760, François-Noel (afterwards Gracchus) Babeuf belonged however to none of these worlds. His godfather was a gardener's laborer of St. Margaret parish; his godmother, Marguerite Divers, could not write her own name and had to make a mark. For that matter Babeuf's mother, Marie Cathérine, was also illiterate. Very little certain is known about the family background of the future revolutionary leader and what is known is obscured and complicated by the survival of contradictory traditions. On the one hand, avowedly relying on "family papers" and "family tradition" Advielle attempted in the nineteenth century to present Babeuf's father, Claude Babeuf, as a man of substance, a former major in the Austrian army and an ex-tutor of Emperor Joseph II of Austria. The source of these and a number of other fantasies appears to have been Robert Babeuf, eldest son of François-Noel, whose memoirs were characterized by a pervading anxiety to elevate the social status of his immediate ancestors.[2]

On the other hand, in an account written in December 1793, with a Jacobin readership in mind, Babeuf himself stated flatly that he was "born in the dirt" (*né dans la fange*) and stressed the general wretchedness of his family circumstances. Subsequent socialist and communist biographers have been at pains to paint the picture of Babeuf's youth as darkly as possible, in order to document the rise of an impeccably proletarian leader of the people. The reality, as far as we may judge, seems to lie somewhere between the two extremes.

Claude Babeuf was certainly an old soldier; in fact he was an old deserter. According to the details of a royal pardon granted in 1755 "Claude Babeuf dit L'Epine" deserted in November 1738 from the Compagnie d'Estrade of the Régiment Dauphin, at the age of 26, remaining abroad for most of the next 17 years. It is quite possible that he served in the Austrian army and probable that he served at any rate in some army for most of this time, but there is no evidence that he did so as an officer, despite one biographer's pleasing sketch of the aging warrior treasuring a fading but still splendid uniform and taking down his trusty sabre for a polish from time to time.[3]

On Babeuf's baptismal certificate his father is described as an employee of the royal tax farm. Since Colbert's reforms of 1681 the collection of all royal indirect taxes had been farmed out to a corporation of financiers, the Compagnie des Fermiers Généraux. The "General Farmers" were responsible for the administration of the royal domain, the *gabelles* (or taxes on salt), the *traites* (or customs duties), the *aides* (excises mainly on drink but also on some foods and manufactured articles) and the *tabac* (the state tobacco monopoly).

To discharge these wide responsibilities the General Farmers were compelled to become the largest employers and organizers of manpower in France apart from the Royal Army. The tax farm itself was auctioned to fresh partnerships from time to time, but the bureaucracy became permanent. Critics of the tax system spoke in terms of "hordes" and "armies" of tax gatherers; a moderate recent assessment places their numbers at about 36,000. Of these the corps of Gardes des Fermes et des Gabelles, to which Babeuf's father belonged, made up the largest single element. These were the excisemen who policed the taxes. Organized in brigades of from two to eight men, in their relentless war against smuggling and fraud the *gardes* exercised an almost unlimited right of search over places and people, without warrant, and they were authorized to call on the *maréchaussée* and the army when necessary. The *gardes* were generally unpopular: penalties for smuggling were heavy, including whipping, branding and exile, the galleys, and, for offenders bearing arms, breaking on the wheel.[4]

As a simple *garde,* Claude Babeuf belonged to the very lowest rank of the tax administration. According to the *Encyclopédie méthodique*, salaries of the *gardes* varied from a minimum of 260 livres a year to a maximum of 300 livres, plus a share of fines. Babeuf said that his father received from nineteen to twenty-three livres a month (228-276 livres a year), although other evidence suggests that he finished his career, about 1780, as a *brigadier des gabelles*, with a consequently higher salary.[5] In 1790, the last year before revolutionary inflation makes the comparisons unreliable, ordinary town laborers in Saint-Quentin were reported as earning one livre five sous a day, which was considerably more than Claude Babeuf's salary. Skilled workers were still better off. Although agricultural laborers in the Somme received considerably less than 250 livres a year cash wages, their income was normally supplemented by provisions, so that the Babeufs were certainly little better off than the laborers and poor peasants of the surrounding countryside.[6]

There can be no doubt that François-Noel Babeuf knew the bite of poverty as a child, as his parents struggled to rear thirteen children on such a meager income. Yet it is questionable whether such origins may properly be called "proletarian." Employment by the General Farmers was permanent and carried with it a certain status. The *gardes* were royal officials and as such technically *privilégiès:* they carried a sword, they possessed some judicial immunity and they were exempt from the most onerous direct taxes. There was even, after 1768, a pension fund. According to the ordinance of 1681, although they were to be "drawn from among the people," the *gardes* were supposed at least to be able to read and write sufficiently well to draw up reports.[7]

Although there were thirteen children in the Babeuf family, only four survived, of whom François-Noel was the eldest son. A younger brother, Jean-Baptiste, born in 1769, was living at Cerisy-Gailly in 1782, together with his widowed mother; and in 1797 Babeuf asked that his mother and sisters should be told the news of his execution.[8] What became of the other infants is not revealed. There can be little doubt, however, that Babeuf's later insistence on the duty of the state to ensure adequate nourishment, medical attention and education for all children must have owed something to childhood recollections of this "slaughter of the innocents."

Babeuf's own education was received, quite literally, at the hands of his father. Although the "family tradition" depicts Claude Babeuf as a cultivated man, a reader of Plutarch, skilled in German, Latin and astronomy, François-Noel himself described his father as only barely able to read and write. This semi-literate ex-soldier undertook his children's education personally, making up for any possible academic deficiency by the vigor of his physical punishments so effectively that by the age of eight Babeuf's calligraphic skill was reputed the wonder of the neighborhood, and he was presented by the "abbot of Saint-Quentin" with a copy of the life of Emperor Charles V as an encouragement. Before long however the adolescent boy rebelled against the strict paternal regime, and for the next four or five years, from the age of twelve or thirteen to seventeen, he "touched neither pen nor book" while he earned his living by laboring.

Nevertheless it looks as though Babeuf received at least a firm grounding in the three R's from his father. Whether his education went any deeper than this is unclear. There is absolutely no evidence that he knew or read German, and the evidence for a knowledge of Latin is ambiguous. From a study of some notes completed in 1790 or 1791 one biographer deduces for Babeuf "a fine knowledge of Latin,"[9] and many of his later writings during 1794-6 certainly reveal a close familiarity with Roman history. On the other hand this knowledge could easily have been culled from translations, and unlike his fellow conspirator Brutus Magnier, Babeuf never displayed the habit of interlarding his writings with Latin quotations. Perhaps he did receive the foundations of Latin grammar from his father, with deeper studies following in later years. But while his contemporary Maximilien de Robespierre was composing prize Latin orations at the Collège Louis le Grand, Babeuf was destined for a very different kind of "secondary education."

In 1732 the Picardy Canal, or "Canal Crozat," had been completed, joining the Somme and the Oise via Saint-Quentin and opening a route for the transport of wheat from the granary of the Santerre to Paris and Le Havre. In 1769 work was begun on an extension of the canal north to Cambrai and the Scheldt over a route which required a great deal of tunneling, and François-Noel Babeuf was among the laborers taken on for the work. It seems likely that he worked on the canal between 1772, when he reached his twelfth birthday, and sometime in 1776, when a major section of the new extension was completed. Nothing can be learned from the Babeuf papers about conditions on the canal, and so we can only imagine the impact on a young boy of the months of relentless toil amid the mud. By the age of 17 Babeuf had decided to try for something better, and he applied for a job as a clerk with a surveyor at Flixécourt, near Abbeville.

Henri Joseph Hullin, Babeuf's new master, was a man of rising importance in his small community. His profession was that of *feudiste*, or notary specializing in the legal aspects of the administration of feudal estates. In the second half of the eighteenth century pressures of rising costs and increasing expectations compelled the owners of feudal *seigneuries* to rationalize the administration of their holdings and, wherever possible, to increase their incomes from feudal dues and incidents. The investigation of feudal archives and the revising of the *terriers*, as the formal surveys of obligation for each estate were called, provided work for an expanding army of experts. Such men worked chiefly for aristocratic landowners or for the priors of religious houses, although there were also many *seigneuries* owned by bourgeois, no less keen to maximize their incomes from feudal sources.

By May 1779, at the age of 18, Babeuf had begun an apprenticeship with Hullin and was living in with the family. The tone of a letter he wrote to his father at the time suggests that he had not long left home. In this Babeuf expressed his embarrassment at his ragged clothing, since his work forced him to be "often in castles." His father had given him 3 livres, but some of this was already spent and more was urgently needed. As yet, and for almost a year more, the apprenticeship carried no salary, but Mme. Hullin had agreed to wash his things once every six weeks "not only in water, but with soap." At Easter 1780 Babeuf was given some clothing and a pair of shoes, and soon after he began at last to receive a regular salary—of 3 livres a month—a pittance even by eighteenth-century standards.[10]

Meanwhile, life and work at Flixécourt provided an invaluable training for a rising *feudiste*. A tiny "bourg" of 600 or 700 inhabitants, Flixécourt was typical of many such communities in the marshy lands of the Somme: hardly more than an oversize agricultural village dominated by the great local landlord, the marquis de Louvencourt, but with two annual fairs, a weekly market, and a certain independent communal life. Babeuf's employer, Hullin, was both *receveur* for the marquis and secretary of the commune, so that his apprentice was in a unique position to acquire a knowledge of the workings of the kind of rural community in which his early life would be spent, first as a *feudiste* and afterwards as a revolutionary agitator. Babeuf had been brought up in a town; this was his first real experience of the life of the peasants who made up the majority of the population of Picardy under the Ancien Régime.

By the end of 1780 or the beginning of 1781 Babeuf evidently felt that he had learned enough from Hullin to justify branching out on his own account. In June 1781 we find him living in Grivillé, near Roye, and working for Aubert de La Merrye, canon of the Chapter of Saint Florent of Roye. Babeuf performed his duties so well that La Merrye had no hesitation in recommending his new *feudiste* to two more landowners in the same neighborhood, Mme. Audoy and M. Saint-Sauveur, as *"un très honnête homme et intelligent."*

In three years Babeuf had climbed literally "out of the mud" of the Picardy Canal to reach the threshold of an independent professional career at the age of twenty, without any kind of outside help. It was a remarkable achievement, giving evidence of a characteristic quickness of intellect and capacity for steady and concentrated work. Perhaps through another recommendation from La Merrye, Babeuf was soon afterwards commissioned by another local seigneur, Louis Aubé de Bracquemont.[11]

The Bracquemont château of Damery, where Babeuf now spent more than a year, lay in a tiny hamlet just outside Roye. During 1781 he received letters addressed to the *"feudiste* in the château of Damery," although his position may possibly have been rather less grand than this. In 1791 one of Babeuf's enemies was to remind him of time spent "herding turkeys" for the Bracquemonts before he was allowed to get in amongst the dust of the archives. In his reply Babeuf did not actually refute the charge of "herding turkeys," contenting himself with protesting that if he did so he also spent his time reading "Frémenville and Bourdaloue, Voltaire and Plato, Aristotle and Jean-Jacques." The library of the château must have afforded him for the first time an opportunity to broaden his reading and perhaps to begin the intensive course of self-education the progress of which is recorded in his notes during the years that followed.

Among the other servants at the château Damery was a 24-year-old chambermaid of Mme. Imbert de Bracquemont, Marie-Anne-Victoire Langlet, the daughter of an Amiens ironmonger. Already, in July 1781, a friend was writing to warn Babeuf against the dangers of early marriage. Mme. Hullin (if the family tradition is accepted) had found him an attractive young man, making something of a pet of her husband's apprentice and finding pleasure in dressing his light chestnut locks in ribbons.[12] Descriptions on police warrants and other documents in the 1790s confirm the chestnut hair and tell us that Babeuf at his full height was 5 feet 6 inches, about average for Frenchmen of that day, and that he had blue eyes and an oval face with well-formed features and a good brow.[13] Unattached and rising in the world, such an addition to the staff of the château must have caused some speculation "below stairs."

On 13 November 1782 François-Noel Babeuf and Marie-Anne Langlet were married in the Damery parish church. Babeuf's mother and his brother were present (his father had died at the end of 1781). None of the Langlet family attended the ceremony, although the father, Antoine Langlet, had given his assent in October. The rather hasty circumstances of the marriage may have been the reason for this boycott: within a month Marie-Anne gave birth to a daughter, Sofie.

There is no portrait and no description of Marie-Anne Babeuf. She wrote little and inarticulately, and was plainly a "woman of the people." Yet a study of the Babeuf papers helps to build an impression of a woman of character and immense loyalty. Between 1782 and 1797 Marie-Anne bore her husband five children, of whom three boys survived.[14] To begin with, in the 1780s there were a few years of relative comfort; afterwards only a constant battle against poverty and even starvation. During Babeuf's six imprisonments it was Marie-Anne who fought to keep the family together, trudging to the doors of a succession of jails to carry the additional clothing and supplies which made a prisoner's existence barely tolerable in the eighteenth century, tirelessly organizing lobbying and agitation campaigns for her husband's release, even facing her own arrest bravely when it came. François-Noel may have seemed a "good catch" to a chambermaid in 1782. Perhaps he may have still seemed so to Marie-Anne as he mounted the guillotine at Vendôme in May 1797. How far she really understood her husband's revolutionary ideals is another matter. Marie-Anne was barely literate in 1782 and remained so. In the 1780s and afterwards Babeuf spent much thought and much ink on the education of his daughter and of his sons; he is completely and strangely silent on the question of the education of his wife. Theoretically a believer in the intellectual equality of women, he was clearly unconvinced of the intellectual equality of the one woman closest to him. He saw her instead as another Thérèse Levasseur to his own Rousseau: it was perhaps the rôle she was best fitted to fill.[15]

Soon after his marriage at the age of 22 Babeuf left the château at Damery and set himself up as an independent *feudiste* in the little town of Roye close by. The first two years at Roye are badly documented, but it is known that Babeuf's first clients included Aubert de Montoviller, a nephew of Canon La Merrye, whose estates were at Grivillé, and that he was also concerned with properties of the Louvencourts at Domfront (Oise), Le Fretoy and Courcelles-Epayelles. Babeuf's reputation grew and commissions became more numerous. By April 1785 he was in a position to turn down an offer of employment from Bucquet, a *feudiste* at Noyon, with the boast that he had "two years' work" in hand, although he agreed to take on some *terriers* as a subcontractor and sent Jean-Baptiste, his 16-year-old brother, to work for Bucquet instead. Encouraged by the receipt of a small inheritance from an uncle and by his growing business success, in August 1785 Babeuf leased a former ironmonger's shop in the rue de Paris, the best street in Roye, with permission to convert the shop into an office; the lease was for 150 livres a year. The Babeufs moved in just in time for the birth of a son, Robert, on 29 September.[16]

The next two years seem to have been years of success and domestic happiness as François-Noel and Marie-Anne occupied themselves with building a circle of friends and raising their young family. This last task Babeuf took very seriously indeed, so that first Sofie (until her death in 1787), and afterwards Robert, was the subject of a concentrated attention which amounted to a personal cult on the part of the father, and in which we may perhaps detect the neurotic purging of anxieties stemming from Babeuf's own tragic and insecure childhood. As a disciple of the author of *Emile*, Babeuf naturally followed the prescribed Rousseauist methods of infant-rearing: light clothing, free kicking time, and breast feeding. According to local tradition Robert was given a daily bath in the Avre throughout the year, even when it was necessary to break the ice. As his daughter, his first "masterpiece of nature," grew older Babeuf sought and received the most advanced specialist advice, among others from M. de Fourcroy, celebrated author of *Les Enfants élevés dans l'ordre de la Nature*. He would, as he said, have consulted Jean-Jacques himself had not the Genevan's death made that impossible. What is less clear is whether he ever consulted Marie-Anne Babeuf about their children's education.

The death of Sofie after a painful illness in 1787 affected Babeuf very greatly. If the local tradition is to be believed (there is some corroborative evidence) the grieving father, in a gruesome display of *sensibilité*, cut open his dead child's body and removed the heart, swallowing one portion and placing another in a locket which he hung round his neck.[17]

Henceforth, all paternal enthusiasms were focused on Robert. Determined to educate his own children personally, Babeuf continued in the main to follow the precepts of Rousseau, with certain common-sense reservations, and it was no accident that the new "revolutionary" name he chose for Robert after 1789 was "Emile." In 1795 Babeuf would publicly declare his happiness at discovering in his nine-year-old son "all the moral and patriotic virtues that the great Rousseau could only attribute to his fictional Emile." Such virtues were fostered by a very deliberate and intensive parental education—continued, when necessary, even from the prison cell. So abnormally anxious and possessive did Babeuf become about his son that during two imprisonments, in 1790 and again in 1796, he actually petitioned (unsuccessfully) to have Emile allowed to join him in his cell.[18]

Despite such occasional aberrations, the family correspondence shows Babeuf to have been an affectionate parent, with a close and informal relationship with his son. His educational experiments, as far as one may judge, appear to have been successful enough in providing Robert/Emile with a sound basic education, adequate at any rate for a future career as a bookseller and journalist, and with an independence of spirit which would lead to trouble with the police under Bonaparte and the Restoration.

Like Marie-Anne Babeuf, the Babeuf children, while their father lived, struggled along in poverty, hunger and misery. In a farewell letter, written in the shadow of the guillotine, Babeuf would express the most bitter paradox of his existence. "I know no other manner of making you happy," he wrote, "than through the common happiness. I have failed and I have sacrificed myself. I also die for you. . ."[19] The mainspring of his being was concern for the welfare of his own children and their right to a good life. Yet the vicissitudes of his career as a revolutionary brought them only suffering and despair.

Two

Roye

Despite its smaller size, the town in which Babeuf chose to begin his professional notarial career as a *feudiste* had much in common with that in which he had been born. Like Saint-Quentin, Roye was a small town, set amid the chalk slopes and peat marshes of the Somme valley. Seen from the Faubourg Saint-Gilles to the south, where the Babeufs finally settled, its streets rose steeply from the banks of the Avre river where the tanners of the faubourg worked, a scattering of windmills thrusting out amongst the close-built houses.

With no more than 3,000 inhabitants, Roye was still half agricultural and an early nineteenth-century chronicler, Grégoire d'Essigny, could remember nostalgic summers when the air filled with the singing of the "*herbionnes*," women culling weeds from the harvest fields for their beasts. To the northwest, beyond the Faubourg Saint-Médard, there were still unenclosed commons belonging to the town, while in 1740 only six houses in the Saint-Gilles and Saint-Médard faubourgs had tiled roofs. For all that Roye was a town and not a village. The seat of a *sous-délégué* of the intendant of Amiens, it was also (like Saint-Quentin) the center of a royal bailliage, which in this case extended over eighty parishes, to include Péronne and Montdidier. The court, the municipality and the *grenier à sel* were housed at the new Hôtel de Ville, completed in 1776. There was also a *bureau des fermes*, under a *directeur*, in the rue de Paris. There were five churches, of which the most important was the collegiate church of Saint-Florent; the Feast of Saint-Florent was celebrated on 22 September with a procession and a fair. There were three monastic houses—Minimes, Cordeliers, and Frères de la

Charité—and two convents, housing the Soeurs de la Croix and the Religieuses de l'Annonciade.

Within the limits of its size Roye was also a busy commercial and industrial center. Situated at the point where the main route from Paris to Lille crossed the Noyon-Amiens road, the town was an important grain market, collecting grain from the Santerre for dispatch to Paris and Amiens. Industrially, Roye was traditionally noted for its woollen cloth and hosiery, with some bonnet making. In 1718 there were said to be fifty stocking-weavers, with an estimated seven or eight hundred workers in ancillary trades, such as combing and spinning. During the eighteenth century the Roye drapers had a bureau at Paris. In 1760 the intendant of Picardy established a free school to teach girls cotton spinning, and in the second half of the century cotton began to challenge the older woollen industry.[1]

Despite these developments the hub of the life of this small provincial town remained the bailliage court at the Hôtel de Ville. The work of the court and the social life of Roye were dominated by a small group of legal families. The Billecocq family, for example, had a family history of legal office dating back to 1493. In the 1780s one brother, Louis-Charles Billecocq, held the important office of *lieutenant civil*, while another, Louis-François, was *procureur du roi*. Another closely related family, the Prévosts, had furnished the court with *avocats du roi* since 1699; in the 1780s the office was held by Marc-Florent Prévost. The legal business of the court provided the livelihood for several other notarial families of somewhat lesser status, such as the Longuecamps, the Grégoires d'Essigny, and the Thoquênes.[2]

The example of Babeuf's patron, Pierre-Louis-Florent Aubert de Montoviller, illustrates the way in which the local aristocracy was firmly based on the triple supports of the land, the church, and the law. The nephew of a canon of the Chapter of Saint-Florent, Aubert was seigneur of Grivillé; from 1786 he was also *lieutenant particulier assesseur criminel* of the bailliage court. Municipal office also tended to be retained in the hands of the same families. Thus Louis-Charles Billecocq was mayor of Roye from 1757 to 1759, and Marc-Florent Prévost from 1768 to 1771. Another *avocat*, Pierre-Florent Masson, held the office from 1783 to 1787 and Louis-Charles Billecocq returned for a second term in 1789. Beyond the clergy and the lawyers, cultivated society scarcely reached down beyond the principal of the *collège*, the doctor and the three surgeons, and the family of M. Goret, *receveur de la ville*.[3]

As a mere *feudiste* of quite plebeian origins Babeuf was well out-side the charmed circle of *avocats du parlement, conseillers du roi,* and *procureurs.* He could hardly aspire, as yet, to membership of the Société des Dinants, for example, the polite literary salon founded in 1777 in which the Billecocqs, the Prévosts, the Auberts and their wives and daughters shared the salt with one or two selected ad-vocates and notaries, and diverted themselves with amateur theatricals, publishing a little news-sheet and circulating their literary efforts in a manuscript volume. He tried twice, unsuccessful-ly, to join the Masonic lodge, a branch of the Orient, which met in the tower of the old château de Roye, and which included among its members two Bracquemonts, Louis-Charles Billecocq and Pierre-Florent Masson.[4]

At the end of 1785, however, Babeuf's recognition as a correspon-ding member of the Academy of Arras provided solace. In 1773 the Société Littéraire of Arras had transformed itself into the Académie Royale des Belles Lettres, and in the 1780s, thanks to the energy of its new secretary, Ferdinand Dubois de Fosseux, and to the support of the royal minister Calonne and the intendant of Flanders and Ar-tois, the academy helped to make the garrison town of Arras a center of cultural life for northeastern France.

The nucleus of the academy comprised the ordinary members, who were able to take part in the formal sessions at Arras. There was also a less eminent category of honorary members and a wider circle of corresponding members, both of which groups were allowed to at-tend meetings of the academy by a resolution of 1786. With these the secretary conducted a highly organized correspondence rather after the fashion of the extramural department of a university, circulating information about the progress of the humanities and the sciences and raising questions for discussion.

The academy also offered an annual essay competition with a prize worth 500 livres. The subject set for 1786, published in April 1785, was one which touched, if only marginally, on Babeuf's pro-fessional interests and experience and attracted his attention. The academy sought to know: "Is it useful in Artois to divide up lease-hold farms, and if the answer is yes, what limits ought to be fixed in such a division?" Babeuf's entry, one of at least twenty, was completed in November 1785 but was unfortunately not received by the academy until after the closing date of 1 December. On 15 December, however, Dubois responded with a gracious and friendly letter urging Babeuf to put in an entry for the 1787 competition, on a subject connected with the roads of Artois. Meanwhile, he enrolled Babeuf as one of the eighty or so regular corresponding members, entitled to receive weekly circulars and summaries of the proceedings of the academy.[5]

The association with Dubois opened a door into a wide and glittering world of intellectual cultivation compared with which the transactions of the exclusive small town *littérateurs* of Roye might well have seemed pretentious and petty. Recent research has revealed that the polite and flattering terms which appear in Dubois' letters to Babeuf were merely part of a system of automatic formulas which were used in all his secretarial correspondence, and that for the most part Babeuf was no more to Dubois than "correspondent 24X" and "22K." From time to time, however, Dubois was accustomed to add a few personal remarks and comments which were sufficient to reinforce Babeuf's conviction that he had a close and friendly relationship with a cultivated and powerful patron. Moreover Dubois was often directly helpful, passing on books, journals and essays as loans or outright gifts by way of the royal postal service, which Calonne allowed the academy to use free of charge.[6]

Invaluable for his intellectual development and satisfying to Babeuf's self-esteem as it was, even the Arras correspondence was not without its disappointments. In May 1786 Dubois sent a tantalizing account of the latest session of the academy, a social occasion "honored by the presence of the most distinguished citizens of our town, of a great part of the officers of the three regiments garrisoned there, of many fine ladies and several inhabitants of the neighboring towns." Among other things this splendid assembly was treated to a two-hour discourse on bastardy by a prominent member of the academy, the distinguished Arras lawyer M. de Robespierre. Babeuf, of course, was not present.

At first suitably humble and deferential, as the correspondence progressed Babeuf became more confident both of his own talents and of the sympathy and friendship of the secretary, until, in June 1787, he felt that the time was ripe to ask Dubois to support his application for honorary membership of the academy. The result was a deafening silence on the part of Dubois. Honorary membership of the Academy of Arras was a much sought after social prize; indeed of fifty-six applications made at the beginning of 1786 only twenty-one were successful. The three full members admitted during the same period included two advocates of the Conseil d'Artois and a major in the engineers.[7] Babeuf was out of his social depth, and his realization of this fact doubtless contributed to the rapid loss of interest in the affairs of the academy which became evident soon afterward.

Biographers have been at pains to show how quickly Babeuf was repelled by the values of the feudal landlords he served and the small-town pettifoggers among whom he lived. Yet it is clear that at the start of his career Babeuf was ambitious and eager to make his way in the world, driven by the curious mixture of confidence and insecurity which belongs to the self-made and self-taught. The way ahead lay clearly through success and renown in his profession. With a good number of commissions in hand Babeuf could expect to go on building up a local practice as he gained in experience and reputation. But such a route to fortune seemed too slow and uncertain. At twenty-five Babeuf was convinced that he was potentially one of the national leaders of his profession and that he had ideas capable of revolutionizing estate administration.

The central problem for those who sought to introduce more rational methods into the collection of feudal dues and rents was the introduction of a ledger system in which the details of payments and services due could be precisely recorded, together with any alterations. Existing estate records were generally unsuited to this purpose since they were based on the accumulation of different and unrelated classes of obligations, some personal, some connected with feudal tenure, others with more modern types of lease or rent. In 1785 the feudal specialist Charles-Louis Aubry de Saint-Vibert published the first two sections of an edition of his book *Les Terriers rendus perpétuels,* a description of a new method of keeping accounts based on "a single and invariable principle" and one which made significant use of cartographic plans. During the autumn of 1785 a copy of this work came into Babeuf's possession, and in November he wrote a letter to the author containing certain criticisms which he used soon afterwards as the basis of a short publication of his own, the *Mémoire pour les propriétaires des terres et seigneuries, ou idées sur la manutention des fiefs.* The first copies of this pamphlet were put out by a Noyon printer at the beginning of April 1786. It was intended partly as a prospectus for a larger work which was to be published later in the year, but chiefly as a circular advertising the services Babeuf was ready to offer to seigneurial patrons.

While it was an advance on the existing confusion, in Babeuf's view Aubry's method was still unnecessarily complex. It required the maintaining of ten different ledgers and divided records into four distinct classes: by estates taken as a whole, by parishes, by fiefs, and by *chapitres,* or miscellaneous feudal acts such as fealty, homage, *aveux* and *dénombrements.* Babeuf proposed to simplify matters by re-garding the fief, or feudal holding, as the unique and basic unit, com-piling complete inventories of obligations for each separate fief, and ignoring all other territorial or qualitative classifications. The result would be a genuinely uniform and efficient system requiring the maintaining of four ledgers only.[8]

After 1789, during the revolutionary years, Babeuf found his prerevolutionary career as a "lackey of the *ci-devant*" something of an embarrassment, and in one document compiled in 1794 and in-tended for Jacobin eyes he preferred to describe his profession as that of *"archiviste et géomètre."* Not long afterwards a public denuncia-tion by the deputy Dubois-Crancé forced Babeuf to grasp the nettle more firmly. "I was a *feudiste* under the old régime," he was com-pelled to admit, "and that is the reason I was perhaps the most for-midable scourge of feudalism in the new. In the dust of the seigneurial archives I uncovered the horrifying mysteries of the usur-pations of the noble caste. From the dawn of the revolution I un-veiled them for the people in burning words." Thus Babeuf himself claimed no more than that the sins of the *feudiste* had been atoned for by the good works of the revolutionary.[9]

However, in their zeal to "rehabilitate" Babeuf as a "communist without taint" from the earliest possible date, some modern scholars have gone to absurd lengths to explain away the sin itself. One of the advantages claimed by Babeuf for his new system was that by clarify-ing and simplifying obligations it would be fairer for the peasants as well as more useful to the seigneur, and that the seigneur would not be in danger of "involuntarily making unfounded demands." With this claim as the only concrete basis Professor Dalin and A. Pelletier have both gone on to argue that Babeuf's true sympathies lay at all times with the peasants, even if they had to be concealed in his dealings with the seigneurs. Another historian, Professor Saitta, manages to wax indignant that a feudal seigneur should have had the impertinence to make use of Babeuf's "technical work" to increase the oppression of the poor.[10]

The facts are that Babeuf was always, and naturally, careful to ex-plain that his methods would prevent unnecessary losses to his seigneurial patrons and would increase their revenues, and that he did not fail to request the customary clause in his contracts which allowed the *feudiste* to claim one-third of all arrears collected from the peasants as a result of his skill.

The best that can be said of Babeuf as a *feudiste*, therefore, is that he sought to replace inefficient and arbitrary exploitation by efficient and scientific exploitation. But even this "defense" requires some qualification. However humanitarian his personal attitudes might be, Babeuf could not escape the iron logic of his situation, summed up in the stony instructions of his client the comte de Castéja: "not to allow any grace at my expense towards any individual, nor any interpretation which might be disadvantageous to me, or to the people who handle my affairs."[11]

In the light of this evidence the influential thesis advanced by Lefebvre and Dommanget that Babeuf's communism was derived from his social identification with the peasants of Picardy, and the more recent version of Dalin that, from the beginning, he reflected the aspirations of the proletariat of the Picard countryside, both seem to require a careful scrutiny.[12]

Most of Babeuf's life before the revolution was spent in the two small towns of Saint-Quentin and Roye, and while his profession certainly took him into the rural villages, it was one hardly calculated to establish a bond of solidarity with their peasant inhabitants. As a *feudiste* Babeuf worked in and from the seigneur's château, and whatever his personal sympathies, a great social gulf inevitably separated him from the tenants.[13] Moreover, as an inhabitant of Roye, Babeuf's aspirations before 1789 were clearly to achieve acceptance by the bourgeoisie rather than to lead the proletariat. Whereas his mother had spun linen "night and day" at Saint-Quentin, it was Babeuf's boast that his own wife never once had to take in work in the years before the revolution, a most significant index of social status and aspiration in a province in which the labor of women and children was the foundation of the burgeoning textile industry.[14]

That Babeuf did become, after 1789, the spokesman of the peasants and proletarians of Picardy is perfectly true, but this was due to causes more subjective and accidental than class origins or association. Even before the revolution there were quarrels with aristocratic clients which threatened to destroy his faith in the possibilities of the profession of *feudiste*, and left a simmering hatred against the arrogance of the seigneurs. The revolution of 1789 completed the destruction of "feudalism" and with it the profession of *feudiste*, leaving Babeuf free to follow to their logical conclusions developing personal convictions about democracy and social justice that might in other circumstances have remained purely speculative and abstract.

In May 1785 Babeuf had boasted that he had two years' work in hand. Nevertheless, in the summer of 1786 he began prudently to seek new commissions. On 29 June 1786 he wrote to Galoppe, seigneur of Armancourt, offering to renew the *terriers* of his properties for the modest fee of 300 livres, plus a third of all arrears recovered, and citing his achievement at Grivillé, where the seigneur, Aubert, would be "a hundred times better off" than the cost of the *terrier* now that Babeuf had put his affairs in order. However, checking privately, Galoppe discovered that Aubert had paid the flat rate of 300 livres only, and he insisted on the same terms. The figure of 300 livres is significant of the relatively small scale of Babeuf's operations at this time, but there was hope that the circular advertising the new methods would bring in more lucrative commissions.

That same month of June Dubois had written some words of encouragement, after glancing at the *Mémoire . . . sur la manutention des fiefs*, and Babeuf set to work to gather material for the extended treatise by which he hoped to make his name in the profession: *L'Archiviste terriste, ou traité méthodique de l'arrangement des archives seigneuriales et de la confection et perpétuation successives des inventaires, des titres et des terriers d'icelles, des plans domaniaux, feodaux et censuels*. The prospectus of this work, offering prior subscribers a 10-livre discount, was completed at the end of October and in January 1787 Dubois brought it to the notice of the Academy of Arras, with a favorable comment, but in fact the work itself never saw the light. This was partly because of a poor response to the appeal for subscriptions, but perhaps chiefly because during 1787 Babeuf's enthusiasm was diverted by a fresh notion, that of applying his new surveying and recording techniques instead to the problem of preparing uniform land tax records.[15]

In June 1786 Dubois had warned Babeuf in a friendly fashion against a too ready optimism in his attempts to innovate in an old profession, even though his methods were clearly efficient and advantageous: "The most useful things become accepted with difficulty. Everywhere people hold fast to ancient usages, and the light of reason penetrates only fitfully to prejudiced eyes." Meanwhile, Bucquet, the Noyon *feudiste*, was more bluntly predicting the early ruin of his colleague. The flashy new methods of a self-educated upstart

were hardly likely to win much support from established prac-
titioners.[16]

Moreover, Babeuf's deliberate apotheosis of the feudal fief as the
basic unit of accounting may well have seemed quite wrong-headed
to landowners and specialists concerned with the day-to-day administration of property in Picardy, a province where capitalist
relationships were already well advanced and on the eve of their final
triumph in the countryside. For whatever reason, by the summer of
1787 Babeuf's affairs were in a state of crisis. He was forced to
abandon his office in the rue de Paris and move to a poorer house in
the Faubourg Saint-Gilles, and the family only survived thanks to
small loans from Jean-Baptiste, Babeuf's younger brother, who was
still working under Bucquet at Noyon.[17]

Yet there were a few hopeful signs. In March 1787 the comte
Biaudos de Castéja, *maréchal du roi* and seigneur of Framerville,
sent a courteous letter explaining that he had been impressed by
Babeuf's circular and agreeing to discuss a possible commission. A
tough bargainer, Castéja countered Babeuf's proposed terms of
"1,600 livres for lands of 1,000 arpents" by an offer to pay by the
hour. Nevertheless, sometime in July or early August, Babeuf began
to work at Framerville.

Before long there was a serious quarrel. Castéja resented Babeuf's
criticisms of his other servants and, above all, the "ridiculous pride"
which led the *feudiste* to demand to dine at the count's own table
while working at the château. Babeuf was reminded that the proper
place for his kind to eat was with the servants or, if that did not suit
him, in the village; and he was forced to swallow his pride.[18] The hint
of differences with Castéja's other servants over professional and
social status was an ominous anticipation of a far more catastrophic
quarrel which disrupted Babeuf's relationships with another client,
the marquis de Soyecourt, the following year.

The Belleforières de Soyecourt were one of the most important
families of the local nobility. Briefly the inheritors of the domain of
the counts of Roye in the seventeenth century, they retained extensive properties in the vicinity of Roye in the eighteenth, and for the
last thirty years of the Ancien Régime the Bailli d'Epée, or honorific
president of the Bailliage of Roye, was a member of the Soyecourt
family.[19]

Sometime in the year 1787 Babeuf approached Louis-Armand
de Seiglières de Soyecourt, offering to renew his *terriers*. Babeuf
pointed out that no survey of the Soyecourt lands at Tilloloy and

elsewhere had been made since 1732. Even then the method had been faulty. A notary had merely called together the inhabitants and collected their declarations; the *terrier* entries for many who had failed to attend had not been revised, and subsequently the marquis's revenues from the feudal *cens* or quitrent had fallen by half, a situation which could only be restored by a thorough reorganizing of the *terriers*.

At the beginning of October 1787 Babeuf and Soyecourt signed an agreement. This was Babeuf's largest and most important commission yet, and he felt obliged not only to take on two assistants to cope with the work, but also to appeal to his brother and to a specialist in surveying from Paris to join him. At last he seemed on the threshold of professional success.

Within a few months, however, the marquis had begun to have doubts about the competence of his new *feudiste*. Babeuf himself blamed the difficulties that followed on a conspiracy of persecution by the legal aristocracy of Roye. Soyecourt's bailiff, Thoquêne, was one of Roye's most prominent notaries; and, according to Babeuf, Thoquêne and Dantier, another of Soyecourt's agents, were determined to use the reorganization of the *terriers* as an excuse for harassing the tenants with a salvo of profitable legal cases in the bailliage court. His opposition to this course earned Babeuf not only their hostility, but that of the other legal "vampires" of the court. There seems no reason to doubt that there was a conflict of this kind over tactics, and that it served to embitter relationships. There is equally some evidence that the task he had undertaken was in fact beyond Babeuf's competence. In June 1788, Soyecourt himself complained that Babeuf had failed to observe the proper formalities in letters to his copyhold tenants. He had written to the parish priest and the duc de Mailly indiscriminately in the same style, incorrectly summoning both to appear with their proofs at his own house, whereas the priest might be summoned only to the *caput* of the seigneurie and Babeuf should attend on the duc de Mailly and not vice versa. "M. Billecocq" of the bailliage court had understandably found such a circular comic; however Soyecourt was prepared to put such mistakes down to the inexperience of youth.

By September Thoquêne was less inclined to be charitable. "Even if the opinion of the whole world were on your side," he wrote to Babeuf, "this would not help you at all. I have said that everything that you have done has been done badly and I intend to repeat this about everything you do in the future. No one will succeed in refuting the opinion of a man who has been for 28 years the bailiff of the marquis de Soyecourt." Moreover Thoquêne refused to endorse Babeuf's accounts, and the marquis refused to pay. At the end of 1788 Babeuf claimed 12,000 livres to cover his fees and expenses of more than 7,000 livres, which, he said, had exhausted his savings. Soyecourt admitted liability for only 2,370 livres, of which the greater part had already been collected, and expected Babeuf to settle for 953 livres.

In January 1789 Babeuf committed the extraordinary folly of suing Soyecourt in the bailliage court for breach of contract. Billecocq senior presided and Billecocq junior, as *procureur royal*, decided the case for the marquis.[20] The president of the court was, after all, a Soyecourt, and the Billecocqs were friends of the family. Even a less sensitive plaintiff than Babeuf might have been forgiven for crying persecution. Taking their cue from the marquis, other clients now also refused to pay.

Babeuf would later claim that at the outbreak of the revolution he was owed 30,000 livres by aristocratic landowners, and 6,000 livres by the church, for work completed. While these figures seem suspiciously rounded there is evidence for the reluctance of aristocratic clients to settle Babeuf's charges; indeed some of the proceedings dragged on for several years. In February 1794 the district court of Montdidier was still discussing a claim by Babeuf for fees owed for his work on the *terriers* of the Célestins of Saint-Croix at Offrement, along with a claim for 314 livres by Grégoire d'Essigny, the Roye notary, for defending Louis Joseph Brunol, the prior of Saint-Aurin, near Roye, against Babeuf's demand for payment for work on the priory *terriers*.[21]

Naturally enough in the circumstances, new clients were slower than ever to come forward. Thus even before 1789 Babeuf was facing personal ruin in his career as a *feudiste*.

There is a nineteenth-century tradition, followed by some modern biographers, that the revolution of 1789 now gave Babeuf the opportunity to break with his feudal past in a dramatically satisfying manner: by a public *auto-da-fé* of feudal records in the main square of Roye.[22] The truth is rather more prosaic. There were times during 1789 when Babeuf lost all hope in the future of his profession, and there are even letters in which he seemed to rejoice with perfect altruism in the end of feudalism. Yet there is other evidence which shows that he continued his work as a *feudiste* throughout the year and even employed an assistant.[23] The decrees of August 1789 "abolishing feudalism"—in reality outlining the procedures for the abolition and commutation of feudal obligations—even revived Babeuf's hopes for the restoration of his fortunes, as he circularized the seigneurs once again, to offer his services for the new and urgent task of justifying and clarifying title to the dues which were now to be commuted.[24]

Babeuf may well have thrown seigneurial archives into the flames along with the other "feudal relics" he certainly did burn in a public demonstration at Montdidier in January of 1793. In 1789 such documents still represented his bread and butter and he would hardly have been capable of anything so foolish. Yet before long Babeuf was to place his specialist skills at the service no longer of the seigneurs, but of the peasant communities of Picardy, as they struggled to free themselves from feudal domination. Babeuf's renunciation of feudalism was a fact, but it was a complex process in which private misfortunes, national politics and the ripening of a personal ideology all played a part, and not a sudden conversion celebrated with bright bonfires and dancing in the streets of Roye.

Three

Utopian Speculations

Laying bare his soul to Coupé de l'Oise in August 1791, Babeuf claimed for himself a "rare virtue," the possession of "that pride, that species of private vanity by which we are persuaded that we are better than many of our brothers, which makes us take pleasure in the notion that for the world's greater advantage we are called upon to govern it. . . ." "This passion for the public welfare," he reflected, "can only sustain itself on illusions, but I shall always look upon it as the most praiseworthy thing here below, for it is plain that without it good will never exercise influence among mankind."

In the later years of the revolution this "private vanity" came increasingly to dominate Babeuf's personality. "I have to a certain degree the character of a philosopher," he wrote in a letter drafted at the beginning of 1793. ". . . I reflect and I meditate, just as Rousseau did in his day. The search for a means of accomplishing universal happiness is for me, as for him, a ceaseless study."[1]

Like Marx in the British Museum, or Lenin in exile in Zurich, Babeuf came eventually to see himself as a man capable of overturning the world from his study desk, with the Word as his lever. In the years before 1789 the conviction of a messianic vocation was as yet undeveloped. Yet even in the midst of his professional researches and polite debates with the secretary of the Arras Academy on such subjects as "why Negroes are black" and Roman agriculture, it is clear that "the means of accomplishing universal happiness" were already Babeuf's central intellectual concern, and that he had begun to speculate on the possibilities of communism in such a connection.

The problem of the origins of Babeuf's communism is, however, not a simple one. The theoretical merits of utopian communism were a commonplace in eighteenth-century thought. The discovery that Babeuf toyed with notions which had attracted the sympathetic attention of Morelly, Rousseau and Mably, of Fénélon, Prévost or of Restif de la Bretonne is of itself of little significance. One of Babeuf's most cogent arguments at his trial in 1797 was that in arraigning the Equals for preaching communism the Directory was placing the entire philosophy of the eighteenth century in the dock.[2]

If the private scribblings and occasional correspondence of Babeuf have become an essential source for the history of the development of modern communist thought, it is because they have been studied not in the context of the mainstream of eighteenth-century political theory, but through the distorting lens of 1796 and the Conspiracy of the Equals. Scholars have deliberately sought to find in them the earliest traces of a communism that was practical rather than utopian, and revolutionary rather than speculative. The result has been a virtual competition to establish the earliest possible date for Babeuf's conversion to revolutionary communism, often to the detriment of a sensible evaluation of the development of his ideas. Thus, in 1884 Advielle concluded from a study of Babeuf's correspondence that "the idea of Babouvisme was in germination from the age of twenty-five," or from about 1785. In 1902 Albert Thomas found that "the idea of communism had begun to haunt Babeuf's thinking" by about 1787.

In 1935 Lefebvre and Dommanget established in *Pages choisies de Babeuf* the first sketch of an orthodox or generally accepted periodicization. According to this—as it was outlined in full definition in 1946 in Lefebvre's study of the Directory—Babeuf's sympathy with the peasants of Picardy and his reading of the classics of the Enlightenment led him by 1787 to a theoretical espousal of communism. However, only the experiences of the revolutionary years that followed transformed this, through several mutations, into the practical program of revolutionary communism of 1796.[3]

In 1960 this "orthodox" periodicization was challenged by the Soviet scholar Dalin. He had become convinced, by a reconsideration of certain unpublished notes, that Babeuf had already become a collectivist and revolutionary communist by the summer of 1786, and that he had arrived at this position as a result of a critical evaluation of the developing capitalist society in which he lived rather than through a familiarity with the ideas of the Enlightenment.[4]

Thanks to the publication (in 1961) of Babeuf's correspondence with the Academy of Arras we can now place both the "orthodox" interpretation and Professor Dalin's revisions in a new perspective. It is possible, for example, to learn from the correspondence with Dubois something about the kind of books Babeuf was reading during the years 1786 and 1787 and those with whose contents he was already familiar.[5] The impression emerges of a much narrower intellectual life than has usually been attributed to Babeuf, although one more in keeping with the practical restrictions of life in a small provincial backwater like Roye.

In August 1786 Dubois wrote to ask Babeuf what journals he read. Babeuf, in some embarrassment, parried by explaining that as he was away in the country a great deal he did not always get to see the journals, but that he did have a "co-subscription" to the *Mercure de France*. The current subscription to the *Mercure* alone was thirty-two livres in the provinces. Despite Dubois' sneers—the political section was *"bien froide"* and the literary section *"bien faible"*—it was probably through the *Mercure* that Babeuf kept abreast of movements in the world of letters and picked up a smattering of general culture. From 1786 Dubois began to send him also the *Journal de la langue française*, founded by Urbain Domergue of Lyons in 1784, in which the bias was heavily towards belles lettres.

The general emphasis of the correspondence of the Academy of Arras tended also in the same direction, and Babeuf entered readily into the spirit, adopting a private reformed spelling system, offering critical comments on verses and style, and even correcting another of Dubois' correspondents for using the wrong subjunctive tense. In cultural matters he adopted a classicist and conservative standpoint, scathingly dismissing the contemporary experiments with balloons and Mesmer's "electricity" and "animal magnetism" as unworthy of serious attention; he strongly defended formal standards in literature against innovation. The prize essay topic set by the Besançon Academy in 1787, *"Le Génie, est-il au-dessus de toutes règles?,"* produced an outburst against the proposition in which Babeuf was careful to range his views alongside those of the equally conservative editor of the *Journal de la langue française*.[6] Perhaps one should see no more in these reactions than the attitudes of an autodidact seeking to ingratiate himself with his cultural betters. They are, however, perfectly consistent with the general emphasis on form and rigorous logic in Babeuf's written work in later years.

There was little in the curious ragbag of reading matter passed on by Dubois to Babeuf from time to time capable of playing a significant rôle in the conversion of a communist, or indeed of exciting anyone's interest in profound social questions. Crignon's *Voyage de Suède,* de la Coudraye's *Théorie des vents,* the Abbé Reynard's *Tableau des différents espèces d'air et de gaz*, the program of the Academy of La Rochelle, a "relation of Louis XVI's visit to Le Havre" in June 1786, a grammar by de Tournon, M. Roman on *Le Sexe des fleurs* and Marie Le Masson Le Golft's *Lettres sur l'éducation* were among the most substantial items. Occasional remarks in the correspondence on the subject of slavery and the Americas suggest that Babeuf had already absorbed Raynal's *Histoire philosophique et politique . . . dans les Indes*, but apart from this there is little indication of much in the way of any deeper penetration into the general culture of the Enlightenment.[7]

In the prize essay on the roads of Artois, submitted in November 1786, Babeuf was able to display a certain professional erudition, demonstrating his familiarity with the Custom of Saint-Omer, the General Custom of Artois, the Code de la Voirie, and Mellier's *Traité du droit de voirie*. However the only evidence in this work of any wider cultivation was a single quotation from Rousseau's *Discourse on the Origins of Inequality*. This is the only concrete evidence that Babeuf had read Rousseau before the revolution. In a letter written on the subject of the education of his children in 1787 Babeuf paid tribute to Rousseau and showed an apparent familiarity with the substance of *Emile*, and in one other letter there are remarks which appear to be based on a confused appreciation of the argument of the *Social Contract*.[8] But there is no reason to question the conclusion that the sum total of Babeuf's acquaintance with Rousseau before 1788 amounted to no more than a rapid reading of *Emile* and perhaps the *Discourses* and that the *Social Contract* was possibly not even available to him in Picardy. There is also a complete absence of any hint that Babeuf was directly influenced by any of the great classics of eighteenth-century utopianism. Neither in the published correspondence nor in the private notes, for example, is there any indication that Babeuf had read Morelly's *Code de la Nature* or Mably's *Entretiens de Phocion* or any other works by these authors before 1789, and his notes on Mercier's *L'An 2440* date from 1790-91.[9]

In fact, as far as Babeuf's published correspondence is concerned, the evidence for his adoption of the standpoint of utopian communism before the revolution turns mainly on a single letter, written in July 1787 to comment on a secondhand summary of the ideas of a quite obscure minor utopian pamphleteer from Alsace called Claude-Boniface Collignon. In October 1786 the secretary of the Société de Physique of Orléans sent Dubois, as secretary of the Arras Academy, a copy of Collignon's prospectus for a proposed eight-volume work entitled *"L'Avant-coureur du changement du monde entier par l'aisance; la bonne éducation et la prospérité générale de tous les hommes, ou prospectus d'un mémoire patriotique sur les causes de la grand misère qui existe partout et sur les moyens de l'extirper radicalement."*

On 26 October Dubois brought this publication to the notice of his correspondents as a work of singular whimsy, but without identifying the author and without giving any significant further details. On 19 March 1787, however, he sent out the first of a series of six circulars in which he summarized the contents of Collignon's pamphlet, attributing it to an anonymous "reformer of the whole world" and concentrating chiefly on the author's vision of the future reformed society, rather than on his critique of existing conditions or any practical suggestions as to how to achieve the desired transformation.

According to Dubois' summary, Collignon advocated a clean sweep of existing French towns, villages and farms and the rebuilding of a completely new society in fifty years, with "1,000 cities, 100 technical colleges, 16,000 villages and 330,000 farms." In this society everything would be communally owned and administered and all citizens would receive, free of charge, meals, clothing, housing, lighting and heating, with free support and education for all children from the age of four to twenty. The details of the resultant utopia were lovingly documented. Men and women were to receive ordinarily not just lunch but a thick and well-conditioned soup, an entrée, either stew or a substitute, and a dessert consisting more or less of the same fruit as at breakfast. On fast days a well-seasoned soup; a dish of lentils, peas, haricots, vegetables, eggs, rice, turnips, cauliflower or other products according to the season; a dish of river or lake fish, cod, herring, salmon or some other; and dessert. The evening meal was to be washed down by an allowance of a half bottle of wine for men and a quarter bottle for women (doubled on feast days).

Newly married couples were to receive an issue of furniture worth 4,000 livres: two twin beds—each with palliasse, eiderdown, and mattress—three pillows, six pairs of sheets, twelve pillowcases, six stuffed-bottom chairs, two fine armchairs, a sofa in silk, two tables, a desk, a wardrobe, and two fine chandeliers.[10]

No doubt Babeuf, with his recollection of childhood poverty, found this kind of thing rather less amusing than Dubois, the wealthy seigneur of Fosseux; and it is conceivable that the quite detailed lists of benefits accruing to individuals joining the communist community put out by the Equals in 1796 reflect in part a distant echo of speculations stimulated by Dubois' account of Collignon's utopia nine years before.[11]

After a delay of some weeks, on 8 July 1787 Babeuf dispatched a long comment on the ideas of the anonymous "reformer." The letter was drafted in the form of a polite essay comparing a project to rationalize systems of law internationally (on the model of the Prussian Code as reformed by Frederick the Great in the spirit of the Enlightenment) with the complete remodeling of the world (as envisaged by Collignon). But it rapidly developed into a personal, radical and passionate denunciation of inequality. The proposition to replace the chaos of individual customaries by a common universal code elicited a fierce attack on "the astonishing feudal system," in which the origins of feudal property were attributed to conquest, pillage, and usurpation by lucky brigands, and those of feudal law to the "ridiculous pride" and "swollen vanity" of the victors, who sought to legitimize and perpetuate their triumph by means suited to a time of ignorance and barbarism.

The function of the feudal codes, Babeuf argued, was to perpetuate a class division originally founded on violent conquest and to ensure that the position of the dominant class would never be challenged by the inferior class: "Hence the origins of the so-called nobles and that of revolting distinctions in all orders of society." A mere rationalization and unification of local codes after the Prussian pattern would, consequently, provide only the most meager of palliatives while leaving the great central evil of inequality untouched. "It would not prevent my children from being born poor and deprived while, from the moment they open their eyes, the children of my neighbor the millionaire will be choked with a superfluity of everything."

Babeuf then went on to point the contrast with the egalitarian society sketched by "the reformer," in which, inevitably, all titled and privileged persons would have to give up their distinctions and privileges and work alongside the others, and in which all useful vocations would be regarded as equally worthy of respect. "If, as is the case here, I should work as a writer, I would be enchanted to find myself no longer disdained by those who, through belonging to professions which pretended to greater distinction, believe themselves authorized to look upon me as a *protégé* [*se croient autorisés à me donner des regards qui semblent anoncer la protéxion*], and for my part, I will not find any difficulty in treating as an equal my barber or my shoemaker."

With the social hierarchy of Roye doubtless in mind Babeuf devoted a final paragraph to denouncing the pretensions of the legal and magisterial caste to social precedence over the honest artisan.

So far, in using the ideal arrangements of a utopia to contrast the imperfections of the existing society, Babeuf was doing no more than adopting a common device of eighteenth-century writing, however vigorous and original his critique. It is clear, however, from other sources that his interest in utopian speculation went much deeper. On 21 March Babeuf had sent Dubois three suggestions for the prize essay competition for 1788, each on a topic on which he claimed already to have a reserve of developed personal ideas. Suggestion number three raised the following question: "According to the sum total of present knowledge, what would be the condition of a people whose social institutions were such that the most perfect equality reigned without distinction in each individual member, in which the land on which he lived was nobody's property but belonged to all, where, in fact, all was in common, even including the products of all kinds of industry? Would such institutions be authorized by natural law? Could such a society exist, and would the means of observing an absolutely equal distribution be practicable?"[12]

The topic was politely declined. But in the central section of his letter on Collignon's project Babeuf seized the opportunity to air some of his own "reserve of ideas," as he strove to demonstrate that the principles of equality implicit in the "reformer's" utopia, far from being the product of mere whimsy, were in fact in accordance with nature and human reason. In order to do this he appealed, firstly, to the evidence of the remote past, in which inequality was unknown; and, secondly, to accounts of the primitive equality of the native Americans before the fall from grace occasioned by the European conquest. Then followed a very brief exposition of Rousseau on the origins of inequality. "The first man who enclosed a patch of ground, says the author of *Emile*, and took it upon himself to say *'C'est à moi,'* was the prime author of all the ills which afflicted humanity." Rousseau, however, was condemned on the erroneous grounds that he sought to send humanity back into the forests to enjoy a life of primitive equality in the state of nature. The reformer, who offered four square meals a day, elegant clothing, and charming

1,000-livre houses for fathers of families, was much to be preferred.

His correspondence with the Academy of Arras reveals that Babeuf's awareness of the theoretical currents of eighteenth-century utopian thought was, at best, no more than superficial. The letter of 8 July was nevertheless a remarkable personal manifesto. Writing to Dubois, a seigneur of the Old Régime and a municipal magistrate of Arras, Babeuf declared himself openly the enemy of feudal and magisterial privilege in the name of absolute social equality. While Dubois, the wealthy dilettante, might put aside his utopian "dreams" of "paradise on earth" with a sigh and pass on to new and more interesting speculations, for his correspondent equality was a vital matter of personal dignity and of survival itself.

Henceforth Babeuf would live and move in two worlds: a public world in which he pursued his profession as *feudiste*, accepting, in practice, the assumption that the arrangement of things as they were was permanent, and that one must strive to make the best of one's lot, and a private world of speculation in which all the foundations of the public world were already demolished and the search for a new and more just order seemed the true reality.

Thanks to the explorations of Professor Dalin among Babeuf's personal papers we know more of the outlines of that "private world" than is revealed in the correspondence with Dubois. In particular, the essay competition of 1786 on the advisability of splitting up farms in Artois, which was the occasion of the start of the correspondence, is now known to have inspired original and radical reflections on the related questions of property and poverty which Babeuf kept to himself, even while commenting much more conventionally on the topic in his correspondence. Unfortunately the manuscript of Babeuf's own submission for the competition has not survived. The prize went to a certain Delegorgue, an *avocat au conseil d'Artois*. His *Mémoire*, printed in 1786, shows him to have been a strong partisan of large and concentrated farms, which he regarded as more suitable for the application of new and advanced techniques of agriculture, and a decided opponent of "the sectaries of the system of dividing up farms" (among whom the *accessit,* Délestré du Terrage, was apparently numbered).

Babeuf was not able to read Delegorgue's *Mémoire* before January 1787. However, more than six months earlier Dubois had sent him, in the circulars of the academy, an analysis of the positions of both Delegorgue and Délestré, and in June 1786 Babeuf confessed to Dubois that he was more in favor of Délestré's "system of equality and proportion in fortunes" as closer to "the institutions of nature."[13]

At the same time he drafted a much longer letter devoted to the same subject, which on reflection he decided not to send.[14] In this draft Babeuf ranged himself very decidedly among the opponents of the *"coqs du village,"* the substantial tenant farmers who were constantly striving to build up their individual holdings at the expense of the smaller peasants. Studies of the Département du Nord and of Picardy, Babeuf's own province, have demonstrated the extent to which the development of capitalist agriculture produced a class division in the villages of northeastern France during the eighteenth century, as capital from trade and office-holding was steadily invested in land and as the demands of the Paris grain market grew.

In the Nord the twin pressures of developing capitalism and overpopulation resulted, as Lefebvre has shown, in a doubling of leaserents in the eighty years immediately preceding the French Revolution. A small section of the peasants, by improving techniques of production and marketing and by intensifying the exploitation of hired labor, was able to prosper in such conditions; the remainder faced steady impoverishment and often outright starvation.[15] That the issue of the concentration of leasehold property in the hands of the bigger farmers was a vital social and political concern of the countryside is demonstrated by the numerous petitions for some legal restriction of the size of leases submitted to the various revolutionary assemblies after 1789. A *mémoire* read to the provincial assembly of Picardy against *fermiers forts* on 4 December 1787 complained of the way in which the "farmers" formed a closed caste, selling, bequeathing, settling and subletting their leasehold properties only amongst their own kind.[16]

In his undispatched letter of June 1786 Babeuf analyzed with feeling the sufferings of the struggling small peasants and the landless, displaced by a situation in which three or four main cultivators in a parish held in their hands the exploitation of an entire territory and could manage everything with the aid of a few hired laborers. He painted a grim picture of a Picardy where the roads were marred by the sight of "old beggar women, filthy and emaciated so that they are frightful to behold, herding on the roadside verges skinny, scabby cows from which they hope to get a little milk." It was a province where in the shadow of the splendid châteaux of rich seigneurs the majority of the villagers subsisted on dirty water, onions and sour black bread among their peat marshes, and where starving mothers were aged before their time through selling their breast-milk to feed town children. It was a province where some had fifty thousand times as much as they needed, and others one thousand times as much, yet "others, who are almost beyond count, have considerably less than they need, or almost nothing."

To explain the origins of this monstrous system of inequality Babeuf turned to a version of Rousseau. The first and overriding right of mankind was the right of survival: "The natural right, the right to live, exists from birth, it is an absolute right; all the remaining rights are only conditional." The birth and early development of the institution of property had not, at first, threatened the recognition of the basic right to survive. But when all land had been appropriated, it was no longer possible for the propertyless individuals to provide for themselves independently. The monopolizing of property by some did not, and could not, mean the surrender by the others of their most essential natural rights.[17] History (or, rather, an abstract model of history) thus provided a sanction for the natural right to survive as well as an account of its derivation. But history was not, for Babeuf, the only or necessarily the most important sanction. Over the next five years he would offer a variety of rational constructions in support of the same basic moral principle. In 1786 it was self-evident, "sacred and imprescriptible"; in 1789, mathematically demonstrated by a comparison of the cultivable area of the land and the size of the population; in 1791, the clear and evident intent of the Creator in the act of creation.[18] The important thing for Babeuf was that the fact of the "right to survive" and the primacy of this right over all other rights, including the right of property, should be acknowledged. In this he was neither more nor less inconsistent than the framers of the Declaration of the Rights of Man of 1789, who insisted on defending the right of property as "natural, imprescriptible and sacred" while all other rights were simply "natural and imprescriptible."

The corollary of the principle of the natural right to live was that the owners of property were morally bound to give the propertyless the opportunity to support themselves, either by leasing them land or by giving them work. If they failed in this duty, then the starving would have the clear right to take what they needed by force. Dalin sees in this passage a deliberate justification of revolutionary expropriation, at least in principle. Babeuf, however, did not in 1786 propose the expropriation of the landowners; the time for that, he said, was either past or had not yet come. Instead, he argued for a reduction in the size of leases, thus making more farms available. At the same time he offered another, completely original suggestion. In order to maintain the undoubted advantages of large-scale farming, groups of peasants should come together to bid for leases collectively, working the leased property in combination.[19] On the basis of this suggestion Professor Dalin has hailed Babeuf as a pioneer of collective farms. But there is a semantic difficulty. The term Babeuf used—*"ferme collective"*[20]—means "collective lease" not "collective farm"; but from other evidence it is clear that Professor Dalin is in complete earnest when he argues that contrary to all received opinion, and to all other accessible evidence, the draft letter of June 1786 shows that fully ten years before the Conspiracy of the Equals Babeuf was already a partisan, not of a primitive distributivist communism, but of a communism based on the collective ownership and use of the means of production.

According to Dalin's summary, in Babeuf's plan "fifty, forty, thirty or twenty people" would come together to live in association (*en associés*) on the leasehold, working under a management chosen by themselves. There would always be ample labor available at the proper times for the major tasks of agriculture like digging pits, draining, pruning, sowing, mowing, harvesting, and straw-gathering, and a collective responsibility for care of the herd and the fowlyard. After the rent had been paid and reserves set aside for sowing and subsistence, the remainder of the production of the enterprise would be sold or exchanged and the product distributed among all the interested parties, apparently on a basis of equality. The technical advantages of such large-scale collective production would be such that all would be guaranteed a life of plenty. A doubling, or even a tripling, of the population could be supported without difficulty.[21]

That Babeuf speculated on the establishment of something resembling a collective farm in the 1780s seems incontrovertible, and it is a remarkable fact in itself. The construction erected upon it by Dalin, however, appears somewhat exaggerated. Firstly the letter, after all, was *not* sent off or published, but remained among Babeuf's private papers along with other speculative scribblings. Secondly Babeuf never returned to his 1786 collective lease project in any of his subsequent writings, neither in those centered on the "agrarian law" (the redistribution of property), nor in those advocating the abolition of property and the collective ownership of the products of the soil and the workshops. Finally, it is impossible to join Professor Dalin in his interpretive leap from the fact of Babeuf's abstract moral justification of violence by the expropriated to the conclusion of a practical conversion to revolutionary communism. The letter of June 1786 was, in point of fact, no more than a misfire, a brilliant flash of light anticipating the ideas of utopians like Charles Fourier in the following century. It was of no deeper significance for the development of Babeuf's ideas, other than as an illustration of the vigor of his questing mind as it sought and discarded alternative formulas for achieving the great goals to which he was already dedicated: social equality and the vindication of the right to live.

The more general thesis that two or three years before the revolution of 1789 Babeuf's theoretical sympathy for communism had begun to evolve into a determination to accomplish a practical communist reorganization of society must also be rejected.[22] Such a view becomes plausible only when Babeuf's processes of thought are considered in isolation, and abstracted from the general context of eighteenth-century thought on social questions.

In the unpublished letter of June 1786 and in the correspondence with Dubois the following year, Babeuf contrasted his private ideal world, based on the natural rights of man and equality, with the existing public world, in which the rights of man were denied and inequality and injustice prevailed. He declared a clear personal preference for absolute equality and absolute justice, but he accepted the necessity, for the time being, of some compromise for the practical achievement of a more equal and more just world here and now.

It is many years since Lichtenberger, in his study of *Socialism and the French Revolution*, demonstrated that this same mode and sequence of argument was almost obligatory for social reformers in eighteenth-century France. "Commonplaces shaped a paradox," he wrote; "in order to demand the most modest reforms, people believed it necessary to establish the most subversive principles, and to set forth the most formidable denunciations." Such was the fashion of the age that nobody who sought a practical remedy for the prevailing evil of poverty could escape a preliminary excursion into the abstract realms of the origins of the right of property—in order to prove that it was not absolute, as the Physiocrats taught, but conditional. To deduce the primacy of the "right to live" from the conditions of an abstract "state of nature" was a frequent device, and one adopted, for example, by such contemporary pamphleteers as Gosselin, Leroy de Barincourt, Dufourny de Villiers and even Jean-Paul Marat.[23]

The corollary was generally an invocation of the "social contract" which, by creating civil society, established the right of property, and by the same token could modify and limit that right. The demonstrable right of society to impose conditions on the tenure of property was then used to justify a variety of more or less radical reforms. In Gosselin, for example, after a formal recognition of the impracticable ideal of pure communism, it was invoked to legitimize the state seizure of wastes and uncultivated land, the leasing out of the lands of the crown and the church to small cultivators, and state purchase of the estates of the great proprietors for redistribution, financed by a progressive tax. In Restif de la Bretonne's *Thesmographe*, it meant a redistribution of property every five years. In the case of Babeuf, the much less radical solution of the breakup of large farms and the adoption of collective leases was involved.

While rejecting the Rousseauist argument from the "state of nature," Helvétius and Holbach (the representatives of a different stream of Enlightenment thought) also relied on a "social contract" theory to establish the conditional nature of the right of property. Yet the utilitarian principle they adopted, that men come together in society to seek the greatest happiness of the greatest number, also presupposes a natural equality. One man's happiness is assumed to have the same "value" as another's. What must follow is state action to secure a wider distribution of property by taxation and inheritance duties, and a guarantee of subsistence through property or labor to every citizen. Their conclusions were closely comparable.[24]

The most serious theoretical obstacle to such programs (apart from the unfashionable argument from prescription) was the defense of the absolute natural right of property along Lockeian lines by the Physiocrats and their disciples, especially Chastellux, Turgot and the Abbé Baudeau. This provided the rationale for the vindication of the right of property contained in the Declaration of the Rights of Man in 1789. According to this thesis, property was a natural and imprescriptible right of man, established by the investment of personal toil in improving nature's original patrimony. Babeuf's counter was that, in practice, existing property had originated in theft and fraud during the epoch of feudal barbarism and not in honest toil. Despite its ultraradical implications, this was neither unique nor original, but another commonplace of the age, for which support could be derived from Rousseau's *Discourse on the Origins of Inequality*. In context, its purpose was to serve as a practical legitimization of measures attacking or restricting existing property rights.

In general, thinkers and reformers in eighteenth-century France shared a remarkable consensus about ends. Civil society must provide a guaranteed subsistence for all, and some redress for gross inequalities. But this consensus presents a curious contrast with the proliferation of individual speculative systems invoked to justify the various means selected to achieve these ends. The conclusion must be that, in the case of many reformers, the ends dictated the system; the legitimizing system was an embellishment rather than an essential part of the argument. Only in terms of such a perspective can the evolution of Babeuf's political thought be properly understood. His end remained always constant: "universal happiness" through the triumph of equality. The practical program advocated changed with the lessons of experience, and the theoretical justifications were amended or reconstructed to fit the current practical needs.

To suppose that Babeuf was a doctrinaire communist from 1786 or 1787, seeking to impose a preconceived utopia on mankind by revolution, reveals a misunderstanding of the contemporary function of utopian speculation in providing the moral sanction for comparatively moderate practical measures of reform. Only the repeated failure of such "palliatives" in the course of the revolution drove him finally to recognize the speculative extreme as the only truly practical policy.

Four

A Practical Program

If the "reformation of the entire world" could still be dismissed as a utopian dream in July 1787, the same did not hold true of the reformation of France. In terms of the political awakening of France, 1786 was the last year of the Ancien Régime and 1787 the first year of the revolution. In August 1786 Calonne, the royal comptroller-general, set out his plan to tackle the impending financial collapse of the kingdom through the imposition of a universal tax based on land, administered by new local assemblies elected by the taxpayers. By both threatening the fiscal immunities of the privileged classes and undermining the traditional political preeminence of the nobility in the new assemblies, Calonne's reforms aroused the bitter opposition of the nobility and the upper clergy, which was expressed through the Assembly of the Notables, convened in February 1787 to discuss his proposals. In the pamphlet war that followed, aristocratic propaganda attacked the despotism of the crown while the government exposed the selfishness and arrogance of the *privilégiés*. This was preparing the ground for the great explosion of 1789, when the people of France would rise impartially against both tyranny and privilege.

The impact of this political struggle was felt even in Roye when Prévost, the royal *avocat au bailliage*, was summoned to the Assembly of Notables. In August 1787 Prévost would sit as a member of the new departmental assembly at Montdidier, part of the reformed local government system created by the royal edict of June 1787, in company with Aubé de Bracquemont, Galoppe d'Armancourt and the dean of Saint-Florent.[1]

By May 1787 Babeuf himself had become involved in the campaign against the *privilégiés*. He returned from a visit to Paris with an armful of pamphlets, even seeking in his enthusiasm to enroll Dubois and the Academy of Arras as agents for the dissemination of reform propaganda. In September he himself tried his hand at compiling a political pamphlet. But the publisher found his attacks on the *privilégiés* too dangerous and refused to print it.[2]

The man responsible for Babeuf's recruitment into the "radical underground" was Jean-Frédéric-Alexis Devin, a Noyon printer and bookseller with whom he had made contact through Jean-Baptiste Babeuf at the beginning of 1786, in connection with the printing of a professional circular. In November 1786 Devin was busy with another of Babeuf's brochures, the prospectus for *L'Archiviste terriste*, which was held up by the royal censor in Paris. On 25 November he invited Babeuf to Noyon to see a timely performance of Beaumarchais' *Marriage of Figaro*, and to enjoy the playwright's mordant satire on the Noblesse de la Robe. Devin now began to supply Babeuf with books and pamphlets from Paris, not all of which had passed under the eye of the royal censor. On 9 December, for example, he sent a tract attacking the existing constitution of the Royal Army. In March 1787 Babeuf wrote to Dubois asking for his help in disseminating this piece. But Dubois declined the privilege; none of the Arras booksellers would handle the publication for fear of the police, and as a municipal magistrate he himself could hardly oblige.[3]

In particular Devin let Babeuf have a number of works by Rutledge, a Parisian journalist and novelist of Irish extraction for whom he had acted as a publisher. In 1786 Rutledge had published (in London) a republican, anticlerical and quasi-revolutionary tract, the *Eloge de Montesquieu*, with especially harsh words reserved for the exactions of the tax-farmers and *"les fers de l'esclavage féodale."* Babeuf may or may not have read this particular tract, but he certainly read others by the same author, and he passed them on to Dubois in the summer of 1787.[4]

The debate on Calonne's proposals at the beginning of 1787 suggested a means by which Babeuf might profitably combine business and politics. By January it was clear that his earlier project—to write a substantial book outlining his revolutionary new methods of keeping feudal records—had run aground. The censor was continuing to be difficult, and the work itself was still no more than a collection of notes. The imminence of the new land tax, however, seemed to suggest another outlet for the talents of a specialist in surveying. Not only would Calonne's tax make necessary a universal mapping out of the ownership of the land, but it would also require a breakdown of landed property into several classes according to productivity, a technical operation of some complexity. On 13 April Babeuf wrote to Dubois canvassing the advantage, in the circumstances, of a "general and perpetual" land survey. On 4 May he wrote again, offering to let Dubois have a "piece after my fashion touching a very useful subject." This, though it was never sent, was the first draft of the *Cadastre perpétuel*, an original manual describing a method of compiling a land survey and then of keeping it up-to-date by methods similar to Babeuf's techniques of feudal administration, but based on a general parish survey of real property and not of separate fiefs.

During May Babeuf spent several weeks in Paris seeking support for the promotion of this new project. Probably through Devin's good offices he was able to make the acquaintance of Rutledge, who read the manuscript, approved, and undertook to bring it to the attention of Delessart, the *intendant-général des finances,* who was a member of the committee appointed to consider proposals for tax reform.[5] While in Paris Babeuf also met another of Devin's connections, J.-P. Audiffred, a merchant and amateur scientist from the rue Quincampoix, and he agreed to help Audiffred to publicize his latest invention, a surveying instrument for measuring distances on trigonometrical principles. On his return to Roye Babeuf wrote off immediately to Dubois with details of Audiffred's *grafomètre trigonométrique*, which (he said) he had personally seen successfully tested in the Champs Elysées "in the presence of a multitude of spectators." Dubois' expression of polite interest led Babeuf, on 19 July, to suggest that the Arras Academy should be asked to arrange for a formal examination of the instrument; but Dubois did not oblige.

Meanwhile, at the beginning of June, Babeuf had also sent Dubois details of the *Cadastre perpétuel*. On 7 June he wrote again, betraying a somewhat naive impatience. The government committee had considered his project a month before but he still had heard nothing. Should he bring it to the attention of the new provincial tax assemblies, or perhaps have a précis printed and made public? With his usual urbanity Dubois parried these attempts to engage the active help of the Academy of Arras in publicizing the *Cadastre*, by suggesting that Babeuf should try an approach to the intendant of Picardy, d'Agay de Mutigny. However the intendant did not answer Babeuf's letter, and an announcement in the *Affiches de Picardie et d'Artois* produced such a disappointing response that the whole project had to be shelved.[6] The manuscript of the *Cadastre perpétuel* was now to gather dust for eighteen months until the political excitements of 1789 and the revived debate on taxation reminded Babeuf of its existence and gave him fresh hope that it might find a profitable market.

The year 1788 was to be his busiest as a *feudiste*, as he took on the *terriers* of the marquis de Soyecourt. Partly for this reason, but no doubt partly also because Dubois had responded coldly to his efforts at personal advancement, Babeuf's correspondence with the academy became less frequent and finally ceased. We have no evidence for his political attitudes or activities during 1788; he certainly published nothing in this period, and it seems probable that his energies were absorbed chiefly in professional activities and (in the second half of the year) by the quarrel with Soyecourt and his agents. But soon the elections to the Estates-General at the beginning of 1789 ensured the revival of the political debate in every corner of France. How could Babeuf stand aside at a time when so many opportunities for the achievement of "universal happiness" seemed to be opening up?

The first preliminary at Roye was the publication on 12 February of an ordinance by Antoine-Adolphe de Soyecourt, the Bailli d'Epée, calling on the towns and villages of the Bailliage of Roye to meet as soon as possible to elect and mandate delegates to the general assembly of the Third Estate at Péronne. The elections, which were held in March, proceeded through several stages, beginning with separate town meetings at which the guilds and the unattached citizens of Roye, Montdidier, and Péronne elected delegates and drew up cahiers, or mandates. In the second stage, representatives of each town met with delegates of the villages of the dependent *bailliage secondaire* to agree on a combined cahier and to select delegates to attend the assembly at Péronne. During the final proceedings at Péronne, which began on 30 March, four deputies of the Third Estate were chosen to go to Versailles, among them Prévost from Roye, and four "substitutes" (of whom Masson was one). A final form for the cahiers of each of the three orders was also agreed.[7]

In practice, due to the influence of the duc de Mailly, Charles and Alexandre de Lameth, and other liberal nobles, the nobility and the Third Estate were able to agree on a common formula and drew up a single joint cahier with a strongly liberal flavor; the comte de

Castéja, Florent Masson and Louis-François Billecocq were among the *commissaires* responsible for preparing the agreed version.[8]

A year after these events Babeuf was to claim that he had attempted to put forward several propositions for inclusion in the cahier during the transactions at Roye, but that the "viziers of Roye," the legal officialdom which dominated the affairs of the town, had refused to listen. It seems most likely that this intervention occurred at the town meeting which convened sometime before 9 March to choose and mandate Roye's delegates to the intermediate *bailliage secondaire* assembly.

According to Babeuf's summary of his proposals he spoke in favor of the abolition of fiefs, the commutation of feudal dues, and the suppression of primogeniture. He defended one plan (based most probably on the *Cadastre perpétuel*) for a single and equal tax, and another for the creation of a national system of education.[9]

Babeuf's suggestions were all "spurned" by the "viziers of Roye," and the proceedings at the general gathering of his aristocratic clients and their legal hangers-on at Péronne were hardly more satisfactory. Three clauses in the cahier of the nobility and the Third Estate of Péronne did express the spirit of at least some of Babeuf's suggestions. Clauses XXIV and XXV of the second section demanded the introduction of a single proportional tax with no exemptions; and clause XXI of the third section pleaded for the suppression of primogeniture. The cahier did not, however, contain any recommendations about feudal dues. Babeuf was careful to note that Alexandre de Lameth's remarks on this subject showed that beneath his liberal sheep's clothing the aristocratic wolf remained, as always, an aristocratic wolf.

From Roye Babeuf followed the events in Paris as the Estates-General met at the beginning of May, metamorphosed itself into a National Assembly and challenged the royal authority; he noted in particular that Prévost, the deputy from Roye, consistently figured among the most conservative of the representatives of the Third Estate. When finally it became known in June that Prévost, alone of the Péronne bailliage deputies, had refused to adhere to the Tennis Court Oath, Babeuf took the lead in a campaign to secure his recall, which was, however, quashed by the Billecocqs.[10]

The revival of the national political debate had encouraged Babeuf to take another look at the manuscript of the *Cadastre perpétuel* and to revise it by adding circumstantial political reflections more appropriate to 1789. At the end of March he also wrote to Audiffred and to Devin to suggest the incorporation of an additional section expounding the use of Audiffred's surveying invention.[11] In July he set off once again for Paris full of renewed hopes for the success of the *Cadastre perpétuel*. Thanks to the generous hospitality of Audiffred, Babeuf was able to spend the summer of 1789 completing his revision and preparing the volume for the press.

According to Advielle's biography Babeuf arrived in Paris in good time to take part in the capture of the Bastille on 14 July. However, the historical evidence confirms only that he was in the capital by 22 July, when he witnessed the aftermath of the murders of Foulon and Berthier, two officials of the Ancien Régime who had been accused of a plot to starve the people. The sight of a procession carrying the heads of the murdered men through the streets of the Faubourg Saint-Martin affected Babeuf strongly. It inspired horrified reflections (in a letter to Marie-Anne at Roye) on the brutalization of the people by the barbarities of the Ancien Régime and the dire consequences to be anticipated from a poor harvest. There was, however, the consolation to be drawn from the fact that the National Assembly was safe, thanks to the vigilance of the people in scotching the intrigues of the duc d'Artois; and Babeuf took a keen pleasure in promising to send a revolutionary cockade for Robert.[12]

As soon as he arrived in Paris Babeuf set out to try to restore his personal fortunes, ruined by the quarrel with Soyecourt and the failure of his suit in the bailliage court, which had brought a swarm of small creditors about his ears.[13] By personal lobbying he managed to gather a few livres from one of the brothers of the Abbé Maury, and the promise of more work, including the *terriers* of Saint-Quentin in Beauvais, of which yet another of Maury's brothers, the prince de Broglie, was *abbé commendataire*. Nevertheless recent events suggested that income from such sources could no longer be relied on. However bravely Babeuf might declare himself "disposed to give a good pat on the back to encourage those seeking to upset his cooking-pot," the imminent demise of feudalism clearly threatened him with personal catastrophe. During the summer of 1789 the Babeuf family was again, as in 1787, on the threshold of destitution. Babeuf himself was only able to survive by lodging and eating at Audiffred's house in the rue Quincampoix. By borrowing sums of money from his host, from time to time he was able to send back a pitiful handful of livres to Roye to buy bread for the family.[14]

In August Babeuf pinned his hopes on an anonymously published pamphlet that took Mirabeau to task for some remarks in one of his speeches. Babeuf apparently hoped that mention of the famous name would guarantee a good sale, but the work produced no profits, and, for that matter, contained very little that was worth reading.[15]

All the while work on the text of the *Cadastre perpétuel* continued as Babeuf read through the books and pamphlets collected for him by Audiffred: works by Linguet, Necker, Voltaire, Mirabeau, Condorcet, Raynal and others on the tax question. At the beginning of September Babeuf and Audiffred visited Versailles as spectators at a meeting of the National Assembly. Babeuf was introduced to Mirabeau, who charmed the visitors with his informality and promised to say something on behalf of the *Cadastre perpétuel* in the assembly. Then the party visited the château and gardens with Constantini, the Corsican deputy from Bonifacio. Babeuf suddenly spotted Soyecourt's carriage and ran after it shouting, but without gaining any satisfaction.

On 21 September Babeuf and Audiffred signed an agreement as joint authors, according to which Audiffred was to bear the entire expense of publication (in a letter of 4 September this was put at 6,000 livres); Babeuf undertook to meet half of any losses if sales had failed to cover expenses within a year.[16] Babeuf now spent nearly all his time seeing to the final stages of preparation. The book was in proof by 4 October, and Constantini read it and summarized the contents in an address to the Jacobin Club on the 6th. On 16 or 17 October Babeuf was able to leave Paris to return to Roye taking the first printed copies with him. He had "worn out three pairs of shoes" walking to and from the printing shop to supervise the workmen. Fifty copies were set aside as complimentaries for members of the National Assembly, and there were presentation copies for the king and for Necker.[17]

The *Cadastre perpétuel* was published ostensibly as a practical guide to local authorities charged with the administration of taxes on land and personal revenues. When sales proved slow Babeuf suggested that the 40,000 communes of France should all be circularized with a prospectus outlining its utility.[18] The volume contained instructions on the drawing up of land plans at the village level, the division of land by classes, details of how to adjust the records whenever land changed hands, and a suggested means for the assessment of annual income for the purposes of the personal tax. In essence, however, the *Cadastre perpétuel* was a political tract rather than a technical manual. In the eighteenth-century manner, what Babeuf discussed in his forty-six-page "Discours préliminaire," and even in important sections of the text itself, was not so much the bureaucratic details of tax administration, but the principles by which the replacement of existing imposts by a single and equal tax might be justified and the uses to which money raised in this way might properly be put, all in terms of the social contract. The *Cadastre perpétuel* was, in fact, Babeuf's first attempt at a practical political program to achieve "the common happiness of the peoples."

The essentials of this program may be summarized quite briefly. In order to redress the existing social inequality, the state should finance certain essential services from general taxation: religious services like baptism and burial, which should be free to all; poor relief through the establishment of a national subsistence fund; medical aid by a salaried public service of doctors, apothecaries and surgeons; education, free and open to all; and a salaried magistracy, dispensing justice without charge. Only in the case of the national educational system did Babeuf go on to outline his proposals in greater detail. Babeuf's remarks reveal the strong influence of Condorcet and in particular of Condorcet's *Essai sur la constitution des assemblées provinciales*, especially by their insistence on the practical value of education in restoring equality to a society divided into an educated master class and an ignorant slave class.

The appointment of parish schoolmasters, Babeuf argued, should no longer be left to uncultivated villagers, whose choice was often almost as ignorant as they were themselves. Instead, the state should appoint teachers and pay them salaries sufficiently high to attract competent scholars. Unlike Condorcet, whose generous vision included an elementary syllabus incorporating technical skills, general science, and civics as well as the three "Rs," Babeuf insisted on the almost exclusive importance of his own special academic interest, language studies, as the key to all other knowledge. We know that in 1794 Babeuf briefly toyed with the idea of a career as a local schoolmaster; it is conceivable that he was already casting himself in the same rôle in 1789.[19]

The other practical proposals in the *Cadastre perpétuel* are less detailed. When, at the end of 1789, Babeuf took up the question of poverty, he drafted a projected petition on the relief of beggary which may give some indication of the way he hoped the national subsistence fund would work. According to this, each commune was to keep a list of paupers and to guarantee "all whose resources are not adequate to their needs" a dole of five sous per day, supported by a levy on the wealthier inhabitants in proportion to their wealth.[20]

The major reform defended in the *Cadastre perpétuel* was, of course, a reform of the tax system, explicitly intended to lift the burden from the shoulders of the poor. Consistently, Babeuf reserved an especially strong attack for indirect taxes, which bore most heavily on the poor, for the "disastrous régime of the *gabelles* and the *aides*," and for contemporary proposals to impose a tax on corn. All taxes on articles of consumption must be abolished, and the legions of "bloodsuckers" and "vampires" employed by the tax-farmers must disappear with them.

At the same time Babeuf turned his attention to the other special and unequal charges on the poor: feudal dues and the church tithe. After demonstrating at some length the injustice and illegitimacy of *"cens, lods et ventes, quints, droits de rachat, déshérences, etc.,"* he concluded with the relatively mild recommendation that "at the very least" such dues ought to be abolished through commutation. Tithes also should be abolished, and the upkeep of the church, instead of remaining a special charge on the land and on the peasant, should henceforth be borne by all classes of society. In place of all the existing and inequitable direct and indirect taxes Babeuf proposed a single tax, graduated according to wealth, bearing both on land and on personal income. The land tax would be assessed by local communes on the basis outlined in the *Cadastre perpétuel*. The income tax would require an annual declaration to be vetted by citizens' committees drawn from all classes.[21]

The text of the *Cadastre perpétuel* bears the marks of its origins as a manuscript constantly revised over two years. There is a tendency to go over important ground again and again, and to break up the major argument with asides on matters of general principle or of topical interest. In particular the sections on feudalism are strictly irrelevant to the question of taxation. Taken as a whole, however, the work has a unity. On the one hand, money is to be raised by taxes bearing most heavily on those best able to pay; on the other hand, it is to be spent to the advantage of those most in need. Later generations have been satisfied that this prescription carries its own pragmatic justification in terms of human solidarity. For the eighteenth century this was not enough. Babeuf was compelled by his own rational methods of argument to face up to the inevitable objection that his proposed system involved upsetting the natural order by confiscating the lawful property of the rich to distribute it among the poor.[22]

To answer this objection it was necessary to demonstrate that the right of property was conditional and subject to regulation. In the *Cadastre perpétuel* Babeuf used four distinct arguments for this purpose. The first was a Rousseauist exposition of the social contract, beginning with the axiom "In the natural state all men are equal." If in practice men were found to be not actually equal in intelligence, industry, or strength, then it was the function of human reason through the *"pacte social"* to redress the balance by good laws— instead of encouraging the tendency to inequality by sanctioning the accumulation of property in the hands of the few.

The second argument began by hypothesizing a state of natural equality in which all the cultivated land in France, sixty-six million arpents, was divided equally among the nation's six million families to produce an ideal situation in which the average holding of eleven arpents (about fourteen acres) would be perfectly adequate to enable every family to live a decent life of plenty. By making provision for a frugal sufficiency for all, nature had thus established a natural right among men to that sufficiency. Nature was, however, economical. If there was enough for all it was demonstrable that there was only *just* enough. Hence, if some were to enjoy a superfluity others must be deprived of necessities. Equality of consumption was, therefore, a self-evident law of nature and individual opulence was a violation of natural justice. Henceforward this conception of the natural right of all to an equal share of the adequate but restricted bounty of nature, here outlined in detail for the first time, would become the fundamental axiom of Babeuf's political thought. It became the underlying moral sanction for the successive practical revolutionary programs by which he sought to restore an ever greater measure of the ideal, or absolute, equality to the conditions of everyday life.

The third argument used in the *Cadastre perpétuel* to demonstrate the conditional nature of property derived from an examination of the origins of feudal rights. Here Babeuf began by demolishing the argument from prescription or *"respect des propriétés."* The mere buying and selling of rights could not establish them as "property," exempt from the conditions imposed by the prior and imprescriptible rights of man. But in incidentally pursuing the argument that feudal property derived originally from usurpation and fraud, Babeuf was challenging the legitimacy of all property, as he himself cheerfully recognized.

The final argument for the conditional nature of the right of property was of a quite different, and more pragmatic, quality. The poor were in a majority, and, once conscious of their strength, were in a practical position to abolish existing property altogether. Of twenty-four million Frenchmen fifteen million were entirely without property. It was inconceivable that this majority would continue to respect the "right" of the nine million property-owners to allow them to starve at will. In Rome, when the plebeians had demanded the equal redivision of the land, the patricians had managed to hoodwink them into the conviction that they, the patricians, were in possession of the superior force. But this was no longer the case, since now power lay unquestionably with numbers. The people now had the strength, if they wished to use it, to overthrow the feudal usurpation of the land and divide up the big landed estates among the majority of the inhabitants of the countryside, thus securing a decent sufficiency for all.[23]

The enthusiastic and vigorous language of this section of the *Cadastre perpétuel* led Professor Dalin to the conviction that Babeuf had already become by 1789, in deadly earnest, an advocate of the redistribution of property. But even the most apparently revolutionary paragraph is deliberately left in the hypothetical case, and Babeuf's conclusion—"We shall leave those who appreciate the principles of natural law to pass the proper judgment on these ideas"— is ambiguous. What this postscript actually means may be best appreciated by reference to another passage of the *Cadastre perpétuel* where Babeuf explains that he has no intention of "pretending to reform the world to the extent of wishing to restore exact primitive equality." His intention, he says, is only "to demonstrate that all who have fallen into misfortune have the right to demand" such a restoration "if opulence persists in refusing them honorable assistance, and the way in which they should be treated as equals."[24]

The purpose of the appeals to general principle in the *Cadastre perpétuel* is to provide an absolute standard of social justice against which to measure the injustice of existing conditions and the adequacy of ameliorating reforms. It is true that, using the identical principles of natural right and the social contract laid down in the *Cadastre perpétuel*, it would be perfectly possible to provide a theoretical justification for either pure communism or a general redistribution of the land. In the context of 1789 it was Babeuf's intention to use them instead to justify a much more moderate program of redistributive taxation and a program of state welfare for the poor, for the great majority of Frenchmen.

There was also a clear secondary aim: to make a profit from the publication of the *Cadastre perpétuel*, and, hopefully, to secure a post in the administration of the national survey which (it was recommended) should accompany the imposition of the new tax. "After this work is completed," Babeuf boasted in private correspondence, "it will serve for ages. . . . Its permanent form will make it just as applicable in a hundred years' time as it is today, despite the innumerable changes which will inescapably take place." It is surely running against common sense to argue that the man who wrote that was already thinking in imminent terms of the complete abolition of property through social revolution.

In practice, if social revolution were to come about, it would scarcely be as a result of any inflammatory message from the *Cadastre perpétuel*. It would be dramatic to picture Robespierre, Pétion and Brissot drawing reinforcement for their developing radicalism from a careful reading of their complimentary copies, but somewhat fanciful. There is no evidence that anybody apart from Constantini ever took Babeuf's book seriously. Certainly it did not sell; on 28 January 1790 Audiffred wrote in disgust to his co-author that he had received hard cash for only four copies.[25] The *Cadastre perpétuel* would appear to have been a catastrophic failure, both as a commercial venture and as a political manifesto. More than the publication of the Word was required to make a revolution.

Five

The Tax Rebellion of 1789-1790

S ome recent disturbances have taken place in this city, for want of bread," an English traveler wrote from Amiens, the chief town of Picardy, in September 1789, "a plea, I fear, that has much truth in it, as I never remember to have seen so great a number of beggars in any city I have passed through: they flock through the streets in immense crowds and are sometimes exceedingly riotous on being refused their request, or rather demand."

That same summer the municipality reported that 11,500, or more than a quarter of the town's population of 40,000, were in extreme poverty, making Amiens a fitting capital for a province notorious for the wretchedness of its inhabitants during the closing years of the Ancien Régime. An investigation in 1790 yielded an estimate of 52,-000 poor in the Amiens tax district in 1788, or one in twelve of the population; the figure for the adjoining Soissons tax district was one in six or one in seven.[1]

Both in the *Cadastre perpétuel* and in his notes on collective leases, Babeuf had included passages of indignation at the plight of the poor in his native province, and condemned the prevalence of unemployment and low wages. But up to now the solutions he proposed had been "solutions of the study," based on appeals to the Mirabeaus and the Dubois of the world through the universal language of reason. Now, confronted with a general and spontaneous uprising of the people of Picardy, he would turn to experiment, for the first time, with the practical possibilities of organized mass political pressure as a means to achieve concrete reforms.

The crisis of the Ancien Régime was particularly acute in Picardy for a number of reasons. Thanks to the capitalization of farming and to eighteenth-century increases in population Picardy was not a land of self-sufficient peasants; already, quite early in the century, three-quarters of the population of the province did not own or lease enough land to satisfy their needs. To survive, the majority of peasant families had to rely to a greater or lesser degree on industrial earnings. Picardy had become one of the chief textile regions of France, with perhaps a quarter of a million men, women and children engaged in wool, linen and cotton manufacture. Established centers like Amiens, Abbeville, Saint-Quentin and Beauvais continued to possess their working-class suburbs; and the spread of industry into the countryside accelerated, as entrepreneurs from these centers organized the putting out and collection of work to take advantage of cheap labor in the villages.

Because of these developments Picardy was hard hit by the general depression of the French textile industry in the 1780s. The royal intendant, Tolozan, maintained in 1789 that the Eden treaty for freer trade (negotiated with Britain in 1785) had resulted in unemployment for 200,000 workers in the textile districts. Arthur Young, on his visits to Amiens, Abbeville and Beauvais, found the manufacturers united in blaming the treaty for the severe recession in trade. Whether or not the Eden treaty was responsible, the recession was a fact; and it created great hardship throughout Picardy, throwing 36,000 out of work in Amiens and Abbeville alone.[2]

Other parts of France, notably Normandy and Lyons, felt the effects of the crisis in textiles as badly or worse. In Picardy, however, the crisis was aggravated by a special local catastrophe. In July 1788 the wheat harvest, already unpromising after a nationwide drought and severe winter frosts, was halved by unseasonal hailstorms which swept across the province. Industrial staples like flax and hemp were decimated at the same time. The bad harvest of 1788 contributed to the effects of unemployment by reducing the demand for seasonal labor in the dependent trades, and it intensified the miseries of the unemployed and the poor by driving up the price of grain, as speculators cornered supplies in anticipation of scarcity in the spring of 1789. On top of all this the winter of 1788-9 was unusually cold in northern France, with eighty-six days of frost; the rivers froze over and the mills stopped work, aggravating both unemployment and the shortage of flour.

The double crisis of unemployment and scarcity prices resulted in a widespread movement of popular revolt in Picardy during the spring and summer of 1789. As always in times of dearth the grain trade became a target for popular violence. Rioting crowds invaded the markets and attacked convoys along roads and rivers, seeking to impose "popular" prices and to prevent grain export. Individual *accapareurs* (or grain-cornerers) were also occasionally attacked. In May 1789 there were riots in the markets at Roye and at Montdidier close by; and the countryside around Saint-Quentin was terrorized by bands of two to five hundred peasants who marched around imposing fixed prices on bread and grain, ransacking seigneurial and church granaries, and preventing the movement of grain on the roads.[3]

In July there was a second wave of outbreaks of which the most significant was in the province capital, Amiens. Concerned at the growing threat of famine a group of Amiens merchants and financiers had formed a consortium to import more than three-quarters of a million livres' worth of grain from England and Holland—to be sold without profit for the duration of the crisis. On 14 July, however, the population of Amiens intervened, when a vast crowd, armed with cudgels, surrounded the intendant's residence and forced him (before fleeing the city) to cut the selling price by a half. The mob then stormed the Hôtel de Ville and compelled the municipal government to agree to this regulation, which remained in force for several months, during which time not only the inhabitants of Amiens but crowds of peasants from the surrounding countryside flocked in to buy cheap supplies. The movement spread across the province, as villagers banded together to intercept Amiens-bound convoys and to demand grain at the "Amiens price."[4]

Outside the Amiens region, violence was chiefly directed against attempts to export grain to Paris or via the ports. At Péronne, for example, crowds stopped flour wagons on the way to Paris on 31 July; on 31 January 1790 they seized four cartloads of grain destined for Valenciennes. On 28 October 1789 the inhabitants of the village of Desvres in the Boulonnais stopped a grain export convoy, sold the grain, and also the horses and the wagon, and threatened to hang the carters. At Ham, in December, the population negotiated a truce with the local farmers, agreeing to release grain for export only on condition that the growers agreed to stock the local market with enough grain to last until August the following year.[5]

These disturbances, like the Amiens outbreak, reflected one aspect of a general determination of the peasants and laborers of Picardy to impose their desperate will to survive on a collapsing society. At the

same time a wider and more sustained popular revolt was directed
against the royal excise administration of the General Farmers. Particularly hated targets were the collectors of the *gabelles* (the salt taxes) and the administration of the *aides*, duties which raised the cost
of food and alcoholic drinks and such items as soap, iron, leather,
and wood. The depots of the *tabac* (the state tobacco monopoly) and
the collectors of the *entrées* (local tolls levied at the gates of the
towns) were also frequently attacked.

The resentment felt by the French people against the burden of
taxes in 1789 was general and universal. Professor Marion has shown
how, as a nationwide movement, the "tax rebellion" of 1789-90 affected places as far apart as Roussillon and Artois, or Arles and
Caen, reducing receipts from direct taxes by a half to two-thirds, and
those from indirect taxes sometimes by as much as 80 percent.
However, because of various historical accidents, popular grievances
seem to have been more strongly felt in Picardy than elsewhere. With
Paris and Normandy, Picardy is generally conceded to have been one
of the three most heavily taxed regions of France in terms of the
burden per head of the population. In particular, the province (as
pays de grande gabelle) was subjected to an especially heavy salt tax.
Only four generalities of France were subject to both the *gros* and the
augmentation on wine—sales taxes on both price and quantity. The
boundaries of two of them, Amiens and Soissons, included most of
Picardy. Moreover, some parts of Picardy were more heavily taxed
than others. The parts of the Generality of Amiens subject to the
jurisdiction of the Rouen Cour des Aides, for example, paid the
quatrième, a retail duty of 25 percent on brandy and beer, and 20
percent on wine, while those subject to the Paris Cour des Aides paid
only the *huitième*, a smaller duty.[6]

In the spring of 1789 the bitter popular feeling against the indirect
taxes found some expression in the cahiers drawn up for the Estates-
General at Versailles. Thus the parish of Ayencourt and Le Monchel
(close to Montdidier and in a countryside well known to Babeuf),
after fairly curtly demanding the end of the salt tax since "peasants
live chiefly on soup," went on to append a tirade against the *aides*.
On top of other taxes the weight of the *aides* reduced most wine-
growers, "who have no other resources, to the most frightful misery,
forcing them to beg for bread during most of the year." The same exactions "place hindrances in the way of commerce and ruin those artisans whose trades they affect." Moreover, the excise agents, "by
their frequent and unjust prosecutions, keep the people in a state of

slavery." Furthermore, why did Montdidier pay the *quatrième* when other parts paid only the *huitième*? The petitioners concluded that the king should abolish *aides* on necessities like "wine, meat, drink and other foodstuffs," retaining duties, if unavoidable, only on luxury fabrics like silk and gauze (*gaze*), and on nonessential comestibles like brandy and coffee, thus dispensing with the unnecessary army of tax officials.[7]

The same bitterness is distilled in the cahier of the parish of Grécourt, in the neighboring Bailliage of Noyon, drawn up by a hamlet in which all twenty households were composed of agricultural laborers and their dependents, eking out a miserable existence in a marshy and infertile hollow. The laborers of Grécourt may perhaps be allowed to speak for the generality of laborers and peasants of the twenty-seven rural parishes of Noyon, every one of which demanded the suppression of the *aides* and the *gabelles:*

"It is a hard thing when a wretched workingman who dies of hunger if he misses a day's work, who has only a few fruit trees from which he has made a drink, cannot make some money from that drink to buy bread without losing half the value of the drink, and if ever a *commis* catches him carrying a pint of cider in his hand to his neighbor to exchange it for bread, he is dragged off pitilessly to prison, for failing to pay the fine. Poor workingmen are happy enough when they manage to gain twelve or fifteen sols per day to support themselves and their families. Bread! that is their cry. Soup! that is the summit of their desires. . . .

"But is this soup a thick soup, or a chicken in the pot? No, only boiled water but with at least a little salt in it, bought more dearly than bread: at least this commodity ought to be cheaper for these unfortunate people. . . ."

The inhabitants of another parish in the Noyonnais, Pont l'Evêque, offered a more general but equally heartfelt condemnation of "the insatiable avidity of the General Farmers, who have always and at all times suggested special methods for bleeding the people and making them carry the weight of imposts of every name and of every kind and on all products, whatever, and above all on drink."[8]

So universal and deeply felt was the resentment against the burden of indirect taxation in Picardy that the demand for the abolition of the *aides* and the *gabelles* found expression in the cahiers of the clergy and the joint cahier of the nobility and the Third Estate of Péronne, even though many of the clergy, nobles, and bourgeois who were responsible for their drafting were privileged and personally

The destruction of the Paris excise barriers, 12 July 1789

more or less exempt from the full weight of the *aides* and the other taxes.[9]

The signal for the first attacks on excise barriers and officials in Picardy was given by Paris. As early as 10 July 1789, four days before the fighting round the Bastille, bands of Parisians had begun the systematic destruction of the excise posts which surrounded the capital. In the course of four days' rioting no less than forty of the fifty-four posts were burned down and the officials driven out. Traveling along the major routes to the northeastern frontier the news from Paris reached the cluster of small Picard market towns to which Roye belonged. Almost immediately riots broke out at Roye, Péronne, Saint-Quentin and in the neighborhood of Noyon.[10]

The events at Péronne, a town of about 5,000 people, may be taken as characteristic of the outbreaks. On the morning of 18 July a mixed crowd of peasants and "some workers and apprentices from the town" marched on two guardhouses and the customs house in the Faubourg de Bretagne. They sacked and pillaged the buildings, destroying the furniture and chasing out the officials. At Roye the *bureaux de déclaration* at the gates of the town were destroyed, and de Larabit, the *directeur des aides*, was forced to suspend the collection altogether. While order was restored fairly rapidly at Péronne and Saint-Quentin, Roye became a center of the most stubborn resistance. Wagonloads of dutiable goods continued to be met at the town gates and escorted in by triumphant crowds. Contraband salt and tobacco were sold openly in the town and the surrounding countryside. New cabarets sprang up, opened on the strength of the duty-free wine, beer and spirits, and the local peasants, looking to the future, began to plant tobacco.[11]

From Péronne, Roye and Saint-Quentin the rebellion spread to the other towns of the province and also to the peasant villages. On 16 August rioters attacked and burned the house of Morillot, *directeur des aides* at Doullens, and made a bonfire of his papers in the middle of the street. The following day the offices of the collector of customs and the *gabelles* and the tobacco depot were similarly treated. On 12 October the furniture and effects of the excise agent at Hervilly were thrown into the street by the inhabitants. On the 25th four to five hundred peasants from several villages gathered to attack the customs house at Fins, a few miles from Péronne, breaking up the furniture, cutting and tearing the clothes of the local officer, and threatening fire and blood if the *aides* were restored.

Sporadic violence continued into 1790. According to Lambert (the controller-general of finance), Marduel, the parish *curé*, was behind two attacks on the houses of excise agents at Airanes in January and February 1790. In March the agents were finally driven out of the township with jeers and stones. In mid-January there was fresh trouble at Doullens, where an attempt to destroy the new house of the *directeur des aides* was defeated. Yet another riot was reported from Mareuil, near Abbeville, on 26 February, when a party of excisemen, protected by troops, descended on an inn to inspect the stock. The tocsin was promptly rung in the neighboring village of Coubert, and peasants from all the adjoining parishes gathered, armed with scythes and sticks.[12]

Doubtless in many cases the spearhead of the movement against the *aides* was provided by detachments of professional smugglers, for whom the collapse of royal authority heralded a period of general carnival. At the same time there is no doubt that the movement represented a genuine popular rebellion against the hated régime of the General Farmers and their *commis*.

Nobody understood better than Babeuf, the son of a *gabelou*, the depth of the popular feeling against the *aides* and the *gabelles*. In the *Cadastre perpétuel* he voiced a personal condemnation of the "bloodsuckers" and "vampires" of the excise administration; and while he remained in Paris he followed closely the spread of the national movement of rebellion against the *aides*. On 4 September 1789 Babeuf wrote home to Marie-Anne from Paris eagerly requesting the latest news from Roye about the fate of the *aides* and the *gabelles*. During 1789, however, he played no personal part in the movement. Ironically enough, he had remained in Roye during July just long enough for the Paris rioting to die down, only to set out for Paris just before the riots spread to Roye.

After his return to Roye in the middle of October, Babeuf was at first very busy with an attempt to restore his personal fortunes through a journalistic enterprise. In September he had entered into an agreement with the editor and publisher Panckouke to provide regular correspondence on the debates of the National Assembly, and on the general news of Paris and the provinces, for the *Courrier de l'Europe*, published in London under the editorship of de la Tour. The arrangements were particularly attractive to Babeuf, since he was to receive twelve livres a week for work he could easily do at Roye. Babeuf's papers contain a completed manuscript correspondence for the week 1 to 8 October. There are also notes for further contributions for the rest of October, culled chiefly from

Marat's *Ami du peuple*, Mercier's *Annales patriotiques*, and Prudhomme's *Révolutions de Paris*; but nothing by Babeuf was ever published in the *Courrier de l'Europe*, nor did he receive any money for his work. On 14 November, Audiffred—the universal provider —wrote to say that de la Tour had defaulted on money he had lent to him, and had suspended the journal for lack of funds; and he advised that Babeuf should discontinue his connection.

In growing desperation Babeuf now tried to interest an Amiens bookseller, Caron-Berquier, in the projected publication of a *Journal des assemblées de la province*, apparently to report the proceedings of the Estates of Picardy. In the first days of 1790 he even wrote to Van der Noot, leader of the anti-Austrian rebellion in the Austrian Netherlands, offering to edit a journal dedicated to his Belgian cause. All this came to nothing, as did a contemporary intrigue to try to secure the post of secretary to the municipality of Amiens, through Caron-Berquier's good offices.[13]

The year 1789 had ended bleakly for Babeuf. His aristocratic clients continued to default on their debts. His career as a *feudiste* lay in ruins. The *Cadastre perpétuel* was a failure, and the *Courrier de l'Europe* had proved a weak reed.

His personal and political enemies, the "viziers of Roye," continued to dominate the affairs of the town undisturbed, as if the revolution had never been.

At the beginning of 1789 the municipality of Roye consisted of the mayor, two *échevins,* two *assesseurs*, the *procureur du roi*, a secretary and a treasurer. The chief officers were elected by a college of eleven deputies representing the clergy, the nobility, the bourgeois and the different corporations and guilds. The regulations of 1773 laid down that important questions of finance should be referred to a general assembly, called by the secretary. During 1789 elements of the old municipality continued to govern the town, meeting as a *comité permanent* of twelve members. On 7 and 9 February 1790 elections were held under new general regulations introduced by the National Assembly. Louis-Charles Billecocq was confirmed as mayor, his brother Louis-François Billecocq du Mirail became *procureur-général syndic*, and a municipal council was elected which included the *avocat* Masson and the notaries Grégoire d'Essigny and Longuecamp. The first elections for the Somme departmental administration in May-July would follow the same pattern; among the seven second-degree electors chosen for Roye were the two Billecocqs, Masson and Aubé de Bracquemont from Damery. In

July 1790 Louis-Charles Billecocq completed a remarkable record of successful adaptation when he accepted election as president of the directory of the new District of Montdidier, within which the town of Roye was included. His successive offices—president of the bailliage and mayor of Roye under the Old Régime, president of the *comité permanent*, mayor of Roye and president of the district under the new—were a symbol of the continuity of the old patterns of life in Roye despite the revolution. The "legal aristocracy" continued to dominate the town and its affairs almost unchallenged.[14]

Only the continued difficulties of de Larabit, the *directeur des aides*, and J.B. Goret, the president of the *grenier à sel*, upset the smoothness of the transition. After the violence in July 1789 the *comité permanent* of Roye had made little attempt to restore the excise collection or the domestic visits by inspectors on which the administration of the *aides* on wine, cider and beer depended. They preferred to wait (their spokesman afterwards explained) until the good harvest of 1789 had brought the people to a better frame of mind. Before long, however, Paris began to prod local administrations into taking more positive action. On 23 September the National Assembly published a decree declaring the continuing liability of all citizens to the existing indirect taxes, with certain modifications for the time being; and on 22 October the minister of finance circularized the administration at Roye drawing the members' attention to this decree.

On 12 and 25 December Lambert, the controller-general of finances, sent letters couched in stronger terms to remind the members of the *comité permanent* of their duty and to urge immediate and effective action to restore the *aides*.

Apart from the menace of popular violence the chief resistance to this "counteroffensive" came from the innkeepers and brewers and other drink-sellers, of whom there were more than a hundred in business at Roye. While they were prepared to compromise over other matters, the *cabaretiers* and *aubergistes* of Roye were adamant in their refusal to agree to the restoration of domestic visits and the inspection of their stock, for this would have opened the way to a demand for arrears of duty. After a series of conferences at the Hôtel de Ville only three *cabaretiers* could be persuaded (on 17 December) to agree to allow the excise inspectors to carry out their functions. The remainder offered to pay a single tax at the gates of the town instead of the previous complex series of charges.[15]

Babeuf followed the negotiations closely. He had returned from

Paris in October determined to shake the hold of the Billecocq clique over Roye; and he was quick to realize the value of the excise issue as a means of isolating the administration from the general body of the citizens. At the beginning of January 1790 he drafted a petition criticizing the September decree, attacking the attempt to restore the *aides* and *gabelles* and advocating the imposition of a supplementary direct and proportional tax in their place.

Nothing appears to have come of this project immediately. But on 20 February the Communauté des Marchands de Vin, Aubergistes et Cabaretiers de la Ville de Roye commissioned Babeuf to draw up a petition to the National Assembly in which they withdrew their earlier compromise offer and now absolutely rejected the proposal to restore the *aides* in any form. In defense of this stand they cited the assembly's decree of 7 October 1789 which established the general principle of equal and proportional taxation for all citizens.

The attitude of the administration had also hardened. On 25 January the National Assembly published a further decree ordering the restoration of the existing tax machinery, pending the long-term general reorganization of the tax system. On 23 February yet another decree followed, ordering municipal authorities to support the tax and excise agents in their operations up to the hilt. Together these decrees gave the signal for a general counteroffensive by the authorities during the next few weeks. At Roye, Larabit secured the support of the municipal administration for a complete restoration of the excise machinery, including the reopening of the *bureaux de déclaration* and visits of inspection to determine arrears due since 18 July 1789. On Sunday, 28 February, the *cabaretiers* were called to the Hôtel de Ville to hear the bad news. On Monday a town crier with a drum visited the three gates of the town to make a public announcement. He was not prepared to penetrate the Faubourg Saint-Gilles and only stood on the bridge to shout his news.

On Tuesday the excise agents began their work with the support of the *maréchaussée*, which was, however, deliberately sent out without guns to prevent bloodshed. Almost immediately a riot broke out at the Cheval Blanc. A crowd from the Faubourg Saint-Gilles and from the town chased off a party of inspectors, and the entire operation had to be abandoned. On the following Sunday, Babeuf attended a session of the municipality at the Hôtel de Ville, most probably together with a crowd of supporters; and he delivered a general attack on the record of the administration. In an impassioned speech he warned the authorities that the final veto on unjust laws belonged to the people. He promised personally to lead armed resistance if troops were sent in to enforce the collection of the *aides*.[16]

By directing his appeal for resistance over the heads of the municipality to the people of Roye, Babeuf had for the first time assumed the rôle of popular spokesman or tribune. A new phase of his life had begun.

For the moment, his following was restricted to Roye and to the Faubourg Saint-Gilles in particular. Immediately, however, he began to make plans for a wider campaign of popular resistance against the *aides*. In Paris (in the autumn of 1789) and since his return to Roye Babeuf had followed closely the developing techniques of popular organization and direct democracy pioneered by the sixty Paris districts through popular meetings and joint petitions.

When liberty had been recovered at Paris (as he explained in a brochure published in May 1790), it had become the custom for a citizen to sound public opinion, to draft a motion and to seek support for his motion at the district meetings. By this means, when the majority of the districts adopted the motion, the "general will" could become known and thus the task of legislators in putting that will into effect would be facilitated.[17]

At the end of March 1790 Babeuf wrote to friends at Péronne, one of the chief centers of resistance to the *aides*, commending a recent success of the Paris districts in organizing a united petition campaign and proposing that the local patriots should make use of the same technique in their fight against the *aides*. "Let us set an example—and who can doubt that the province will follow us?"

At the beginning of April he visited Saint-Quentin, Noyon and Péronne to gather support (and funds) for a general petition to be printed by Devin. The plan was to send a copy of the petition to every parish, firstly of the Péronne region, later of all Picardy, ultimately of the entire kingdom. The petition was ready for distribution on 16 April, and by the end of April the campaign was beginning to make itself felt. On 23 April "half the *cabaretiers*" of Montdidier signed at a public meeting.

On 26 April the municipal administration of Péronne wrote to the National Assembly formally disavowing the agitation and indignantly and disingenuously denying that Péronne was its center. The petition had then been circulating in the countryside for some days. About the same date the *directeur des aides* at Amiens reported that the Péronne brewers and the *cabaretiers* of Péronne and Roye had approached their opposite numbers at Amiens, and that the petition was winning some support. The *aubergistes* of Péronne were equally held to be responsible for the appearance of the petition at Guise—where the campaign was enlivened by the presence of a wandering street singer, or *marchand des chansons*, who went from village to village, heralded by a drum, to "sing the suppression of the *aides*." The same singer turned up at Ham and also at Noyon, where he was refused permission to sing or to hand out the words of his songs.[18]

A special effort was made in the campaign to gain the support of the parish priests, as the natural leaders of the village community, and not without some success. On 29 April, for example, Veret, for thirty-four years *curé* of Villiers-les-Roye (a village of about 300 inhabitants not far from Roye), signed a copy of the petition together with a dozen of his parishioners—despite some cautious reservations as to the intemperance of its language. "One Sunday in May" Pierre Vasseur, *curé* of Longueval, read out Babeuf's petition from the pulpit. Then he himself issued a spirited call to his parishioners to massacre the excise agents without mercy and to refuse to accept the assembly's decrees; Vasseur then signed the document, together with many of those present. Two months later he was arrested for organizing a riot and for urging that the mayor and some others (who had retracted their signatures) should be lynched.[19]

On 13 May, when Babeuf forwarded a copy of the petition to the National Assembly, he claimed the support of "a thousand communities." No doubt this was an exaggeration. But there can have been few villages and no towns of any size in Picardy where the petition was not received and discussed by the municipality, the *curé*, or the regulars at the local taverns.

Babeuf's part in the campaign against the *aides* has been seen by some writers as a mercenary arrangement in which Babeuf acted as a hired propagandist for the liquor trade lobby. In so far as the initial financial support and much of the organizing initiative came from the brewers and innkeepers, there is an element of truth in this interpretation. It is equally true that Babeuf's contribution was not entirely altruistic. He certainly hoped and expected to make some money out of the sale of copies of his petition. He even sent three hundred copies to Audiffred, asking him to put them on sale in Paris.[20] It is quite clear, however, that profit was very much a secondary consideration. To Babeuf the question of the *aides* was not a matter of local significance which concerned one special-interest group only, but a matter of general principle for the people as a whole, and his chief concern was to use the petition as a vehicle for the general political education of the population of Picardy.

Thus, at the same time as he rehearsed the practical grievances of the victims of an unjust tax system and an arbitrary administration, Babeuf was careful to explain the political principle which lay behind the use of the right of petition itself. In this way the inhabitants of the remote villages and working-class faubourgs of Picardy were introduced to the same principles of direct democracy on which the advanced revolutionaries of the Paris districts were currently basing their campaign for political autonomy: that is, to the notion of a representative system limited by popular mandate, referendum, and veto.[21]

For Babeuf the Rousseauist jargon used to justify the popular defiance of the National Assembly over the *aides* had a deeper political significance as the foundation for the development of a general democratic program.

"A man who gives power of attorney to another does not sanction anything to which his mandatory may agree which may be to his detriment, when it has not been authorized by the mandate. . . . The people do not forget that it is they who have given you representative power, that every representative ought to act according to the will of his principal, that the whole is greater than the part, that the constituent is higher than the constituted, and that often when it is a question of particular interests—and always, when it is a question affecting the whole nation—the sanction of the former is necessary to confirm the operations of the latter."[22]

In another section of the petition Babeuf ingeniously managed to smuggle in some personal ideas on the social question which had nothing whatsoever to do with the interests of the liquor trade. At the end of 1789 the National Assembly had nationalized the lands of the French church. At the time Babeuf was writing, arrangements were under way for selling the land. In his petition Babeuf raised the question of the church lands ostensibly only as a practical solution to the problem of the resettlement of excise officers thrown out of employment by the abolition of taxes. At the same time, however, he hinted at a much more general redistribution of this land among the landless and needy, and he promised to publish details later.

Babeuf never did publish these promised details; but the general outline of his projected scheme is indicated by references in his correspondence in June and July 1790. What Babeuf had in mind was an arrangement by which the lands of the church would not be sold to capitalists and speculators but would instead be leased by the state to peasants on long leases. The April petition did not spell out the terms of any such proposal. It did include a clear invitation to the landless and the needy to think hard about the future disposal of the church lands as a possible solution to their hardships.

In September 1789 Babeuf had been particularly impressed (while following the debates on the Declaration of the Rights of Man in the National Assembly) by the contribution of Pétion, deputy for the Third Estate of Chartres. He now invoked a proposed additional "right" which Pétion had then put forward, as a justification for the use of the church lands to solve the social question.

"Each citizen ought to have an assured existence, be it from the revenue from his properties, be it from his labor and his industry. And if infirmities or misfortunes reduce him to misery, society ought to provide for his subsistence." This might easily have served as a summary of Babeuf's own program as advanced in the *Cadastre perpétuel*. Now it was linked for the first time with practical prescriptions for realization through popular political pressure.[23]

There is no way of measuring the impact of such ideas on the hundreds, and perhaps thousands, of persons who read Babeuf's pamphlet. There was certainly a wide response to its more immediate appeal to "cut, slice, smash, break these cursed *aides* and *gabelles*."

The circulation of the petition was accompanied by a revival of violence throughout Picardy. At Péronne the municipality reported on 26 April that the inhabitants of the Faubourg de Paris had ordered the employees of the tax farm out of the town "in twenty-four hours" and that those of the Faubourg de Bretagne were preparing a similar demonstration. At Landisaye a small civil war broke out when excisemen tried to interrupt a consignment of untaxed beer from the Cambrésis. A riot over a cask of cider at Saint-Valéry on 3 May led to the complete abandonment of the *aides* on cider, wood, and meat there. At La Fère on 12 May the soldiers of the garrison themselves encouraged the retailers to resist inspection and to refuse to pay duty. At Montreuil-sur-Mer the inhabitants armed themselves with canes and sticks and drove out the officials after threatening to drown them in the harbor. Similar riots and disturbances were reported from many other places during 1790.[24]

In one of the biggest outbreaks, at Saint-Quentin on 21 May, four or five hundred "brigands" pillaged the house of the *directeur des fermes*. On this occasion the "tax riot" was combined with a riot directed against a grain speculator, de Lartigue, a canon of the collegiate church. After sacking de Lartigue's house the rioters seized a convoy of grain and invaded the market. Order was not restored for a week, until the local National Guard had been reinforced by the *maréchaussée*, a detachment of the National Guard from Ham, and a troop of regulars from the Bourbon-Dragons, who made twenty arrests.

On 28 June the controller-general of finances, Lambert, addressing the National Assembly, painted a grim picture of virtually the entire province of Picardy given over to anarchy, and he forecasted a reduction in expected local receipts from the *aides* from 3,800,000 to 800,000 livres, a fall of approximately 80 percent.[25]

At the end of March the assembly had formally abandoned the *gabelles* and some other taxes as unenforceable, but it remained determined to salvage the *aides*, and the national credit along with them. Between this determination and the sharpening hostility of the Roye municipality Babeuf was about to be caught and crushed.

On 10 March Billecocq sent an account of the previous week's troubles at Roye, together with a copy of Babeuf's inflammatory speech of 7 March, to Paris. A few days later this packet was followed by a copy of a somewhat ambiguous placard posted by Babeuf on 15 March appearing to incite armed rebellion. This evidence was forwarded by the minister of finance to the Cour des Aides on 3 April, and it decreed Babeuf's arrest.[26]

The Cour des Aides was not the sole master of the situation however. Since it was an institution of the Ancien Régime, its ways of proceeding and its own existence were under constant and critical scrutiny (especially since a committee of the National Assembly was engaged at the precise moment in a general investigation of the tax system). The deputies of the National Assembly were compelled to weigh their actions very carefully. On the one hand, the dignity of the assembly had to be upheld and the national revenue assured. On the other hand, the assembly was revolutionary and its leaders could not afford to take too strong a position against the leaders of the revolutionary movement in the country. The Comité des Rapports decided, in effect, to try persuasion first rather than repression.

On 3 April Grégoire (as secretary of the committee) sent a reasoned reply to the Roye *cabaretiers'* petition of 20 February, refuting Babeuf's arguments. He appealed to the petitioners to pay their lawful taxes as good citizens. On 5 April he wrote a further conciliatory letter to Roye arguing that Babeuf might have been led astray by nothing more than an excess of revolutionary zeal and he should be given a chance to mend his ways. For the moment, therefore, no action was taken to execute the warrant of the Cour des Aides. But by the beginning of May the development of the petition campaign had made it clear that Grégoire's optimism was misplaced and another committee of the assembly, the Comité des Recherches, decided to take action. Babeuf's petition was now denounced as subversive of the public order, and the municipal administration of Noyon was ordered to ban its printing and circulation. On 10 May Babeuf sent the Comité des Recherches an indignant protest, with much flourishing of the Declaration of the Rights of Man; and this, too, was printed and circulated. On 13 May he wrote to Mounier, president of the National Assembly, demanding that the assembly should discuss the banned petition.[27]

The response was dramatic. At 8 p.m. on Tuesday, 18 May, a bailiff of the Cour des Aides (with two *cavaliers de robe courte*) arrived in Roye. They went first to the Billecocqs' house to obtain witnesses and more men, and then they waited until after dark. A party of ten men broke into Babeuf's house, where he was asleep (sharing a bed with Robert). After hearing the warrant read, Babeuf submitted; his hands were fettered, and he was led away. He was then escorted to Paris on the mail coach. He was put into the Conciergerie prison at 2 a.m. on Friday, 21 May.[28]

Six

"The Marat of the Somme"

The Conciergerie prison on the Ile de la Cité, where Babeuf was to remain for seven weeks, was the old prison of the Parlement de Paris. It was close by the Palais de Justice, where the Cour des Aides also held its sessions. Like the other common prisons of the Old Régime (the Châtelet, La Force, the Abbaye), it was noted for overcrowding and filth. During 1790 there were normally about five hundred prisoners "in residence," many of them lodged in the *chambres de paille* in the gloomy and damp cellars. Once a fortnight the inmates were provided with a clean shirt by a charitable organization.

The procedures of judicial torture had been only recently abolished (in 1787-8). A miasma of cruelty and terror still clung to the building. Prisoners were still kept shackled in their cells, as they awaited the harsh and as yet unreformed punishments of the Ancien Régime: hanging, breaking on the wheel, the galleys, the whip, the ax. As late as 11 August 1790 the Parlement de Paris upheld the sentence passed by a royal court on Louis Tonnellier, a murderer (and Babeuf's fellow prisoner), that he should have his arms, legs, thighs and back smashed by the executioner before being left on the wheel "for as long as it should please God to preserve his life."[1]

The days of the Cour des Aides might be numbered—it would be abolished in September—but the court still formed part of an immensely powerful machinery of repression. As its prisoner Babeuf was now compelled to begin a bitter struggle: possibly for his life, certainly for his liberty. He decided on an aggressive campaign, attacking the Cour des Aides on several fronts, both judicial and political, seeking always to exploit the ambiguity of the position of this relic of the Ancien Régime. His legal defense was to deny the continuing competence of the court. If he was accused of "armed revolt," he argued, he should have been prosecuted by the Châtelet; if it was a matter of "resistance against taxes" the proper court was now the court of first instance, the tribunal of the newly constituted District of Montdidier.

His first act after his imprisonment had been to contact the journalist Rutledge and to enlist his aid in lobbying the National Assembly. Rutledge was by this time an influential figure in Paris revolutionary circles. At the end of 1789 he had himself spent two months in the Châtelet prison for a press attack on Necker. Defended by Marat in the *Ami du peuple*, he had emerged with a halo of martyrdom, to become one of the leaders of the Cordeliers District. Now Rutledge undertook to use his influence with the Comité des Recherches to get Babeuf's prosecution quashed.

Babeuf also appealed for support from his friends in Picardy. After the arrest, Marie-Anne and Robert had followed him to Paris; and they visited the Conciergerie on 26 May. Babeuf gave his wife a list of persons to contact in Noyon, Montdidier, Péronne, and Saint-Quentin who might cooperate in gathering signatures for a petition. At first things looked promising. The members of the Comité des Recherches responded quite favorably, and Marie-Anne returned to Paris around 7 or 8 July with the petition to strengthen Babeuf's case.[2]

Unfortunately at this point the committee members began to have second thoughts. A thousand copies of Babeuf's letter of protest to the committee on 10 May had been printed and were still circulating. Worse still, a version of the letter now appeared in an issue of Rivarol's royalist "underground" newspaper, the *Actes des apôtres*, and the members of the committee were not satisfied with Babeuf's explanations. In fact there was rather more to explain away than Babeuf cared to acknowledge. On 25 May he had written to the comte de Lauraguais to appeal for help; and Marie-Anne had visited Lauraguais in his château at Manicamp, near Noyon, on her way back to Picardy.

Louis-Léon-Félicité de Lauraguais, a patron of the theater and an amateur scientist, had played a leading part in the "aristocratic revolt" before 1789. (Ironically he was destined himself to finish up in the Conciergerie, in 1794, during the Reign of Terror.) In 1790 Lauraguais' position was ambiguous. As an aristocratic critic of the "bourgeois" National Assembly, he appeared to be playing both sides against the middle. That Babeuf expected his support so confidently suggests that Lauraguais had already contributed towards financing the campaign against the *aides*, probably through Devin. Certainly from May to August 1790 this unabashed aristocrat conducted a friendly correspondence with Babeuf—at a time when he was providing sanctuary at Manicamp for the royalist journalist Rivarol and, presumably, supporting the publication of the *Actes des apôtres* and other of Rivarol's "counter-revolutionary" publications. Whether Babeuf was using Lauraguais or Lauraguais Babeuf, it was a politically compromising relationship and enough to make the Comité des Recherches lose interest in Babeuf's case.[3]

While the Babeuf prosecution was under way, Clément de Barville (*procureur* of the Cour des Aides) had begun to develop a general offensive aimed at crushing the tax strike and restoring the authority of the tax administration. From the end of February he had been gathering evidence against persons suspected of complicity in the destruction of the Paris customs barriers in July 1789. On 10 May eighty warrants were prepared, but it was not until 16 June that the first eleven arrests were made; more followed on 18 June. The implications of this new offensive were not missed by the revolutionary leaders of the capital. "If they can seek out citizens for having burned the barriers, what is to stop them from seeking out those who demolished the Bastille?" Marat's *Ami du peuple* asked.[4]

During May the ever-watchful Marat had been carrying on his personal vendetta with the police administration of the Châtelet. He printed letters from inmates attacking conditions in the prison. On 16 June the *Ami du peuple* also published a furious outburst against a report of the assembly's Comité des Finances which proposed to retain the Cour des Aides as part of a general refurbishing of the old tax-collecting machinery of the General Farmers.

The same day Babeuf wrote to Marat to applaud his attack on the proposed reforms, and to denounce the arrests and the subsequent ill-treatment of the prisoners, who had been chained up in separate cells. In this letter, which Marat published on 19 June, Babeuf called on the Paris districts and the popular societies to bring pressure to bear on the Conciergerie to secure better treatment for the prisoners. On 25 June Marat summarized the contents of another letter from Babeuf about the second wave of arrests of 18 June.[5] Babeuf seems also to have been responsible for drafting a short brochure about the arrests which began to circulate in Paris about this time.[6]

The letters in the *Ami du peuple* and the brochure were anonymous; now, however, encouraged by Marat's support, Babeuf made arrangements to publish a personal news-sheet, compiled in jail, partly to reinforce the general campaign against the Cour des Aides but also with the hope of founding a new and permanent journal. The first number of this *Journal de la confédération* (so named in honor of the anniversary celebrations planned for 14 July) appears to have been published in the last few days of June; two more numbers rapidly appeared (no. 2, dated 3 July, and no. 3, 4 July) and the manuscript of a fourth exists. Each of the published issues contained eight pages of text. Apart from continuing and documenting the theme of his attacks on the "frightful conspiracy of the General Farmers and the Cour des Aides," Babeuf carefully identified the *Journal de la confédération* with the contemporary protest of the leaders of the Paris districts against plans to reorganize the municipal government, plans that threatened their autonomy and their political cohesion.[7]

The sixty Paris districts, so active in influencing the course of the revolution since July 1789, were in fact approaching the end of their career. During July they were to be replaced by forty-eight newly delineated sections, whose powers were much more clearly defined and limited than those of the former districts. The liberation of the "victims" of the Cour des Aides, attributed by Babeuf to the initiative chiefly of the Nazareth District, was the Parthian shot of those militants who over the last few months had confronted the Châtelet in a number of successful actions in defense of Marat, Danton, and other popular leaders.[8]

Babeuf's public lamentations over the deliberate dismantling of the machinery of popular pressure which had made these triumphs possible served the practical purpose of drawing the attention of the leaders of the districts to his own predicament. At the same time they provided a peg on which to hang a general declaration of faith in the principles of "direct democracy" on which the action of the districts had been based and to which he had already paid tribute during the campaign against the *aides* in the previous months.

No. 3 of the *Journal de la confédération* was largely devoted to contrasting the practice of the Paris districts (which allowed every citizen to play a direct part in public affairs) with the situation in the provinces, and at Roye in particular, where power was in the hands of a delegated municipality. Babeuf pressed for the rejection of the reforms abolishing the districts, urging the continued vigilance of

JOURNAL
DE
LA CONFEDERATION.
(Nº. I.)

APPEL AU PEUPLE

Sur l'effroyable conspiration des fermiers-généraux
& de la cour des aides de Paris, contre tous les
bons citoyens de la capitale & du royaume.
Noms de tous les citoyens déjà emprisonnés, &
vexations criantes exercées à leur égard. Bar-
baries incroyables envers les malheureux prison-
niers. Régime de la Bastille perfectionné dans
les prisons ordinaires de la capitale. Nargue à
la fédération prochaine du 14 juillet. Insou-
ciance ou aveuglement du peuple français sur
tous les attentats formés contre sa liberté.

CE n'est point ici, citoyens, une de ces
annonces bourdonnantes, semblables à celles pour
lesquelles la politique aristocratique s'est plue,
à l'aide de quelques folliculaires soudoyés, à
vous donner mille fausses alertes, qui bientôt
vous ont habitués, ainsi que vos ennemis l'a-
voient prévu & desiré, à prendre tous les avis
pour des terreurs paniques, & à ne vous mettre
plus en garde sur rien. Il est vraiment question
ici d'un plan horrible, & dans lequel vous devez
appercevoir les mêmes tramés, & de plus mons-
trueuses peut-être, que dans celui qui se cimen-

A

Title page of no. 1 of the *Journal de la confédération*

these tried champions of democracy as essential to check the inevitable tendency of the people's representatives to shrug off popular control. At the same time he proffered certain more general guiding political principles for democrats.

"Always, in political administration, administrators tend to encroach on the rights of the administered. . . . It is in the nature of every man to wish to dominate. Let us then so arrange things that everyone dominates at once, and no person dominates in particular. . . . Above all do not lose sight of this holy maxim, *The People are the Sovereign* . . . If the people are the Sovereign, they should exercise as much sovereignty as they absolutely can themselves . . . to accomplish that which you have to do and can do yourself use representation on the fewest possible occasions and be nearly always your own representatives."

To these themes—the fatal natural tendency of men to dominate, and the need for constant vigilance and participation by the people in political life—Babeuf would return repeatedly in the course of the revolution.

Meanwhile, the practical matter of his own personal liberation remained to be arranged. In general terms Marat's campaign produced rapid and satisfactory results. To begin with, conditions in the cells were improved, the shackles were taken off, and the prisoners were allowed to communicate with one another and with outsiders. Then, in a debate of 1 July, the National Assembly ordered the freeing of all those imprisoned for their part in the events of July 1789, and the prisoners arrested in June were immediately released.

However this still left Babeuf behind bars, and there he might well have remained indefinitely, once the districts had taken care of their own, if Marat had not loyally come to his rescue. On 4 July the greater part of an issue of the *Ami du peuple* was devoted to Babeuf and his plight. Marat acknowledged Babeuf's contributions to the *Ami du peuple* in June, summarized the content of his petition against the *aides*, condemned his continued imprisonment and called upon the deputies Soulet, Paquin and Bentabole to "pay a patriotic visit to our brother Babeuf" to keep his spirits up. Two days later, on 6 July, Marat appealed directly to the Paris districts to give the same support to Babeuf as they had rendered to other prisoners.

Behind this cryptic appeal there lay a threat of violence which was effective in securing Babeuf's prompt release. On 20 July Babeuf wrote to Lauraguais, sending him fifty copies of Marat's 6 July issue, and commenting: "People were already saying that several thousand brave men would open the doors of the Conciergerie for me. The vampires of the treasury, noting these quite serious preparations, did not dare to await their fulfillment. . . ." The "vampires of the treasury" seem to have released their grip about 6 or 7 July; but they did not do so completely. Babeuf was freed *"en état de prise de corps,"* which meant that he was released only conditionally and was liable to rearrest by the court without formality. The apparent intention of this treatment was to prevent him from returning to Picardy and reviving the agitation against the *aides*.[9]

Until the beginning of August Babeuf remained in Paris trying unsuccessfully to secure more satisfactory terms and even some compensation for his imprisonment. During this time he published a *Lettre d'un député de Picardie*, an anonymous eight-page commentary on the Fête de la Fédération on 14 July, which attacked Lafayette, the commandant of the National Guard, for his conceit and reflected sourly on the general antidemocratic atmosphere of the ceremony.[10] He appears also to have prepared another pamphlet which pilloried Marie Antoinette (who had promised, uncharacteristically, to unbend by mingling with the people at another Paris festival on 25 July). Both these items would have been suitable for the *Journal de la confédération*, and the decision to publish the *Lettre d'un député de Picardie* anonymously instead suggests that the discontinuance of the *Journal* was an explicit or implicit condition of Babeuf's liberation. No. 4 of the *Journal*, which would have publicized a feminist project for a Confédération des Dames, also remained unpublished.[11]

After the stimulation of his and Marat's campaign Babeuf found the atmosphere in Paris anticlimactic and depressing. In the end the districts acquiesced peacefully in their dissolution, and the spirit of Parisian radicalism melted temporarily away in the fraternal glow of the Fête de la Fédération. The *Journal de la confédération* had proved a failure; and the *Lettre d'un député de Picardie* brought in no money. There remained the ever-present threat of fresh arrest for a too open, or too direct, participation in revolutionary politics either in Paris or in Picardy (where the campaign against the *aides* was still being bitterly fought out). A return to Roye under such conditions might seem particularly dangerous. In the end Babeuf did nevertheless decide to leave Paris and to go back to Picardy.

Different motives contributed to this decision. In the first place, there were the practical demands of domestic life: it was necessary to find some regular occupation and to make some money, and Paris had proved a disappointment. In the second place, the campaign against the *aides* in the spring of 1790 had made Babeuf more than ever conscious of his vocation as a revolutionary leader. In Paris he was at best a temporary hero; in Picardy he was already a recognized figure with a general reputation and the beginnings of an organized following.

Before his imprisonment in May, Babeuf had discussed with Devin the notion of founding a journal to provide a rallying point for revolutionary opinion in Picardy; it would draw its material from a network of correspondents in the various towns and villages of the province.

The original idea of publishing a local journal of this kind was apparently borrowed from the Le Tellier brothers of Chartres, who had begun (at the beginning of May 1790) to print the first numbers of *Le Correspondant, ou Journal du Département d'Eure et Loir*, a weekly which lasted for thirty-nine numbers.[12] Soon after his release from jail Babeuf decided to revive his own project; and on Saturday, 7 August, he set out alone for Roye and Noyon on foot to see to the launching of a prospectus. At Pont Saint-Maixent, where he stopped for breakfast at 6:30 on Sunday morning, Babeuf's solitary trudge began to turn into a triumphal procession, as he passed around copies of Marat's journal to crowds of well-wishers. From Pont Saint-Maixent Babeuf traveled in the coach of a tobacco merchant from Aire in Artois as far as Tilloloy. There a local innkeeper recognized him and organized an impromptu lunch and celebration at which the wine flowed, the company sang "Vive Henri Quatre" in honor of the guest, and most of the village insisted on viewing the "apparition."

In the evening a party set out with Babeuf to Roye, where, though it was the middle of the night and despite his (probably genuine) protests, there was another celebration at the Auberge Saint-Martin, with much shouting of "Vive la nation" in the streets and many pledges of support for the new journal. On the following day, 10 August, peasants from the countryside around began to flock in to greet Babeuf and to seek his advice and help. He promised them that his new publication would look after their interests too. It was a splendid homecoming—marred only by the fact that the day before the notary Longuecamp (another of the "viziers of Roye") had been elected mayor in place of Billecocq, who was now president of the district.[13]

On 14 August Babeuf wrote to Marie-Anne, who had remained in Paris, claiming that the landowner Galoppe d'Armancourt had undertaken to pay for the printing of the prospectus of a journal to be called *Le Correspondant Picard*. He had promised to send a copy to Audiffred, and Babeuf urged her to try to borrow "yet a few more écus" from his long-suffering friend by a kind of confidence trick. Once before, when faced with complete destitution in 1789, Babeuf had imposed on his partner by getting his wife to copy and send to him at Audiffred's address a letter containing fictitious details of promised payments for his services as *feudiste*. This time he hinted at a "place" promised by *M. le procureur-général* which might or might not suit him. Whether the ruse succeeded it is impossible to say; but we do know that when Marie-Anne finally left Paris for Roye she left behind an unpaid bill for accommodation.[14]

For many years a certain amount of mystery surrounded the history of *Le Correspondant Picard*. In 1884 Advielle reported the existence of a collection of forty issues of the journal; yet scholars subsequently failed to unearth a single complete number, and part of the contents of one issue only was known. Recently, however, Professor Dalin has discovered manuscript notes of three, and possibly four, issues. From Babeuf's correspondence he concludes that no more than five numbers were ever published.[15]

In fact *Le Correspondant Picard*, like Babeuf's earlier journalistic ventures, turned out to be a practical and financial catastrophe. Babeuf hoped for a circulation of a thousand, but halfway through September (in an optimistic letter to Devin) he could claim only fifty local subscriptions. The actual conduct of the enterprise quickly ran into difficulties which ended in acrimonious disputes between the three partners, Babeuf (who acted as editor), Devin (the printer), and Gouban (a Roye merchant who provided the financial backing). The first issue, promised for 1 September, did not appear until 8 October, after complaints from the subscribers had been received. Devin found it impossible to get the material from Babeuf on time. By December the partnership was finished and the journal ceased to appear.

Babeuf now published a prospectus for a continuation under a different title. In this he admitted that there had not been an adequate number of subscriptions to support the *Correspondant Picard*. He proposed to broaden the scope of the proposed substitute, the *Scrutateur des Décrets,* in order to turn it into a publication for "all parts of the empire." For the moment subscribers were offered (in lieu of nos. 6 and 7 of the *Correspondant Picard*) a lengthy petition by the "commune and municipality of Montigny," near Clermont, against the feudal dues and privileges of the local seigneur, but nothing else whatsoever. A further number was promised. But there is no evidence that it ever appeared or that the *Scrutateur* was ever actually launched. It seems unlikely.[16]

Despite this sorry story of failure the *Correspondant Picard* adventure was not without significance as a courageous attempt at a new style of radical journalism. The purpose of the journal was not merely to instruct from above, but also to act as a vehicle for pressures from below. During the campaign against the *aides* Babeuf had become impressed by the value of the mass petition as an instrument of democratic agitation. In the prospectus of the *Correspondant Picard* he promised to set aside a section for "petitions, addresses and instructions to different administrative bodies." He also opened a section for local correspondence, intended as a free forum for the discussion of ideas. To fill these sections Babeuf made a point of seeking to recruit local correspondents. He made a special approach to the parish priests, "those honorable pastors of the countryside, whose interests are so particularly identified with those of the flock that they direct."

Whether or not the *curés* were impressed, there is evidence that Babeuf's appeal to local activists produced some response. The contents of no. 3 of the *Correspondant Picard,* for example, included a petition from the commune of Gournay asserting the right to collect fruit from roadside trees claimed by the seigneur of Gournay; and in November Babeuf received a request from Boulogne to publish a petition against the appointment of a local official.[17]

Another section of the journal was reserved for personal comment by Babeuf on political matters of the day. Thus much space in no. 1 was devoted to advocating an egalitarian national educational system, enlarging on a theme already broached in the *Cadastre perpétuel*. When on 23 October a debate was reopened in the National Assembly on voting qualifications under the new constitution, Babeuf prepared a strong and ironical attack for no. 4 of the *Correspondant Picard*. It denounced, in the name of equality, the decree of 2 December 1789 for reserving the franchise for taxpayers only, and it criticized the higher qualifications demanded for second-degree electors and deputies.

The *Correspondant Picard* had an ambitious secondary title: it was intended to be (as well as everything else) *"le rédacteur des cahiers de la seconde législature."* Its intended role was to guide and coordinate a general demand by the people for a democratic revision of the constitution by the deputies soon to be elected to the new Legislative Assembly.

The influence of the journal was, in fact, much more modest. Nevertheless, the first number ran to five hundred copies, and at least two subsequent members of the Convention, Coupé de l'Oise and André Dumont, were among the subscribers. The *Correspondant Picard* was obtainable in Amiens and Montdidier, in Saint-Quentin, Ham, Senlis, Beauvais, Noyon, Vervins and Laon, and even as far afield as Boulogne and Paris. If the subscribers were few, the readership was not necessarily equally restricted. For it was customary for circles of friends to share joint subscriptions, and for issues to be passed from hand to hand. Journals were often made available also in taverns and coffeehouses.[18]

Later, writing to Dumont in 1793, Babeuf boasted of his rôle as the "Marat" of the Somme Département during these months.[19] The launching of the *Correspondant Picard*, with its deliberately popular and "crusading" style, was indeed one aspect of a conscious attempt to emulate the example of the "watchdog of the people." In the columns of the *Correspondant Picard* and in the petitions which he drafted between 1790 and 1792, Babeuf sought to act as a spokesman for the peasants and laborers of his native province.

During the autumn of 1790 one issue above all began to occupy the attention of the Picard peasantry: the struggle against "feudalism." It had been abolished, in theory, by the decrees of 4 and 5 August 1789, but in fact was still strongly manifested in the countryside in economic arrangements surviving from the Ancien Régime.

At the time of the 1789 decree, Babeuf had offered to place his technical expertise at the service of the seigneurs, who were faced with the complexities of the commutation arrangements then foreshadowed. In 1790, instead, it was the peasant communities who increasingly sought his aid in legal battles with the noble landowners. The crowds of villagers who flocked to his door in the triumphant days of August 1790 to seek advice were a tribute to Babeuf's growing reputation as the "scourge of feudalism."

By the autumn of 1790 a peasant offensive was under way on three main fronts. In one series of actions peasant communities sought to vindicate their rights to common lands against seigneurial encroachments, and often, too, against those of the bourgeoisie of the corporate towns, where common pasture and meadows had often been diverted to private use and profit. Although the decrees of 1790

entitled peasant communities to claim back commons in certain circumstances, they applied only where there had been encroachment
within the last thirty years, and the onus of proof lay with the
peasants. In another series of actions the peasants challenged the
right of the seigneur to exercise *"voirie,"* planting and cutting
timber along roads and highways, or to exploit fruit trees in the same
manner. In July and August 1790 the National Assembly published
details of compromise arrangements which caused widespread dis-
satisfaction. While the seigneurs were forbidden to carry out any
further plantings, not only were they promised compensation at the
expense of the peasants, but they were permitted (pending such compensation) to gather fruit and even to chop down trees, on giving
proper notice to the peasant community.

Finally, the peasants began a resistance movement against the
continued, if temporary, collection of the main feudal dues, the *cens*
(or quitrent in cash), the *champart* (or quitrent in kind), and *lods et
ventes* (mutation or succession dues). The August decrees of 1789, by
forthrightly declaring feudalism abolished, had produced a temporary pacification of the countryside after the attacks on châteaux,
the burnings and violence of the summer of 1789. But from October
1789 the Comité des Droits Féodaux—under pressure from the
propertied classes, noble and bourgeois—strove to salvage as much
from the ruins as possible. In March 1790 it was decreed that while
certain "personal" feudal rights were abolished without compensation, quitrents were to be commuted, on the basis of twenty or
twenty-five years' purchase, with a fixed sum for mutation or succession dues added; meanwhile, until commutation had been completed,
the peasants were to continue to pay the dues. Equally, although the
dîmes (the church tithes) had been "abolished" in August 1789, the
effective date was fixed at 1 January 1791. In 1790 and 1791 Babeuf
acted as the representative of the peasants in the legal disputes which
developed out of the interpretation of the assembly's decrees and the
peasants' refusal to accept the unfavorable compromises they
represented.

The apple harvest of August and September resulted in a general
"war of the trees" in Picardy, in which peasants seized the fruit from
seigneurial trees along the roads and on the commons. Among the
leaders of this rebellion were the villagers of Gournay-sur-Aronde in
the Oise Département—for whom Babeuf drew up a petition to the
National Assembly. At the end of August the inhabitants of Gournay

decided to gather the fruit from the apple trees, to fell the trees, and to divide out the land on which they were planted. Troops and a National Guard detachment from Compiègne had to be sent to recover the fruit, which was claimed by the seigneur's farmers or lessees, and several villagers were arrested. In a similar episode at Montigny, near Clermont, when the tenant-farmers collected the fruit, even though negotiations for redemption were under way, the commune seized the harvest, and the National Guard again intervened on behalf of the tenants. The villagers retaliated by turning out 500 strong to chop down the trees. On 5 December 1790 the council of the Commune of Montigny sent Babeuf to Paris with a delegation to plead the case, and he drew up a petition which was published.[20]

Babeuf was also busy with another petition, for the municipality of Méry, near Clermont, also in the Oise Département. In this Babeuf set out to justify a refusal of the peasants of Méry to pay feudal dues. But he did so by way of a general attack on seigneurial property which echoed his earlier denunciations in the correspondence with Dubois and in the *Cadastre perpétuel*. By now, however, his researches (and particularly hints culled from C.J.F. Henault's *Nouvel abrégé chronologique de l'histoire de France*) had led him to a more empirical and historical perspective of the origins of feudalism, which he traced back to the Frankish and Carolingian epoch. In Frankish times, he argued, there had existed both salic property (peasant land) and military benefices (fiefs, seigneuries); but towards the close of the Carolingian dynasty the feudal lords had succeeded in transforming fiefs and seigneuries, originally held only on life tenure from the king, into heritable possessions. Feudal property and all feudal rights had, thus, been established by fraud and usurpation.

As an *ad hoc* defense of a refusal to pay *champart* and *cens* this was not particularly extravagant, considering the kind of analysis which was being canvassed with increasing frequency in the second year of the revolution. Babeuf went on, however, to draw certain quite original conclusions of exceptional radicalism. Since feudal property had originally belonged to the "nation," the time had now come (he argued) to end the age-old usurpation and to reclaim "for our children that which had belonged to their forefathers." The National Assembly must nationalize all fiefs and seigneuries. And after the abolition of feudal dues without compensation, the domain land belonging to the seigneuries should be sold by the municipalities along with the already nationalized church lands, and the proceeds used to meet the nation's debts.[21]

Not only was this program for the expropriation of the feudal landlords advanced almost two years before the first sequestrations of the property of the *émigré* nobles, but by attacking the position of an entire economic class, it went beyond even the most extreme Jacobin measures (such as the Ventôse laws of 1794) in its implications. It helped to earn for Babeuf the growing reputation, of which he complained—somewhat disingenuously—of an advocate of the "agrarian law," a general redistribution of the property of the rich among the poor.[22]

In the petition on behalf of the inhabitants of Méry—as in the other petitions in which he acted as a spokesman of the peasants in 1790 and 1791, and in the petitions on the *aides*—Babeuf revealed an almost instinctive genius for linking the theoretical and the practical. This was his strength as an agitator. His invariable technique in tackling any specific local issue was to shift the discussion immediately to the plane of general principles, and in drafting a petition to a specific body, such as the National Assembly, to appeal to the public at large through propaganda and publicity, partly to secure immediate practical support but also (and more importantly) to educate and proselytize.

Even so, at the time, the Méry petition did not form part of a general revolutionary program for the peasantry. Babeuf continued, as always, to live in two worlds: the world of speculation, where all things were possible, and the world of everyday affairs, in which he could offer hardheaded and practical advice to peasant communities at grips with concrete problems. Thus, as late as October 1791 he was still circularizing the "citizen property-owners" of Picardy to offer his professional services for the handling of negotiations over the redemption of the very feudal dues whose existence he had long since demonstrated to be unjust and indefensible.[23]

Babeuf's return to Picardy coincided with a new phase in the struggle over the indirect taxes. The local administrations began a final effort to crush the surviving centers of resistance and to restore the collection of the *aides*. After Babeuf's arrest in May the innkeepers of Roye had been, at last, compelled to agree to a restoration of the barriers and the inspection system; but despite the presence of a detachment of cavalry of the Berry regiment, popular resistance was still so strong that no practical action was taken for some weeks.

In the second half of August, however, a determined attempt to restore the tax machinery developed in the neighboring town of Péronne, backed by Swiss mercenaries and the National Guard. On 30 September the Directory of the Somme Département began a new initiative with a general circular to the district and municipal administrations urging firm action. At Roye the new administration (elected at the beginning of August) took prompt action, and a meeting of innkeepers on 9 October was persuaded to agree to the restoration of the machinery of the *aides*.

At the time of this meeting (and for a week or so previously) Babeuf had been out of Roye, probably in Noyon seeing to the printing and distribution of the first number of the *Correspondant Picard*, which saw the light on 8 October. On the afternoon of Sunday, 10 October, he returned to Roye and immediately called a meeting, which rejected the previous day's arrangements and demanded that the matter be submitted to a new town meeting the following Sunday. At this, Babeuf was able to present a *"pouvoir"* signed by sixty-three persons which named him as the official spokesman for the *cabaretiers* and *aubergistes* of Roye. A tumultuous assembly of 400-500 people heard him deliver a fiery speech which rehearsed most of the arguments of his April petition.

In a rhetorical (and, I fear, untranslatable) outburst Babeuf ridiculed the incredible complexity of the archaic burdens of indirect taxation to which the inhabitants were subjected: "des anciens et nouveaux cinq sous, des sols pour livre, des subventions à tant par muid, des droits à tant par tonneau, des inspecteurs aux boissons, des inspecteurs aux boucheries, octrois municipaux, octrois royaux, courtiers-jaugeurs, jaugeurs-courtiers, dix sols pour livre, droits réservés, six sols pour livre, sol pour livre des octrois, droit de douane, droit de jauge, composition, huitième et quatrième composés, prix principal, huit sols pour livre, quatre sols pour livre et encore dix sols pour livre. Et le trop-bu? et le droit de remuage? et le droit de revente? les annuels sur le vin, annuels sur la bière, annuels sur le cidre, annuels sur l'eau de vie et les liqueurs."

The speech was acclaimed, its publication ordered; and the municipal administration was forced to retire discomfited. There was little the new mayor, Longuecamp, could do except to appeal through the district administration at Montdidier to the departmental administration at Amiens.[24]

At the beginning of November the administrators of the Somme Département suggested that the District of Montdidier should begin another prosecution against Babeuf by way of a denunciation to the

Ministry of the Interior; but the minister, Delessart, suggested a further attempt at persuasion first. As earlier in the year, the Paris government faced an awkward dilemma. Babeuf was regarded as the inspiration of the continuing resistance movement in places like Airanes, Oisement, and Albert, as well as Roye and Péronne.[25] In a situation in which local municipalities, National Guard and even regular troop detachments were frequently unreliable or lukewarm, it was clear that violent repression might be counterproductive—especially if, instead, Babeuf himself could be brought to listen to reason. Developments during November seemed to offer the promise that Babeuf might, in fact, become more vulnerable to pressure from above. On 14 November 1790 elections were held to renew half the municipal council at Roye, and Babeuf succeeded in gaining election as one of the *notables* of the new municipality, despite the objections of his enemies on the municipality that he had not met the tax requirements for eligibility.

The position of *notable* offered neither great responsibility nor great reward; but it was a potential steppingstone to higher political honors. On 23 November Babeuf was entrusted with a public funeral oration for P.-F. Masson, the Roye *avocat* and member of the administration of the Somme Département. On 14 December, however, the *département* directory drew attention to the legal provision that officeholders must be free of all public taint. The writ of *prise de corps* of the Cour des Aides, which still applied to Babeuf, was technically a disqualifier from public office. His enemies decided to make use of this technicality, a writ from an abolished court, either to drive him out of municipal politics or (possibly) to compel him to offer to abandon his support for the tax rebellion as a *quid pro quo*.

At the beginning of December Babeuf went to Paris to try to get his legal disability lifted, only to find that there was no way of getting a judgment rescinded by a nonexistent court. On his return he found himself excluded from the transactions of the municipality, despite his indignant protests.[26] In January the election of a *juge de paix* provided the occasion of a trial of strength between the entrenched municipal faction and Babeuf's followers. On 16 January (the election day) the National Guard, the garrison, and a detachment of the *maréchaussée* were placed on the alert; the election hall was guarded, and Babeuf was forcibly excluded while Longuecamp gained election to a post which Babeuf coveted. Although this maneuver was successful, the municipal administration of Roye was now fighting with its back to the wall against a rising tide of opposition. Even the meeting of 16 January, restricted to the wealthier "active" citizens, had protested by electing Babeuf president of the electoral meeting in his absence.[27]

Meanwhile, the *département* administration at Amiens had finally lost patience with the continuing tax strike. On 12 January the Montdidier district administration politely refused the honor of leading a mission of peaceful persuasion to Roye. The *département* authorities now sent an armed force to Roye instead and ordered the municipality to restore the *aides*. Taking advantage of a temporary absence of Babeuf from the town (on 24 January), Longuecamp persuaded a town meeting to agree to the reopening of the *bureaux d'entrées*; but duty-free cider continued to enter the town, escorted by crowds of armed men, and Longuecamp was compelled to ask for more reinforcements from Amiens. His plan, submitted to the *département* on 11 February, was to quarter forty or fifty troopers on the more recalcitrant innkeepers until they yielded.[28]

The previous day Babeuf had managed to get into the General Assembly of the Commune of Roye, where he made a defiant speech, promising to resist the troops at the entrance of the town with anyone who would join him. On 13 February he was present at a gathering which collected at the Grand Vainqueur in the rue de Paris to support the refusal of Lambin, the innkeeper, to pay duty. Lambin was arrested by the *sergent de la ville* and two troopers, and taken before the mayor, who reproached him for riotous and illegal assembly. Meanwhile, Colbert, the son of Widow Colbert of the Auberge Saint-Martin in the Faubourg Saint-Gilles, had rung the tocsin to rally the faubourg for a march on the Hôtel de Ville to free the prisoner, and, even more alarming, Mme. Lambin arrived and gave the municipality the rough edge of an innkeeper's wife's tongue. Lambin was hastily released with a warning but the mayor issued a warrant for the arrest of Colbert and another leader of the Faubourg Saint-Gilles uprising. On 15 February, he wrote to the Somme Département administration at Amiens begging to be allowed to send the prisoners there for safety and demanding that the existing garrison at Roye of twenty-eight troopers of the Berry regiment should be reinforced by a further seventy. In the end the *département* sent sixty troopers from Abbeville, who arrived at Roye about 23 February.[29]

These determined measures did not bring permanent peace to Roye. Sporadic battles in the streets between waggoners and troops supporting the collection of the *entrées* (or town dues) continued well into 1792.[30] But the struggle over the *aides* was now effectively over. It remained far from clear who had won. Although the authority of the financial administration had been technically vindicated, it was no more than a Pyrrhic and symbolic victory. On 2 March 1791 the National Assembly abolished the *aides* as from 1 April—yielding to a complex of pressures of which Babeuf's campaign in Picardy was not the least effective.

Seven

Toward the Agrarian Law

Victors (albeit temporarily) in the struggle over the *aides*, the Roye administration enjoyed only an uneasy security under the protection of the military garrison. Deeply embittered by the blocking of his civic and political ambitions, Babeuf was now more than ever determined to bring them down. During February and March 1791 he prepared a fresh attack on the municipal party on a new front.

In the eighteenth century the inhabitants of Roye still retained commoning rights over certain surrounding territories. According to Babeuf's researches the *échevins*, or aldermen, of the prerevolutionary municipality had usurped a wide tract of land containing more than 250 acres of arable meadow and pasture which were rightly the property of all the inhabitants. By various pretexts (he alleged) the members of the new constitutional municipality were continuing to divert the revenues from the commons into their own pockets.

The dispute chiefly concerned the Marais de Bracquemont, a low-lying patch of land planted with trees, on the north side of the town, next to the Faubourg Saint-Médard. In 1757 the *marais* had been the subject of an unsuccessful lawsuit in which the town claimed possession (and the right to exploit the timber) from the Priory of the Célestins of Amiens. The decision favored the Célestins' lessee, but the commoning rights of the townsmen were recognized.[1]

The title to the *marais* was still in dispute in 1791, but the scales had tipped in favor of the municipality as a result of general revolutionary sequestration of the church lands.

In villages like Gournay and Montigny the "war of the trees" was a three-cornered struggle—with the feudal landlord, the *fermiers* (or "rural bourgeoisie") and the poor peasants each having conflicting interests. In Roye three parties were also involved: the Célestins of Amiens, the dominant "bourgeois" elements of the town and the mass of the artisans and laborers.

In his research into the historical origins of feudalism Babeuf had begun also to formulate a general theory about the fate of the commons. Some notes made in 1792 contain an outline sketch of the general evolution by which common lands (in Frankish times genuinely the common resource of villages of equal and independent peasant households) had, with the passage of time and the depression of a section of the peasant class, become increasingly monopolized by a narrow group of richer owners, who alone were able to keep and breed cattle. Once again, as in the case of feudal property, the logical corollary was that it was now legitimate for the present generation of peasants to reclaim their birthright.

With or without the benefit of Babeuf's theoretical insights, in the spring of 1791 the inhabitants of Roye certainly began to "reclaim their birthright" by cutting timber on the Marais de Bracquemont. On 27 March, Longuecamp called a public meeting to explain the illegality of these encroachments. After a challenge by Babeuf, the municipal administration agreed, in order to pacify the angry citizens, to call an assembly made up of two *commissaires* from each *quartier* of the town to examine the matter.

The result was a virtual revolution at Roye. On 4 April the elected *commissaires* occupied the Hôtel de Ville, supported by a large crowd gathered in the market square, and forced the mayor to attend the meeting. Longuecamp found the *commissaire* for the Quartier Saint-Gilles, namely Babeuf, firmly in control, with a pocketful of prepared "decrees." Longuecamp and the *procureur-syndic*, Lefebvre, protested, left the meeting, and were encouraged on their way by threats of hanging and crucifying, and by the sound of the tocsin calling larger crowds into the streets.

The assembly then acclaimed Babeuf's "decrees," which ordered the division of the land and timber of the Marais de Bracquemont among the townspeople and the resumption of other lands, buildings, and gardens on the south and west sides of the town (leased out long since by the municipality, but declared by Babeuf to be still properly common lands). In fear and trembling Longuecamp ordered the Orléans and Berry cavalry detachments of the garrison

to guard the *marais* and to break up any large crowds. At 7 p.m. on 5
April Babeuf was arrested with two other *commissaires* at the
Amiens gate. The party had actually been out with a surveyor to
measure the *marais*.[2]

Longuecamp and Lefebvre determined to prosecute Babeuf. But
they insisted that he should be taken immediately to Montdidier to
be held for trial, since otherwise his party might be expected to attack the jail and free him.

The new prosecution of Babeuf might easily have had very serious
results for him. But it was rapidly swallowed up in a general atmosphere of farce, with a constant and ineffective to-ing and fro-ing
of the parties between Roye, Montdidier, and Amiens. On 12 April
the municipal administration decided to send twelve witnesses to
Montdidier, together with an officer, to attend the trial; they also
resolved that, whatever the result, Babeuf should be detained under
their summary powers for eight days, his imprisonment to begin on 8
April. Longuecamp and Lefebvre set out for Amiens to seek the support of the Directory of the Somme Département for the strongest
action against Babeuf, threatening to resign if he were allowed to
return to Roye. On 14 April the *département* instructed the District
of Montdidier to open an investigation of Babeuf's activities since the
previous October, while holding him behind bars.

Longuecamp and Lefebvre hastened to Montdidier with a copy of
this instruction only to find that their bird had already flown. The
procureur of the district, Billecocq, had acted with a surprising im-
partiality and correctness. On 12 April he had opened a formal hearing, only to find that not one of the twelve witnesses from Roye was
prepared to testify against Babeuf. At least one had been threatened
with "crushing" by Marie-Anne, and there was a general atmosphere
of intimidation, with Babeuf's friends from Roye and his local partisans shouting for him in the streets. However, it seems likely that
Babeuf's personal popularity also contributed to the witnesses'
silence. On leaving Roye one of the party had been moved by a
shouted appeal in the street urging him to "paint Babeuf white from
head to foot! Bring him back to us! This is our Mirabeau—he
deserves crowns!"

Since the prosecution had presented no evidence, Billecocq released Babeuf immediately, whereupon the accused, his wife, and most
of the witnesses adjourned for a celebration drink. The following
morning they arrived back in Roye amid general rejoicing, and a
triumphal procession escorted Babeuf to breakfast at the house of

Sulpice Dercheu, a local cloth merchant. After breakfast the triumph continued with Babeuf's welcome back to the Faubourg Saint-Gilles, where he set up headquarters at the Auberge de Saint-Martin once again. Some men and women brought him a bouquet, a laurel branch decorated with a tricolor ribbon, and a laurel wreath was placed in the window of the hostelry. Roye's "Mirabeau" was safely home again, and plainly immune (for the time being) from further prosecution.[3]

Despite their threats, Longuecamp and Lefebvre did not abdicate; and despite their fears, Babeuf did not, after all, have them "crucified." Instead the Roye municipality continued in office peacefully enough for the rest of its term, with Lefebvre as the new mayor after Longuecamp had resigned to take up his post as justice of the peace.

The Marais de Bracquemont affair had confirmed Babeuf's position as the leader of an opposition party supported (according to Longuecamp) by "the workers and the greater part of the poorest class" of the town. In a naive tribute the mayor assigned Babeuf's success partly to his skill in appealing to the populace's material interests, and partly to the vigor with which he "ceaselessly assured the people that they were sovereign, and that they could exercise all their rights for themselves." Appropriately enough this was the time (the end of 1790) when Babeuf adopted the name "Camille" after the champion of the Roman plebeians.

As far as the Marais de Bracquemont was concerned, nothing was settled. In August 1791 there were fresh troubles, and again in March 1792, when it was rumored that the Montdidier district tribunal had adjudged the pasture land to the inhabitants and that they were entitled to divide it up. The *marais* was again invaded, despite a prohibition by the Roye municipality and the Somme Département.[4]

Before long Babeuf's name would be linked with yet another uprising against the "relics of feudalism." In prison at Montdidier after his arrest in April he had met a group of prisoners from the village of Davenescourt, a place of about 160 households situated not far from Montdidier, who were awaiting trial for an attack on the château of Davenescourt in February 1791. He promised to take charge of their defense. The essential facts of the Davenescourt affair were indisputable; on 25 February an armed mob from Davenescourt had broken into the château, seized and burned the estate archives, and compelled the countess de la Myre, by physical threats, to sign a number of papers abandoning rights over the commons and feudal rights disputed by the peasants. Although the countess and her two children escaped with only minor scratches, one of the household servants was shot and killed during these transactions, and the château was pillaged.[5]

In July 1791 seventeen persons were brought before the district tribunal at Montdidier, after the four ringleaders had spent several months in prison. Babeuf's official connection with the case was as the defense counsel for these four principal defendants (Alexis Bailli, his wife and his two sons). As always, he sought to make political capital out of the case with a general pamphlet published on behalf of all the defendants, and it began to circulate at the beginning of August.[6] By then the Davenescourt affair had become something of a test case nationally and locally, both for the protagonists of "law and order" and for those peasant elements who were determined to force through the completion of a social revolution in the countryside. The peasants of Davenescourt and the neighboring communities demonstrated their complete solidarity at the beginning of May 1791 by a march on Montdidier, one to two hundred strong, to demand the speeding-up of the trial. Later a small peasant army was gathered for a fresh siege of the château, which had to be garrisoned by a battalion of gendarmerie from Amiens, stiffened by a detachment of Swiss regulars. The actual trial of the Davenescourt men at Montdidier was held under the threat of hostile crowds who intimidated the witnesses.[7]

Babeuf's published defense of the rioters, cast in the form of an appeal to the National Assembly, was, in fact, a telling indictment of the countess de la Myre as a feudal tyrant who had finally goaded the peasants into justified violence. Although the defense was an ex-parte statement, none of the major accusations it contains was convincingly refuted by a counter-pamphlet which was probably the work of the countess's chaplain, Pierre Tournier. It is clear that (during the 1780s) the countess, aided by Tournier and her steward, Vincent Lesueur, had turned the screw of the seigneurial reaction as hard as possible whenever and wherever the opportunity occurred. She had enforced the seigneurial monopoly of the mill rigorously, with the aid of an unusually grasping miller. She had exploited the *droit de voirie* to the limit by actually planting on the highways and not merely along the verges. She had seized and enclosed one-third of the village commons under the right of *triage*, making the remainder of the commons unsafe for the village cattle by drainage works. A new *terrier* had also been introduced enforcing the tenants' responsibility for the upkeep of the highway and the bridge. A number of contesting legal actions by the villagers had all been defeated, leaving a heavy burden of costs. In addition, there were certain personal aggravations, notably the idiosyncratic tendency of the Abbé Tournier to take potshots at village lads who strayed in the direction of the countess's garden or the maids' quarters.

However, the bringing of all this to light—though an excellent propaganda justification for the subsequent *jacquerie*—was, of course, hardly a defense at law. There seems little doubt that (as Babeuf believed) the defendants would have gone to the scaffold for all his efforts, but for a timely accident. On 14 September 1791, having completed its self-imposed task of providing France with a constitution, the National Assembly paid a parting tribute to the spirit of fraternity by declaring a general amnesty for all under prosecution for acts of rebellion or revolution. Babeuf immediately forwarded a *mémoire* to Duport, the minister of justice, together with his published account of the background. It supported the contention that the *jacquerie* at Davenescourt was an act of justifiable rebellion and not an ordinary crime. Duport eventually agreed that the amnesty did apply to the Davenescourt case; and on 15 October 1791 the Montdidier tribunal convened a final session to liberate the prisoners.

For Babeuf it was a moment of sweet triumph. As it was a market day at Montdidier, the place was crowded with peasants and citizens who collected in the square to cheer the liberated prisoners and their defender. Then a triumphal progress to Davenescourt began. "All the villagers greeted us a league before Davenescourt," Babeuf wrote. "On our arrival in the village the tocsin was rung, and everyone set out for the church, and they ... played "We Praise Thee, Lord" and then dancing began; this continued all the following day, the Sunday. The festival was concluded by fireworks. Citizens of all ages assembled, to complete the celebration of a victory over hated feudalism."[8]

For several months Babeuf had been almost totally involved in the Davenescourt affair. He had even neglected to contest the municipal elections held at Roye in June to renew the commune council. He did, however, find time to attend meetings of the newly founded Jacobin Club at Noyon, one of whose leading spirits was his old associate the printer Devin. During 1790 and 1791 a network of political clubs had begun to spring up across Picardy, often in correspondence with the Jacobins of Paris. At Roye Babeuf himself had

been associated since the autumn of 1790 with the Amis de la
Révolution, who met in the Eglise des Minimes; by October 1791
there was also a Jacobin Club at Montdidier. The Société des Amis
de la Constitution at Noyon was amongst the most vigorous shoots
of this new growth, and it quickly established corresponding
relationships with both the Cordeliers and the Jacobin clubs at Paris
and with sister clubs at Compiègne, Beauvais, and Amiens, and even
more distant places like Cherbourg, Rochefort, and Bordeaux.

On 3 April Devin printed the foundation address of the club. In
May Babeuf made a maiden speech in which he deplored the decay of
the institutions of direct democracy, the Paris districts and the permanent committees and general assemblies of sections and communes in the provinces. He regretted that the new constitution
prohibited electoral mandates or cahiers and appealed to the "last
bastion of liberty," the patriotic societies and clubs, to demand that a
review of the constitution should accompany the summoning of a
new assembly. Babeuf was too radical for the other members of the
club, however, and in July, following the king's flight to Varennes, he
was unsuccessful in an attempt to win their support for a
republican petition. On the other hand, in the schism which followed
the secession of the right-wing Club des Feuillants from the Paris
Jacobins, Noyon followed the policy favored by Babeuf, and maintained its connection with the Robespierrist mother society.[9]

During the summer of 1790 Babeuf established a close and friendly
relationship with another of the leaders of the Noyon club, Jacques-
Michel Coupé, the *curé* of the parish of Sermaize, situated between
Roye and Noyon, and the president of the Noyon district administration. Coupé was a vegetarian and an amateur scientist, and
he has been characterized as a humble village priest suddenly out of
his depth in revolutionary politics. Yet, a man of more than fifty, he
had served as professor of rhetoric at the Collège d'Amiens, and in
1787 the bishop of Noyon had recommended him for the position of
principal of the Collège de Saint-Quentin.

Coupé and Babeuf began to meet together to discuss the
philosophes, politics, and the course of the revolution. When in
August 1791 elections were held at Beauvais to choose the Oise
Département's deputies to the new Legislative Assembly, it became
evident that Coupé was likely to be chosen; and Babeuf devoted his
energies to backing his friend's candidacy. His motives were not entirely altruistic. The *Correspondant Picard* had failed; for understandable reasons no further work or payment could be expected from

the seigneurs; and there are indications that even peasant clients were growing reluctant to entrust their cases to a notorious agitator. Meanwhile family responsibilities were growing. The birth of a son in October 1790 meant that there were three Babeuf children: Robert, five, Sophie, two, and the baby, Jean-Baptiste-Claude. In a despairing letter written on 16 August Babeuf confessed that nothing was coming in and he could not last another month.[10]

In these circumstances Coupé's friendship seemed to offer the only ray of hope, and Babeuf began to cherish the dream of going back to Paris as Coupé's secretary. On 20 August, as the elections drew near, he wrote a massive 7,000-word letter to "brief" the candidate on the political platform he should adopt, at the same time laying out his own innermost convictions so that Coupé might assess his qualities as a future colleague.

When the electoral assembly began to meet at Beauvais on 29 August, Babeuf was present; and he was probably responsible for drafting an address by the Noyon club outlining the kind of candidate the electors should favor. The model bears an even more striking resemblance to Babeuf than to Coupé, and it is quite possible that Babeuf hoped that someone would draw the obvious conclusion. But he played his part in the informal lobbying which rallied 345 votes to Coupé and ensured his election to the Legislative Assembly.[11]

On 10 September (while still in Beauvais) Babeuf sent Coupé a second letter, this time of some 4,000 words, in the form of a virtual ultimatum which demanded an answer "after 24 hours." In this he outlined the principles on which the new deputy should base his parliamentary strategy and tactics. He explicitly offered the services of a secretary who, like Coupé, could "live on vegetables, fruit and milk" and who would be willing to handle his correspondence, draft his speeches, and help him edit published *Lettres à mes commettants* after the style of Mirabeau. The new deputy may well have begun to wonder just who had really been elected to go to Paris. In any case, while he maintained a friendly correspondence with Babeuf, Coupé had no intention of putting on the kind of double-harness his correspondent had in mind. In a letter of 30 September he hinted that he might be able to do something for Babeuf in Paris; and Babeuf eagerly responded, swallowing his pride and giving Coupé the full story of his desperate situation. In the end, however, nothing came of it, once Coupé discovered the tremendous pressure of place-hunting in the capital; and in February 1792 Babeuf broke off the correspondence.[12]

His letters to Coupé had, nevertheless, provided an opportunity to summarize his main political ideas as they had developed by the end of 1791. Professor Dalin's analysis of his personal notebooks shows that, despite his many practical preoccupations, during 1790 and 1791 Babeuf had embarked on a program of private study in the principles of political philosophy. Among the works he read at this time were Adam Smith's *Wealth of Nations*, Condorcet's life of Turgot, Rousseau's *Social Contract* and *Confessions*, and Mercier's utopia, *L'An 2440*. He made notes from Pierre Bayle's *Dictionnaire*, from the *Grande encyclopédie*, and from Livy's history of the Roman Republic. At the same time Babeuf examined the ideas of feudal theorists like Ducange, Grotius, and Pufendorf. Much of this study was based on secondary popularizations, on dictionaries and other summaries, and there were significant gaps. There are no references, for example, to Morelly or Diderot, and there is little indication that Babeuf had any familiarity with the works of Mably, Holbach, Helvétius or Quesnay. Nevertheless, Babeuf's notes made in these years for "a treatise on the principles of the laws of nature, which are called natural rights," and his collected *Lueurs philosophiques* represent a remarkable achievement for a self-taught and isolated thinker.

Babeuf's speculative enquiries were concerned with two major themes: social equality and political power. While his attack on the issue of social equality was abstract and theoretical in form, the basic datum was always the continuing practical problem of desperate poverty for the great majority of Frenchmen. In seeking a theoretical justification for practical measures of relief Babeuf was forced once again to reopen the crucial question of the origins and the legitimacy of property and its relationship to the natural right of survival. By now he was beginning to find his earlier reliance on a crude social contract theory unsatisfying. In fact the notes reveal an imperfectly resolved internal debate on this question.

At one point Babeuf reproduced and appeared to accept the standard Lockeian derivation of the right of property from the application of labor to unappropriated land, with the corollary that society was created to protect the enjoyment of that right. Yet elsewhere he was positive that all rights derived from society, and he denied the existence of natural rights outside or prior to the foundation of society. Since logically this must abolish the essential natural right to survive, as well as the natural right to property, Babeuf was forced to wrestle with a subtle distinction between natural rights and natural laws (self-preservation remaining a "law of nature," if no longer a "natural right"). This reliance on the concept of *loix naturelles* appears to reflect the influence of English empiricism; in this case we must assume that Babeuf meant that self-preservation was an observable and verifiable fact of nature. Yet at the same time he introduced another concept, that of a universal morality based on mutual aid and assistance. This seemed to imply innate qualities in men and to owe more to the inspiration of Rousseau.

It would be unreasonable to expect consistency in a collection of unedited notes made over a period of time, especially as (whatever the mode of argument) the conclusions Babeuf drew were always the same and indeed identical with those he had been drawing ever since the correspondence with Dubois in 1786 and the publication of the *Cadastre perpétuel*. All men were entitled to a subsistence, either from property in land or from their productive labor; and if the rich denied this entitlement by monopolizing land and refusing employment, then the poor might justly resort to violence to redress the situation. However, the practical proposals outlined in Babeuf's notes fell well short of this ultimate extreme. They amounted chiefly, on the one hand, to a program for an "agrarian law," resettling propertyless peasants on common and waste lands; and, on the other, to the establishment of a committee to encourage an expansion of employment by reviving staple trades, in which many hands would be employed to satisfy the needs of many, at the expense of luxury production, in which a few worked to satisfy the whims of a few. Such a committee would also devote itself to spreading and encouraging new techniques in industry, like the steam flour-mills that Babeuf defended as more reliable and more economical in their use of farming land than water-mills or windmills.

In *Lueurs philosophiques* Babeuf attacked some of the central practical problems of democracy and of representative government in particular. Deliberately rejecting revolutionary rhetoric and "the deceptive dreams of metaphysics," he set out to examine instead the practical mechanism of democratic government, and its failings, in passages refreshingly skeptical and free from cant. For Babeuf—as for all aspiring political leaders—one of the most depressing features of democracy was the repeated tendency of the people to make the wrong choice. In his remarks on this subject Babeuf revealed a certain élitist contempt for the masses that at first sight seems to justify some of the strictures of J.L. Talmon in *The Origins of Totalitarian Democracy*. Suggestible and inexperienced, the people had tended to follow a succession of demagogues, from Catiline's time onward.

"The earth must be cleansed" of such demagogues. Yet if very few were truly fitted to be representatives of the people, the electoral process (influenced by factional pressures and special interests) was a very imperfect means of ensuring the selection of such representatives. The pretended inherent right of popular sovereignty was, therefore, "purely ideal and imaginary," since it could "never be made use of by the people."

Continuing his reflections on the "obstacles to good government" Babeuf turned to another major difficulty. It was an observed fact that while reason was rare and scarcely influential among the people, the power of habit and of the passions was universal and strong. It followed that there must be some restraint on absolute liberty in order to maintain a rational purposiveness in human affairs and to prevent degeneration into arbitrariness and license. This led to the recognition of a very serious contradiction. Since there had to be some rational order and some subordination in human society some men needed to be invested with power over their fellows. "Sooner or later, but always and unavoidably, the majority is subordinated to the arbitrary use of power of the one, or of those, who must rule."

Moreover, there was in men an inherent love of domination and an irresistible striving for power. Hence, humanity was doomed to an endless civil war between those who govern and those who are governed. Babeuf described this situation as a chronic moral disease of society. But while the disease was incurable it might nevertheless be treated. At this point, despite his promises, Babeuf did trespass into the realm of metaphysics—by introducing the concept of "the force of the people" as the appropriate treatment. By the continuous application of the "force of the people" in politics, the *esprit dominateur* could be controlled, and rights might be established and preserved. The proper application of this force might even for long periods of time ensure, if not the complete happiness, at least the general health of human societies. By "force" Babeuf did not appear to mean simply violence, but a force in the Newtonian sense, translated into the realms of political science. Presumably such a force might act through a riot or an insurrection, but equally through an election or a petition.

At this point Babeuf returned from metaphysics once again perforce to the practical question: "To whom ought the responsibility for organizing the force of the people be given?" Although his notes left this question unsolved there was a concluding note of optimism. "I do not consider that this cannot be overcome." His practical advocacy of the mechanisms of direct democracy (the popular initiative, mandate, referendum and recall) indicates the region in which Babeuf believed the solution might be found.[13]

Babeuf's letters to Coupé revealed the same preoccupations as his private notes: social equality and democracy. During 1791 his thoughts on social equality had begun increasingly to center on the notion of the *loi agraire*. Since the end of 1790 this concept had been the subject of general and heated discussion among revolutionaries. Formally, the notion derived from the familiarity of most educated Frenchmen with the history of the Roman Republic, and in particular with the attempts of Tiberius and Caius Gracchus to carry out some measure of land redistribution by the *lex agraria*. It had become a matter of popular controversy ever since the Abbé Claude Fauchet had been accused of advocating a version in a series of lectures delivered in the cirque of the Palais Royal at Paris between October and December 1790. These lectures had been given under the auspices of the Confédération Universelle des Amis de la Vérité, a revolutionary group with strong Masonic affiliations, of which the journalist Nicolas de Bonneville was the leading spirit.

In point of fact the measures advocated by Fauchet were quite moderate: a progressive tax, the suggestion that waste lands should be put under cultivation, marriage and inheritance laws to prevent the formation in future of estates worth more than 50,000 livres annually, and the equal division of inheritances.[14] The abstract principles cited in the defense of such moderate, concrete measures were characteristically extreme and absolute: "Every man has a right to the land and ought to possess there the domain property of his existence. He takes possession of this by labor, and his portion should be circumscribed by the rights of his equals. All rights are placed in common in a well-ordered society. The social sovereignty ought to delineate matters so that everybody has something, and nobody has too much. . . . If every man in every place is not guaranteed by the constitution the enjoyment of a sufficiency, there is no constitution at all—nature is violated, liberty does not exist."

Fauchet was vigorously denounced in the Jacobin Club and in the press for preaching the agrarian law, and it is significant that Babeuf should have paid a visit to Paris during December 1790 while the controversy was at its height. It is even more significant that Babeuf should have chosen to sign a copy of a petition drafted immediately on his return to Roye as "Babeuf, de la Société de la Confédération Universelle des Amis de la Vérité," even though he afterwards struck out this qualification. While Professor Dalin is positive that Babeuf owed nothing ideologically to Fauchet and the Amis de la Vérité, it seems difficult to avoid the conclusion that his interest in the agrarian law was aroused by his familiarity with Fauchet's ideas.[15]

In the opening months of 1791 the stock-taking of the achievement of the revolution which preceded the impending dissolution of the National Assembly stimulated a revival of the discussion of the agrarian law, which Babeuf followed with keen interest. In particular he made notes from the files of Prudhomme's *Révolutions de Paris*, in which, from the beginning of February, there was defended a program for settling peasants on small properties created by the division of waste lands and by the voluntary self-denial of the rich.

Writing in the *Mercure de France* in April 1791 La Harpe took Prudhomme severely to task for propagating "the absurd chimera of an agrarian law." In May the *Révolutions de Paris* published a rejoinder: "The French Revolution is a veritable agrarian law put into effect by the people. The people have recovered their rights: one step more and they will have recovered their property. . . ." During the spring and summer of 1791 the works of a handful of bold pamphleteers were circulating which defended more explicitly the principles of absolute equality and implied more or less directly a redistribution of property (notably Rutledge's *Questions sur les lois agraires* and the Abbé Cournand's *De la propriété, ou la cause du pauvre* . . . , with both of which works Babeuf was probably familiar).[16]

Occasionally in the past (in the correspondence with Dubois, and in the pages of the *Cadastre perpétuel*) Babeuf had been compelled to admit that the logical conclusion of his arguments in defense of absolute equality was the redistribution of property. Always, however, he had stopped short of drawing this logical conclusion on the grounds of its impracticability. Now, however, in his correspondence with Coupé, he was to cross this threshold, with an open advocacy of the agrarian law as a political program. Writing to the newly elected deputy on 10 September, Babeuf took it for granted that both he and Coupé were in complete agreement on the long-term goal of complete equality. He painted a picture of an idyllic future society of independent peasant householders, each firmly anchored in security to a basic inalienable patrimony of land large enough to ensure a minimum subsistence, and for the satisfaction of the rest of their needs exchanging the fruits of their labors on the basis of the equal valuation of all work.

For the rest, the outlines of the shape of this new world were left vague. Anxious, however, to "defend" Babeuf against the charge of advocating "petty peasant proprietorship," his chief Marxist biographers have argued that even while seeming to endorse the universal petit-bourgeois dream of his day he remained "fundamentally" a communist. The peasant holdings (it is pointed out) were to be non-heritable, held only on life tenure, and to revert to the state at death for redistribution according to need.[17] Much has been made of one passage of the Coupé correspondence in which Babeuf appears to be advocating a collective economic administration devoted to improving production, as well as to redistributing wealth and equalizing consumption:

"The Constitution must be a national patrimony in which may be found at the same time for the people the bread of the spirit and the bread of the body, in which a stipulation for the complete intellectual and material life shall be not only clear, precise, positive, but in addition immediately sanctioned by the putting in common of all resources, indefinitely multiplied and increased by means of skillfully combined organization and wisely directed labor."[18]

This passage certainly appears to represent a theoretical endorsement of communism. What it meant to Babeuf in practice in 1791 is another matter. At the minimum, Babeuf's stipulations could have been met by nothing more radical than the program of redistributive taxation and social welfare advanced in the *Cadastre perpétuel*, together with the activities of a version of the advisory committee for industry which had appeared in Babeuf's notes during the summer of 1791. At the maximum the passage might be seen as an anticipation of the complete abolition of private property and of the fully controlled and directed economy advocated by the Equals in 1796. What seems most likely in the context is that while Babeuf had avowedly already begun to think in terms of the "maximum program" as the final goal, he was still prepared to accept the temporary necessity of something nearer to the minimum program as a transitional measure. The two aspects of Babeuf's thought, the speculative and the practical, were now closer and more directly linked; but they still remained separate and distinct. The acid test of formulating a practical program showed that Babeuf was still capable of postponing his dreams of a communist utopia while he devoted his attention to the immediate tasks of concrete reform. In this he did not greatly differ from contemporary Jacobin thinkers like Saint-Just or Robespierre.

Indeed, in his letters Babeuf urged Coupé to begin to work practically towards the ultimate goal of the agrarian law by rallying a party to his side in the Convention, and by giving a lead to such underground agrarians as Robespierre and Pétion. Thus, by the twin means of a surface campaign of short-term moderate measures and an undercover conspiracy of the converted, it would be possible eventually to arrive at the "final end and the crowning of good legislation: equality in landed property."[19]

On the subject of the practical details of such legislation Babeuf was strangely reticent, apart from a general recommendation of the example of the classical precursors (Lycurgus, Camillus, Gracchus, Cassius and Brutus) and an indirect reminder of the continued availability of the church lands. He did not choose this opportunity to revive any of the schemes of the past: collective leases, the subdivision of the church lands into leaseholds, the sequestration of seigneurial estates, or the occupation of the common lands. Instead he concentrated all his attention on what was for him the first and crucial step, the achievement of a truly effective democracy through which the people's will could be expressed.

Just as Blanqui, a half-century later, was to pin his faith on an insurrection which would inaugurate proletarian power, leaving the details to look after themselves, and Bakunin was to trust the instinctive socialism of the revolutionary Russian peasantry, so the essence of Babeuf's program was the seizure of power by the people through reformed democratic institutions. Since the people must will their own interests, it was inevitable that they would will the agrarian law, a conclusion which was expressed by Babeuf almost with the rigor of a mathematical equation when he listed "the great principles on which society is established: primitive equality, the general interest, the common will which decrees the law, and the force of all which constitutes sovereignty."[20]

In his letter to Coupé of 20 August Babeuf outlined a coherent series of practical reforms of the French constitution which would make possible the expression of such a common will. Taken together his proposals amounted to a formal and organized vindication of the principles of direct democracy. Firstly, however, it was necessary to sweep away one significant obstacle: the existing constitution of France, only recently completed after the expenditure of much labor and ingenuity by the "founding fathers" of the National Assembly. This was disposed of brusquely enough by invoking the general theory of the mandate. Every assembly existed as a result of a specific mandate from the people; the new Legislative Assembly was the result of a new mandate, and could not be bound by the mandate of its predecessor. The constitution was not a closed question, and could therefore be revoked or amended at will by anybody truly representative of the sovereign—or almost so. For apparently without noting the inconsistency, Babeuf declared that the legislative could have no power to modify the constitution in a sense restrictive to liberty. But the new Legislative Assembly was not, and could not be, the true repository of sovereignty. Sovereignty was reserved to the people, and with it the right of veto over any decision, any law, or even any procedural rule the assembly might adopt.

The popular sovereignty might be exercised by the machinery of the referendum and the initiative. The referendum was represented in Babeuf's system by the obligation binding the National Assembly to refer all important laws, including those of the constitution, to regular assemblies of citizens meeting in their municipalities or communes. They would vote approval or disapproval. After six months the total of such votes would be counted in the capital and the acceptance or rejection of the law would be declared on the basis of a majority decision. The initiative was represented by formal arrangements for the reception and consideration of petitions.

Individuals or groups wishing to have their voices heard would first submit their petitions for endorsement by the local municipal or communal assemblies, which would forward them to a local deputy, who in turn would hand them to a central bureau of petitions. The function of the central bureau would be, firstly, to give the petition a public reading and, secondly, to publish daily summaries of petitions received for the information of deputies, who would thus have a ready and up-to-date means of gauging the movement of public opinion in the country. Furthermore—considering the fate of past petitions—there must be no more debating petitions in secret committees, only open public debates by the full assembly.

Should the deputies prove unresponsive, or untrue to their mandate, there would be provision for recall. Every *département* would have an elected board of twenty-one "curators," independent citizens not in government employ, who would meet at three-month intervals to examine the record of the local deputies. By a majority vote the curators could declare a deputy to have lost the people's mandate and call for new elections. Babeuf was convinced that the mere existence of such machinery would be enough and that it would seldom be used. He did not explain what would happen if the curators lost the people's mandate.

Other reforms dealt with democracy at the grass-roots level. The franchise was to be universal, although women were not specifically mentioned. All citizens were to be permitted to attend municipal assemblies, at which the officers would exercise only temporary presidial functions; and special efforts must be made to encourage the attendance of marginal elements such as beggars, vagrants, vagabonds and the very poor, and to turn them into stalwarts of democracy by looking after their needs. As a further safeguard all fit citizens were to be admitted to serve in the National Guard and bear arms, and the standing army was to be reduced and reformed until it was no longer a danger to liberty. In his prescription for the army Babeuf clearly sought to create a pilot model for the new democratic future. The officers were to be elected, all ranks were to receive equal but greatly increased pay, and social distinctions between ranks would vanish. In time of peace the army would play an important economic role in public works, building canals and roads, draining marshes, and bringing wastes under cultivation.[21]

Much of Babeuf's program for the institutional realization of the principles of direct democracy was original and unique. It was hardly surprising that Coupé, when he arrived in Paris, should have made no attempt to impose such an idiosyncratic and complex system on the Legislative Assembly, but should have remained then, and in later years in the Convention and the Council of Five Hundred, apparently content with orthodox representative democracy. It would be wrong, however, to regard Babeuf's brave attack on the problems of "the spirit of domination," and the expression of the "force of the people," as the isolated outburst of a crank: the ideas of direct democracy were very much in the air in 1791.

In writing to Coupé Babeuf acknowledged his own debt to a pamphlet entitled *Discours sur la nécessité de la ratification de la loi par la volonté générale.* The author of this was the marquis de Girardin, an old soldier and an eccentric aristocrat who had seen Jean-Jacques Rousseau die on his father's property at Ermenonville, and had become ever after a fervent disciple of the master. In June 1791 he had delivered his *Discours* before the Cordeliers Club in Paris, defending (with Rousseauist chapter and verse) the referendum, the recall and the right of petition. The Cordeliers Club had agreed to print Girardin's work and to send copies to all the patriotic societies in France. By the end of July it was being circulated among members of the Jacobin clubs of the Oise Département, so that Babeuf probably received a copy through his connection with the Noyon club. In lobbying Coupé with his scheme, Babeuf was therefore expressing not merely an isolated piece of speculation but rather the current preoccupations of the general stratum of advanced democrats to which they both belonged.[22]

The impracticality of Babeuf's detailed program will be readily conceded. At the same time the basic elements, stripped of their institutional embellishments, were and remained part of a continuing democratic program which offered an alternative to the parliamentary authoritarianism of the successive revolutionary assemblies. The popular watchwords or slogans of this movement—"mandate," "popular veto," "recall"—would find a mature echo in the challenge to the Convention of the Enragés and the *sans-culotte* movement in 1793. Professor Talmon has depicted this movement for direct democracy as merely a façade to conceal the totalitarian ambitions of a Rousseauist minority.[23] Yet it is difficult to see in such speculations, at least those of theorists like Girardin and Babeuf, anything other than an honest attempt to tackle the central problems of a truly effective and broadly based democracy. To conclude, as Talmon does, that "ultimately Babeuf trusts the people no more than he trusts the National Assembly" is to fall into the same error as those who seek to anticipate Babeuf's conversion to revolutionary communism: to view the years before 1796 from the perspective of the twentieth century, and through the distorting prism of the Conspiracy of the Equals. It was not "the people" that Babeuf distrusted in 1791, but the demagogues and politicians who misled them. Granted the proper democratic machinery, he had every faith in the triumph of a pure and beneficent people's will.

Eight

The Servant of the People

"Politics and meditations on the true principles of the laws, and on putting them into practice, have so irresistible an attraction for me," Babeuf wrote to Coupé in August 1791, "that I am inclined to think that there is my unique vocation."[1]

The failure of Coupé to respond to the suggestion of a political partnership was a disappointing conclusion to a year of general frustration, both public and private. Yet the tide had already begun to flow, however imperceptibly, in Babeuf's direction. The victory in the Davenescourt case at Montdidier in October marked the turning point. Babeuf's prestige as a "people's advocate" was now restored; the Commune of Hangest, which was the immediate neighbor of Davenescourt, was the first to offer Babeuf a new commission to negotiate over feudal dues. At another level the peasants' triumph in the Davenescourt affair reflected the beginning of a general shifting of the balance of power leftward in the Picard region, which continued and became more pronounced as 1792 progressed. By the autumn the swing was strong enough for Babeuf to win personal electoral successes and to begin to rebuild a career in revolutionary politics.

The peasant communities continued at least to send enough work his way to enable his family to eat. An agreement concluded with the Commune of Beauvraigne in May 1791 indicated the terms under which such work was completed. Under this agreement Babeuf undertook for four livres a day to compile a list of peasants and of their obligations; he was to begin work at 6 a.m. and work through until 8 p.m. with a midday break of two hours.

In the same month Babeuf received another commission which must have afforded him ironic satisfaction: "The women, mothers and sisters of the citizens of Tilloloy" sought his aid in a dispute with the lessee of his old enemy the marquis de Soyecourt, who was preventing the village women and children from gathering forage and herbs in the park around the château. From the end of June to the middle of August Babeuf's time was almost exclusively taken up in representing a group of peasants from Bulles, near Clermont, in the Oise Département, who had invaded the common meadow and cut hay belonging to the municipality. In this case Babeuf played the part of a conciliator, persuading the peasants to accept the municipality's claim, yet at the same time working for the release of the imprisoned ringleaders.[2]

Two main factors contributed to the growing radicalization of northeast France during 1792—inflation, due to the depreciation of the revolutionary paper money, and the effects of the war with Austria and Prussia which began in April. The year opened with a sharp and general economic crisis as farmers, corn factors, and other provision dealers sought to corner supplies of grain in the anticipation of rising prices later in the year. In many parts of France the population responded with a wave of riots reminiscent of the troubled months of the spring and summer of 1789. Crowds gathered to seize stocks and to force sales at fixed maximum prices. One of the most dramatic of such outbreaks occurred in the Oise Département, where (on 6 February) a small army of three to four thousand armed men from communes along the river, led by their municipal officers, seized four boatloads of grain at Pont L'Evêque. The grain was taken to Ourscamp, unloaded and stored under guard at the former abbey there. On 11 February the movement spread to Noyon. Crowds of peasants and townsmen marched on the municipality to demand an ordinance fixing the price of grain at six livres the bushel, and then imposed their own "popular maximum" on the market by the threat of violence.

Meanwhile General Gouy, the commandant of the National Guard at Compiègne, had begun to threaten an expedition to Ourscamp to "liberate" the grain, only to find himself faced with a general insurrection of the entire region. By the afternoon of 13 February it was estimated that ten thousand men had rallied to the defense of Ourscamp. Several municipalities, including the Noyon administration, had been swept along with the tide; and there was a kind of *ad hoc* revolutionary parliament, 200 strong, meeting in a hall at the abbey to try to concert action. On the 15th a delegation from the Legislative Assembly was received by rebels claiming to speak for 60 to 80 municipalities able to call out 25,000 men. The insurgents refused to disperse and drew up a petition to the Legislative Assembly, and price control was again imposed on the Noyon market on 18 February.

Ultimately the Paris government gathered a powerful force with detachments from three regiments of the Paris garrison and National Guards from half a dozen *départements*, and on 25 February General Victinghoff succeeded in dispersing the Ourscamp "parliament" and in seizing the grain at last.

Although Coupé defended the rebels in the Legislative Assembly, there is no direct evidence that Babeuf participated in this movement. However, at the beginning of March he prepared an "address" to the municipalities of the Oise Département, defending the rebels, voicing their complaints against paper money, depreciation, unemployment and grain cornering, and proposing a petition to the Legislative Assembly.[3]

The preparations for war against Austria and Prussia, which began in the spring of 1792, resulted in a sharp polarizing of political forces in the French countryside. As the volunteers gathered and prepared to march to the frontier, a wave of patriotic enthusiasm reinforced the growing tide of revolutionary sentiment. Elements which had been hostile or lukewarm towards the revolution—the families of *émigré* nobles, priests who refused to accept the revolutionary church settlement, moderate local administrations—all now became doubly suspect as potential traitors and counter-revolutionaries.

At the beginning of May the second battalion of the Volunteers of the Aisne brought the new spirit to Roye as they marched through on their way to the front. The cross of St. Andrew in the market square was overturned and a Tree of Liberty planted in front of the Hôtel de Ville. On 3 May the mayor (now, once again, the former deputy Prévost) was summoned by a lieutenant in a red cap of liberty and ordered to remove the "gothic filth," the coats of arms and other heraldic material which still "disfigured" the town. Babeuf joyfully wrote to the editor of the *Annales patriotiques* in Paris to detail the fate of the "rosettes, garlands, crowns, toads, serpents, grass-snakes, and dogs, so artistically carved from stone, and glorifying all the stupidity and swagger of the *échevins* and governors!" The "purge" was carried out in a festive atmosphere, with much singing of the "Ça ira," while Prévost went into hiding. To complete the day, on the urging of the Roye inhabitants, the volunteers paid a visit to Montdidier, where they conducted themselves with comparable violence, dragging individuals from their houses and making them kiss the Tree of Liberty in the central square, smashing statues and carvings, slashing the fleurs-de-lis and the donors' coats of arms from pictures in the Lady Chapel, and tearing apart books whose bindings displayed coats of arms.[4] Despite the growing pressure, the "viziers of Roye" held on stubbornly, and Roye remained the only town of the district to refuse to take part in the Bastille anniversary celebrations in July. At the beginning of October there was an even more terrifying visitation, this time by a division of the Gendarmerie Nationale from Paris, with two companies of *canonniers*, also on their way to the front. The Parisians turned their attention this time to the "relics of superstition," attacking the Church of Saint Pierre and compelling Prévost to preside in a red bonnet as they forced the Soeurs de la Croix and the Annonciades to dance with them on the town square. They also threatened to train cannon on the Hôtel de Ville and "aristocrats' houses," before moving off with 30 requisitioned horses. The *canonniers* also gave the lead to a popular movement (in which women were especially prominent) to impose a maximum price for grain on the Roye market.

The extremists did not have things all their own way in Picardy, however. Following the events of 20 June in Paris, in which revolutionaries stormed their way into the Tuileries and threatened the royal family, there was a rallying of the royalist and moderate ranks. Many local authorities (including the districts and municipalities of Amiens, Péronne, and Abbeville) sent addresses to the throne expressing their indignation. The Somme Département administration also declared its loyalty to the crown in the same manner.[5]

The elections to the Convention and the accompanying municipal elections in the autumn of 1792 became the arena of a bitter power struggle between the rival factions. After 20 June Babeuf, in his lonely and self-styled role as the "Marat of the Somme," had made a point of taking each of the moderate administrations to task, with a campaign of counteraddresses, proclamations, and letters of protest. When, on 10 August, the *fédérés* and militant *sectionnaires* of Paris stormed the Tuileries and put an end to the monarchy, his claim to radical leadership in Picardy was thus triumphantly vindicated.[6]

On 26 August the citizens of Roye were called together for the first stage of the elections to the National Convention. They were charged by the Paris insurgents with the task of replacing the Legislative Assembly and formulating a new constitution. For the first time, in the new conditions following the uprising of 10 August, all citizens (and not just the élite of wealthier "active" citizens) were able to take part in the elections. Although, in the event, only about a quarter of the adult male population turned out, Babeuf's party was in a majority. Babeuf was chosen to go as a second-degree elector to the *département* electoral assembly at Abbeville, which would elect the Somme Département deputies to the Convention, and renew the *département* administration. While his old rival Longuecamp was also elected, the Roye electors agreed to mandate all five second-degree electors in terms proposed by Babeuf.

In a carefully moderate and practical electoral address Babeuf had urged that the meeting should avoid offering any detailed judgments on either the fate of the deposed and imprisoned Louis XVI or the structure of the new constitution. He also made it quite clear that he personally stood for a republic and for "pure democracy," with referendum and recall. Although the Legislative Assembly had called for the election of deputies with unrestricted powers, Babeuf argued that "the Nation," as sovereign, was nevertheless entitled to follow different counsels. He proposed as a general mandate the Declaration of the Rights of Man, but with three "supplementary clauses," which were accepted by the meeting. The first demanded universal suffrage, the abolition of the distinction between active and nonactive citizens. By the second the electors endorsed free state education adequate to fit any citizen for government service on a basis of equality: human knowledge was declared "a national property." Finally, Babeuf won support for the additional clause proposed by Pétion to the Constituent Assembly in 1789 (he had already quoted it in his petition on the *aides* in April 1790), which guaranteed every citizen the right to a subsistence from his property or his labor, and "society" was held responsible for meeting the guarantee in case of ill-fortune or sickness.[7]

The proceedings of the Abbeville assembly opened with a mass in the church of the Saint-Esprit on the morning of Sunday, 2 September. Babeuf arrived at Abbeville with high hopes. He intended to persuade the assembly to agree to a mandate on the lines of the democratic program brought from Roye, and he hoped to win a personal seat in the National Covention. He took with him the drafts of an address which he planned to deliver, broadly restating the essentials of the Roye mandate, but with some further elaboration. Pétion's declaration of the right of subsistence was enlarged by an additional clause vesting in society the duty not only to guarantee work for all, but also to fix wages in accordance with prices, so that all families could provide for their needs.

Babeuf also proposed to advance a democratic program containing the same elements as those summarized in his correspondence with Coupé a year before, giving the right of recall, replacement, and popular veto to the primary assemblies. The laws adopted by the Convention should be provisionally in force for a year before being submitted for ratification by the people in their primary assemblies. The votes would then be forwarded via the districts and *départements* to Paris, where they would be totaled and the true people's will declared. There was no mention in any of this of "communism" or the "agrarian law." As in his address to the Roye electors Babeuf strove to present himself as a practical, down-to-earth reformer who could be trusted with the people's mandate. However, there was nothing to stop his partisans among the electors from dropping hints in the Abbeville cafés that there was a much more radical secret program. One of the electors who recorded such rumors was Louis Pierre Croissy (*vicaire* of the parish of Hangest, hard by Davenescourt). Two years later, arrested and himself charged with preaching the agrarian law, Croissy even admitted that some such project—the redistribution of large leasehold farms among the poorer peasants—had in fact been canvassed in at least one Picard village about this time.[8]

How much, or little, Babeuf's friends at Abbeville knew of his personal commitment to the agrarian law must remain a matter of conjecture. What is certain is that his overt political campaign was based on the broader ground of democratic republicanism, rather than on social revolution. He still believed that the way to the achievement of the ultimate goal lay through a limited political reform.

At first the opportunities for furthering such a reform at Abbeville seemed not unhopeful. The full assembly should have numbered 780, but the exclusion in the course of the proceedings of almost a quarter as signatories of protests against the events of 20 June and other "anti-patriotic" petitions increased the potential power of the Left.

It soon became clear, however, that the strongest party belonged to the followers of André Dumont, an administrator of the Amiens

District, who was able to rally 365 votes for his election as deputy. At the very beginning, on the afternoon of 2 September, Dumont blocked Babeuf's chance of having his projected mandate discussed; he successfully moved that the assembly should restrict itself formally to the business of the elections and eschew the discussion of any other questions. Encouraged by this lead, Longuecamp launched on the following day a bitter attack on his colleague Babeuf as an agitator and a "teacher of evil principles," and Babeuf was prevented from replying. On 5 September the balance was somewhat redressed by the arrival in Abbeville of Parein and Corchant, *commissaires* of the Revolutionary Commune of Paris, who addressed the assembly and whose obvious ultrarevolutionary sympathies forced the moderates to go cautiously.

The situation now began to be complicated by the strain of the long, drawn-out procedures of the electoral assembly. Initially responsible for choosing twelve deputies, the electors soon found themselves compelled to vote again to replace five who chose to accept their election by other *départements*. They also had to select four *suppléants,* two high court jurors and thirty-six members of the *département* general council. Proceedings dragged on for more than a fortnight, and voting attendance fluctuated considerably as some electors were excluded and others were called away by business or domestic pressures. Thus while Saladin, the first deputy to be elected, received 535 votes, by 13 September 174 votes were enough to secure the election of Sillery, the fourteenth choice.[9]

By 14 September, despite their energetic beginning, it was clear that Babeuf and his friends could not compete with the Dumont faction for control of the shrinking assembly. Babeuf unsuccessfully proposed to shorten procedures by adopting the method of vote by acclamation for certain posts. On 15 September Babeuf was passed over in the election of the four *suppléant* deputies, although Longuecamp collected a few votes and was elected high court juror.

The following day was a Sunday, so that the assembly did not get down to the *département* elections until Monday, 17 September. When the session began, at six in the morning, it was decided to meet continuously until midday on Tuesday in order to complete business. The electors were now evidently under some pressure from extremists. Dumont had complained about the surrounding of the electoral hall, the church of the Saint Sépulcre, by the National Guard. Under these exceptional conditions, what Babeuf himself described as a "miracle" occurred, when he was elected one of the

thirty-six members of the General Council of the Somme Département. Babeuf received 225 votes, the second highest total for a councillor, but well below the 377 votes collected by an old enemy,
Thierry, the successful candidate for the post of *procureur-syndic* of
the *département*.[10]

Still at Abbeville on 20 September Babeuf wrote to Roland,
the minister of the interior, who had been chosen as one of the
Somme deputies, partly to explain away his own failure to support
Roland's candidature (he was convinced, he said, that it was an
aristocratic plot to compel the resignation of a patriotic minister),
but chiefly to enlist Roland's moral support in the fierce struggle he
anticipated with his counter-revolutionary colleagues at Amiens.
Already attempts were being concerted to prevent his election to a
post on the (well-paid) *département* directory. The hope was that his
continuing poverty and domestic cares, many miles from the
département capital, would free the reactionaries from his embarrassing surveillance.

Nevertheless, Babeuf had every intention of taking up residence in
Amiens and keeping a watchful eye on the maneuvers of the
aristocrats. "I will do what I can for my family, but *la Patrie* comes
before all." On 21 September he set out from Abbeville for the Pied
de Boeuf at Amiens, to prepare for the opening session of the
département general council on 25 September. Two days later, as
Babeuf had anticipated, he failed to win a place in the elections to the
département directory.[11] Yet despite his almost paranoiac denunciations at the time and afterwards, a study of the minutes of the
département council leaves the impression that during the autumn of
1792 the Somme administration was, after all, far more interested in
fighting the Prussians than in fighting Babeuf. In their desperate efforts to stiffen republican resistance to the advancing Prussian armies they were ready to use any and all competent assistance
available, and on 25 September Babeuf found himself elected immediately to an important subcommittee charged with military affairs. A few days later, on 30 September, he was sent off with a
colleague on a special mission to Péronne, to speed the mobilization
of men for the war front. The imminent capture of the frontier fortress of Lille was expected to herald a general invasion of France.[12]

A fortnight before, the general in charge of the defending armies,
Marassé-Bourdonnaye, had ordered from his H.Q. at Douai a
general call-up of a sixth of the National Guard infantry, and a half
of the élite corps of grenadiers and chasseurs, to provide the bulk of a

reserve corps based on Soissons. During the third and fourth week of September this mobilization had proceeded in the face of growing logistical problems. The main bottleneck was Péronne, a town through which many of the new units of *fédérés* would have to pass. On 24 September the members of the Péronne district administration sent off a representative, Gaudefroi, to explain their difficulties. Already 400 men had been stationed at Péronne for ten days, and a further 1,200 were hourly expected to join them. The daily passage of troops through the town would raise the total of billets required to two or three thousand, an impossible burden. Gaudefroi appealed to the *département* directory to provide the means to lodge, pay, dress and equip the volunteers, and to act against the neighboring municipalities who were refusing to pull their weight. Meanwhile Marassé-Bourdonnaye himself paid a flying visit to the Péronne district administration to express his anxiety about food supplies for the army. Apparently what he discovered was so disheartening that he wrote to Amiens to countermand the mobilization of the National Guard detachments altogether.

It was at this point that the *département* administration decided to dispatch Babeuf and a colleague, Devaux, to Péronne to supervise the lodging and feeding of the volunteers, to stir the local officials to more effective action and, ominously, to reassure themselves about the political disposition of the inhabitants. Arriving in Péronne on 1 October, the two men went straight to the municipality and demanded the minutes of the general assembly of the commune, which they scrutinized. Then followed an inspection of the convents of the Clairesses and the Ursulines (then being converted into barracks and a military hospital) and the town prison and the Hôtel Dieu, which were being used as emergency quarters; Babeuf and Devaux also visited the district administration.

What the two *commissaires* found (though they did not report this) was a very commendable record of local initiative. Since 22 September the Péronne municipal government had requisitioned the two convents as barracks and the church of Saint-Jean as a forage store. They had requisitioned sheets and bed coverings from the citizens and seized the houses of *émigrés* as officers' billets. They had completed a census of the town's bakers as a step towards ensuring the food supply. On 1 October (but before Babeuf and Devaux arrived) the municipality had taken the further step of requisitioning bedding from the inns for the officers' billets. Artisans had been hard at work turning the ironwork of the churches and convents into pikes to arm the volunteers. The only additional measure attributable to the intervention from Amiens was, possibly, a renewed appeal for bedding for the Clairesses on 4 October.[13]

On 5 October the *commissaires* returned to Amiens, where two days later Babeuf tried to present a report which described how he and his colleague had thwarted an aristocratic plot. It would have opened the front to the Prussians, who would then have been invited to march on Paris through Péronne. The details of this "plot," as published in 1794, linked Marassé-Bourdonnaye with Bouteville Du Metz and Tattegrain, administrators and members of the old "legal aristocracy" of Péronne. Unconvinced, the *département* general council passed (with some irritation) to further business, after a sharp rebuke to Babeuf by Thierry and other members. Babeuf naturally regarded this treatment as no more than an indication of the probable complicity of his enemies on the *département* administration in the "aristocratic plot" and he appealed to Paris, sending a report to Roland which was also ignored.[14]

Whether a plot existed at all must remain an open question, in the absence of Babeuf's report. It seems likely that this contained a recital of the circumstantial evidence: the protests of the Péronne district administration against the burdens of mobilization, which were seen as culpable delaying tactics; and an account of Marassé-Bourdonnaye's visit to Péronne and the sudden cancellation of the mobilization that followed, plus observations on the "well-known" aristocratic tendencies of both the general and the district administration. In the hectic circumstances of 1792, and in the shadow of General Lafayette's recent defection, there was certainly material enough here to lead even a less enthusiastic revolutionary than Babeuf to scent deliberate treachery.

On his return to Amiens Babeuf discovered that he had been elected, in his absence, to the third bureau of the administration; this was responsible for a curious variety of "welfare" functions including public assistance, the encouragement of commerce and agriculture, the administration of common lands, the control of fires and epidemics, the repair of churches, and the price of grain and forage. The work of this bureau might have seemed to offer admirable scope for his reforming zeal, touching as it did on so many areas of past interest and commitment. But even better prospects were opening up. On 13 October Babeuf wrote to his family at Roye to express pleasure at his election as archivist of the *département*, at a starting salary of twelve to fifteen hundred livres. After so many vicissitudes he seemed at last to have arrived at a safe berth, and he even began to make plans for his son Emile (Robert) to join him in Amiens. In the meantime money was still desperately short. Pending the first installment of his salary he was forced to borrow from a friend, and to move out of his hotel into a cheaper furnished room. Even his salary as a councillor, three livres per session attended, was paid in arrears. For forty-one sessions from September to November he ultimately received 123 livres. On 9 October the *département* directory had authorized expenses of 99 livres, 11 sous, 6 deniers for Babeuf and Devaux's mission to Péronne, but little of this is likely to have remained as profit.[15]

There are few details of Babeuf's personal life at Amiens. About this time he appears to have adopted a revolutionary presence appropriate to the majesty of a people's representative. He was wearing his hair long and cut low on the brow in the Jacobin style, and had a long grey cloak and a huge sabre.[16] On Sunday, 21 October, he took his place, along with other civic functionaries, at the foot of the Altar of the Fatherland in the Place du Marché aux Herbes for the public celebrations of the first republican victories in Savoy, despite the pouring rain, joining in the performance of the "Marseillaise" by a choir of forty voices.

Babeuf also visited the Amiens theater to see a performance of the *Héros français*—only to be scandalized when the actors followed up this patriotic opening piece with Desforges' *Le Sourd, ou l'Auberge pleine*, an Ancien Régime farce in which the usual barons and chevaliers frolicked about on the stage making a mock of a virtuous and industrious citizen. It was all too close to home for at least one of the spectators. The fleurs-de-lis and coats of arms on the stage curtain had been painted out, and the orchestra instructed to play only "the divine chants" of liberty; but the content of the performances still plainly needed a purifying scrutiny. On 29 October Babeuf posted a placard (subsequently published in the *Affiches de la Somme*) in which he attacked the actors of the theater and demanded that in future the French theaters should become "truly and uniquely schools of good morals and *civisme*" in which philosophy and reason should hold exclusive sway. The only saving grace in this humorless and philistine outburst was the recognition that "almost all of Molière is still acceptable." It contributed to the growing conviction of the *département* directory that Babeuf was an impossible colleague.[17] At the end of October they sent him away on another mission.

During the autumn of 1792 the continuing inflation, the threat of invasion, and the exceptional demands of the army conspired together to empty the markets of grain and to arouse lively fears of famine. Despite a predilection for free-trade principles, the Girondin administration in Paris had been forced to accept the necessity of some regulation of the grain trade by ordering a census of supplies. On 29 October the Somme Département council decided to send Babeuf to Abbeville to check on the apparent dilatoriness of the authorities in carrying out this census. Having arrived at Abbeville Babeuf predictably discovered a *"complot de famine,"* a deliberate conspiracy by the administration to withhold supplies and starve the people.

Whatever the real causes of the shortage, Babeuf acted on the spot in a levelheaded and vigorous way to counter its effects. On 2 November, for example, he wrote a letter to the administration of St. Valéry, seeking information and advising them of his powers: to supervise the grain census and to requisition such supplies as were necessary to see that the markets were stocked. On 4 November he ordered the mayor and the municipal officers of the Commune of Abbeville to begin a careful accounting of all grains henceforth received, with a record of sales, a weekly summary to be forwarded to the *département* through the district administration. On 6 November the same instructions were sent off to the municipalities of Ault, Saint-Valéry, Crécy and Rue. Returning to Amiens, Babeuf presented his report (including a denunciation of the Abbeville administration) on 9 November. This time there were apparently no difficulties, and the report was heard and acted upon. The report on Abbeville was, however, to be Babeuf's "swan-song" as a member of the *département* general council, for he attended no further meetings.[18]

On Sunday, 11 November, he once again found himself in Péronne, this time in his capacity as a second-degree elector, to take part in the election of officers of the criminal tribunal of the *département*. Proceedings began with the choice of a bureau for the conduct of the elections, and Babeuf was named vice-secretary. However he received only forty-three votes as against 174 for the president, the "aristocratic plotter" of Péronne, Bouteville-Du-Metz. In the election of scrutineers Babeuf collected 101 votes and topped the list, and as vice-secretary he played a prominent part in the proceedings.

On 14 November the assembly listened to an uncontroversially patriotic address to the Convention, drafted by Babeuf, and then voted its approval. The minutes of the Péronne assembly imply indeed that everything went off perfectly smoothly and without conflict. The president and secretary of the existing tribunal were reelected by 349 and 360 votes respectively. Nevertheless there must have been at least one jarring note, for Babeuf used the platform of the Péronne assembly to launch a public attack on the Somme Département Directory. Its members, he said, were infected with an exclusive spirit. Decisions were made at private back-room meetings after 6 p.m., and the general council was kept deliberately in the dark. The actual administrative cadres were riddled with officials of the royal intendancy, whose bureaucratic spirit they were still preserving.[19]

In fact Babeuf had already decided to give up the unequal struggle at Amiens. On Sunday, 18 November, he turned up at the church of the Saint-Sépulcre at Montdidier for the opening of the election of the Montdidier district administration, determined to seek office nearer home. Here, too, there were difficulties, for Babeuf's old enemy Longuecamp was also at Montdidier, with ambitions of his own. In the first clash, the Longuecamp party showed its strength by capturing the presidency of the electoral assembly, with thirty-one votes for Longuecamp against fifteen for Babeuf; there were about fifty second-degree electors present.

Worse was to follow when the important and lucrative post of *procureur-syndic* went to Longuecamp by forty-nine votes, after Babeuf had rallied only twenty-seven for his own candidature. In the afternoon, however, he managed to scrape in as one of three members of the district directory, elected with twenty-three votes, the lowest figure, after his enemies had challenged both the counting of the votes and Babeuf's eligibility (he was a member of the *département* general council).

Clearly it would be necessary for the new administrator to go cautiously. His old enemy Longuecamp held the strategic post of *procureur-syndic*. Of his two colleagues on the directory, one (Lefrançois) had been a member of the old administration, while the other (Hallot) was an honest but uninspired peasant farmer. The remaining members of the council were mainly Longuecamp supporters. Already a too obvious and too incautious extremism had forced Babeuf to resign the prospect of 1,200 livres a year at Amiens for the 900-livre salary of a district administrator, and there was nowhere else to go.

All these considerations may help to explain the care and moderation with which Babeuf now strove to reinforce the new image he had chosen for himself as a hard-headed, reliable republican administrator. Such a policy was, of course, perfectly consistent with the Machiavellian tactic of surface public moderation to conceal a long-term aim of social revolution that Babeuf had defended in his correspondence with Coupé a year earlier. Yet from a study of his conduct as an administrator of the Somme Département, no less than of Montdidier, it is difficult to avoid the conclusion that Babeuf's dedication to his new rôle was anything less than entirely genuine—and that, caught up in the exciting day-to-day challenge of winning and holding revolutionary power, he had, for the moment, relegated the ultimate dream of social revolution to the distant future.

In the tense, embattled days that followed the overthrow of the monarchy the "short-term" objective, the democratic revolution, was beginning to develop its own mystique as its Jacobin defenders glimpsed the distant prospect of the Reign of Virtue on the horizon. "We shall be able to tell our descendants," Babeuf assured a meeting of his colleagues at Montdidier, "that we have had the advantage of playing our part in administration in the finest days of the Republic: in those times when all the prejudices disappeared to give place to the laws of pure philosophy that were soon to become the code of all the nations."[20]

At the morning session of 20 November Babeuf delivered an address of gratitude to the Montdidier electors in which he pledged his faith as a democratic administrator. He promised to remain always accessible to citizens and to treat their petitions with promptness, and he listed the major preoccupations of the new administration: collecting taxes for the war effort, lightening the burden of taxation and the promulgation of laws to consolidate the well-being of the people, above all of the peasants.

An inaugural speech to the first full meeting of the new district council on 3 December presented an opportunity to develop the same themes. The urgency of infusing revolutionary vigor into the routine of administration had already led Babeuf (on 26 November) to persuade Hallot and Lefrançois to join him in moving into office a week before the legal date. Now he stressed the necessity of speeding up the completion of the tax-rolls and the collection of outstanding taxes. While it was true, he explained, both that the Somme Département was carrying an unfair burden of taxation and that within the *département* the District of Montdidier was too heavily assessed also, the correct procedure was to collect the taxes nevertheless and only then to request an adjustment from Amiens.

Next, Babeuf turned his attention to the question of the property of counter-revolutionary *émigrés*. Here, once again, administrative delays were evident. Many communes had yet to draw up a list of properties now liable for confiscation under the decree of 14 August, and the administration had to press ahead with uncovering these resources, which were needed by the nation. There was no mention of any plan to redistribute such lands among the landless. Only when he came to discuss the alarming food situation did Babeuf allow his deeper preoccupations to become apparent. The most grave and immediate crisis, he declared, was the present desperate spectacle of general famine at a time of actual abundance. "How can the public welfare [*le bonheur public*] exist when the greater part of the children of the great family are suffering? Can citizens view in cold blood their brothers weeping with hunger? . . . Public order, the security of person and property, can only be ensured when all members of the common society live in adequate comfort."

In 1786, 1789, and 1791 the same essential principle had been used to justify the most radical social policies. Now it was invoked to sanction no more than the administration's intention vigorously to enforce the grain census and the compulsory sale of stocks necessary to provision the markets, in accordance with the existing decrees.[21]

On 20 December the district council elected its committees: the Public Weal (Bien Public), Procedures (Règlement), Taxes and Finance, and National Domains. Babeuf found himself seconded to the Procedures Committee, with Councillors Dubois and Delahoche. With remarkable dispatch, the committee tabled its thirty-two-page report, in which Babeuf's special expertise had enabled him to prescribe a new and more orderly system of maintaining the district archives. The hours of work for the administrators and their three clerks were fixed at 7 a.m. to 8 p.m. in summer, with a break from 1 p.m. to 3 p.m., and a later start in winter months. Babeuf recommended that the clerks should be given an increase in salary, to avoid the scandal of their being wined and dined by the purchasers of state lands or by other petitioners. There was a special recommendation for alterations to the district offices and to the style of correspondence. The existing coat of arms must be removed and replaced by a republican device with an appropriate motto: *"Egalité, Liberté, Publicité, Sauvegarde du Peuple."* Parishes should be henceforth referred to as communes, and *impositions* as *con-*

tributions. Citizens were expected to wear the red bonnet of liberty on visiting the district building (though they need not remove it in the presence of the administrators). Babeuf served as an administrator at Montdidier for just over two months, until the beginning of February 1793. Although Roye was within the boundaries of the Montdidier District, during this time he stayed in Montdidier, actually living in the district offices (in the buildings of a former priory) and taking his meals at a hôtel run by the ex-cook of the archbishop of Rheims.[22]

The records of Babeuf's activities at Montdidier during these crowded and busy weeks are not plentiful. He seems to have interested himself chiefly in four aspects of the work of the administration: poor relief, the completion of a purge of outlying municipal authorities, the sequestration of *émigré* lands and "the extirpation of the outward signs of feudalism." Poor relief, probably for reasons of convenience, had been placed within the competence of the Procedures Committee, and Babeuf lost no time in circularizing the municipal authorities to urge them to take prompt action to tackle the crisis of poverty: he reminded the administrators that the Constituent Assembly had twice allocated funds for public works. Small though the amounts might be, such funds would assure the needy of bread, if only for a few days.

Although the Paris authorities had ordered the renewal of all elected authorities where such a renewal had not already taken place since the overthrow of the monarchy on 10 August, some of the old administrations were still clinging to office. In places like Goyencourt and Beauvraigne popular meetings were now organized to oust the diehards, with the encouragement of the district directory. Elsewhere, as at Crémery, a republican administration was sustained against a "counter-revolutionary" challenge from below.

The enforcement of the laws against *émigrés* naturally afforded Babeuf the liveliest satisfaction. Many of his most hated aristocratic enemies had sent one or more members of the family to join Condé and Artois abroad; to circumvent the charge of emigration other members remained in France, outwardly—and in some cases genuinely—loyal to the Republic. The breaking of such "alibis" was a function for which Babeuf was particularly well qualified, and in 1794 he was able to boast that he had persuaded the Montdidier district council to agree to sequestrate nearly 20,000 acres of land, worth more than ten million livres, belonging to local aristocrats like the duc de Liancourt, the marquis de Nesle, the comte d'Herly, and, inevitably, the comtesse de la Myre (the tyrant of Davenescourt), despite the resistance of the Longuecamp faction. Babeuf was also able to throw the weight of the administration behind the struggle of the villagers of Chavatte with a member of the Bracquemont family over the perennially vexed question of seigneurial timber rights, even though he was eventually overruled by his enemies in the Somme Département.[23]

Despite his studied republican orthodoxy, Babeuf continued to stand out very much as a lone Jacobin figure, battling against the apathy and hostility of the reactionary district. Nowhere was this more so than in his iconoclastic outbursts. On 12 December, soon after he took office, the district directory ordered the Montdidier municipality to join in the destruction of "the signs of ancient servitude." Anything burnable was to be handed over for a public bonfire at the foot of the Tree of Liberty, in the market square, after proper provision had been made for "fuel for the poor." It was not, however, until the end of January that Babeuf—acting alone, and amidst the jeers and menaces of a hostile crowd—was able to carry out his *auto-da-fé*. To the fleur-de-lis tapestries from the tribunal and the town hall he added "twelve superb portraits of kings," garnered from the same places and from the district offices. The demonstration had been staged with the intention of celebrating the execution of Louis XVI on 21 January. But all it seemed to show was that the majority of the inhabitants of at least one Picard town were still royalists at heart.[24]

A few days later the "reign of philosophy" at Montdidier came to an end, when Babeuf was suspended from his functions and driven into flight by Longuecamp. The cause of Babeuf's downfall was the discovery by Longuecamp of an irregularity in the recording of a sale of national property which was regarded as a deliberate fraud.

Among the church lands on the market at Montdidier in 1792 was an extensive *commanderie* of the Knights of Malta at Fontaines. In the normal course of business the directory of the district auctioned this land on 31 December to a "rich proprietor from Montdidier," a certain Constancien Levavasseur, for 76,200 livres. There were certain peculiarities about the transaction. Levavasseur was old, deaf, feeble of speech and sight (because of syphilis), so that he entrusted the bidding to an agent, Devillasse (the parish priest of Etelfay, who was also president of the Montdidier District and who was himself a practiced speculator in church lands). The sale was correctly recorded as having been made to Devillasse, with a note to explain that the purchaser had been acting for Levavasseur. In due course Babeuf provided Levavasseur with an extract of the auction proceedings, correctly drawn up in every particular.

Before Levavasseur had time to collect together the 12 percent deposit required to confirm the purchase, he and Devillasse quarreled, and Devillasse decided to try to sabotage the sale. Apart from personal pique, Devillasse seems to have been motivated by sympathy for the sitting tenant, Debraine, who had been unable to compete with Levavasseur at the auction. Having bought for speculative purposes Levavasseur was now expected to raise the lease-rent beyond Debraine's means. Devillasse and Leclerc de Raineval, a judge on the district tribunal, decided to come to Debraine's rescue by bringing in Leclerc's cousin, Leclerc d'Assainvilliers, a military contractor, to finance a joint purchase in his name and Debraine's.

The conspiracy came to a head on 30 January when Devillasse, Debraine, and Leclerc invited Babeuf to join them at a lunch at the Hôtel Chevrier. They persuaded him that what had happened at the auction was that Devillasse had bought an *option* on the property and that he was free to dispose of it as he pleased. They then asked Babeuf to prepare a certification of sale naming Debraine and Leclerc d'Assainvilliers. Babeuf, thereupon, went to the district offices, took the original auction record from the archive, struck out Levavasseur's name and inserted those of Debraine and Leclerc in its place, calling in another councillor, Jaudhuin, to witness the document.

Since there was no other indication on the document, this meant that Babeuf was technically claiming to have witnessed a transaction at which he had not been present—the auction of 31 December—and authenticating an agreement that he knew not to have been made at that date, an agreement by Devillasse to act as agent for Leclerc and Debraine. To complete the transaction he insisted on a copy of the altered auction record, even though the clerk reminded him that he had already given Levavasseur a copy of the original.[25]

Biographers favorable to Babeuf have generally dismissed these actions as constituting either a very minor peccadillo or no sin at all. Thus, Mazauric affirms that the action was performed "*en tout naïveté*" and that Babeuf's innocence is "generally conceded," while Professor Dalin dismisses it as "a mistake made by Babeuf through inexperience" and a "quite accidental and innocent blunder."[26] But whether Babeuf acted in complete innocence or out of confused sympathy for a working *fermier* in the clutches of a speculator, he had unquestionably falsified a public document in his charge. It was an offense for which the prescribed minimum penalty was twenty years in irons.

With his trained lawyer's mind Longuecamp immediately realized the implications of Babeuf's mistake, and, before the day was out, he had seized and locked away the crucial document. From this point on Babeuf's ruin was a foregone conclusion. On 31 January Levavasseur was turned away, with money in hand, from the district registry; and he promptly appealed to the directory. On 4 February the district council discussed Levavasseur's complaint, confirmed his right to Fontaines, and suspended Babeuf. Details of the case were also sent to the Somme Département council in Amiens. On 7 February the *département* council considered the matter and Babeuf's enemies were not slow to seize their opportunity. Babeuf, who had come to Amiens to protest against his suspension, was horrified to learn that the council had discovered "powerful presumptions" that he was the "instigator" of the entire conspiracy, and had referred the case to the *département* public prosecutor.

Realistically weighing the chances of obtaining a fair hearing under the prevailing conditions he decided to flee to Paris, where a virtuous republican in difficulty might still be able to find influential friends. Babeuf's instincts were sound. In March a Montdidier jury of presentment found a *prima facie* case against him, while absolving Leclerc, Jaudhuin and Devillasse, and ordered his arrest. On 23 August 1793 the Criminal Tribunal of the Somme Département sentenced Babeuf, in absentia, to twenty years in irons.[27]

Nine

Paris and the 'Sans-Culotte' Movement

Paris in 1793 was a place in which a hunted man would find it easy to lose himself. Within this city of half a million people a variety of competing and conflicting authorities strove with only limited success to impose a revolutionary order on a population steadily growing more and more suspicious of any authority and order at all.

The atmosphere of the capital was pervaded by an almost anarchist affirmation of local and individual sovereignties. The autonomous pretensions of the sixty Paris districts, so admired by Babeuf in 1790, had given place to an even more stubborn assertion of independence by the forty-eight sections which had inherited the functions of the districts. After 10 August the sovereignty of the sections had been delegated for a time to the revolutionary commune of Paris, the organizer of the uprising and the watchdog of the new republic. Almost immediately, however, there was a reaction by the sections against both the revolutionary commune and the elected commune which replaced it.

The spokesmen of the sections argued that the sovereignty of the people resided only in the general assemblies of the sections and could not be permanently delegated, whether to a national convention or to a municipal council. Central delegate assemblies of the forty-eight sections continued to meet at the Evêché, the former archbishop's palace on the Ile de la Cité, and to seek to impose policies which reflected more flexibly the changing preoccupations of the *sans-culottes* of the sections, and of the handful of politically active militants who dominated the section assemblies and bureaus. These, in turn, took their lead from the Jacobins and the popular societies, and particularly from the Cordeliers Club and the Société Fraternelle, the meeting place at the Jacobin Club of the "Enragés" (or extreme democrats) of both sexes.

Contact with this developing *sans-culotte* movement introduced Babeuf to a new and unfamiliar world. He knew the life of the villagers and the small towns of Picardy, the sufferings of their peasants, artisans, and laborers. But while many of the inhabitants of the capital were recently uprooted peasants, the dominant tradition and attitudes were essentially urban and industrial. The typical Parisian below the level of the bourgeoisie was an artisan working at a traditional craft at home or in a small workshop alone, with other members of his family, or with one or two other fellow workers. Many of the *quartiers* still preserved their own distinctive industrial character: dyeing, leather trades and brewing in the Faubourg Saint-Marceau; furniture and upholstery in the Faubourg Saint-Antoine; ribbon-weaving and cloth-making in the crowded regions of the center which lay on the right bank; lace-making, weaving and other textile trades on the slopes of the Montagne Sainte-Geneviève, in the Faubourg Saint-Jacques.

There was nothing exclusive about the distribution of most trades, however, and the textile trades were normally represented wherever there was a concentration of population. There were of course tens of thousands who did not fit the "artisan" stereotype: domestic servants, building workers, laborers at the Halles (the great central markets) and at the wharves along the Seine, casual laborers, and the unemployed, the "submerged fifth" of the city population. Crowded into damp cellars along the banks of the river, in the garrets and upper stories of the city center and in the streets of the Faubourg Saint-Antoine, this element (together with the most impoverished layer of artisans) provided the reservoir of the Paris mob, which from time to time erupted to impose its will on the course of events during the repeated *journées*, or popular insurrections, of the revolution.

The economic interests of this Paris population were not uniform. There were strikes by wage-earning journeymen and apprentices against the masters, and there was bitter resentment between established masters and mushrooming *chambrelans* (who took advantage of the decay of the guild system during the decades preceding the revolution, and its legal demolition after 1791, to multiply workshops and to introduce ruinous competition). There was also the perennial and intensifying conflict of interest between self-employed masters and the capitalist middlemen who supplied raw materials and marketed the products. On one important issue the mass of the Paris population was, nevertheless, united. To all—whether master, wage-earner, or laborer—reasonably stable food prices were essential for survival. Wages and the prices of manufactured goods were fixed by custom and competition and were slow to respond to general price movements. Food supplies on the other hand were liable to wild fluctuations, depending on the harvest and on other factors, including speculation.

By the beginning of 1793 the living standards of the great mass of the Paris *sans-culottes* were beginning to be seriously undermined by the effects of the revolution and the war. On the one hand inflation, encouraged by speculation against the assignats, the revolutionary paper money, meant a reduction in the real value of wages and fixed incomes, of the profits of small industries and of savings. On the other hand, the dislocations of war—interrupted supplies and government contracts—offered golden opportunities for speculation in foodstuffs and raw materials, as successful "corners" forced up commodity prices disproportionately.

During the winter of 1792 and the early months of 1793 the growing discontent of the *sans-culottes* began to find expression in the agitation of Enragé leaders. They voiced demands for draconian laws against speculation and for the price control of essential commodities, together with a purge of counter-revolutionary elements and protectors of the rich from the Convention, the army and the administration. The riots of 25-26 February—in which Paris crowds took the law into their own hands, imposed their own price control and cleared out the grocers' shops—were an indication of the growing force of a new popular militancy which would soon challenge the Convention itself for control of France.

In the vanguard of this popular revolution at the beginning of 1793 was a new and disturbing element among the Paris population. Since the summer of 1792 thousands of military volunteers had been flocking to the capital from the provinces and even from abroad, their strong anxiety to serve in proper style sometimes leading to a more or less protracted delay in their actual arrival at the front. In September 1793 Fabre de l'Eglantine offered a somewhat unflattering portrait of these warriors: ". . . men with moustaches, dressed in military uniforms . . . flaunting their great sabres in the streets of Paris and frightening peaceful citizens who pass by, and the women and children who get in their way, with their propositions and their menaces. I have seen them too, in the lobbies of the theaters, suddenly drawing their sabres, to say to people around them, who were minding their own business: I am so and so, and if you look at me like that, I will chop you to pieces. . . ."[1]

It was among such people that Babeuf managed to find sanctuary on his arrival in Paris.

Babeuf's first letter to Marie-Anne from the capital (written on 13 February) shows that his earliest concern was to appeal against his suspension from his post in the Montdidier administration. Through the good offices of Carra he tried to interest Garat, the new minister of the interior, in his fate, only to learn, a few days later, that Garat had merely forwarded his petition to the Somme authorities. By this time Babeuf had already thrown himself into a new venture, the formation of a so-called "legion of people's liberators," an élite corps of revolutionary superpatriots who were to be raised from among the volunteers in Paris. The man behind this project was a 47-year-old adventurer from the West Indies with a somewhat ambiguous reputation, Claude Fournier l'Héritier, known also as Fournier "l'Américain." The former proprietor of a rum distillery in St. Domingo, Fournier had haunted the courts in the 1780s with a protracted lawsuit against his neighbors, whom he accused of ruining his business by an act of arson. Fournier was one of the pioneers in the organization of the Paris National Guard in July 1789, had been prominent in the Champ de Mars demonstration, and had recently distinguished himself in the fighting in Paris on 10 August (and also by his brutal conduct towards a party of priests and nuns in his charge at the time of the September Massacres). He was currently reported by the police to be living in the rue des Fosses M. le Prince (*"aujourd'hui dite égalité"*) with two women: his mistress, described as a woman of "shady reputation," and a reputed marquise de Saint-Giran. This was the protector who became for Babeuf "the most excellent heart that I know."[2]

For about two months, until the middle of April, Babeuf acted as Fournier's secretary. He drafted several petitions and pamphlets for him, and for six weeks, during February and March, he lived in the Fournier household, in the Tuileries Section. On 17 February the two men visited the Convention, and Babeuf read out Fournier's petition for permission to form his "liberators' legion," which was taken under consideration by the Comité de Guerre. On 24 February Babeuf wrote home to Roye of his high hopes of obtaining a good position in Fournier's legion. But the Convention moved only with painful slowness, and no serious progress had been made when Fournier alienated any immediate chance of official support by taking part in the abortive Parisian uprising of 9-10 March.

In allying himself with Fournier, Babeuf had sought out, almost as if by instinct, the center of the most radical agitation in Paris. Since the beginning of January a close alliance had been formed between the military "superpatriots" of the republican volunteer groups in Paris and the militant leaders of the forty-eight sections. The main military organization involved was the society of the "Defenders of the Republic," of which Fournier was one of the leading lights. The Defenders of the Republic met under the same roof as the Jacobin Club in the rue Saint-Honoré, and in close collaboration with the Société Fraternelle.[3]

During January and February the Defenders of the Republic collaborated with the Paris sections in staging patriotic festivals. They acted in general as revolutionary "storm-troopers," stopping "unpatriotic" theater performances and forcibly evicting "suspect elements" from the cafés of the Palais Royal. Politically the Defenders threw their weight behind the developing Enragé campaign for action to check inflation and punish speculators. They were represented in the joint delegation of the commune and the forty-eight sections which arrived at the Convention to demand the death penalty for *agiotage* (exchange speculation in paper money). Delegates from the Defenders also collaborated in drawing up a petition for the fixing of maximum food prices, which was presented to the Convention in the name of the forty-eight sections on 12 February.

The closing stages of the king's trial had seen the beginning of a major division between rival groups in the Convention, which was already polarizing into the conflict of "Girondin" and "Jacobin," or "Montagnard," factions. Popular propaganda readily identified a "liberticidal faction" in the Convention, centered on Roland and Brissot, which was to be recognized by its "contempt" for the sufferings of the people, its stubborn resistance to demands for economic regulation, and by a "counter-revolutionary moderation" which had become evident in the attempts to prevent or postpone the execution of Louis XVI. As early as 18 January some of the Paris sections had begun to agitate for a "recall" of the Appelans, almost 300 members of the Convention who had voted in favor of a referendum, or an "appeal to the people," to decide the king's fate. At the same time agitation for the eviction of "Rolandistes" and "Brissotins" from the ministry began. On 17 January the

Defenders of the Republic and the section militants burned Roland's pamphlets on the Place du Carousel. In the weeks that followed the Defenders continued their vendetta against Roland, even after he had been forced out of office, and they also made a special target of "counter-revolutionary" journalists like Brissot and Gorsas.

In the first few days of March the worst suspicions and wildest accusations of the Defenders and the Enragés suddenly seemed to be borne out when Paris learned of serious defeats suffered by the French armies engaged in the invasion of Holland under the command of the Girondin protégé Dumouriez. The first reaction of the minister of war, Buernonville, seconded by the Girondin press, was to play down the reverses. But on 8 March everyone knew that Dumouriez's invasion had been turned back, his army was in danger of encirclement, and a march on Paris by the enemy armies might be imminent. In an atmosphere of mounting panic the commune, enthusiastically backed by Marat in the *Publiciste*, called for a general mobilization of the *sans-culottes* of the sections and a mass march to the frontiers.

But for many the lesson of the French defeats in the field seemed to be that the patriotic warriors of the Republic had been "betrayed by treason" in the high command, aided and abetted by a nucleus of Girondin ministers, particularly by Buernonville, Clavière, and Lebrun (ministers of war, finance, and foreign affairs, respectively). A feeling grew that before setting out for the front it was imperative first to deal with "the traitors in the rear."

Thus, a group of deputies from the Convention who attended a meeting of the Poissonière Section on 8 March to rally support for the emergency mobilization were greeted by the president of the section with an address which demanded the arrest of Dumouriez and his high command and of Roland, the removal of Buernonville from the War Ministry, and a general purge of former aristocrats from administrative office. Clavière received harsh treatment as a protector of speculators and financial corruption. The address concluded by demanding the closing of the Bourse, and severe action against exchange speculation and food-cornering. The demands of the Poissonière Section summarized the program of those elements who during the next few days strove to organize an uprising to purge the Convention and the government.

The first call for insurrection came from the Defenders of the Republic. On 8 March the Defenders published a pamphlet calling for the recall and execution of "faithless deputies" in the Convention.

At 2 a.m. on 9 March a so-called *comité de surveillance* of the Defenders of the Republic issued an appeal to the *"sans-culottes* of the sections" to rally to the club's headquarters at 5 a.m. in order to march on the Convention and deal with the "factious" deputies. An attack on the pro-Girondin press was also threatened, with particular mention of Brissot's *Patriote français* and Gorsas' *Courrier des départements.*[4]

Although this first insurrectionary plan was abandoned because of an inadequate response by the sections, the threat of an uprising grew steadily during the day as hostile crowds gathered around the Convention. Fournier meanwhile organized an assembly of the Defenders of the Republic on the Champ de Mars. Although the stalwarts of this party seemed chiefly inclined to rally rather to the inns of the *quartier*, some elements at least were preparing to take more definite action. In one incident on the Terrasse des Feuillants, at which Fournier was present, a couple of hundred men put the Girondin deputy Pétion in fear of his life.[5] Others among the Defenders concerted plans for an attack on the presses of Fiévée's *Chronique* and Gorsas' *Courrier.* This took place in the evening, and both offices were completely wrecked.[6]

On 10 March the center of the revolt shifted to the Cordeliers Club, where a new lead was provided by Jean Varlet, veteran Enragé leader of the Droits de l'Homme Section, who was acting as a delegate of the Société Fraternelle. On Varlet's initiative, the Cordeliers issued an appeal for concerted action to compel the Convention to submit to a purge of its members by a specially convened session of the Paris electoral assembly. According to Vergniaud, the version of the appeal for which Varlet won the support of the Quatre-Nations Section included, as well as the demand for a recall of deputies, an accusation of "treason" against Dumouriez, and denounced certain leaders of the Gironde by name: Roland, Brissot, Gensonné, Pétion, Barbaroux, and Louvet.[7]

Towards evening on 10 March Varlet and Fournier and another delegate arrived at the Hôtel de Ville in an attempt to win the commune's support for the planned uprising. By this time a large and dangerous crowd had gathered around the building, reinforced by a party who, led by Desfieux, had earlier tried to force the Jacobin Club to give its formal support to the insurgents' program. But despite this pressure Chaumette, the *procureur* of the commune, and Hébert, his assistant, refused to budge, and Fournier was prevented from addressing the general council. Instead, the commune circulated an official warning to the sections against joining the agitation.[8] Leaving the Hôtel de Ville, Fournier now returned to the Cordeliers Club, which remained, for a time, the headquarters of the insurrection. Later, a final appeal to the sections was decided on at the Cordeliers and the insurgents dispersed to carry this to the sections. Fournier went first to the general assembly of his own section, the Tuileries Section, and then home to bed. By now the commune's firm stand was beginning to take effect and the majority of the sections refused to take any action, so that by the morning of 11 March the insurrection had petered out.[9]

There was to be a curious epilogue. The Convention was debating the news from the front on 12 March when, to the sound of martial music, the "Volunteers of the Poissonière Section" arrived to announce their readiness to march off to join the battle. The president of the section began to read out the section's address of 8 March, complete with its attacks on the commander-in-chief and the minister of war. An immediate storm broke as the Girondin deputies launched a furious attack on this "counter-revolutionary intrigue." Then, to everybody's astonishment, Marat, the bitter enemy of the Gironde, rose to add his denunciation of the hidden plotters responsible both for the Poissonière Section's demonstration and for the recent disturbances in general. In the course of his speech Marat singled out Fournier for a particularly vitriolic attack, and he persuaded the Convention to decree his arrest. The same evening Billaud-Varennes and Dufourny, president of the Paris Département, echoed Marat's denunciation at the Jacobin Club, and Marat again resumed the offensive in the next number of the *Publiciste de la Révolution française*.[10]

There was sound political logic behind Marat's sudden and apparently paradoxical attack. The Jacobin leadership had already begun to count on mobilizing the popular movement against speculators and for a "plebeian" purge of the army and the administration, as a major gambit in their power struggle with the Gironde. But their attitude towards the movement continued to be ambiguous. There were implications of the *sans-culotte* program that went beyond anything the Jacobins could possibly concede: a general and all-out war on the rich (whether unpatriotic or not), a haziness about the outlines of the category of "aristocrats" to be purged (which left the way open for a universal and permanent challenge to all constituted authority). Thus it was necessary to encourage the rhetoric of the popular movement, but at the same time to resist the emergence of an independent Enragé leadership.

From their vantage point on the frontier between Jacobin organization and popular agitation, Chaumette and Hébert, the leaders of the commune, Dufourny of the Paris Département administration, and Marat, the leftist deputy and popular journalist, grasped the demands of the situation perfectly. Already, after the grocery riots in February, Marat had begun his break with the extremists with an open breach with Jacques Roux, the most influential of the Enragé leaders. His quarrel with Fournier also dated from a clash in the Cordeliers Club inspired by the February riots.

On 13 March Fournier managed to win a hearing at the bar of the Convention. The Committee of General Security had searched his papers without finding anything incriminating; and he was able to explain away his activities on 9-10 March with enough plausibility for the Convention to decree his release. There remained, however, the task of restoring his reputation after the savaging it had received from Marat in the Convention and in the Jacobin Club. It was Babeuf who was commissioned to draft a formal vindication. Carrying the publication date 14 March, this comprised an eight-page pamphlet, *C. Fournier (Américain) à Marat*. It took the offensive by implying that though Marat might "still impose on a few citizens" he was a spent force. It concluded that as a true *ami du peuple* he should now rally to the new program put forward by Duchosal and Tallien in the *Ami des sans-culottes*, which was based squarely on the well-being of the poorest class ("*l'aisance de la classe indigente*").[11]

Marat was a dangerous man with whom to pick a quarrel. On 3 May the Cordeliers Club announced that it had expelled Fournier on account of an address attacking Marat "full of immoralities and anti-republican principles." On 9 May the *Publiciste*, Marat's journal, printed a renewed attack on Fournier, in order to block his appointment as commandant of a force of 12,000 volunteers recruited for a campaign against the Vendée uprising. Fournier's published rebuttal, in the form of a placard and a pamphlet, has been attributed, like the earlier pamphlet, to Babeuf. It was unsuccessful in its aim, for the Vendée command did not go to Fournier but to Santerre.[12]

Several historians have reflected with some asperity on Babeuf's ingratitude in launching an attack in 1793 on the very man who had opened his prison doors in 1790.[13] But neither Marat nor Babeuf was the same man in 1793 as in 1790. In 1790 Marat himself had been an Enragé, a spokesman for the most militant elements in Paris. In 1793 he was fast becoming a man of the Jacobin establishment, at a time when Babeuf was building the closest personal connections with the most *enragé* among the popular leaders. Babeuf's disillusion with Marat was, therefore, perfectly genuine, and indeed showed a clear grasp of political realities.

How far Babeuf personally participated in Fournier's activities as a leader of the Defenders of the Republic and during the quasi-insurrection of 9-10 March must remain conjectural. Surely it is inconceivable and entirely out of character that he could have remained academically aloof in the midst of such stirring events. As a potential officer of Fournier's legion, his place would have been by the side of his chief, on the Champ de Mars and on the Terrasse des Feuillants, at the Cordeliers Club, the commune and in the Tuileries Section.

In general, Babeuf's collaboration with Fournier is an aspect of his revolutionary career which has been surprisingly neglected in view of the undoubted importance of these contacts for his political education.[14]

Until the beginning of 1793 the center of Babeuf's agitation had been the small towns and villages of Picardy. His attitudes and his political programs had been formed against a background of rural poverty. Land—its just distribution, and the just distribution of the product of land—was still central to his thinking. On his arrival in Paris Babeuf had been confronted with a revolutionary movement based on a quite different rationale. It was the rationale of an already sophisticated tradition whose central theme was the protection of the interests of city workers as consumers, through economic action directed against speculators, food cornerers, and the rich in general.

Towards the end of April Fournier revived his attempt to form an élite volunteer corps. In a pamphlet entitled *Où en sommes nous?* (composed by Babeuf), he appealed for volunteers to enlist in a *"phalange des sans-culottes,"* which would then demand recognition by the Convention.[15] The pamphlet was also a stirring piece of *sans-culotte* propaganda, a plea on behalf of the "great national mass," "the innumerable phalanx of the poor, the most *sans-culotte* of *sans-culottes.*" As yet, the poor, the mass of the people, had gained nothing materially from the revolution except unemployment and excessively high prices which made it impossible to live. Under the shelter of the revolution the "voracious race of *accapareurs*" was engaged in "pumping" the last remaining denier from its victims. Why should the volunteers go to war to protect the property of the rich, and even of the *accapareurs*, haters of liberty who, wherever they could, would open the gates to the enemy? The revolution must offer its defenders a real and tangible return for their sacrifices. First, the promise of an agrarian law: "Moses promised the land of Canaan to the army of Israel, Caesar distributed the fields of the conquered to all his soldiers. Your efforts must also be rewarded."

To complete the logic of the argument, the proposed distribution of land should be at the expense of the denounced *accapareurs* and *Crésus égoistes*. However, on 18 March the Convention had formally decreed the death penalty for anyone preaching the agrarian law. It was necessary to go cautiously. Could anybody object to an apparent proposal to confiscate and distribute the land of foreign invaders of the Republic? Yet it should be remembered that the "Canaanites" whom Fournier's volunteers were expecting to fight in the spring of 1793 were in the Vendée, and not on the Rhine; they were French counter-revolutionaries and not Prussians or Austrians.[16] For Babeuf and Fournier the dream of the peasant soldier—returning, garlanded with flowers, to his own cottage and farm—may have had sentimental overtones of Canaan, Sparta, and ancient Rome; but it was firmly rooted in the land-hunger of the French peasant.

But the end of the war was a long way off and not all soldiers were peasants. There were immediate practical measures which might ease the lot of the *sans-culottes*. Thus, *Où en sommes nous?* demanded pensions after each campaign for all soldiers, and a tax on the rich to subsidize bread in order to establish "an exact proportion between the price of bread and that of the labor of the *sans-culottes*."

The pamphlet drafted for Fournier represented yet another variant of Babeuf's program for the achievement of practical equality. This time the driving force of the *sans-culotte* movement was to be harnessed to achieve the supreme goal of the agrarian law. Even while the political expediencies of 1792 and 1793 made an overt avowal of this goal impractical, it yet remained central to Babeuf's thinking. At the beginning of May 1793 he would assume for the first time the name "Gracchus," after the most famous protagonist of the agrarian law in the ancient world, in place of Camillus, the tribune of the plebeians.

Babeuf was still working for Fournier as late as 17 April, and he still had hopes for a place in Fournier's legion. Long before this, however, he had begun to send out feelers in other directions. Fournier himself was short of money; he had so many enemies that the eventual success of his project was problematical, and Babeuf's financial needs were becoming even more than usually pressing. His flight from Montdidier and Amiens at the beginning of the year had only been made possible by loans from friends which remained unrepaid. Although Fournier's hospitality kept him alive, his own personal circumstances were miserable. In a letter to Marie-Anne (on 3 March) he confessed that he would shortly be unable to afford even the paper on which to write to his family.[17] For her part Marie-Anne was desperately fending off creditors hounding her for Babeuf's debts incurred at Montdidier, trying to keep the children fed by sewing shirts for the army, and even sending some of the proceeds to her husband in Paris. On 6 March all that was of any value among the household furniture went in a forced sale to satisfy the creditors: one wooden bed with a straw mattress; two cloaks, one silk-lined, one wool; one table and one small writing table of stained wood with drawers; six chairs with straw-stuffed seats; and a quilt of violet cotton.[18]

On 1 April, too late, the Somme Département finally decided to pay Babeuf's salary and expenses, 158 livres due since the previous November (but only after stopping 24 livres to cover the value of seven volumes of laws the ex-councillor had allegedly carried off with him). At the same time the citizens of Hangest and Beauvraigne also were reminded of fees totaling more than 200 livres still owing to Babeuf for services rendered, but with uncertain results.

Snatching at straws, Babeuf wrote to the journalist Sylvain Maréchal asking for a job in the printery of Prudhomme's *Révolutions de Paris*, but without success.[19] He had begun to sound out the possibilities of one of Fournier's rivals in the business of "liberating the peoples," Noe Makketros, a Dutchman who was busy organizing a "Batavian Legion" to support the French invasion of the Netherlands. Colonel Makketros agreed to take Babeuf on as a secretary, provided the necessary dispensation for a Frenchman joining a Dutch corps could be obtained. At the beginning of April, Babeuf moved into the Batavian Legion's barracks in the rue Babylon and began to draw his allowance of twenty-five sous per day.

The prospect of marching with Makketros fired Babeuf with a sudden enthusiasm. He pictured himself drafting the revolutionary manifestos and appeals which would rally a grateful nation to its liberator. It was not long, however, before his enthusiasm cooled;

although Makketros agreed to make him quartermaster the salary was not enough for the father of a family.[20] Moreover, Babeuf was becoming increasingly caught up in the extraordinary current of confidence and optimism which had begun to flow through the *sans-culotte* movement in Paris as the revolution reached its central crisis. The commune and the Jacobin leadership were being swept along by the campaign of the Enragés and the section militants. Suddenly everything seemed imminently possible, even the great goal of perfect equality. To leave Paris at such a time was unthinkable.

Ten

Jacobin Collectivism

S oon after 17 April 1793 Babeuf moved out of the barracks of the Batavian Legion, leaving the fate of the Dutch nation to be decided by others. He was motivated by a new determination to throw himself fully into the central struggle of the revolution in Paris. The logic of his association with Fournier, his disillusion with Marat, and his personal temperament and political program might have dictated that he should join the ranks of the Enragés, the followers of Jacques Roux and Jean Varlet, whose independent pressure for *sans-culotte* economic policies was the real driving force of the growing revolutionary movement. Instead, on 7 May, Babeuf chose in a letter to Chaumette (the *procureur* of the commune) to offer his allegiance direct to the Paris Commune and the leaders of the Jacobin party.

A number of contemporary events contributed to this decision by convincing Babeuf that the Jacobin leadership was perfectly genuine in its defense of the people's cause. On 18 April Chaumette signaled the commune's adhesion to a central demand of the *sans-culotte* program when he joined Lullier (*procureur-syndic* of the Paris Département) in a deputation to the Convention to demand the "*maximum*," or controlled prices for food grains. The same day the commune general council declared itself in a state of revolution "as long as the food supply remains uncertain." This demonstration by the commune, supported by a petition from the Faubourg Saint-Antoine, was one of the important pressures behind the Convention's decrees imposing price control on 3-4 May.[1]

Another event which greatly impressed Babeuf was Robespierre's emergence as a fierce critic of the unlimited right of property during the contemporary Convention debate on the new French constitution. On 21 April Robespierre won the unanimous approval of the Jacobin Club for his own draft Declaration of the Rights of Man, which he presented to the Convention three days later and which subjected the right of property to the limitation that "it might not prejudice the existence of fellow citizens." In addition Robespierre once again echoed Pétion's formulation of the right to subsistence, which had become so central to Babeuf's thinking: "Society is obliged to provide for the subsistence of all its members, whether by providing them with work, or by assuring the means of existence to those who are not able to work. . . ."

The "underground agrarians" at last seemed to be declaring themselves and rallying for the final struggle. On 17 April Babeuf noted with special interest another contribution to the constitutional debate by the deputy Harmand de la Meuse, who defended complete social and economic equality (*égalité de fait*) as a "most natural and most active desire" stemming from political equality (*égalité de droit*). He condemned political equality by itself as "a cruel illusion" and a "Tantalus torture" for the great mass of the citizens.[2]

Just as in August-September 1791, the revolution seemed to have reached a new threshold, awaiting only enlightened and heroic leadership to begin some great leap forward. In 1791 Babeuf had singled out Coupé for the role of leader. This time the responsibility was to be Chaumette's. In his letter to Chaumette on 7 May Babeuf reviewed the recent victories of the *sans-culotte* movement and congratulated the *procureur* on his part in the achievement of the *maximum* of 3 May. The *maximum* was only a half-measure, however. The price of bread was still too high, and a further campaign was needed, this time based on Robespierre's declaration of rights. In his appeal to Chaumette to rally the *sans-culottes* of Paris and of the nation behind Robespierre's program, Babeuf's language took on again the apocalyptic overtones which had been first hinted in his letters to Coupé in 1792. He urged Chaumette onwards towards the revolutionary conquest of "a general happiness unknown throughout the ages and to all the nations whose deeds are known to us."

The messianic note was even more marked in the conclusion. Babeuf offered, as a new guide to the road ahead, a book he was in the act of writing on the subject of equality. "Sophists," he declaimed, "by this book I shall destroy all the false reasonings by the aid of which you have misled, enchained, and caused endless suffering to the Universe; and in spite of you, men shall know the full extent of their rights, Nature's intent shall be no longer deceived, and they shall all achieve happiness. . . . "

Babeuf's letter brought an immediate and favorable response from Chaumette. Apart from the generally flattering role for which it cast Chaumette personally, the text reflected the contemporary standpoint of the *procureur* and his associates at the Hôtel de Ville, Hébert and Pache (the mayor), perfectly. On the one hand, while paying tribute to Robespierre and the Jacobin minority, it condemned the Convention in general for its class bias and failure to understand the needs of the poor. On the other, it depicted Chaumette and his associates as genuinely sharing the idealistic dreams of a *sans-culotte* revolution which they alone were qualified to lead. At a time when the struggle for the control of Paris and the revolution was rapidly intensifying, a propagandist who could so skillfully blend passionate idealism and political astuteness was a welcome discovery.

Through the intervention of Sylvain Maréchal, Chaumette interviewed Babeuf and promised to secure the immediate publication of his letter in the *Ami des sans-culottes*. Shortly afterwards Chaumette and Maréchal got him a post on the commune's Food Administration, which was worth 166 livres a month. On 27 May Babeuf wrote to Marie-Anne to express an understandable satisfaction at his new situation: "My friends here are the most important people in Paris: Chaumette, the *procureur* of the commune; Pache, the mayor; Garin, the chief food administrator; Robespierre; Sylvain Maréchal, the editor of the *Révolutions de Paris*." He was still living virtually in a garret and dressing in rags, but he was now a welcome dinner guest at the houses of all these people.[3]

Even as Babeuf wrote, the fortunes of the political faction with which he had thrown in his lot were being decided in the final crisis of the Girondin-Jacobin conflict. A Girondin committee of the Convention, the "Committee of Twelve," had launched a counteroffensive against the Enragés, the leaders of the sections, and the Paris Commune, arresting Varlet and Hébert and other popular leaders. Several days of turmoil followed. They culminated in the massive uprising of 2 June, in which the Convention, overawed by 80,000 armed *sans-culottes,* was compelled to expel the Girondin leaders and accept the hegemony of the "Montagnards," the followers of Robespierre. The deuxième juin decided more than the control of the

Convention. A great deal of the running during the early stages of the uprising (from 30 May onward) had been made by the Enragés and a central committee of the forty-eight sections, whose demands went far beyond what was eventually conceded. A massive purge and renewal of the Convention, the commune, and all constituted authorities was almost the minimum program of these elements. The maximum program included a general massacre of deputies and a merciless war on the rich. Only by a mixture of maneuvering and good luck was it possible for the triumphant alliance of Robespierrist Jacobins and the Paris Commune to check the Enragés and finally to emerge from this challenge masters not only of the Convention but of the capital also.[4]

There is no evidence that Babeuf played any significant part in these crucial events, and certainly nothing to suggest that he took his place alongside Enragé leaders like Varlet, Roux, Théophile Leclerc and Claire Lacombe, however closely their demands seemed to echo his own thinking. His main preoccupation during the crucial days at the end of May seems instead to have been a private guerrilla war against the Catholic Church. The *casus belli* was a placard demanding the restoration of the annual Corpus Christi festival and procession—on the grounds that the constitution guaranteed freedom of worship. In a letter to the general council of the commune Babeuf expressed his opposition in strongly anti-Christian language, which was no doubt suitably gratifying to his anti-clerical patrons Maréchal and Chaumette. The "god of the Nazarenes" must have no more privileges than the others. Christ was no longer the God of everyone, and was therefore not entitled to an exclusive homage in the streets. The sectaries of the Christian religion should shut themselves up in their perfectly convenient and suitable temples, where they might hold whatever festivals they wished.

When on 2 June, at the height of the insurrection, Babeuf wrote home to Marie-Anne, it was chiefly to complain that the disturbances had interrupted the payment of his salary. Although he expressed his pleasure at the imminent victory of *"la sans-culotterie"* the passage was almost incidental in a letter which was concerned chiefly with domestic matters. The hope that it might be possible "this time to take a great stride towards the supreme goal of holy equality" found a rather incongruous place alongside another hope—that Babeuf might shortly expect a raise to 250 or 300 livres a month. For the moment (and oddly in the context) the practical, commonsense aspect of Babeuf's character was again in the ascendant, and the visionary thrust below the threshold.

With a reborn confidence in the future Babeuf set about restoring his disrupted domestic existence. It was fully nine months since he had said goodbye to his family in Roye before setting out for the Abbeville assembly. It was less likely than ever that he would return to Picardy. He told Marie-Anne to forget the debts she had been trying to collect on his behalf, to abandon the remnants of the furniture, and to bring the children to make a new home in Paris.[5] Soon afterwards the Babeufs moved into the house of Etienne-François Garin, the chief food administrator, at Porte Honoré no. 27, in the bourgeois Champs-Elysées Section, not without some embarrassment for Babeuf at the ragged appearance of his family. Garin was fraternal and understanding, lending the family the essentials for their new home without fuss, and with a kindness that Babeuf never forgot.[6]

The task of secretary to the Food Administration, to which Babeuf now devoted himself, was exacting and difficult. From early May until the end of August he acted as a kind of chief clerk, a "number three" to Garin and Defavanne, the two administrators, conducting the administration's register of correspondence and with responsibility (if Robert Babeuf is to be believed) for the oversight of some eighty underlings.

From its headquarters (in the Cour Lamoignon, on the Ile de la Cité), the administration sent out a stream of protests, instructions and orders to local authorities who might hamper the free transit of grain to Paris. Special agents scoured the countryside to buy supplies to stock the administration's warehouses. Garin's overwhelming concern was to maintain the continuity of arrivals of wheat and rye, the staple food grains of the capital. In normal times the Paris population consumed about two pounds of bread per head per day, or a million pounds per day. Four thousand mills in the Paris region alone were employed in milling the flour. The Paris grain market drew heavily on two zones: an inner granary comprising the valleys of the Seine, the Marne, the Loire and the Oise, with the plateaus of Brie, Beauce, Valois and Vexin; and an outer hinterland, of which Picardy, Champagne and the Orléannais were the chief resources. The three *départements* of Aisne, Oise and Somme were of supreme importance, since together they provided more than half of Paris's needs.

The problems faced by Garin and his associates in 1793 in feeding the capital were daunting. The war had interrupted foreign supplies; the entire Somme Département had been "allocated" to supply the Army of the North; an unusually dry summer made navigation impossible on the Oise from May to October.[7] The greatest difficulties, however, resulted from the attempt to apply the first law of the *maximum*, promulgated in May. This legislation had entrusted the district administrations with the control of the grain trade and thus made it possible for them to hold back supplies for local use at will. (Another effect of the price-control regulations was to starve the markets by encouraging a flourishing black market.) Matters were to become particularly desperate during the summer months of 1793, when the seasonal shortage in anticipation of the new harvest coincided with the disruption of the "Federalist" revolt and civil war, and milling was hampered by drought and a shortage of labor.

Politically, the Food Administration was in a very delicate situation. It was balanced precariously between, on the one hand, the population—with its pathological distrust of grain-dealers, millers, bakers and indeed anybody who had anything to do with the bread supply, and its hysterical suspicions of counter-revolutionary famine plots—and, on the other hand, the granary areas, resentful of the *maximum* and politically hostile to the pretensions of the capital. Indeed one of the major preoccupations of the Food Administration during 1793 was simply to defend its political life against attacks from both sides.

The most serious and sustained challenge came from below, from the Paris sections. As a baker, Garin had once earned a special tribute from Marat for his zeal in lowering bread prices. Once appointed chief food administrator (in February 1793), he found himself faced with the implacable hostility of the same self-elected "people's watchdog," always ready to listen to charges of corruption and nepotism and to believe the worst of those in authority. As his first piece of work for Garin, Babeuf was employed to edit a refutation of Marat's attacks, which was published jointly with Fournier's protest against his own renewed denunciation by Marat in the *Publiciste*. This was one of several indications that Garin and Fournier were close associates politically. On 24 May Garin published a further detailed vindication of his own conduct, and at the beginning of July yet another defense of Garin appeared (under the name of Defavanne, the second administrator).[8]

The popular suspicion of Garin fed chiefly on his alleged undue penchant for secrecy. Shortly before his appointment his predecessors had closed the doors of the administration's storehouses to the *commissaires* of the sections, and Garin steadfastly rejected repeated demands that he should reopen them to inspection. Under these conditions dark suspicions burgeoned that behind the closed doors not only were stocks much closer to famine level than was admitted, but clandestine adulterations were being practiced, with barley-flour and worse being mixed with good wheat. Whenever bad bread appeared, the administration was held solely responsible. Meanwhile everyone "knew" that Garin was lining the pockets of his relatives and his friends, the bakers and the millers, with millions of livres in subsidies and commissions.

In point of fact there was some substance behind this last charge. During the desperate weeks of the summer Garin sent out agents to scour the countryside for supplies for Paris, guaranteeing them heavy commissions on purchases. As they crossed one another's trails these independent operators inevitably tended to drive up prices. Garin also encouraged the Paris bakers to forage on their own account, without regard to price, by guaranteeing subsidies to hold the price of bread at the controlled level of three sous a livre. By September, it was alleged, these policies had cost the government as much as fifteen million livres.[9]

Conscious that their policies, whatever their deficiencies, were at least successfully keeping Paris fed, the administrators nevertheless realized the necessity for an effective political defense against the accusations of both inefficiency and corruption. On 16 June they wrote to Dominique Garat, minister of the interior, protesting against his policy of *laissez-faire* whenever local administrations defied the agents of the Food Administration and held back supplies. In a fury Garat wrote to Pache, the mayor of Paris, to demand a general conference; and when this was convened, he threatened to denounce Garin to the Convention. There was a sharp quarrel, which Pache tried to appease by tearing up the administrator's letter, but the conference agreed that Garin should press the Convention to adopt a general *maximum* for the whole Republic, thus removing one of the most serious of the anomalies created by the first *maximum*. Garat got in some telling counterblows. He pointed out that he was responsible for ensuring supplies throughout the whole country, and not just in Paris, and that while Garin had been pillorying him for leniency towards local administrators, the *procureur-syndic* of the Corbeil municipality had attacked him for showing Garin too much favor and for over-protecting his agents. Shortly afterwards Defavanne reopened hostilities with a pamphlet which openly charged Garat with responsibility for the growing food crisis. On 26 July the walls of Paris were placarded with a further attack, edited by Babeuf (and based on the administrators' protest of 16 June), denouncing a plot to starve Paris in which Garat was implicated.[10]

As a tactical device the attack on Garat proved a dangerous gamble. The Committee of Public Safety was bound to rally to the defense of a minister, while the sections were not convinced. The Amis de la Patrie Section called for the arrest of Garin and Defavanne; on 29 July Garin actually was arrested, on the orders of the Committee of Public Safety. Freed the following day, after representations from the commune, he now had to face a direct challenge from the Evêché, where a meeting of delegates of thirty-nine out of the forty-eight sections agreed to demand a general account "within three days" of the state of the food supply, the opening of the warehouses, and the right of the section *commissaires* to inspect stocks and examine registers. The struggle which was now joined continued throughout the whole of August, with the Evêché committee maintaining its pressure while the commune and the Paris Département parried the Evêché demands first with delaying tactics and finally with an outright refusal.

More was at stake than the fate of the Food Administration. The state of the food supply was indeed critical. It was the eve of the new harvest, normally a difficult period, and the disruptions caused by the "Federalist" revolt were at their peak. By 6 August flour supplies to several sections had been cut by a half. The fate of the Jacobin revolution hung on the maintenance of confidence in the administration among the Paris *sans-culottes*, and that confidence might have been destroyed if Pache and Chaumette had given way to the Evêché committee. Both Mathiez and Soboul have seen the hidden hand of anti-Jacobin moderates in the August agitation (Cauchois, the chief spokesman of the Evêché committee, was notoriously a friend of the Rolands). The campaign was also a fresh trial of strength by the Enragés, in disarray since their tactical defeat in the 31 May - 2 June insurrection. Faced with the refusal of the commune and the *département* administration to act, Cauchois invoked the dangerous Enragé principles of direct democracy. He warned the authorities that "the people having declared their will, their mandatories become here simple spectators of the developments which will follow. . . . It only remains for you to obey."

It was Jacques Roux who led the denunciation of the mayor and the commune administration in the Gravilliers Section. By 23 August the Observatoire and Poissonière sections had reached the stage of proposing the arrest of Pache, Chaumette, Hébert and Réal, and on the 24th the Popincourt Section called for the replacement of the commune and the municipal authorities by the *commissaires* of the sections. The Hôtel de Ville rallied for a counterattack. Jacques Roux was arrested and silenced. Loyal addresses began to come in from the Muséum, the Croix Rouge, the Luxembourg sections; finally on 25 August, on the motion of Tallien, the Convention ordered the dissolution of the Evêché committee and the agitation collapsed. The authority of the Jacobin-municipal alliance had been vindicated. In the process, however, certain tactical sacrifices had been deemed advisable. Garin and Defavanne were removed from office, arrested, and replaced by three new administrators. Garat was gone from the Ministry of the Interior, replaced by Paré on 15 August.[11]

Babeuf's role in all these events seems to have been ambiguous. According to his own account, at the beginning of August he delivered a long report to the Evêché committee in which he denounced not only Pache and Garat, but Barère and "the whole Committee of Public Safety," for a counter-revolutionary conspiracy to starve Paris and provoke an uprising. The Evêché committee then took Garin and Defavanne under its protection and ordered the publication of Babeuf's report. From fragments among his notes and other evidence it is clear that Babeuf did associate himself with the Evêché committee's campaign, and in this way sought to deflect the *sans-culotte* hostility away from the Food Administration and toward the government and the municipal leaders.[12]

It is probable that in choosing this tactic Babeuf was motivated by a genuine respect for the *bona fides* of the Evêché committee's claim to represent "the will of the people." Even so, to follow such a line was to show an extraordinary and dangerous disloyalty towards Chaumette and his other friends at the Hôtel de Ville. It is surprising that Babeuf did not, in the denouement, share the same fate as Garin and Defavanne. However, despite the disgrace of his powerful friend and protector, the new administrators (Champeaux, Louvet and Dumetz) continued to employ Babeuf for another two months, even if in a less responsible position. Moreover, when he left the commune's Food Administration in October, it was only to go to a better post with the new national Commission des Subsistances.

The national Commission des Subsistances was a logical consequence of the steady extension of economic controls by the Jacobin government in the autumn of 1793 to cope with the massive demands of the army and the home front in time of inflation, economic disruptions and civil war. On 9 September (on the initiative of Leonard Bourdon) the Convention had decreed the establishment of a network of *greniers d'abondance* (or national food granaries), to be stocked by requisition if necessary. On 29 September the general *maximum* had extended price control to a wide range of essential foodstuffs and raw materials. The commission's officers were charged with supervising the administration of these decrees and with a wide range of other functions, including the feeding of Paris, the grain census, the requisition of supplies for the army, the import of raw materials, and the even distribution of available supplies between *départements*. The commission was also made responsible for supervising sowing, for stimulating improvements in agriculture and manufacture, and for overseeing timber procurement, transport, and mining.

On 7 November Babeuf was successful in obtaining an appointment as a secretary of this new "ministry of economic warfare" at a comfortable salary of 4,000 livres.[13] His good fortune was to last for only a single week, before he was suspended and imprisoned in the Mairie, the jail of the commune police administration.

During the course of 1793, while Babeuf had been deep in the preoccupations of *sans-culotte* politics and the Food Administration, far away at Montdidier and Amiens the wheels of justice had been slowly but inexorably revolving. At the end of March a Montdidier jury of presentment had rejected the charges against Leclerc, Jaudhuin and Devillasse in connection with the fraud over the Fontaines property. Not unreasonably, Babeuf had concluded that the "acquittal" of his "fellow conspirators" meant that his own prosecution was now a meaningless formality. It seems likely indeed that he did not learn of the sentence of "twenty years in irons" (passed on him in absentia by the Somme tribunal in August) until the moment the Paris police administration arrested him, at the request of Varin, the public prosecutor of the Montdidier District.[14]

Nevertheless, however apologetic and sympathetic his colleagues in the Commission des Subsistances and the Paris police might be, Babeuf's career as a republican administrator was at an end. The Reign of Terror and Virtue was beginning. Servants of the people must be free from suspicion and the corrupt must not escape their just punishment. These were surely sentiments with which Babeuf himself would hardly have quarreled.

Eleven

Thermidor

After his arrest in November 1793 Babeuf was to spend more than eight months in various prisons at Paris and Laon, before his release the following July. Throughout this time he continued to protest his innocence by a series of appeals to the legal and political authorities, sustained by the faith and steadfastness of a small group of friends and the courage and resourcefulness of his wife and his eldest son.

The lynchpin of Babeuf's case was his contention that he was not a common criminal fleeing from justice, but a revolutionary martyr relentlessly hounded by aristocratic persecutors for a trivial and honest error. In the circumstances of 1793 and 1794 there was enough plausibility in this to sow honest doubts in the minds of the revolutionary officials who were successively involved in the case. After all, in the autumn of 1793 André Dumont, the sole Montagnard deputy from the Somme Département, had found it necessary to "purge" the *département* and municipal administrations of "aristocrats," among them Babeuf's enemies Longuecamp at Montdidier and Thierry at Amiens.[1]

These residual doubts about the political overtones of his prosecution were eventually to provide the key to Babeuf's liberation, but not without a long and arduous struggle. This was not so much against deliberate malevolence as against the professional habits of legal officials who preferred to allow the law to follow its proper course, even in a time of revolutionary upheaval.

The first skirmish led to the easiest victory of the campaign. The police administration of the Paris Commune had acted correctly in arresting Babeuf on the application of Varin, *procureur-syndic* of the Somme. Yet they had done so reluctantly. Babeuf was in good standing as a revolutionary and the accusation of petty fraud did not seem to fit. On the day of the arrest the police *commissaires* Menessier and Dangé said as much in a letter to Varin, in which they demanded that he forward the evidence to Paris so that they could scrutinize it, in case it should turn out that the Somme authorities and not Babeuf were the real culprits.

Varin, who was Dumont's protégé, refused to be intimidated, and he even counterattacked by reporting the commune police to the Somme Département, and the complaint was forwarded to the minister of justice, Gohier. On 22 December Gohier conceded the correctness of Varin's demand—Babeuf should be handed over to the Somme tribunal. But the commune police, having by then received no reply from Varin, had already released Babeuf on bail. This was done on the guarantee of Silvain Maréchal and two former colleagues from the commune's Food Administration, Thibaudeau and Daube (who was now chief accounts clerk of the national Commission des Subsistances). After his release Maréchal found Babeuf a job in Prudhomme's printery.[2]

During his three weeks in the commune's prison at the Mairie Babeuf had busied himself with drafting appeals to potential sympathizers: to Chaumette and Menessier, and above all to André Dumont, through whom he hoped to influence the all-powerful Committee of Public Safety. At the end of November he forwarded a long *mémoire* about his case to Dumont, together with a covering letter which reminded the deputy of their mutual struggle against the aristocrats of the Somme. Babeuf admitted the political clash between the two men at the time of the electoral assembly at Abbeville, but it was naturally glossed over. Dumont did not reply to Babeuf's letter.

When Gohier ordered the commune police to rearrest Babeuf and hand him over to the Somme tribunal, there was nothing for it but to submit. On 31 December Babeuf surrendered himself and was locked up in the Abbaye prison.[3] His friends, however, were not prepared to give up without a fight. Garin continued to allow Marie-Anne and the three children to live in his fourth-floor apartment on the rue Saint-Honoré; Thibaudeau appointed himself Babeuf's official defender; and Maréchal deployed his considerable influence with prominent Jacobin officials and deputies.

Thibaudeau wrote to Silvain Maréchal (on 2 January 1794) to outline the tactics he had decided upon. Appeals must be made to Gohier and to the Committee of Public Safety. The Committee of Legislation of the Convention must be approached and asked to settle Babeuf's case *révolutionnairement*, and not to allow him to fall into the hands of the Somme Département again. The first step must be therefore to collect and present evidence of the "aristocratic conduct" of the Somme Département. Thanks probably to Maréchal's intervention, Gohier decided to hold Babeuf in Paris for the time being, and at the beginning of February 1794 he requested details of the case from Amiens.[4]

The wretchedness of the Babeuf family had now reached new depths. Outside the Abbaye Marie-Anne struggled through the bitter January and February days (as the revolution entered one of its worst food crises), saved from starvation only through Daube's constant help. Possibly through contact with the prison, the three children all contracted smallpox; and Marie-Anne was forced to spend her days nursing them before visiting the Abbaye in the evening with the meager supplies which made her husband's prison diet tolerable. Later, although still weak, the 8-year-old Emile was able to help with the visiting, but on 28 February Babeuf complained that his son had been refused entry to the prison and had been wandering the streets, cold and hungry, until ten in the evening.[5]

Soon after this it was Babeuf's turn: he became so ill and depressed that his friends despaired of his recovery. The cells in the three-story Abbaye prison were all damp, and the worst were the common cells on the ground floor reserved for prisoners without means, dark and noisome with the stench of the prison lavatories. Under these conditions, with Babeuf in fetters, Thibaudeau and he toiled in the prison over a mass of personal papers in order to compile an effective defense.

Copies of a printed *mémoire* were sent to Gohier and to the members of the Committee of Public Safety, outlining both Babeuf's own impeccable career and the black record of the Somme Département. The revival of interest in his case (which led to Babeuf's arrest in November) was ascribed to the malevolence of aristocrats stirred up by his vigorous activity as secretary of the Paris Food Administration. The appeal concluded with a demand for a trial before the Revolutionary Tribunal, on the grounds that the alleged fraud involved national domain land, and was therefore a political offense.[6] The minister of justice, at least, was impressed by these arguments. On 11 March Gohier told Emile that he was going to put his father's case before the Committee of General Security, and the following day Gohier's wife received Marie-Anne and Emile with kindness. For a subsequent visit to the Gohiers, Emile composed a petition, and then learned it by heart, for the minister's benefit.

Babeuf was transferred to the Saint-Pélagie prison, and in growing impatience with the slowness of his friends' efforts he resolved to launch an independent campaign of his own. The Ventôse decrees of 8 and 13 March provided fresh machinery for speeding up trials in political cases. Babeuf therefore appealed directly to the Committee of General Security (by way of the Champs-Elysées Section) for his immediate release, but without any result. The weeks dragged on, with Gohier due to retire on 20 April and no concrete progress apparent. Toward the middle of April Daube lobbied the Legislation Committee, accompanied by eight friendly members of the Convention; but the committee refused to be hurried.[7]

A new plan was now adopted, according to which the Committee of Public Safety would pass the matter on to the Legislation Committee, who would refer it to the Cour de Cassation, the supreme court of appeal. But despite desperate appeals by Babeuf it was 8 May before the Legislation Committee considered his case. On 13 May it was formally referred to the Cour de Cassation, and the whole process of lobbying began again, as Daube, Thibaudeau, and the *conventionnel* Desrues worked to influence members of the court on Babeuf's behalf.

Marie-Anne became desperately ill and she nearly died; when she finally managed to drag herself to the prison on 22 June after a long absence, the journey took her some six hours to complete. The Babeuf family continued to survive only because Babeuf passed on his own prison subsistence allowance of 50 sous, leaving himself only bread and water.[8]

On 9 June the Cour de Cassation at last reviewed Babeuf's case. The court had no difficulty in discovering a flaw in the original proceedings at Amiens and in setting the verdict aside. Technically, the prosecution of an administrator for a crime committed in the course of his functions required the prior sanction of the Convention, and this had not been obtained. But instead of simply quashing the conviction, the court ordered a fresh presentment before the tribunal of the Aisne Département at Laon (probably on the grounds that Babeuf was a native of Saint-Quentin, in that *département*). The chief concern of Babeuf's friends was now his health, as they sought a lightening of his régime, and permission for him to travel to Laon by coach. Their fears were well-founded. After leaving Saint-Pélagie on 27 June Babeuf was passed from police brigade to brigade before finally arriving at Laon on 4 July. The whole distance, normally a three-day journey, was covered on foot, with Emile trudging beside his father.[9]

At the rue Sainte-Geneviève prison in Laon, where Babeuf was now to remain for a fortnight, the prisoners were either crowded into dark, airless rooms or kept in damp, underground, fever-infected cells. Weakened by his long imprisonment, Babeuf found the preliminaries of the new trial an unexpected ordeal. The officers of the Aisne tribunal refused to be distracted by political issues and concentrated instead on the details of the alleged fraud. Except for his indignant rejection of the charge of taking bribes, Babeuf's explanations tended to be tired, repetitive, and unconvincing. However, there was one gleam of hope. Polycarpe Pottofeux (the *procureur-syndic* of the Aisne Département) was a fervent Jacobin and a disciple of Saint-Just. Moreover he was, like Babeuf, a native of Saint-Quentin. It is not impossible that the two men had known one another as children; it is hardly likely that Pottofeux was unaware of Babeuf's political reputation. The local Jacobin Club and the Laon Commune began to bring pressure to bear on behalf of the prisoner.[10]

The Aisne tribunal reviewed the evidence on 16 July and concluded that the Cour de Cassation had erred in sending Babeuf for retrial without the other accused (Devillasse, Leclerc, Jaudhuin and Debraine). Pottofeux refused to proceed with the prosecution until a further body, the Commission des Tribunaux, had resolved this anomaly. Babeuf might well have been remanded now for a few more frustrating and miserable months had it not been for Pottofeux, who made the point that, if innocent, he had already been in prison far too long. On 18 July Babeuf was released on a bail of ten thousand livres, put up by "two citizens of Laon." A few days later he set out on the journey back to Paris, once again accompanied by Emile.

In his own view the Aisne tribunal had cleared his name. In fact, it had done nothing of the kind, and throughout the remaining months of his life the threat of a renewed prosecution was never absent. Had Babeuf not been arrested for conspiracy in 1796, he would almost certainly have been compelled to serve out his twenty-year sentence for fraud.[11] After his return to Paris Babeuf's first concern was to find a job and to support his family, and he managed to persuade the

Paris Food Administration to take him on once again. Throughout the month of August he worked quietly at his post, and strove to reorient himself to the new and confusing political situation in Paris.[12]

When the gates of the Abbaye had closed behind him in December 1793, revolutionary politics had been dominated by an uneasy combination of two forces: the Robespierrists in the Convention, with their Jacobin followers, and the Paris Commune, at the peak of its influence. In March 1794, however, Robespierre had turned on the "Hébertists," executed the commune's leaders (including Babeuf's protector Chaumette) and replaced the elected officers and councillors by a newly nominated commune subordinated to the Committee of Public Safety. In the succeeding weeks the Robespierrists had proceeded with the consolidation of a centralized revolutionary dictatorship, acting against the surviving Enragé leadership and completing the emasculation of the *sans-culotte* movement by imposing restrictions on the activity of the sections and the popular societies.

Yet even while Babeuf and Emile were still on the road from Laon to Paris, by the coup of 9 thermidor (27 July 1794) a strange alliance of frightened terrorists and reacting moderates had risen against Robespierre and his closest associates, in the name of the dignity and liberty of the Convention. As an ironical consequence of his imprisonment Babeuf had escaped the danger of proscription under the Jacobin terror or at the hands of the anti-Jacobin Thermidorians. Equally he had escaped the pressure of the corrupting expediencies which had led other democrats to accommodate themselves to the rationalizations of the "revolutionary government" and the "Terror," the instruments of Jacobin dictatorship.

Indeed, preoccupied with organizing his legal defense, Babeuf had found little time or inclination even to comment on current events during his imprisonment. Essentially his political outlook remained unchanged since 1793. In some correspondence with Sylvain Maréchal and Prudhomme (both noted "priest-eaters"), Babeuf confirmed the sharp personal hostility to Christianity which had been revealed by his campaign against the celebration of the Corpus Christi procession in May 1793; yet this was never a central concern of his political program at other times. Otherwise the only significant political piece dating from this period is a moving letter to Emile (written from the Abbaye in February 1794) in which Babeuf outlined the essential values of his personal political faith: from each according to his ability, to each according to his needs, but on the basis of an absolutely equal share of the common product *(jouissances)*—a society without rich or poor, and without wage-slaves driven to work for rich masters. "Perfect equality" remained, as always, the goal.[13]

Yet after Thermidor who would lead the revolution towards that goal? Chaumette and Robespierre, in whom Babeuf had placed his trust in 1793, were both vanquished and discredited. The *sans-culotte* program of price control, requisition, and squeezing the rich with which they had become identified was equally in disrepute. And there was no immediate sign of a new lead from the Convention.

The victors of Thermidor seemed determined to behave as if nothing more significant than a "palace revolution" had taken place. The surviving Montagnards on the two committees—Barère, Collot and Billaud on the Committee of Public Safety; Amar, David, Montaut, Voulland and Vadier on the Committee of General Security—clung to their positions of power at the heart of the undamaged machinery of the revolutionary government. Outside the Convention thousands of Jacobin functionaries, *commissaires* and administrators closed ranks and rallied to the Jacobin Club in a defense of the status quo.

By September 1794 the outlines of a fundamental conflict within the Thermidorian régime had nevertheless begun to emerge. In the Convention the moderates of the "Plain" were beginning to stir themselves against "Robespierre's tail": the embattled Montagnard remnant and the continuators of the revolutionary government. Outside, in the country generally, there was a growing movement of reaction against the local tyranny of petty Jacobin agents, and it gathered momentum as the prisons opened to release victims of the Terror from both the Left and Right oppositions.

A rational calculus of self-preservation had been one of the chief motives of the plotters of Thermidor. The same reasoning now drove one section of the Montagnard leadership openly to desert the standard of the revolutionary government and seek a reconciliation with the "silent majority" of moderate and anti-Jacobin France. The leaders in this "schism" were Fréron (the journalist and one-time terrorist scourge of Provence), Tallien (the ruthless purifier of Federalist Bordeaux), Barras, and Lecointre.

The strategy of this group was to rally the opposition to "Robespierre's tail," whether from the Right or the Left, behind a campaign to dismantle the revolutionary government and to restore the personal and political liberties curtailed during the Terror. The ground on which they chose to fight first was that of the liberty of the press. On 21 August Merlin de Douai opened discussion on a new press law in the Convention, and soon lines became clearly marked out between a party of unlimited freedom (led by Fréron, Tallien, and Lecointre) and the defenders of continued restriction (who followed the lead of Barère, Billaud, Cambon, Bourdon de l'Oise, and Collot). The division became definitive on 3 September with the formal expulsion of Fréron and his two associates from the Jacobin Club.

One of Fréron's close friends and supporters in the Convention was the journalist and printer A.-B.-J. Guffroy, deputy for the Pas-de-Calais Département. After Marat's assassination in July 1793 Guffroy had begun to publish an ultrarevolutionary journal, *Rougyff*. It was subsidized for a time by the War Ministry for distribution to the army, but "terrorist excesses" and links with the Hébertists eventually brought about the editor's expulsion from the Jacobins and the collapse of *Rougyff*. Now, after Thermidor, Guffroy began to print a stream of pamphlets by "Felhemési," a pseudonym for Méhée de la Touche, who was a protégé of Tallien. Felhemési flailed "Robespierre's tail" vigorously and supported the "Fréronist" opposition.[14]

On 3 September Guffroy published the first issue of a new regular journal which followed the same general Fréronist line, the *Journal de la liberté de la presse*. The editor was Gracchus Babeuf, who became Guffroy's partner in the enterprise. For the next month Babeuf would devote all his energies to this new enterprise, slaving day and night, with the help of Marie-Anne and Emile, to meet the deadline of daily publication, and to organize the subscription and distribution side. The two younger children found themselves locked up for long periods in the Porte Saint-Honoré apartment, and normal domestic life was suspended while the family lived on bread, raisins, and nuts. The venture was a gratifying success: some of the first numbers ran to two editions, there were soon eight hundred subscribers at four livres apiece, and the average printing was twelve hundred copies per issue.[15]

For many historians and biographers Babeuf's brief association with Fréron at this time represents a puzzling and disturbing episode. Fréron and Tallien were soon to epitomize the "Thermidorian Reaction," rallying to their side the *jeunesse dorée*, cynical young profiteers of the revolution determined to consolidate their administrative and military careers and defend their new "bourgeois" comforts by a demonstrative anti-Jacobinism and a violent contempt for the *sans-*

culottes. Albert Mathiez, the diehard Robespierrist historian, even went so far as to christen Babeuf "one of the first chiefs of Fréron's *Jeunesse dorée*." More recently some Marxist historians—committed to the positive interpretation of the Jacobin revolutionary dictatorship as a historical stage in the development of Leninist revolutionary doctrine—have been equally severe. Mazauric, for example, condemns Babeuf's naiveté and argues that in acting as an agent of Fréron he "disoriented the popular masses." Similarly Professor Tønnesson, while conceding Babeuf's "good faith," argues that the "effect of his action" was "to contribute to the success of the bourgeois reaction." Professor Dalin concedes that Babeuf allowed himself to be enrolled in the "Thermidorian camp," only "because he had not yet understood the role of the revolutionary dictatorship." After a few months he would come to recognize "the great historic role of Robespierre" and of the Jacobin dictatorship.[16]

To interpret Babeuf's position in this way is once again to fall into the error of reading history backwards. If, by 1796, he had come to take a more favorable view of the Jacobin dictatorship than in 1794, it was for purely circumstantial reasons, and not because the dialectic of history which led to the Conspiracy of the Equals made this inevitable. Indeed the evidence of his contemporary writings indicates that Babeuf "understood the historic role of the Jacobin dictatorship" very well indeed, and he rejected it quite deliberately as wholly inconsistent with his own democratic philosophy. Years before (in 1791), Babeuf had isolated as a central problem of politics the universal presence of the *esprit dominateur* in men, the tendency of those who govern to seek to impose their arbitrary will on the governed. The solution he advanced then—the continuous application of *la force du peuple* through the creation of democratic institutions—he regarded as equally valid in 1794.

In the pages of the *Journal de la liberté de la presse* Babeuf attacked the establishment of the Jacobin revolutionary government as a counter-revolution against the freedoms which had been won in 1789, and he hailed Thermidor as a new revolution in which the lost ground might be recovered. On 15 September, in a critical examination of the *ad hoc* arguments for a "temporary" dictatorship, he demolished specious parallels drawn from ancient Rome. Roman dictators, he pointed out, had been entrusted with executive power and not legislative power. Their tenure had been short: six months at a maximum, once (in Cincinnatus' case) sixteen days only. Rome had resorted to dictatorship only in times of extreme military danger,

Babeuf c. 1794

whereas in the autumn of 1794 French troops were sixty leagues across the frontier inside enemy territory. Moreover, in France it was not a question as in Rome of the temporary appointment of one man as dictator, but of the continuing rule of a multitude of dictators, of "our one hundred and one *commissaire*-dictators," through the machinery of the revolutionary government.

Writing on the same theme on 8 October, Babeuf emphasized that the revolutionary government could no longer be explained away as a bloody personal aberration of Robespierre. Instead it must be seen as a device for perpetuating a particular clique in power and providing places for their protégés and friends. On 29 September he had used a quotation from Mably to make a similar point: "On the pretext of avoiding cabals among the people and of making a better choice, never permit the magistrates to appoint to vacant magistracies or you will be opening the door to great abuses to prevent small ones. The magistrates will not fail to favor their relatives and friends. Instead of concerning themselves with the general good they will busy themselves with the particular interest of their magistracy."

In February 1795 Babeuf would complete his critique of the harmful effects of the revolutionary government with some reflections on the dangerous consequences of a successful dictatorship for the survival of democracy. "The majority of citizens naturally like repose," he conceded, and "only ask to take flight from public affairs and to live in tranquillity close to the domestic hearth: as long as they can find there a pleasant and easy life they will willingly let anyone govern who can preserve such an order of things."[17]

From his comments on the Roman precedent, and from other remarks, it is clear that Babeuf was prepared to recognize the necessity for a short-term dictatorship in exceptional circumstances. "It was necessary to permit ourselves to be led by our great legislative physicians for as long as the crisis of the political fever by which we were attacked lasted." But on pragmatic grounds, and even more so on grounds of principle, a prolonged and institutional dictatorship was decisively rejected. Babeuf had always consistently argued (with Rousseau) that sovereignty is inalienable, and cannot be represented or permanently delegated. The premise on which the revolutionary government was based, that sovereignty might be surrendered in the present in order that it might be enjoyed more securely at some indeterminate future date, he regarded as completely unacceptable. Liberty was something every citizen was entitled to enjoy here and now. "The republican is not a man in eternity, he is a man in time. His paradise is this earth; he deserves to enjoy there liberty and happiness, and to enjoy it for as long as he has being, without postponement, or at least with as little as possible. All the time he spends outside this condition is lost for him, he will never recover it again."[18]

Babeuf's critique of the Jacobin dictatorship was, therefore, neither naive nor ill-considered, but a mature evaluation which was completely consistent with all that he had written or said previously on the central problems of democracy. The fact remains that Babeuf's position was one that fitted very closely the needs of the Fréron-Tallien faction, in their anxiety to mobilize the surviving forces of intransigent *sans-culottisme* and range them alongside the moderates against the Jacobin machine. Whether Babeuf may be properly described as Fréron's "agent" is another matter. Certainly some kind of a bargain was struck. The floating of the *Journal de la liberté de la presse* required funds; Guffroy says that "some patriots" undertook to underwrite the first month's publication. It is not difficult to guess the probable identity of these "patriots." Particularly in his earlier issues, Babeuf followed the Fréronist line closely. Fréron and Tallien were portrayed as the leaders of a democratic revival, and their enemies, the chief ornaments of "Robespierre's tail," were specifically and savagely pilloried. At the same time, while demands were voiced for an end to the revolutionary government and a return to the election of "magistrates" (or local administrations) by the people, one particular demand—for new elections to replace the Convention—was muted.

Toward the end of September, through the medium of Lanthénas, the government party tried to buy off Babeuf with the offer of a post in the Commission d'Instruction Publique, suggesting that he might continue to bring out his journal under the auspices of the commission and of the Committee of Public Safety. In return he was to declare a three-month truce on attacks on the Convention and attempts to agitate the people.[19] Though this deal was rejected, it did not merely mean that Babeuf was already in Fréron's pocket. In fact the hard question "who was using whom?" is not so simply answered as is sometimes supposed.

With the same naive arrogance with which he had once briefed Coupé and Chaumette, Babeuf also issued his "marching orders" to Fréron. Fréron and his supporters in the Convention were to provide the spearhead of the reconquest of liberty, supported by the rank and file of a revived *sans-culotte* movement.[20] Hindsight shows the casting of Fréron for this role to have been a bizarre delusion, but this was hardly so obvious in 1794. At the worst, Babeuf knew Fréron, Tallien, and Guffroy as opportunists; at the best, their record showed them to be men of the Left, and not of the Right. If one of the lessons of Thermidor was that it is precisely such men who make the most savage and successful reactionaries in the aftermath of revolution, this was a lesson yet to be learned.

Moreover, the bargain was far from one-sided. In return for his qualified support, Babeuf obtained control of a popular and successful journal in which the demands of an independent and developing third force could be aired: the demands of a reviving democratic *sans-culotte* and *sectionnaire* movement, whose program surpassed that of Fréron and the moderates. The first stirrings of this democratic revival had begun even before the fall of Robespierre, in the Muséum Section, where Legray (one of the revolutionary *commissaires* of the section) began an agitation for the end of the revolutionary government and the immediate adoption of the Constitution of 1793.

After the overthrow of Robespierre, on 17 August the General Assembly of the Muséum Section appealed to the forty-eight sections to support a petition vindicating the people's right to elect their "mandatories" and magistrates. The rallying point of the movement quickly shifted however to the Evêché, where a collection of veteran Enragés, Hébertists, and militants of the popular societies had organized a new central popular society, the so-called "Club Electoral," which met in the former assembly hall of the electors of the Paris Département. Among the more prominent leaders were Varlet (of the Droits de l'Homme Section), Crespin (of the Popular Society of the rue du Vert-Bois in the Gravilliers Section), Bodson (of the Révolutionnaire Section), and Legray.

The Club Electoral ordered the publication (on 19 August) of an address which supported similar demands to those of the Muséum Section. Babeuf's own section was the Champs-Elysées, and there is no evidence that he was in any way associated with the initial launching of the Muséum Section's petition. He did, however, attend meetings of the Club Electoral; and from 8 September he began to give extensive reports of the club's activities in his columns, beginning with an account of a petition (on 6 September) to the Convention in favor of unlimited press freedom and the restoration of the popular election of magistrates.[21]

A few days later the *Journal de la liberté de la presse* protested against the arrest of the orator who had delivered the 6 September petition. In a series of numbers beginning on 14 September Babeuf reviewed the political developments of the preceding weeks. The address of the Muséum Section, he explained, had become the manifesto of a party, the "Faction des Défenseurs des Droits de l'Homme." Despite the organized and violent intervention of Jacobin agents, the "Faction" was gaining support. Fifteen sections had adopted the Muséum Section's petition, and others had initially given their support only to be forced to withdraw by pressure from above.

On 16 September a delegation from the Club Electoral addressed the Convention and pledged itself to continue the democratic campaign.[22] Nevertheless, the defenders of the revolutionary government were beginning to move inexorably against the leaders of Babeuf's faction. On 21 August the Convention had imposed new restrictions on the freedom of action of section militants. During the summer of 1793 the section general assemblies had met daily, but in September 1793 the Convention had restricted meetings to two per week. After the adoption of the revolutionary calendar they had been further restricted to two per *décade*, or one each five days. Now they were cut to one every ten days.

On 5 September the Committee of General Security arrested Varlet, after he had defended publicly a demand by Lecointre for the indictment of the surviving Montagnards. About the same time Bodson was also arrested. On 16 September (and again on 28 September) the Club Electoral petitioned for Varlet and Bodson's release but without success.

The club's own days were numbered. On 29 September a party of workmen moved into the club's hall in the Evêché, tore out the benches, the president's desk and the tribune, smashed the stove, and began preliminaries for converting the place into a hospital. Only the previous day, with Legray acting as president, the members had launched yet another petition for the restoration of an elected Paris commune and the withdrawal of the new restrictions on section meetings. Printed and circulated to the forty-eight sections, this program was to become the rallying point for a counteroffensive by the democratic forces. If Babeuf was not the editor he certainly had a hand in the preparation. The printer was Guffroy; one paragraph contained an extract from the same Mably quotation Babeuf used in his number for 29 September, and the *Journal de la liberté de la presse* published what amounted to a call for an insurrection by the sections to reclaim their lost liberties.[23]

The Club Electoral's demonstration began with an open air meeting on the Place Notre-Dame ("Place du Temple de la Raison"), after which a procession to the Convention formed up behind the Table of the Rights of Man. At the Convention the petitioners were roughly received by the president, André Dumont; but there were cheers from the spectators, and during the day seventeen section general meetings came out in support. On 2 October the Révolution-naire, Cité, Temple and Muséum sections organized another dem-onstration at the Convention in favor of the Club Electoral's peti-tion; and several other sections sent delegations to demand the restoration of the banned "midweekly" section meetings. But 2 Oc-tober 1794 was an immeasurable distance from 2 June 1793. There was no new massive rising of the *sans-culottes*. Instead, the only im-mediate result of the campaign was a wave of arrests of popular leaders, which effectively destroyed the movement for the time being. Legray was sent to the Madelonnettes prison on 12 October, Babeuf to the Luxembourg prison on the 13th.[24]

The events of the first fortnight in October marked a turning point in the revolution. On 6 October the Convention removed the last three Robespierrists from the Committee of General Security. The strategy of the Fréronists had succeeded. From now on the momen-tum of the reaction against Jacobinism would steadily accelerate. As long as the issue was in doubt, Fréron and Tallien had deliberately kept the democratic movement in play, thus preventing any possibili-ty of the re-establishment of a Jacobin power base in the sections. Now, the triumph of the "Thermidorian" opportunist-moderate alliance in the Convention meant that the democratic revival had out-lived its usefulness, and might well become an embarrassment. Thus the democratic leaders found themselves jettisoned suddenly and without ceremony.

Babeuf had begun to sense, already at the beginning of October, that something was going terribly awry with the strategy of the democratic campaign. It was true that in the *Orateur du peuple* for 30 September Fréron had proclaimed his enrollment in the "Faction des Défenseurs des Droits de l'Homme." But a few pages later he had outlined a new theory of *"souveraineté en miniature,"* according to which the people had delegated their authority irrevocably and completely to the Convention. It was, in effect, a naked justification of a new dictatorship by the Convention majority. Further (on 7 October) Fréron had come out in support of the deputy Bourdon de l'Oise's motion for a purge of the popular societies. Meanwhile, in the *Journal de la liberté de la presse*—renamed *Le Tribun du peuple* on 5 October—Babeuf was following a steadily more decided anti-Convention line, invoking the Constitution of 1793 and declaring the need for new elections.

On 8 October he issued a last desperate appeal for "two or three mandatories" to take the lead in a genuine program for the restoration of democracy. When this produced no response, he launched for the first time an open attack on Fréron. This brought about an immediate breach with Guffroy, who stopped the printing of the offending issue, broke off the partnership, and threatened to denounce Babeuf to the Committee of General Security.[25] In his next number, completed in hiding while waiting for his own arrest to follow that of Legray, Babeuf expressed his bitter recognition of the confidence trick of which he and his fellow democrats had been the victims. "Tyranny is on the point of gaining a complete triumph and overthrowing forever the republican system." In an acute but belated analysis of Fréron's and Tallien's tactics, he pointed out that the two journalists had relied on denunciations of the terrorist excesses of the past only to cover up their lack of principle in the present; and that they had always deliberately stopped short at the palisades without taking the principal fortifications by assault. In particular they had shown their true colors by the contempt with which they had ignored the struggles of the Club Electoral. In order finally to clarify the situation, Babeuf challenged Fréron to take a definite stand on Legray's arrest.

The copy for this first "underground" number of the *Tribun*, no. 27, was passed on to the Club Electoral, which was now meeting in one of the halls of the Louvre (and it was published by the club, by a decision taken on 18 October). Babeuf had been set free on 17 October after spending only four days in the Luxembourg. Such lenient treatment suggests that he may have agreed to abandon his attacks, as a *quid pro quo* for his release. Publication of no. 27 quickly hardened the attitude of the Committee of General Security, however, and on the 24th fresh warrants were issued for the arrest of Babeuf and the president and secretaries of the Club Electoral. On 28 October the *Courrier républicain* reported the arrest of the president and secretary of the club, but Babeuf escaped.[26]

For the next three months he existed "on the run," in hiding from the police.

If Babeuf's "no. 27" was intended as a challenge, the response was clear and unequivocal. No excuse could remain for any further illusions. Already the Convention had followed up the "taming" of the sections by the beginnings of an offensive against the popular societies. New regulations were decreed requiring popular societies to declare a list of their members, and forbidding them to form federations or to carry on correspondence as collective entities. A few weeks later (on 11 November) the Jacobin Club was formally closed down, after two days of rioting outside the building and violent attacks on the members.

In a brace of clandestine pamphlets Babeuf greeted the downfall of the Jacobin Club with uncompromising joy. The recent bitter infighting in the sections still rankled strongly, and he saw the breakdown of the exclusiveness and the arrogance of the Jacobins as a necessity if the democratic party were to rally and to close its ranks. Yet there are hints that Babeuf's attitude to the Jacobin Club was not as entirely negative as might appear. Most of the members, he conceded, were probably misled rather than personally evil. Once they had rallied again to the defense of the rights of the people the Jacobins might even become acceptable recruits to the battalions of the "Defenders of the Rights of Man."[27]

From the point of view of practical achievement, the democratic campaign of the autumn of 1794 was a disastrous failure. Yet from another point of view it represented an important "breakthrough" during which new political strategies emerged and were tested for the first time. Throughout the earlier years of the revolution, democratic political thought—or at least the rhetoric through which that thought was expressed—had been dominated by naive Rousseauist conceptions of popular sovereignty and the general will. According to these ideas, the undifferentiated mass of the people, in its natural goodness, could be relied upon to impose its will through the machinery of section and commune assemblies, and, in the last resort, through "holy insurrection." In practice, both the Enragé leaders of the Paris sections and the Jacobin Club had developed highly sophisticated faction techniques of manipulating the transactions of the sovereign people. Still, democratic theory was permeated by Rousseau's distrust of faction and of the distortion of the general will by the deliberate machinations of the particular wills of individuals or of parties.

Thus Babeuf's open avowal of support (on 8 September) for "a faction which demands the holiest of the rights of man" represented the beginning of a significant personal reappraisal of democratic theory. "Our party is strong," Babeuf declared on 14 September; "I do not conceal the fact that we have one." On 22 September the *Tribun du peuple* proudly proclaimed its support for the "Faction of the Defenders of the Rights of Man." They were engaged in a struggle for control of the revolution against "the party of the protectors of the Robespierrist system," or the "Thermidorian sect."[28]

At first it was little more than a phrase or a metaphor. But by the middle of October the "Faction of the Defenders of the Rights of Man" had come to represent for Babeuf a concrete organization with the essential attributes of a democratic political party. While the "Faction" could count on support in some of the Paris sections and even in the Convention itself, it was to the popular societies that Babeuf looked as the fundamental cells of the democratic organization.

In his correspondence with Coupé in 1791 Babeuf had depicted the ultimate democratic power as an emanation from the primary assemblies of the whole and undivided people. Now, in 1794 the practical expression of that power was attributed, instead, to the popular societies. Babeuf proceeded to publish (on 13 September) an outline of the role of the popular societies in a democratic order. They must keep a vigilant eye on the agents of the administration, to watch that they did not exceed their mandates; and they must keep the people's mandatories informed of the latest expressions of the general will. "In this way the whole people will cooperate at least indirectly in the formation of the law, and in this manner the people will give the lie in a large degree to the principle of Jean-Jacques which states that representative government is entirely aristocratic because the people play no part in the making of the laws."

In the letter in which he broke off his association with Babeuf, Guffroy was to make the telling point that to argue thus was to claim for a *sectarian group* a sovereignty that properly belonged to *the people as a whole.* Yet this was to oversimplify Babeuf's position. Nobody was better aware of the narrow basis of support for the democratic program in the disillusioned and cautious aftermath of Thermidor. On 1 October Babeuf sadly contrasted the current mood with the spirit of 1789-90, and the triumphs of Marat with his own failures (as he confessed) "preaching in the desert."[29]

Reflecting on the history of the Club Electoral at the beginning of November, Babeuf noted that out of 400 members of the club only thirty or forty could be counted on to attend sessions and only a dozen were ready to sign their names to declarations or protests. The vital battle for control of the sections in September and October 1794 had been a matter of violent engagements between mere handfuls of partisans: democrats, moderates, Jacobins. The masses remained aloof and apparently unmoved.

There was nevertheless a paradoxical element in this situation. While the section meetings were virtually deserted and the popular societies haunted only by a few diehards, there was still a revolutionary crowd in existence. Thousands of spectators, if not indeed the "20,000" claimed by Babeuf, frequented the public galleries of the Club Electoral during the Evêché period, and the onlookers were ready enough to cheer the club's delegates at the Convention.[30] The essential organizational problem was to enroll this broadly sympathetic public opinion behind the banners of "the Defenders of the Rights of Man."

Babeuf's solution involved the frank recognition of the guiding rôle of a party élite. Already, three years before, in his reflections on democracy during the summer of 1791, he had been greatly exercised by the tendency of the people, in their ignorance and irrationality, to be misled by demagogues. Now (on 14 and 27 September) Babeuf published some reflections on an even more serious danger which had been underscored by the experience of the Jacobin dictatorship and its aftermath. It was the inveterate tendency of the wielders of power and the ambitious to mold public opinion, indeed to create a manufactured public opinion (*"opinion factice"*). Because of this "the opinion of the moment was never good opinion."

Yet public opinion was the most important of all political forces. "One can do anything by means of public opinion, and when one has managed to direct it toward any system whatever, one is quite sure of causing that system to prevail, for the opinion of the people (as has been well said) is the force of the people, and the force of the people is everything." Since the political conflict between the "chiefs of the Faction of the Rights of Man" and the "Thermidorian sect" was essentially a struggle to capture this force, the democratic party must challenge the monopoly of those who controlled the state power and must consciously and deliberately seek to create a public opinion favorable to its cause. Inevitably, Babeuf saw the rôle of journalists in such a campaign as crucial. "Wise Argus-eyes" like Marat and Loustalot (and by implication himself) could spot trends and tendencies six months before they were revealed to the mass of the ordinary people.[31]

In other contexts—the history of the British party system, or even of the political conflicts of the French monarchy of the Old Régime—Babeuf's "discovery" of the tactics of party organization and party propaganda might seem a banal achievement. In the context of democratic political thought during the French Revolution it represented a novel and significant break with the dominant and constricting Rousseauist modes of the day.

The strategy had been clarified: the tactics remained unsettled. How, in practice, were the democrats to break out of the iron ring of isolation in which they found themselves? Babeuf believed that the answer lay in the adoption of a new organizational style by the popular societies. During the discussions which led to the adoption of the petition of 28 September the Club Electoral had attempted a new experiment. The "citizens of the tribunes" (the spectators in the public gallery) had been invited to speak and to vote, and even to name half the delegates charged with bringing the petition to the attention of the general assemblies of the forty-eight sections.

Babeuf became convinced that the salvation of the democratic cause lay in a further development of this breaking down of the barrier between "members" and "spectators" in the popular societies. He drafted two addresses to the Club Electoral (on 24 October and 2 November) outlining the reforms which would transform it into a "Club du Peuple." All formalities of entry, membership and organization must be abandoned. The general public must be invited to sit, speak, and vote in complete equality, and it would be sufficient to elect *ad hoc* officers for each session. All citizens must be allowed and encouraged to participate regardless of wealth, age, sex, or even capacity. Just as in 1791, when Babeuf had urged that special efforts be made to persuade the "marginal" people (vagrants and beggars) to attend popular assemblies, now he recommended the greatest patience with diffident and timid speakers in order to allow their talents to develop.[32]

In insisting on the equal status of women, Babeuf was taking a stand against a current of prejudice which remained strong even in the most democratic cadres. To Babeuf's chagrin the Club Electoral itself had only recently refused to allow a woman to take part in its deliberations. Yet, as he reminded the members, she belonged to a sex "which had never been unserviceable in revolutions." Babeuf printed a letter in his journal (on 13 October) from Albertine Marat, Jean-Paul Marat's sister, protesting against Legray's arrest. In a preface the readers were reminded of the revolutionary rôle of the women of Paris in the "October days" of 1789. Might they not help once again in the reconquest of liberty? Yet even Babeuf was bound to a certain extent by the clichés of his time. Women, he explained to the Club Electoral, should be allowed to have their say, because it was they who were responsible for the earliest education of men. "How will they be able to bring men up to be heroes if you crush them down?"[33] Babeuf's was thus, at best, a rather conditional acceptance of feminine equality, on a purely political level. Yet his offer of fraternal comradeship in a common cause would prove enough to win for the conspiracy of 1796 the devoted support of a number of idealistic women.

The Club Electoral dutifully adopted Babeuf's revised rules on 2 November. In his earlier address, Babeuf had urged the members to attempt a proselytizing campaign by approaching other popular societies and by house-to-house visits to gain individual converts. Taken together with the adoption of the new popular style of organization, he confidently predicted that this campaign would produce new petitions with thousands of signatures to take the place of the present pitiful addresses signed only by a courageous handful. In the event no such revival took place. The Club Electoral continued to linger on until the middle of November, when it was ejected from the Louvre meeting place.[34] Thereafter nothing more was heard of it. As an experiment in democratic tactics the "Club du Peuple" was no more successful than the "Faction of the Defenders of the Rights of Man." Something more compelling than a passion for pure democracy was needed to stir the Paris masses into action again after the repeated disappointments and disillusions of 1793-4; and it was not until the bite of cold and hunger made itself felt during the winter of 1794-5 that the mood of the *sans-culottes* began to change at last.

Yet Babeuf could draw certain valuable lessons from the defeats of 1794: the folly of relying on opportunist deputies of the Convention to provide honest leadership for the people; the need for the determined and deliberate organization of a democratic party; the need to prepare for the conquest of power by a propaganda campaign to "direct" public opinion; above all, the need for a new dream to provide a fresh inspiration for a people made jaded and cynical by repeated betrayals.

Twelve

"The Party of the Plebeians"

Despite the illusions of the summer, it was clear by November
1794 that Thermidor meant not simply a reaction against the
distortions of the revolutionary government, but a rejection of the entire democratic phase of the French Revolution. By a curious irony,
the post-Thermidorian political struggle had been fought out under
the only conditions which could have guaranteed the victory of the
moderates, conditions which were at the same time a direct consequence of the successes of the overthrown Robespierrist régime.
Throughout the revolution "extremism" flourished under two circumstances: whenever the people were forced to go hungry through
economic crisis; and whenever there was a threat of war and invasion. By July 1794 the economic policies of the Jacobin government
had checked inflation and guaranteed the food supply, and the victory of Fleurus had removed the threat of invasion. Thus the post-
Thermidorian debate had been carried out in an atmosphere of
relative social harmony, aided by the Convention's *maximum* decree
of 9 August, which permitted wages to rise to approximately 50 percent above the level fixed shortly before the overthrow of Robespierre.

Under these circumstances the Jacobin rump had gone down to
defeat even while continuing to take its stand on the popular social
and economic policies of the revolutionary government. By another
paradox, the movement for a democratic revival led by the Club
Electoral included in its program a condemnation of the collectivist
and restrictive controls on commerce imposed by the Jacobin dictatorship. Even though he protested against this condemnation in the

Journal de la liberté de la presse, Babeuf had tacitly accepted the need to mount his campaign on the purely political plane. Not until his final address to the Club Electoral (on 2 November) did he launch a new slogan in which political and economic demands were linked once more in the Jacobin manner: "Liberty, bread—and good bread—all essential commodities of good quality and in abundance."

It was true that on 13 October the *Tribun du peuple* had begun to sound a new note, as Babeuf reminded his readers of "the cry of mothers of families, obliged to devote entire days to prevent us from dying, to snatch by grace or charity a quarter of what we need of the worst possible provisions." Yet this note was instantly muted. After 13 October the *Tribun* failed to appear for nine weeks. Although Babeuf published three pamphlets during this period, these were concerned solely with political reflections on the closing of the Jacobin Club or the trial of Carrier, the notorious terrorist deputy.[1]

When Babeuf began to publish a new series of the *Tribun* the tone was quite different from that of the old. Between mid-December and the beginning of February five numbers appeared which set out to express the demands of the Paris workers and artisans and to advocate a revival of the most popular aspects of Jacobin economic policy. From the end of October onward Babeuf lived in hiding in Paris, moving from one refuge to another. As winter approached, the economic situation was steadily worsening. "Complaints and murmurs are continually heard," a police agent wrote in late November. "The long delays in obtaining unrationed bread; the shortage of flour; the high prices, in markets and squares, of bread, firewood, wine, coal, vegetables and potatoes, the price of which is increasing daily in the most alarming manner, are plunging people into a state of wretchedness and despair that is easy to imagine. . . ."

The *maximum* had been amended in October to allow the prices of controlled items to rise; the prices of goods on the free market soared as inflation took hold again. By mid-December the revolutionary paper money was worth only half its July value. In January the members of the Convention felt obliged to double their own salaries from eighteen livres a day to thirty-six livres. For the wage-earner or the artisan things were less simply arranged, and their real incomes fell sharply. At the end of December the *maximum* was abolished completely, and a number of other factors promised to make the winter of 1794-5 a particularly bleak time for the French people. The 1794 harvest was poor, and the demands of the army had grown to absorb an even larger share of the surplus. In Paris the easing of the military crisis made it possible for the Convention (on 6 December) to threaten to disband the national arms workshops and thus throw hundreds out of work; this operation was finally accomplished at the beginning of February 1795, after stiff resistance from the militant employees. After 26 December the Seine was frozen over, interrupting the supply of food, fuel, and raw materials for the workshops.

The poorer classes were plunged once more into economic misery. At the same time special groups began to flaunt a new-found affluence in ways which would not have disgraced the Ancien Régime. The leaders of the Thermidorian reaction in the Convention lived in style; their splendid wives and mistresses reopened salons; they bought estates in the country, shared boxes at the Opéra. In the streets and at the Palais Royal the *jeunesse dorée* paraded, the actors were playing farces again, and prostitution emerged above ground after the puritanical repression of the Jacobin régime. The Reign of Virtue and Terror was over.

In September Babeuf could still view the contemporary power struggle in terms of a purely political conflict between the "Faction of the Defenders of the Rights of Man" and the "party of the protectors of the Robespierrist system." By January 1795 he had come to recognize the existence of a much more profound conflict at the very heart of society. "I distinguish two parties diametrically opposed by their system and their plan for the public administration," he wrote in no. 29 of the *Tribun du peuple,* reviewing the conduct of members of the Convention. "I am ready to believe that both desire the republic, but each wants a republic after its own fashion. One wants it to be bourgeois and aristocratic; the other believes that they have achieved it, and it should remain wholly popular and democratic. One wants the republic of a million which was always the enemy, the dominator, the exactor, the oppressor, the bloodsucker of the twenty-four other millions, of the million which has disported itself in idleness for centuries at the expense of our sweat and our labor; the other party wants the republic of those other twenty-four millions, who have laid down its foundations and cemented them with their blood, who are defending it and dying for its safety and its glory."

This declaration formed part of a general manifesto of a new "plebeian party" dedicated to a struggle to wrest power from the "patricians." Yet even as late as December 1794 it was still necessary to begin such a manifesto by justifying the idea of "party" itself. Revolutionary experience, as Babeuf explained, had shown that those who had argued in the past for vesting the unity of the people's will in their delegates had been misguided. In political life there were always two parties in conflict: one desiring good for its own sake, the other pursuing only self-interest. Wherever there was an appearance of harmony, this meant no more than that the triumph of the party of self-interest was unchallenged.[2]

Arguments on such an abstract level were not, however, characteristic of the pages of the *Tribun*. Instead, from the first number of the new series the basis of the plebeian party was clearly identified with the interests of a concrete social class. On 18 December Babeuf declared himself spokesman for *"le pauvre ouvrier"* on four livres or a hundred sols per day, and for the *"classe des sans-culottes"* menaced with starvation. He denounced (on 8 January) the attempt to drive workers out of the section assemblies and committees on the pretext of their "ignorance"; he warned (on 23 January) the toughs of the *jeunesse dorée* to expect a counterattack by working-class Paris if they persisted in harassing democrats and provoking civil war: "our workers, our faubourgs are already assigned. . . . " Essentially the objective of the *Tribun du peuple* was to rally two forces against the dominant coalition of the wealthy *"millionistes"* and the Thermidorian opportunists: the political vanguard of Jacobin and *sans-culotte* militants and the great mass of working-class Paris, whether wage-earners or artisans.[3]

Babeuf's analysis of the political situation in terms of class was elaborated in greater depth in a lengthy pamphlet published on 3 January. Deliberately disguised as an ephemeral squib written to capitalize on the public interest in the current trial of Carrier, this study, *Du système de dépopulation . . . de Carrier*, contained important "contraband": a review of the goals of the social revolution which had been interrupted at Thermidor, and the establishment of the theoretical basis for a new advance by the plebeian party.[4]

The description of such material as "contraband" is Babeuf's own. During the difficult days of November, disillusioned by the collapse of the Club Electoral campaign, he had resolved to experiment with a new technique of propaganda by stealth. In the prevailing political climate democratic publications faced two main hazards: seizure and suppression by the hostile authorities, and rejection by a jaded and disillusioned public. Babeuf's solution was to compose works which superficially seemed to follow the fashion of the moment in decrying Jacobins and terrorists, but which nevertheless contained a hidden anti-Thermidorian message. In this way the government agents could be outflanked and the unsuspecting reader seduced. The technique was openly admitted. "One must accommodate oneself to the French frivolity if one wishes to be read," Babeuf wrote. "A pamphlet cannot be launched unless it bears a piquant title which leads to an expectation that the contents will occasion laughter. These premises are only contraband. The publication is in people's hands, and that is all I want. . . ." He explained in December to Jacobin readers of the reborn *Tribun du peuple,* who might have been offended by his apparent apostasy, that the object of the recent series of pamphlets had been only "to smuggle through the recall to principles in the form of contraband . . . and to take a long circuit to arrive at a few words of reason."[5]

The *Système de dépopulation* was the most ambitious of Babeuf's pioneer experiments in "black propaganda." In form the pamphlet was an attack on Carrier's personal cruelties during the suppression of the Vendée, which were linked with the "discovery" of a Jacobin plot to tackle the problem of poverty by a simple but atrocious device, namely, by deliberately decimating the population and dividing available wealth among the reduced number of citizens. However, in pillorying Carrier, Babeuf was able to raise the general questions of the escape of "the people's mandatories" from democratic control during the Terror, and of the general responsibility of all the members of the Convention for the crimes which were now being ascribed only to a few scapegoats.

The alert reader could hardly have experienced any difficulty in applying Babeuf's condemnation of the dangers of vesting arbitrary power in the "proconsul" Carrier, and attributing to him so much "idolatrous prestige," to other "proconsuls" like Fréron and Tallien, who were now safely entrenched within the Thermidorian régime. At the same time, in the exposé of the details of the "depopulation plot," every argument for equality attributed to the Robespierrists was expressed with such cogency that the satirical intent of the accompanying description of the Jacobin final solution of general massacre is inescapable.

The Robespierrist plan, according to Babeuf, was essentially a version of the agrarian law, but turned upside-down in its reasoning. Convinced that a true regeneration of France could only be accomplished by a redistribution of land according to need, the Robespierrists (he explained) had set out to accomplish Rousseau's ideal in which "all citizens had enough, and nobody had too much." Like Lycurgus at Sparta, they had sought to endow every citizen with an inalienable domain guaranteeing his basic subsistence, but calculated on the basis of the relationship of the total population to the total production of the land.

In practice, since property had fallen into a small number of hands, the great majority of Frenchmen possessed nothing. If this state of affairs were allowed to persist, equality of rights would remain an empty word, as against the reality of an aristocracy of property-owners. The masses, the majority, would always be the slaves of the tyrannical minority. Thanks to their mastery of the resources of industry, the property-owners were in a position to give out or withhold employment from the propertyless or proletarians (*prolétaires*). Thus the same property-owning minority dictated the law, the distribution of employment, the level of wages, and the price of objects of consumption.

According to Babeuf, "Maximilien and his council" had concluded that the only way to break the power of the property-owners was for the government to seize all property. They had been ready to accept the consequence: that such a seizure would only succeed by means of the slaughter of the large landowners (*les gros possesseurs*) and by terrorizing the others into submission. Such interim measures as the *maximum*, the adoption of requisition, and the introduction of the national Commission des Subsistances represented the "first act" of the seizure of property, and the distribution of aid to the wives and children of combatants the first installment of "the agrarian redistribution."

In commenting on the details of this program Babeuf carefully took exception only to the alleged Machiavellian scheme of the Robespierrists to reduce the population by encouraging endless civil and foreign wars. Here more "contraband" was smuggled in. Babeuf explained that he himself was not convinced, like the Jacobins, that the produce of the soil of France was inadequate to meet the needs of the inhabitants. Should there be a shortage, the laws of nature decreed rationing rather than depopulation: an equal sharing out of what was available. Finally, for the benefit of the exceptionally obtuse reader, he provided extensive footnotes explicitly defending the Jacobin policy of taxing the rich for the benefit of soldiers' dependents, and Jacobin measures to bleed the "child of fortune" for the benefit of returned soldiers (a reminder of the Ventôse laws of February 1794, which had promised to place the property of "suspects" at the disposal of *sans-culotte* patriots).

At the same time Babeuf made it clear that his own prescriptions went beyond the wartime collectivism of the Robespierrists. "I say that ... whether they are combatants or not, the soil of a state ought to assure the existence of all the members of that state." Whatever the old administration had left undone to tackle the abuses of inequality must remain imperatively on the agenda of the new. There was nothing in the least cryptic or satirical about Babeuf's conclusion: the government's duty was to put every man to work, and to guarantee in return for the labor exacted "a subsistence for all [*le nécessaire à tous*], ... an equal education, and the independence of every citizen from every other." The government must also guarantee an unconditional subsistence to the child, to the weak, to the infirm, and to the aged.[6]

The parallels between the argument of the *Cadastre perpétuel* of 1789 and the *Système de dépopulation* of 1795 are close. In each case an agrarian ideal—the natural right of every party to the social contract to an equal subsistence from the common patrimony, the land—is held to form the basis of a civic right to subsistence for the citizens. In each case the principle of an equal right to the produce of the soil is advanced to justify certain specific practical measures of redistribution. In 1789 it was progressive taxation and a general welfare program, in 1795 the Jacobin economic policy of *maximum*, requisition, and rationing. But whereas in 1789 Babeuf was still only toying with the agrarian law in a purely speculative way, by the end of 1794 he had come plainly to accept land redistribution as a practical policy, or, at any rate, the seizure of the land of the rich for division among veteran defenders of the fatherland.

As always, Babeuf's "program" in January 1795 combined the visionary and extreme with the immediate and the practical. In the *Tribun du peuple* the emphasis was on the immediate and the practical. The columns of no. 29 (published a few days after the *Système de dépopulation*) outlined essentials of the new program of the plebeian party. The party must stand not only for equality of rights, equality on paper, but for the legal guarantee to all of a fair sufficiency in satisfaction of physical needs, and equal access to the advantages of society in return for the labor every man contributed to the common toil.

The popular party in the Convention was reminded of its promises of land to the returning soldier; of assistance to the sick, to children, to the aged and poverty-stricken; of its promise of work for both sexes in all industries. Babeuf argued that many deputies who were not yet corrupt might still be rallied in defense of the Le Peletier plan for a national education, of the laws against food hoarding, and of the Constitution of 1793. By maintaining a dole of bread and wood at a controlled price in Paris, the Convention had up to now protected the Parisians from the extremes of misery to which the French countryside had become a prey. After giving horrifying details of the plight of the starving village of Verneuil, Babeuf urged the Convention to generalize and extend the Paris *maximum* arrangements throughout the provinces.[7]

The strategy of the *Tribun du peuple* during the early weeks of 1795 was twofold: to strengthen the morale of the remaining *sans-culotte* and Jacobin cadres, and to appeal to the working-class faubourgs, Saint-Antoine and Saint-Marceau, for another 31 May, for a general march on the Convention to demand a return to a "Jacobin" economic and political program of "bread and the Constitution of 1793." A prerequisite for the success of this strategy was the existence of a nucleus of allies in the Convention itself, as yet untouched by the prevailing Thermidorian degeneration. It may be that Babeuf had already reassured himself on this point. There is some evidence that a liaison existed between Babeuf and the Montagnard deputy Fouché, notorious for the political violence and collectivist extremism of his policies (while representative on mission at Lyons and in the Nièvre Département); and it has even been suggested that Babeuf was now being used by Fouché almost as he had earlier been used by Fréron.

Sometime during January 1795 Babeuf sent Fouché the proofs of a brochure (which was never printed) defending the heroes of the insurrection of 31 May 1793 against current attacks. Fouché showed the proofs to Tallien. On 29 January Tallien used this confidence as the pretext for an attack on Fouché in the Convention for his relationship with Babeuf; but it was an attack which misfired, since it produced only cheers for Fouché from the public gallery and a rally of the survivors of the Montagne in the body of the Convention. At the same date the *Messager du soir* accused Fouché of sheltering Babeuf. Although Babeuf, like Fouché, denied the existence of any close connection, a letter which he wrote to Fouché from jail in April 1795 suggests strongly that both a personal and a political understanding existed between the two men. Babeuf called Fouché *"mon ami"* and revealed the names of a number of political associates to whom he had entrusted a clandestine no. 33 of the *Tribun*.[8] If such an understanding did exist, Babeuf was destined for yet another disappointment. As the insurrection of Prairial was to show in May 1795, there was a small group of old Montagnards prepared to reform the old alliance with the *sans-culottes,* but, from motives of prudent calculation, Fouché was not among them.

In practical terms the "Party of the Plebeians" had no formal existence outside the pages of the *Tribun du peuple.* At best it was only a convenient description for a loose coalition of *sans-culotte* diehards. After the collapse of the democratic campaign in October and November most of the Paris sections and popular societies succumbed to the general reaction, as bourgeois and moderate elements seized control of their bureaus and committees. Yet despite the repeated arrests of the leading militants and the street violence of the *jeunesse dorée,* the last embers of resistance were not yet stamped out.

In the working-class faubourg of Saint-Antoine, the Society of the Defenders of the Rights of Man (meeting in an orphanage in the Quinze-Vingts Section) remained a rallying point for elements who continued to count for something in the meetings of the Quinze-Vingts, Montreuil and Popincourt sections. In the Faubourg Saint-Marceau the Society of Republican Virtues in the Observatoire Section filled the same rôle. In the center of Paris, after the collapse of the Club Electoral the democrats had fallen back on the Society of the Friends of Liberty and Humanity (the Popular Society of the rue du Vert-Bois), from which they were able to dominate the General Assembly of the Gravilliers Section; the Muséum Section also remained in militant hands.[9]

Working from a series of "underground" hideouts, Babeuf composed the *Tribun du peuple* as the guide and spokesman of this opposition movement. Despite the difficult conditions—and despite Babeuf's disavowal of any claims to be a "gazetteer" of daily news—the developing skill with which he strove to act as a "sentinel of the people" is impressive. No. 29, for example, contained a hard-hitting chronicle of the first fifteen days of nivôse (21 December 1794 - 4 January 1795). It was in the best tradition of Babeuf's avowed models, Marat and Prudhomme. One by one a succession of "anti-republican and anti-democratic" measures were held up for critical scrutiny: the purging of *sans-culotte* justices of the peace, the closing of the state arms workshops, permission for the export of specie, the suppression of the *maximum,* the purge of *sans-culottes* from government offices, acts relieving *émigrés* and making the return of counter-revolutionaries from abroad easier. Particularly telling passages pilloried the personal failings of individual Thermidorians and their "traitorous nymphs": Tallien for his weakness for the aristocratic courtesan Thérèse Cabarrus; Bentabole for his marriage to the comtesse Choiseul-Gouffier and "300,000 livres a year." Legendre was taken to task in another number for his relations with "the actresses Comtat and Raucourt."[10]

Together with Lebois' Jacobin *Ami du peuple*, Babeuf's journal played a very important part in maintaining the morale and the cohesion of the surviving revolutionary opposition in Paris during the winter of 1794-5. Decimated by arrests, terrorized by the *jeunesse dorée*, disillusioned by the persistence of popular apathy, only a hardy handful of *sans-culottes* were prepared to declare themselves openly in the sections and the popular societies. The overt opposition was measured in dozens and half-dozens rather than hundreds or thousands. However, the success of Babeuf's journal provided a reassurance of the stubborn persistence of a much wider army of hidden sympathizers. He warned the Thermidorians that the closing of the Club Electoral and the Jacobins, far from crushing the organized opposition, had merely changed its tactics. Now every garret and every slum tenement would become its own popular society. Public readings of the *Tribun* in such garrets and in the popular cafés provided the rallying center for the "hidden opposition," and Babeuf's circulation rose until printings of 2,000 were inadequate to meet the demand.[11]

Sensing the beginnings of a revival of popular support, the popular societies of the Quinze-Vingts and the rue du Vert-Bois launched a new agitation for the immediate introduction of the Constitution of 1793. On 23 January Babeuf welcomed the support of several sections for this campaign; but in his next number, five days later, he was compelled to report a serious set-back. On 9 January the Gravilliers Section General Assembly had agreed to petition the Convention for the "democratic Constitution of 1793." The following day the two chief leaders of the democratic faction, Petit and Camelin, were arrested and consigned to Le Plessis prison, where they remained despite a protest demonstration at the Convention on 19 January. Babeuf's response to this new repression was to issue a call for an insurrection on the pattern of 31 May 1793. The people of Paris must stage a peaceful mass approach to the Convention to protest present griefs, impose a new mandate on the deputies, and lay down a program for the future. Even though Babeuf insisted that there must be "no torrents of blood and no heaps of corpses," this was a challenge which could hardly be ignored by the Convention majority. The police were ordered to close in on Babeuf and the *Tribun*.[12]

Babeuf had been "on the run" for three months, since the end of October. However, until the reappearance of the *Tribun du peuple* in mid-December, the police appear to have shown little energy in tracking him down. At the beginning of January Naftel, a police agent, received orders to arrest Babeuf, and he called at a wine-merchant's house on the rue des Champs-Elysées where Marie-Anne and the three children were now living. Not only did Naftel fail to find Babeuf, but he was afterward alleged to have given his quarry advance warning. The police were able to pull in the printer of no. 28 of the *Tribun*, Jean Robert Carin (proprietor of the Imprimerie de Franklin), without any difficulty. But all they got out of Carin was an admission that he had printed a couple of pamphlets by Babeuf, including the *Système de dépopulation,* which was due to be published that day (3 January), and that Babeuf and Marie-Anne occasionally visited him together. Incredibly enough, the police then allowed the *Système de dépopulation* to appear without interference. They also arrested Marie-Anne and subjected her to interrogation, but without learning anything important. According to Marie-Anne, Babeuf had lived away from home since October but she had no idea where, and he only kept in touch through Emile (his mother called him Robert!) by catching up with him in the street. During this time she had been living on the proceeds of sewing work commissioned by the Champs-Elysées Section, apart from some money collected from Carin.[13]

The publication of no. 29 on 8 January—with its personal attacks on Fréron and Tallien and its appeal to the opposition to rally behind a Jacobin program—caused fresh disturbance in high places. In retaliation Fréron saw to it that the streets were placarded with the findings of the Somme tribunal convicting Babeuf of forgery and fraud. Meanwhile steps were taken to reactivate Babeuf's prosecution before the Laon tribunal.[14] Then came Babeuf's general call for an insurrection contained in no. 31, published on 28 January. On 2 February Boursault (representative on mission in Brittany) added still more fuel to the flames by a report to the Committee of Public Safety in which he explained that the influence of Babeuf's journal and other Jacobin papers had been leading the people of Rennes to riot over the price of bread.

By 6 February the police had tracked down Babeuf's new printer,

Jean Divernois (of the rue des Vieux Augustins), and seized no. 33 of the *Tribun* while it was still on the presses. They also discovered that Divernois had sent his copy to a shop in the rue Nicaise, probably Parein's. An informer led a police inspector to a house on the corner of the rue Antoine and Passage Lesdiguières, not far from the Place de la Bastille. At 8 p.m. on 7 February an armed detachment found Babeuf in a small back room on the second floor and arrested him without any disturbance. The following day, Mathieu, a member of the Committee of General Security, was able to announce triumphantly to his colleagues that Babeuf was at last powerless "to call on the citizens to revolt." Two days later (on 10 February) the *jeunesse dorée* held their own celebration at the Théâtre de la Montagne. A bust of Marat was thrown out of the building and replaced by a bust of Rousseau, which was given a civic crown. Then a copy of Babeuf's journal was ceremonially burned "as an expiatory sacrifice," to the accompaniment of general applause.[15]

The Thermidorians had reason to celebrate. The régime had weathered a serious crisis, and with the arrest of Babeuf the last serious organized opposition from the *sans-culottes* was nearing its end. On 8 February the popular society of the Quinze-Vingts was closed down, to the accompaniment of a general roundup of popular leaders in the Faubourg Saint-Antoine. The Gravilliers Section had been in the hands of the moderates since 29 January, and the days of the Society of the rue du Vert-Bois were numbered. On 18 February, the militants were literally "kicked out" of the Muséum Section assembly. By this date the Quinze-Vingts Section had also been captured by the moderates, along with those of the Lombards, the Marchés and the Faubourg du Nord. Before the end of February the Arsenal and Cité sections had also fallen. Only in the Bondy Section, alone among the forty-eight, was the *sans-culotte* party able to stand fast against the general reaction for a few more weeks.

Yet even as its generals were vanishing from the scene, by a strange irony the popular army began to reconstitute itself ever more strongly. During the spring of 1795 the economic crisis steadily worsened, and under the scourge of poverty and hunger the Paris workers and artisans at last began to shed their year-old mood of apathy in preparation for a last desperate uprising. In the five months between December 1794 and May 1795, accelerating inflation doubled prices yet again. Inflation and scarcity drove the price of bread on the free market up to 16 livres a pound at a time when a good day's wage was no more than 8 livres: a day's work for half a pound of bread. The government continued to provide Parisians with a ration of bread at a fixed low price, but by the end of March supplies were running out and daily distributions had to be cut to half a pound a head or less, sometimes failing altogether. Attempts were made to persuade the Parisians to eat potatoes and a distribution of rice was tried, but there was no fuel to cook it in domestic grates. Households sold furniture, clothes, and bedding, and then resigned themselves to starvation. Professor Tønnesson cites the example of Tailleur, a vermicelli-maker and the former president of the Quinze-Vingts Section. When the police arrived to arrest him in April 1795 they found his wife and five children huddled together naked, in "the most frightful misery and the most absolute poverty."[16]

By the end of March Paris was ripe for a rebellion. But the tried machinery of the sections and the popular societies was no longer available. For the two uprisings of Germinal (1 April) and Prairial (20-22 May) the *sans-culottes* relied instead on a version of Babeuf's peaceful mass insurrection. Babeuf himself had been transferred from Paris to a prison in Arras before Germinal and thus bore no direct responsibility for the uprisings. The real "agitator" responsible for setting the faubourgs in motion was, in any case, the impersonal and relentless spur of hunger. Even so, these last popular *journées* of the revolution represented a vindication of the campaign of the *Tribun du peuple* for an effective alliance of the workers and the *sans-culotte* militants of the sections and the popular societies. Even the tactics followed in Germinal and Prairial were an indirect tribute to Babeuf's new prestige as a leader of the Jacobin-democratic alliance.

There is considerable evidence to show that the insurgents looked for ultimate guidance to the imprisoned *sans-culotte* leaders locked away in the Paris jails, and inevitably much of the discussion inside and outside the prisons about tactics centered on ideas launched by Babeuf in the *Tribun du peuple*. In a manifesto smuggled out of Plessis before Germinal, for example, Brutus Magnier urged the people to descend on the Convention peacefully, but armed with guns and cannon ready to defend themselves. "The majestic movement of a people saying to its mandatories: do that, because that is what I wish." On the eve of Prairial another influential pamphlet, *L'Insurrection du peuple* (attributed to the prisoner Claude Fiquet), called on the people to "surge on the Convention in a fraternal disorder."[17]

In the event, the two uprisings of Germinal and Prairial were nothing if not spontaneous. Street riots, meetings in workshops, *ad*

hoc unofficial section assemblies, all fused together in a mass movement. Yet, in the end, the lack of formal organization was fatal. Both
in Germinal and in Prairial the insurgent crowds were able to break
into the Convention. In Prairial the force of armed rebels from the
faubourgs and from the center of Paris was briefly strong enough to
overcome the Convention and to compel the deputies to vote assent to
their new "mandate": the release of Jacobin and militant prisoners,
steps to implement the Constitution of 1793, and an improvement in
the food supply.[18] In effect the Prairial rebels had successfully accomplished Babeuf's program of "peaceful insurrection" at the cost
of the head of only one unfortunate deputy.

But the sequel showed that something more was needed. The
rebellion had no organized central leadership and it had no common
agreed program. Consequently, once the Thermidorians and the
moderates had recovered their courage they were able to restore
order and to hunt down the revolutionary militants without difficulty, thus turning a momentary triumph into permanent catastrophe
for the *sans-culotte* movement.

Far away in the cells of Arras, Babeuf and his fellow-prisoners
learned the news and put aside their naive dreams of a "revolution of
fraternal disorder." Insurrections in the future would have to be
carefully planned and responsibly led by an organizing cadre of
professionals: the "Party of the Plebeians" must have a high command.

Thirteen

Communism

On the evening of 7 February, immediately after his arrest, Babeuf was given a preliminary interrogation and taken before the Committee of General Security. But he refused to reveal any information, or to give any details of those who had helped him to evade the police for so long. About 2 a.m. he was sent to Les Orties prison and thrust into a room with twenty other prisoners, who gave him a hero's reception. Les Orties prison was situated in the center of Paris, close to the Tuileries. It had been recently opened, and it contained only a handful of prisoners: twenty-three on 27 February, about thirty on 6 March. As political prisons went, it was regarded as fairly comfortable. From the first, however, Babeuf determined to make his jailer's life as difficult as possible during his fifth imprisonment.

He began his protest campaign with a nine-page letter (on 9 February) to the Committee of General Security justifying himself and indignantly rebutting the charge that he had attempted to bribe one of the arresting officers with 30,000 livres. On his arrest he had had six livres in his pocket; and the total value of the clothing, furniture and other possessions belonging to the family was less than 800 livres. Babeuf refused to cooperate in a second police interrogation (on 12 February), demanding instead to confront a member of the Convention. He drafted a letter to Bentabole (on 17 February) complaining that he was being held in solitary confinement and that Marie-Anne had been refused permission to visit him. At the same time Babeuf was busy seeing to the publication and distribution of a pamphlet refuting the damaging slanders which had been spread by

Guffroy and Tallien about his part in the Montdidier forgery case.[1]

Babeuf's stay at Les Orties was characterized by increasingly strained relations with Besse, the governor of the prison, and Besse singled him out (on 27 February) as the most intractable among two dozen prisoners. The previous day had been marked by a particularly violent quarrel when the governor had ordered windows to be closed through which the prisoners had been trying to talk to their wives and families outside. (Visiting hours for Marie-Anne Babeuf had been fixed at once every five days.) Besse asked for Babeuf to be transferred to a safer prison, since (according to an informer planted among the prisoners) he had acted as one of the ringleaders in an escape plot for which hidden ropes had been collected. The other leader was Lebois, editor of the *Ami du peuple*, who had been arrested and sent to Les Orties on 1 March, and who was said to be "close to Babeuf in everything."[2]

Babeuf, Lebois, and a third prisoner were promptly transferred to La Grande Force, a much less eligible prison and a former debtors' jail of the Ancien Régime. Babeuf set to work at La Force to prepare a new version of number 33 of the *Tribun du peuple*, to replace the copy seized in the police raid on the printers at the beginning of February. But before he had time to arrange for publication, he and Lebois were moved again, this time to a prison at Arras, 120 miles northeast of Paris—the first of a stream of particularly dangerous agitators the Committee of General Security felt it safest to remove from the possibility of contact and rescue by Parisian activists still at liberty.[3]

Babeuf was to remain in exile at Arras, cut off from the possibility of seeing his wife and children, for six months (from 15 March to 10 September). During the whole of this time he was locked up in Les Baudets prison, an ancient, crumbling stone building originally built in the Middle Ages for the princes of Melun Epernay. Before the revolution the municipality of Arras had used the building partly as a prison, partly as a madhouse. At the height of the terror of 1793-4, Joseph Le Bon (the representative on mission charged with securing the rear of the northern armies) had kept up to 192 prisoners there.

On their arrival Babeuf and Lebois found conditions extremely primitive. The prisoners were accommodated in pairs in cold, damp cells into which the sun scarcely filtered during the day. There was only straw to sleep on, and the prison rations amounted at first to only bread (a pound a day) and water. Additional meals had to be provided by the inmates at their own expense, through negotiations with a private contractor. After enduring this régime for a month, Babeuf and Lebois sent off a formal complaint to the Committee of General Security; and the responsible authorities at Arras were ordered to take action to improve conditions. Babeuf listed the prisoners' "demands" in a letter (on 17 April) to the General Council of the Commune of Arras: a bed each and a water pot; dinner and supper to be provided, together with two cups of coffee with milk in the morning; a bottle of wine a day; and some means of lighting the cells. The prisoners of the committee at Paris, Babeuf pointed out, "were fed, lodged and treated with distinction and regard," as were those at the other special prison for political exiles at Ham.[4]

In a letter smuggled out to Fouché (on 8 April) Babeuf had remarked on one of the peculiarities of the Thermidorian régime. Having "made humanity the order of the day," its leaders had substituted exile for the death sentence; but "one may return from exile, and one may return glorious and triumphant." Of course, more—or rather less—than mere humanity was involved in this reasonable treatment of political prisoners of the Left, as Babeuf recognized. The Thermidorian stance represented an increasingly unstable balancing act between the Jacobins on the one flank and resurgent royalism on the other. The Thermidorians of the center, preoccupied with desperate infighting on the committees and in the Convention, preferred to keep as many pieces in play as possible (including some, like Babeuf and Lebois, locked away safely in reserve). Thus the prisoners had some bargaining power, and Babeuf and his fellow-prisoners were determined to use this to the full.

Similar considerations may help to explain why Babeuf thought it worthwhile to write on 28 April to his one-time partner Guffroy, offering, in effect, to strike a bargain with the Thermidorian center and to attach himself to a democratic faction which (he persuaded himself) was currently gathering around the deputy Cambacérès. After promising to send along his own reflections on the contemporary constitutional debate for Cambacérès' edification, Babeuf concluded with a naive and insolent reminder of the terms of the quarrel between Guffroy and himself. "You also know what influence over the people I have managed to get hold of latterly. You know of it, because you are one of those who were most frightened by that influence, since with the other members of the government you took such great measures to stop its effect."[5]

Needless to say Cambacérès (if Guffroy ever showed him the letter) displayed no haste in rushing to unlock the door of Babeuf's cell, and there is no evidence that the letter received any reply. Had he managed to attach himself to Cambacérès, Babeuf would have found himself in very strange company indeed. He had misjudged his new hero here even more completely than all the other "heroes" on whom he had pinned his faith since Coupé—for Cambacérès' leanings were much more towards an accommodation with moderate royalists than one with extreme democrats. The letter to Guffroy may, however, have represented no more than a Machiavellian ruse by Babeuf to regain his liberty and his freedom of action.

At the same time as he wrote to Fouché and to Cambacérès, Babeuf also began a secret correspondence with imprisoned former Jacobins throughout the northeast of France. Les Baudets was only one of seven prisons at Arras linked by an "underground" network of communication. Two of the prisons (La Providence and L'Hôtel Dieu) were so close together that their prisoners could even talk to one another. Other links were provided by bribed couriers —sometimes the jailers' children—and by visitors. From early June Babeuf carried on a regular correspondence with a contact in La Providence, who passed on news from Paris culled from Duval's *Journal des hommes libres*, which was received by the prisoners there. At Les Baudets, Lebois composed manuscript editions of the *Ami du peuple* for circulation among the prisoners.[6]

Outside the prisons Arras still contained a strong cohort of Jacobins and former associates of Joseph Le Bon (even though Le Bon himself had been under arrest since shortly after Thermidor). At the beginning of his stay at Arras, Babeuf had established a close relationship with two fellow prisoners, Cochet and Taffoureau, disciples of Le Bon's with whom he continued to correspond later in the year, as they were moved from prison to prison in the northeast. Babeuf also wrote to Le Bon's wife, Elisabeth Regnier, and to other ex-followers of the imprisoned terrorist leader (Caubrières, Fontenier, Goulliart). According to Babeuf, Le Bon's brother Henri was also imprisoned in Les Baudets for a time; and another brother, Léandre, used to visit the jail (but this must have been after the beginning of August).[7]

The most important among the inner circle of Babeuf's confidants was his correspondent in La Providence, Charles Germain. It seems probable that Babeuf's close friendship with Germain had begun in Les Orties. Germain had been sent there after his arrest in January 1795 for brawling with an anti-Jacobin in the public galleries of the Convention. After the Prairial insurrection he had been transferred first to Plessis prison and then to Arras. On 9 June Germain wrote to Babeuf from La Providence as his "brother and friend," in response to unsuccessful efforts by Babeuf to smuggle notes through. Thus began a long correspondence between the two men. It was a relationship which quickly developed into that of master and disciple, as the correspondents debated the details of a new revolutionary program for the final achievement of complete equality.

Although Charles Germain deferred to Babeuf, he yet remained a strong personality with original ideas of his own to contribute to the discussion. Germain was a southerner, born at Narbonne in 1770, a man of ready wit and a volatile temperament, capable of fervent loyalties and sudden rages. The son of a minor royal official, he had been brought up in the Calvinist religion, for which he still retained a certain apologetic loyalty in 1795. Despite this background he had been encouraged to study by Dillon, the archbishop of Narbonne, who obtained a scholarship for him at a Paris college. At the age of seventeen, however, Germain threw up his studies and joined the army as a private. During the revolutionary wars he saw service in the Alps and the Pyrenees and was wounded. In December 1793 he was made an officer in a new regiment of Hussars, and held the rank for six months before being stripped and imprisoned by a Jacobin representative on mission for an injudicious political speech in a popular society. He was released, but not reinstated, at the end of August 1794.

Germain's attitudes to politics and social morality were essentially religious, though not in the sectarian sense. He was aware of the Anabaptist experiments in communism during the sixteenth century; he knew of the Essene tradition in Jewish history; and he professed a high regard for "the sublime Nazarene legislator" as an honored pioneer of the creed of equality. Still only 25 (in 1795) Germain retained a taste for philosophy and a thirst for knowledge which led him to rise at five o'clock in the morning to read Helvétius as the first rays of the sun struck the pillars of his cell. To such a man (at some time in mid-July) Babeuf offered the new revelation of his "agrarian doctrine," and he found his correspondent taking fire with a sudden enthusiasm.[8]

Unfortunately Babeuf's letter itself has not been discovered and we can only surmise its contents from the subsequent correspondence. According to Germain, it contained "an agrarian code," the code that the Gracchi themselves would have promulgated had they not been murdered. It thus seems reasonable to suppose that the essence of Babeuf's plan was a variant of the system he had first defended in his correspondence with Coupé in 1791—the acquisition of the land by the state and its allocation to the peasant farmers in equal lots on a basis of life tenure. On 23 July Germain sent back a long commentary in reply. In this he envisaged a two-stage revolution: first a forcible seizure and redistribution of the land among individuals, and then the melting of such individual holdings into "the common domain," with cultivation directed for the good of all and the ultimate aim complete equality through the equal distribution of the products of the soil.[9]

Babeuf in turn sent back (on 28 July) an essay of 5,000 words in 13 quarto pages for further comment; it was a first draft of a public manifesto. Germain had cast his letter of 23 July in the form of an examination and refutation of certain common objections to the agrarian law. Babeuf's reply systematically took up the points raised by Germain as a basis for a deeper analysis. The first objection dealt with was the allegation that the establishment of absolute equality would "destroy commerce." Germain's answer to this charge was to admit its validity, and to launch into an attack on the evils of luxury in the common style of the eighteenth century. Lycurgus, the Spartan lawgiver (and the first founder of "a true republic of brothers"), had been the first to recognize the poisonous influence of commerce and to establish the fatal connection between commerce, a taste for luxury, and the growth of tyranny. The fall of Carthage and the decay of Tyre were historical object-lessons in the evils resulting from the triumph of the commercial principle in the state.

While Babeuf did not reject Germain's arguments, his own condemnation of commerce was firmly rooted in an appreciation of the history of his own country and the facts of contemporary economic life. Whereas according to its defenders it was supposed to benefit everyone, from the first-stage producer to the large manufacturer and the merchant, in practice (Babeuf argued) commerce represented no more than a façade for the exploitation of the productive majority by the idle minority, thanks to the workings of the "very old plot . . . by the aid of which one is able to set a multitude of arms in motion, without those who move them receiving the intended fruits."

The failure of commerce to live up to its promises was an irrefutable fact of common observation. The greater part of those who grew linen and hemp—and almost all who worked with wool or silk, spun or made cloth, tanned leather or made boots—were without shirts, clothing, or footwear, while those who worked with their hands (making furniture, trade tools, or household utensils) or as building workers were similarly deprived of their basic needs. Far from providing an equal subsistence to all its agents, in practice commerce discriminated against the original producer, whose work (although the most essential) was incomparably less well rewarded than the purely subordinate operations of distribution. Babeuf explained this central injustice of society as the result of a conspiracy between the speculators and the merchants to keep the producer at their mercy. On the one hand, the "criminal speculators" used their monopoly of capital and their control of the allocation of work to force down wages and keep up working hours. This was "the barbaric law dictated by capital." On the other hand, the merchants used all kinds of devices to force up prices: concealing stocks, spreading rumors of scarcity, even sometimes destroying goods, until only they and their speculator confederates could afford to buy. In this way commerce served only to "suck forth the sweat and the blood of almost everybody to turn them into lakes of gold to the profit of a very small number."

Some reflections on the charge that his system would "destroy industry" provided Babeuf with a further opportunity to develop his critique of existing economic institutions, and in particular of the harmful effects of competition. In the existing unorganized world of industry, competition meant either the suppression of new inventions or a flood of new production driving down standards and forcing producers into bankruptcy. The competition of manufactured items with one another also meant the swindling of the public by the marketing of shoddy goods "dressed up" for the customer, and the waste of raw materials and labor which might be better used elsewhere. Competition was, finally, a system in which only the richest could win out and the small man must go to the wall.[10]

When Charles Germain turned to discuss what form of economic organization was to replace the commercial system, he was deliberately vague. He preferred to pin his faith on the spontaneous inventiveness of the liberated people, in a visionary passage which seems to foreshadow the spirit of nineteenth-century anarchism. "There are enough resources in the people's heads. Whatever we have not been able to discover will be discovered by them. The true way to return to nature, both social and individual, to re-enter into fraternity and never to leave it again, will be assuredly revealed in the midst of the common tendencies and common efforts to discover it. We shall only direct the movement. Our task is to give the impulsion for the shock." Nevertheless, the clear implication of Germain's letter is that ultimately both agriculture and industry were to be centrally organized, administered, and directed.[11]

Babeuf's reflections on the same subject were much more detailed and explicit. For Babeuf, in the new regenerated society there would be neither money nor individual trade. All would work for "the common storehouse" (*le magasin commun*), to which they would send the product of their individual labor. Then assigned agents would distribute to each citizen an equal portion of the total production in return for their contribution. It is not clear whether Babeuf envisaged at this time an actual physical network of storehouses. He seems rather to have been thinking in terms of a national *commission des subsistances* after the pattern of 1793, which would have requisitioning powers. "Every workshop," he wrote, "will be a part of the great workshop, every product, every merchandise will be accounted for in the great storehouse and listed in the total of the resources of the Republic. . . ."

In return for his labor every citizen would receive "every necessary object" of consumption. At the same time the dependent and nonproductive classes would also be entitled to an equal share: "For society, having an interest in being just, binds itself to take an equal care of children, of invalids, and the aged. This is an advance made to the first group, so that they may render service at an age when they are strong. As regards the others, if they have served her, society repays a debt. If they have been incapable of making themselves useful, society repays the debt of humanity. . . . "

As in all his previous projects of social reform Babeuf regarded this humane guarantee of social security for the helpless as a particularly important provision. But he had other than the purely material aspects of the rearrangement of society in mind. Germain had argued, somewhat optimistically, that even the rich would come to see the advantages of merging their private fortunes in an egalitarian commonwealth. Such fortunes, after all, were impermanent, and provided no guarantee of the future happiness of their descendants to match that offered by the new society. Developing the same theme, Babeuf argued that the provision of security for children and dependents would have a powerful moral effect on society. Individuals would no longer feel driven to accumulate private wealth and would be able to reconcile themselves readily to the régime of absolute equality.

Both Germain and Babeuf were less than specific about the details. Who would be responsible for organizing the collection and distribution of the produce of the community? Babeuf thought in terms of a central administration both of the "great storehouse" and of the "great workshop," and he specifically allowed for "governmental industry" as an acceptable contribution to the common good. Indeed, his vision seems to have included a far-reaching collectivist direction of manufacture as well as the management of distribution.

The tasks assigned to the government of "the association" thus included the regulation of production in industry according to a rational calculation of present and future need. It would assign a fixed output to each producer, determine the number of workers to be employed in a particular craft, and exercise a control over the number of young men allowed to enter any craft or profession. By dint of such planning the evil effects of competition could be avoided and industry conducted more efficiently. At the same time "the association's" agents would be responsible for collecting and spreading the knowledge of new inventions capable of simplifying and lightening labor in industry—so that the workers in general might enjoy more leisure, and so that labor saved could be transferred to trades where it could be deployed more usefully. Babeuf also implied that "the association" would see to the general dissemination of the advanced techniques of regions of large-scale farming, with the use of agricultural machinery and the rational division of labor (*la bonne distribution des travaux*).

Other sections of Babeuf's letter dealt with minor criticisms of the projected agrarian society. He was concerned, for example, to deny the allegation that the new system would mean the death of the arts and the end of science. No, the arts and sciences would receive a new stimulus in the direction of the general good, as a result of their being harnessed to the project of increasing the sum of satisfactions for all. Freed from their dependence on private patrons, artists would be able to achieve new and splendid conceptions worthy of a true civilization based on a common happiness.

Another objection (that abolishing property would destroy international trade) had produced a xenophobic outburst from Germain. France was self-sufficient, foreign imports were unnecessary; much of the grain actually imported from Holland had previously been surreptitiously exported from France. Moreover, while the revolution was in progress and until the "agrarian institution" was firmly established, any contact with the foreigner and with disturbing foreign ideas would be dangerous. In the interim it would be better to erect an "impassable barrier of steel" between the foreigner and the French people.[12]

With all these arguments Babeuf declared himself in general agreement. Commerce between nations would certainly have to be suspended for the duration of "the regenerative enterprise" and it would not be a necessity even afterwards. France could be self-sufficient so long as her citizens were sober enough, and moderate enough, to dispense with "foreign superfluities." Such imports would be in any case harmful in themselves, for they tended to bring back the fatal taste for the sweet life and luxury, and to revive the mercantile spirit. However, despite all this, Babeuf rejected the notion of a "Chinese wall" between revolutionary France and the outside world. The peoples of Europe would be allowed free access, and even a certain amount of trade would be permissible provided that it represented only the free gift of France's "surplus" in return for whatever other nations might wish to give.[13] Babeuf also showed more confidence in the universal appeal of the new revolution than did Germain. If, for a time, the nations might "continue to be infected by prejudices and crimes by despots, and plunged into wars contrary to their interests and mortal to their liberty," nevertheless "the circle of humanity would grow, and step by step, frontiers, customs posts and bad governments would disappear." Finally, "the great principle of equality or universal fraternity would become the sole religion of the peoples."

Towards the end of his letter Babeuf considered, almost reluctantly, the objection that the system of absolute equality would "consecrate idleness." His reply was to declare, in effect, that "he who does not work, neither shall he eat." Whoever failed to contribute to the common storehouse so far as he was able, granted his natural faculties, would not share in the distribution. There would be no difficulty in establishing a system of supervision. Indeed willful idleness would be the only crime for which a penal code would be needed, the sole cause for the existence of tribunals. While this solution might appear extraordinarily naive and optimistic, it must be remembered that Babeuf (like all subsequent communists) counted on a general moral reformation of humanity following the introduction of the new order. "In the regenerated society," he wrote, "there will be neither high nor low, neither first nor last; the efforts, like the intentions, of all the associated . . . will constantly converge on the great fraternal goal, the common prosperity, the inexhaustible and perpetual mine of individual well-being. Equity, loyalty, probity, sincerity—at all times and in all places. Everyone shall have his function which he exercises conscientiously, and which shall cause him to live happily, and no more, for the need is for happiness for all equally shared by all. . . . " The *"égalité parfaite"* preached by Babeuf was, thus, more than simple economic equality. It was a thorough-going equality of status within a genuinely classless society.

"Everything will be blended together and on the footing of a perfect equality: producers who are agriculturalists and workers who follow a trade, artists and scientists, storekeepers, allocators and distributors responsible for getting material products to the consumers. All distinctions between industry and commerce will disappear, and there will be a fusion of all professions raised to the same level of honor. . . . " In such a society it could hardly be anticipated that habitual laziness could be a serious long-term problem.[14]

The goal thus was defined—it remained to map out the route. For Charles Germain, who lamented the mismanagement of the "imbeciles" of Prairial, the road to the new society lay through a sudden, apocalyptic, and universal explosion (even though it was prepared by propaganda and careful organization). "It will be better to burn closer and closer, and to operate by sure agents in one single night, at a fixed hour, the total destruction of all the *matériel* of the pernicious and false institutions that justice commands us to overturn." Babeuf regarded such a plan as unrealistic. "If I had in my possession a fairy's wand," he wrote in friendly irony, "on the one hand . . . I would make dust of the past, and on the other I should make leap up from the earth everything which demands and permits the establishment of a society of equals." Babeuf's critique of Germain's plan for a sudden uprising was based on essentially practical considerations. Germain himself had insisted that "the essential point to avoid failure" was "to have been properly understood and properly evaluated." But this assumed a freedom to indoctrinate and to catechize openly which did not exist. Under the prevailing conditions, as soon as Germain began to "preach" he would be arrested by those in power. While it was possible that Germain's insurrection might be successful in the first instance, the aftermath—unless the public had been properly prepared—would be catastrophic. The "sacred manifesto" of the insurgents would not be read. Instead the hired hacks and propagandists of the existing régime would be able to represent the uprising as the work of "brigands, incendiaries, gangsters."

Babeuf's solution was quite different. The insurgents should not attempt to overthrow the state overnight, but should instead seek out a "center of population" where the people were known to be generally favorable. There they would launch a "republican Vendée," a purely local movement. Having established this base they could inaugurate their social experiment and allow its fame to spread, thus bringing about a steady extension and consolidation of the social revolution. Only in this way could the uprising be based firmly on the understanding of the people, which was essential.

Commenting on this passage in 1935 the French socialist scholar Maurice Dommanget drew a rather forced parallel between Babeuf's republican Vendée and the pilot settlements advocated by Fourier and Cabet, the utopian socialists, in the nineteenth century.[15] A generation later what appears most striking is rather the way in which Babeuf's chosen revolutionary tactics foreshadow those of Mao Tse-tung in China or of Che Guevara in South America. It is hard, however, to imagine where Babeuf might have hoped to found his Yenan. Perhaps in the depths of his prison the sound of northern accents reminded him of those moments in 1790 and 1791 when the whole of Picardy had seemed ready to follow his leadership, of the uprising of the peasants of Davenescourt against feudalism, or of the general rebellion of the Oise Département against the grain speculators at Ourscamp in February 1792. Perhaps it was his native Picardy which was intended as the site of the republican Vendée.

Some of the propositions outlined in Babeuf's correspondence with Germain in July 1795 were no more than restatements in a systematic form of ideas which had been maturing ever since 1786 with the first speculations on collective organization of agriculture. The principle of the responsibility of society for the welfare of the aged and the infirm had been clearly affirmed in the *Cadastre perpétuel* in 1789, and that of an agrarian redistribution no later than the autumn of 1791. During 1791 Babeuf had already begun to reflect on the possibilities of a committee of experts supervising, guiding and reorganizing industry on a national level. Now, in the summer of 1795, each of these elements was incorporated for the first time within a single coherent general program for the "regeneration" of society.

The enforced opportunity for reflection in the prison cell of Les

Baudets (and the stimulus of Germain's enthusiasm) led Babeuf to a systematization of his thought into what was to be, more or less, its final form. The new formulation represented more than a simple reshuffling of earlier ideas. Babeuf's letter of 28 July contained two quite new propositions—the abandonment of money as a medium of exchange, and the creation of a national economic administration for the collection, allocation, and distribution of commodities.

The Arras correspondence, in fact, represents a breakthrough, a sudden, qualitative leap in Babeuf's thought. No longer is it a question, as in the past, of criticizing and ameliorating existing society by the standards of an ideal, abstract system. Henceforth the practical and the ideal are united, and the achievement of a communist society is regarded as an immediate and practical goal. Speculating on the inspiration of Babeuf's new program, Maurice Dommanget drew attention to a number of striking parallels between Babeuf's "agrarian code" and the *Code de la Nature*, an influential literary utopia published by Morelly in 1755 (and attributed in Babeuf's day to Diderot). The Morelly specialist Professor Richard Coë also argues strongly in defense of the thesis that many of Babeuf's ideas were borrowed more or less directly from the *Code de la Nature*.

"Magasins publics" do serve a similar function in Babeuf's and Morelly's utopias; and Morelly, like Babeuf, exempts "the sick, the aged, the crippled and infants" from the requirement to contribute to "the common store" while reserving for them a share in the general distribution. It is also true that in his general defense before the court at Vendôme in 1797 Babeuf quoted extensively from the *Code de la Nature*. He also cited certain passages from Mably in which there is an even closer parallel with the arrangements foreshadowed in his correspondence with Germain—including both the establishment of public storehouses for the fruits of labor, and the election of "stewards whose task will be the distribution of goods to each in accordance with his needs, the allotment of tasks to be performed by each, and the maintenance of public order."[16]

Even though there is no direct supporting evidence, it is not impossible that the relevant works of Morelly and Mably were known to Babeuf before the summer of 1795. He had certainly read the *Code de la Nature* before the end of the year, and some of Mably much earlier.[17] We cannot rule out the possibility that the final impulse in Babeuf's conversion to communism may thus have been the literary influence of Enlightenment utopianism. It is more likely, however, that the significant influence was the practice and the promise of the Jacobin experiment in collectivist economy during 1793 and 1794. The legacy of Babeuf's experience as secretary of the Paris Commune's Food Administration was a conviction of the practicality of a state system of grain collection and rationing; and though he was never able to take up his post with Raisson's national Commission des Subsistances, he can hardly have been unaware of its ambitious program of state-organized production and distribution during 1793 and 1794. Even during the Thermidorian period Babeuf had shown a keen and critical interest in the operations of the administration responsible for supplying bread and wood to Paris.

It was, thus, no accident that in a further elaboration of his communist program composed in November 1795 Babeuf defined the common storehouse as "a simple administration of distribution," an *administration des subsistances*, while at the same time citing the success of the Commission des Subsistances in organizing supplies for the "1,200,000 men" in the republican army as evidence of the perfect practicality of a collectivist economy.

At the end of 1795 a friend and fellow-prisoner, the former Jacobin firebrand Marc-Antoine Jullien, rejected Babeuf's "agrarian system" as a work of folly, impossible to apply in practice in a world where men were not prepared to live on roots and herbs and to go naked and without shelter. Yet it should be remembered that Jullien was writing at the end of a year in which inflation finally reduced the republican paper currency to complete worthlessness; the resulting collapse of economic organization drove, quite literally, not a few French families to live on roots and herbs, and to wander about the countryside, ragged and homeless. Moreover, if the armies continued to be fed, and if Paris was saved from absolute starvation, it was less through the working of a free market economy than through the efforts of the Commission des Subsistances and other state organizations charged with the collection and rationing of food and vital supplies. Thus while Babeuf's communism may have represented (in Jullien's words) "the elixir of the social contract," a distillation of the fashionable agrarian utopianism of the eighteenth century, it also represented an essentially practical program, a logical and necessary extension of the experiment in collectivism begun by the Jacobins in 1793-4.[18]

For the prisoners of Arras, Babeuf's new dream of a perfect society possessed a special and even quasi-religious significance. It was a vision that gave a meaning to their present martyrdom, strengthened their inner conviction of moral superiority over their jailers, and offered a promise of hope for the future. It was only partly in jest that Germain referred to the new cause as a "holy crusade." On 22 July Germain wrote to another prisoner, his former secretary and friend Guilhem, to say that "the tribune being completely satisfied," he had been busy "initiating" his cellmate Goulliart "into the secret of the holy and apostolic doctrine." In a letter to Babeuf written soon afterwards he gave an account of Goulliart's initiation into "the sacred mysteries of agrarianism."

On 15 August Germain wrote again to Babeuf: "I have executed your orders. Goulliart is a knight of the Order of the Equals; he has pronounced vows with all the fervor and piety that are appropriate to the mission which we hold from justice and reason. . . . " About the same time Goulliart himself sent a letter to offer congratulations to his "dear tribune" for a project which "could not be better developed." "I send you the fraternal accolade," the new convert concluded, "and it will not be until I have received yours that I believe myself in truth a fully fledged knight" (*armé chevalier*).[19]

The extravagant language of this correspondence may have reflected no more than a jeu d'esprit on the part of Germain, suitable for enlivening the tedious prison hours. Yet there are hints that some of those involved took it more seriously. In 1797 Germain testified that even after their return to Paris, Babeuf and he regarded themselves as members of a kind of sect like the Epicureans and the Stoics. The language in which Babeuf wrote (in January 1796) to his "dear equal" Simon, a one-time fellow-prisoner at Les Orties, as a member elect of "the holy league of the equality of the common happiness" (*la sainte ligue de l'égalité du bonheur commun*) implies that there were others who felt the same way. In February the "Equals of Arras" wrote to offer their "brother tribune" the proceeds of a patriotic collection, with a covering letter addressed to "Citoyen Gracchus Babeuf, notre bon paire."[20]

The campaign of the *Tribun du peuple* in the winter of 1794-5 had already made Babeuf's name known, and marked him out as a leader of the irreconcilables. Henceforth, for an inner circle, his leadership would take on an additional personal significance as that of the prophet of a new creed.

At the moment, in the summer of 1795, there was a demand for leadership on a different and more practical plane from a wider circle of "oppressed patriots" inside and outside the prisons. After the *journées* of Germinal and Prairial, as the "White Terror" developed, most provincial towns in France acquired their own *jeunesse dorée*, harassing and sometimes (especially in southern France) ambushing and murdering the local Jacobins. At Lyons in May dozens of "ex-terrorists" were murdered by an attack on the prison in which they were locked away; and at Aix, twenty-nine prisoners were killed. In June there was more slaughter in the prisons of Marseilles and Tarascon. The situation was less threatening in the north, but even Arras had its band of anti-Jacobin brawlers under leadership of the son of the comte de Béthune. They turned out in force at the Arras theater on 6 August for a performance of *Lodoiska*, dressed in their usual "uniform" of green cravats, with long hair hanging in free tresses, and armed with *fouette-coquins,* special brawling sticks.

The result was a riot in which, for once, the "partisans of Le Bon" gained the upper hand, and de Béthune and several other "green-cravats" were arrested and subjected to a brief and terrifying im-prisonment in Les Baudets in the midst of the "blood-drinkers." On his release one of the anti-Jacobin prisoners published a pamphlet in protest and sent a copy to Babeuf. Babeuf riposted with a satirical account of the riot and its sequel, holding up the "green-cravats" to ridicule. "Les Terroristes aux Furoristes d'Arras" was probably in-tended for clandestine publication outside the prison, for Germain wrote to Babeuf (on 27 August) to discuss a plan to smuggle out pamphlets and publish them at Bapaume. Soon after Babeuf com-posed another attack on de Béthune and the Compagnie de Jésus (the terrorist gang over which he presided) under the title "Lettre à l'Armée infernale et aux patriotes d'Arras."[21] This was followed on 4 September by a second "Lettre," which offered some critical reflec-tions on the Convention's proposals for a new constitution. During the summer of 1795 the deputies had been busy tearing up the Constitution of 1793 and elaborating the details of new and less democratic arrangements whose final form was sanctioned on 22 August.

For the Thermidorian leaders the task of shedding the dictatorial powers of the Convention and returning to normal constitutional processes was beset with difficulties. The experiences of 1793-4 had left behind a compelling fear of the mob. Universal suffrage, as em-bodied in the 1793 constitution, was seen as an invitation to demagogy and a threat to social stability. Consequently the deputies opted for substantial property and educational qualifications for the franchise, with an upper chamber (the Council of Ancients) as a further safeguard. On the other hand, to place power so unreservedly in the hands of the propertied classes was not only to expose the whole work of the revolution to a challenge from the royalist Right, but to place the lives of the regicide majority of the Convention in jeopardy. The Thermidorians solved this problem by decreeing that two-thirds of the members of the two new houses (the Council of Five Hundred and the Council of Ancients) must be elected from the outgoing deputies of the Convention, with arrangements for co-option should the electors fail to oblige. There remained one outstanding difficulty: the Constitution of 1793 had been "accepted by the people" in a national referendum. In order that the Constitution of the Year III might have the same moral authority, it too required the seal of the people's will. Accordingly arrangements were made to submit the Convention's project to the primary assemblies during the month of September.

Babeuf's commentary was clearly drafted for the benefit of the voters in this referendum, and not for the adepts of the "Order of Equals." It criticized the new constitution not for failing to create a communist utopia, but on more prosaic grounds: it excluded the majority of Frenchmen from voting. The franchise was made dependent on literacy, but there was no constitutional provision for public education. Through the institution of the Executive Directory the constitution restored five kings instead of one, while the reorganization of local government established the rule of five intendants instead of one in each *département*. The Convention's self-perpetuating ordinance was also given particularly scathing treatment.[22]

Before the underground press campaign had time to develop further, the Arras center was broken up and a number of the most important prisoners (including Babeuf, Germain and Lebois) were transferred to Le Plessis prison in Paris. The move was ordered by the Committee of General Security on 2 September, and the prisoners left Arras on the tenth, traveling by wagon and arriving at the Paris prison four days later. The motives for this transfer are not clear. Government spies were regularly intercepting the prisoners' correspondence; and the police may have felt that their contacts with the local "patriotic" network were beginning to present a significant danger. Alternatively, the return to Paris may have been arranged as a first step towards liberation. For some time now the Jacobin and radical prisoners had been speculating on the possibility of an amnesty. The Thermidorians, concerned at the growing strength of royalist reaction, were already beginning to make the opening moves towards a reconciliation with the Left. On 24 August Réal sounded the new note strongly with an appeal to "patriots of 1789, constitutional monarchists, Jacobins, moderates, *exagérés*, democrats, republicans" to choose between "liberty and death," and to close ranks in defense of the newly consolidated Republic.[23]

The move to a Paris prison enabled Babeuf to see his family again, but it was a reconciliation darkened by a personal tragedy. Marie-Anne had written a brave letter (on 8 August) telling Babeuf that Thibaudeau was again working to secure his release and reassuring him that although things were tight she was earning a little money, the family was getting by, and the children were well. Emile was a big boy and growing fast. Yet by the time Babeuf actually managed to see his family a few weeks later, his seven-year-old daughter, Cathérine-Adélaide, was dead from starvation, and the two boys were so altered by privation as to be barely recognizable.[24]

Le Plessis prison, where Babeuf was now to spend the last four weeks of his imprisonment, contained perhaps 2,000 prisoners, mostly dedicated *sans-culottes*, Jacobins and ex-terrorists. Their fanaticism, sharpened by persecution, was deepened and consolidated by the collective psychology of prison life. At one time or another during 1795 Le Plessis accommodated, as well as former leaders of the Paris sections, the members of the revolutionary tribunals of Arras, Cambrai, Angers, Rennes, and Brest, and the *commission populaire* of Orange, together with the personnel of the revolutionary committees of Paris, Nantes, Nevers, and Moulins.

Richard Cobb has commented on the process by which the police persecutions of the Thermidorians and their successors served to knit together and to preserve a freemasonry of Jacobin irreconcilables in the political prisons. Outside the prison walls public opinion abandoned the revolutionary cause in growing cynicism and despair. But inside Le Plessis life took on an almost monastic, quasi-religious quality, exalting the values of frugality, fraternity, honorable poverty, work and study. One of the Le Plessis prisoners, Buonarroti, describes how crowds of citizens would gather round the prison walls each evening to listen to concerts of revolutionary songs sung by the prisoners.[25]

Under such conditions the "Equals" inevitably attracted many recruits. Buonarroti lists more than twenty of the "principal actors" in the conspiracy of 1796 who were Le Plessis veterans. At Le Plessis, however, Babeuf was no longer the unqualified chief of the Equals. There were other revolutionaries of stature among his fellow-prisoners: men like Jullien, Bertrand, the ex-mayor of Lyons and a former disciple of Chalier, and Buonarroti himself, the Italian-born revolutionizer of Corsica and a former Jacobin *commissaire* in northern Italy.

Ever since the end of April or the beginning of May the veterans of Le Plessis had been meeting in Jullien's room to concert action and to discuss the tactics to be adopted by a militant counterattack once they were free again. They were not likely to defer unduly to the recent arrival from Arras; and for that matter Buonarroti's account of the Conspiracy of the Equals never conceded to Babeuf more than an executive rôle in what other contemporaries were content to recognize as the "Babeuf plot." To Buonarroti the Equals represented, in retrospect, not so much Germain's vision of an organized order (with Babeuf at its head) as a loose and voluntary confederation of individuals united by their common commitment to a fairly vague concept of equality, and their refusal to compromise with the Thermidorians.[26]

Yet before long the pressure of events was to thrust Babeuf into a position of leadership among his fellow prisoners. The referendum campaign for the endorsement of the Constitution of the Year III neared its climax during the course of September, and the danger of a royalist reaction appeared more threatening. The desirability of closing the ranks of moderate and democratic republicans became more and more apparent. Negotiations began between the prisoners and certain deputies in the Convention. At the beginning of October, Barras (entrusted with organizing the defense of the Convention, and desperately aware of the strength of royalism in the Paris sections) relaxed the prohibition on ex-terrorists carrying arms, and he sanctioned the formation of an armed force of the "Patriots of 1789," composed of dedicated republicans and democrats.

On 13 vendémiaire (5 October) the royalists of a number of the Paris sections struck back. They rose in protest against the new constitution and the rearming of Jacobin "blood-drinkers." Several thousand armed insurgents attacked the Convention, only to be repulsed by Barras' defense forces, effectively deployed by General Napoléon Bonaparte. By nightfall the revolt was virtually over. For the prisoners in Le Plessis the noise of gunfire in the capital was terrifying, and the ominous quiet that succeeded the guns even more so, as they hourly awaited the general massacre they knew would follow a royalist victory.

In this terrifying situation it was Babeuf who took the initiative, with an appeal to the concierge of the prison, Haly, to allow the prisoners to arm themselves and march to the defense of the Convention. The four chief signatories to the appeal were Pierre Philip (a Bordeaux sea-captain and one-time member of the Club Electoral), Germain, Jullien, and Babeuf (who wrote out the text of the appeal). There were also a number of supporting signatures, chiefly of former section militants. Haly received the prisoners' deputation and immediately passed their request on to the Committee of General Security. But he refused to allow them to send a further deputation to the Convention.

In the middle of the night a second deputation approached Haly only to find themselves coldly received, and the following morning the concierge threatened to denounce Jullien and Babeuf as the organizers of the movement. Babeuf promptly drew up a second address. This time it was destined for the Convention, and the prisoners protested at being left to die at the hands of the "friends of Tarquin." The moment, however, was past: a government which already had Bonaparte had no need of Babeuf, and hopes of an early release died. The majority of the Le Plessis prisoners had to wait until the general amnesty of 4 brumaire (26 October) before they were freed. However, certain prisoners who had influential friends—or who were regarded by Barras and his entourage as potentially valuable agents for marshalling Jacobin support for the new constitution—were given favored treatment. Jullien was set free on 13 October, and Babeuf on the eighteenth. The order for Babeuf's release bore Barras' own signature.[27]

Fourteen

The People's Tribune

While still in prison Babeuf and Jullien (together with other radical and Jacobin leaders) had already begun to make plans for a counteroffensive to take advantage of the momentarily favorable climate following the suppression of the Vendémiaire uprising. Babeuf wrote impatiently to Jullien from Le Plessis (on 14 October) urging him to press ahead—to get on with the formation of a committee of influential sympathizers to negotiate a speeding up of the release of prisoners with the Committee of General Security, to get in touch with a printer, and to establish contact with the surviving remnants of the *sans-culotte* cause in Paris. Immediately after his own release Babeuf set out on a "tour of the faubourgs" to sound out the climate in the working-class quarters of Saint-Antoine and Saint-Marceau, only to return (as Jullien noted in his journal) "discontented and without hope." On 22 October the two men met and discussed the situation in a mood of despair. The spirit of the faubourgs was plainly broken and the chances of reviving the *sans-culotte* party problematical. Jullien threw up the fight on the following day and left Paris for the countryside.[1]

Yet while the 21-year-old Jullien was away "looking for cows" and trying to exorcise the memory of his months of imprisonment, there was a sudden, dramatic change in the situation. As almost their last corporate act, the members of the Convention offered (on 26 October) a sweeping amnesty for political offenses. Hundreds of Jacobin terrorists and *sans-culotte* militants began to re-emerge from the cells in which they had spent the weary months since Thermidor and Prairial. Other factors combined with the amnesty to produce a considerable strengthening of the Jacobin party in the capital during the first days of November. Many provincial Jacobins, on their liberation, made straight for Paris as a refuge from the White Terror bands which were still active in many parts of France. Many also hoped to make their peace with the Directory and to find a niche in the reorganized republican administration.

Like Jullien and Babeuf, many of the released prisoners found themselves disoriented on their release. They were isolated figures in a world whose outlines were barely recognizable. The fraternal élan of popular society, section and revolutionary committee was gone, and the sustaining consciousness of belonging to a movement and a cause firmly rooted in an insurgent people had vanished with it. The emerging prisoners found public affairs dominated by bourgeois notables, and they felt abandoned by a disillusioned and apathetic population. In many cases careers and businesses had been irretrievably ruined, homes abandoned, and families broken up. In the closing weeks of 1795 this remnant of a "lost generation" of revolutionaries reacted to its isolation by drawing closer together; and the sectarian tendencies of prison existence were thus reinforced by experience of the outside world.

Certain rallying centers of the Jacobin remnant quickly became notorious. On 18 November a police report described assemblies of about sixty "ex-terrorists" at the Café Chrétien in the rue Neuve Saint-Marc (close by the Comédie Italienne) and as many again at the Café des Bains Chinois (on the rue Marivaux in Montmartre). The Café Cauvin (on the rue du Bac) was another gathering point of similar elements. Of the three, the Café Chrétien was perhaps the most significant center. The proprietor, Pierre-Nicolas Chrétien, was an ex-member of the Paris Revolutionary Tribunal and of the revolutionary committee of the Lepeletier Section. Among the habitués were numbered former Montagnards like Marc Vadier, Leonard Bourdon, and Claude Javogues, and veterans of the Vendée campaign like Brutus Magnier and Jean-Antoine Rossignol. The Café des Bains Chinois tended to attract a more radical clientele, the adherents of René Lebois.

In their revulsion against the precedents of the Jacobin Club and the *sans-culotte* popular societies of 1793-4, the framers of the Constitution of the Year Three had placed a number of obstacles in the way of popular political organization. The freedom of association was guaranteed; but the formation of "corporations and associations" contrary to public order (and specifically of *sociétés populaires*) was forbidden. Political societies were prohibited from corresponding or affiliating with one another, and from holding public sessions; they were not allowed to impose special conditions of membership or to adopt distinctive emblems. It was also a crime to advocate the democratic Constitution of 1793 or to criticize the Constitution of the Year Three.

Despite all these restrictions political life began to stir again. By 16 December a central *"société de la réunion des amis de la République"* was in existence in Paris. It met in the Faubourg Saint-Germain, in a former convent (close to the Panthéon) which had been converted into a dance-hall; when the main hall was needed for dances the members of this "Panthéon Society" had to adjourn to the cellar.

Before long the Jacobin leadership of the political revival began to strive to build up a popular base once again. A police report on the Café Chrétien warned that the *sociétaires* were sending emissaries into the faubourgs to agitate among the workers. Another report (filed on 2 January) contains an account of a canvass of workers in the Faubourg Saint-Martin by Panthéonists, who went about handing out membership cards and invitations to the society's meetings.[2]

Two tendencies quickly became apparent among the former militants. There were "the Patriots of 1789," who were eager to compromise with the new republican régime as the lesser evil, or at least to arrive at an accommodation with the Directorial Left, which was more or less dependent on Barras. The tactic of this group was one of "permeation," a comfortable doctrine which enabled consciences to be salved while journalistic subsidies were pocketed and jobs distributed among the Patriots. The other tendency was represented by the unreconciled democrats and the Equals of Arras and Le Plessis. According to Buonarroti, "at the beginning of brumaire" Babeuf, Jullien, Augustin-Alexandre-Joseph Darthé, and Fontenelle attempted to create a "directing center" for this party. In view of Jullien's absence from Paris between 22 and 31 October, these discussions must have taken place at the beginning of November. They are said to have been concerned with rival proposals either for the formation of a kind of quasi-Masonic secret society (dependent on a central group of directors) or for the creation of an insurrectionary committee. But there was no agreement, and the discussions were abandoned.

At the same time a rather wider circle of "patriots" was more successful in planning the preliminaries for the organization of the

Panthéon Society. The first meeting of this group took place (apparently on 3 November) at the house of Mathurin Bouin, a militant of the Marché-des-Innocents Section, at no. 14 rue Saint-Denis. Darthé, Jullien, Buonarroti, and Fontenelle were all present at this meeting. Babeuf does not seem to have attended, although Germain was there. Once again there were disagreements. This time it was over the question of whether the organization should take the form of a single central political society which could be readily guided along safe and judicious paths, or a proliferation of local societies which would be likely to escape from the control of the organizing committee. After further meetings during November the decision turned in favor of a single central society. It seems probable that this was a defeat for the policy Babeuf favored, but there is no evidence that he played any part in the foundation of the Panthéon Society.

A further division had become apparent among the Equals: between those who were prepared to maintain a deliberately moderate stance in order to avoid driving the Directory into a fresh reaction, and Babeuf, who virtually alone remained completely intransigent and irreconcilable. One of the earliest "defectors" to the moderate ranks was Jullien, who accepted a secret government subsidy for his new journal, the *Orateur plébéien*, which began publication on 12 November. Before the end of November Jullien was brazenly negotiating with the Directory for a diplomatic appointment, which would satisfy all parties by removing him from the dangerous political temptations of the capital. Henceforth he seems to have acted as a go-between for Barras, keeping open the lines of communication and patronage between the Directory and the veterans of the Jacobin and radical Left, a service which ultimately brought him (in March 1796) an important appointment in Merlin's Ministry of Police.[3]

Jullien's was one way of adapting to the political climate of 1795. Babeuf's was the other. Whatever had been agreed in the discussions inside Le Plessis, Babeuf had resolved by the beginning of November to follow his own path and to resurrect the *Tribun du peuple*. The text for no. 34 was in fact ready for printing on 5 November, when Babeuf received a visit from Joseph Fouché. Acting for the Directory, Fouché allegedly offered a bribe of 6,000 government subscriptions for Babeuf's new series in return for the right to make any "necessary" alterations in the copy. Babeuf protested, and Fouché pointed out that several of his colleagues (for example, Mehée and Réal of the *Journal des Patriotes de 1789*) had already come to an arrangement with the government. The interview, which lasted two or three hours, ended unpleasantly.

Babeuf went ahead and published the unaltered text (on 6 November). It was greeted by a curiously concerted storm of abuse in the remainder of the press, and an "insurrection" against the distribution of his journal, organized by Fouché. More than half of the copies of the second number in the new series (no. 35, which appeared on 30 November) were confiscated by the police.[4]

Fouché's rage and the sharp reaction of the Directory's police were a tribute to the importance of Babeuf's uncompromising stand. Politics after Vendémiaire were in a precarious state of balance. Socially, the Directory represented an unstable alliance between the property-owning classes, reacting against Jacobinism, and the "professional republicans," men whose survival and prosperity depended on the régime's success in holding at bay the growing royalist reaction. The survival of this precarious system depended largely on the success with which able and energetic revolutionaries could be brought to abandon the "impractical" social doctrines of 1793-4 and to rally to the fact of the "bourgeois" republic of 1795. The refusal of even one influential journalist to be harnessed to the Directorial chariot was thus a matter for serious concern.

During 1794 the standard size of the *Journal de la liberte de la presse* had been eight pages, while the largest issue of the *Tribun* had reached thirty pages. Between them the first two numbers of the new series amounted to no fewer than 160 pages: fifty-two pages for no. 34, 108 pages for no. 35, a combined total of almost fifty thousand words. In these numbers Babeuf declared himself less concerned with purveying news or even comment on immediate events than with the exposition of "first truths" and the promulgation of a "manifesto of the plebeians," which was the fruit of his collaboration with Germain since the preceding July.

In the opening paragraph of no. 34 Babeuf began by declaring war on the government which had released him from prison. Immediately afterwards he advanced his claim to be regarded as the commander, the "Achilles," of the "plebeian army," reminding his readers of his unique services during the winter of 1794-5, when he had turned the *Tribun* into the scourge of the Thermidorian government. There followed an analysis of the existing political situation in which he rejected the "republican" policy, advocated in certain quarters, of rallying to the Directory. Vendémiaire, Babeuf explained, had changed nothing in depth. Those who had rallied to the Convention had done so for personal motives, such as individual revenge against the royalist reactionaries, which could have no appeal to the mass of the people. The plebeian majority was still suffering from economic "strangulation." Prices were higher than ever and people were beginning understandably to listen to the royalists who reminded them of the comparative plenty that had prevailed in the days of the monarchy. To counter this propaganda the old political slogans of liberty and equality were no longer adequate. Instead, an effective republican polity could now only be based on a new spirit and on the recognition of the one great truth: "That happiness belongs to all among men, that the object of their social coming together is to guarantee to each in perpetuity his sufficient portion of happiness; that institutions suitable for establishing this marvelous order are infinitely easy to found; and that it is only by way of the republican government that this may be done."

At this point Babeuf turned to a summary investigation of the political first principles which must guide the new party and provide the basis of its policy: a clear but commonplace exposition of the traditional Rousseauist argument for equality on the basis of natural right. All men are born equal in rights and needs; this primitive equality is imprescriptible and precedes the formation of society. "Civil establishments" must not, therefore, interfere with the enjoyment of the right to equality but may only guarantee it. The next step was to test theory by practice: "After having examined what ought to be, we shall examine that which is." By such a test the existing order had palpably failed to secure elementary justice. The majority of citizens did not receive their due, and the missing provision was in the hands of a small minority, a caste of hoarders and usurpers, robbing their brothers under a cloak of legality provided by "horrible institutions consecrated by governments." Inequality and injustice were therefore laid squarely at the door of bad government, protecting a malevolent conspiracy of the "patricians."

Examining the history of the revolution against the yardstick of the natural right to equality, Babeuf discovered the existence of a protracted civil war between the two classes of plebeians and patricians. Since 1789 the poor had been in rebellion against the laws which consecrated the violation of equality, as they sought to "reestablish the holy institutions which assure forever to every member of the great family the totality of his rights and of his needs." The struggle had been essentially a moral one: between "the plebs," whose cause relied on justice, philanthropy and selflessness, and the "patriciate," whose resources were cunning, duplicity, perfidy, pride and ambition. Despite all obstacles, Babeuf concluded, the period up to 9 thermidor and the fall of Robespierre had been one of advance; but ever since, the revolution had only been in retreat. The time was now ripe for a rally by democrats, "soldiers of liberty" and "people's mandatories" to provide a new lead for the "plebeian masses" and the *sans-culottes*.[5]

In the pages of no. 35 of the *Tribun* Babeuf offered a more precise definition of the nature of the "plebeian institutions" by means of which the goal of equality might be attained. In a section devoted to the "Manifesto of the Plebeians" he drew in the outlines of a communist state identical in its configuration with that which he had sketched for Charles Germain four months before in Arras. This would be founded by the establishment of a "common administration" (*l'administration commune*). Private property would be suppressed, and every man put to work according to his talent and his trade. The product of each man's labor would then be collected by the "common storehouse," where "a simple provision administration" would keep a register of people and goods, supervise the rationing of everything "according to the most scrupulous equality," and see to the delivery of "each citizen's share to his domicile." This was the essentially simple central program of the "Manifesto of the Plebeians." In its defense, after a passing tribute to "*le juif Jésus Christ*," Babeuf cited learned precedents of Greek and Roman history, buttressed by extensive quotations from the philosophes, and from revolutionary leaders like Robespierre and Saint-Just (and even Fouché and Tallien).[6]

In one respect Babeuf's ideas as expressed in his new "manifesto" differed significantly from those he had expounded to Germain at Arras. Since the summer Babeuf had completely and explicitly abandoned the projected first stage of the revolution: the stage of agrarian redistribution.[7] The "agrarian law," now and henceforth, formed no part of his doctrine, and indeed there was little in the new program which was specifically relevant to the peasants or the countryside. The revolution was to proceed by a single uniform step to the universal abolition of property and to the establishment of "*le bonheur commun*" by the pooling of all resources. Significant changes in emphasis also appear in Babeuf's treatment of the central theme of the "manifesto": the necessity for an uncompromising acceptance of a completely immaculate system of absolute equality.

"*L'égalité parfaite*" had now taken on for Babeuf something of the

Le Tribun du Peuple,

OU

LE DÉFENSEUR

DES

DROITS DE L'HOMME.

Par Gracchus BABEUF.

Le but de la société est le bonheur commun.
Droits de l'Homme, (de 93.) art. Ier.

Conjuration contre le Tribun. Fouché de Nantes es
à la tête. Elle a pour objet de faire perdre au Tribun
la confiance dont il a besoin pour servir le Peuple.
Sous ce rapport il envisage cette attaque comme une
affaire majeure, et il donne à sa défense des soins
et de la latitude.
Causes de cette conjuration. Elle procède du refus qu'a
fait le Tribun de se vendre au ministère, pour
écrire selon son esprit, et sous sa censure.
Moyens de Fouché pour faire insurger contre le n.º 34
du Tribun du peuple, les cafés, les grouppes, et
les journaux de tous les partis, savoir : populaires,
ministériels, patriciens et royalistes.
La vérité à l'ex-député de Nantes. Un mot à Charles
Duval, qui, tout en reconnaissant le Tribun pour

Tome II.   L

Title page of no. 35 of the *Tribun du peuple,* in which the "Manifesto of the Plebeians" appeared quality of an obsession. Where previously it had been the essential moral value by which existing institutions might be judged, now "absolute equality" became the keystone of the entire structure of an ideal universe. In the past Babeuf had been content to find an explanation for the origins of inequality in historical or economic processes, in the original brigandage of feudal usurpers, or (as late as summer 1795) in landowners and speculators making use of their monopoly of the ownership of wealth. Now he was determined to demonstrate that inequality originated solely in an act of will, in the deliberate rejection of the fundamental moral principle of equality. If a clockmaker was paid twenty times as much for his labor as a ploughman, it was not because his labor was worth more in any absolute sense, but because it was regarded so by a common prejudice. "The difference in value and merit in the product of the labor of men rests only on the opinion that certain among them have attached to it and have caused to prevail." By the same token, all proletarians (*prolétaires*) had become so only as a result of "the difference in value established between things by the sole authority of opinion."

Babeuf was particularly scathing about the special value claimed for brainwork. "There is absurdity and injustice in the pretended attribution of a greater recompense for whoever works at a task that demands a higher degree of intelligence and more application and stretching of the mind . . . for this does not in any way extend the capacity of his stomach. . . . It is the intelligentsia [*les intelligens*] who have fixed such a high price for conceptions of their brains." His insistence on the absolute equality of the division of the common product also compelled Babeuf to confront the problem of the unusually strong or unusually skillful worker who might be able to produce perhaps four times as much as his fellow citizen. Such a man, he declared, must be repressed as a threat to social harmony, and compelled to produce no more than an ordinary worker.[8]

The curious and even ludicrous fixation on a literal and exact physical equality of recompense revealed by these passages reflects the degree to which, in the isolation of prison existence, Babeuf had retreated into an abstract world of absolutes. The task he had set himself—the elaboration of a moral system of equality—seemed to demand such violations of common sense in order to maintain internal consistency. Babeuf was convinced that, according to the logic of his system, once it was conceded that *any* individual contributed more to the common storehouse than any other, it would be necessary to concede that he had thereby established a moral right to a greater share in the general distribution. Hence certain individuals would be entitled to accumulate a surplus, to amass property, and the division of society into two opposing classes of propertied and propertyless would begin its fatal history over again.

Such reflections, however, were no more than marginal details in a manifesto which opened up a new vision for weary revolutionaries of a perfectly attainable world in which their highest moral aspirations could be realized: a new world of equality and fraternity, freed from the crimes and vices of the old. It would be a world without boundaries, hedges, walls, locks, disputes, litigation, theft, murder, courts, gibbets, punishment, jealousy, pride, fraud or deceit; and, most important of all, without perpetual personal anxiety about the morrow, about old age, and about the future of one's children and grandchildren.

How many of his readers understood Babeuf's vision of a communist society or took it seriously it is impossible to judge. A police report noted (on 3 December) that the Café Chrétien had listened to a reading of Babeuf's no. 35; but what seemed significant to the police was not the preaching of communism but the fact that the *Tribun* had openly praised Maximilien Robespierre and Joseph Le Bon. It seems probable that this was a fair measure of the public impact of Babeuf's manifesto. Another agent noted (on 10 December) the lively eagerness with which the circle at the Café Chrétien awaited the appearance of the next number, which was expected to "uncover the conspiracy of 9 thermidor and indicate to the people who are the scoundrels who assassinated Robespierre and his courageous partisans."[9]

In 1794 Babeuf had bitterly attacked the needless cruelties of Carrier's suppression of the Vendée, as well as the savagery of Le Bon, the "executioner of the north." His position had every appearance of strong personal conviction. Now, from the very first number of the new series, he was to take up the defense of terror as a necessary revolutionary weapon. "In order to govern judiciously," he declared, "it is necessary to terrorize [*terrifier*] the evilly disposed, the royalists, papists and starvers of the public . . . and one cannot govern democratically without this terrorism." In no. 40 of the *Tribun* (published in February 1796) Babeuf even went so far as to offer an enthusiastic justification of the September massacres of 1792. He regretted only that "a wider, more general 2 September" had not taken place "to bring about the disappearance of the totality of the starvation-mongers, the despoilers and massacrers who have since . . . developed all the energies of their atrocious souls."[10]

Babeuf was a skilled and sophisticated propagandist, fully aware that he was writing for a public of Jacobins and ex-terrorists, and that the only hope for a revival of the radical democratic cause lay in abandoning old feuds and closing the ranks of Jacobins, Enragés and Hébertists to form a common front. There was certainly an element of expedient calculation in his new public defense of the Reign of Terror.

At the end of February 1796 Joseph Bodson (one-time Hébertist, former fellow-member of the Club Electoral, and Le Plessis prisoner) wrote to Babeuf to protest against his apparent apostasy. In his reply Babeuf showed himself completely unrepentant, stressing the importance of the name of Robespierre and the memory of his régime as a rallying point for radical democrats throughout France: "Robespierrism is in all the Republic, in all the judicious and far-seeing class and naturally in all the people. The reason for this is simple, Robespierrism is democracy, and these two words are perfectly identical: thus in reviving Robespierrism you are sure to revive democracy." By contrast, he argued, Hébertism was a sect with only a local Parisian appeal. As for Robespierre's revolutionary government, it could no longer be denied that it was "devilishly well conceived." Later, at his trial in 1797, Babeuf agreed that his letter to Bodson was a genuine expression of his ideas at the time; and that he had indeed come to regard the revolutionary government as a necessary evil, as a quite moderate installment of revenge against centuries of oppression by the possessing classes, and as a positive step towards achieving "the lasting happiness of the majority of the people."

Babeuf's reflections on the fate of Robespierre's Hébertist victims were of a different order. Even if (as he told Bodson) Hébert and Chaumette were innocent of the plot with which they were charged, he would still justify Robespierre. Robespierre was right to liquidate "these ridiculous if well-intentioned rivals" if he believed that they were plotting against him. "The welfare of twenty-five million men ought not to be balanced against the accommodation of a few equivocal individuals."

The correspondence with Bodson has been frequently cited by those who seek to prove that during 1794 and 1795 Babeuf abandoned the "democratic illusions" of his post-Thermidorian period, going on to embrace the thoroughgoing advocacy of revolutionary dictatorship which is attributed to the Conspiracy of the Equals. In fact this is to oversimplify the situation. "My opinion has never changed on principles," Babeuf himself explained to Bodson, "but it has changed on certain men." Even in 1794 Babeuf had allowed for the necessity of a temporary dictatorship in exceptional circumstances. The force of his critique of the idea of dictatorship had been directed against a permanent or institutional dictatorship, and there is no reason to suppose that he ever abandoned this position.

Some valuable light is thrown on this question by an exchange between Babeuf and the Jacobin journalist René Lebois in November 1795, immediately following the appearance of the first of the new series of the *Tribun du peuple*. Babeuf and Lebois had quarreled in Les Baudets prison during the summer of 1795—possibly because Lebois had been unable to forgive Babeuf's violent anti-Jacobin campaign during the post-Thermidorian months. After his liberation Lebois greeted with some natural indignation the attempt of the revived *Tribun du peuple* to compete with his own *Ami du peuple* as the mouthpiece of Jacobin orthodoxy. The man who was now praising Robespierre and Le Bon, as Lebois pointed out in his own journal, had been among the bitterest enemies of the Jacobin cause in 1794. Babeuf replied to Lebois in the columns of the *Tribun*. He admitted frankly that he had been misled by his colleague Guffroy about the character of Le Bon; but while in jail at Arras he had discovered the truth, and had even offered to go to Amiens to defend this "just avenger of an oppressed people." As for his general attitude towards the Jacobins, he had attacked the Jacobins so long as they refused to support his campaign for the application of the democratic Constitution of 1793; just as soon as they had rallied to the Constitution of 1793 he had become their defender.[11]

The Constitution of 1793 was no longer, during 1795-6, at the center of Babeuf's program. What was important, he explained in no. 35, was *institutions*, not constitutions. Once satisfactory plebeian institutions had been established, then a satisfactory constitution would follow. Thus the Constitution of 1793 was only valuable to the degree that it afforded the opportunity of founding plebeian institutions and creating a society based on "*le bonheur commun.*" For all that, from the very first number of the new series the *Tribun du peuple* vigorously and unequivocally defended the 1793 constitution, based on universal suffrage and freely elected national and local governments, as the true constitution of the French people; and it continued to do so without faltering until Babeuf's arrest in May 1796.[12]

Once again, expediency entered into the adoption of such a stand-point. "The Constitution of 1793" was a valuable rallying cry for elements who might not understand the *Tribun's* communism, or who might refuse to take it seriously, but who were nevertheless determined to dislodge the Directorial régime. There is, however, no reason to doubt Babeuf's continuing commitment to democracy.

In the pages of the *Tribun du peuple* it is possible to detect the reflection of an internal conflict over tactics among the Equals: between Babeuf and those who (like Jullien and Buonarroti) were still thinking in terms of striking a bargain with the Directory, using the "force of the people" only as a bargaining counter in their negotiations. Babeuf's stance was, by contrast, quite without am-biguity. "Eternally persuaded that one can do nothing great except with all the people," he wrote in November in his prospectus for the *Tribun*, "I believe that it is again necessary to do something with them, to tell them everything, to show them tirelessly what it is necessary to do, and less to fear the inconveniences of a publicity from which the schemers [*la politique*] may profit, than to count on the advantages of the colossal force which always negates scheming [*déjoue bien la politique*]. . . . One must take into account all the forces one loses in leaving opinion in apathy, without sustenance and without an objective, and all those one gains in activating opinion, in enlightening it and showing it a goal."

The *Tribun* returned to the same theme on 21 December in no. 37. "The true tactic of the defenders of liberty, of equality, of all the rights of the people is to seek to grow, to let everyone know *how things are*, and what it is necessary to do, to speak to all of evils and remedies, and to get everyone interested in cooperating in putting things right. . . . Nothing is more detestable . . . more foolishly and visibly inept than to isolate oneself, to reduce oneself to a handful of activist patriots, to separate oneself from the people, to abandon their opinion and their force, to try to accomplish good without them, without that opinion and that force."

The *Tribun* was thus launched in a mood of confidence in the peo-ple and the imminence of a resurgence of the democratic forces. Before the end of the winter, however, the hard facts of a continuing public apathy drove Babeuf to a disillusioned reappraisal. In his no. 39 (published at the end of January 1796) he was forced to come to terms with some unpleasant facts. "Thanks to the horrible cunning of the patriciate" the majority of the people were the enemies of liberty, and the contemporary struggle was one between "a handful of consistent and energetic republicans and a coalition of the government, the well-to-do [*les gens comme-il-faut*] and the multitude." It seemed that, after all, a handful of patriots must act for the people, even if it meant braving the temporary prejudices of the multitude. In the succeeding weeks Babeuf reconciled himself to the inevitability of a *coup d'état,* to be followed by a period of revolutionary dictatorship in order to consolidate the seizure of power.

Half a century later another revolutionary Frenchman, Auguste Blanqui, would propose as a solution to the same problem of the "corrupt majority" a seventy-year dictatorship, during which the people might be re-educated to the values of a new communist society. In the twentieth century, Lenin's dictatorship of the "vanguard of the proletariat" was conceived in terms of a time scale of at least the same order. It is perhaps inevitable that Babeuf's rôle as a precursor of this "élitist" current should be seen by most historians as his claim to historical significance. "It was probably in this idea that Babeuf's historical importance lies," Professor Lefebvre wrote in 1946. "He arrived at a clear concept of that popular dictatorship of which Marat and the Hébertists had spoken without defining it. Through Buonarroti, he bequeathed it to Blanqui and then to Lenin, who turned it into reality. . . ."

Such a view is no longer tenable. The evidence shows that the revolutionary dictatorship that Babeuf endorsed in 1796 had relatively little in common with those advocated by Blanqui or Lenin. It was of a strictly limited and provisional character, even more so indeed than Robespierre's revolutionary government, which was devised to last indefinitely, until the peace. By contrast, Babeuf's plan (as outlined in his personal papers) was for a dictatorship of no more than three months' duration, during which the Republic would be purged of royalist influence and its public opinion enlightened, in preparation for the handing of power back to the people through the application of the Constitution of 1793.[13]

Fine distinctions between legitimate and illegitimate terror—between the democratic Robespierre of 1793 and the dictatorial Robespierre of 1794, or between short-term and long-term revolutionary dictatorship—were, for the most part, of no consequence to Babeuf's readers. Enragés, Hébertists, and Jacobins could welcome with equal enthusiasm the one journal which squarely confronted the opportunists of the Directorial party, which took its stand on the democratic and egalitarian ideals of 1793, and which spoke up fearlessly for the martyred heroes whose names had been calumniated and whose partisans had been persecuted ever since

Thermidor. By the beginning of December there were already more than five hundred individual subscribers to the *Tribun,* while the number of copies sold probably ran to four times this figure.[14] Police reports paint a vivid picture of the enthusiasm with which the "soldiers and workers" at the Café Chrétien greeted the appearance of each new issue. "They know that they are threatened by the royalists," one report concluded on 30 December, "but they are ready to fall upon them, with the aid of the workers." Soon there were ten café subscriptions, each representing a nucleus of partisans, including one from the "*citoyens réunis*" of the Café des Amis de la Patrie, in the heart of the Faubourg Saint-Antoine. An "exiled" democrat from Lorient wrote home that it had become a custom for him to read the *Tribun* aloud to the ex-Montagnard deputy Prieur de la Marne, who had opened his Paris apartment as a refuge for old Jacobins.

Outside Paris the isolated, embattled Jacobins of the provinces grasped with eagerness at the new lifeline thrown out from the capital. At Cherbourg, the watchmaker Pierre-Louis Fossard read about the revival of the *Tribun* in the *Journal des hommes libres*, and he collected a circle of four or five friends who took out a joint subscription. At Metz, Bouchotte (who had been minister of war in 1794) presided over a similar group of subscribers. On 29 January the bookseller Cormier (former leader of the Jacobin Club of Autun) wrote to Babeuf from Autun to say that despite having been disarmed and imprisoned after 9 thermidor he was now active again: "There are meetings at my house . . . what a pleasure it would be to you if you could be present each evening in the midst of our reunion. With what avidity they listen to the readings of your journal! When I announce a number, the greatest silence descends, joy is depicted on every face, our spirits are enlivened, courage is reborn, and we are ready to fall on the enemy." Ten subscribers at Arras and twenty in the Pas de Calais Département bore witness to the persistence of a Jacobin network in the northeast. There were twenty-one subscribers in the Var in the southeast of France, four at Lorient in Brittany, ten at Avignon. There were even subscribers as far afield as Zurich, Genoa and Brussels.

In Paris the list of subscribers included a knot of thirty-two ex-deputies of the Convention and two generals, Fyon and Laronde (as well as Turreau, who was living at Conches). There was also a group of "distinguished widows" of Jacobin and *sans-culotte* leaders, Citoyennes Le Peletier and Marat, Citoyenne Goujon (widow of the martyr of Prairial), Citoyennes Lazowski, Ronsin, and Brochet. For the most part the Paris subscribers seem to have been ordinary *sans-culottes*, however, after the style of 1793: chiefly shopkeepers and artisans. As a general rule subscribers from the provinces were drawn from higher social strata and included a sprinkling of merchants, together with many representatives of the professions.[15]

The reaction of the government to the reappearance of the *Tribun* was immediate and savage. Soon after the distribution of no. 34, Merlin, the minister of justice, wrote off (on 23 November) to Laon to revive the fraud case once again. As soon as no. 35 appeared a fresh prosecution was begun, this time for a political crime against the 1795 constitution. A warrant was issued for Babeuf's arrest on 4 December, barely more than five weeks after his release from Le Plessis. At 3:30 p.m. the following day Pernet, a police inspector, arrived at the apartment in the rue Saint-Honoré, hoping to catch Babeuf at lunch. In fact Babeuf was at home, but he refused to surrender and there was a struggle, which soon turned into a small riot when some of the neighbors came to his assistance. Finally Babeuf was able to break away. Pernet raised a hue and cry, pursuing him along the rue Saint-Honoré as far as L'Assomption, a former religious house now used as a food warehouse. Here the grain porters of the warehouse intervened and took Babeuf under their protection. While they were busy giving the inspector a rough time, beating him and covering him with mud and ordure, Babeuf was guided to a hiding place in the nearby Maison de la Conception (another monastic building now converted into apartments). At nightfall one of the residents of La Conception, Jean-Baptiste Didier, came for Babeuf and escorted him to his own rooms. Didier was a locksmith, a former juryman of the Revolutionary Tribunal and a veteran of Le Plessis.[16]

At the Didier apartment Babeuf shared a room with the regular lodger, Augustin Darthé (Le Bon's brother-in-law and one-time public prosecutor of the revolutionary tribunals of Arras and Cambrai). At the trial of the Equals in 1797 the prosecution produced a register of expenditure kept by Mme. Louise Aubert Didier for Darthé and Babeuf until 16 April. Darthé maintained that Babeuf used his room for only ten days, until 18 December; but this evidence was colored by an anxiety to protect the Didiers, so that the balance of probability is that Babeuf lived with the family for some weeks.[17]

On 11 December, while Babeuf was still at the Didiers, no. 36 of the *Tribun*, the first of a new series of clandestine numbers, was published. Eight numbers appeared from the beginning of December to the end of May, with an average gap of a fortnight to three weeks between each. None was of comparable length to no. 35, and the last three numbers were of sixteen or twelve pages only; the average was about twenty pages. Babeuf had promised in his prospectus five or six numbers each month (for a subscription of 125 livres for three months). In December the subscription was raised to 500 livres, but the *Tribun* was soon in financial straits, and both the numbers published in January contained appeals for money to keep the paper going. In December Inspector Pernet discovered Marie-Anne and the children still living "in the most frightful poverty."

Irritated by Pernet's failure to arrest Babeuf, Merlin was now more determined than ever to silence him by any available means. The minister of justice published in the press (on 11 December) a Directorial minute which yet again summarized the details of the Montdidier forgery case and announced the reopening of proceedings. On 20 December the Cour de Cassation quashed Babeuf's liberation by the Laon court. The case was then transferred to another court at Compiègne in the Oise Département, which duly found that there was a case to answer; and on 9 March it issued a warrant for Babeuf which ordered his imprisonment at Beauvais.

The press prosecution also went ahead in Paris. Babeuf was indicted before the Jury of Presentment of the Seine Département on 18 December, in the carefully selected company of Richer-Sérizy, the royalist editor of *L'Accusateur public*, who was also in hiding. The obvious intention was to link both men in a "royalist" conspiracy. This stratagem proved overripe, however, for the bourgeois jury insisted on accepting the charge against Babeuf, while finding no case against Richer-Sérizy. As a result Merlin was forced to concede that, technically, the Babeuf prosecution had also collapsed.[18]

Merlin did not reach this conclusion, however, until 16 February, and in the intervening period there was no relaxation of pressure. The Directory ordered Lebois' arrest (on 24 December) for printing Babeuf's account of his escape from Pernet in the *Ami du peuple* and for "advocating the agrarian law"; Lebois spent a week in jail. No. 39 of the *Tribun* was denounced at a meeting of the Directory on 2 February, and an instruction (signed by Letourneur, Carnot, and La Revellière-Lépaux) ordered Merlin to arrest Marie-Anne Babeuf for distributing the *Tribun*. Marie-Anne was seized on 5 February and she was held for two days without food before being interrogated by Lamaignière, a justice of the peace from the Champs-Elysées Section. Persisting in her refusal to give any information about the whereabouts of either her husband or of the press on which the *Tribun* was printed, she was finally locked away in the Petite-Force prison in the rue Pavé. Emile sought out his father on the morning of 6 February, evaded the police watch and passed on the news.[19]

Merlin quickly discovered that the arrest of Marie-Anne was another tactical error. On 8 February he wrote to the police central bureau to demand full details, and in particular an account of the alleged starvation treatment (which was already causing "much noise and even a certain agitation"). Moderate enough by the debased standards of the twentieth century, the harshness of the Directory's treatment of Citoyenne Babeuf was greeted with horror even among the substantial party of revolutionaries who still clung to the hope of a working compromise with the Directorial republic.

On the evening of 11 February a third-floor neighbor of the Babeufs came to the magistrate Lamaignière with a strange and disturbing story. Before being taken away by the police, Marie-Anne had handed over the 4-year-old boy, Camille, into her care. Ever since, there had been a constant procession of people to see the child; and "a well-dressed woman" had given her money for his keep, and collected certain personal effects from the Babeufs' room. Finally, on 10 February there had been a special visit by some of the "Patriotes de '89 de la réunion aux Bains Chinois," who were very angry indeed, breathing riot and predicting revolution.

The agitation gathered momentum. The *Journal des hommes libres*, which normally advocated a policy of collaboration with the government, condemned (on 21 February) the persecution of Babeuf and demanded his wife's immediate release. Charles Germain raised the matter of Marie-Anne's arrest at the Panthéon Society (on 23 February), a collection was taken up, and the members drew up a petition to Merlin protesting both against the arrest itself and against the linking of Marie-Anne's name with that of Richer-Sérizy and the Vendémiaire conspirators. Babeuf put on more fuel by publishing an account of his wife's arrest and ill treatment in no. 40 of the *Tribun* (24 February)—the following day Darthé was greeted with cheers when he read out its contents to the Panthéon Society. As a result of this campaign Marie-Anne was released on 26 February, after a three-week imprisonment. But by this time the damage was irreparable from Merlin's point of view: her "martyrdom" had "traced a line of demarcation" between the Directory and republican public opinion.[20]

The alliance on which the Directorial system was based had, in any case, been developing increasing strains for some time. While the *Tribun du peuple* led the attack on the policy of compromise from the Left, other elements were working to undermine it from the Right. The general line of the Panthéon Society—that the Directory itself was pure, but that the government and the councils contained hidden royalists—was disquieting to powerful elements in the government who had played a leading part in the Thermidorian reaction. Equally alarming was the tendency of the Panthéon members to discuss radical social measures which seemed to have been given a decent burial at Thermidor, and in particular to raise the question of the implementation of the Ventôse decrees of 1794 and the distribution of land among military veterans.[21] Moreover, the club appeared to be attracting a dangerous type of agitator. A police report (24 January) described the members as for the most part badly dressed and seemingly workers; and it noted that they were generally armed with clubs.

Pierre Bénézech, the minister of the interior, tried to have the club shut down at the end of December 1795 by persuading Faypoult, the finance minister, to cancel Cardinaux's lease of the premises. The Panthéonists were given twenty-four hours' notice to quit, but were allowed to remain after a protest, probably because the Director Barras overruled the minister. During the first weeks of 1796 the Directory was finding it expedient to lean on the Panthéon—for support not only against the rising tide of royalism in the country, but also against quasi-royalists amongst the ministers (such as Bénézech and Faypoult) and against powerful leaders of the Right on the councils (like Rovère, Boissy d'Anglas, Saladin and Lanjuinais).

The Directors began a leftward tack in policy on 8 January. They issued decrees which enjoined the singing of the "Ça ira" and the "Marseillaise," and even banned the Thermidorian anthem, "Le Réveil du Peuple." They also pressed Bénézech for an account of the progress of his measures to stop the massacre of republicans in the south, and urged him to put into effect the mandatory exclusion of royalists from public office.

The Panthéon Society responded by demonstrating an ostentatious public support of the Directory. After some difficulties, the society was finally persuaded to commit itself to an address (on 4 January) declaring its loyalty to the Constitution of the Year Three. A new republican festival, the celebration of the anniversary of Louis XVI's execution, provided the opportunity on 21 January for a further demonstration which marked the culmination of the Directorial phase of the Panthéon's alignment, with members of the society providing an escort for the Directors' carriage in the public procession to the Champ de Mars.[22]

From the beginning, Babeuf vigorously attacked the policy of the compromisers, the "*faction des prudens.*" No. 36 of the *Tribun* (on 11 December) contained a scathing analysis of the notion of permeation, the alibi of those who argued that "other things being equal" it was better for posts in the administration to be in the hands of "patriots" rather than "royalists," pointing out the inescapable conflicts of interest and conscience involved. Ten days later no. 37 returned to the same theme. This time Babeuf emphasized the demoralizing effect on the people of the spectacle of its leaders accepting government jobs and ridiculed the excuse that the time was not yet ripe for revolution—with the bread ration down to two ounces and the streets filled with walking skeletons. In his first reference to the Panthéon Society (in no. 38), Babeuf recorded with approval the society's initial refusal to endorse the proposed address of loyalty to the Constitution of the Year Three. On 30 January (no. 39) he denounced the ultimate success of the "government agents" Feru and Roussillon in snatching a majority for the loyalty address from a packed meeting, and he condemned the Panthéon Society's rôle in the 21 January celebrations. The *Tribun* painted an evocative picture of a silent and joyless ceremony shared by the Directors, isolated in gilded splendor on the balcony of the Ecole Militaire, and the military detachments drawn up on the Champ de Mars below, with the people relegated to the rôle of mere spectators on the fringes.[23]

The struggle for the sympathies of the Jacobin remnant intensified during February as the Panthéon Society continued in a state of delicate balance between the Patriots of 1789 and the Equals of 1792. An influx of new recruits brought the membership to nearly three thousand, and reflected a general revival of radical democratic activity. (On February 26 the Lorient Jacobin Ollivier wrote home from Paris: "In most sections, clubs are forming like that of the Panthéon Français, to which I belong.") To add to the growing alarm in government circles, Babeuf's no. 40 printed an extensive documentation on 24 February of the spread of democratic ideas and organization in the provinces—in the Moselle, in Mont-Blanc, the Pas de Calais, La Manche, the Var—and in the army.

From the Directorial point of view the continued patronage of the

Panthéon was thus already rapidly becoming an embarrassment when the furor over the arrest of Marie-Anne Babeuf produced a decisive leftward swing of opinion within the society. As late as 23 February the society was still divided: Charles Germain's appeal on Marie-Anne's behalf met serious opposition, and the form of petition agreed on represented a compromise with the moderates. Two days later the issue was no longer in doubt, and the members applauded as Darthé read out Babeuf's attack on the Directors as tyrants and his thinly veiled appeal to the army to intervene in favor of equality.

The army did intervene. On 27 February, on the order of the Directory, the commander of the Army of the Interior, General Bonaparte, supported by heavy patrols of cavalry, personally supervised the closing of the Panthéon Society. Soon afterwards (on 17 March) the Directors ordered a fresh purge of the administration, dislodging many of the radical democrats who had infiltrated since October. Thereafter nobody could entertain any illusions about the possibility of a broad republican alliance and a peaceful and gradual democratization of the Directorial régime. Other methods would have to be found.[24]

Fifteen

The Conspiracy for Equality

The closing of the Panthéon Society meant the end of the uneasy republican alliance behind the shelter of which the Directory had consolidated the new régime after Vendémiaire. Following closely on the moral shock of Marie-Anne Babeuf's arrest, this new act of repression compelled radical republicans to recognize that only two choices henceforth lay open to them: unconditional submission or uncompromising resistance. From the beginning of March it was clear that some, at least, had decided to make a fight of it, and that a desperate, last-ditch challenge to the Directory was being prepared by the diehards of the Jacobin and radical democrat party.

The concept of a clandestine, underground "conspiracy for equality" which was now revived was not new. It dated back at least to the prison discussions in Le Plessis before Vendémiaire. Even though the attempt to found a permanent guiding committee of released militants after Vendémiaire had failed in November 1795, throughout the succeeding months the leaders of the party had continued to meet together informally to discuss strategy and tactics, as well as the more profound questions of the ultimate goal and direction of the revolution.

From December 1795 one of the chief centers of discussion was André Amar's house in the rue Cléry. Amar was a former Montagnard deputy of the Convention and a member of the Committee of General Security in 1794; despite his active rôle in the overthrow of Robespierre at Thermidor, he had spent several months in prison during 1795.

The founders of this "Comité chez Amar" were Darthé and

Guillaume Massard, an army officer who had held the rank of adjutant-general; the regular frequenters soon included Buonarroti, Germain, Debon (a veteran of Le Plessis who had established a close relationship with Babeuf before Vendémiaire), and Félix Le Peletier (a member of a wealthy family of the Robe Nobility and the younger brother of the revolutionary martyr Michel Le Peletier, the deputy assassinated by royalists at the time of the king's execution in 1793). There is no evidence that Babeuf belonged formally to this group, although hints dropped in the *Tribun du peuple* as early as the middle of January confirm that he was aware both of its existence and of its purpose.[1]

According to Buonarroti the "Comité chez Amar" debated the most fundamental questions of politics: the right of property, equality, the agrarian law, insurrection against tyranny, dictatorship versus democracy. A division rapidly became apparent between Amar and the "neo-Jacobins" (who argued essentially for a return to the Robespierrist program of 1793-4) and another group which followed Debon, Darthé, Le Peletier and Buonarroti in advocating the newer doctrine of "community of goods and labor." Similarly, while there was general agreement on the need to overthrow the Directory, there were divergent views on the kind of régime which should be installed in its place. Amar wanted to see power entrusted to a restored National Convention. Debon argued for a dictatorship. But the majority were for some kind of provisional revolutionary government.

Toward the end of the winter the committee moved to a new meeting place in the rue Neuve-Egalité, where they began serious preparations for an insurrection. The new home of the committee was probably Massard's apartment, on the third floor of a house on the corner of the rue des Filles-Dieu. The owner of the house, Barbe Audibert, the Widow Sergent, was a notorious Jacobin militant and a veteran of Le Plessis. She was also a one-time associate of Hébert and the former mistress of "Coupe-tête" Jourdan, the terrorizer of Avignon and Marseille. In May 1796 Massard would boast that the whole idea of the conspiracy had been thought up by a circle over which he presided and which met at the Café Philpin, opposite Saint-Roch. Before long the growing conflict of views—and the general distrust of Amar as a "Thermidorian"—made continued close cooperation between the original conspirators impossible. The committee finally broke up on Le Peletier's initiative.[2]

There followed a period during which radical agitation continued on a more informal pattern. The former Panthéonists dispersed and regrouped around the "Jacobin" cafés—the Bains Chinois, the Café Chrétien, and the Café Bournand, near the porte Honoré—and the Couvent des Cathérinettes in the rue Denis, where Valentin Haüy conducted his school for the blind.

All over Paris radical leaders presided over separate private circles of militants. As well as Massard's group, others were associated with Didier, Bouin, Trinchard, Deray, Mittois, Dufour and Chapelle, and with Pierre-Antoine Antonelle (the ex-marquis and one-time mayor of Arles, who was an influential member of the editorial committee of the *Journal des hommes libres*). Babeuf seems at first to have had the closest relationship with the Didier group. Didier (the 37-year-old locksmith who had given Babeuf asylum at the beginning of February) was an intimate of the Duplays, for whom he worked, and of Darthé; and he also knew Antonelle. Babeuf probably continued to share Darthé's room at the Didiers' until some time in March, when he took refuge briefly with Félix Le Peletier, presumably at his house in the rue Culture-Cathérine. Babeuf and Didier were certainly still in close contact as late as 11 March, for Didier was then busy in organizing the distribution of copies of the *Tribun du peuple*.[3]

No issues of Babeuf's journal were printed for a month after 24 February; but in the meantime (on 2 and 9 March) the first two numbers appeared of a new journal with a similar style, entitled *L'Eclaireur du peuple*. The editorship of *L'Eclaireur* was attributed to a certain "S. Lalande, soldat de la patrie." Lalande was later identified by Buonarroti as Simon Duplay, the nephew of Robespierre's old landlord, who had been wounded at Valmy and now stumped around on a wooden leg. In May 1796 the police found a printing press belonging to the Duplays at Didier's apartment. *L'Eclaireur* appears to have been a collective enterprise, and Babeuf later admitted responsibility for "two or three numbers," specifically for no. 5, of which the manuscript is in his hand.[4]

The first number of *L'Eclaireur*, in the form of a prospectus, was notable for a glowing tribute to Robespierre, printed in large capitals. No. 2 (published on 9 March) was more explicitly "Babouvist" in spirit, and contained an account of Marie-Anne's imprisonment and a summary of the events which had led up to the closing of the Panthéon Society. There was also an exhortation to rally and counterattack: "Already the sacred battalion which marches under the standard of *le bonheur commun*, raised by the intrepid

Tribun du peuple," was "growing day by day." Democrats were urged to meet the new repressive measures against popular societies by rallying to "100 reunions in each section," centered on cafés and private houses. Guides, instructors, and "enlighteners" would be provided who would organize and unify this dispersed activity so as to prepare for the forthcoming Jour de Peuple. The watchword of the new insurrectional movement was Babeuf's: *"L'égalité réelle, le bonheur commun, ou la mort!"*[5]

A few days earlier Babeuf had written privately (5 March) to reassure a correspondent that already "great political doctors" were working "on a general purge which would cure at once all the evils of the body politic." In fact, now that all the alternative programs lay in ruins, the diehards began to turn for leadership to the *Tribun du peuple*, to the one figure who had remained absolutely irreconcilable during the ambiguous post-Vendémiairian period. Charles Germain sent an appeal to Babeuf on 16 March to take up the challenge. Germain (who had been sharing quarters with Guilhem in the rue du Carême Prenant) was now himself in imminent danger of arrest for his part in organizing the final campaign of defiance at the Panthéon Society. For this reason he was reluctant to visit Babeuf personally; it could give the police a lead. Nevertheless the insistence of "one of the coteries of democrat patriots" compelled him to make contact and to urge the "tribune" to come forward. His group contained several avowed Equals and friends of Babeuf and his doctrines, but (as Germain explained) the members were not united. Some wanted "the laws of '93," some a compromise between 1793 and 1795. Most wanted a new convention and another revolutionary government. Meanwhile all were working and conspiring together for an uprising. In such a situation it was Babeuf's duty to give a lead to "the party which desires the reign of pure equality," to "outline to the people" (or at least to those who were in a position to be intermediaries between Babeuf and the people) "the plan, the mode of attack." Otherwise the patriots would yet again tend to fall out among themselves as they drew near to the great goal.[6]

Although Germain gave no indication of the membership of his "coterie," it seems reasonable to suppose that it contained at least some of those elements once connected with the Comité Amar who had acted as a caucus in the Panthéon: Darthé and Buonarroti, who were both now under the eye of the police for their part in the club's protest against the persecution of Babeuf and Marie-Anne; Le Peletier, who had defended Babeuf and attacked Marie-Anne's arrest in anonymous articles in the *Journal des hommes libres*; and Antonelle, who had published a protest against the closing of the club.[7]

Babeuf was formally enrolled toward the end of March in a new central coordinating committee of four; the other members were Le Peletier, Antonelle, and Silvain Maréchal (the former editor of the *Révolutions de Paris*). Sometime before 30 March these four constituted themselves an "Insurrectional Directory" and began to issue instructions to subordinate agents. Didier persuaded the original "Directory" during the first days of April to add Darthé and Buonarroti to their number; and on Buonarroti's recommendation Debon was also co-opted. The full committee of seven was complete on 8 April, when a meeting was held at Babeuf's current hideout, an apartment belonging to the tailor Lambert Clerex (in the rue Babille, close to the corn market). By now the structure of the insurrectional conspiracy was already firmly established. At the center was the Insurrectional Directory, soon to adopt the title of "Insurrectional Committee." At the periphery were the "principal agents" in each of the twelve Paris *arrondissements,* charged with coordinating the activities of all the democrats living within their *arrondissement.* In theory the identity of the members of the Insurrectional Committee was kept secret even from the *arrondissement* agents, liaison being provided by Didier, who acted as an "intermediary agent." Military agents were also appointed, of whom Germain was the most active, charged with agitation among the various military units stationed in the capital.

The details of the appointment of *arrondissement* agents supplied by Buonarroti suggest that the practical organization of the conspiracy was in the hands of a smaller subgroup of the full Insurrectional Committee. Thus, of the twelve agents, three were nominated by Darthé, two each by Babeuf, Germain and Debon, one by Buonarroti, and another by Buonarroti and Babeuf jointly. Neither Antonelle nor Maréchal appears to have had much of an active organizing rôle after the first launching of the conspiracy, while Le Peletier's contribution seems to have been chiefly the provision of funds and facilities for the organizational work of the conspirators.[8]

The short-term aim of the conspirators was simply to overthrow the "tyranny" of the Executive Directory and to seize power. Their long-term aims are less easily established, for in the nature of things, they were still incompletely defined in detail when the conspiracy was smashed in May 1796. According to Buonarroti, the members of the

Insurrectional Committee were in "perfect unanimity" in their dedication to communism: to the achievement, that is, of "the equality of labor and of consumption" (*l'égalité des travaux et des jouissances*). The contemporary evidence provided by the committee's propaganda is less definite. The walls of Paris were placarded on 9 April with a manifesto in fifteen sections authorized by the committee, the so-called *Analyse de la doctrine de Babeuf.* Despite its title, this piece was not written by Babeuf himself, although he approved it as a summary of his teachings.

The *Analyse* began by stating as an axiom the equal right of all to the enjoyment of the bounty of nature. Society was then defined in Rousseauist fashion as an institution whose purposes were to defend primitive equality against the attacks of the strong and evilly disposed, and to increase the communal resources of well-being (*les jouissances communes*). Such practical proposals as the *Analyse* contained for realizing these purposes were expressed in very vague terms. Exclusive property in land or of the means of production was described as a crime; the rich were ordered to "renounce their surplus" in favor of the poor. The goal of the revolution was affirmed as "to destroy inequality and to restore *le bonheur commun*." Each was to contribute an equal share of labor to society and draw out an equal share of *jouissances* in return, and all were to have an equal right to education. There was no hint of the collectivist economic organization long since outlined by Babeuf in the *Tribun de peuple.* The committee was, thus, endorsing a somewhat incomplete version of the "doctrine of Babeuf." Indeed the *Analyse* concluded with a call to rally to the Constitution of 1793 so strongly emphasized as to imply that the route towards the desired goal of *le bonheur commun* must lead in the first instance through the restoration of the status quo of 1793-4. There was nothing, in fact, in this carefully ambiguous document to which the most orthodox Jacobin could take exception.[9]

However, the agents of the conspiracy began to distribute on 18 April another publication which penetrated rather more deeply into the practical mechanism of *le bonheur commun*. Attributed to Buonarroti, this work was cast in the form of a reply to certain criticisms of Babeuf's doctrines made in an open letter from "M. V." at the beginning of February. In this, "M.V." (who seems to be identifiable as Marc Vadier, the ex-Montagnard deputy) had posed the problem of the fate of the arts and sciences in general, and the position of the artist, the musician, and the scientist in particular, in the model of a communist society advocated by Babeuf in the *Tribun du peuple.* How was it possible, Vadier demanded, for a violinist or a singer and a soap-maker to deposit their produce at "the general storehouse of real equality" in exactly the same manner?

Although Buonarroti's "reply" offered at best only an unsatisfactory and largely rhetorical answer to Vadier's query, the pamphlet provided an opportunity for a general restatement of the essential features of the ideal society to which the insurgents were formally pledged. The *Réponse à ... M.V.* was thus a much fuller statement of Babeuf's doctrine than the *Analyse* itself; indeed it is the most complete version of the ultimate shape of *le bonheur commun* for which they were striving which was ever actually published by the conspirators. The organizers of the new insurrection declared themselves opposed to the *loi agraire* as no more than a temporary palliative which left the root evil of property firmly entrenched. In their alternative program all kinds of existing wealth were to be sequestrated by the Republic, and the labor of the citizens was to be given a rational direction by its rulers. All the products of the land and of industry would be collected in "public depots" and distributed equally by "the public authority."[10]

From this it is clear that at least two of the most active members of the Insurrectional Committee, Babeuf and Buonarroti, shared a common dream of a communist society without private property and with the collective administration of the production and distribution of goods, and that these ideas were approved at least in general terms by the committee as a whole. Babeuf and Buonarroti worked closely together during much of April and the beginning of May 1796, organizing and publicizing the insurrectional campaign, often sharing the same secret retreat, and all the while discussing and elaborating the plan of the future communist commonwealth in greater detail.

In 1828 Buonarroti reconstructed and published from his personal papers and his own recollections a "fragment of a projected economic decree," from which (after making allowances for the distortions of an old man's memory and imagination) the main gist of these discussions may be pieced together. In general the proposals incorporated in the "projected economic decree" conformed closely to the "administered economy" first outlined by Babeuf at Arras in the summer of 1795. In return for their labor the citizens of the "community" were guaranteed a modest sufficiency of food, clothing, housing, lighting and heating, medical attention and education. Provision was made for the old, the young, and the infirm to enjoy the same equal share in this distribution. What was new in 1796 was the detailed attention given to the function of the administrative machinery in what was deliberately constructed as a bureaucratic society.[11]

At the base of the economic system the supervision of production was to be entrusted to a corps of magistrates elected by the members of "classes" (or groupings of trades and professions); they were to be responsible for ensuring the delivery of produce to the public warehouses. The warehouses themselves were to be under the control of magistrates elected in each commune, whose duties included the keeping of records and the distribution of goods. All this machinery was to be subject to the authority of a higher administration at the national level with the responsibility for conducting overseas trade and for maintaining a balance in supplies between the different parts of the country. To facilitate the work of the higher administration the nation was to be divided into a number of regions, into which *départements* were grouped according to the nature of their production and resources, with a subadministration in charge of each region. A further body of magistrates was to undertake the organization of transport between the different regions at the orders of the higher administration and on the basis of information supplied by the *départements*. The higher administration was also to be entrusted with the dissemination of the knowledge of mechanical inventions and new techniques. At the commune level it was proposed to vest the task of spreading knowledge and improving techniques in councils of elders representing the various occupational "classes." Such councils of elders would form, in effect, a parallel structure to the established political representation, itself elected according to the prescriptions of the Constitution of 1793.

Some further details may be gleaned from Buonarroti's general account of the conspiracy. Thus, the economic administration was to have the right and duty to dispose of labor in the most effective way (even to the extent of the direction of workers to meet shortages and the consignment of the idle to forced-labor camps). On a long-term basis it was also intended to plan the "production" of skills through the regulation of admissions to the different vocational courses in the public schools. The curriculum of the schools was to be overwhelmingly vocational.

Much of this detail is perfectly consistent with the general tenor of Babeuf's earlier speculations. What Buonarroti seems to have contributed personally (whether in 1796 or in 1828) was an emphasis on the moral organization of the projected community. Buonarroti's vision of the new communist order was of a pseudo-Spartan utopia, well endowed with councils of elders laying down the law to respectful, patriotic, and athletic young men and women, with a calendar of civic festivals for every conceivable occasion, all staged against a background of stern grandeur provided by splendid public architecture. Another of Buonarroti's preoccupations (clearly evident in his writings at the time of the conspiracy) was a marked Rousseauist revulsion from the evils of city life and the apotheosis of the virtues of rustic simplicity. Buonarroti's ideal state was an overwhelmingly agricultural community.[12]

It is difficult to assess the extent to which such ideas or the details of the projected economic decree represented the consensus of the Insurrectional Committee. Most probably the agreed goal of *le bonheur commun* represented something different to each of the leaders of the conspiracy. To Buonarroti it meant a kind of idealized Sparta; to Babeuf, a land of well-fed children and of equal dignity for all; to Maréchal, to judge from his projected *Manifeste des Egaux*, a virtual anarchist utopia modeled on Morelly's *Code de la Nature*. For what it meant to the others there is less evidence. For old Robespierrists like Darthé and Debon the essential was probably a return to the morality of 1794, to the Reign of Virtue, in which all things were placed in common for the survival of the Republic and the well-being of the virtuous citizen, with an immediate practical redistribution of wealth to ease the harsh pressures of destitution and starvation on the poor.

Partly as a tactical expediency (in order to broaden the base of the revolt) but partly also as a matter of conviction, the committee was prepared in fact to sanction as an immediate aim of the uprising an instant *ad hoc* redistribution of property which amounted to little more than authorized pillage and looting. Babeuf's notes specified the prompt provision of food and lodging for "the people of the garrets and the attics," a "guarantee" of the property of *émigrés* and counter-revolutionaries to soldiers and their dependents, and the free distribution of food.

Draft instructions were prepared by Buonarroti ordering that badly housed "poor citizens" should be installed in houses belonging to counter-revolutionaries, and provided with furniture at the expense of "rich conspirators." The revolutionary committees of the sections were to be revived on the model of 1793-4, and were to take over clothing shops and shoe shops and to provide free clothing for "indigent citizens left naked by tyranny." The revolutionary committees were also to seize all food in public and private stores and to begin an immediate distribution. Similar measures were officially endorsed in the collectively authorized Act of Insurrection, prepared by the Insurrectional Committee for distribution on the "Day of the People." This promised the immediate return of all pawned items free of charge, the prompt rehousing of "the wretched of all the Republic," free bread from the bakers for everyone, other foodstuffs distributed gratis in public places, and the immediate confiscation of the property of *émigrés*, conspirators, "and all the enemies of the people" for the benefit of soldiers and the poor.[13]

The primary political goal of the new revolution was declared by the Act of Insurrection (and by several other publications of the conspiracy) to be the restoration of the Constitution of 1793. Buonarroti, however, argues that there was a strong consensus that even the democratic arrangements of 1793 would require some improvements in order to extend popular control over the government. It was intended to place more emphasis on the powers of referendum and initiative vested in the primary assemblies, and to create a national corps of people's watch-dogs, or *conservateurs de la volonté nationale*. The *conservateurs* were to have the function of declaring the people's will, as ascertained through referenda held on either governmental or popular initiative. They would also be empowered either to suspend a recalcitrant National Assembly or to initiate an appeal to the people to withdraw their mandate; no final decision had been taken on these alternatives.[14]

Thus, the ultimate political goal of the conspirators was not, as is generally supposed, an élitist dictatorship, but rather a form of representative government leavened by a strong infusion of direct democracy. Between the immediate and the ultimate there is often, of course, a very long and difficult road to travel. It is not surprising that, in preparing to venture forth into the dangerously unmapped territory of the final great revolution of humanity, the leaders of the insurrection should have found it hard to agree on the precise degree of the length and the difficulty to be anticipated. All were agreed formally that (in the words of the Act of Insurrection) the "Insurrectional Committee of Public Safety should remain in permanence until the total accomplishment of the revolution." This meant, at the very least, that the committee should on its own authority accept responsibility for preparing, planning, and carrying out the practical task of destroying the existing government and establishing itself at

LE COMITÉ INSURRECTEUR DE
SALUT PUBLIC, AU PEUPLE.

Acte, d'Insurrection.

ÉGALITÉ,   LIBERTÉ,

BONHEUR COMMUN.

DES Démocrates Français, considérant que l'oppression et la misère du Peuple sont à leur comble, que cet état de tyrannie et de malheur est du fait du gouvernement actuel;

Considérant que les nombreux forfaits des gouvernans ont excité contre eux les plaintes journalières et toujours inutiles des gouvernés;

Considérant que la constitution du Peuple, jurée en 1793, fut remise par lui *sous la garde de toutes les vertus*;

Qu'en conséquence; lorsque le Peuple entier a perdu tous ses moyens de garantie contre le despotisme, c'est aux vertus les plus courageuses, les plus intrépides, à prendre l'initiative de l'insurrection, et à diriger l'affranchissement de la masse;

Considérant que les Droits de l'Homme, reconnus à la même époque 93, tracent *au Peuple entier, ou à chacune de ses portions, comme le plus sacré et le plus indispensable des devoirs, celui de s'insurger contre le gouvernement qui viole ses droits*; et qu'ils prescrivent *à chaque homme libre, de mettre à l'instant à mort ceux qui usurpent la souveraineté*;

Considérant qu'une faction conspiratrice a usurpé la souveraineté, en substituant sa volonté particulière à la volonté générale, librement et légalement

A

The insurrectional proclamation

the conclusion of the uprising as the sole executive power. But even this inescapable measure of *ad hoc* and temporary usurpation of the people's sovereignty was assumed uneasily. "It is not the same in times of crisis as in ordinary times," the committee explained in the preamble to its first circular to the *arrondissement* agents. "When the people are in full possession of their rights . . . he who . . . clothes himself on his own authority with whatever title as public magistrate, on the pretext of desiring to improve the situation of his fellow citizens, would be a usurper, even supposing his intentions to be, in the last analysis, perfectly altruistic [*très droit*]."[15]

In assessing the probable duration of the "total accomplishment" of their revolution it is likely that the conspirators were thinking in terms of days rather than months. Their models for revolution were the great *journées* of 1789, 1792, and 1793, each of which had accomplished crucial political changes in a matter of a few hours. But after the *journée*, what? Darthé and Debon argued the merits of a personal dictatorship by a "lawgiver" in the classical and Rousseauist tradition, who would lay the foundation of the new order. In opposing this proposal Babeuf repeated the arguments he had used against personal dictatorship in 1794. But he now declared himself in favor of "the dictatorship of authority but not the dictatorship of a man." In an unfinished review of the course of the revolution he noted, in a commonsense way, that the revolutionary situation itself would be likely to determine the measures to be adopted; he plainly leaned personally towards the resurrection of a revolutionary government on the Robespierrist model. But a revolutionary government exercised by whom? Buonarroti says that on the eve of the uprising the Insurrectional Committee of Public Safety—"after long hesitation"—had "almost" decided to ask "the people" to invest them with the sole power of initiating and enforcing the law. This passage must surely be interpreted as meaning that the matter had been the subject of controversy, and that it still remained unsettled. What was decided, and indeed proclaimed in the Act of Insurrection, was that at the earliest possible moment the Insurrectional Committee would convene a mass meeting of the insurgent people of Paris, which would, on the committee's nomination, appoint a provisional national convention. This would comprise ninety-seven deputies, one for each *département*. The committee probably saw itself as filling the rôle of a committee of public safety towards this provisional convention, and some of its members also intended to serve as deputies. Babeuf, for example, was named as candidate for the Somme Département.[16]

There is some evidence of a last-minute hardening of attitudes as the Day of the People approached. No sooner did the growing strength of the popular support for an uprising against the Directory become apparent than all kinds of interested parties began to fish in the troubled waters. In particular a group of former Montagnard deputies, as a price for their support, sought and won a recognition of their right to sit as *ex officio* members of the new provisional convention, thus maintaining a thread of continuity with the Convention of 1792.[17]

One consequence of this alliance between the original conspirators and the Montagnards was an amendment to the Act of Insurrection, the effect of which was to withdraw the exclusive right of the In-surrectional Committee to nominate members of the provisional convention and to vest it instead in "the delegates of that portion of the people who shall have taken the initiative in the insurrection." This arrangement would have left it open to the Montagnards to put forward their own nominees.

In the face of this very real threat that the control of the revolution would pass prematurely into other hands, the Equals were forced to seek security in a new formula. They declared, in turn, their deter-mination to retain "the title and the power of Insurrectional Com-mittee of Public Safety . . . until the whole people are perfectly hap-py and tranquil." What sort of period was this new formula intended to cover? At the time, the leaders of the conspiracy seem to have been generally sanguine. Babeuf, as has been already noted, believed that about three months of provisional government might be adequate. In an insurrectionary proclamation the committee asked the people for "*some months* of calm, courage, patience and docility." Buonarroti affirms that it was intended to promise that the provisional conven-tion should report back to the people within a year.[18]

Whatever speculation may suggest about the hypothetical out-come of an uprising had it ever materialized, there is no contem-porary evidence that the leaders of the conspiracy thought, as a group, in terms of a substantially longer period of provisional dic-tatorship than these few months. Only from the remote perspective of 1828, reviewing his own state of mind and those of his fellow con-spirators after a gap of some thirty years, did Buonarroti suggest otherwise. In one passage of his *History* he declares that the committee was determined to maintain its dictatorship until the ultimate social revolution, the founding of a communist "national community," was completed—only then would the Constitution of 1793 be fully implemented. Even accepting their own optimistic terms of reference, such a decision would have committed the Equals to at least five or ten years—perhaps even a generation—of dictatorship. During this time (in Buonarroti's version) power would have been relinquished only gradually by a governing communist élite, in proportion as the people's re-education and reconditioning progressed as a result of the consolidation of the new communist society.[19] Such a vision is certainly important evidence of Buonarroti's state of mind in 1828, and it is even possible that it represents a summary of his innermost convictions in 1796. As evidence for the collective attitude of the conspirators of 1796 it must be regarded as suspect.

Yet, with all reservations made, it is clear that the committee was agreed on the necessity of a period of revolutionary dictatorship to follow the uprising to consolidate power and to prepare the way for the triumph of ultimate communism and true democracy. The institutions of this provisional dictatorship, it was anticipated, would be modeled closely on the precedent of Robespierre's revolutionary government of 1793-4. Indeed it was decided, as a rule of thumb, that wherever possible, all authorities should be resurrected and restored to the *status quo ante* Thermidor. In Paris, for example, the restored section revolutionary committees were expected to seize the initiative from the earliest moments of the uprising, and similar committees would re-form in the provinces.

The seizure of power was expected to be violent and to involve bloodshed. Not all the conspirators necessarily shared General Rossignol's pathological desire to see "heads falling like hail and tripes and bowels scattered about the pavement," but for most, inevitably, the Day of the People would also be a day of revenge. For the cold-blooded Darthé, slaughter had value as a strategic weapon: the people were to be urged on to a bloodbath in order to ensure their irrevocable commitment to the revolt, for there could be no turning back after a new Septembrisade. Darthé marked down the following for summary execution: the five Directors and the seven ministers; the general commanding the Army of the Interior and his headquarters staff; anybody who fought for the old administration; all foreigners found abroad in the streets; bakers who refused to bake bread (they were to be "strung up from the nearest *lanterne*"); and all citizens who refused to surrender their flour or were found to be hiding other foodstuffs.

According to Buonarroti, it was also intended to liquidate the members of both the Council of Five Hundred and the Council of Ancients. A special humiliation was planned for Fréron and Tallien: they were to be set to work personally to rebuild the old meeting-hall of the Jacobin Club. As soon as the insurrection was proclaimed, special emissaries were to be dispatched to rouse the provinces and to subject selected strategic cities like Arras, Dijon, Montpellier and Metz to the same régime of terror. Darthé and Massard also planned to send out armed columns to Orléans and Beauvais to secure the Paris food supply.[20] As soon as possible the planned repression was to be given a more formal structure at Paris by the creation of a special court or popular commission. This would be made up of reliable representatives of the Paris sections named by the *arrondissement* agents.

Once in control of Paris, the Insurrectional Committee proposed to secure the sanction of the people for a "projected police decree" institutionalizing the repressive aspects of the revolutionary dictatorship. This would have established a special category of *étrangers*, persons deprived of political rights and subject to arbitrary deportation and imprisonment. Virtual concentration camps for enemies of the people were projected, to be sited on convenient islands off the Mediterranean and Atlantic coasts. The category of *étrangers* included "all not employed in useful labor," the determination of status being left to the revolutionary committees, who were authorized to issue or withhold *certificats de civisme*. As a general rule, all persons in prison on the eve of Robespierre's fall would have automatically found themselves behind bars again. The same decree authorized the creation of twelve strategic armed camps in important provincial centers, garrisoned by dedicated republicans hand-picked by local revolutionary committees throughout the land. Safeguarded by such measures, a campaign would then be launched to win the enthusiastic support of the nation for the new régime. "*Commissaires-généraux*" from the provisional convention would go out from Paris on the model of the representatives on mission of 1793, encouraging the revival of popular societies. At the same time a central propaganda "college" in the capital would be opened to instill the principles of the new revolution into delegates from the provinces.[21]

Germain's and Babeuf's first vision (in 1795) of the communist revolution had been apocalyptic: a sudden holocaust heralding the birth of a new age. "Everything must return to chaos," Babeuf declared in the *Tribun du peuple,* "and a new and regenerated world must emerge from the chaos." Even in their Arras days, however, both men (in calmer moments) had pictured the new world as growing more or less gradually out of the old: Germain by way of the development of cooperation between individual peasants made free and independent by the *loi agraire,* Babeuf through the progressive expansion of the republican Vendée as the advantages of the new system became obvious through the example of the liberated areas.

The conspirators of 1796, similarly, did not expect to establish communism overnight. Instead, in the first instance it was intended to return to a compromise or "ultra-Jacobin" social policy. All payments in cash were to be suspended, and all taxes on the poor abolished. The rich would be subjected to a progressive tax in kind; the rents of state leases were also to be collected in kind. The pressing needs of "public agents," of the families of soldiers' dependents, of the aged and the infirm, were to be a first charge on such receipts. The rich were to be "exhorted," for fear of worse, to yield up their "surplus" voluntarily to the people.

Meanwhile, the projected economic decree would have established the foundations of a distinct communist sector, a "great national community," within which the transition to communism would be made immediately. The basis of the national community would be various classes of land already in social ownership: such nationalized church lands and confiscated property of *émigrés* as had remained unsold at Thermidor, the property of "enemies of the revolution" sequestrated by the Ventôse laws of 1794, together with other lands and properties used or owned by the state, by local authorities, or by public foundations for charity or education. To these it was proposed to add uncultivated private land, the property of those found guilty of enriching themselves as public officials, and the accommodations seized *ad hoc* from the rich to provide housing for the poor. Individual citizens would also be invited to surrender their personal property as a condition of admission to the community, in return for a guarantee of an equal and adequate subsistence to all working members and their dependents.

An appeal would be made, in the first instance, to "small proprietors, poor shopkeepers, day-laborers, peasants, artisans, and all the wretched" to join the community. But it was anticipated that within a generation (at the most) the great national community would extend to cover the entire land and the entire population, since with the abolition of inheritance all land would revert to the community on the death of the existing owners. Certain mounting pressures would help to persuade the reluctant or hostile laggards. They would bear the entire weight of increasingly heavy taxation; they would be excluded from civil or military office; and they would be boycotted by citizens as suspect *étrangers*. Life outside the community would soon become intolerable for the resisters.[22]

A summary of the aims of the Conspiracy of the Equals of 1796 inevitably tends to systematize what was not systematic, to institutionalize what was provisional, and to clarify artificially what was obscure. Yet the broad outlines are plain. The conspirators seem to have seen the conspiracy as involving three stages. Firstly, there would be the Day of the People, accompanied by an orgy of primitive popular justice, of slaughter, revenge and looting. This would usher in a return to a rigorous version of Robespierre's revolutionary government, which would prepare, within as short a time as possible, the triumph of the principles of pure democracy and pure communism, and establish the reign of *le bonheur commun*. There seems no reason to doubt Buonarroti's assertion that all the members of the Insurrectional Committee shared a general commitment to such a program. In the nature of things some, like Darthé, were inclined to dwell more lovingly on the details of present revenge while others, like Babeuf and Buonarroti, preferred to spend their time dreaming of the utopian future.

Such evidence as we have suggests that a rather more marked difference of emphasis existed between the rank-and-file supporters of the conspiracy and the membership of the central committee. Of the twelve *arrondissement* agents only two have left any evidence (in their surviving correspondence) of a personal understanding of the nature of the ultimate goal of the uprising. On 8 April Pierre-François Pâris (appointed agent of the Seventh Arrondissement on Darthé's nomination) wrote to Babeuf to declare his long-established enthusiasm for *l'égalité réelle* and *le bonheur commun*, yet without offering any more precise definitions. Nicolas Morel (Babeuf's nominee for the First Arrondissement) alone thought it proper to add occasional notes on the extent to which the reliable *sans-culottes* in his sections shared the ostensible central doctrines of the conspiracy. Thus we learn that La Vicomterie (of the rue de l'Echelle) was "something of a poltroon, but virtuous and capable of undertaking great measures to bring about pure democracy, even though he is not for *le bonheur commun*, since he regards it as impossible." Piorry (the ex-deputy) was "somewhat Directorial, with no love for the tribune's doctrine." Curiously the only "patriot" described without qualification in all the papers of the conspiracy as "a friend of the tribune's doctrine" was the deputy François-Pierre Ingrand, a member of the Council of Five Hundred and a subscriber to Babeuf's journal.

Without doubt there were many more disciples of *le bonheur commun* on the fringes of the conspiracy. But what, exactly, they understood by the phrase can be anybody's conjecture. During the trial of the conspirators in 1797 one of the accused, Jean-Baptiste Goulart, offered one man's interpretation. For Goulart *le bonheur commun* meant "a reduction in the price of all commodities necessary for the survival of the poor, and the recognition of paper money."[23]

It is highly probable that most of the rank-and-file supporters of the conspiracy saw the struggle for *le bonheur commun* in similar terms, as an attempt to resurrect the vanished "golden age" of Robespierre, when the poor man could eat and speak his mind, rather than as the prelude for a new and universal utopia. The prevailing winds were Jacobin rather than communist.

Sixteen

Organizing the Day of the People

At the end of March 1796 Juste Moroy (a 45-year-old jeweller and former member of the revolutionary committee of the Finistère Section and of the Paris Revolutionary Army), like many other former militants, was facing a desperate personal crisis. Orphaned at eleven and the son of a "simple worker," he was not un-used to hardship; but now, jobless since his removal from the municipal administration of the Tenth Arrondissement, he had been driven by soaring prices into the deepest poverty. The house in the rue de l'Oursine in which he lived with his 71-year-old sister was empty: the furniture had all been sold and the two occupants were sleeping on heaps of straw.[1]

On or about 30 March a stranger handed Juste Moroy a package which he opened to find a commission, formally sealed with an im-pression on red wax, appointing him revolutionary agent for the Twelfth Arrondissement (a district more or less co-extensive with the Faubourg Saint-Marceau). There were also eight pages of instruc-tions from an anonymous and presumably hitherto undreamed-of "Insurrectional Committee." Trustingly, and without apparently even wondering whether an *agent-provocateur* might be at work, Moroy accepted. Either he knew more than he was supposed to, or he was exceptionally foolhardy. In either case, he had nothing very much to lose.

About the same time a similar packet found its way into the hands of Jean-Baptiste Cazin (of the rue des Postes, in the Quinze-Vingts Section). Pastry cook before the revolution to the cardinal de Rohan, at forty-eight Cazin was also facing a bleak future. After a brief period as an inspector of works of the artillery of the Paris arsenal, he had been imprisoned during the Thermidorian reaction, spending (like Babeuf and Germain) several months in exile in the prisons of Arras. He was unemployed and without a profession, penniless, ragged, and semi-literate, and at first Cazin found his commission as revolutionary agent of the Eighth Arrondissement an overwhelming honor. His first reaction was to write suggesting politely that perhaps the committee might really prefer to look for someone else. Babeuf replied personally on 3 April to assure Cazin that there had been no mistake: the committee had every confidence in him; there would be ample supplies of money and plenty of help; he must not refuse to take charge of operations in the all-important Faubourg Saint-Antoine. His personal loyalty appealed to in this way, Cazin thereafter became one of the most sturdy and effective agents of the conspiracy. Pierre-François Pâris (who acknowledged his own commission as agent for the Seventh Arrondissement on 8 April) warned Babeuf that Cazin's tongue was liable to loosen with drink; but in the end it was not Cazin's tongue that wagged too often, and the Directory's police got no lead on the conspiracy from him.[2]

All twelve *arrondissement* agents had been appointed by the end of April. At the beginning of the month the "Hébertist" veteran Joseph Bodson had agreed to serve for the Eleventh Arrondissement, although only after demanding guarantees from Babeuf that the old Robespierrist suspicions of Hébert's followers were dead, over and done with. The Fifth Arrondissement was in the charge of Germain's friend the Lyonnais Guilhem, another one-time Arras prisoner; the Third under Claude Menessier, a former gardener and Babeuf's friend and protector as a police official of the commune in 1793. The First Arrondissement was entrusted to Nicolas Morel (a leader of the Bains Chinois group) and the Second to Baudement (of the Muséum Section). The Fourth Arrondissement was assigned to Mathurin Bouin, the Sixth to the builder Claude Fiquet (an ex-member of the revolutionary committee of the Temple Section), and the Ninth to Deray. On 27 April responsibility for the remaining Tenth Arrondissement was offered to the actuary Pierron after an earlier appointment had proved unsatisfactory.[3]

Not all the appointed agents took their commissions with equal seriousness. The Insurrectional Committee (on 23 April) administered a sharp rap on the knuckles to Morel, who had been "inactive," guilty of "light conduct" and too absorbed in a private law suit; the committee threatened revenge if there should be no improvement. In fact Morel did begin to take his duties more seriously after this. But as late as 9 May, when a meeting was called at Massard's to finalize last-minute arrangements for the insurrection, only six out of the twelve *arrondissement* agents turned up. Even so the most important revolutionary centers (the Faubourgs Saint-Antoine and Saint-Marceau and some of the militant sections of the center) were safely in the charge of a group of dedicated revolutionaries: Cazin, Moroy, Pâris, and Fiquet.

As outlined in their original commission the task assigned to the *arrondissement* agents was both propagandist and organizational. They were to organize meetings, give readings from the radical press, and direct discussion along revolutionary channels. Their attention was directed, in the first place, to the existing neighborhood café groups as centers for further expansion; but they were warned to avoid attempting too formal a style of organization. The groups must not attract the attention of the authorities by constituting themselves as "clubs" or "popular societies," or by growing individually too large. Instead the militants were to be urged to associate informally in as large a number of separate "domestic" gatherings as possible. In addition to their agitational work the agents were instructed to observe and report back on the daily climate of opinion, and to make a note of the most likely supporters of "the movement to be produced" and the most useful "revolutionary task" to which each supporter might be assigned. A special note was also to be made of the activities of the "intriguers" and "false brothers" who managed to insinuate themselves into popular gatherings.

In all these activities the maximum of secrecy was recommended. At the organizational level, not only was the identity of the Insurrectional Committee kept secret from the twelve *arrondissement* agents, but the agents were not even told the identity of their fellow-agents. The "intermediary agents" (or couriers) who carried messages between the committee and the *arrondissement* agents were supposed to remain ignorant of the contents of the packages. In their agitational work the agents were urged to strive to do good by stealth, working from the midst of the rank and file rather than openly taking the lead in organizing and leading meetings and discussions.

These original arrangements were the product of the central committee's naive intoxication with the idea of conspiracy rather than the result of a practical evaluation of the possibilities. "Nothing can be more internally satisfying," the agents were comfortingly assured, "than to reflect that one is the invisible instrument by which great forces are set in motion."[4]

Following on the formation of the enlarged Insurrectional Committee during the first week of April, the agents began to receive a new series of directives which added considerably to their organizational burdens. On 6 April the central committee asked for lists of sympathizers among the *canonniers* of the National Guard in each section, men who held the key to success or failure of any Paris uprising. On 8 April another circular detailed a further daunting series of tasks. The agents were now requested to carry out a census of accommodations for "brothers from the *départements*" arriving in Paris; to organize companies of bill posters and tearers-down of royalist and governmental placards; to compile a census of workshops, listing the number of workers in each and how employed; to supply details of arms depots and shops; and to indicate police agents and spies. They were urged to form *groupes*, small squads of picked men to frequent public places, especially the Tuileries gardens. Such squads would make it their task to spread propaganda and to influence the public arguments which were beginning as the spring weather brought Parisians out of doors again. On top of all this the agents were also to try to collect funds from well-to-do sympathizers (all apparently in return for a "salary" of two francs a day in specie).

On 16 April the Insurrectional Committee again requested annotated lists of *canonniers*, together with a census of pikes and a list of "*bons et mauvais citoyens*." The following day yet another circular demanded details of the location of all kinds of stores in each *arrondissement*, whether located in private houses or commercial premises. In the nature of things the simplest of the assigned tasks of the *arrondissement* agents was the drawing up of lists. On the basis of the information so supplied Buonarroti and Germain were able to compile a register of more than 1,500 names of potential supporters. It later proved very helpful to the Directory's police after it had been seized at the time of the uncovering of the conspiracy—an ironical commentary on the elaborate initial security precautions prescribed by the Insurrectional Committee.[5]

How many of the *canonniers*, the citizens "worthy of command," or the other militants on the committee's lists had actually been sounded out it is impossible to say. Consequently any general conclusions based on an analysis of this rank-and-file roll call of the supporters of the conspiracy must be tentative. Professor Soboul has emphasized two conclusions of significance which may properly be drawn from this evidence. Firstly (and surprisingly) many of the names listed are new names. In the Seventh Arrondissement for example, only a quarter can be shown to have played an active part in *sans-culotte* or Jacobin politics in 1793-4. The second point is that although the individuals had changed, the social character of the movement had remained the same. Thus the "Babouvists" of 1796 cannot be described as "proletarians." They belong to essentially the same social strata as the *sans-culottes* of 1793-4. "The revolutionary vanguard on which Babeuf and the conspirators believed themselves able to count was still constituted, in the year IV," Professor Soboul concludes, "not by a factory or workshop proletariat, but by . . . a coalition of small masters and journeymen, working and living together." In such a milieu communism was hardly likely to have taken serious root. "The social mentality of these men at the bottom, patriots and democrats, remains incontestably in the main stream of *sans-culotte* ideology, characterized by an attachment to small property, founded on personal labor."[6]

Even so, despite Professor Soboul's caution, it is clear that there were stirrings of a new spirit in the agitation launched by the Babouvists. A conscious attempt was made by the Insurrectional Committee and its agents to rouse the genuinely proletarian elements of the faubourgs. Thus, according to Cazin, the political "reunions" he formed in the Faubourg Saint-Antoine were simply natural assemblies of workers in the workshops, where the employers were "pure enemies of their working people." Cazin would provide such groups with literature which they read at breaks and lunchtime. Rossignol, Lamy, Placet and other agitators were also accused of trying to rouse the workshops of the Faubourg Saint-Antoine.

In the Faubourg Saint-Marceau, Juste Moroy at first expressed the point of view (perhaps surprising to the historian with twentieth-century preconceptions) that little support could be expected from his *arrondissement* precisely because the inhabitants were mainly workers and therefore easy for enemies of the people to lead astray. The greater part of the employers of the district, tanners, leather manufacturers and dyers, were royalists, and the workers followed their employers' opinions, for "their livelihood depends on it."[7] Of all the agents Moroy seems, nevertheless, to have taken his commission to make contact with the workers most seriously. During the second or third week of April he actually carried out the required "sociological" survey of the Faubourg Saint-Marceau and reported on the result. There were no workshops in the Observatoire, Panthéon and Jardin-des-Plantes sections except for small artisan concerns with two, three or perhaps four workers; in the Panthéon Section the workers at the wood and wine warehouses of Port Bernard were sound, but their employers were "absolutely rotten for royalism and aristocracy." In other reports Moroy praised the favorable spirit of the other riverside workers, the stevedores and grain porters and the laundrywomen. Only in the Finistère Section did he discover anything in the nature of real "workshops" with substantial bodies of workers. However, the largest concern, the Gobelins tapestry, proved a disappointing prospect. Although there were 100 workers, they were simply for any government which could be expected to preserve their specialist manufacture. Nevertheless, Bille (one of the leaders of the Gobelins workers) was noted down as a potential insurgent leader. The workers at the Julienne dye-works were all *sans-culottes*, but accustomed to "follow the crowd"; some were already sympathizers. The same was true of the thirty workers at Verité's dye-works, and Moroy had also a good word to say for Verité himself. For the rest, there were about twenty tanneries (each with 15 to 20 workers) and as many leather-dressers, where the usual strictures applied: the employers were royalists, the workers *sans-culottes*.

Moroy's conclusion was that the best tactic would be a campaign to win over the two classes of small tanners, who were being squeezed out by the bigger entrepreneurs, and "discontented workers." Already, by 10 April, Moroy had formed his agitators' cells and he was able to report that the workers were stirring "from the torpor in which they had been held by the tanners, the leather-dressers, the blanket-makers and the other manufacturers." His method was to start with cells of five or six members and allow them to grow until twelve, when a second group would hive off.[8]

While the *arrondissement* agents confronted their proliferating tasks with varying degrees of enthusiasm and competence, Babeuf and Buonarroti set up a small "insurrectional" factory at the central headquarters of the conspiracy, tirelessly turning out circulars and propaganda publications and compiling their lists of democratic sympathizers. Babeuf's hideout and the headquarters of the conspiracy were shifted at the end of April to an apartment near the Halles Centrales (in the rue de la Grande Truanderie) belonging to Pierre-François Tissot, who had been secretary of the Commission des Subsistances in 1794.[9] Among the papers later seized by the police at the rue de la Grande Truanderie was an orderly program of agitation, apparently drawn up by Buonarroti (about the time of the meeting in Clerex's apartment on 8 April) with marginal entries by Babeuf indicating various actions taken (down to 19 or 20 April). As the conspiracy's "director of public opinion," Babeuf was responsible for the astonishingly concentrated propaganda campaign which was now launched.

A pamphlet in defense of the Constitution of 1793 appeared on 12 April, followed on 13 April by the pamphlet *Lettre de Franc-Libre*, directed towards the military garrison. On 14 April no. 42 of the *Tribun du peuple* and *Doit-on obéissance à la Constitution de 1795* were published, and on 16 April two more pamphlets aimed at the soldiers: *Soldat, arrête encore* and *L'Adresse du Tribun du peuple à l'Armée de l'Intérieur*, an extensive reprint from no. 41 of the *Tribun du peuple*. The sixth number of *L'Eclaireur du peuple* and the *Réponse à . . . M.V.* were distributed on 18 April, followed on 20 April by yet another pamphlet, *Le Cri du peuple français contre ses oppresseurs*.[10]

The printer who was responsible for the most important of these publications was Théodore Lamberté, one of the leading members of the Café Chrétien group. Babeuf received Lamberté's bill (on 23 April) for more than 17,000 livres for work which included 2,000 brochures and 300 placards of the *Analyse de la doctrine de Gracchus Babeuf*, 200 brochures and 400 placards of Le Peletier's *Soldat, arrête et lis*, 3,000 copies each of the *Tribun* and the *Eclaireur*, and 2,000 of the *Réponse à . . . M.V.* Although Lamberté lived in the *enclos* Martin, Gravilliers Section, his press was somewhere in the Fidélité Section.[11]

From the point of view of public impact the Insurrectional Committee could not have launched their propaganda offensive at a more favorable moment. During the winter of 1795-6 the economic policies of the Thermidorians had run their course and had produced an almost complete collapse. By 19 February, when the printing of assignats was discontinued, the paper currency had lost so much exchange value that the revolutionary money was quite literally not worth the cost of printing. A new paper currency, the *mandats territoriaux*, began issue on 18 March, backed once again by the security of state-owned lands. But within a fortnight inflation had taken hold again, and at the beginning of April the mandats were passing at 80 percent discount; within three months they too would be no more than waste paper. The government's grudging dole of flour at a controlled price fell to a sixth of a livre a head, and it was supplemented by ground rice. Plans to discontinue the ration at the end of February were temporarily shelved in view of the growing popular discontent, but even so prices were raised on 25 March. Almost immediately afterwards rents, which had become meaningless with the collapse of the assignat, were declared payable in the new mandats after 4 April, when they would thus become a financial burden once again.

Moroy described the circumstances which led him to join the conspiracy. Bread (on the free market) at 80, 150, even 200 francs the livre, at a time when a day's work was paid at a rate of 100 francs. In a worker's household, three-quarters of a livre of bread, all eaten at breakfast, with nothing left but potatoes at the end of the day. The result: everything of value sold or pawned, down to the sheets from the beds.[12] Against such a background the conspiracy's propaganda made rapid headway. On 5 April young Emile greeted his father cheerfully, assuring the "general in a waxcloth hat" (*Général à chapeau ciré*) in a letter that no. 41 of the *Tribun* had made a great impression in the "Faubourg Hentoine." The following day Pierre Robin, one of Babeuf's associates from the Arras prison days, was spotted by the police reading out the *Tribun* to a public gathering.

The major propaganda battle was joined soon after with the distribution of the conspiracy's manifesto, a placard version of the *Analyse de la doctrine de Babeuf.* From the Faubourg Saint-Marceau Moroy reported posting up eighteen copies on the night of 10-11 April, of which all except two were torn down by government agents the following morning.[13] A "poster war" developed between posters-up and tearers-down. Moroy's detachment would begin operations at 4 to 5 a.m. so that the people could have a chance to read the placards on their way to work at 6 a.m. "before the royalists got up." Then a second wave would have posters ready to greet the workers at their breakfast break, about 9 a.m. However, on 12 April Bodson complained that his posters in the Saint-André des Arts quarter had been torn down before 6:30 a.m.; evidently at least some "royalists" were early risers. Another agent, Baudement, organized a counterattack by children, who tore down the Directory's proclamations in the rue Denis. The other end of the working day was also taken care of. Claude Fiquet reported (on 13 April) that he had organized groups to meet the workers at dusk at the Porte Saint-Martin and Porte Saint-Denis on their way home from work. The handing out of pamphlets also went ahead, often when groups had gathered to read the placards, with women particularly active. Even Emile Babeuf made himself useful by distributing copies of the *Analyse*.[14]

The *Courrier républicain* noted the posting up of the *Analyse* "in the faubourgs" and in the Place de la Grève on 11 April, and described a scene in the Tuileries gardens, where a woman climbed onto a chair to give a public reading of the manifesto, afterwards only just succeeding in escaping from the police. The formation of open-air *groupes*, apparently spontaneous and informal assemblies for discussion, also went ahead. Moroy reported (on 14 April) some successful gatherings on the Seine bridges, despite the unseasonal cold weather, "where the name of Robespierre was heard" and his régime regretted. On the 15th Darthé pointed out to a recent recruit to the conspiracy a group of patriots on the Terrasse des Feuillants resisting police attempts to disperse them. On 19 and 20 April larger crowds began to gather on the Pont au Change and along the river around the apple-sellers' stalls, and attempts by cavalry patrols to clear the pavements were met with threats to disembowel the horses. During the morning of 26 April the cavalry proved powerless to disperse a crowd of 2,000 who had gathered in the rue Saint-Antoine around a placard copy of *Soldat, arrête et lis*.[15]

The previous day, however, the Insurrectional Committee had ordered a change of tactic. It circularized the *arrondissement* agents to advise them that the *groupistes* who had been active in public places would be better employed distributing literature to gatherings in private households, since such cells were more valuable than the larger, more open assemblies in the cafés and the public squares. Certain of the cafés, nevertheless, continued to be important meeting places for the insurgent activists, above all the Bains Chinois, which became the overt center of the agitation. On 9 April Georges Grisel, who would later be recruited by Darthé at the café as a military agent, paid the Bains Chinois a visit: he found it crowded, and joined the thirty or forty habitués who were listening to Babouvist songs sung by the seamstress Sophie Lapierre. A new song written by Maréchal and published in the *Eclaireur* was wildly applauded in the Bains Chinois and in the Café Madeleine, another radical rallying point. Before long the open "Jacobin" resurgence had produced street brawling outside the Bains Chinois, in which, predictably, Charles Germain became embroiled with the *jeunesse dorée*, and some of the windows of the café were smashed.[16]

There was a reaction in official quarters too. The Directory pushed through a series of decrees (on 16-17 April) to contain the rising tide of popular discontent. These measures, the decrees of 27 and 28 germinal, introduced new penalties for forming public assemblies or posting illegal placards and made it a capital offense to advocate the Constitution of 1793. The new repressive laws, together with the rebirth of street violence, were in a sense a tribute to the success of the Equals in blowing the dying embers of *sans-culotte* militancy into a new life. But the key to a successful insurrection, as the conspirators were only too keenly aware, remained the attitude of the troops garrisoned in and around Paris.

From the beginning a great deal of the propaganda effort of the Insurrectional Committee had been expended in this direction. Special military agents were appointed to take charge of agitation among the different corps: General Joseph Fyon for the Invalides garrison, Charles Germain for the special security corps, the Police Legion, General Massey for the detachments quartered at Bourg Franciade, or Saint-Denis, and Georges Grisel for the large force encamped at Grenelle. Jean-Baptiste Vanheck, ex-commandant of the National Guard of the Cité Section, was given a roving commission. No special arrangements were made for work among the 4,000 troops garrisoned at Vincennes. In the event neither Massey nor Vanheck appears to have played an active part in the conspiracy, and on 30 April the military committee had to be strengthened by the addition of Massard and General Rossignol.[17]

Darthé handed Georges Grisel his commission as a military agent on 15 April in the kitchen of the Bains Chinois, together with a lengthy set of instructions from the Insurrectional Committee. Grisel was the son of a master tailor from Abbeville, and a man with a varied career behind him. An old regular soldier of the Royal Army, he had first joined the Royal Comtois in 1782, in hopes of taking part in the Gibraltar campaign. Then, in 1784, he had suffered the humiliation of being discharged from the regiment on account of his short stature (he was little more than five feet tall). For the following two years Grisel worked at home with his father at Abbeville before running away to Paris in 1786 (allegedly "with the family savings"). The revolution found him still in Paris, living the hard life of a tailor's apprentice and sleeping twelve in a room with the other apprentices; but at the end of 1790 he found himself jobless and without a sou, and soon after went back to Abbeville and his family. Grisel rejoined the army in September 1791, as a volunteer in the first battalion of the Somme regiment, and he was commissioned captain in the autumn of 1793. In 1796 he was attached to the 21st half-brigade, with his quarters at the Ecole Militaire.

According to Grisel, his involvement with the conspiracy was the result of a perfectly accidental encounter (at the end of March) with an old comrade from his apprentice days in Paris. This friend introduced him to one of Darthé's associates and, eventually, to Darthé himself.[18] Grisel's instructions from the Insurrectional Committee reproduced to a large extent those which had been passed on to the *arrondissement* agents. But certain passages were added dealing with the special problems of propaganda among soldiers. The military agents were to play on particular military grievances: the low pay and poor conditions which made the French soldier "worse off than Uhlans," equipment shortages which left many without shoes or cloaks, the high price of laundry ("thirty francs for washing a shirt"). Discipline was also a target: "a mass of tortures worse than under Louis XVI," the caprice of subalterns, the reduction of the rank and file to automatons. A special effort was to be made to drive a wedge between the veterans and the political appointees commanding the Paris garrison.

At a different level the agents were directed to play on the contrast between the promise of 1793 ("a milliard of land for the returning warriors") and the reality of 1796, when at least 300 milliards would be needed to meet this promise and the land was meanwhile steadily falling into the hands of "enemies of the Fatherland." Going back to his native village the soldier of the revolution could expect to find that nothing had changed except for the worse. "The defender of the Fatherland, returning to his cottage, ought not to find it still dominated by the keep of the insolent would-be gentleman who, with all the land in his possession, once made his father work like a slave, treating him so in every respect, half starving him and keeping him in rags. . . ." Only by rallying to the people's cause could the peasant-soldier escape a hopeless future as the despised and suspect serf of the victorious *émigré* and royalist landowners—while from the moment of joining the people a future of plenty and contentment would be guaranteed. The instructions concluded with a reminder of the classic revolutionary appeal to the troops not to fire on wives and sons and brothers and fathers, to remember the great days of July 1789 and the glorious example set then by "Capet's" mutinous regiments.[19]

A propaganda campaign specifically directed at the Paris garrison was launched at the beginning of April by Le Peletier and Babeuf. A section of no. 41 of the *Tribun du peuple,* subsequently off-printed as a pamphlet, was set aside for an "Address from the Tribune of the People to the Army of the Interior," which promised an immediate distribution of land among soldiers' dependents, raised the specter of a return to beggary after demobilization, and denounced the corruption and conceit of "newly arrived" generals like Bonaparte, concluding with an appeal to the troops to refuse to fire on the people. The third number of the *Eclaireur du peuple* carried a similar message, stressing again demands for land redistribution and for pensions for the war-wounded, and urging a strike by the soldiers until these demands were met. The language of these publications, for both of which Babeuf was probably responsible, was fairly simple. They did not, like Le Peletier in his *Soldat, arrête et lis,* expect peasant soldiers to follow literary allusions to Xerxes and ancient Greece. They were nevertheless put together in a style which, while appropriate to the politically sophisticated *sans-culotte* élite of Paris, must have been largely incomprehensible—hence boring and doctrinaire—to an illiterate conscript from the Auvergne or from Brittany.[20]

As a career soldier of plebeian origins, Grisel drafted a commentary (on 15 April) on the "instructions" for the benefit of the Insurrectional Committee. In it he demolished some of Babeuf and Le Peletier's illusions. The rank and file, he explained, were no longer revolutionary veterans in whose hearts an appeal to the sacred memory of 1789 would strike any kind of chord. Instead, by and large, they were "conscripted rustics, serving liberty like convicted criminals serve the galleys." Because of the greater skill of literate townsmen in evading the draft perhaps only 40 out of a battalion of 400 might be able to read and write. The one serious "political" ambition of the majority was to get back home: "Thousands of them think so little of the revolution that they would willingly give away the Republic for a taste of home cooking [*un gâteau de leur village*]. . . ." Perhaps a third of the men were good soldiers whose lead was followed by the others, but such men were left unmoved by "fine long discourses." To win the support of this group "wine and the hope of pillage" were quite sufficient.

Captain Grisel's own practical proposals were, first, to drop the attempt to drive a wedge between the troops and their junior officers, for the situation was quite different from 1789. The officers were now much closer to the men and almost as poverty-stricken. The attempt to isolate the reactionary generals and headquarters of staff should, however, be continued. Broadly speaking the conspiracy should en-

courage the growth of indiscipline and even the dissolution of particular corps. Propaganda for the insurrection should stress the opportunities it would offer for the pillage of the rich and for desertion;
as for "absolute equality," there were strong prejudices against this,
thanks to the counter-propaganda of the authorities. Tactically, what
was really important was to encourage dancing in wine-shops close to
the barracks and to keep the drink flowing freely.[21] Meanwhile
Grisel had turned his hand to devising a style of propaganda more
likely to reach the "natural leaders" of camp and barracks. On 10
April he gave Darthé the manuscript of a pamphlet, *Lettre de Franc-
Libre, soldat de l'Armée circo-parisienne à son ami la Terreur,
soldat de l'Armée du Rhin*, full of *foutres* and *bougres* and other
colorful expletives in the best tradition of Hébert's *Père Duchesne*.
This was the message of the *Tribun du peuple* translated into
barrack-room language for the benefit of ordinary soldiers.

Grisel's pamphlet was immediately printed and circulated, and indeed the papers of the conspiracy show that his advice was treated
with respect. Darthé in particular seems to have been impressed by
the value of an immediate promise of pillage and the disbanding of
regiments as an effective tactical device for neutralizing the Directory's military superiority in Paris. Darthé's notes contain a suggestion that all soldiers should be offered the chance to return to their
homes, and that they should be paid for each item of military
supplies brought over, including horses, uniforms and weapons.[22]

The Equals continued to develop their original attack on the
political front. There was at least one important military unit among
whose rank and file Babeuf and Le Peletier's style of propaganda
might be expected to find a response: the Police Legion, an élite
corps of about 7,000 men responsible for guarding the Directory, the
legislative councils, and the arsenals, prisons and law courts of the
capital. The Police Legion had originally been created in the reaction
which followed the Prairial uprising in 1795 as a special security
force to protect the Convention against the threat of popular revolution. After Vendémiaire, however, its political orientation had been
dramatically reversed when Bonaparte had personally purged anti-
republican elements and replaced them with *sans-culotte* recruits,
some of them veterans of the Revolutionary Army of 1793. In contrast to the line regiments, its rank and file was predominantly urban
and artisan; perhaps a fifth of the effectives were Parisians and most
of the legionaries were literate. Provided with a distinctive uniform
with red facings instead of the blue of the line regiments, they were

well-paid and, fortified by incursions into speculation and petty crime, they "enjoyed their war," in which most of the engagements took place in the Parisian cafés.

The *"collets rouges"* of the Police Legion were a thorn in the flesh of the civilian police; from as early as 19 February 1796 police reports began to mention "dangerous tendencies" among the legionaries. The police central bureau complained on 21 March of an outright refusal of the legion to render aid when requested. A legion patrol was reported on 14 April to have fraternized with a "gathering of workers" in the Faubourg Saint-Antoine, and to have declared: "Fear nothing, the soldiers are with you." Responding to pressure from the minister of police, the Directory decided on 23 April to order the legion out of Paris and to the front, and the movement order for five battalions was made public the following day. The result was an outburst of disaffection. It culminated in an outright mutiny by the legion and an insurrectional opportunity which might, had it been seized, have resulted in a serious threat to the government's control of Paris.[23]

The conspiracy had had agents working among the legionaries for some time. The most important agitator was Jean-Noel Barbier, a 22-year-old soldier in the second battalion who, like other soldiers, had been recruited by the Equals during a spell in the Ripaille military prison at Versailles. On his return to Paris, Barbier established close contact with Antoine Fiquet, the brother of the agent for the Sixth Arrondissement, who gave him pamphlets and copies of the *Tribun* and introduced him to Germain. Claude Fiquet was able to report on 25 April that there was serious disaffection among the sections of the legion quartered in the Courtille barracks, and Barbier collected signatures for a petition to the Directory against the removal of the legion from Paris. On the critical morning, on 28 April, the Courtille men refused to march out and to surrender their barracks to a line unit. Germain was quickly on the spot, and he sent his first report to the central committee at 11 a.m. in a mood of some excitement: the *collets rouges* were fraternizing with the *collets bleus,* and there was talk of a joint march on the camp at Vincennes to persuade the garrison there to join a general mutiny.[24]

The crisis of 28 April found the members of the Insurrectional Committee in a state of indecision. The previous day Germain and Antoine Fiquet had gone so far as to promise that in view of the legion's difficulties the Day of the People could be brought forward from the nineteenth to the ninth of May. An immediate uprising—when all the reports had not been carefully tabulated, all the detailed arrangements not yet made and, most important, the attitude of the line regiments was as yet ambiguous—was another matter. Nevertheless at 12:30 p.m. Pillé, acting as secretary for the committee, penned what almost amounted to a call for insurrection, and the *arrondissement* agents were warned to get the banners ready and hold on for one more day in order to give time for a clearer evaluation of the situation. Rumors of an imminent rising spread rapidly to the Bains Chinois and elsewhere. In the Faubourg Saint-Antoine, Jean-Louis Eudes, the fire-eating *canonnier* of the Droits de l'Homme Section, spent the night with a party wandering about the streets waiting for the action to start. But by midnight the opportunity had been let slip, and the Directory was in full control of the situation.

Carnot had reacted sharply and decisively to the news of the mutiny, summarily disbanding the most disaffected second and third battalions and ordering the arrest of the ringleaders. The next day (29 April) the first battalion was also disbanded.

The key to the failure of the police mutiny was the hostile attitude of the Flanders regiment and other line regiments. Over a number of days the Directory had been carefully cultivating selected units by a distribution of pay arrears and free drink, clinched by the promise of a move from tents into the newly vacated legion barracks. In the end such practical considerations proved more persuasive than the propaganda of the Equals; and by 8 p.m. on the 28th, Germain was reporting back bitterly that the combination of a show of strength and the disbanding of the legion battalions had broken resistance. Too many of the reluctant warriors among the legionaries were only too delighted at this early termination of their service.[25]

Eventually, on 21 May, 96 legionaries faced a court-martial at the Ecole Militaire for their part in the mutiny, and Barbier was given ten years in irons; seventeen others had been sentenced and shot before 5 May in the immediate aftermath.

Hidden away in the homes of "patriots," hundreds of legion deserters remained a potential reserve army for the conspiracy. Of one detachment of 1,250 "reliable" men actually sent off to the front, almost 600 had melted away before the column got as far as Metz; many of them probably filtered back to Paris.[26] Nevertheless, what was probably the most favorable opportunity for an insurrection in 1796 had passed without any decisive action by the Equals.

Seventeen

The End of the Conspiracy

Following their break with Amar, the Equals had abandoned any idea of alliance or compromise with the group of former Montagnard deputies who continued to form a half-secret opposition to the Directory in Paris. On the other hand there was one actual member of the Council of Five Hundred who was not (like the other Montagnards) suspect either as a Thermidorian or as an opportunist seeking to climb back into office over the backs of the insurgent people. Jean-Baptiste Drouet was the celebrated postmaster who had stopped Louis XVI's flight to the frontier at Varennes in June 1791. Elected to the Convention in 1792, he had been captured by the Austrians while on a mission in 1793, and spent the next two years in a fortress prison at Fribourg. At the end of 1795 he was returned to France in an exchange of prisoners, after an ingenious and nearly successful escape attempt.

Because of these accidents Drouet was free of the stigma of participation in Thermidor or the repression after Prairial. Partly because of his personal sympathies, and partly because of his resentment of the active persecution of a member of his family after Thermidor, Drouet found himself very much the odd man out in the Council of Five Hundred—a radical Rip Van Winkle, returning to life in an alien world to find all the old Jacobin landmarks of 1793 destroyed. The returned hero, prudently enough, kept his more extreme opinions to himself (and some of them were decidedly odd).[1] But on one occasion (towards the end of March), having drunk too much at a dinner, he broke out in a furious denunciation of the Thermidorians which left no doubt either in police or in Jacobin quarters about his true affiliations.

Babeuf seized the opportunity to recruit Drouet as a candidate for the mantle of his earlier heroes, Coupé, Chaumette, Fréron and Bentabole. The first approach seems to have been made through Emile, at the beginning of April, and was confirmed by a letter written by Babeuf on 6 April. Later Babeuf provided Drouet with a fiery draft speech defending popular societies, and he was predictably angry when Drouet decided to adopt a less intransigent tone in the council. Despite his disappointing tendency towards caution, Drouet was now nevertheless part of the conspiracy.[2]

As the popular effervescence rose during April and the possibility of some kind of uprising began to seem more real, so other political figures and groups began to make the necessary accommodations. Within the Directory itself growing tensions were developing between Barras, who continued to cling to the platform of the broad republican alliance, and Carnot, who began (in the spring of 1796) to work for a régime more firmly based on the bourgeois center, with the shedding of the Directorial Jacobin hangers-on. Before long, almost by reflex, Carnot's rival began to seek to underpin his own position within the Directory by making contact with the growing democratic opposition. Charles Cochon de Lapparent, the new minister of police and Carnot's man, appointed on 3 April, was soon noting that a certain "Louis dit Brutus," who was Barras' secretary, was also a frequenter of the Café Guilloché, along with Rossignol, Cazin, and Pierre-Mathieu Parein, "Germain's warmest friends." Barras actually summoned Germain to the Luxembourg Palace on 19 April in order to explain his general sympathy, but for a new Vendémiaire and not the new Prairial which the plotters seemed to have in mind.

To Babeuf the thought of the Day of the People ending in another triumph of the corrupt Barras was intolerable. As early as 30 March (in no. 41 of the *Tribun*) he declared, "Barras shall not have my confidence, and . . . I shall do all in my power to prevent him from insinuating himself into the confidence of the patriots [*de surprendre celle des patriotes*]." Babeuf alerted the *arrondissement* agent Bodson (on 10 April) against the intrigues of Tallien and his friends, who were in close liaison with Barras. The Barras-Tallien faction, he warned, were hoping to use Rossignol as a go-between and to channel the popular discontent into a paltry movement against their parliamentary enemies of the Right, led by "Isnard and Co." On 15 April the Insurrectional Committee sent out a general warning to all *arrondissement* agents, warning them against the attempt by Tallien, Legendre and Barras to capture the insurgent movement and to pose as its leaders, "to save their heads."[3] An attack on the conspiracy's virginity was developing from yet another quarter. On 13 April the agents were put on their guard against the maneuvers of a reconstituted Comité Amar, whose chief members were now the ex-Montagnard deputies Amar, Vadier, Laignelot, Javogues, Choudieu and Ricord. A similar warning went out on 26 April, after the Directory had ordered the expulsion of seven Montagnards from Paris (including Amar, Choudieu and Vadier). Efforts were to be made to persuade the proscribed men to defy the expulsion order as a moral gesture; but they were to be allowed no further importance in the plans of the conspiracy.

Freezing out the Montagnards proved a much more difficult operation than fending off Barras. Several of these former leaders of the Jacobin Convention continued to enjoy the respect and loyalty of some of the leading members of the conspiracy (notably of the military agents Rossignol and Fyon). Following the collapse of the Police Legion mutiny, a joint council of war was held by the Insurrectional Committee and the military agents (on 30 April), at which Rossignol and Fyon pressed strongly for an understanding with the Montagnards. When, shortly afterwards, Ricord and Laignelot made a formal proposition to Germain for a fusion of the two groups, it became obvious that the two agents had reported all the details of the conspiracy to the Montagnard committee.[4]

Rossignol had an important following in the Faubourg Saint-Antoine, and his "advice" could hardly be treated lightly. Drouet was also in favor of an accommodation with his former colleagues from the Convention. The Montagnard initiative was, nevertheless, greeted with alarm and anger by the majority of the Equals. While the tactical value of an alliance with the diehards of the Jacobin Convention, men who still reflected the glory of the Constitution of 1793, could not be denied, it would bring with it a serious danger that the leadership of the insurrection might fall into the hands of opportunists who did not share the Equals' ultimate ideals of absolute equality and *le bonheur commun*.

In the resulting discussions Debon was for abandoning the conspiracy altogether. Darthé cynically argued that the Montagnards should be promised everything before the uprising—but then "sacrificed" on the day itself. Eventually, it was decided to negotiate. On the morning of 4 May Germain led the Montagnard delegate Jean-François Ricord to the conspiracy's headquarters in the rue de la Grande Truanderie to hear the Insurrectional Committee's terms.

These were that the Convention should be recalled, by which was meant the Montagnard rump, comprising about sixty deputies who had not taken office under the Constitution of 1795, but with the addition of one radical democrat per *département,* chosen by the people from a list presented by the Insurrectional Committee on the day of the revolt. Two other clauses bound the Montagnards to agree in advance to the nationalizing of all public and private property (*"sous la sauvegarde du peuple"*) and to the acceptance of "the mandate of the people" on the day of the insurrection.

Such a compromise would have left all real power in the hands of the triumphant Insurrectional Committee. On the following day Ricord returned with counterproposals which rejected the "election" of the additional democrat members of the Convention and refused to be bound by the mandate of the insurgent people. While accepting the seizure of housing and goods as a tactical device to secure popular support, the Montagnards formally rejected the confiscation of private property as a political principle. To sweeten the dose the members of the Insurrectional Committee were promised ministerial places in the new Montagnard government. Agreement on such terms was impossible, and Ricord was given a sharp reply to carry back to his principals.

While these negotiations were under way, the inexplicable delay and the apparent faltering of nerve of the Insurrectional Committee, following closely on the missed opportunity of the Police Legion mutiny, were producing ominous signs of a falling-off of morale amongst the rank and file. On the evening of 6 May there was a stormy meeting at Ricord's house, attended by Darthé, at which, thanks to the intervention of Amar and Robert Lindet, the Montagnards decided to accept the Equals' terms with only slight modifications. On the evening of 7 May the Insurrectional Committee was able finally to circularize the *arrondissement* agents to reassure them that the political crisis was over. It remained only to finalize the tactical details of the insurrection. The terms of the alliance were incorporated in an amended version of the Act of Insurrection.[5]

Following the general council of war attended by the Insurrectional Committee and the military agents (on 30 April), the military committee began to meet daily to work out a plan of campaign, at first at the saddler Jacob Reys' apartment in the rue du Montblanc, and then, after 2 May, at Clerex's apartment. Massard gave a report on the military committee's progress to a general assembly of the Insurrectional Committee and the Montagnards (they met at Drouet's house in the rue Saint-Honoré, close to the Place Vendôme). There was general agreement on the broad tactical outlines.

The insurrection would begin in daytime with a call to arms signaled by the ringing of the tocsin and a trumpet call. This would be accompanied, hopefully, by a military mutiny and the "showing of the heads of their enemies" to the people. The insurgents would then rally to their designated chiefs and platoon commanders, who would be grouped in three divisions, each commanded by a general. Care would be taken to provide each unit with political commissars, *démocrates ardents,* to ensure that the revolution stayed on course to the end.[6]

The immediate targets of the insurrection were fixed as the legislative councils, the Luxembourg Palace (headquarters of the Directory), the army headquarters and the ministries, and the military camps at Grenelle and Vincennes. The soldiers were to be approached in the first instance by patriotic citizenesses bearing civic crowns and refreshments. But if this experiment in distaff psychological warfare failed, sulphuric acid and brickbats were to be held in reserve to bar passage through the streets to counter-revolutionary detachments. Most of these details were included in a circular of instructions to *arrondissement* agents, drawn up chiefly by Buonarroti.

Darthé's notes provide some supplementary details of the conspiracy's tactical plans. They stress the importance of seizing the optical telegraph terminals at the Louvre and on the heights of Montmartre, the Treasury, the artillery camp at Meudon, the powder magazine at Grenelle, and the eighteen cannons and 12,000 muskets at the Feuillants arsenal, which were to be the special responsibility of the architect Lefranc. The Act of Insurrection also named the post office as a primary target, together with all food stores.[7]

Another meeting was fixed for the evening of 9 May at Massard's apartment, located in the rue Neuve Egalité, for a joint review of arrangements by the military agents and the *arrondissement* agents. This produced some further tactical suggestions, chiefly from Cazin, who seems to have anticipated a rather tougher struggle than the others. Cazin's most original proposal was the construction of a boat bridge across the Seine at the Jardin des Plantes. This would provide for ready communication between the two democratic fortress-faubourgs of Saint-Antoine and Saint-Marceau. This proposal implied a tacit assumption that the bridges might remain in government hands. Cazin also urged the preparation of a contingency plan for a retreat to the heights of Montmartre should the first assaults fail.

The members of the Insurrectional Committee made their own private arrangements for a kind of final heroic Götterdämmerung should the people be defeated. At the outset a special picked guard of 8 *sans-culottes* from each *arrondissement* were to report to the committee, prepared "in the last extremity" to be buried with their chiefs "beneath the ruins of liberty." In general, however, the conspirators were enthusiastic and optimistic. After all, had not the *arrondissement* agent Pâris reported that for every sympathizer he had managed to list in the Seventh Arrondissement there were at least ten others who could be counted on? In 1828 Buonarroti reproduced a carefully calculated tabulation on which the conspirators based their strategy, which listed 17,000 direct and immediate supporters, "not counting the numerous class of the workers." The count included 4,000 "revolutionaries" from Paris and 1,000 from the provinces; 1,000 *canonniers* of the sections; 1,500 Jacobins purged from administrative posts and 500 Jacobin ex-officers; 6,000 members of the Police Legion; and 3,000 men from other military units.[8]

Despite such sanguine calculations, as the Day of the People approached nagging suspicions and doubts remained. Even in April, another agent of a less trusting disposition than Pâris, Joseph Bodson, had sceptically urged that, human nature being what it was, promises to turn out should be cut by at least half. He also went on to point out some irritating facts to upset the tidy symmetry of the insurrectional plan. Some of the soldiers he had personally sounded seemed in "the most perfect ignorance" about the constitutions of '95 and '93. Moreover, all the bells in the Théâtre Français and Pont Neuf sections had been taken down—so that there were none left to sound the tocsin and signal the start of the uprising. Juste Moroy was also encountering unexpected difficulties. While the military committee counted on an average of about 400 firearms per *arrondissement* in the hands of patriots, Moroy could find no more than 30 in the Faubourg Saint-Marceau (and very few cartridges). On the other hand, the supply of civic crowns happily provided no problem: Moroy's female shock-troops were armed with twenty each, and spares "could be made in half an hour from trees in the garden."[9]

Perhaps most disturbing of all was the discovery that only six out of the twelve *arrondissement* agents had turned up at the crucial meeting of 9 May at Massard's. There was no means of judging how far the support of the others could be relied on, and how far their preparations had progressed. After a somewhat stormy session—the wine flowed freely and brought out the worst in Cazin and Germain—the 9 May meeting finally broke up without fixing the date of the uprising. Instead Germain called for further and more detailed reports from each *arrondissement* on the precise numbers of hard-core militants who would be prepared to rally to form the nucleus of the insurgent force before the tocsin was rung, on how they would be armed, and on the roll call of sympathizers and of "royalists." Another joint meeting of military and *arrondissement* agents was called for 11 a.m. on the following day (10 May) at François Dufour's apartment in the rue Papillon to consider these final reports.[10]

This meeting might have decided on a final plan and fixed a date for the uprising—had not the police intervened and arrested the participants. Perhaps, instead, there would have been further delays and postponements. Ever since the collapse of the Police Legion mutiny the revolt had shown every sign of having gone off the boil. The more closely the Insurrectional Committee scrutinized its lists of effectives, the more the certainty of the necessary mass support seemed to melt away.

"Something seems to be about to happen," noted a police report of 10 May. "We cannot fool ourselves that the number of anarchists scattered and hidden about Paris are not working away quietly or that they do not have their police, their Directory, their bureaus. But the question is, where are their armed forces, where is their support?" If the police had as yet no satisfactory answer to that question, neither, despite their activity and their planning, did the conspirators.

To a number of other important questions the police already had some quite clear and useful answers. On 3 May the Director Carnot had received the first of a series of letters signed by a certain "Armand," warning him of the existence of the conspiracy and offering to provide further details in a personal interview. Since "Armand" was in fact Georges Grisel, the conspiracy was doomed from this moment on. In his evidence at the conspirators' trial (and in other statements) Grisel maintained that he had never been a loyal member of the conspiracy at all, but from the beginning had only allowed himself to become involved in order to discover as much as possible about the plotters before revealing everything to the proper authorities. In return for Grisel's valuable cooperation as the main prosecution witness, the Directory was prepared, officially, to accept this alibi. But, as with many double agents, residual doubts persisted. After the arrest of the leaders of the conspiracy the members of the Directory awarded Captain Grisel a sabre and belt as a token of their gratitude; yet in the years that followed preferment came only with painful slowness to this "savior of the Republic." He was ultimately promoted garrison adjutant at Nantes in 1800, and he died in the same rank twelve years later.[11]

In point of fact the only corroborating evidence Grisel was able to advance in support of his version was a claim that he had kept his immediate superior officers informed of his activities from the beginning. Although their evidence would have immensely strengthened Grisel's credibility as a witness, the officers in question were not called upon to testify in court, nor are their depositions preserved in the court papers. On the other hand there are quite strong indications that Grisel began as a genuine sympathizer and only betrayed the conspiracy in the end to save his own neck.

There was, for example, his reputation as a known associate of "terrorists" at Abbeville. There was also the readiness with which his first contact with the conspiracy, the tailor Meunier, who had known him before 1791, accepted the genuineness of Grisel's radical sympathies, and the success with which this "innocent" who "had never heard of Babeuf" persuaded men like Darthé and Germain to accept his *bona fides*. For Grisel was not, after all, a professional secret agent trained and experienced in dissimulation, but only a simple career soldier. Similarly, his valuable and practical advice to the Insurrectional Committee on the best propaganda approach to the troops and Grisel's own pamphlet, *Franc-Libre . . . à son ami la Terreur*, read more like the product of a genuine commitment than of a deep Machiavellian cunning.[12]

Grisel's conduct in the period immediately following his recruitment as conspiratorial agent is glaringly inconsistent in one important respect with that of a loyal officer seeking information about the extent and aims of a dangerous subversive organization. According to Grisel, Darthé gave him his sealed commission as military agent at the Bains Chinois Café on 13 April. After that he again met Darthé, who introduced him to Germain, on 15 April. There were two further meetings with Darthé and Germain on 16 and 17 April; but from then until 30 April, when Darthé sent a messenger to contact him at the Ecole Militaire, Grisel apparently made no attempt to maintain contact with the organizers of the dangerous conspiracy he alone had uncovered, even during the crisis over the Police Legion mutiny, which occurred during this period. Grisel's explanation, that he was busy with military duties, is hardly acceptable considering his rank; captains can usually find a way in most armies. That he was undergoing an agonizing crisis of indecision seems more likely.

It may well be that, by the end of April, Grisel had had second thoughts and would have liked nothing so much as to have extricated himself from the conspiracy altogether. A curious and completely fortuitous accident now intervened to make such a course impossible. On receiving his military agent's commission, for security's sake Grisel unpicked the mattress of his bed in his quarters in the Ecole Militaire, placed the commission inside, and sewed it up. A few days later he was dismayed to discover that his mattress (with the commission) had been taken in as part of a routine collection by the forage stores of the Ecole Militaire.

After the arrest of the conspirators the story of the "lost commission" leaked out, and many people drew the natural conclusion that Grisel's decision to betray the conspiracy must have been the product of his resulting panic. By this time, however, Carnot and Grisel had agreed on the official version, according to which Grisel had to be presented as a loyal patriot from the very beginning. Grisel was, therefore, forced to concoct a refutation for public consumption. The loss of his mattress (as he explained in a letter to the mayor and municipal officers of Abbeville) had caused him no concern whatever. Taken in and piled with two to three thousand others, it might have remained unexamined for two or three years; nor was there any way in which it could be traced back to Grisel. The commission document itself is said to have carried no names or signatures, and might have belonged to "anybody."

On examination neither of these alibis turns out to be satisfactory. For all Grisel knew, at the time his mattress might have been examined on the spot, for any number of chance reasons. (When Grisel and an accompanying party visited the stores on 16 May, they had no difficulty at all in identifying the mattress and pulling out the commission!) Most damning of all, the *commissaire* in charge of the expedition clearly recorded that the commission did, in fact, name Grisel as "principal agent attached to the line battalions," and this was probably why the document was conveniently "lost" again soon afterwards and could not be found at the time of the trial of the conspirators.[13]

Darthé's message to Grisel on 30 April plunged him immediately back into the very center of the conspiracy's operations. In response, he first went to Darthé's apartment, where he was introduced to Didier; soon afterwards Buonarroti arrived, and Grisel and Buonarroti shared a drink before Buonarroti led him at about 2 p.m. to a back room at no. 27 rue de la Grande Truanderie, where the joint meeting of the Insurrectional Committee and the military agents was in progress. Those present included Babeuf (whom Grisel now met for the first time), Germain, Buonarroti, Didier, Fyon, Rossignol, and Massard. In the course of the meeting Babeuf read out the Act of Insurrection, and the names of sixty potential insurgent leaders were considered. The meeting broke up at 7 p.m., but not before Grisel had been seconded to the military committee. The following day (1 May) he attended the meeting of the military committee at Reys' apartment, and on the morning of 2 May he was also present at the session held at Clerex's home. It was at this point that Grisel decided to write to Carnot, explaining that he had chosen this direct approach because of his fears of being betrayed by contacts at any lower level. On 3 May Carnot replied, fixing an interview at the Luxembourg for 9 p.m. on the 4th, and Grisel now revealed his true name.[14]

On 4 May Grisel attended another meeting of the military committee at Clerex's apartment. He left about 6:30 or 7 p.m. to go to his uncle's apartment in the rue Bourtibourg. He spent half an hour making notes in a café in the Faubourg Saint-Germain before presenting himself at the Luxembourg about 9 p.m. Carnot found Grisel's information so interesting that he arranged for him to return at the same time on the following day (5 May) to meet all the other members of the Directory, with the significant exception of Barras. At this meeting the Directors relieved Grisel of military duties; and the next day he drew 10,000 francs expenses to assist his operations.[15]

Over the next few days Grisel was very busy indeed, attending meetings of the military committee and general assemblies of the conspirators in various places, reporting to Cochon de Lapparent, the minister of police, and in between times secretly tracking down some of the leading conspirators and arranging "chance" social meetings with others to pump them and to discover the exact location of Babeuf's hideout. Grisel was not convinced that the venue of the 30 April meeting, no. 27 rue de la Grande Truanderie, was the permanent headquarters of the conspiracy, even though he suspected (rightly) that Babeuf was living somewhere close by.[16]

The Directory debated what use should be made of Grisel's information. Cochon de Lapparent, whose nerves were excellent, argued (with some support from Carnot) that the best tactic was to allow the insurrection to ripen and then to crush it and thus smash the radical opposition once and for all. But he was overruled and ordered to track down and arrest the leaders of the conspiracy as soon as possible. All five Directors signed the order: Carnot first and Barras last. Barras' reaction was entirely characteristic. Recognizing that the conspiracy was irretrievably doomed, he let things take their course, allowing no hint of Grisel's activities to filter through to the Insurrectional Committee. The source of such a leak would hardly have been in doubt in the circumstances. At the same time Barras prudently hedged his bets: he sent his household silver into the country and slept outside Paris each night.[17]

Despite their excellent intelligence, Cochon and Inspector Dossonville of the police central bureau opened their operations against the conspiracy with a series of extraordinary blunders which would have alerted any less complacent band of plotters to their danger. On 7 May, for example, Grisel (having imperfectly understood some remarks of Massard's) warned Cochon that an important meeting of the leaders of the conspiracy would take place at Ricord's house in the rue Saint-Florentin; the police mounted a raid at 11 p.m., but found nobody there. The following day (8 May) Grisel learned that there would be a general assembly of the conspirators at Drouet's that evening, and he arranged with Carnot for a police raid at 9:30 p.m. Grisel arrived at the meeting at 8:45, and found Darthé, Lindet, Ricord and Laignelot present. At 9:15 Babeuf arrived, followed shortly by Massard, Fyon, Rossignol, Massey, and three or four others. About the same time a regular mounted patrol stopped outside the house—but then moved on, to Grisel's astonishment. In fact, on Carnot's orders, the police did not arrive until 11:15, a quarter of an hour after the meeting had broken up. They found Drouet and Darthé alone, splitting a friendly bottle of wine together and no incriminating evidence around to justify an arrest; Grisel learned this news an hour after midnight.[18]

There were other strong hints that the secret conspiracy was now an open secret as far as the police were concerned. One of the most trusted secondary agents, Lefranc, took a chance and discussed the military plan of operations with a friend, Adjutant-General Valory, hoping to enroll him; but Valory immediately went to the police and on 8 May warrants were issued for Lefranc, the *arrondissement* agent Pâris, Parein, and another suspect. Pâris and Parein went into hiding, but Lefranc was arrested. The following day Antoine Fiquet (the brother of another *arrondissement* agent) arrived at Guilhem's apartment in pouring rain to find it under guard, and was himself arrested together with a soldier recruit for the conspiracy, who railed against him as a police spy all the way to the lock-up. The same day Germain wrote to Babeuf to explain his absence from the recent meetings, which had aroused some suspicion: he was being closely followed and was determined not to offer a lead to the police.[19]

Incredibly, despite all these ominous signs, both the Insurrectional Committee and its military committee decided to go ahead with the last-minute finalization of their plans. After leaving the joint meeting of the military committee and the *arrondissement* agents at Massard's on 9 May, Grisel went along to the rue de la Grande Truanderie to continue his search for Babeuf's hideout. He met there a surprised but unsuspicious Didier, joined him in a drink, and tried to loosen his tongue. About 11 p.m. he reported to the Directory, and it was agreed that all the conspirators named by Grisel should be arrested, and also that a special attempt should be made to capture Babeuf and to seize the papers at the insurrectionary headquarters. It still remained to discover exactly where the central headquarters was. But Grisel had hit on a ruse which he hoped would solve the problem.

Grisel went to Clerex's apartment (at 8 a.m. on 10 May) and gave Mme. Clerex a letter addressed to Babeuf. In it he proposed that he should bring some sympathizers from the Grenelle garrison to meet the military committee, and asked for the address of the day's meeting. He explained that he would be too late to keep an assignment with Darthé, who was to lead him to the committee. At the same time Grisel arranged for an agent to follow Mme. Clerex when she left to deliver the message. The agent bungled the job, and Grisel had to report his failure to the officer in charge of the operation, General Jacques Blondeau.

Grisel now tried a desperate improvisation. Returning to the rue Babille at about 8:15 he told Clerex that he had forgotten to include a vital detail in his letter, and he asked him directly for Babeuf's address. In fact Clerex did not have the street number; but he was able to describe the position of the building. Hurrying over to the rue de la Grande Truanderie Grisel identified the house as no. 21, and he immediately passed the information to a police agent. Between 9:30 and 10 a.m. he went back a third time to the Clerex apartment and met Mme. Clerex. She passed on a note from Babeuf which rejected Grisel's suggestions but obligingly gave the address of that day's meeting of the military committee—Dufour's apartment in the rue Papillon.

Grisel and General Blondeau (in mufti) went immediately to the rue Papillon to position their forces and complete the arrangements for a raid. After this Grisel called on Darthé at about 11:45 a.m., only to find that Darthé had grown tired of waiting (he had gone on to Dufour's, leaving the address with Mme. Didier). Thankfully, Grisel rejected the chance to be "in at the kill." According to his own account, having had "about two hours' sleep in a fortnight" (and none for the last two days) he went back instead to his quarters and "fell senseless," only re-emerging to receive the congratulations of the Directory on the day after the arrests. On the 14th he pocketed a further 40,000 francs "for expenses."[20]

Grisel's information had left Cochon's police with two major tasks: the seizure of the military committee at the rue Papillon, and the capture of Babeuf and the insurrectional headquarters in the rue de la Grande Truanderie.

François Dufour spent the morning of 10 May collecting payment for some cotton spinning work before returning home with some radishes for lunch. He found his house surrounded by 700-800 soldiers. Germain, Didier and Drouet were under arrest (together with several others, including the Montagnards Ricord and Laignelot). Darthé was also in the net, having allegedly been discovered hiding "between two mattresses." The arrested men were promptly transferred to the Abbaye prison under heavy guard. A curious and potentially dangerous crowd which had gathered had been pacified by the explanation that the arrested men were desperate criminals responsible for a recent outrageous robbery of the Lyons mail.[21]

As the police were closing in on the rue Papillon, at the rue de la Grande Truanderie Inspector Dossonville was busy perfecting his plans for the capture of the insurrectionary headquarters. At about 9 a.m., as soon as he heard from Grisel, Dossonville posted mounted guards in the neighboring streets. To avoid arousing the suspicion of the crowd it was explained, again, that the police were trying to arrest a gang of desperate and violent criminals. Dossonville's next step was to recruit a justice of the peace to assist in the arrest, as the law prescribed, a task which proved much more difficult than he had anticipated.

The first officer who was approached (he was from the Brutus Section) declared himself ready to resign rather than take part in an operation of the nature proposed. The second (from the Bon Conseil Section) also refused point blank. The justice from the Mail Section could not be found, and his colleague from the Contrat-Social was "ill." Discouraged, Dossonville did not even bother to tackle the justice from the Bonne-Nouvelle Section since his principles were notoriously suspect. Instead, after wasting an incredible two hours in such negotiations, he finally decided to dispense with formalities. Accompanied by Etienne Renel, *commissaire de police* of the Brutus Section, Dossonville entered no. 21 and climbed up to the Tissot apartment on the third floor. When the unsuspecting Mme. Tissot opened the door the police party burst in—and found Babeuf seated at a table, writing, with Buonarroti and Pillé in the same room. Although the place was a small arsenal, with loaded pistols and sabres scattered about, there was no attempt at resistance. Buonarroti tried desperately to hide papers; Babeuf bitterly upbraided Dossonville; and Pillé tried to protest legalistically that his name was not actually included in the warrant.

Before leaving the apartment Dossonville collected together the most obviously incriminating papers, placed seals on the rest, and posted two guards. Then the three prisoners were taken by carriage under cavalry escort to the Police Ministry for preliminary interrogation, amid the jeers of an immense crowd, still convinced that they were witnessing the well-deserved humiliation of a gang of common cut-throats.[22] To the arrested men it was a puzzling and demoralizing conclusion to the great conspiracy for the universal happiness of mankind.

Eighteen

Grenelle

After his arrest on 10 May Babeuf was taken to the Abbaye prison, within whose familiar walls he was soon joined by thirteen other chief suspects. On official orders all the prisoners were kept in solitary confinement while the preliminary investigations were conducted. Babeuf's first interrogation took place about 2 p.m. and produced some damaging admissions, which Cochon reported immediately to Carnot. While refusing to name any of his accomplices Babeuf personally admitted conspiring to overthrow the government and to re-establish the Constitution of 1793. A second interrogation on 11 May was concerned chiefly with the identification of papers seized by the police.[1]

Throughout Cochon found his prisoner unexpectedly cooperative. In a scrawled note to the police minister (on 12 May) Babeuf even offered to make further "declarations of the greatest utility to the government," provided Cochon would grant him an interview the next morning. In a further note Babeuf hinted that his revelations were really for the ears of the Directory alone; but Cochon (well aware of Barras' ambiguities over the past few weeks) scented political danger and thought it best to maintain a rigidly correct attitude. Babeuf was, accordingly, given writing materials and told to write down anything he wished to communicate.

The result was a remarkable letter in which the admitted chief of a murderous conspiracy offered a political deal to its intended victims. The Directors must realize, Babeuf argued, that the conspiracy was a much bigger affair than they had at first suspected; and so they would do well to proceed with great caution. Any attempt to prosecute the captured leaders would be unpopular and dangerous, and could only strengthen the opposition. On the other hand, any serious attempt to round up the rank-and-file supporters would also be impolitic; the consequent destruction of the *sans-culotte* party would incidentally destroy the Directors' own party in the country and leave them at the mercy of the royalists. There was, however, another possible path open. If the Directory would agree to abandon its present course and "govern popularly," Babeuf promised to use his influence to persuade the "patriots" to rally to the government once again and to set aside their differences.[2]

Babeuf's extraordinary offer to treat with his captors on an equal basis must not be interpreted as a lapse into some manic delusion, but as a tactical gamble to try to save the necks of all the conspirators by an appeal to the political opportunism of the Directory. The month, however, was floréal and not vendémiaire. Barras might have appreciated the arguments put forward, but Barras was too practiced a politician to risk offering any comfort to a party so plainly and crushingly defeated. His only concern now was to cover his tracks by a show of solidarity with the dominant triumvirate of Carnot, Le Tourneur, and La Révellière.

There was even less hope that Carnot would take Babeuf's offer seriously. He had been personally responsible for uncovering a dangerous and fanatical conspiracy against constitutional legality and the safety of life and property. The prosecution of the guilty and the vigorous rooting out of their accomplices could only strengthen his desired new image as the man of order and blur still further the old one as the colleague of Robespierre.

Babeuf sent a further agonized and cryptic appeal to Cochon on 15 May, but even then he must have already begun to realize that his gamble had failed.[3] After listening to Cochon's report on 13 May, the Directory had ordered proceedings against Babeuf, Buonarroti, and thirteen others under the law of 27 germinal (16 April). The accused were charged with planning to overthrow the Constitution of the Year Three in order to reintroduce that of 1793, and with plotting the destruction of the two legislative councils and the Directory. The following day Carnot, Barras, and Reubell signed an order together for the arrest of 110 persons for alleged implication in the conspiracy, 62 from Paris and the rest from the provinces. On the 15th orders for the arrest of René Lebois, of Lecointre (the printer of the *Journal des hommes libres*), and General Ganier followed.[4] Communication between the Abbaye cells and the streets outside was notoriously easy, and rumors of this developing manhunt must have rapidly made it clear that hopes of negotiating any kind of agreement with the Directory were utterly chimerical.

The inadequacy of security at the Abbaye was a matter of serious concern to Merlin, the minister of justice, and he began to explore alternatives. Ultimately, second-rank suspects were housed in Le Plessis, Saint-Pélagie, and the Petite-Force as well as the Abbaye; but there was a pressing need for a maximum security prison for the chief conspirators. Merlin's first choice was the Madelonnettes prison, but the building turned out to be under repair and unavailable for a month at least. Eventually it was decided to reopen the Temple, the medieval fortress in which Louis XVI and his family had been locked away in 1792 and 1793. The prisoners began to be moved across to their new quarters on 19 May, and Babeuf's turn came on the 21st. The other prisoners transferred at this time were Germain, Darthé, Didier, Massard, Buonarroti and Moroy. Cazin later made up a complement of eight who were held at the Temple.[5]

Situated in the heart of the northeast of Paris, the Temple had been built as a fortress of the Knights Templar at the beginning of the fourteenth century. A surrounding wall (some thirty-six feet high) enclosed two courtyards, within one of which was a central keep 120 feet tall with walls thirteen to fourteen feet thick and separate turrets at each corner. The whole was topped by an enormous bonnet of liberty on a flagpole. The prisoners were each locked in separate cells in the keep and were kept in solitary confinement, without news, writing materials, or contact with the outside world, while their interrogations were completed.

The walls were so thick that no sound penetrated, and the windows were barred and boarded up in such a way that no more than a patch of sky could be seen. Charles Germain (who was transferred separately from the others) believed himself to be completely alone for several days, until he heard Didier singing; afterward the prisoners communicated by shouting across from cell to cell and from floor to floor.[6]

The natural defenses of the prison were strengthened by a picquet of forty to sixty grenadiers in addition to the six jailers. The chances of escape seemed very remote—but evidently the inmates did not despair. All kinds of ruses were tried to communicate with the outside world. Relatives and friends were not allowed to visit the prisoners, but they were permitted to bring food and drink, to provide clean linen, and mend clothes. Emile was caught on 1 June attempting to smuggle a message to Germain concealed in a coat button. Darthé also advised his contacts to conceal letters in clean linen or in a bottle of wine, protected by a ball of wax. While the prisoners were still at the Abbaye Mme. Didier had tried to use a similar method with a pot of soup. Germain wrote his notes with a carefully trimmed fingernail dipped in ink concocted from crushed charcoal dust and sugar.[7]

Later, when the prisoners' interrogations were completed, they were allowed out of their cells to talk together and to walk in the gardens for two hours in the morning and the evening. One consequence of this relaxation was a series of escape plots. At the end of July Etienne Lasne, the concierge, caught a whisper of a forthcoming escape plan and ordered a general search. A knotted rope made from sheets was discovered in Didier's mattress; and files, wires and strings were also found. Didier, as befitted a former locksmith, had manufactured a master key of the Temple and there were signs of file work on the bars of a window.

The stationing of a permanent guard of grenadiers at the Temple reflected another fear of the jailers—the possibility of a rescue attempt by partisans from outside. The roundup of 10 May and the following days had effectively broken up the headquarters staff of the conspiracy and neutralized most of the active agents of the second rank; but many of the rank and file and a few quite important leaders continued to evade the police for weeks. Among those still at liberty, for example, were Antonelle, Le Peletier, Maréchal and Rossignol, together with Bouin, Bodson and Parein. Meanwhile the social discontents which had produced the crisis of the spring of 1796 intensified as the summer wore on and the revolutionary paper currency entered its final agony. On 29 June a series of food-riots broke out all over the capital which seemed to re-enact the scenes of February 1793.[8]

In a letter written from prison in December 1796 Babeuf looked back on a year of lost opportunity, and he commented on the "wretched cowardice" of the second-line chiefs, who had failed to step into the breach and carry the insurrectional plans to a successful conclusion. But if the "high command" betrayed the trust of the "plebeian phalanxes," here and there a scattering of minor leaders proved themselves more courageous than Babeuf was prepared to allow.

The most vigorous efforts to pull the strings of the conspiracy together on the morrow of the arrests were made at first by Joseph

Monnard (a hatter and an old soldier of the Revolutionary Army). For a few days Monnard moved easily about the Faubourgs Saint-Denis and Saint-Antoine, surrounded by a tough and determined bodyguard which made his casual arrest improbable. Together with Sophie Lapierre, the revolutionary singer from the Bains Chinois Café, and her friend Marie Adélaide Lambert, Monnard organized a "rescue" operation for deserters and discharged soldiers of the Police Legion. "La fille Lambert" was credited alone with the recruiting of some 2,000 ex-legionaries, working from her apartment in a former convent near the Boulevard du Temple.

Monnard's final plan (concerted with Moroy and a few others) was for an uprising of the Faubourg Saint-Antoine to take place on 16 May. Agents scattered around the cabarets of the faubourg would rally separate parties to the army camp at Vincennes, where the mutinous troops (worked on by Fournier l'Américain and Fyon) would provide the necessary arms. Rossignol, who was in hiding, refused to sanction an uprising and when Monnard tried to go it alone, it turned out that police agents had penetrated this minor conspiracy as effectively as they had the main organization. Thus the attempted rally of the faubourg on the 16th was greeted only by another wave of arrests.[9]

The rôle of activist leader now seems to have passed to Cazin, who continued to organize resistance for a few weeks more from his stronghold in the Faubourg Saint-Antoine. Mme. Sergent provided another rallying point for the Babouvist underground at her house in the rue Neuve Egalité. A denunciation even claimed that she was in possession of a small arsenal of three dozen guns, and another (on 9 June) accused this "*jacobine enragée*" of acting as the treasurer of a collection taken up for the prisoners of the Temple.

Some of the agitation which continued to disturb Paris to the end of May and during the first days of June seems to have been the work of a "jury-rigged" revolutionary organization set up by Cazin and some of the other survivors. A police report of 4 June somewhat wildly credited the rebels with the possession of 20,000 guns, and claimed to have uncovered evidence of the existence of four revolutionary committees, one based on the Halles, one each for the Faubourgs Saint-Marceau and Saint-Germain, and another centered on the rue Montmartre.[10]

As the shock of the initial wave of arrests wore off, some of the rank-and-file agitators began to recover their spirit and to re-emerge into the streets. An agent on 21 May found about forty persons gathered in an angry group at the Porte Saint-Martin, an old center of Babouvist agitation, grumbling about the cost of food, the collapse of the assignats and the mandats, and the incompetence of the government. The sentiment of the crowd was that Babeuf must not perish; but if he did, many members of both councils would go with him. The following day there was a riot at the former Church of Saint-Elisabeth du Temple, now a workshop, where several hundred women were employed in the manufacture of sacks. According to one version of this incident, forty or fifty men armed with pistols and sabres broke into the workshop and harangued the workers to the effect that they were fools to go on toiling when, according to the Constitution of 1793, they had the right to divide up the property of the rich and live in leisure. The women immediately declared a strike, and armed detachments had to be called in before they were finally pacified.

Other evidence shows that there were determined attempts to stir the workers into action. Babouvist agitators were out at 6 a.m. on 24 May on the Pont Notre-Dame distributing pamphlets urging the overthrow of the government to men on their way to work. Another pamphlet was reportedly circulating on the 25th which called for the rescue of Babeuf and the completion of the insurrection; and on the 26th the police noted the presence of Babeuf's long-time disciple Robin in another group at the Porte Saint-Martin. By 7 June the agitation had developed a regular pattern, with crowds gathering at the Porte Saint-Martin during the day and in the evening along the river at the Pont au Change, and with continued attempts, especially by women, to win over the troops. A crowd at the Porte Saint-Martin threw stones at a police detachment sent to disperse them, and the police arrested the Babouvist militant Crespin (one-time president of the Club Electoral) as a ringleader.[11]

In the early hours of 9 June Cazin organized a secret conference of delegates from various parts of Paris in the rue Verte, off the boulevard de la Porte Antoine. It seems probable that this was yet another attempt to coordinate action for an uprising. However the following day Cazin was finally tracked down by the police and dispatched to the Temple. A fresh wave of arrests followed, as a result of which a further 300 "brigands" were picked up in the space of a month. By mid-June the last remnants of the Babouvist agitation appeared to have been crushed, and the government could proceed confidently with its plans to make an example of the ringleaders.[12]

For the moment the main weight of responsibility for the legal counterattack rested on the shoulders of André Gérard, director of the jury of presentment of the Canton of Paris. A man in his late thirties and a former *avocat au parlement* under the old régime, Gérard had served in the first months of the revolution as president of the District du Petit Saint-Antoine and as a member of the General Council of the Paris Commune. Disappointed in his political ambitions by the elections to the Legislative Assembly and out of sympathy with the Jacobin phase of the revolution, he had begun to lay the foundations of a new professional career after Thermidor; and he owed his appointment as judge on the Civil Tribunal of the Seine Département to the Directory. It was Gérard's task to piece together an indictment from the papers of the conspiracy and from the progressive interrogations of the accused and of witnesses. The accumulating material ultimately grew until it filled a whole carriage. As the investigation proceeded fresh names were steadily added to the list, until Gérard's final indictment covered fifty-four persons. The paperwork took Gérard's two assistants two months to complete, often working night and day.[13]

There seems little doubt that Gérard's task was made easier by the admissions Babeuf had already volunteered to Cochon immediately after his arrest. On 23 May, for example, Gérard was able to open his first interrogation of Babeuf by confronting him with his letter offering to negotiate with the Directory. Faced with this evidence, Babeuf probably would have done best to adopt a plan of reserving his defense and refusing to offer any further assistance to the inquiry. Instead, adroitly encouraged by Gérard, he plunged into justifications and explanations. Yes, there had been a conspiracy to overthrow the government; yes, he Babeuf had been a party to it; but he was prepared to defend the conspirators' motives in public and before the "jury of the centuries." Gérard, however, was mistaken to suppose that he, Babeuf, had acted as the chief of the conspiracy or had even played a leading rôle. He had been recruited simply to take charge of propaganda as *"directeur de l'esprit public."* Thus he had had no knowledge of any insurrectional plans, and no part in receiving agents' reports, drafting proscription lists, or naming members of the new government. In all things he had acted as a subordinate of the leaders of the conspiracy, whom, however, he refused to name. In short Babeuf's defense was that what he had personally done was justified; what others had planned and done was not his responsibility.

Such a position presented an obvious opportunity to break the unity of the defense, and Gérard was quick to respond. With every appearance of sympathetic interest he began to probe the delicate area of the conspirators' plans for an insurrectional dictatorship. How was it, he asked, that such true and pure democrats had managed to bring themselves so blatantly to propose to usurp the inalienable and imprescriptible rights of the sovereign people?

Babeuf's response was revealing. Firstly, he dissociated himself from the decision. He was, he explained, only a "writing member" and not a "deliberating member" of the rebel organization. Secondly, he declared that those who had adopted the principle of dictatorship had done so as a provisional measure, effective only as long as the majority of the people remained apathetic and misguided.[14]

In his eagerness to exculpate himself individually and to vindicate the purity of his own democratic convictions, Babeuf had thus volunteered a valuable piece of evidence which could be used against the defendants as a group. Few of the other defendants were so cooperative. Darthé refused to answer Gérard at all, and he counseled the others to do the same. Germain, Buonarroti, Didier and Massard denied everything, as did Laignelot, Vadier, Amar, Lamberté, the Duplays and most of the other chief suspects. Moroy alone followed Babeuf's example by admitting almost everything, while refusing to name his accomplices. Cazin admitted his own part in the conspiracy but denied that there was any intention of spilling blood. Pierre Philip agreed that he knew of the conspiracy's existence, but declared that he was not a party to it. Only one of the prisoners broke down completely before Gérard and agreed to turn state's evidence: Nicolas Pillé, who had acted as secretary and copyist for the Insurrectional Committee. Together with that of Grisel, Pillé's testimony provided the cornerstone of the prosecution's case.[15]

Grisel himself was proving something of a problem. Having already betrayed both sides, he now trusted nobody, and he began to panic in case he found himself betrayed in turn by the Directory once he had served his purpose as a witness. He wrote to Carnot on 2 July to seek reassurance, complaining that rumors were circulating that he had been a convinced member of the conspiracy and had only hastily denounced its existence after losing his agent's commission. Carnot responded with a public declaration of confidence in Grisel and a refutation of these "slanders," which was printed in the *Rédacteur*; he also, apparently, arranged that the commission would disappear permanently from the evidence. Reassured, Grisel continued to cooperate with Gérard; and on 16 July, after the jury presentment was completed, he received a further 3,000 livres in mandats for his services.[16]

Grisel's testimony was read over to Babeuf, who this time did reserve his defense. He demanded to confront all hostile witnesses personally (as provided by the operative law code of 3 brumaire). On 10 July Babeuf drew up a formal but unheeded protest on the same lines on behalf of Cazin, Moroy, Buonarroti, Didier, and Massard. Germain had already made a similar point. Darthé, always consistent, had simply refused to listen to the witnesses' testimony.[17]

By 11 July Gérard was ready to present his indictment, and a special jury of eight was convened at the Palais de Justice. Early on the morning of the 12th, after deliberating overnight, the jury declared its findings: there had been a conspiracy, and there was a case to answer against all the defendants. The jurors had clearly taken a very formal view of their functions; there had hardly been time to question the thirty-one witnesses adequately, or to review the mass of written evidence against more than fifty defendants. The defendants would eventually protest against this apparently lighthearted and uncritical acceptance of the government's case. They were also able to point to a number of technical flaws in Gérard's procedure: his refusal to allow the confrontation of witnesses by the accused; the illegal citing of Grisel as a witness in a case in which he was the denunciator; the completion of formal detention orders against all the accused dated 23 messidor (11 July), when the jury did not pronounce until 24 messidor. It was charged also that some jurors had been intimidated by the "prevalence of bayonets," and others swayed by bribery (two sumptuous "orgies" laid on by the prosecution). At the time, however, the prisoners could hardly have expected a different outcome and, indeed, it is hard to see how any jury not composed of hand-picked Jacobins would have arrived at any other decision.[18]

The normal procedure after the verdict of the jury of presentment would have been for the prisoners to be sent for trial before their "natural judges," in most cases the Criminal Tribunal of the Seine Département. The implication of Drouet in the conspiracy, however, raised a difficulty. Drouet was a member of the Council of Five Hundred; and the Constitution of the Year III provided that members of the two legislative councils should be tried before a specially convened high court presided over by a panel of judges from the Cour de

Cassation, the highest national appeals court. Since it would be necessary to set up such a court for the one defendant, the Directory decided to maintain the unity of the prosecution by sending the rest of the accused before the high court as well. After some debate in the councils, the proclamation establishing the court was published on 7 August.

To ensure that proceedings would be free from political and popular pressures, the constitution had provided that the high court be convened at a locality not less than 120 kilometers from Paris. The place chosen was Vendôme, a small provincial town on the Loir river, about 150 kilometers southwest of the capital. Arrangements were put in hand to transport the prisoners there towards the end of August.

The decision to resort to high court procedures was not made on technical grounds alone. Not only would it have been possible to have tried the defendants in separate courts; but after the middle of August it would have been more logical to have done so. On 17 August Drouet escaped from the Abbaye under suspicious circumstances, and it was generally rumored that Barras had helped to arrange his escape.[19] Thus the principal defendant, for whom the entire proceedings had been arranged, never appeared before the court at Vendôme at all. The government went ahead with the high court trial nevertheless. From the standpoint of Carnot and the government, a "show trial" of the conspirators seemed to offer many solid political advantages. It would demonstrate to the propertied classes that the Directory was determined to act as a bulwark against "anarchism" and to hold the remnants of Jacobin fanaticism firmly in check. The agony of the defendants would also act as an object lesson to the many ex-Jacobins who had rallied uneasily to the Directory after Vendémiaire. The age of wild and millenarian fantasies was past, and the Directory was now the only possible alternative to a royalist restoration. There was also another aspect to Vendôme. By adhering to the legal forms in such a demonstrative and public manner, the Directory was making an important political statement. The era of the Terrors, both Jacobin and Thermidorian, was over. The rule of law, firmly based on the Constitution of the Year III and defended by a scrupulous executive, had now been at last securely established. Thus the proceedings at Vendôme were intended to consolidate the reputation of the Directory as a régime of property, order, law, and liberty.

Rather less delicate methods were invoked to stamp out the last embers of the revolutionary movement in Paris. Throughout the summer of 1796 popular discontent continued to smolder in the faubourgs; and despite a steady stream of arrests, remnants of the Babouvist party remained active. The garrison also continued to provide cause for alarm, particularly the camp at Grenelle, where the ten thousand troops, bored, inactive, and chronically short of money, offered a ready target for agitators, whether Babouvists or government *agents-provocateurs*.

As always, members of the former Police Legion provided the nucleus of discontent. Louis-Jacques-Philippe Blondeau, the former ringleader of the Police Legion mutiny, attempted at the end of June to take up the threads of the conspiracy once again, working the cafés near the Invalides barracks. On 25 and 26 June he was busy canvassing a plan for an attack on the Directory and the councils, to be spearheaded by the Invalides garrison, with the support of "thirty thousand workers." Grisel wrote to the Directory on 15 July to warn that a dangerous situation was developing at Grenelle. He also offered a soldier's solution—less guard duty and more leave. The police had other ideas. The *Courrier républicain* reported (on 23 July) that the leaders of the sedition at Grenelle had been arrested (and one had suicided by jumping in the Seine). A hundred and eighty soldiers had been discharged and sent home under guard, but all had reputedly escaped at Versailles and for the most part made their way back to Paris. According to the *Courrier*, the crisis had been caused by the refusal of some troops to accept their pay in mandats, the new paper currency, and of others to carry out the execution of convicted men sentenced to the firing squad.[20]

The Grenelle deserters helped to strengthen the ranks of the Babouvist supporters in Paris, who now began to appear openly in public places again. On 22 and 24 July parties of *"anarchistes"* armed with sticks were reported to be gathering on the riverside Terrasse of the Tuileries gardens, with Marie-Anne Babeuf prominent among the leaders. Copies of a continuation of the *Tribun du peuple* (under the title *Le Décius français*) were allegedly distributed at the Terrasse gatherings. On 26 July the *Messager du soir* reported crowds once more at the Porte Saint-Martin, as well as the Terrasse; and these two localities continued to be centers of anti-government agitation throughout the remaining weeks of the summer.[21]

The proclamation establishing the high court on 7 August, foreshadowing the imminent removal of the prisoners from Paris, directed the attention of the Babouvists to the urgent task of rescuing

The skirmish at the Grenelle encampment

their imprisoned leaders. Almost immediately, the police received a report of an attempt planned for the following day. False orders were to be presented at the Temple and the Abbaye, and the imprisoned leaders were to be spirited off to Grenelle, whence a new "Tenth of August" would be mounted against the government. Nothing came of this plan, whether it was real or imaginary. But at the end of August the Babouvist "underground" learned of plans for the immediate transport of all the prisoners to Vendôme. A desperate attempt was staged to intercept the convoy from the Temple. The central feature of this plan was a simulated royalist plot for a general massacre of revolutionaries. Royalist standards were planted in various parts of the city, and a number of bombs were prepared which were to be set off in the small hours of the morning of 30 August at a prearranged signal. Under cover of the inevitable confusion a picked party of several hundred men would attack the convoy guards and rescue the prisoners. There was some attempt to carry out this plan. One of the flag-planters was arrested and Arnoux (one-time member of the revolutionary committee of the Arcis Section) blew half his head away with one of the bombs. But apart from these alarms the convoy left on its way to Vendôme without incident.[22]

Despite the pitiful fiasco of the "royalist plot" and the exile of their leaders, the Babouvists were not yet completely disheartened. The Grenelle camp remained as a last reserve. While disaffection persisted among the garrison, the Babouvist diehards could continue to dream of an apocalyptic *journée* in which the workers of the faubourgs and the defenders of the Fatherland would march, shoulder to shoulder, to put an end to the rule of the tyrants of the Luxembourg.

The reality was to differ sadly from this splendid vision. A small army of *sans-culottes* from all over Paris, variously estimated at from 400 to 800 strong, gathered on the evening of 9 September in a group of cabarets and drinking shops in Vaugirard, close to Grenelle. The headquarters of the operation appears to have been the Soleil d'Or in the rue Vaugirard, and the leaders included Babouvist stalwarts like General Fyon and Bertrand (the ex-mayor of Lyons) as well as veteran section militants like Jacques Eudes (of the Droits de l'Homme Section) and Sandoz (of the Unité Section). They also included a considerable sprinkling of police agents, who had given ample warning that an attempt to rouse the camp would be made that night.

The insurgents appear to have hoped to begin by winning over the 21st Dragoons, a cavalry detachment which had formerly served as the cavalry of the Police Legion. When they broke into the camp shortly before midnight they chose this unit's lines as the point of entry. Their appeals for a fraternal rally to the Constitution of 1793 were greeted by shots and a sabre charge. Twenty were killed on the spot and fifty captured; and the others withdrew behind the cover of the walls and hedges of the gardens of Vaugirard, carrying some of their dead and wounded. About the same time an appeal to the Invalides veterans in the heart of Paris was reputedly thwarted by the cool nerve of a sergeant, who arrested the rebel leader in front of the men.[23]

Some historians, following Buonarroti, have attributed the entire Grenelle affair to the work of *agents-provocateurs* in the pay of Barras, Carnot, or Cochon. All three certainly knew what was afoot and *agents-provocateurs* were very active in the preparations. It is most likely, however, that the Grenelle episode was not entirely a manufactured affair, but that this time the plan of allowing the conspiracy to come to a head was followed. In the resulting wave of arrests more than 130 survivors were picked up and consigned to the Temple prison. The government wasted no time on protracted legal proceedings for these "rank-and-file" conspirators. Instead, they were tried during September and October before military commissions (a form of summary procedure originally introduced to deal with the royalist rebels of the Vendée and the Chouans). Thirty received death sentences, while the remainder were put behind bars "until the peace."[24]

Alone among the 132 prisoners included in an official list, two sergeants from the fourth battalion of the Aisne regiment represented the participation of the Grenelle garrison. Put to the test, the defenders of the Fatherland had refused to move. They were duly rewarded by being allowed to divide out the cash of the dead and the prisoners. It worked out at 21 livres each.[25]

Nineteen

Vendôme

T he pace of the proceedings against the principal conspirators was in marked contrast to the summary treatment of the Grenelle rebels. By the end of August they had already spent three months in prison under a strict régime, with visits even by close relatives forbidden. In the end the majority of those tried at Vendôme were acquitted, but it was not until May 1797 that the court reached its verdict. Thus guilty and innocent alike were compelled to endure a year's imprisonment in the shadow of the guillotine, for the charges on which they were arraigned carried the death penalty. The discovery that the government was determined to adhere to the legal formalities was small consolation to defendants acutely conscious that theirs was a political trial, with the scales heavily weighted against them by prejudice throughout.

The circumstances of the transfer to Vendôme were a cruel reminder that, whatever the legal pretenses, the authorities regarded the prisoners more or less as a species of dangerous wild beast in need of restraint and punishment. The prisoners traveled in two convoys. The first convoy, comprising about two dozen of the less important captives, set off from the Abbaye on 27 August and arrived in Vendôme on the evening of the 30th. The second convoy left the Temple two days later with Babeuf, Buonarroti, and the other principal leaders, together with five women prisoners. Germain has left a graphic account of the progress of this second convoy.

On the evening of 27 August a general arrived at the Temple with a strong escort, bearing a message from Bénézech (the minister of the interior) which promised to attend to any complaints and to treat the prisoners with humanity. Unimpressed, the prisoners responded by inviting the general to visit the stinking *tourelle* in which one of them slept, a cell eight feet square into which light penetrated only at midday. Next Mme. Lasne, the concierge's wife, handed over the pitifully small sum of money scraped together by relatives and supporters to ease the hardships of the journey. The prisoners were not allowed to receive any visitors or to bid farewell to their families. However on the following day (28 August), the precincts of the Temple were crowded with the prisoners' relations and friends, who joined in the singing of revolutionary songs, and discipline was relaxed enough to allow for demonstrative scenes. The prisoners were still singing in the early hours of the following morning when the representatives of the police central bureau arrived to supervise the departure. Before leaving, each prisoner was subjected to a humiliating public search, which elicited several morsels of bread and also some secreted weapons: a brick, two tiles, and a piece of copper piping.[1]

In the 1790s the 150-kilometer journey from Paris to Vendôme normally took two full days by coach. The two wagons by which the prisoners were to travel were much slower and, inevitably, much less comfortable. They were a kind of four-wheeled cart, without springs and with wooden seats, enclosed on all sides, pulled by a team of horses. The windows were barred but there were blinds which could be closed by the inmates. The convoy left the Temple about 3 a.m. after Dossonville had tried to bid each prisoner a formal farewell. Almost exactly a year later, after the *coup d'état* of Fructidor, Dossonville would find himself inside one of the same wagons, on his way to exile to Cayenne.

Babeuf was in the leading wagon with Buonarroti, Germain, Darthé, Didier, Massard, Moroy, and Cazin. The second was occupied by Sophie Lapierre and four other women, together with the two Duplays, Pottofeux, and one other. There was also a guard in each wagon. According to Germain, Pesnant (the commander of the escort) was ill-disposed towards the prisoners and determined to make their trip as unpleasant as possible. He must also have been somewhat on edge in view of the rescue plot which had been discovered.

Leaving the heavily guarded streets of Paris the convoy was soon rolling along the rue de Chaillot on the way to Versailles, where there was another heavy turn-out of troops. With the dawn the prisoners began to sing again (encouraged by the cavalry guard, to Pesnant's irritation). The commandant retaliated by refusing to stop to allow the prisoners to relieve themselves and, to the disgust of the troops, mocking the men and women as they performed their functions in public. When the convoy halted for lunch at Trappes about noon Pesnant became drunk and decided to stage a political occasion; but the crowd which gathered to hear his denunciatory speech cheered when the prisoners struck up a revolutionary anthem, and it had to be dispersed.

The first day's journey ended at Rambouillet, a royalist town, where the prisoners were in fear of massacre and where Pesnant personally selected the filthiest cell he could find for them in the municipal jail and refused to provide mattresses or to allow adequate ventilation. The following morning one of the prisoners was so ill that he had to be carried out. A local official, a retired officer called Saint-Victor, quarreled with Pesnant and insisted on accompanying the convoy all the way to Vendôme to check on their future treatment. By lunch-time on the 29th the prisoners had traveled as far as Maintenon, where a party of wives had already arrived on their way to Vendôme. Pesnant, however, refused to allow any contact. Dinner that evening was at Chartres; a party of *jeunesse dorée* turned out to jeer, but the municipal officers were friendly. Sleeping quarters were arranged at the "gothic habitation of the duc de Luynes" at Châteaudun.

The following day relations between Pesnant and his men, never good, became even more strained when they reached Pézou for lunch. They found that no provision had been made for either men or horses, and some asked for the words of the songs the prisoners had been singing along the route. As a result the last stage of the journey, from Pézou to Vendôme, took the form of a strange triumphal procession, with prisoners and troops joining in the choruses of seditious songs as the prison wagons creaked along. The convoy finally entered Vendôme at 6 p.m. via the rue Chartraine and the rue des Hommes Libres (rue du Change), making its way to the former Benedictine abbey of La Trinité, where the prisoners were locked in cells built into the old refectory hall. The town's inhabitants, who had witnessed the arrival of the first convoy two days earlier, crowded the streets and balconies to enjoy the new spectacle, but they greeted the passage of the convoy with silence.[2]

With a population of scarcely more than six thousand, Vendôme was a sleepy market town and administrative center close enough to the Vendée to ensure republican orthodoxy, yet with few active native Jacobins. Nervously, on 15 August, the Directory had laid down a list of security measures in preparation for the trial: a garrison of at least 1,000 infantry and 100 cavalry (with two cannon) to reinforce the gendarmerie, together with a detachment of the Paris fire-brigade (with two pumps). All visitors were to register with the municipal administration, and no resident was to leave town without an official passport. There were further restrictions exiling several broad categories of dangerous "Jacobin" suspects to a distance of at least thirty miles from the town.

During the first weeks of September the Vendômois were astonished to see the town take on a siege atmosphere. Military picquets appeared on the three bridges and in the public squares, all boats which could not be moved were sunk in the channels of the Loir, and the town gates were closed and guarded every night. Later, during the winter months, the streets were illuminated by powerful oil lamps at dusk. Soon, from his headquarters in the château, Chef de Brigade Lestranges commanded a force of two battalions of infantry and a squadron of cavalry, not to mention the gendarmes and the pompiers.[3]

The prime target of the exile order was the leader of the local Jacobins, Pierre-Nicolas Hésine, who had served until recently as *commissaire* of the Directory to the cantonal administration of Vendôme. Hésine was a former professor of mathematics at the military school of Pontlevoy, and had first established a reputation as a Jacobin militant at Blois during 1793 and 1794. After a period of imprisonment as a terrorist in Paris in 1795, he had been released after Vendémiaire. Sent back to Vendôme to consolidate the Directory's control over the town and to keep the resurgent royalism of the surrounding countryside in check, in his zeal in rebuilding the National Guard and arming his Jacobin friends Hésine had overstepped the mark; and at the beginning of June 1796 he had been removed from his post.[4] Driven from Vendôme by the exile order, Hésine went to live with a sister at Pontlevoy; his wife remained in Vendôme, and the Hésine house in the rue du Mail became a rallying center for the relatives and friends of the Babouvist prisoners. It was here that Babeuf's third son, "Cassius Graccus," was born on 28 January 1797.

Five months pregnant, and accompanied by the 10-year-old Emile, Marie-Anne had made her way on foot from Paris with a party of wives at the beginning of September, to begin yet another prison-gate vigil. The little "Babouvist" community at Vendôme included Citoyennes Didier, Duplay, Pottofeux, Vadier and Laignelot, and Buonarroti's mistress Thérèse Poggi. Later Vadier's son was also allowed to stay in Vendôme as his father's defense counsel, as was Henri Jaume, who was defending Ricord. The Hésines provided a link with a group of local sympathizers who included the Ballyers, father and son, who voluntarily acted as unpaid defense counsel for some of the accused, and Catherinet (*ex-commissaire* of the Directory to the Canton of Villiers), who represented Pillé. Until his arrest in March 1797 Hésine himself continued to act as a kind of Jacobin "scarlet pimpernel," turning up in Vendôme in disguise from time to time, organizing contacts between the prisoners and the outside world, printing their protests, and even bringing out a journal of the trial, which ran to seventy-three numbers.[5]

The prosecution was also setting up its unofficial headquarters. At the beginning of 1797 Dufort de Cheverny paid a visit to Vendôme out of curiosity, and he was invited to breakfast with an old friend, Charles Pajon, one of the five judges of the high court. He discovered that Pajon was sharing the same lodgings, and indeed a common table, with Gandon, the president of the court, Lalande, one of the *suppléant* judges, and Viellart, the chief public prosecutor, an arrangement which no doubt assisted in the smooth settlement of procedural difficulties, but was hardly in the best interests of the defense.[6]

Vendôme was situated on an island formed by a division of the Loir into two arms, which later rejoined beyond the town. The Abbaye de la Trinité, more recently known as the Palais National, the building in which the Babouvists were imprisoned, marked the point where the river divided. The abbey gate was on the west side, leading on to the Place des Armes, beyond which lay the town. The south side overlooked a terrace and gardens sloping down to the river, in normal times a favorite Sunday promenade where the citizens of Vendôme could listen to musicians playing from a bandstand. The opposite bank of the river was dominated by the "Montagne," a steep hill crowned by a ruined castle, another popular recreation spot.

The abbey was intended to serve as the seat of the high court as well as a prison, and extensive alterations were necessary on both counts. The architect, Lemit, had descended on Vendôme from Paris, gathered a scratch team of workmen and begun operations on 15 August. Within the shell of the old buildings room had to be found for the principal audience chamber, two smaller council and deliberation rooms for the judges' use, and a suite of three rooms for the jury. At the same time separate individual cells had to be built into existing rooms for forty to fifty prisoners, and the whole place made safe from escape or rescue attempts. Even with the men working in three shifts round the clock (and the authorities exerting maximum pressure), the necessary alterations took several months to complete.[7]

Lemit planned a main audience chamber on the first floor 100 feet long by 30 feet wide, approached by a specially built public stairway from the abbey churchyard, next to the Place des Armes. The prisoners were to be accommodated on two levels. The least salubrious and first-occupied cells were on the ground floor, some of them damp and close to the latrines, but on 14 September most of the prisoners were moved to the first floor and henceforth relegation to the ground floor was used as a punishment for the exceptionally recalcitrant. On each floor the main suites of cells were aligned along a central corridor, but there were also intermediate divisions so that the ground floor had an eastern and a western corridor; and there was a separate women's section. Under the normal régime the prisoners were free to use their corridors during the day from 8 a.m. until about half an hour before nightfall. They were then allowed candles to enable them to work on their defense in their cells until "lights out" at 9 p.m. The former abbey cloister provided an exercise yard, where small groups were allowed out for up to an hour at a time. At the beginning of 1797 Dufort de Cheverny saw some of the prisoners there playing a form of quoits. On 21 January another exercise group celebrated the anniversary of the king's execution by dancing a *carmagnole* in the cloister.[8]

Compared with the prisons of the Terror or with a contemporary English jail, the abbey was in many ways a model prison. Provision was made for regular medical inspection and for the issue of clean linen. Staff were allocated to clean out the cells and corridors, and kitchens were set up to feed the prisoners. To some of the inmates, including Babeuf, the rations must have seemed almost sumptuous: a basic ration of a pound and a half of bread per day, with another four ounces given out with soup, a thick soup at midday for lunch, a stew or a roast with salad or vegetables and a half bottle of wine for supper at 7 p.m. Dufort de Cheverny made a point of visiting the kitchens, inspecting the meat and tasting the wine, and noted that the chef was a former royal cook. Needless to say this last consideration did not prevent the prisoners from complaining about the quality of the food from time to time. It was, however, probably a great deal

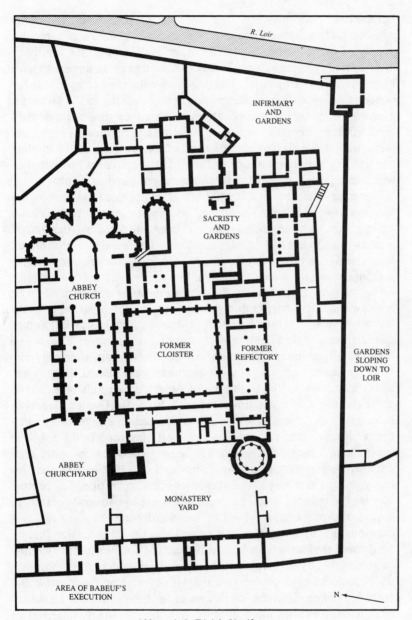

R. Loir

INFIRMARY
AND
GARDENS

SACRISTY
AND
GARDENS

ABBEY
CHURCH

FORMER
CLOISTER

FORMER
REFECTORY

GARDENS
SLOPING
DOWN TO
LOIR

ABBEY
CHURCHYARD

MONASTERY
YARD

AREA OF BABEUF'S
EXECUTION

N

Abbaye de la Trinité, Vendôme

better than working-class families ate in the town. By doing without certain items Babeuf was even able to send out a regular supply of bread, wine, meat, and other provisions to his family.[9]

The prison régime at Vendôme does not, in general, appear to have been unduly strict or cruel. The prisoners continued to assemble for concerts of revolutionary songs, music and dancing in the evenings. Meanwhile, planning escape attempts or concerting the defense's legal strategy kept the prisoners busy and their morale high. Yet there was also a darker side of the picture: wearied by the endless frustrations and humiliations of their life the prisoners lost patience with their jailers, defied them, and were punished in return.

Germain was the first to suffer, after threatening one of the warders with a bench. The attack took place soon after Germain learned that his young wife, Julie, had been murdered by "brigands," leaving his 3-year-old child parentless. The result of the attack was a sentence of ten days' solitary in irons (although some of the sentence was afterwards remitted).[10]

Babeuf was punished for the first time on 31 January, when he was awarded five days' solitary for joining a prohibited party in the women's quarters together with Blondeau; the hostesses, Sophie Lapierre and Adélaide Lambert, were also punished. The prison medical officer insisted that Babeuf be allowed out after only two days for health reasons: only the corridors were heated. Babeuf was again in trouble at the beginning of March as a result of a quarrel arising out of a long standing feud with the cook. The feud seems to have begun in December when Babeuf, placed on a vegetable diet by the medical officer, refused the cook's offerings and broke a dish in the ensuing struggle. Subsequently he caused difficulties more than once by deliberately smashing dishes and other objects to vent his frustration. There was a final tragi-comic confrontation. The routine was for the cook to set off each evening for the prisoners' quarters in a kind of procession, followed by two warders and two sentries and accompanied by a boy carrying a great pot. On this occasion Babeuf announced that he had broken his plates. The cook impatiently refused to supply any more, and in a fury Babeuf tendered his chamberpot, which the cook promptly filled with everything (soup, stew and entrée), then received the lot thrown at his head in return. In the sequel Babeuf was awarded another five days' solitary, deprived of wine for the duration, and restricted to wooden plates henceforth.[11]

Other prisoners were occasionally punished with solitary confinement, in one case for as long as sixteen days. But there was no deliberate brutality or torture, and in general the conduct of the prison was as civilized as was possible in the circumstances.

For many of the prisoners the continued separation from their families, after the stringent régime of the Temple, was the harshest aspect of prison life at Vendôme. Soon after the transfer the abbey was opened for visits for an hour a day, but this concession lasted for only two days before the concierge announced on 10 September that the visits would be discontinued until a new round of interrogations had been completed. Babeuf in particular took the new separation hard, as he joined other prisoners in pathetic attempts to spot Marie-Anne (and Emile) as she walked with the other wives on the Montagne on the other bank of the river. On 4 October he wrote to say that he had at last made both of them out, with the aid of a borrowed lorgnette.[12]

Babeuf was particularly anxious about Emile, who seemed to be running wild in the streets, and he devoted several letters to arrangements for his son's education. He was not to attend the public school, but to study at home; he was to send the exercises to his father for correction, together with a daily account of the way he spent his time. For exercise and distraction he might try taking his mother for occasional walks. But such adjurations were far from solving the problem satisfactorily, and in the end Babeuf proposed a remarkable remedy—Emile should join him in the abbey, so that his father could supervise his schooling personally. Babeuf explained that he had a well-sited and airy room, there was a long corridor to walk or even run in, and more than enough food for two. What Emile and Marie-Anne thought of this suggestion is not recorded, but nothing came of it; and Babeuf did not see his wife or his son again until 5 November, when he was at last allowed routine visits. During the next month Marie-Anne was given passes to visit every other day, from noon until 2 p.m. For some of the other prisoners, whose interrogations had been completed earlier, visits had been permitted since the middle of October, in a specially built *parloir*. The visiting hours were always a headache for the guards, with inevitable attempts to smuggle messages and occasionally riotous behavior by the visitors.[13]

Maintaining the security of the prison demanded unremitting vigilance from the authorities. One of Cochon's special agents, Bourdon, arrived in Vendôme from Paris on 3 September, and he lost no time in writing back for reinforcements. While the reconstruction was under way the prison was unsafe, he reported; the 15-year-old

adopted son of the concierge was in the pay of the prisoners and
carrying their correspondence; one window had been carefully constructed by an artisan sympathizer so that the spaces between the
bars were wider than the prisoners' heads; a locksmith must be sent
from Paris. On 18 September, after a first escape attempt, the prison
windows were strengthened by the addition of horizontal to the existing vertical bars.

In a very successful smuggling operation the workmen employed
on the building alterations were steadily passing over a useful supply
of tools to the prisoners. Babeuf's corridor was responsible for a
major escape attempt, discovered only after the prisoners had
driven a tunnel through a stone wall which would have led out to the
roof of the cloisters and thence to the walls of the abbey church. The
tunnel was discovered on 19 January, but only a day or so later
Babeuf was smuggling out code instructions to Marie-Anne to try to
bribe one of the guards. During February several of the bars in the
women's quarters were discovered to be loose, with one removable at
will. Even though these escape plans never quite worked there was
always the alternative hope of a rescue attempt from the town.
Daude, the concierge, complained of the skill of the Babouvist sympathizers who were agitating among the workers and soldiers, playing on delays in pay for the workers at the abbey and demoralizing the soldiers on guard outside the building by spreading ghost
stories.[14]

Dufort de Cheverny was convinced that the infantry garrison,
despite two changes, had been "worked on" by the hand of "a
master" and was completely unreliable. Only the gendarmes and the
20th Regiment of Cavalry stood between the court and the uncertain
loyalties of the Vendômois.[15] Such reflections may have made the
authorities extra cautious in their treatment of the prisoners in open
court; but they do not seem to have been based on any material
possibility of a rising in the town or an attack on the abbey. Although
there were rumors from the capital from time to time, the Grenelle
fiasco made the likelihood of a revolution in Paris opening the doors
of the prison quite remote.

Failing escape, rescue, or political revolution, the only course
remaining open was to take the legalistic preoccupations of the
Directory at their face value, and to organize a formal defense which
would sabotage and discredit the prosecution's case. The problem
here was that it soon became apparent that different groups of
prisoners had varying interests which could not be easily reconciled.

The evidence against Babeuf, Darthé, Buonarroti, Germain, and some of the other leaders of the original conspiracy was strong. From their point of view the best strategy was to fight every legal point to the death and to use obstructive tactics to prolong the trial as long as possible. In the meantime events outside the court might move in the defendants' favor. The elections of the spring of 1797 might produce a swing to the left; the balance of power in the Directory might shift to their advantage; perhaps, even, the Jacobin party might in the end revive and overthrow the government.

At the other extreme, there were a number of defendants conscious of their own innocence and convinced that the court could only vindicate them. The only desire of this group (as of the traitor, Pillé) was for the least possible delay in the proceedings and their inevitable subsequent acquittal. Of equal significance was the conflict of interest between the nucleus of the original Equals and the Montagnards, whose involvement in the conspiracy had been a matter of momentary political tactics rather than of shared ideals. For Babeuf and those closest to him the Vendôme trial presented a valuable opportunity for propaganda, and their intention was not to admit conspiracy as a crime but to proclaim it as a civic duty, to justify their political stand, and to defend the principles of communism.

For the Montagnards, on the other hand, to admit participation in a communist conspiracy would have been the height of folly. The general propaganda line of the survivors of the republican Left since May had been to ridicule the "Babeuf plot" as a fantastic invention of the Directory, and to explain away evidence of communist aims as no more than utopian speculation. It was possible that a successful development of this line might save the necks of a great number of prisoners who would be doomed if Babeuf's tactics of open avowal were followed. The Equals themselves were sharply divided on this question. Antonelle, who joined the other prisoners at the end of November, published several pamphlets which dismissed the speculations of the Equals as "castles in Spain," not to be taken seriously. Babeuf's anger and disgust at this "betrayal" were expressed in a letter to Hésine, and Germain made it painfully clear that he was determined that the Montagnards should be forced to face the music along with the others. Buonarroti, on the other hand, took his cue from Antonelle and ranged himself with the Montagnard party.[16]

Such divisions did not make for friendly relations in the prison corridors, and the first few months at the abbey were in fact marked by dissension and controversy. According to the police agent Bourdon the prisoners customarily met together in separate small groups of no more than four, six, eight or twelve at the most. Bourdon also took pleasure in reporting the details of a particular quarrel in which the mutual distrust of the different groups of prisoners was clearly revealed. On this occasion the prisoners had sent back their meal in protest, declaring that they would only eat the bread. When the Montagnards then bought themselves another supper, Babeuf's group declared that they "did not find this astonishing" since the others "had always belonged to the party only for themselves."[17]

Despite these tensions there was nevertheless a considerable amount of effective cooperation in the preliminary legal skirmishing which preceded the opening of the formal public trial. The first session of the court was held on 5 October 1796 after workmen had worked all night, by the light of flares, to prepare a provisional courtroom at the abbey and to tidy up the public approaches. To dignify the proceedings "a spectacle of majestic symmetry" (as a contemporary observer described it) was staged: a procession of administrative and legal dignitaries, escorted by cavalry, gendarmerie, infantry, the National Guard, and the Paris pompiers. The cortege moved through the Place Saint-Martin to the Place des Armes, where the members of the court were saluted by a salvo of artillery before entering the abbey. The first day's proceedings were held in public, and were concerned with formalities. The president, Gandon, and his four co-judges heard an opening address by Viellart; the *greffier*, Jalbert, read out the laws and decrees establishing the court and regulating its procedure; and the oaths were taken. Then the court adjourned, with more shooting of cannon and yet another procession to wind up the ceremonies. In all this the prisoners had played no part.

The first important business before the court was the examination of a formal protest against its competence drawn up by the prisoners immediately on their arrival at Vendôme and adhered to by almost all of them. The central argument of this submission was that the resort to high court procedure for accused who were not members of the councils or of the government violated the constitutional provision which guaranteed the citizen the right to trial before his natural judges, in this case the ordinary tribunals established under the Constitution of the Year III. In setting up a special court after the offense, the Council of Five Hundred had been guilty of *ex post facto* legislation which violated both the letter and spirit of the constitution.

Some of the consequent legal anomalies were explored in detail. It was planned that contumacious fugitives apprehended after the high court had been dissolved would be sent before their natural judges, and would have the normal recourse of appeal to the Cour de Cassation, whereas there was no appeal for the main body of the accused who were to appear before the high court. How was this to be reconciled with the basic principle that the law was equal for all citizens? The only jury of presentment competent to establish a *prima facie* case against a defendant in the high court was the Council of Five Hundred and the Council of Ancients. But none of the defendants, except Drouet, had in fact been indicted before the councils. Whereas the constitution guaranteed appeal from *all* tribunals to the Cour de Cassation, the Council of Five Hundred had arbitrarily ruled out an appeal from the high court, partly on the grounds that this might take up to three years to complete. Men's lives, it was protested, were not counted for nothing in this way in England—where Warren Hastings' trial had lasted for seven years. The text of this protest was smuggled out of the abbey and published by Hésine and later by René Vatar in Paris.[18] Its critique of the bastard offspring of the Directory's attempt to crossbreed normal and special legal procedures was cogent and well argued, even if the appeal to the independence of the judiciary and to the sanctity of the constitution on behalf of a band of unrepentant terrorists and advocates of revolutionary dictatorship had a certain irony. To succeed, however, such an appeal would have required a remarkable bench of judges, prepared to take a stand against the Directory, the councils, and their own prejudices, in favor of the "enemies of civilization" they were called upon to judge.

The high court was presided over by five judges elected from a panel chosen by lot from the members of the national appeals court, the Cour de Cassation. The president of the court, Yves-Marie Nicolas Gandon, a former *avocat* of the Parlement of Rennes in Brittany, was in his early fifties at the time of the trial. (He died in 1834 at the respectable age of 89, having achieved according to one biography "nothing but a few anecdotes.") Although he owed his elevation to the Cour de Cassation to the Directory, Gandon was to prove himself a man of ready political accommodation under future régimes. Bonaparte made him a senator and gave him a Légion d'Honneur; yet this did not prevent him from rallying to Louis XVIII. Throughout the Vendôme trial, while preserving the forms, Gandon showed consistent hostility towards the defendants.[19]

Of the other four judges Joseph Coffinhal (whose brother Pierre-

André had been guillotined after Thermidor as a member of Robespierre's Revolutionary Tribunal) was the only one tainted with "Jacobinism," and was probably doubly cautious in consequence. Charles Pajon de la Chambaudière was an aristocrat who had first emerged into the public eye as a member of the provincial assembly of the Orléannais in 1788; Audier-Massillon was a former high legal official of the Royal Sénéchaussé Court of Aix-en-Provence.

The judges' ruling on the defendants' protest was delivered on 10 October: all the defendants' submissions were rejected, and the court declared itself competent. An appeal was allowed, but on 20 October the Cour de Cassation judges supported their Vendôme colleagues without reservation, thus finally blocking the defense's opening gambit.[20] The court was now able to proceed to its first task, the individual examination of each of the accused in camera. The first interrogations began even before the appeal decision from Paris had been received, and by 23 October thirty-seven interrogations were complete. Babeuf's examination was left until last and occupied six sessions of several hours each, beginning on 25 October and finishing on 3 November, after two interruptions due to the prisoner's exhaustion. The discomforts of the onset of winter, added to the prolonged imprisonment, had begun seriously to undermine Babeuf's health, along with that of several other prisoners.[21]

His formal judicial examination brought Babeuf into confrontation for the first time with his chief adversary, the public prosecutor appointed by the Cour de Cassation. At 42, René-Louis Marie Viellart was an able and ambitious former lieutenant of the Royal Bailliage Court of Rheims who had been born into the same stratum of provincial officialdom as Babeuf's old enemies the Billecocqs and the Prévosts of Roye. As deputy of the Third Estate in 1789 he had taken a special interest in the Constituent Assembly in questions of public order. Viellart was fully alive to the political significance of the Vendôme trial, and was determined to use it to advance his personal career. In March 1797 (after Letourneur's retirement) he is even said to have aspired to the vacant position on the Directory. As a result of such ambitions he was an enthusiastic prosecutor, perhaps even over-enthusiastic. The prosecution's eagerness to convict the least likely defendants and to paint the conspiracy in the blackest possible colors was an error of strategy that contributed to the ultimately sceptical response of the jury.

During his interrogation Babeuf raised a major legal point which required a formal decision by the court before the trial could proceed further. Babeuf's contention was that Gérard's refusal to allow the confrontation of witnesses; his illegal citing of Grisel, a denunciator, as witness; his anticipation of the jury's decision when making out the detention orders; and the perfunctory nature of the final jury deliberations all made the proceedings of the Paris jury and the findings of 12 July invalid. If this was accepted it would mean, at the least, a postponement of proceedings for several months while a new presentment was completed. After Viellart himself had asked for guidance, the court considered Babeuf's objections and disallowed them (in a ruling handed down on 13 November). A similar protest by Germain was also disallowed on 18 November. At the same time the court rejected a submission by several other defendants that the warrants under which they were being held were illegal, since these had not specified the law under which they had been issued, as required by the constitution.[22]

Babeuf had launched another delaying tactic on 6 November. Until this date he had maintained his original position, refusing to recognize the competence of the court. Now, suddenly, he changed his mind and formally gave notice that he would enter a defense after all. He also asked to call four witnesses. One, Leblanc, was the French government's commissioner in the West Indies; the second, Lesage-Senault, was Leblanc's secretary. Jeanbon Saint-André, the third, was the envoy of the French Republic to the Bey of Algiers, while the fourth, Aubert Dubayet, was currently the French ambassador at Constantinople. Babeuf had faced the court with a delicate problem. The choice of such a bizarre panel of witnesses was obviously a delaying tactic; but, committed as they were to maintaining the appearance of a scrupulous legality, Gandon and his colleagues were bound to take the applications seriously. On 16 November, therefore, they listened while Viellart solemnly explored the points of law involved, and then as solemnly rejected Babeuf's demand in respect of each witness.[23]

One of the most difficult and time-consuming operations necessary for the constitution of the high court still lay ahead. The law provided for a jury of sixteen, together with four *adjoints* and four *suppléants*, all selected by lot from a special body of eighty-seven jurors, one chosen by the electoral assembly of each *département*. The defense was allowed a week in which to challenge up to thirty of the jurors without explanation and any further number showing due cause. The effective use of this right was of supreme importance to the defendants, since they needed only four of the sixteen jurors to vote for innocence for the trial to produce an acquittal.

The regulations for the court made a generous provision for the jurors' expenses. They were to receive the same salary as members of the legislative councils and to receive an additional allowance of wheat flour—a significant commentary on the collapse of the Republic's finances during 1796. Even so, the greatest difficulties were experienced in collecting together a full panel. Many jurors were clearly reluctant to place themselves in an exposed position in the essentially political battle which was to take place at Vendôme. When the court met on 17 November to draw up a definitive list of jurors in order to begin the selection procedure, they were faced with twenty-four excuses, of which they were forced to accept thirteen. One prospective juror was dead, three were ill, six were *émigrés* or relatives of *émigrés,* one had served on the jury of presentment, another was secretary to the Directory, and the thirteenth was himself in custody.

At a session of the court on 19 November the names of the sixteen jurors and their eight substitutes were drawn from an urn and made public, leaving fifty in reserve. Provided they were allowed to meet together it was possible for the defendants, by pooling their information, to arrive at some useful conclusions about the probable prejudices of the jurors. Permission for the necessary contact was in fact given on the morning of 21 November, with the prisoners moving freely in the corridors. There was trouble in the afternoon, however, when they refused to separate again, and the gendarmerie had to be called in to enforce the order. On 23 November the initial concession was withdrawn, and for the remainder of the operation the prisoners were allowed to communicate only by deputations.[24]

During the court session the following day a deep rift in the defense strategy became apparent for the first time. Thirty-six of the defendants, including Buonarroti and all the *ex-conventionnels,* presented a joint challenge rejecting twelve jurors, two *adjoints*, and three *suppléants*. The remaining ten tendered a note in which they restated their refusal to recognize the competence of the court and declined to take part in its proceedings. The ten protesters seem to have been the essential nucleus of Babeuf's "party": Darthé, Germain, Moroy, Cazin, Blondeau, Cochet, Toulotte, Sophie Lapierre, Marie-Adélaide Lambert, and Babeuf himself. In these circumstances Gandon and his colleagues refused to accept the joint challenges made by Buonarroti's group, and insisted on adopting the procedure of individual challenges, to be made by each prisoner in turn until the complement of thirty had been accounted for.

The order in which the forty-six defendants might challenge was to be settled by lot. Babeuf (and the others) remaining recalcitrant, an usher drew for them, but there was no effective way of making them cooperate further. Darthé was dragged struggling into court on 23 November and presented with the jury list, but he refused to speak. It was Babeuf's turn on 25 November to refuse to leave his cell. He sent up a defiant note denouncing the proceedings as "a ridiculous piece of play-acting," a *"pantalonnade"* played before a packed courtroom; and he appealed, not for the last time, to "the justice of impartial posterity."

By the 26th there were only four survivors of the original jury left unchallenged: Rey-Pailhade of the Hérault Département, whose impartial skepticism in cross-examination would stand the defendants in good stead during the trial, and three others. Hulin, Babeuf's one-time employer and now high juror for the Somme Département, was one of the challenged.[25] The defense having failed to make any challenges for cause, the final jury list was declared on 3 December. Another act of the "comedy" now began as the court waited impatiently for the jurors to assemble at Vendôme.

Viellart complained on 29 December that three jurors and one *adjoint* had written to say that it was "physically impossible for them to come" despite the prescribed sentence of three months' jail for such a refusal. Since the law provided for the replacement of jurors only by the four *adjoints*, it needed only one more excuse and there would be no jury. The fifth excuse arrived in fact on the very next day; and the court decided to fill the vacant places by drawing five more names from the urn. The defendants immediately reacted by lodging a protest, pointing out that they had been given no opportunity to challenge these replacements. At the hearing, on 9 January, Viellart countered charges of attempting to "pack" the jury with allegations that the jurors were being pressured by threatening letters (including some from Hésine at Pontlevoy) and urged an end to delaying tactics. "The interest of the Republic" demanded that the full details of the conspiracy should be made public before the forthcoming national elections to the Council of Five Hundred.

The court felt the wind blowing from Paris and obediently rejected the protest. Even so, Viellart's difficulties were only just beginning. By 20 January, the date originally fixed for the public trial to open, only ten out of the twenty-four jurors, assistants, and substitutes had put in an appearance. Two of the recent replacements had not been heard from; one original juror had sent a valid medical excuse; one had not replied to any letters; and another, André Boreldat, had written to demand 1,200 livres for a carriage and traveling expenses before he was prepared to stir from the Aude Département. To make matters more complicated, Jean Duffau (one of the original jurors who had sent an excuse and had been replaced) had finally decided to put in an appearance. The court held yet another drawing to provide replacements for Boreldat and for the invalid, and ordered proceedings against Boreldat.[26]

By the middle of February the tally of jurors and *adjoints* had at last reached the required minimum of twenty; but at this point yet another difficulty arose. The Directory had published in December a selection of extracts from the papers of the conspiracy for propaganda effect, and as a result one of the jurors, Pierre-Jean Agier, discovered that he was listed by the defendants as a *"royaliste contre-révolutionnaire,"* and thus, in his own view, marked out for death. Accordingly he now asked to be excused on the grounds of natural prejudice against the defendants.[27] In the circumstances the court had by now no sympathy left for tender consciences among the jurymen, and Agier's plea was brusquely rejected. Even so, when the public trial opened on 20 February the jury was still two *suppléants* short, with consequent embarrassments for the prosecution.

In all decisions concerning the composition of the jury the court had shown a consistent bias against the defense. The same was true of the other representations from the accused, the most important of which was a demand for a full documentation of the evidence to be made available to the defendants. During December each of the accused had been provided with the indictment, with two volumes of documentation of the procedure "common to Babeuf and his co-accused," and with a separate documentation of the particular case against himself. The defendants were quick to point out that this left a serious gap. To prepare an adequate defense each prisoner needed to have access to all the other individual indictments. While it was possible for defense counsel to arrange for this material to be copied out, several of the accused (including Babeuf) had no defense counsel, and therefore no way of getting hold of the necessary documents save by borrowing them from fellow-prisoners. The court formally rejected this protest on 13 February, completing a pattern of decisions uniformly weighted against the defendants which seemed to justify the contention of Babeuf's circle that the Vendôme trial was a prearranged farce in which it would be humiliating and distasteful to take part.[28]

For the majority of the prisoners, however, the battle still seemed one worth fighting. As the opening sessions of the public trial approached, Buonarroti and the Montagnards busied themselves in trying to persuade the Babeuf group to close ranks and organize a firm and unified defense which would prejudice nobody's chances of acquittal. The Directorial journal, the *Rédacteur officiel*, published a well-informed account on 11 February of the bitter and sometimes violent controversy amongst the prisoners, hoping to fan the flames still further. As a countermove Buonarroti collected forty-three signatures for a pre-trial declaration of solidarity which was circulated to the press. Babeuf added a special personal declaration that, despite the fables being disseminated, he was no more the leader of a party in Vendôme than he had been in Paris. About the same time Antonelle got the Babeuf group to swear to "behave themselves" in court and "not to insult anybody." However, on the eve of the trial, the prison concierge reported that Babeuf was having trouble "keeping up the comedy" and that the basic rift between the two groups of defendants had not been bridged.[29]

The prosecution could thus approach the opening sessions with a well-based confidence. A friendly bench, a carefully documented case, and a divided defense seemed to augur a speedy and successful conclusion to the trial.

Twenty

The Trial

From the indictment on 20 February to the verdict on 26 May 1797, the public trial of Babeuf and his fellow-conspirators lasted just over three months. As the first trial in which a verbatim record was kept by stenographers, the Vendôme proceedings made legal history. But there were other ways in which the conduct of the trial was remarkable, not least in the extent of the publicity it received. Throughout, the Directory tolerated the continued existence of Hésine's journal of the trial, published in the interest of the defendants, in addition to the official *Journal des débats du procès*. The Vendôme trial was also exceptional, for a political trial, in the freedom allowed to the defense substantially to destroy the prosecution's case. Emerging, as it did, from the strains and stresses of a revolutionary era, the conduct and results of the trial were something of a tribute to the new spirit of French justice.

The technical problem of the orderly and effective conduct of the court rested on the shoulders of its president, Gandon. By February the prosecution had expanded the conspiracy to include sixty-four accused, of whom forty-nine were present in court, many of them insubordinate and irrepressibly vocal. Together with their defense council each of these was entitled to intervene in the proceedings in order to question witnesses, and so were the two dozen jurors and their assistants. Among the spectators a band of relatives and friends of the accused were always ready to join in the fervent demonstrations of republican enthusiasm initiated from time to time by the prisoners. Moreover, in handling such outbursts and in his treatment of the prisoners generally, Gandon was forced to take account of a volatile public opinion, torn in this era of transition between respect for the veterans of the conquest of liberty in the dock and a heartfelt yearning for a return to order and stability.

The task before the prosecution, despite its initial advantages, was not an easy one. To prosecute an "anarchist" conspiracy with ramifications all over France made good propaganda for the spring elections. To make an effective case against the considerable number of suspects who had been added to the list for political rather than evidential reasons was another matter. After eight years of revolution the moral distinction between legitimate opposition to a government and subversive conspiracy had inevitably become blurred in the minds of Frenchmen, whatever the legal and political realities. The jury could not be expected to accept government definitions tamely.

By the same token, a jury trial offered significant advantages to the defense. While it was not to be expected that many members of a jury elected under the Constitution of the Year III would have much sympathy with the egalitarian ideals of the accused, some at least might be expected to be sincere republicans, anxious to avoid an outcome of the trial which might give comfort to resurgent royalism, skeptically sensitive to the politically motivated exaggerations of the prosecution's case, and more resistant than the judges to pressures from Paris.

Every appeal to the court since October had been blocked through the legal formalism or political prejudice of the bench. Neither factor would be likely to operate to the same extent within the jury. However, the defense's approach to the jury demanded a different strategy from that which had been followed in the trial preliminaries. The defendants must appear cooperative where they had been intransigent and moderate where they had been extreme; and they had to avoid outbursts of wild utopianism calculated to raise the hackles of the bourgeois jurors. Because such a prudent restraint was entirely out of character for Babeuf, Germain, and for one or two of the others, the result of the trial was always genuinely in the balance.

The proceedings opened in the crowded main audience hall at 10 a.m. on 20 February. The judges sat at one end of the room. On one side were benches for the jury; on the other the defendants sat, each accompanied by a gendarme. Facing the judges, at the opposite end of the room, were benches reserved for counsel and privileged observers (including members of the municipal administration of Vendôme), and behind these space was left for the general public. Grisel was the last to find his way to the yellow velvet seats reserved for witnesses, and he was greeted by a chorus of threats and invectives. The court was so arranged that the witnesses sat with their backs to the prisoners.

The first clash came almost immediately after the opening formalities: Babeuf responded to Gandon's routine request to state his name by protesting against the competence of the court. In the minutes that followed the outlines of the two parties into which the defendants were divided emerged clearly. The majority followed Buonarroti and the Montagnards in making orderly reply to Gandon's questions, while a minority took their cue from Babeuf and protested against either the legitimacy of the court or the conditions of the trial. Babeuf's group comprised twelve prisoners and included Darthé, Germain, Didier, Cazin, Moroy, Blondeau, Sophie Lapierre, Adélaide Lambert, and three Equals from Saint-Omer, Taffoureau, Toulotte, and Cochet.[1]

The swearing-in of the jury provided the first of many embarrassing moments for the prosecution. One juror, Vignalet, who had failed to turn up, was sentenced in absentia to three months' jail. Another, Baudin, was discharged at the prosecution's request as a relative of *émigrés*. This left the jury short of two *suppléants*, as several defendants were quick to point out. Even more embarrassing, Agier at first refused (consistently with his earlier protest) to take the oath, and finally did so on Gandon's insistence only after the defense had made noisy capital out of the episode.[2]

Once the formalities had been completed, Babeuf immediately took practical charge of the conduct of the trial. He insisted on reading a written discourse, two to three hours long, in which he rehearsed the history and circumstances of the various earlier protests against the competence of the court, and urged the jury to stop the case on the spot, or, alternatively, to postpone the hearings until the accused had been provided with adequate documentation. In the latter event, Babeuf explained, he had decided to take part in the trial after all, in view of his faith in the integrity of a jury elected by the people. About 3:15 p.m. with Babeuf desperately tired, the session was closed; and the prisoners sang the first verse of the "Marseillaise" before filing out to their cells. The following day there was a short afternoon session in which Germain renewed the initiative, echoing Babeuf's attacks. Viellart countered by reminding the jury that they were there to judge facts, not procedure; the court rejected both Babeuf's and Germain's protests and the session broke up to the accompaniment of more singing by the prisoners.[3]

The next session (on 22 February) was concerned with the formalities relating to the prisoners in contumacy, and the court did not meet again until 24 February. Once the court had reassembled, Viellart launched the prosecution's case with a set-piece denunciation of the accused as monsters of hypocrisy, of ambition and irreligion, of murder and pillage, in a speech delivered against a background of angry outbursts and interruptions from the prisoners and defense counsel, partly spontaneous and partly deliberately calculated to spoil the elocutionary flow of Viellart's presentation. Babeuf proved a particularly vigorous interrupter and clashed on several occasions with Gandon, who threatened at one point to remove him from the court. The session of 24 February was also noteworthy for the first intervention of Pierre-François Réal (the defense counsel for Drouet, Antonelle and Fyon), who would soon emerge as the master-tactician of the defense.

Réal stood out among his legal colleagues on a number of counts. Most of the others (apart from Jaume) were locals. Réal was a Parisian and a man of wide experience. The son of a royal gamekeeper, he had graduated under the old régime from the Royal Bailliage Court of Chatou to the service of the king as *procureur au châtelet* in Paris, and thence to that of the Republic, as *substitut-procureur* of the Paris Commune in 1793. In 1794 he had acted as defense counsel when Carrier was tried for his terroristic excesses.

Réal's professional strength lay in his capacity to analyze the contradictions in the opposition's case, and his skill in gently leading a hostile witness into catastrophic ambush. There was, however, another and more important aspect to Réal's intervention, for he was a man of considerable influence. As a leader of the "Patriots of 1789" and the editor of the *Journal des Patriotes de '89*, Réal was known to be a close ally and protégé of Barras, and a political enemy of Carnot and of Merlin (the minister of justice). Thus he was, in effect, Barras' representative at the trial, as Viellart and (to a lesser extent) Gandon were Carnot's. So long as the Directorial struggle for dominance remained in the balance, the judges could not afford to browbeat and overrule Réal as if he were an insignificant provincial lawyer. This was a factor of immense value for the defense generally.

Réal used his first intervention at Vendôme (at the close of the session of 24 February) to demand more convenient facilities for the defense counsel, protesting that the arrangement of the court prevented counsel from free and regular discussion with the accused and from a proper view of the witnesses and the jury. He refused to

Anti-Babouvist satire: anarchy forestalled by republican vigilance

be satisfied until Gandon had agreed to take immediate action to seat him in front of the accused. It was not surprising that the concierge at the abbey reported that the session had raised the prisoners' morale and that they were singing together again.[4]

The prosecution's case, as outlined by Viellart, was not complicated. The defendants were not on trial for their political opinions but for participating in a conspiracy, organized by Babeuf, whose object was to overthrow the lawful government of the Republic by violence. The existence of the conspiracy was attested both by written and published documents and by the evidence of witnesses. To destroy this case it was necessary for the defense to challenge either the authenticity of the documents or the interpretation placed upon them, and either to exclude or to discredit the witnesses.

The first major clash over the validity of the documentary evidence occurred on 2 March, the tenth day of the trial. In order to strengthen their case the prosecution decided to call in an expert graphologist, Alexis-Joseph Harger, a one-time member of the pre-revolutionary Bureau Académique d'Ecriture. The intention was that Harger and Guillaume, another graphologist, would positively identify a number of damaging pieces as being in the handwriting of the leading defendants. These included one item in particular, a by now notorious outline of a tactical program for insurrection written out by Babeuf and subsequently widely publicized by the Directory which began with the words "*Tuer les cinq*," i.e., "kill the five Directors." Viellart had made this document a central pillar of his indictment on 24 February. In fact, as Babeuf pointed out, challenging the admissibility of the graphologists' evidence, the words *Tuer les cinq* were crossed out; and the prosecution's case thus apparently rested on the experts' opinion of what lay under the crossing out. But this specific issue, though important, was only incidental to a more general challenge to the admissibility of Harger and Guillaume.

Expert witnesses are always fair game in court, and Babeuf was able to make much capital by contrasting the generally recognized lack of precision of graphological science and the pompous and sometimes quite tautological certainties adduced by Harger and Guillaume. Although the court finally decided to allow the witnesses to be heard, seeds of doubt had been sown in the right place, and the following day the chairman of the jury, Rey-Pailhade, displayed a particular interest in the processes by which the documents presented by the prosecution had been identified.

Several days later, a fresh appearance of Harger allowed another of the jurors, Jean-François Gaultier de Biauzat, to emerge for the first time in the virtual rôle of an auxiliary counsel for the defense.[5]

Biauzat, high juror for the Puy de Dôme Département and a former mayor of Clermont-Ferrand, was a man with an ambivalent political reputation. Throughout the Jacobin period of the revolution and the Thermidorian reaction, he had consistently followed a moderate line, which had embroiled him first with the followers of Couthon, Robespierre's ally, and afterwards with the royalist reaction. His biographer, Mège, makes it clear that Biauzat was no Jacobin, but in the circumstances of 1797 he saw the royalists as the real danger to a moderate republican policy, and also to his own political survival at Clermont. Writing home from Paris just before he left for Vendôme Biauzat had expressed his concern at the spread of royalism and declared himself on the side of the patriots "known as Jacobins." As the trial progressed his partiality soon became unmistakable.[6]

The demolition of the state's experts began on 7 March when Réal cross-examined Harger, and got him to contradict himself and to lapse into unconvincing bluster when his discrepancies were pointed out. Réal also demonstrated to the jury that in different parts of his evidence Harger had attributed the *Tuer les cinq* piece to both Darthé and Babeuf. Biauzat next intervened to demand who had told Harger to guess the words that lay under the crossing out. Réal followed up by getting the witness to admit that he had discussed his original report with the prosecutor Gérard before putting it on paper. Finally, Lamberté challenged the prosecution counsel, Viellart and Bailly, to declare whether they could read *Tuer les cinq*, and Bailly had to admit that he could not.

Worse was to follow. The next day Harger stumbled over his evidence, and, to Réal's delight, actually declared that the first word was clearly legible as *Tout* (all) and not *Tuer* (kill). The jury demanded to see the document; and Biauzat got Harger to admit that Gérard "could have" asked him if the phrase read *Tuer les cinq*, that he had been expecting to find *Tuer* and that *Tout* would have done just as well.

The turn of the other graphologist, Guillaume, followed shortly afterwards. After the new witness had, improbably, identified seventeen items in two minutes, ruthless probing by Réal and Biauzat made it clear that he was repeating schooled evidence and not acting as an independent expert at all. In fact it was demonstrated that Gandon and Viellart had thrown Guillaume into the fray in a desperate attempt to fill up the blanks left in Harger's testimony. Guillaume's evidence continued over the next two days, in the course of which the defense elicited the fact that he and Harger shared the same lodgings and must therefore have influenced one another's evidence, and got the witness to admit that the crucial document might even read *Tirer les cinq* (Pull the five).[7]

The prosecution's case was now in serious disarray. On the one hand, the "experts" had been discredited so effectively that no specific document could be convincingly attributed to any particular prisoner. On the other, since the prosecution had been shown to be capable of concocting important evidence on one occasion, its credibility would be in question for the remainder of the trial. Even so, the defense still had to account for a great mass of documentary evidence brought forward by the prosecution. It would have been an insult to the common sense of the jury to deny the authenticity of much of this material; and, indeed, during the session of 3 March Babeuf had frankly admitted responsibility for many of the papers found at the rue de la Grande Truanderie. These were not, however, the papers of a conspiracy, he declared, but the transactions of a small club or "circle" of democrats. Nor was Babeuf the leader of the group, but only its propagandist; it was for this reason alone that a large number of items were in his hand. Later, in the course of the trial, he would add the further explanation that he was the "archivist" of the "circle of democrats" and that some of the items had been copied by him from dictation.[8]

The strategy of the defense was now clear. The validity of any really dangerous piece of evidence like *Tuer les cinq* would be disputed as manufactured or doctored evidence; the remainder would be explained away. Thus on 18 March Babeuf declared that the manuscript of "The Creation of an Insurrectional Committee" was no more than a philanthropic dream; the prosecution had not established that he or any other among the accused had composed the "Act of Insurrection." Babeuf's own letter to Cochon, offering to negotiate as the leader of the conspiracy, was dismissed as a tactical device to frighten the Directory into releasing the prisoners, with no basis in truth.

Buonarroti adopted the same line on the 19th, again explaining away many of the projects of the conspiracy as "philanthropic dreams" discussed as possibilities only in case the government should fall. Germain's problem was to account for a bundle of papers belonging to Guilhem, the agent for the Fifth Arrondissement, which had been found in his possession. He told the court on 31 March that they were pieces brought to him by a worried patriot, who thought them the work of an *agent-provocateur*. Germain had himself subsequently dictated and made a number of copies, and this was why some of the material was in his own handwriting.

A couple of days later Buonarroti offered an ingenious general alibi covering the highly incriminating check-lists of royalists and "trustworthy patriots." These lists, he explained, had been drawn up about the time of Vendémiaire, when the present authorities needed help against the royalists, and thus had no connection with any alleged conspiracy. Taking their cue, Cazin and Moroy subsequently both fell back on the same explanation to account for lists they had compiled as *arrondissement* agents.[9]

Such alibis were hardly convincing. The best that could be said about them was that, for a juror who might be well disposed towards the defendants for other reasons, they provided a reasonable excuse to discount a mass of uncomfortable evidence.

The deployment of the chief witnesses provided the prosecution with more serious difficulties. By the spring of 1797 the events on which these witnesses would be cross-examined were a year old. It had not been an easy year for Grisel. Like all traitors he found himself isolated, despised and distrusted by both sides, unable to return home to Abbeville for fear of vengeance, completely in the power of Cochon and the Directory. Things must have been worse for Pillé, locked up with the others in the abbey and (once the details of his evidence had been handed over to the defense) faced by their daily contempt.

Grisel's evidence was the most dangerous, and the first major battle of the trial was joined in the last few days of February, when the defense made a determined attempt to exclude him altogether. The attack was led jointly by Buonarroti and Réal, relying on the principle of Roman law that a denunciator may not appear as a witness against the denounced. There was a wealth of precedent and authority for this challenge, and the prosecution found itself in some real difficulty. Bailly attempted to counter by advancing a general contention that the precedents of Roman law were no longer applicable since the revolution. But it was pointed out, in rejoinder, that the operative republican Code des Délits et Peines explicitly followed the Roman precedent by excluding denunciators from giving evidence as witnesses when the act of denunciation was rewarded by law, or when the denunciator could profit in any other manner from the act. The prosecution then fell back on the argument that Grisel had not technically *denounced* the conspiracy by swearing a statement before a justice of the peace, but instead had *revealed* it by making a declaration before the president of the Directory. On the basis of this casuistry the court formally decided for Grisel's admissibility on 2 March. The prosecution had won its point, but such a cavalier overriding of precedent and authority can hardly have appealed to a jury composed largely of professional lawyers.[10]

Grisel's first appearance as a witness was hardly auspicious. It took place after lunch on 12 March: Grisel appeared to be drunk, and the session had to be hastily wound up. The following morning he reappeared and spoke for more than two hours, but his evidence was confused, repetitive, and badly arranged. The process of discrediting began immediately, when the defendants demonstrated that Grisel could not identify Dufour, whom he had claimed to have seen conspiring with Darthé. At the next session (on 15 March) when Gandon asked Grisel to identify the prisoners he failed to recognize Ricord and he picked out Fiquet as Laignelot. Germain then took command of the attack, pointing out that in 1796 Grisel had waited thirteen days before "revealing" what his own evidence indicated as a fearsome and imminent conspiracy. He then examined Grisel's three published depositions (before Cochon, before Gérard, and before the court at Vendôme) and drew attention to a number of inconsistencies and contradictions, before concluding that where the evidence was accurate it was insignificant, and wherever it was significant it was manufactured.

When the court next assembled (on 16 March) Babeuf, in the course of a three-hour tirade, contributed the suggestion that Grisel had acted as an *agent-provocateur* (which could hardly be denied), and that all his evidence must be scrutinized with this in mind. While all those present caught their breath to recover from Babeuf's oratorical outburst, Réal fired three rapid questions at Grisel which caught him off balance and won an admission that the names of Buonarroti and Darthé had been added to his original deposition by Carnot "after discussion." Gandon hurriedly suspended the session and Grisel did not reappear the following morning. The damage had been done: the defense contention that the state had manufactured some of Grisel's evidence had been publicly vindicated.[11]

Not until 23 March did the prosecution venture to introduce further witnesses. The intention was to document the existence of a conspiracy to suborn the Police Legion and the military garrison. The session brought Viellart little comfort. In the first place, five of the witnesses listed could not be produced, either because they were ill or because they had absconded. One former legionary, Lescot, was available, since he was himself in custody. However, Réal's cross-examination brought out the fact that Lescot's evidence purported to refer to a session at a cabaret at which sixty bottles of wine were drunk by ten or twelve diners, and under questioning by Biauzat the witness was made to contradict himself. Biauzat also established that Lescot, like Grisel, was a denunciator and a witness at the same time. The chairman of the jury, Rey-Pailhade, the two jurors Biauzat and Pierre-Marie Pajot, and even the president of the court himself joined (during the sessions of 23-25 March) in the savaging of a string of minor and incompetent witnesses in a growing atmosphere of skepticism.[12]

The final disaster for the prosecution came on 25 March with the appearance as a prosecution witness of Jean-Baptiste Meunier, a twenty-year-old *chasseur* from the 21st Dragons. When called, Meunier entered the court singing a Babouvist song, turned to the jury, professed his admiration for the accused, and declared that he would sooner sit beside them than play the part of a Grisel. He then refused to testify, claiming that Gérard had dictated his original testimony and compelled him to sign under threat of ten years' imprisonment for possession of seditious literature. Since arriving at Vendôme he had written to Gandon to complain that the prosecution had offered to provide a copy of his evidence in order to school him. Meunier remained obdurate even in the face of a threatened prosecution for perjury, and the next witness had to be called.

Jean-Noel Barbier was a twenty-three-year-old former legionary of the second battalion of the Police Legion. Before his appearance Barbier must have learned that the court had just ordered Meunier's arrest on the perjury charge. Nevertheless he too refused to testify, and denounced Gérard for making him sign a bogus deposition while he was half dead with fever in the Bicêtre prison infirmary. According to the stenographic record of the trial Gandon's response to Barbier's evidence was to exclaim *"c'est fini"* (it's all over) in disgust. He had every justification. Meunier and Barbier's freely volunteered statements threw Gérard's entire procedure into doubt and raised even more questions about the credibility of the prosecution's unconvincing procession of witnesses. More than that, the jury could hardly have remained unmoved by the heroism of two young men openly braving ten-year sentences for perjury to make their protest.

The prosecution never recovered from the fiasco of 25 March. Even so, Viellart and his colleagues had not yet tasted the dregs. One witness remained, Nicolas Pillé, whose evidence should have been damning for Babeuf, Buonarroti, and Le Peletier. Pillé's testimony was heard on 2 April. All went reasonably smoothly until Pillé insisted on telling the president of the court about the influence of evil spirits on his own conduct and giving a description of personal demons belonging to Philip and Nayez, two of the defendants. After this Réal had no difficulty in demonstrating that the state's second most important witness had gone mad, and the session had to be wound up hurriedly once again.[13]

Even before the time of the Pillé incident the atmosphere of the trial had begun to undergo a remarkable change. During the first few weeks, the defendants had continued their earlier delaying tactics, seizing on every possible technicality to hold up or prolong the proceedings. Now, most of the prisoners began instead to show an eagerness to cooperate with Gandon in his attempts to cut short formalities and speed things up.[14] This change in attitude was a reflection of the growing realization that the prosecution's case had collapsed, and that the jury was going to acquit all or most of the accused. The general strategy of the defense had succeeded. The authenticity, and the validity of the state's interpretation, of the documentary evidence had both been placed in doubt; the prosecution's chief witnesses had been shown up as unreliable; and the state had been proven guilty of manufacturing evidence.

There was a price to be paid for these achievements, however. To deny the existence of a conspiracy meant to renounce the attractive alternative of using the Vendôme trial as a public platform from which to justify great aims and noble motives. Those of the prisoners who had been at the heart of the conspiracy thus faced a troublesome crisis of conscience. Darthé resolved his by continuing to refuse to acknowledge the court throughout the trial, as did Sophie Lapierre and several others. Antonelle and Buonarroti both made a clear and definite choice and decided to concentrate on saving the necks of as many of the accused as possible. For Babeuf the dilemma was most painful of all. His strongly developed messianic streak prevented him from following Darthé's example by remaining silent and thus allowing the forces of evil to triumph by default. To avow everything openly would bring personal satisfaction and a martyr's halo, but only at the cost of condemning several dozen good republicans, democrats, and Equals to execution or imprisonment. Yet to follow Buonarroti's lead meant to compromise with his most deeply felt convictions.

The need to choose between such alternatives threatened a complete disruption of Babeuf's personality. Already physically ill with dropsy in the legs as a result of his long imprisonments, he repeatedly drove both himself and the court to the point of exhaustion with long rambling tirades read from previously composed texts. Self-contradictory and unconvincing on matters of fact, these excursions frequently approached closely enough to a political vindication of the conspiracy to stir up dismay and anger among the rest of the defendants.[15]

For Babeuf, too, the trial reached a watershed at the end of March. During the first few weeks his conduct was aggressive and defiant, and there were repeated clashes with Gandon as he strove to dominate the court and to deliver orations for the benefit of the spectators, the guards, and posterity rather than the jury. Babeuf's personal cross-examination at the end of March proved to be an anticlimax.

The prosecution's main offensive was launched by Gandon in the opening moments of the session of 17 March, when, without warning, he suddenly confronted Babeuf with his own open avowal of the conspiracy before Cochon and Gérard, and demanded an explanation. Completely at a loss, Babeuf was forced to take refuge in silence while Gandon drove home his advantage: "Up to now you have been running the trial—from now on it is going to be me." By the following morning Babeuf had recovered his balance, only to be tripped again by a formal judgment which blocked his attempt to use the court for a propaganda defense of the Constitution of 1793. After this Babeuf refused to answer further questions and demanded to be taken back to his cell. During the next few days he struggled unconvincingly through the remainder of his personal trial, explaining away incriminating documents as best he could. He begged to be allowed to remain in his cell on 20 March because of the physical distress caused by the dropsy, but the gendarmes dragged him into court notwithstanding, and he received a reprimand by Gandon for his "spirit of revolt and obstinacy." By 22 March Babeuf's trial was petering out, with Gandon mocking the wretched prisoner for his stumbling attempts to answer questions verbatim. Deprived of the opportunity to prepare written explanations, Babeuf cut a very poor figure in court. After the painful and deflating experience of his personal trial Babeuf did not intervene again in the sessions for more than three weeks, until 14 April, and even then he had little to say. On 17 April he offered a few remarks and answered some questions put to him by Gandon, before the court recessed until 27 April for the prosecution's final summing up.[16]

. The task of sticking the scattered pieces of the prosecution's case together was undertaken not by Viellart, but by his colleague, Nicolas Bailly, who spoke for thirteen hours during three sessions extending from 27 to 29 April. Bailly reaffirmed the prosecution's main contentions. A conspiracy to overthrow the government had been planned for the beginning of May 1796; the main instigators and their agents were present in court and must be punished according to law. A section of the address was devoted to refuting three alternative counterarguments which might be raised by the defense: that the evidence indicated only a legitimate association of citizens for innocuous ends; that the conspiracy was a fabrication by *agents-provocateurs*; that the actions of the conspirators were justifiable.

The extent of the prosecution's failure only became apparent when Bailly turned to the task of assessing the guilt of each individual defendant in turn. Not always clearly stating a demand for a conviction, but instead often merely summarizing the evidence, the prosecutors appeared to be virtually throwing themselves on the mercy of the jury. When the tally was complete it became evident that the case had been abandoned against thirty-seven persons, or more than half of those arraigned. Four more indictments were left at the discretion of the jury. This left a total of twenty-three for whom a verdict of guilty was sought, of whom nine were in flight and only fourteen in court. Of Babeuf's closer associates, Germain, Darthé, Didier, Moroy, Cazin and Blondeau were marked for conviction; but the cases against Sophie Lapierre and Marie Adélaide Lambert were abandoned. Laignelot and Ricord were arraigned as leaders of the Montagnards, and Buonarroti, Massard, Fyon and Lamberté were also included in the final list of conspirators for whom a conviction was sought.[17]

According to the procedure of the trial, time was now allowed to the accused to present their personal defenses. For Babeuf this represented an opportunity at last to address the court and the public from a prepared text and without interruption. At the same time, the course of the trial had shown that while the prosecution might have lost its grip on the proceedings in general, Babeuf himself could expect little mercy in the final outcome. His "general defense" therefore was likely to be his last opportunity to address the people and posterity. He requested on 29 April an adjournment of eight days to prepare himself: the court was prepared to allow him four.

In fact, Babeuf began his defense on the morning of 3 May and continued throughout the entire sessions of the 4th, 5th and 6th, concluding only on the morning of 7 May. The text of his address (as published by Advielle in 1884) extends to more than 120,000 words, yet it was received with the maximum of patience and tolerance by the court. Only on one occasion (on the morning of the 5th) was Babeuf interrupted and ordered to abandon a line of argument which equated elections held under the Constitution of the Year III with a royalist conspiracy.[18]

As the longest connected piece of political writing from Babeuf's pen that survives, the "general defense" is an important document, and it was subsequently published as Babeuf's "political testament," in accordance with his own wishes. Nevertheless, the argument of the "defense" bears the unmistakable imprint of the immediate circumstances. The fundamental dilemma posed by the trial could not, even now, be avoided: How to deny the existence of the conspiracy and yet, at the same time, justify its motives and its aims? Babeuf's defense was not therefore a defiant, open call to communist revolution so much as an unconvincing alibi, with occasional democratic and communist propaganda smuggled in as "contraband."

The greater part of Babeuf's plea comprised no more than an elaborate restatement of the general strategy of the defense as it had emerged in the course of the trial. The jury must draw a distinction between the perfectly legitimate activity of a group of democrats in the months after Vendémiaire, seeking to put new heart into the republican cause by propagating the discussion of *le bonheur commun* and equality, and truly conspiratorial activity. To prove the latter, evidence of an attempt actually to put the wilder theoretical speculations into effect had to be presented. This the prosecution had failed to do. Its documentary evidence was doctored and wrongly interpreted, its witnesses worthless, its case fabricated. As far as Babeuf's personal involvement was concerned, his role had been as publicist and archivist only. Allegedly incriminating documents in his handwriting were merely copies made at the instruction of the "democratic circle" to which he belonged. Where there were crossings out and rewriting, this was not evidence of original composition but simply of an archivist overcome by the tedium of his duties.

All this makes very unconvincing reading, and can hardly have made much impression on the jury. To the majority of his fellow-prisoners, nevertheless, Babeuf's line was an immense relief. Until the very last it had never been certain that he would maintain the solidarity of the defense position, and during these last days the others repeatedly crowded round after the sessions to express their gratitude.[19]

Inevitably it fell to Babeuf to explain away the communist motivation of the conspiracy, and it was in this section of his defense that he came closest to using the courtroom as a propaganda tribune. Babeuf's deliberately ambiguous renunciation of communism as an immediately practical policy enabled him to cite powerful arguments in its defense. The works of the *philosophes*, of Rousseau, Mably and Diderot (in fact Morelly), were pillaged for favorable quotations, and Babeuf, in a rare flash of humor, even suggested that surely Jean-Jacques should properly have been cited in contumacy as a member of the "conspiracy." Yet the *philosophes* had escaped unscathed, even in the days of the monarchy; it was evidently no crime, therefore, to speculate on the theoretical desirability of communism under a republic.

In contesting the imputation of criminal intent made against the *Analyse de la doctrine de Babeuf* and against the *Tribun du peuple*, Babeuf was able for the last time to expound and develop his fundamental communist philosophy from a public platform, nailing his colors to the mast by reading out the essential passages of no. 35 of the *Tribun du peuple*. In the shadow of the guillotine, Babeuf reaffirmed his belief in a society which would abandon private property and class divisions to institute the common ownership of wealth, the collective organization of production and distribution, and a distribution of the product of labor on the basis of the complete equality of all citizens. Yet there was no call for insurrection. Instead the passages of the general defense were heavy with disillusion. "As a matter of fact I was very far from enjoying any measure of popular support. He who thinks that such support is easy to win fools himself . . . ," Babeuf declared; ". . . in the present epoch men are dominated and corrupted by a host of evil passions, so that it is not difficult to see that the chances against the possibility of the establishment of such a project are in the proportion of more than a hundred to one against."

Thus, in his political testament, Babeuf presented a picture of himself as a philosophical gradualist, seeking only to persuade by patient and peaceful propaganda, prepared to move only as fast as the progressive enlightenment of the people would permit. Such a picture fitted the general pattern of the defense strategy perfectly. Whether it reflected something more—a genuine eleventh-hour re-evaluation of revolutionary strategy on Babeuf's part—we have no means of judging. Certainly he was still very far from adopting the position of a political quietist.

Babeuf arrived at his peroration on the morning of 7 May. Permission to bid his family a personal farewell had been refused, but they were present in the courtroom, and Babeuf's final words were directed towards Marie-Anne and the children. They took the form of a moving affirmation of his dedication to the cause of equality and freedom, and a call for continued resistance to oppression and royal tyranny. "I leave you in slavery," he concluded, "and this thought alone will torment me at the last." "I ought . . . to advise you how to bear your chains with greater patience, yet I cannot do so."[20]

Babeuf addressed the court again on 17 May to reply to the prosecution's attacks on his defense, and briefly to recapitulate his earlier arguments. In the meantime Germain and Buonarroti had each presented substantial defenses. Several of the other defendants made shorter speeches to the court, and each of the defense counsel spoke on behalf of his clients. Ballyer *fils* was particularly effective, bringing tears to the eyes of the jury and the audience in his plea for Moroy. There were remarkable scenes in court on 14 May after an emotional address by Antonelle in which he appealed to all republicans for "peace and the forgetting of all hatred." With a fine display of *sensibilité*, Viellart leaped to his feet to second the appeal for "the reciprocal oblivion of all faults." Needless to say, there was no slackening of the vigor of the prosecution during the following days. However, in his summing up for the defense (begun on 18 May) Pierre-François Réal astutely attempted variations on the same theme for the benefit of the jury. "We are tired of the revolution," he declared in his conclusion. ". . . If you declare that there was a conspiracy, patriots will no longer find any shelter, and nobody will be able to sleep easily in his bed. . . ." "Everything tells me that you will close up the wounds of the Fatherland in declaring that there was no conspiracy."[21]

Réal again succeeded in wringing tears from the jury as he drew their attention to the anxious wives and children of the defendants in court. For the rest, the defense's final plea was an able performance: an indictment of the "provocations" suffered by true republicans since Thermidor; an enthusiastic assimilation of the high ideals of Babeuf and his new sect with those of Jesus, Thomas More,

Rousseau and Diderot; a devastating attack on Grisel and the "340" contradictions in his testimony. As for the papers seized at the rue de la Grande Truanderie, the archives of any popular society would yield equally extravagant material. If there was a conspiracy at all it was a conspiracy organized by Cochon and the royalists. The accused were no more than a group of democrats legitimately striving to deflect the Republic from a false and dangerous course.[22]

Gandon began his summing up as president of the court on 21 May. He directed the jury to decide three questions. Firstly, was there in germinal and floréal of the year IV a conspiracy to overthrow the government by arming citizens one against the other? Secondly, was there a conspiracy against legitimate authority? Thirdly, was there a conspiracy tending to dissolve the *corps législatif,* the Executive Directory, etc.? Then, in the case of each defendant in any of these general cases, firstly, did the accused take part and, secondly, did he take part with the intention of aiding the execution of the project? When the jury sought some clarification Viellart confirmed that the penalty on any of the three counts was death.[23] The next two days were taken up with a four-cornered wrangle over not only the precise wording of the direction to the jury but, incredibly after three months of trial proceedings, the actual law under which the accused should be judged and sentenced.

As spokesman of the jury, Rey-Pailhade argued that the indictment for conspiracy alone, as pressed by the prosecution, was too restrictive, since it did not allow the jury to consider other counts under the law of 27 germinal, such as provocation to murder, or to the restoration of the Constitution of 1793, or to the pillage of public or private property. It was desirable to consider the culpability of the accused also under these counts, in case the jury should reject the conspiracy charge. Viellart, for the prosecution, also took issue with the president's direction, stating a preference for a single question which would include each of the president's three. For the defense Réal demanded that the question of intent should be more clearly put, under the terms of an article of the penal code which sought to establish whether the accused had acted "*méchamment et à dessein*" (which left room for a reduced penalty). For similar reasons the defense also agreed to Rey-Pailhade's suggestion that the jury should consider the additional series of questions based on the law of 27 germinal, which allowed the imposition of the lesser punishment of exile as well as the death penalty. Viellart strongly contested both Réal's suggestions, and stuck stubbornly to conspiracy as the sole charge.

Finally, the court formally ruled on the morning of 24 May that the jury should consider culpability under several sections of the law of 27 germinal, but made no ruling on the question of culpability *"méchamment et à dessein."* With unchallengeable logic, Babeuf immediately protested and demanded the right to draft a defense against the newly improvised charges. Ironically, at the very beginning of the trial, the court had rejected his own and Germain's demand for a fuller documentation of the procedure on the specific grounds that they were on trial for conspiracy and not for their writings. Gandon refused to consider the new protest, and the jury retired to consider the evidence.[24]

The jury deliberations were held in secret. But one of the spectators, Dufort de Cheverny, was able (through his friendship with Pajon, one of the judges, and possibly through contact with some of the jurors) to glean the essentials of the course of events in the jury room. According to Dufort's version, twelve of the sixteen jurors were solid for a conviction. Three were determined to acquit: Biauzat (whose sympathy for the defendants was no secret), Michel-Casimir Dubois from the Sarthe Département and Moynier from the Pyrénées-Orientales. In April, a police spy had denounced both Dubois and Moynier to Merlin, the minister of justice, as confederates of Biauzat.

Since four votes were enough to secure an acquittal, the fate of the accused rested in the hands of the sixteenth juror. The jury voted by ballot, so that the identity of the waverer cannot be established beyond doubt. Dufort was convinced, however, that it was Jean Duffau from the Gers Département. Duffau, he suspected, had been bribed, or perhaps seduced by Buonarroti's mistress, since he had shown himself otherwise an "open enemy of the scoundrels," as befitted a man with 15,000 livres a year in *rente*. On the other hand, Babeuf had long since noted against Duffau's name (in his summary of the membership of the jury) that he was "an excellent patriot who loved the people as much as he was loved by them"; and Hésine's journal in January had let fall a hint that Duffau not only "looked like a Jacobin" but had reached an understanding with Moynier. For whatever reason, Duffau's was reputedly the fourth white ball which, dropped in the urn, acquitted the defendants on the conspiracy charge.[25]

At 4 a.m. on 25 May the jury declared that its deliberations were complete. Coffinhal and Viellart were deputed to "receive" the verdict and arrangements were made for the court to reconvene in the evening for the formalities to be completed. At this point the proceedings of the court, always unusual, became suddenly more extraordinary than ever. A strong rumor began to circulate in Vendôme during the 25th that there were to be no capital convictions. However, the scheduled evening session at which the rumor might have been confirmed failed to materialize. Instead a further session of the jury took place, and the full meeting of the court was postponed until the early morning of 26 May. Meanwhile (according to the author of the account in Hésine's journal) during the evening of 25 May Viellart brought strong pressure to bear on the jury to find some at least of the defendants guilty of a capital offense under the law of 27 germinal.[26]

Once the jury had retired, all communication with the outside world was cut off for the prisoners, although they were allowed the use of the exercise yard. Already convinced that he, at least, could expect no mercy, Babeuf busied himself with a farewell letter to his wife and his children, expressing his love for Emile, Camille and Cassius and his grief at parting. "I could conceive of no other manner of making you happy than through the common happiness. I have failed, and have sacrificed myself. It is also for you that I die . . ." In a postscript he begged Marie-Anne to write to his mother and his sisters, to send them his defense once it was printed, and to explain to them that his death was not a dishonorable one. In a letter written in the summer of 1796, he had entrusted the care of Marie-Anne and the children to Félix Le Peletier.[27]

At the first light on 26 May the beating of drums, the crash of cannon and the sound of marching detachments drew the inhabitants of Vendôme and the weary relatives of the prisoners to the abbey for the final act of the trial drama. Still earlier, while it was still dark, the jury had declared its verdict. At 4 a.m., after Rey-Pailhade had declared himself "unable" to fulfill his office as jury chairman, Pajot read out the findings. Seven defendants were guilty of advocating the restoration of the Constitution of 1793 by word of mouth, all with extenuating circumstances: Babeuf, Buonarroti, Germain, Darthé, Moroy, Cazin, and Blondeau. All except Blondeau, but with the addition of Bouin and Menessier, were guilty of advocating the restoration of the Constitution of 1793 in writings and publications. There were extenuating circumstances in all cases, save those of Babeuf and Darthé.

The prisoners found guilty were now brought into court one by one, in a leisurely fashion, until all were present: Babeuf first, then Darthé, then Buonarroti and the others. When all were assembled,

Gandon read out the verdict. There was an immediate last-ditch protest from Buonarroti, and it was supported by Réal. Under the terms of an article of the constitution, the effect of all legislation restricting the freedom of the press (including the relevant sections of the law of 27 germinal) was limited to one year, and the findings on the second charge, which carried the death sentence, must therefore be ruled out since the law had expired some weeks before the charge had been brought. Moroy pointed out that the only evidence advanced against him had related to his activities *before* 27 germinal, so that the 27 germinal law could not apply in his case, and he dismissed the court as a "band of brigands." Gandon cut Réal short and the judges retired to consider sentence. About 9 a.m. the court resumed and Gandon read out the sentences: death for Babeuf and Darthé, deportation for the other seven.[28] Thereupon Darthé and Babeuf both stabbed themselves with daggers they had earlier improvised from brass candle-holders and had concealed in their clothing. The two were quickly dragged in a fainting condition from the courtroom as the horrified spectators poured out of the doors and the guards took precautions against a possible riot.

By their public suicide attempts Darthé and Babeuf had effectively made their final protest against injustice. In point of fact, however, neither was mortally wounded, and the arrangements for execution proceeded as arranged. There was some unavoidable delay, as the guillotine had to be fetched from Blois, and it did not arrive until ten o'clock in the evening, when it was set up on the Place des Armes. The execution was fixed for 5 a.m. on 27 May, by which time many of the acquitted defendants had already been freed and had left the abbey.

Babeuf spent the last twenty hours of his life in agony. The point of the dagger had lodged deep in his chest, but he refused an offer by the prison doctor to extract it. On the morning of the execution Darthé was called first and there was a struggle, during which his wound was opened and a great deal of blood was spilled. When his turn came Babeuf died with courage and resignation. He made a last appeal to be allowed to bid farewell to his family. The bodies were taken to the Vendôme town cemetery and buried close to the chapel.[29]

Martyrdom, as Babeuf and Darthé well understood, is a powerful political weapon. Isser Woloch has described, in his study of the *Jacobin Legacy*, the way in which the legend of the "martyrs of Vendôme" became a rallying point for the surviving Jacobins as they strove to rebuild a party capable of challenging the triumphant reaction ushered in by the conservative victory in the spring elections of 1797. The resurgence had already begun in the course of the Vendôme trial itself. Thanks to the moderate and skillful tactics of the defense, pamphleteers like Antonelle and Pache and journalists like Hésine and René Vatar, the editor of the influential Jacobin *Journal des hommes libres*, were able to present the proceedings as simply the most dramatic and savage episode in a continuing campaign of persecution against honest and patriotic republicans.

Many, perhaps most, Jacobins convinced themselves that Babeuf's communism was, in truth, no more than one man's private fantasy, and the conspiracy mere armchair speculation without any serious existence in fact. The minority who knew better remained expediently silent. Meanwhile, symbols of martyrdom remained to be exploited: Buonarroti, Germain, and the other Vendôme convicts, "deported" to a dank jail in Cherbourg harbor; the impoverished Citoyenne Babeuf, in need of succor by patriotic collections; the three Babeuf boys, demonstratively placed in the care of Le Peletier and General Turreau; legal struggles over the fate of Barbier and Meunier, of Hésine, and of Menessier, who was convicted in absentia at Vendôme but eventually cleared by the Seine tribunal.

A wide popular front formed, reaching from the genuine Babouvist remnants in the Faubourg Antoine across to moderates like Réal and Méhée of the *Journal des Patriotes de '89*, ready to support the Fructidor coup of September 1797 and to capitalize on the shift in Directorial policy that followed. During Fructidor Barras, relying on the army, finally ousted Carnot, reconstructed the Directory, and turned to the Jacobin cadres for support in his determination to safeguard the Republic from royalist encroachment. Merged, more or less, in this popular front, old Babouvists played a part in the events of Fructidor, in the subsequent revival of Jacobin political clubs, and in the electoral campaign of 1798. Despite the renewed repression that followed the Jacobin successes in that campaign, the élan of the party persisted down to its last stand in July and August 1799 in the Manège club, where, on the very eve of Bonaparte's coup, the old Hébertist Marchand scandalized the bourgeoisie with his demand for the erection of a memorial column to Babeuf and Darthé.

Afterwards, the persecutions and deportations of the Consulate were no more merciful to the remnants of Babouvism than to other Jacobins, and it was characteristic that Fouché's vindictiveness could even extend down to Marie-Anne Babeuf: in January 1801 she was imprisoned in the Madelonettes in the general round-up of Jacobin sympathizers ordered after the unsuccessful bomb plot against France's new dictator, Bonaparte. Marie-Anne and Emile would again receive the attention of the police in 1808, at the time of General Malet's conspiracy.

Long before then the Jacobin party had been broken up and dispersed, and the Jacobin tradition, including its Babouvist variant, suppressed and for the most part forgotten. Richard Cobb's exploration of French popular protest from 1789 to 1820 has turned up no more than occasional hints of survival and continuity. (Didier, for example, was identified in a police report as a member of a group of old Paris militants meeting at Versailles in November 1807.) The main thrust of Cobb's argument is that, apart from the isolated activities of a few exceptional individuals and families, there was a massive discontinuity between the Jacobin militancy of the 1790s and the radical revolutionism of the 1830s.[30] Whether the discontinuity in radical leadership was reflected also in a discontinuity in the developing political and social consciousness of the workers of the Paris faubourgs, to which the Babouvists had made their own distinctive contribution, is a question still to be asked, one of many concerning the democratic history of the period 1800-30 which await the historian's attention.

Conclusion

In 1817 a Dutch democrat living in New York, Maria Aletta Hulshoff, published the first English account of the Conspiracy of the Equals and the fate of "that much beloved and respected friend to the people, Gracchus Babeuf." In a pamphlet dedicated to the memory of "names dear to European Democrats," Babeuf and Darthé found their place alongside Robespierre, Saint-Just and Marat as part of a common and unforgotten revolutionary tradition.[1] The Jacobin tactic of ridiculing the Directory's allegations of a communist conspiracy proved so successful that, for at least a generation after the revolution, Babeuf's historical reputation was that of a martyr for democracy and not of a prophet of communism.

Only after Buonarroti published his account of the conspiracy (in 1828) did socialists, Marx and Engels among them, pay any recognition to the significance of the communist objectives of the conspirators. Even then it was still possible for the English Chartist Bronterre O'Brien to publish a translation in which he explicitly disavowed the Equals' extreme views on property and violent revolution, while welcoming their attempt to restore Jacobin democracy. But when "the specter of communism" arose to haunt Europe in the 1840s and the 1850s, conservatives seeking the historical origins of the new movement added their contribution to the tradition which made Babeuf (in Taine's words) "the great apostle of despotic communism."[2]

Consequently, while continuing to honor Robespierre as a great revolutionary democrat, socialists like Guesde and Jaurès were able to recognize in Babeuf the originator of a distinct communist tradition in modern French history. Yet not all historians have accepted this view without qualification. For Alfred Espinas, a French conservative writing at the close of the nineteenth century, as for J.L. Talmon more recently, there seemed little to choose between Robespierre and Babeuf as doctrinaire enemies of property, liberty, and civilization in general. In the opposite camp the great French Revolution scholar Albert Mathiez always obstinately refused to distinguish between the Jacobin tradition and the Babouvist tradition. "Buonarroti's publication was of great importance for the history of French socialism," he declared magisterially in his Sorbonne lectures in 1929, "but the plot which it described was not, properly speaking, a communist plot." "Babeuf was essentially the agent of the amnestied terrorists," he was to add; "his communism is something purely accessory which had little to do with his true political program."[3]

For Mathiez, notoriously, Robespierre would always be the one true precursor of social democracy in the French Revolution; and Babeuf was consequently doomed to remain "purely accessory." Yet there was enough authority behind Mathiez's interpretation to encourage the persistence of historical doubt as to whether the 1796 episode was, in fact, "properly speaking, a communist plot."

In 1958 the issue was explored in the pages of the *Annales historiques de la Révolution française*, by English, French, and Italian scholars.[4] The ensuing debate demonstrated the complexity of the problem, but failed to produce a consensus. Whether Babeuf was genuinely and essentially a communist or whether his communism was no more than incidental to his Jacobinism remains, therefore, the central problem of interpretation in Babeuf studies.

Once Babeuf's communism is conceded, a number of highly contentious secondary problems immediately demand attention. What were the sources of his communist ideas? Did they derive from the utopianism of the Enlightenment? Were they rooted in Babeuf's identification with the traditional communal life of the peasantry of Picardy—or in a critical and materialist understanding of the consequences of the impact of capitalism on the French rural economy? What was the importance of the Jacobin example of a controlled and directed economy in 1793-4 for the final shape of Babouvist doctrine? Was Babeuf's communism in the main utopian, ascetic, and backward-looking—or did it foreshadow the possibility of a collective organization of production and thus anticipate the "scientific socialism" of Marx and Lenin? Did Babeuf act as the conscious spokesman of the proletariat and anticipate the class-struggle analysis of Marxism—or was he the spokesman of an as yet imperfectly differentiated *sans-culotte* amalgam of small masters, journeymen and wage-earners? Did Babeuf's main historical importance rest on his advocacy of the revolutionary dictatorship of an élite—or did it lie in his deep-rooted distrust of the exercise of power and his vindication of the theory and practice of direct democracy?

Viewed from the perspective of a biography of Babeuf, the problem of the objectives of the Conspiracy of the Equals is simplified. It is not necessary to postulate that all who took part in the conspiracy—the Equals, their Montagnard allies, the lesser agents and the rank-and-file supporters—understood or accepted communist doctrines. It is necessary only to show that Babeuf himself had, by 1796, a clear vision of a communist goal and a reasonable expectation that the revolutionary overturn of the Directory would lead by the shortest possible path toward that goal.

It is perfectly clear from the prison correspondence with Charles Germain in Arras and from the pages of the *Tribun du peuple* that absolute equality, which was to be attained through the abolition of property and the collectively organized distribution of commodities, was central to Babeuf's thinking, at least from the summer of 1795 onwards. It is also clear that while he saw the restoration of the democratic Constitution of 1793 as a preliminary for the achievement of absolute equality (and a provisional revolutionary dictatorship as a necessary preliminary for that preliminary), it was these intermediate objectives that were "purely accessory"—communism was the essential. What France needed, Babeuf explained in the *Tribun*, was new institutions, not a new constitution.

How far this attitude was shared by the other participants in the conspiracy of 1796 becomes relevant only when it is asked how far Babeuf may be held to have compromised his essential beliefs in the quest for immediate practical support. That there was some compromise is evident. Manifestly many of the conspirators, particularly the former Montagnards, did not share Babeuf's aspirations for a communist society. The greater part of the conspiracy's propaganda was deliberately addressed to a public accessible to Jacobin but not to communist ideas.

To this extent Mathiez's view is doubtless correct, and in its outward manifestations the conspiracy appears as a Jacobin and not as a communist enterprise. Outward manifestations count for a great deal in history, but not for everything. It has been shown, firstly, that the inner group of the Equals, Babeuf's collaborators on the original Insurrectional Committee, formally accepted the communist program elaborated by Babeuf and Buonarroti; and, secondly, that they were determined to hold on to power after the insurrection, and to resist both an anticipated challenge from the Montagnards and the threat of submergence by the corrupted majority of the population. Our conclusion must be, therefore, that Babeuf's compromise was only tactical: the Conspiracy of the Equals was an attempted communist insurrection in which the central organizing body was determined not to compromise on essentials.

Most of the questions of interpretation concerning the nature of Babeuf's communism have already been raised in these pages. Concerning the sources of Babeuf's political ideas it has been contended that the direct influence of the Enlightenment counted for little. In his "General Defense" (compiled at Vendôme in 1797) Babeuf cited Rousseau, Mably, and Diderot (i.e., Morelly) in support of communism. But it is not to underestimate his achievements as a self-taught intellectual to argue that both the level of Babeuf's general culture, and the lack of opportunity for enriching that culture in a provincial backwater like Roye, make any wide and profound acquaintance with the teaching of the *philosophes* unlikely ten years earlier. Nor is there any convincing material evidence for such a degree of familiarity.

On the other hand, the correspondence with Dubois and the Arras Academy shows that, in a more general sense, Babeuf was certainly alive to the main currents of thought that were "in the air" during the closing years of the eighteenth century. He had some grasp of the notions of primitive equality and the argument from the natural rights of man, which was popularized by Rousseau but was also part of the common currency of political speculation of the age. In this sense the "ideas of the Enlightenment" were undeniably important in influencing the forms taken by Babeuf's speculations. But he is not to be seen as a fanatic, imposing an abstract literary blueprint for utopia on the new material world.

The counterview canvassed by Lefebvre, Dommanget and Pelletier—that the roots of Babeuf's communism are to be found in his understanding of and sympathy with the communal traditions of the peasants of Picardy—must also be, in the main, rejected. It is true that between 1789 and 1792 Babeuf aligned himself closely with the village communes in their struggle with the seigneurs over such issues as feudal dues, commoning rights and the seigneurial trees. It is also true that despite Babeuf's own alibis (and those offered on his behalf by the more naive of his biographers), until the revolution disrupted his life he served the seigneurs as a *feudiste* without any apparent qualms, and lived a life remote from the toil of the fields. There is no doubt that, particularly after his harsh treatment at the hands of some of his noble and clerical clients, Babeuf welcomed the opportunity of transferring his talents to the service of the leaders of the village communes, particularly as it also suited his pocket. But as a source of communist inspiration the peasants of Davenescourt, Beauvraigne and Méry are not convincing.

Dalin's argument—that Babeuf's communism originated in his critical awareness of the sufferings of the peasants and artisans of Picardy as a consequence of the rising and disruptive force of capitalism—seems better documented. Owing to his own experiences in childhood and early youth, owing to his day-to-day contact with the misery of an overpopulated countryside in the throes of economic change and a helpless prey to climatic disaster, Babeuf understood the realities of poverty and insecurity well. There is evidence that, even before the revolution, the central concern of his thought was to make those realities less intolerable. Before the revolution he had already concluded that the source of poverty was the concentration of landed property, and consequently the provision of employment, in the hands of a few, which led to the helpless destitution of the many.

In the struggles of the early years of the revolution, the campaigns against the *aides* and the *gabelle* and the agitation over the commons at Roye, Babeuf identified himself deliberately with the cause of the peasants and artisans, the poor and the propertyless, against the owners of rising bourgeois as well as decaying feudal property. In the midst of the practical preoccupations of political conflict he sought and found a theoretical justification for his conduct in the permeating Enlightenment doctrines of equality. Thus far Dalin is right when he traces the origins of Babeuf's communism to an intensifying class struggle in Picardy.

Dalin's further contention that in the 1780s Babeuf had already come to believe in a fully fledged communism must, however, be rejected. From his first venture as a political publicist, the *Cadastre perpétuel* of 1789, to his imprisonment at the beginning of 1795, Babeuf used the notion of absolute equality to justify a practical program of partial and gradual amelioration rather than immediate social revolution. In the *Cadastre perpétuel* he began by establishing the principle of the abstract natural right of every household to an equal portion of the productive land in France. He then derived from that principle a program of redistributive taxation and state-organized welfare which would establish a minimum standard of living for all, with adequate subsistence and medical, educational and religious services. The solution proposed in the *Cadastre perpétuel* however allowed the perpetuation both of inequality itself and of the unequal distribution of landed wealth on which it was based.

Thus, the *Cadastre perpétuel*, by declaring that the conventional right to property was subordinate to the prior natural right of survival, provided a rationale for *ad hoc* confiscation to meet demonstrable social need. However, it can hardly be said to have put forward a communist program. By the summer of 1790 Babeuf's thoughts had begun to turn towards the "agrarian law" in his quest for a solution to the problem of inequality. By the end of 1791 (in his correspondence with Coupé de l'Oise) he was defending the "equality of landed property" as "the final end and crowning of good legislation," and painting an idyllic picture of France divided out into a patchwork of independent peasant holdings each capable of providing a comfortable subsistence for a family.

Yet the practical means advocated remained moderate and partial: the leasing of church lands to the propertyless; the settling of families on commons and wastes; finally, in 1793, the allocation of the lands of the Vendéean rebels to the defenders of the Fatherland. In so far as it rested on the recognition of the theoretical right of the community to dispose of property at will and redistribute it according to need, this advocacy of the agrarian law was tinged with communism. But despite the special pleading of communist historians like Dommanget and Dalin, its ideal was unmistakably one of petty peasant proprietorship, of a wider and more equal distribution of property, but not of its abolition.

Thus at the moment when he became a Jacobin functionary in Paris in 1793, Babeuf's political thought contained two elements, both of which derived from a simplistic conception of equal natural rights: the notion of the duty of government to redistribute income through the provision of relief and essential welfare services; and the desirability of achieving an ultimate general equality in the possession of land through a program of redistribution.

During 1793 a third element was added. As a result of his involvement with the *sans-culotte* movement in the spring of 1793, and his personal experience of Jacobin collectivism in action (as secretary of the Paris Food Administration in the second half of the year), the focus of Babeuf's ideas shifted. Whereas previously his approach had been dominated by the redistribution of incomes or landed property, now he became increasingly concerned with the distribution of commodities. The pamphlet *Du système de dépopulation, ou la vie et les crimes de Carrier* (published at the beginning of 1795) revealed the persistence of all three of these elements in Babeuf's thought.

Within the restrictions imposed by the Thermidorian reaction, the *Système de dépopulation* praised the defunct Robespierre and his followers for planning to put into effect the agrarian law. It applauded Jacobin measures to tax the rich to provide pensions and allowances for soldiers' dependents. It defended the Jacobin attempt to break the property-owners' monopoly control of the distribution and price of commodities through the *maximum*, requisition, rationing, and the establishment of the national Commission des Subsistances.

The emphasis of the *Système de dépopulation* suggests that, as late as January 1795, Babeuf still regarded the *maximum*, requisition, and the other Jacobin policies of economic control as first steps towards the ultimate goal and superior solution of the agrarian law. Not until the summer of 1795, and his prison correspondence with Charles Germain at Arras, did Babeuf arrive at the conclusion that the simplest system for achieving absolute equality, the total bureaucratic control of the distribution of commodities, would make the institution of landed property redundant. It is from this discovery that Babeuf's espousal of pure communism dates: from his abandonment of the solution of a redistribution of the land, and his adoption of a vision of a society based instead on the complete rejection of private property.

The pages of the *Tribun du peuple* and the publications and the papers of the conspiracy show that from the summer of 1795 *le bonheur commun* replaced the agrarian law as the essential goal of political action, and it remained the central pivot of his thought until his death. The new system of *le bonheur commun* was distinguished by a classic simplicity in structure. All citizens would hand over the products of field and workshop to a corps of administrators, who would then divide out the total on a basis of complete equality. The objectives of this final communist system remained identical with those of the two previous systems: the redistribution of income defended in the *Cadastre perpétuel* and the redistribution of landed property, advocated in its most absolute form in the *Système de dépopulation*.

Throughout, Babeuf sought to assure the provision for all of an adequate share of food, clothing, housing and fuel, and access for all to education and medical care. Throughout, he retained the conviction (first made explicit in the *Cadastre perpétuel*) that since nature was frugal, these objectives could be achieved only by the abolition of the grosser inequalities in consumption between citizens. By the autumn of 1795 (as is evident from the argument of no. 35 of the *Tribun du peuple*), this commonsense principle of relative practical equality had become transmuted into an obsession with absolute equality for its own sake. Thus, in Babeuf's final system no individual must expect to receive any consideration of special needs in the distribution of the common store (every citizen's stomach being more or less the same size)—while no member of the community might contribute substantially more than his neighbor, for fear that he might thereby legitimize a claim to draw more out and thus begin again the fatal descent into the system of inequality, accumulation and destitution, wealth and poverty.

It is difficult not to discern in these pages of the *Tribun* a decline in the quality of Babeuf's thought. In his debate with Germain at Arras (and in some earlier writings), Babeuf had developed an explanation of the mechanism of inequality which depended on an observation of the workings of the economic system. Those who held a monopoly of land were able to withhold employment and force down wages; those who held a monopoly of commerce were able to exploit the consumer by fixing prices at will. These were arguments that related to a real external world, and they dealt with problems that could be attacked through practical political action. By the autumn of 1795 Babeuf was tracing the origins of inequality back to abstract first principles, to the difference in value placed by universal prejudice on different kinds of work (as, for example, the rating of the work of a clockmaker several times more highly than that of a peasant). To treat such fundamental causes of inequality required not a practical political program but a total moral revolution. We are, accordingly, forced to the paradoxical conclusion, quite contrary to the received consensus, that Babeuf began as a practical revolutionary and ended as a utopian dreamer.

It has been argued (particularly by Dommanget and Dalin) that Babeuf's communism was not simply a matter of the equal distribution of commodities, but that it also contained the beginnings of a conception of the progressive rôle of socially organized production. It was thus forward-looking, suited to an age of technological advance, and foreshadowed the true "scientific socialism" of Marx and Engels. This contention appears to rest on three legs. First, there is the evidence discovered by Dalin that as early as 1786 Babeuf was speculating on the advantages of the collective leasing and cultivation of the land by peasant associations. Second, there is Babeuf's correspondence with Coupé in 1791, advocating "the indefinite multiplication of resources" through "skillfully combined organization" and "wisely directed labor." Finally, there are the economic arrangements for the communist community discussed by Babeuf and Germain in 1795 (and reproduced, more or less, in the program of the Conspiracy of the Equals), which imply an extensive collective ordering of the processes of production.

In assessing this evidence it has proved impossible to follow Dalin when he attributes great significance to the fact that Babeuf's papers contain notes apparently advocating collective farms in 1786. Not only were these speculations not made public at the time, but Babeuf made no further public or private references to collective cultivation during the remaining ten years of his life. The notion of collective farms was linked neither with the agrarian law nor with the ultimate communist system of 1795. Moreover, although the evidence as presented by Dalin is ambiguous, the emphasis in Babeuf's notes appears to be in any case on exploitation through collective *leasing* rather than by collective *labor*. Finally, while Babeuf anticipated that the formation of his "*fermes collectives*" would result in a massive increase in productivity, this was to be achieved through the economies of social organization, and not through the application of capital and advances in technology. The most that may be said is that, in certain occasional speculations, Babeuf anticipated the insights of utopian socialists like Charles Fourier and Robert Owen, but hardly those of Karl Marx and Josef Stalin.

In 1935 Dommanget cited Babeuf's correspondence with Coupé as evidence of his commitment by 1791 to the concepts of collective organization and of technological progress. The passage adduced is both obscure and marginal to an exposition of Babeuf's main contemporary concern: an exposition of the agrarian law. Nevertheless, notes made by Babeuf a few months earlier in the year may help to make its significance clearer. In these Babeuf proposed the creation of a national "industrial committee"; its functions would be to encourage the revival of staple trades, which provided employment, in place of luxury trades, and to encourage the dissemination of the knowledge of new techniques. Both these objectives were a commonplace of eighteenth-century thought, and neither was concerned primarily with the increase of productivity in this context. It was characteristic that although Babeuf was in favor of the adoption of steam-powered flour mills it was not because of their potentially higher productivity, but because they were more reliable than water mills or windmills and more economical in the use of agricultural land.

The sketch of a communist order outlined at Arras in 1795 incorporated a far more definite and detailed plan for the centralized administration of production. Yet, once again, the potentialities of technology and the raising of productivity were treated as incidental to the central concern, which was to provide employment for all by balancing available manpower against available resources. The functions of the administrators of the community were to avoid waste by fixing a maximum for the output of workshops in each trade and a maximum intake of new workers, and also to allocate labor to make the most economical use of resources. The administrators were to spread the knowledge of more efficient techniques both in industry and in agriculture. But the explicit purpose of this activity was the husbanding of labor and the increase of leisure and not the expansion of production. Nothing substantial was added to this program by the *Tribun du peuple*, by the publications of the conspiracy, or by Buonarroti's account (apart from some clarification of the details of the administrative machinery).

The conclusion must be, firstly, that Babeuf's overriding preoccupation was always the satisfaction of individual needs through a more just mode of the distribution of the product of labor. When he turned to a consideration of the mode of production it was only as a consequence of his interest in two subordinate problems: the provision of employment for all citizens and the most economical use of the scarce resources made available by a frugal nature. Babeuf certainly had a clear vision of the advantages of the large-scale planning of economic life. He was not unaware of the improvements in efficiency that could be achieved through the application of advanced productive techniques. But he did not possess (and could not have possessed) any conception of the industrial and technological revolution which was to transform the face of Europe over the next half-century.

Babeuf's communism was a system conceived within the context of an apparently static peasant and artisan economy; and its prescriptions were inevitably shaped, and indeed calculated, to preserve the essential outlines of such an economy. The peasants were to continue to till their holdings and the artisans to man their workshops. Only the great landlords and the merchants and financiers were to disappear—to give place to an administrative and technocratic bureaucracy.

The example of the Soviet Union, and perhaps of China, suggests that in certain circumstances, such a centralized bureaucracy may be able to carry through a modernizing economic revolution. In eighteenth-century France those circumstances—the inspiration of existing examples of an advanced industrial economy, the leadership of an organized élite with a world-view founded on the concept of material progress—were absent. It is difficult, therefore, not to see the Conspiracy of the Equals as the most extreme reaction of traditional classes during the revolution against the challenge of accelerating capitalism, rather than as the harbinger of a new, progressive, socialist economic order.

Parallel to the debate over the progressive or backward-looking nature of Babeuf's communism is that which seeks to establish how far the Babouvist movement represented the first stirrings of a new proletarian class-consciousness. The problem is complicated by the fact that Babeuf appears to have been one of the earliest publicists to make use of the term "proletarian" in the modern sense. On the first occasion, at the end of 1795, Babeuf invoked the analogy between the original proletarians of ancient Rome and the contemporary class of "passive citizens" deprived of political rights in practice by their lack of education. Subsequently (in the *Système de dépopulation* pamphlet of 1795, as in no. 35 of the *Tribun du peuple*), the *"prolétaires"* were more clearly equated with a social class, the propertyless masses in conflict with the exploiting property-owners. Evoking the same image, the prosecution at the Vendôme trial in 1797 condemned the conspirators for trying to rouse up the "frightening mass of proletarians" to hurl themselves on "the proprietors."[5] For Babeuf, however, the choice of the term *prolétaire* was exceptional, and it had no precise or ideological connotation. More common in his writings are references to "the poor," to "the people," to "workers," *sans-culottes*, or "plebeians."

Moreover, while it is evident that even before 1789, Babeuf had come to recognize the existence of conflict of classes within society, his conception of that conflict, despite Professor Dalin, was not, and never became in any sense, dialectical. In his correspondence with Dubois in 1787, Babeuf traced the origins of feudal property to an ancient act of violence and usurpation, subsequently legitimized by force and fraud. In the *Cadastre perpétuel* the same explanation was extended to the origins of all property, in order to account for the existing distinction between nine million property-owning Frenchmen and fifteen million who owned nothing. In each case the origins of inequality, as in Rousseau, were conceived as historically remote.

No. 29 of the *Tribun du peuple* contains a trenchant analysis which is often cited to illustrate Babeuf's clear grasp of the realities of contemporary class conflict. In these passages, two parties within the Convention are contrasted: one working for a bourgeois and aristocratic republic, one committed to a popular and democratic republic. One represents a million "patricians," the other is the champion of the remaining twenty-four million "plebeians." The context, however, makes it clear that this class conflict is not of recent origin, for the plebeians are called upon to rally against a "million . . . *which was always* . . . the bloodsucker of the twenty-four other millions, . . . *which has disported itself in idleness for centuries* at the expense of our sweat and our labor." (My italics.)

Exposure to a more sophisticated *sans-culotte* tradition in Paris in 1793 broadened Babeuf's conception of the methods of exploitation, the "very old trick" (as he called it) by which the age-old inequality and oppression were perpetuated. He denounced (particularly in his correspondence with Germain in 1795) the system of commerce by which merchants used their monopoly of commodities to squeeze the consumer and keep him poor, just as he had earlier in the *Système de dépopulation* condemned the owners of landed property for squeezing the proletarians. In neither case, however, was there any hint of a recognition of the dynamic nature of society, or that the intensity or the nature of exploitation had changed and was changing under the impact of a new economic system.

To seek in Babeuf an anticipation of *Das Kapital* or even of the *Communist Manifesto* is plainly to pursue a chimera. Babeuf's conception of class and class struggle was one appropriate to an essentially static economy, in which the nature of the confrontation was timeless, moral and absolute, and not determined by changes in the "mode of production."

This is not to say that the Babouvist movement, or Babeuf himself, contributed nothing to the development of proletarian class-consciousness in France. The recognition (so clearly expounded in the pages of the *Tribun du peuple*) that the crucial political conflict was one of class, and not of opinions or of rights, was of great significance. The *Tribun's* deliberate identification of the radical democratic and plebeian cause with the "workers," the Panthéon Society's invocation of the support of the "workers of the faubourgs" in 1796, and the Equals' deliberate attempt to engage the Paris workers in the preparations for their conspiracy were arguably each part of the first attempt in history to build a specifically working-class party. Professor Soboul is doubtless correct when he points out that the Paris *ouvriers* were not proletarians in the Marxist sense. They remained part of a *sans-culotte* amalgam which included small workshop masters and shopkeepers and was still attached to petit-bourgeois property concepts. The fact remains that the Babouvist agitation was qualitatively different from anything that had happened before, even the *sans-culotte* movement of 1793-4.

Nor is this all. The Marxist usage which made the proletariat the special product of modern industry, steam power, and the factory system was not the only (or even the most influential) analysis current in the French democratic and working-class movement for most of the following century. When Blanqui was asked to give his profession at the beginning of a political trial in 1832, he made the historic reply: "Proletarian . . . the class of thirty million Frenchmen who live by their labor and who are deprived of political rights." Twenty years later, in his correspondence, Blanqui offered a fuller analysis of the class struggle: "The middle class comprises most of the individuals possessing a certain amount of wealth and education: financiers, merchants, proprietors, lawyers, doctors, bureaucrats, rentiers—all those living on their revenues and the exploitation of the workers. Add to these a fair number of landowners who have wealth but not education and you will have a maximum number of no more than four million. There remain thirty-two million proletarians without property, or with very little property, and living only by the product of their hands. It is between these two classes that the bitter war has arisen."[6] Proletarian class-consciousness so defined was derived directly from the experience of the French Revolution rather than the Industrial Revolution, and it found its first clear expression in the Conspiracy of the Equals. Despite the triumphs of Marxism at the close of the nineteenth century, the older tradition remained an important component of French working-class attitudes at least until the middle of the twentieth century.

Across the political spectrum from the far left of Daniel Guérin and Herbert Marcuse, through the more orthodox Marxism of Dalin, across to the conservatism of Talmon, there is a wide consensus among historians that Babeuf's major significance as a historical figure was as the pioneer of the doctrine of the revolutionary dictatorship of an élite, and thus as the direct precursor of Lenin and the Bolsheviks.[7] It has been suggested in this study that this view requires considerable modification. Taking Babeuf's revolutionary career as a whole, we can with equal cogency judge his importance to lie in his contribution to the development of the theory and tactics of a widely based and even libertarian democracy.

Babeuf's vindication (in the correspondence with Coupé) of the principles of direct democracy—his deliberate advocacy of the widest and freest possible involvement of all sections of the population in the immediate exercise of sovereignty through initiative, referendum, and recall—may be regarded as "negative features" by Professor Dalin, or as the stock-in-trade of the totalitarian democrat by Professor Talmon. But these attitudes are, in my view, insupportable. Nor can Babeuf's acute post-Thermidorian critique of the Jacobin dictatorship be dismissed as a temporary aberration. His advocacy (in 1794) of the formation of a democratic *party* on the model of the reformed Club Electoral, laying stress on the participation of women and of the most plebeian elements of the Paris population, must be regarded as one of the major breakthroughs in democratic theory that occurred during the revolutionary epoch in Europe.

One of the central themes of this account has nevertheless been the constant tension in Babeuf between his conviction that the people are essentially wise and capable of government, and his observation that in practice people have a tendency to make the wrong choice and to follow the wrong paths. It is true that Babeuf's solution was an élitist solution. He recognized and proclaimed the necessity of the rôle of the dedicated tribune who would enlighten and guide the people towards the right decisions. Nobody was better aware, however, of the dangers of such élitism. In his speculations (gathered together as *Lueurs philosophiques* in 1790-91), in his denunciation of the revolutionary government after Thermidor, in his rejection of revolutionary putschism during the discussions with Germain at Arras, and in his stand against personal dictatorship in the councils of the Equals in 1796, Babeuf was consistent in his distrust of the innate "spirit of domination" within men.

And yet, in the end, Babeuf came to accept the necessity of a revolutionary dictatorship. It is a decision apparently in contradiction to everything he had previously stood for, and a decision which appears to justify his assimilation within the élitist tradition of Buonarroti and Blanqui, Tkachev and Lenin, and his adoption as one of the "founding fathers" of Soviet communism. It has been suggested, nevertheless, that things are perhaps not so simple as they appear, that there are revolutionary dictatorships and revolutionary dictatorships, and indeed some which may be rather more readily reconcilable with a basic faith in genuine democracy than others.

In particular it has been demonstrated that the dictatorship advocated by Babeuf was one hedged about by many conditions. It was to last no more than three months; from the first it was to be subject to the oversight of the resurgent revolutionary people of Paris, and its function was to usher in an even more democratic constitution than the Jacobin Constitution of 1793. But perhaps more important, from the point of view of the question of the consistency of Babeuf's political thought, were the reasons that lay behind his acceptance of even such a provisional dictatorship.

Babeuf's ideal was a free people enlightened and organized by its altruistic tribunes, exercising its sovereignty as directly as possible. In the conditions of 1796 the realization of such an ideal was impossible. In their eagerness to unearth the roots of "totalitarianism" in the Babouvist movement, historians have been strangely blind to the degree to which the Babouvists' opponent, the Directory, itself exercised a political dictatorship. The Constitution of the Year Three excluded the masses from the exercise of political power. The persecution of the *Tribun du peuple* and Lebois' *Ami du peuple*—and the methodical corruption of the rest of the republican press—made it clear that the Directory was determined not to permit any effective anti-government opposition. The closing of the Panthéon Society confirmed that an open and legal political agitation for radical reform would not be tolerated.

In such circumstances Babeuf was compelled to admit that the majority of the people had been corrupted, and that there was no possibility of winning them back until the apparatus of governmental tyranny was overthrown and its influence destroyed. The biographer of Babeuf is not concerned with what might have happened had the conspiracy succeeded, or with what Buonarroti may have believed in 1828. He is concerned only with what Babeuf believed and advocated in 1796, which was a short-term provisional dictatorship to restore democracy and not a long-term institutional dictatorship to impose communism.

During his sojourn in the Temple in Paris in 1796, Babeuf had leisure to reflect on the theoretical consequences of the position he had finally taken up and to draft a justification. He considered it important enough to smuggle out of his prison at Vendôme for publication in Hésine's journal. In this apologia he examined for the last time the problem of the rôle of the revolutionary vanguard.

To begin with, there was the duty to act as the people's watchdog over the machinations of those in power. "Without continually watchful sentinels," Babeuf wrote, "those who are governed are easily misled by governments which always have the art to color their acts with the appearance and the pretext of the public good." Secondly, there was the right and duty of organizing resistance. "It is impossible for everyone to see an infraction [of the people's liberty] at the same time and to be immediately ready to rise against it. Somebody must begin and give the signal. It is natural that it should be whoever first perceives the infraction. Thus, the initiative for the awakening, for the provocation or, if you will, the insurrection, must belong to all, to each in particular and to the first comer. And one should not reasonably fear any dangerous abuses, since it is not tolerable to suppose an entire nation so inept as to allow itself to be led astray by false visions or extravagant suggestions."[8]

Babeuf's final word on the subject of political power was, in this spirit, perfectly consistent with the rest of his teachings. The only check against the fatal "spirit of domination" in men is the "force of the people," and it is the duty of the clear-sighted leaders of the people to call that force into action whenever it becomes necessary. Babeuf's doctrine was one of constant vigilance and permanent insurrection, not of a closed and final totalitarian dictatorship.

"Babeuf might have been soon forgotten," Professor Robert Palmer wrote in his *Age of the Democratic Revolution,* "if the Directory, on suppressing his conspiracy, had merely imprisoned him, and then released him under police supervision, as it did with other such *exagérés*; if it had not brought him to trial, given him a courtroom forum, made his name a byword and his execution a martyrdom; and if Buonarroti, whose life was spared at the same trial, had not published thirty years later his *Conspiration pour l'égalité dite de Babeuf.* . . ."[9]

An attempt has been made in these pages to show that Babeuf's historical significance does not rest solely on his participation in the conspiracy of 1796 or on the accident of his martyrdom. Before 1796 Babeuf had already completed at least three distinct revolutionary careers, each in its own right worth the attention of the modern historian.

As a democratic agitator and a Jacobin administrator in Picardy, he helped to create a rural base for the revolution by involving the peasant masses directly and consciously in its politics, and by involving the revolution deliberately in the defense of their interests. In 1793 (as an associate of Fournier and of Chaumette), he contributed to the rise and temporary triumph of the *sans-culotte* movement in Paris. As a journalist and pamphleteer after Thermidor, he strove to rally the scattered and demoralized democratic forces against both the remnants of the revolutionary government and the steady political counteroffensive of the bourgeois conservatives.

Perhaps history might have ignored each of these episodes, had it not been for the final denouement at Vendôme. Yet without some conception of the rôle of such middle-rank revolutionaries, and even of those more obscure, the history of the revolution and the revolutionary tradition to which it gave birth is hardly comprehensible.

Even so, in the last analysis, it is the challenge to history represented by the dramatic Conspiracy of the Equals that focuses our attention on Babeuf, his personality and his ideas. The end of the eighteenth century in France was an age characterized by growing social inequality, the rapid increase of economic and political power, and its steady concentration in the hands of the bourgeoisie. Against the pressures of these powerful material forces Babeuf asserted the absolute human right to equality in the important things in life, and the right to control and (when necessary) to resist the exercise of political power. Inevitably, in the end, he was personally broken by the struggle, and he died conscious of failure. Yet he died with a clear conscience. What one man could do to vindicate the ideals of equality and freedom, he had done.

Notes

The following abbreviations are used in the Notes and the Bibliography:

A.D.   Archives Départementales
A.H.R.F. *Annales historiques de la Révolution française*
A.N.   Archives Nationales
B.M.   British Library at the British Museum
B.N.   Bibliothèque Nationale

Introduction

1. Bourgin, G., "Babeuf et le babouvisme," *Cahiers de la Révolution française* (no. 1, 1934), p. 106.

Engels, F., and Marx, K., *Die Heilige Familie* (Literarische Anstalt, Frankfurt-am-Main 1845), p. 186.

Marx and Engels, *Selected Works* (Foreign Languages Publishing House, Moscow 1951), vol. I, p. 58.

2. *The Communist International, 1919-1943.* Documents selected and edited by Jane Degras (O.U.P., London 1956), vol. I, 1919-1922, pp. 46-7.

Dalin, V.M., "L'historiographie de Babeuf," *La Pensée* (N.S. no. 128, 1966), p. 79.

Dalin, V.M., *Grakkh Babef; nakanune i vo vremia Velikoi Frantsuzskoi revoliutsii, 1785-1794* (Izdatel'stvo Akademii nauk S.S.S.R., Moscow 1963), *passim.*

3. Dalin, "L'historiographie de Babeuf," p. 78.

Thibout, G., *La Doctrine Babouviste*. Thèse pour le doctorat de droit (Librairie nouvelle de droit et de jurisprudence, Paris 1903), pp. 1-2.

Thomson, D., *The Babeuf Plot: The Making of a Republican Legend* (Kegan Paul, London 1947), p. 85.

4. *Buonarroti's History of Babeuf's Conspiracy for Equality; with the author's reflections on the . . . French Revolution . . . also his views of*

democratic government . . . and . . . equality. Translated from the French
and illustrated by original notes by Bronterre O'Brien (H. Hetherington,
London 1836).

Bax, E.B., *The Last Episode of the French Revolution, Being a History
of Gracchus Babeuf and the Conspiracy of the Equals* (Grant Richards,
London 1911).

Thomson, D., *The Babeuf Plot: The Making of a Republican Legend*
(Kegan Paul, London 1947).

5. Colloque international de Stockholm, *Babeuf et les problèmes du
babouvisme* (Editions sociales, Paris 1963).

Mazauric, C., *Babeuf et la Conspiration pour l'Egalité* (Editions sociales,
Paris 1962).

Dalin, *Grakkh Babef.*

Bergmann, K.H., *Babeuf, Gleich und Ungleich* (Westdeutscher Verlag
Köln und Opladen, Cologne 1965).

Dommanget, M., *Sur Babeuf et la conjuration des égaux* (François
Maspero, Paris 1970).

Dalin, V.M., Saitta, A., and Soboul, A., *Inventaire des manuscrits et
imprimés de Babeuf* (Ministère de l'Education Nationale, Commission
d'Histoire Economique et Sociale de la Révolution française, Paris 1966),
p. xv.

Dalin, V.M., "Napoleone e i Babuvisti," *Studi Storici* (vol. X, no. 3,
1969), pp. 469-79.

Dalin, "L'historiographie de Babeuf," pp. 99-100.

6. Cf. Scott, J.A. (editor & translator), *The Defense of Gracchus Babeuf
before the High Court of Vendôme* (University of Massachusetts, Amherst
1967), which includes Herbert Marcuse's "Thoughts on the Defense of
Gracchus Babeuf."

7. Brinton, Crane, *The Anatomy of Revolution* (Vintage Books, New
York 1957), p. 200.

Pasternak, B., *Doctor Zhivago,* trans. Max Hayward and Manya Harari
(Fontana Books, London 1961), p. 443.

Talmon, J.L., *The Origins of Totalitarian Democracy* (Mercury Books,
London 1966), pp. 5, 11.

8. Buonarroti, F., *Conspiration pour l'égalité, dite de Babeuf, suivie du
procès auquel elle donna lieu et des pièces justificatives* (Librairie romantique, Brussels 1828), 2 vols. The edition cited below is Buonarroti, F.,
Conspiration pour l'égalité, dite de Babeuf, Edition R. Brécy, A. Soboul
(Editions sociales, Paris 1957), 2 vols.

Dufort de Cheverny, J.-N., *Mémoires sur les règnes de Louis XV et Louis
XVI et sur la Révolution,* publiés avec une introduction par Robert de
Crèvecoeur (Plon, Nourrit, Paris 1886), vol. II, pp. 334-5.

A.N. W³ (Tribunaux révolutionnaires) 559-566.

A.N. BB³20, A.N. BB³21, A.N. BB³22, A.N. F⁷4276, 4278 and 7178, and
A.N. AF III 42.

Débats du procès instruit par la Haute-Cour de Justice, contre Drouet,

Baboeuf et autres, recueillis par des sténographes (Baudoin, Paris [1797]), 5 vols.; *Copie des pièces saisies dans le local que Baboeuf occupait lors de son arrestation* (Imprimerie Nationale, Paris), frimaire-nivôse an V; *Suite de la copie des pièces saisies dans le local que Baboeuf occupait lors de son arrestation* (Imprimerie Nationale, Paris), frimaire-nivôse an V. Dalin, Saitta and Soboul, *Inventaire*, pp. 100-12, lists ten more publications connected with the trial, but this does not exhaust the bibliography.

Journal de la Haute-Cour de Justice établie à Vendôme... Soudry, éditeur propriétaire (edited by Abbé Rouzet), 1 vendémiaire an V to 14 nivôse an V; *Journal des séances du tribunal de la Haute-Cour de Justice établi à Vendôme* (edited by J.B.C. Morard); *Journal de la Haute-Cour de Justice, ou l'écho des hommes libres, vrais et sensibles* (edited by P.-N. Hésine), 13 fructidor an IV to 7 prairial an V.

Tribun du peuple, November 1795 - May 1796, and *L'Eclaireur du peuple*, February-April 1796.

9. Cf. Buonarroti, *Conspiration* (ed. Brécy, Soboul), vol. I, p. 224: "une foule de détails se sont éffacés de ma mémoire; elle n'a conservé le souvenir que des traits les plus saillants et une idée bien nette de la progression successive et simultanée des institutions et de la constitution."

10. Legrand, R., *Babeuf, ses idées, sa vie en Picardie* (Lafosse, Abbeville 1961); Pelletier, A., "Babeuf feudiste," *A.H.R.F.* (no. 179, 1965), pp. 29-65.

Dalin, Saitta and Soboul, *Inventaire des manuscrits et imprimés de Babeuf*, p. xii.

Dalin, "L'historiographie de Babeuf," p. 69.

11. Advielle, V., *Histoire de Gracchus Babeuf et du babouvisme, d'après de nombreux documents inédits* (chez l'auteur, Paris 1884), 2 vols.

Dalin, etc., *Inventaire*, p. xii; Dommanget, *Pages choisies de Babeuf, recueillies, commentées, annotées avec une Introduction et une Bibliographie critique* (Colin, Paris 1935), p. 10.

Archives départementales de la Somme, F129.

Reinhard, M., *Correspondance de Babeuf avec l'Académie d'Arras (1785-1788)* (P.U.F., Paris 1961).

Chapter 1

1. Normand, C., *Saint-Quentin et la Royauté* (H. Champion, Paris 1881), pp. 1-11, 176-80.

2. Babeuf's certificate of baptism, published in Advielle, V., *Histoire de Gracchus Babeuf et du babouvisme, d'après de nombreux documents inédits* (chez l'auteur, Paris 1884), vol. I, pp. 1-2, and in Combier, A.E., *La justice criminelle à Laon pendant la Révolution* (H. Champion, Paris 1882), vol. I, pp. 60-61.

Extract of the parish register of Damery, recording the marriage of François-Noel Babeuf and Marie-Anne-Victoire Langlet, published in Lecocq, G., *Un manifeste de Gracchus Babeuf* (Librairie des Bibliophiles, Paris 1885), pp. 7-9.

Advielle, *Gracchus Babeuf*, vol. I, pp. 3-6.

3. Dalin, V.M., *Grakkh Babef: nakanune i vo vremia Velikoi Frantsuzskoi revoliutsii, 1785-1794* (Izdatel'stvo Akademii nauk S.S.S.R., Moscow 1963), p. 42.

Deserters' pardon, published in Lecocq, *Manifeste*, pp. 1-2.

Advielle, *Gracchus Babeuf*, vol. I, p. 9.

4. Combier, *Justice criminelle à Laon*, vol. I, pp. 60-61.

Matthews, G.T., *Royal General Farms in Eighteenth-Century France* (Columbia University Press, New York 1958), *passim*.

5. *Encyclopédie méthodique* (Panckouke, Paris 1782-1832): *Finances*, by Rousselot de Surgy, J.P., vol. II, p. 352.

Dalin, *Grakkh Babef*, p. 42.

Advielle, *Gracchus Babeuf*, vol. I, p. 9, where it is stated as "probable" that Claude Babeuf got a *"brigade à commander dans les Gabelles"* about 1755. Although the date is clearly inaccurate the statement may be based on a reliable family tradition. A "brigadier" presumably received more than the maximum for simple gardes and less than the minimum for captains-general in the service: i.e., between 300 and 600 livres a year.

6. Biollay, L., *Les prix en 1790* (Guillaumin, Paris 1886), pp. 5, 14-81. Assuming a six-day week, a laborer in full employment could expect 31-33 livres a month as against Claude Babeuf's 23 livres. However, the income of a day-laborer would normally be reduced by the effect of religious holidays.

7. *Encyclopédie méthodique: Finances*, vol. I, pp. 330-1; vol. II, p. 352.

Matthews, *Royal General Farms*, p. 211.

8. Dalin, *Grakkh Babef*, pp. 42, 53 n.

Lecocq, *Manifeste*, p. 8.

Dommanget, M., *Pages choisies de Babeuf, recueillies, commentées, annotées avec une Introduction et une Bibliographie critique . . .* (Colin, Paris 1935), p. 313.

9. Advielle, *Gracchus Babeuf*, vol. I, pp. 9-13; Dommanget, M., "Babeuf et l'éducation," *A.H.R.F.* (no. 162, 1960), pp. 490-91.

Dalin, *Grakkh Babef*, pp. 33, 42-4, 331-2.

Dommanget, M., "Babeuf à Flixécourt," *A.H.R.F.* (no. 194, 1968), p. 536.

10. Fouquier-Cholet, *St. Quentin, Ancien et moderne* (Tilloy, St. Quentin 1822), pp. 144-5.

Dalin, *Grakkh Babef*, pp. 45-6.

Dommanget, "Babeuf à Flixécourt," pp. 534-9.

11. Dalin, *Grakkh Babef*, p. 48; Pelletier, A., "Babeuf feudiste," *A.H.R.F.* (no. 179, 1965), p. 33.

For the Bracquemonts, see Coët, E., *Histoire de la ville de Roye* (Paris 1880), vol. II, p. 42. A François Aubé de Bracquemont, 1738-1806, is here described as living in the rue Bridet in Roye. After serving in the army he "retired to Roye" and married in 1789. Babeuf's employer may have been François' father, Louis, or (more likely) a brother of this name.

12. Dalin, *Grakkh Babef*, p. 49.

Dénonciation à M. l'accusateur public du tribunal de Montdidier et réfutation d'un libelle infâme intitulé Affaire de la commune de Davenescourt Contre Philippine Cardevac, veuve de Gabriel La Myre et Ci-devant Dame de Davenescourt (no publisher or place, [1791]), p. 2.

Lecocq, *Manifeste*, pp. 7-9.

Advielle, *Gracchus Babeuf*, vol. I, p. 10.

13. Passport of 2 thermidor, an II: Combier, *Justice Criminelle à Laon*, vol. II, pp. 93-4. Ministre de la police générale de la république, *Extrait des registres des délibérations du Directoire exécutif, Paris, le 23 floréal* (Morard-Colas, Vendôme an IV), pp. 105-6: *Ordonnance de prise de corps contre Babeuf.* Soboul, A., "L'écrou de Gracchus Babeuf à Saint-Pélagie en l'an II," *A.H.R.F.* (no. 135, 1954), p. 175, makes Babeuf 5 ft. 6 ins. (English equivalent measure) and gives him *grey* eyes. An unflattering warrant of 1793 reduces the height to 5 ft. 1 or 2 ins. (English equivalent measure) and makes the eyes *brown:* Patoux, A., *Le faux de Gracchus Babeuf* (Imprimerie de Guetteur, Saint-Quentin 1913), p. 188. In 1796 Babeuf was interrogated by André Gérard, directeur du jury d'accusation du canton de Paris, and since Gérard cited in his description a "kind of scar on the right cheek close to the mouth" which everybody else missed, we may accept his determining vote for *blue* eyes: A.N. W³559.

14. Lecocq, *Manifeste*, pp. 7-9.

Neither the precise date of birth of the first child nor even her name is known with certainty. Advielle, followed by most subsequent biographers, mentions an (unnamed) daughter who died in December 1787. The same source refers to a daughter, Cathérine-Adélaide, baptized 14 November 1787, who died "aged 4 years and two months": *Gracchus Babeuf*, vol. I, p. 40. Professor Dalin assumes that both these notes refer to the same child. which would imply a birth date in September 1783: *Grakkh Babef*, pp. 121-2. However, a historian in touch with local gossip, Grégoire d'Essigny states that Babeuf's daughter was six years old at death, implying that she was born in 1781 and therefore outside wedlock: *Histoire de la ville de Roye* (Noyon 1818), pp. 400-401. Babeuf's correspondence contributes two pertinent pieces of information: firstly that he called the child "Sofie" (sic), and secondly that she had passed her fourth birthday by 13 December 1786: Reinhard, M., *Correspondance de Babeuf avec l'Académie d'Arras: 1785-1788* (P.U.F., Paris 1961), pp. 39, 147. Professor Dalin has also found an indication that the child was buried before 16 November 1787, although the date given is 12 November: *Grakkh Babef*, p. 122. The most likely reconstruction is that a child was born in late November or early December 1782. She was not then baptized, but was known to her parents as Sofie. In November 1787 Sofie was baptized Cathérine-Adélaide on her death-bed, before attaining her fifth birthday.

In addition to Cathérine-Adélaide, Advielle lists the following Babeuf children: Robert, born 29 September 1785; Cathérine-Adélaide-Sofie, bap-

352   *Notes to Pages 14-15*

tized 5 September 1788, "morte jeune"; Jean-Baptiste-Claude, baptized 28 October 1790, "mort jeune": *Gracchus Babeuf,* vol. I, p. 40. In November 1790 Babeuf "dechristianized" his own forenames, adopting the name Camille: Dalin, *Grakkh Babef,* p. 564. It seems likely that Robert was renamed Emile, and that Jean-Baptiste-Claude also became Camille at the same time. Camille junior was three years old in 1794, which is consistent: Deville, G., "Notes inédites de Babeuf sur lui-même," *La Révolution francaise* (vol. XLIX, juillet 1905), p. 39. Advielle says that Camille committed suicide by throwing himself off the Vendôme column when the Cossacks entered Paris in 1815: *Gracchus Babeuf,* vol. I, p. 342. While this may be unreliable, Camille was certainly alive in 1813, and so can hardly be said to have "died young," assuming the identification with Jean-Baptiste-Claude to be correct: Dautry, J., "Une lettre de Camille Babeuf," *A.H.R.F.* (no. 128, 1952), pp. 421-2. Cathérine-Adélaide-Sofie is clearly identifiable as the 7-year-old child who died while Babeuf was imprisoned at Arras in 1795: Advielle, *Gracchus Babeuf,* vol. II, p. 69; Deville, "Notes inédites de Babeuf," p. 39. In February 1797 Babeuf's third son was born and his names recorded as Cassius Graccus (sic): Bouis, R., "P.-N. Hésine, rédacteur du Journal de la Haute-Cour ou l'écho des hommes vrais et sensibles," *A.H.R.F.* (no. 162, 1960), p. 477n. According to Advielle "*Caius* Gracchus" Babeuf was killed fighting for Bonaparte in 1814: *Gracchus Babeuf,* vol. I, p. 342. Robert/Emile survived at least until the end of the 1820s: Dommanget, *Pages choisies,* p. 317n; Bourgin, G., "Note sur Robert Babeuf, fils de Gracchus et journaliste," *Cahiers de la Presse* (1938), pp. 223-9, 386-95; Advielle, *Gracchus Babeuf,* vol. I, pp. 342-3.

15. Dalin, *Grakkh Babef,* p. 50.
16. Ibid., pp. 51-3.
Pelletier, "Babeuf feudiste," p. 33.
Reinhard, *Correspondance de Babeuf,* p. 1.
Advielle's statement that Babeuf worked for a time in Noyon seems to be unfounded, and has led several biographers astray: *Gracchus Babeuf,* vol. I, p. 16. Cf., Legrand, R., *Babeuf, ses idées, sa vie en Picardie* (Lafosse, Abbeville 1961), p. 6; Mazauric, C., *Babeuf et la Conspiration pour l'Egalité* (Editions sociales, Paris 1962), p. 56; Bergmann, K.H., *Babeuf, Gleich und Ungleich* (Westdeutscher Verlag Köln und Opladen, Cologne 1965), p. 19.

17. Dommanget, "Babeuf et l'éducation," *A.H.R.F.* (no. 162, 1960), pp. 496-500.
Coët, *Histoire de Roye,* vol. II, p. 527.
Reinhard, *Correspondance de Babeuf,* pp. 146-7.
Grégoire d'Essigny, *Histoire de Roye,* p. 401.
Dalin, *Grakkh Babef,* p. 122.

18. G. *Babeuf, tribun du peuple, à ses concitoyens* (Imprimerie de Franklin, Paris 1795).

A.D. Somme F129/70, F129/109, copies of two letters written from a Paris prison in 1794 correcting Emile's style and orthography; ibid., F129/88-99, drafts and/or copies of letters containing advice on Emile's education and corrections to exercises, written from prison at Vendôme in September 1796.

Dalin, *Grakkh Babef*, p. 247n.

A.D. Somme F129/92. Copy of letter to Marie-Anne Babeuf from Vendôme prison, dated 23 vendémiaire an V (14 October 1796).

19. Dommanget, *Pages choisies*, p. 312.

Chapter 2

1. The description of Roye in the 18th century is based on Grégoire d'Essigny, *Histoire de Roye*, and Coët, *Histoire de Roye*.

2. Coët, *Histoire de Roye*, vol. II, pp. 170, 565-6.

Grégoire d'Essigny, *Histoire de Roye*, p. 230.

Dalin, *Grakkh Babef*, p. 138.

3. Pelletier, "Babeuf feudiste," pp. 33, 54.

Grégoire d'Essigny, *Histoire de Roye*, pp. 80-81, 230.

Reinhard, *Correspondance de Babeuf*, p. 135.

4. Coët, *Histoire de Roye*, vol. II, pp. 502-3, 508, 511.

Dommanget, *Pages choisies*, pp. 50-51, 69-70. Bergmann, *Babeuf*, p. 39, states that Florent Masson, "Babeuf's friend," gained Babeuf's admission to the Masonic lodge, but without offering any evidence.

5. Van Drival, E., *Histoire de l'Académie d'Arras* (Académie des Sciences, Lettres et Arts d'Arras, Arras 1872), pp. 59-62; Reinhard, *Correspondance de Babeuf*, pp. v-x, 1, 2n.

6. Reinhard, *Correspondance de Babeuf*, pp. vii, 12.

Advielle, *Gracchus Babeuf*, vol. II (second pagination), pp. 38n-39n.

7. Reinhard, *Correspondance de Babeuf*, pp. 3-4, 4n, 104.

Van Drival, *L'Académie d'Arras*, pp. 60-62.

8. Pelletier, "Babeuf feudiste," pp. 42-5.

Dalin, *Grakkh Babef*, pp. 56-70.

The edition of Aubry de Saint-Vibert cited by Dalin has the publication date 1781; *Grakkh Babef*, p. 56; Reinhard cites an edition in the Bibliothèque Nationale: *Les terriers rendus perpétuels, ou mécanisme de leur confection* (Paris 1787), 6 parties en 1 vol.: *Correspondance de Babeuf*, p. 5n; Pelletier states that "the first two parts" of the work "began to appear" in 1785: "Babeuf feudiste," p. 42n.

9. Deville, "Notes inédites de Babeuf," p. 40.

Tribun du peuple, no. 29, 1-19 nivôse, an III, p. 285.

10. Dalin, *Grakkh Babef,* pp. 59-60: "Babeuf could not to any extent fully disclose his thoughts . . . In documents designed for the seigneurs it was difficult for the archivist-feudist to show in any more clear way his sympathies for the peasants."

Pelletier, "Babeuf feudiste," pp. 46-9, 63: "he is accustomed to hide, or rather, not to reveal any thoughts about his conceptions save those which seem necessary and acceptable to whoever he addresses at the moment." *Le Tribun du peuple (1794-1796) par Gracchus Babeuf, textes choisis et présentés par Armando Saitta* (Union Générale d'Editions, Paris 1969), p. 9.

11. Pelletier, "Babeuf feudiste," pp. 35, 51; Advielle, *Gracchus Babeuf*, vol. I, pp. 523-4; A.D. Somme F129/116.

12. Lefebvre, G., Preface to Dommanget, *Pages choisies,* p. x; "Les origines du communisme de Babeuf," in Lefebvre, G., *Etudes sur la Révolution française* (P.U.F., Paris 1954), pp. 305-314; Dommanget, *Pages choisies,* p. 3: "c'est en travaillant comme terrassier au canal de Picardie, c'est en arpentant les sillons et en observant les conditions d'existence des paysans picards, c'est en fouillant dans les vieux grimoires les origines de la propriété seigneuriale de son pays, c'est en gémissant sur la misérable situation des ouvriers de Roye au milieu desquels il vivait que Babeuf s'est forgé une conscience de classe."
Dalin, *Grakkh Babef,* pp. 62-90.

13. Cf. the conclusion of Pelletier, "Babeuf feudiste," pp. 61-2: "nous n'avons cependant nullement l'intention . . . de prétendre que le feudiste chez Babeuf ait engendré le révolutionnaire; car il n'était nullement nécessaire que le travail le moins révolutionnaire qui fut alors—l'art des terriers seigneuriaux—engendrât un révolutionnaire. A moins que celui ne le fût déjà."

14. Advielle, *Gracchus Babeuf*, vol. I, p. 9.
Dommanget, *Pages choisies,* p. 156.

15. Advielle, *Gracchus Babeuf*, vol. I, pp. 523-6.
Reinhard, *Correspondance de Babeuf,* pp. 6, 53n-54n.
Advielle, *Gracchus Babeuf*, vol. I, pp. 478-80; Pelletier, "Babeuf feudiste," pp. 61-2; Dalin, *Grakkh Babef,* pp. 57-8. No copies of the prospectus appear to have survived.

16. Reinhard, *Correspondance de Babeuf,* p. 6.
In April 1787 Bucquet sought to dissuade Jean-Baptiste Babeuf from leaving his service to join his brother on the grounds that if he did so, "in six months" he "would not have a sou in his pocket." Dalin, *Grakkh Babef,* p. 54.

17. Dalin, *Grakkh Babef,* pp. 53, 162, states that the lease of the house in the rue de Paris came to an end in 1788; but on 26 August 1787 and on 29 September 1787 Babeuf wrote letters addressed to his wife at "rue St. Gilles no. 11": Advielle, *Gracchus Babeuf*, vol. I, p. 61; A.D. Somme F129/37.
A.D. Somme F129/34, F.-N. Babeuf to J.-B. Babeuf, acknowledging "J'ai reçu, mon cher ami, tes 15 francs" and begging "a few sous"; ibid., F129/36, copy of letter dated 19 September 1787, F.-N. Babeuf to J.-B. Babeuf, asking for "small change" again.

18. Advielle, *Gracchus Babeuf,* vol. I, pp. 43-4.

A.D. Somme E100/14: "Aperçu d'estimation des diverses opérations nécessaires pour la rénovation des terriers."

Pelletier, "Babeuf feudiste," p. 51.

19. Grégoire d'Essigny, *Histoire de Roye,* p. 36. Antoine-Adolphe de Seiglières de Belleforières de Soyecourt was appointed in 1759: Grégoire d'Essigny, *Histoire de Roye,* p. 97. The office was held by the same man in February 1789: Ramon, G., *La Révolution à Péronne* (Quentin, Péronne, 1898), 2e série, p. 27.

20. Dalin, *Grakkh Babef,* pp. 141-7.

A.D. Somme F129/116, F129/38.

21. Deville, "Notes inédites de Babeuf," p. 40.

A.D. Somme L2105 (Mémoires et requêtes présentés au District [de Montdidier]), ff. 53-4.

22. Coët, *Histoire de Roye,* vol. I, p. 431; Advielle, *Gracchus Babeuf,* vol. I, p. 52; Thomson, D., *The Babeuf Plot: The Making of a Republican Legend* (Kegan Paul, London 1947), p. 9; Legrand, *Babeuf en Picardie,* p. 18n; Pelletier, "Babeuf feudiste," p. 36.

23. A.D. Somme F129/41, copy of letter of F.-N. Babeuf to Marie-Anne Babeuf, 16 August 1789: "l'état de feudiste est perdu."

Advielle, *Gracchus Babeuf,* vol. I, pp. 53-6: F.-N. Babeuf to Marie-Anne Babeuf, 25 July 1789.

A.D. Somme F129/41; Dalin, *Grakkh Babef,* pp. 159, 205

24. Advielle, *Gracchus Babeuf,* vol. I, p. 58.

Dalin, *Grakkh Babef,* p. 369.

Chapter 3

1. Dommanget, *Pages choisies,* p. 104.

A.D. Somme F129/75.

2. Espinas, A., *La philosophie sociale du XVIIIe siècle et de la Révolution* (Alcan, Paris 1898), pp. 88-93; Chinard, G., *L'Amérique et le rêve exotique dans la littérature française au XVIIe et au XVIIIe siècle* (Hachette, Paris 1913), *passim.*

The Defense of Gracchus Babeuf before the High Court of Vendôme (ed. and trans. J.A. Scott, University of Massachusetts, Amherst 1967), pp. 60-61.

3. Advielle, *Gracchus Babeuf,* vol. I, p. 177.

Thomas, A., "La pensée socialiste de Babeuf avant la conspiration des Egaux," *La Revue Socialiste,* vol. XL (1904), p. 233.

Dommanget, *Pages choisies:* Preface by Lefebvre, Introduction by Dommanget.

Lefebvre, G., *Le Directoire* (Armand Colin, Paris 1946), p. 34; Lefebvre, *Etudes sur la Révolution française,* pp. 305-314; and Godechot, J., "Les travaux récents sur Babeuf et le babouvisme," *A.H.R.F.* (no. 162, 1960), pp. 378-9. A version of the "traditional" periodicization also appears in Tønnesson, K.D., "The Babouvists from utopian to practical socialism," *Past and Present* (no. 22, 1962), pp. 60-76.

4. Dalin, V.M., "Les idées sociales de Babeuf à la veille de la Révolution," in Colloque international de Stockholm, *Babeuf et les problèmes du babouvisme* (Editions sociales, Paris 1963), pp. 55-72, and Dalin, *Grakkh Babef, passim.*

5. And thus to try to discount the catastrophic carelessness of Advielle, who claimed to have examined an "inventaire de livres de ma bibliothèque" drawn up by Babeuf about 1790, but who failed to comment on the contents: Advielle, *Gracchus Babeuf*, vol. I, p. 486.

6. Reinhard, *Correspondance de Babeuf*, pp. 13-15, 45, 51, 73, 138.

7. Advielle, *Gracchus Babeuf*, vol. II (second pagination), pp. 38n-39n. Reinhard, *Correspondance de Babeuf*, pp. 12, 33, 65, 77. Coll. int. de Stockholm, *Babeuf,* p. 34.

8. Advielle, *Gracchus Babeuf*, vol. II (second pagination), pp. 5-9, 39-41, 111.

9. Mazauric, C., "Le Rousseauisme de Babeuf," *A.H.R.F.* (no. 170, 1962), pp. 447-8.

Dalin, *Grakkh Babef*, p. 117. Professor Dalin agrees that there is no evidence for a familiarity with Morelly, but claims to furnish "indubitable proof" that Babeuf had studied the works of Mably "very closely" before 1789. The "proof" turns out to be Babeuf's claim at the Vendôme trial in 1796 that he had borrowed the phrase *"égalité parfait"* from Mably, together with a reminder that Babeuf used this phrase for the first time in a letter to Dubois in March 1787. Dalin also tenders in evidence an obscure note made by Babeuf in 1789 referring to "a quotation from Mably" but without citing it. In fact nowhere in Babeuf's defense at Vendôme did he say that the phrase *"égalité parfait"* was borrowed from Mably. Although he did cite a passage from Mably's *Traité de la législation* which contains the phrase, the context is an attempt to show that the ideas of the Equals *in 1796* could claim the sanction of the *philosophes* and not to explore the origins of his own ideas in detail. See *The Defense of Gracchus Babeuf,* ed. and trans. J.A. Scott, pp. 66-70. The "indubitable proof" is no proof at all.

10. Reinhard, *Correspondance de Babeuf,* pp. 22-3, 69-70, 94-102, 109-112.

11. Cf. Buonarroti, F., *Conspiration pour l'égalité, dite de Babeuf* (Edition R. Brécy, A. Soboul, Editions sociales, Paris 1957), vol. II, p. 208: ". . . une quantité suffisante d'aliments en pain, viande, volaille, poisson, oeufs, beurre ou huile, vin et autres boissons usités dans les différentes régions; légumes, fruits, assaisonnements, et autres objets dont la réunion constitue une médiocre et frugale aisance. . . ."

12. Reinhard, *Correspondance de Babeuf*, pp. 71, 109-112.

13. Delegorgue, *Mémoire sur cette question, est-il utile en Artois de diviser les fermes et exploitations des terres; et dans le cas de l'affirmative, quelles bornes doit-on garder dans cette division?* (no place of publication, 1786), p. 13.

Reinhard, *Correspondance de Babeuf*, pp. 7-8, 44, 50.

14. Dalin, *Grakkh Babef*, pp. 92 sqq; Dalin, "Les idées sociales de Babeuf à la veille de la Révolution," Coll. Int. de Stockholm, *Babeuf*, pp. 56 sqq. This document is preserved in the Marx-Lenin Institute and a critical and independent examination has not been permitted. (Cf. Reinhard, *Correspondance de Babeuf*, p. 69.) The existence of a copy, made by Advielle but unpublished, is indicated by Dommanget, "Tempérament et formation de Babeuf," Coll. Int. de Stockholm, *Babeuf*, p. 46, supported, however, by a reference to his private—and also restricted—collection. I am convinced by an examination of the two summaries of the document given by Dalin, against the general context of Babeuf's writings, that they are reliable, even though reservations are necessary on certain of the accompanying passages of interpretation.

15. Lefebvre, G., *Questions agraires au temps de la Terreur*, Collection de Documents inédits sur l'Histoire Economique de la Révolution française, publiés par le ministre de l'instruction publique (2ᵉ édition, Henri Potier, La-Roche-Sur-Yon), pp. 61-73.

Lefebvre, G., *Les Paysans du Nord pendant la Révolution française* (Rieder, Paris, 1924).

Goubert, P., *Beauvais et le Beauvaisis de 1600 à 1730. Contribution à l'histoire sociale de la France du XVIIe siècle* (S.E.V.P.E.N., Paris 1960), pp. 170-196; Deyon, P., "Quelques remarques sur l'évolution du régime Seigneurial en Picardie" (XVIe-XVIIIe siècles), *Revue d'histoire moderne et contemporaine* (N.S. vol. VIII, 1961), pp. 271-281.

16. Lichtenberger, A., *Le Socialisme et la Révolution française* (F. Alcan, Paris 1899), p. 160; Lefebvre, *Questions agraires,* pp. 61-73.

Deyon, "L'évolution du régime Seigneurial en Picardie," p. 280.

17. Dalin, "Les idées sociales de Babeuf," Coll. Int. de Stockholm, *Babeuf*, pp. 58-65.

Dalin, *Grakkh Babef*, pp. 106-7.

18. Dalin, "Les idées sociales de Babeuf," Coll. Int. de Stockholm, *Babeuf*, p. 65.

Babeuf, G., *Cadastre perpétuel* (chez les auteurs, Paris, 1789), p. xxii.

Dommanget, *Pages choisies,* p. 122 (Letter of Babeuf to Coupé de l'Oise, 10 Sept. 1791): "le grand domaine du monde ou le Créateur a voulu que chaque être possedât le rayon de circonférence nécessaire pour produire sa subsistance."

19. Dalin, *Grakkh Babef,* pp. 98, 107-8.

Dalin, "Les idées sociales de Babeuf," Coll. Int. de Stockholm, *Babeuf,* pp. 60, 63.

358   *Notes to Pages 39-46*

20. Dalin compounds the confusion by using a Russian word that translates as the English word "farm," meaning a territorial unit, rather than the Russian word for a lease: Cf. *Grakkh Babef*, p. 99.

21. Dalin, *Grakkh Babef*, pp. 101, 114.

Dalin, "Les idées sociales de Babeuf," Coll. Int. de Stockholm, *Babeuf*, pp. 60-61.

22. Cf. Dommanget, *Pages choisies*, p. 61n (discussing Babeuf's letter of 8 July 1787): "Le Communisme n'est pour lui ni une simple doctrine morale, ni une rêverie sentimentale ni un amusement de littérateur: c'est un but à atteindre." Dalin, *Grakkh Babef*, p. 112: "The establishment of complete social equality was by this time a basic task for Babeuf, for which it was necessary to strive."

23. Lichtenberger, *Le Socialisme et la Révolution française*, pp. 33-55.

Ibid., pp. 33-43 for summaries of Gosselin, *Réflexions d'un citoyen adressées aux notables* (1787); Leroy de Barincourt, *Le principe fondamental du droit des souverains* (1788), *La monarchie parfaite* (1789); Dufourny de Villiers, *Cahier du quatrième ordre* (1789); Marat, J.-P., *La Constitution, ou projet de déclaration des droits de l'homme et du citoyen, suivi d'un plan de constitution juste, sage, et libre.*

24. Ludd, E.C., "Helvétius and d'Holbach," *Journal of the History of Ideas* (vol. XXIII, no. 2, 1962), pp. 221-38.

Chapter 4

1. Coët, *Histoire de Roye*, vol. II, p. 566.

Beauvillé, V. de, *Histoire de Montdidier* (Firmin Didot fils, Paris 1857), vol. I, p. 326. Montdidier was the seat of one of the eight *départements* into which the province was divided: Darsy, F.-I., *Amiens et le Département de la Somme pendant la Révolution* (Doullet, Amiens 1878), vol. I, p. 20.

2. Reinhard, *Correspondance de Babeuf*, p. 89.

Dalin, *Grakkh Babef*, p. 135; Advielle, *Gracchus Babeuf*, vol. I, p. 52, incorrectly attributes Babeuf's pamphlet to 1789.

3. Dalin, *Grakkh Babef*, pp. 125-7.

Reinhard, *Correspondance de Babeuf*, pp. 66, 69.

4. Dalin, *Grakkh Babef*, p. 126.

Rutledge, J.J., *Eloge de Montesquieu* (J. de Boffe, London 1786), pp. 8-9.

Reinhard, *Correspondance de Babeuf*, pp. 126, 126n, 138, 140-145.

5. Reinhard, *Correspondance de Babeuf*, pp. 53, 78-9.

Dalin, *Grakkh Babef*, pp. 129-132.

6. Reinhard, *Correspondance de Babeuf*, pp. 87-8, 91, 99, 103, 116, 122; Bergmann, *Babeuf*, p. 35.

7. Ramon, *La Révolution à Péronne*, 2ᵉ série, pp. 27-30.

Beauvillé, *Histoire de Montdidier*, vol. I, pp. 330-4; Durand, G., *Documents pour servir à l'histoire de la Révolution française dans le département de la Somme* (Amiens 1888), vol. I, pp. x-xxi; Coët, *Histoire de Roye*, vol. I, p. 429.

8. *Cahier des Ordres Réunis de la Noblesse et Tiers Etat du Gouverne-ment de Péronne, Montdidier et Roye, rassemblés à Péronne* (Paris 1789).

Procès-verbal de l'Assemblée de l'ordre de la Noblesse du Gouvernement de Péronne, Montdidier et Roye, tenue le 31 mars 1789 et jours suivans (Paris 1789).

9. A.N. DXXIX 68; cf. Advielle, *Gracchus Babeuf*, vol. I, p. 52. Deville, "Notes inédites de Babeuf," p. 41.

Dalin, *Grakkh Babef*, pp. 150-151.

Coët, *Histoire de Roye*, vol. I, p. 429.

10. *Cahier des Ordres Réunis . . . rassemblés à Péronne*, pp. 17, 29.

Dalin, *Grakkh Babef*, pp. 151-4.

Advielle, *Gracchus Babeuf*, vol. I, p. 52.

11. Dalin, *Grakkh Babef*, p. 155.

In 1794 Babeuf said that he had conceived the plan of the *Cadastre perpétuel* "depuis la rédaction des Cahiers": Deville, "Notes inédites de Babeuf," p. 41.

12. Advielle, *Gracchus Babeuf*, vol. I, pp. 53-6.

Dommanget, *Pages choisies*, pp. 73-5.

A.D. Somme F129/39, copy of letter, F.-N. Babeuf to Robert Babeuf, 25 July 1789.

Had Babeuf been among the "Vainqueurs de la Bastille" there is no doubt that he would have said so (and repeatedly) afterwards.

13. Egged on, Babeuf alleged, by the Billecocqs: Dalin, *Grakkh Babef*, p. 146. In a letter to Marie-Anne Babeuf dated 25 July, Babeuf wrote "garde tes dix écus, et ne paye pas un sou à personne, entends-tu bien": Dom-manget, *Pages choisies*, p. 75.

14. Dommanget, *Pages choisies*, p. 75.

A.D. Somme F129/39.

A.D. Somme F129/41, copy of letter, F.-N. Babeuf to Marie-Anne Babeuf, 16 August 1789: "Je suis désespéré, ma bonne amie, de voir la détresse où je te laisse."

15. Advielle, V., "Une brochure de Mirabeau restituée à Babeuf," *La Révolution française*, vol. VIII (1885), pp. 889-891; Lichtenberger, *Le Socialisme et la Révolution française*, p. 62; Advielle, *Gracchus Babeuf*, vol. I, p. 60.

16. Dalin, *Grakkh Babef*, pp. 174-6, 202.

A.D. Somme F129/44, copy of letter, F.-N. Babeuf to Marie-Anne Babeuf, 9 September 1789. For Mirabeau's undertaking to promote the *Cadastre perpétuel* see ibid., F129/42, copy of letter, F.-N. Babeuf to Marie-Anne Babeuf, 28 August 1789.

17. Advielle, *Gracchus Babeuf*, vol. I, p. 63.

Aulard, F.-A., *La Société des Jacobins: Recueil de documents pour l'histoire du Club des Jacobins de Paris* (Jouaust, Paris 1889-1896), vol. I, p. 302.

Dalin, *Grakkh Babef*, p. 174.

18. Babeuf, F.-N., *Cadastre perpétuel* (chez les auteurs, Paris 1789), pp. xlvi, 192. The British Museum copy has MS corrections, apparently by Babeuf.

Dalin, *Grakkh Babef*, p. 203.

19. Babeuf, *Cadastre perpétuel*, pp. xxiv, xxxv-xliv.

Condorcet, J.-A.-N. de Caritat de, *Essai sur la constitution et les fonctions des Assemblées Provinciales* (no place of publication or publisher, 1788), vol. II, pp. 226-31.

"Défense préparatoire de G. Babeuf contre un jugement du Tribunal de Montdidier" (MS in Institute of Social History, Amsterdam), f. 10. Advielle, *Gracchus Babeuf*, vol. I, p. 99.

20. Dalin, *Grakkh Babef*, pp. 198-9.

21. Babeuf, *Cadastre perpétuel*, pp. xx-xxi, 9-11, 16-17, 28-30, 130-2.

22. Ibid., p. xxxiv: "A quel titre ceux qui ne possèdent rien, peuvent-ils exiger tant d'avantages de ceux qui possèdent tout? A le compte, le sort des uns ne sera point préférable à celui des autres."

23. Ibid., pp. xxvi-xxix, xxxii-xxxiv, 12-16.

24. Dalin, *Grakkh Babef*, pp. 183-4.

Babeuf, *Cadastre perpétuel*, pp. 16, 34.

25. Babeuf, *Cadastre perpétuel*, p. 189.

Dalin, *Grakkh Babef*, pp. 156, 204.

Chapter 5

1. Ireland, S., *A picturesque tour through Holland, Brabant and part of France, made in the Autumn of 1789* (London 1790), vol. II, p. 176.

Département de la Somme. Ville d'Amiens, *Inventaire Sommaire des Archives communales antérieures à 1790*, vol. I, série AA (Piteux, Amiens 1891), p. 238.

Bloch, C., and Tuetey, A., *Procès-verbaux et rapports du Comité de Mendicité de la Constituante, 1790-1791* (Imprimerie Nationale, Paris 1911), p. 485.

2. Goubert, P., "Les techniques agricoles dans les pays picards au XVIIe et XVIIIe siècles," *Revue d'histoire économique et sociale*, vol. XXXV (1957, no. 1), p. 32; cf. Goubert, *Beauvais et le Beauvaisis*, pp. 170-196.

Dalin, *Grakkh Babef*, pp. 80-7.

Sée, H., *Histoire économique de la France* (2e édition, Colin, Paris 1948-51), vol. I, p. 362.

Young, A., *Travels in France during the years 1787, 1788, and 1789* (ed. Constantia Maxwell, Cambridge 1950), pp. 325-6.

Lefebvre, G., *La Grande Peur de 1789* (Colin, Paris 1932), p. 14.

3. Festy, O., *L'agriculture pendant la Révolution française* (Gallimard,

Paris 1947), p. 87; cf. *Cahier des Ordres Réunis . . . rassemblés à Péronne*, section xxxviii.

Rudé, G., "La taxation populaire de mai 1775 en Picardie, en Normandie, et dans le Beauvaisis," *A.H.R.F.* (no. 165, 1961), pp. 305-26.

Legrand, R., *Grèves et incidents dans le Santerre* (Imprimerie Lafosse, Abbeville 1960), p. 5n.

Lefebvre, *La Grande Peur de 1789*, p. 51; Walter, G., *Histoire des paysans de France* (Flammarion, Paris 1963), p. 348.

4. Société Civique d'Amiens, *Mémoire à l'Assemblée Nationale pour la Société Civique d'Amiens*, Couret [Amiens], 1791; Durand, *Documents pour servir à l'histoire de la Révolution française dans le Département de la Somme* (Jeunet, Amiens 1909: Delibérations du conseil du Département, 1ière partie), pp. 52-8; Ville d'Amiens, *Inventaire sommaire des archives communales*, vol. I, p. 239.

5. Ramon, *La Révolution à Péronne*, 3ᵉ série, pp. 18, 52.

Département de la Somme, *Inventaire sommaire des Archives Départementales antérieures à 1790*, ed. Durand; vol. II: Archives Civiles (Kuypers, Amiens 1888), pp. 46-48.

6. Marion, M., "Le recouvrement des impôts en 1790," *Revue Historique*, vol. CXXI (1916), pp. 1-47.

Matthews, *Royal General Farms*, pp. 88 sqq, 151-3.

7. Beauvillé, *Histoire de Montdidier*, vol. I, pp. 570-6.

8. *Les Cahiers de Doléances des paroisses rurales du Bailliage de Noyon* (Comité Archéologique et Historique de Noyon, *Mémoires*, vol. XIV-V, 1898-9), pp. 320-67.

9. Ramon, *La Révolution à Péronne*, 2ᵉ série, pp. 92-5.

Cahier des Ordres Réunis . . . rassemblés à Péronne, p. 17.

10. Rudé, G., *The Crowd in the French Revolution* (O.U.P., Oxford 1959), pp. 48-9.

"Annexe à la séance de l'Assemblée Nationale du 30 juin 1790. Lettre du controleur-général des finances sur la situation des perceptions de la Régie Générale des Aides dans les villes des ci-devant généralités d'Amiens et Soissons," *Archives Parlementaires de 1787 à 1860* (Paris, 1867-1914), vol. XVI, p. 582.

Ramon, *La Révolution à Péronne*, 3ᵉ série, pp. 11-12.

"Annexe à la séance de l'Assemblée Nationale du 30 juin 1790," *Arch. Parl.*, vol. XVI, p. 585.

Mazière, L., *Annales Noyonnaises: Noyon de 1789 à 1795* (Comité Archéologique et Historique de Noyon, *Mémoires*, vol. XV, 1899), p. 6.

11. Ramon, *La Révolution à Péronne*, 3ᵉ série, pp. 14-15.

A.N. DXXIX 68: "Extrait du registre des délibérations de la ville de Roye, le 3 mars 1790"; Babeuf, *Pétition sur les impôts adressée par les habitants de* [Villiers-les-Roye] *en* [Picardie] *à l'Assemblée Nationale* (no publisher or place, [1790]), B.N. LK⁷10437, p. 21.

12. "Annexe à la séance de l'Assemblée Nationale du 30 juin," *Arch. Parl.*, vol. XVI, pp. 583-4; Warmé, A.J., *Histoire de la ville de Doullens* (Grousilliat, Doullens 1863), pp. 304-5.

Durand, G., and Estienne, J., *Inventaire sommaire des Archives Départementales de la Somme, 1790 - An IV*, vol. I, sér. L (Amiens 1925), p. 37.

Ramon, *La Révolution à Péronne*, 3ᵉ série, pp. 44-5.

13. Dalin, V.M., "Babeuf et Marat en 1789-90," *A.H.R.F.* (no. 150, 1958), pp. 17-19, 26.

Dalin, V.M., "Un inédit de Babeuf: sa Correspondance de Londres, 1-8 octobre 1789," *A.H.R.F.* (no. 151, 1958), p. 31.

Dalin, *Grakkh Babef*, pp. 190-1, 272, 274.

14. Coët, *Histoire de Roye*, vol. I, pp. 119-20, 425, 435-6.

A.N. DXXIX 68: "Extrait du registre des délibérations de la ville de Roye, le 3 mars 1790."

[Durand], *Documents pour servir à l'histoire de la Révolution française dans le Département de la Somme*, vol. I, pp. iv, xxii.

Dalin, *Grakkh Babef*, pp. 209-10.

15. Coët, *Histoire de Roye*, vol. I, p. 436.

A.N. DXXIX 68: "Extrait du registre des délibérations de la ville de Roye, le 3 mars 1790."

"Annexe à la séance . . . du 30 juin," *Arch. Parl.*, vol. XVI, p. 582; Advielle, *Gracchus Babeuf*, vol. I, pp. 525-7, 534.

A.D. Somme L374: Letter, Longuecamp to Directory of Somme Département, 15 Feb. 1791.

16. A.N. DXXIX 68: "Adresse de la communauté des marchands de vin, aubergistes et cabaretiers de la ville de Roye, 20 février 1790." "Discours prononcé à la séance de la Municipalité de Roye . . . 7 mars 1790" for Babeuf's avowal of his authorship.

"Extrait du registre des délibérations de la ville de Roye, le 3 mars 1790." Dalin, *Grakkh Babef*, p. 217.

17. Babeuf, *A messieurs du Comité des Recherches de l'Assemblée Nationale. Roye, le 10 mai 1790* [1790].

18. Dalin, "Robespierre et Danton vus par Babeuf," *A.H.R.F.* (no. 162, 1960), p. 406.

A.D. Somme F129/46. Copy of letter, Babeuf to Devin (5 April 1790). F129/47, copy of letter, Babeuf to "M. Bégin, juré priseur à Péronne" (11 April 1790).

Dalin, *Grakkh Babef*, p. 235.

Beauvillé, *Histoire de Montdidier*, vol. II, p. 468.

A.N. DXXIX 68 bis 6, dr. 81, no. 4, extract of *Procès-verbal* of Bureau and Council of Péronne (26 April 1790); no. 3, letter of Municipality of Péronne to Comité des Recherches (21 May 1790). Ramon, *La Révolution à Péronne*, 3ᵉ série, p. 62.

"Annexe à la séance . . . du 30 juin," *Arch. Parl.*, vol. XVI, pp. 584-6.

19. Babeuf, *Pétition sur les impôts*, p. 29.

A.N. DXXIX 68 bis 14/152, pièces 17-18; ibid., 17/184, pièce 2: papers relating to the prosecution of Pierre Vasseur.

20. A.N. DXXIX 68 bis 5, dr. 76, no. 10: Letter of Babeuf to the president of the National Assembly, 13 May 1790. Dalin, *Grakkh Babef*, p. 238.

Walter, G., *Babeuf (1760-1797) et la conjuration des égaux* (Payot, Paris 1937), pp. 36-47, had a section entitled "Au service des cabaretiers de Roye." Thomson, *The Babeuf Plot*, writes, p. 13: "In 1789 these innkeepers employed Babeuf to promote their interests and he was accused of promoting agitation when the inhabitants of the town refused to pay local imposts."

Cf. A.D. Somme F129/46, copy of letter, Babeuf to Devin (5 April 1790): "la pétition est accueillie partout, et j'espère que vous en vendriez beaucoup."

21. Foubert, L., "L'idée autonomiste dans les districts de Paris en 1789 et en 1790," *La Révolution française* (vol. XXVIII, 1895), pp. 141-61; Garrigues, G., *Les Districts de Paris pendant la Révolution française* (Editions Spes, Paris 1932), *passim*.

22. Babeuf, *Pétition sur les impôts*, pp. 11, 23. The original reads: "Un homme qui donne à un autre sa procuration, ne ratifie point ce que son mandataire a pu souscrire à son détriment, quand le mandat ne l'y avait autorisé." "Les peuples . . . n'oublient pas que ce soit eux qui vous ont donné des pouvoirs; que tout fondé de pouvoir doit agir selon le gré de son commettant, que le tout est plus grand que la partie; que le constituant est audessus du constitué; et que souvent quand il s'agit de particuliers, et toujours quand il est question d'une Nation entière, la ratification du premier est nécessaire pour assurer les opérations du second."

23. Ibid., pp. 29-30.

Dalin, *Grakkh Babef*, pp. 265-8.

24. Babeuf, *Pétition sur les impôts*, p. 37.

Ramon, *La Révolution à Péronne*, 3ᵉ série, p. 63.

"Annexe à la séance . . . du 30 juin," *Arch. Parl.*, vol. XVI, pp. 583-6.

Marion, "Le recouvrement des impôts en 1790," p. 39n.

Durand and Estienne, *Inventaire sommaire des Archives Départementales de la Somme, 1790 - An IV*, vol. I, pp. 28-32: references to outbreaks at Airanes, Albert, Nesle, Vignacourt, Rubempré, Domart, etc.

25. "Annexe à la séance . . . du 30 juin," *Arch. Parl.*, vol. XVI, pp. 581-7; Lecocq, G., "La Garde Nationale de Ham à Saint-Quentin," *La Révolution française*, vol. V (1883), pp. 332-5; Lemaire, E., "Une émeute populaire à Saint-Quentin en 1790" (Société Académique de Saint-Quentin, *Mémoires*, vol. IX, 1889), pp. 345-7. Lecocq says that Babeuf was helping to suppress the riot, but Babeuf was already in the Conciergerie prison at this date.

26. A.N. DXXIX 68: "Extrait du registre des délibérations de la ville de Roye, le 3 mars 1790."

Ibid., "Avis important à tous les citoyens. Le 15 mars 1790."

"Annexe à la séance . . . du 30 juin," *Arch. Parl.*, vol. XVI, p. 583

27. Advielle, *Gracchus Babeuf*, pp. 527-30.

Dalin, *Grakkh Babef*, p. 243.

A.N. DXXIX 68 bis 5, dr. 76, no. 11: Letter of Babeuf to the Comité des Recherches of the National Assembly (10 May 1790); Babeuf, *A messieurs du Comité des Recherches de l'Assemblée Nationale. Roye, le 10 mai 1790* [1790].

A.N. DXXIX 68 bis 5, dr. 76, no. 10: Letter of Babeuf to the president of the National Assembly (13 May 1790).

28. Dalin, *Grakkh Babef*, p. 244. Dalin has Tuesday, 19 May, which is incorrect.

Chapter 6

1. Seligman, E., *La justice en France pendant la Révolution* (Plon, Nourrit, Paris 1901), p. 57.

Pottet, E., *Histoire de la Conciergerie* (3ᵉ édition, May et Motteraz, Paris 1895), pp. 61-5.

2. Dalin, *Grakkh Babef*, pp. 244-8; "Lettres inédites de Babeuf," *Franzuskii Yezhegodnik* (French Annual) (1960), pp. 255-7.

Las Vergnas, R., *Le chevalier Rutledge, "gentilhomme anglais," 1742-1794* (Paris 1932), pp. 187-97.

A.D. Somme F129/49, copy of letter of Babeuf (25 May 1790); ibid., F129/50, copy of letter of Babeuf (25 May 1790). Ibid., F129/51, copy of letter of Babeuf to Comité des Recherches (27 May 1790).

Ibid., F129/52, copy of a general letter thanking persons who have interested themselves in Babeuf's fate (31 May 1790).

3. Dalin, V.M., "Rivarol et Babeuf," *A.H.R.F.* (no. 171, 1963), p. 70. *Actes des apôtres* (no. 117, May-June 1790), pp. 6-12.

Dalin, *Grakkh Babef*, pp. 247-52.

4. *Complot horrible, tramé par la Cour des Aides de Paris, pour faire périr sur l'échafaud tous les auteurs de la Révolution* (de l'imprimerie patriotique, Maison du Café Liègois, Porte Saint-Michel, Paris 1790) (John Rylands Library, French Historical Tracts). *Journal de la confédération*, nos. 1 and 2.

Dalin, "Babeuf et Marat en 1789-90," pp. 29-30.

Ami du peuple, no. CXXXVIII (19 juin 1790); no. CXLIV (25 juin 1790).

5. *Ami du peuple*, no. CXV (27 mai 1790), pp. 7-8; no. CXVII (29 mai 1790), *passim*; no. CXXXV (16 juin 1790), pp. 3 sqq; no. CXXVIII (19 juin 1790), pp. 1-8; no. CXLIV (25 juin 1790), pp. 1-2.

6. *Complot horrible, tramé par la Cour des Aides de Paris*. The attribution to Babeuf rests on a general similarity of content to that of no. 1 of Babeuf's *Journal de la confédération* and some specific similarities in

language. Thus, the brochure speaks of a "Complot horrible tramé par la Cour des Aides de Paris pour faire périr sur l'échafaud tous les auteurs de la Révolution . . . pour narguer la fédération projetté le 14 juillet prochain." The *Journal de la confédération* refers to "l'effroyable conspiration des fermiers-généraux et de la Cour des Aides de Paris contre tous les bons citoyens de la capitale et du royaume . . . Nargue à la fédération prochaine du 14 juillet." The brochure was written after the arrests of 16 June but before those of 18 June. It is, of course, possible that Babeuf borrowed from it for his own journal.

7. The John Rylands Library, Manchester, possesses nos. 1 and 3. Nos. 1-3 have been reproduced in facsimile by E.D.H.I.S. (Editions d'Histoire Sociale, Paris 1966).

Dalin, *Grakkh Babef*, p. 263n, refers to the MS of no. 4.

8. Garrigues, *Les Districts de Paris*, pp. 128-60, 198-215.

Journal de la confédération, no. 2, pp. 14-16.

9. *Ami du peuple*, no. CLIII (4 juillet 1790), pp. 3-8; no. CLV, p. 1.

Dalin, *Grakkh Babef*, p. 259.

"Lettres inédites de Babeuf," *Franzuskii Yezhegodnik* (French Annual) (1960), pp. 261-2: Babeuf to Lauraguais (20 July 1790).

10. Dalin, *Grakkh Babef*, pp. 265-6.

Lettre d'un député de Picardie (no publisher or date, John Rylands Library, French Historical Tracts). Attributed to Babeuf by Advielle, *Gracchus Babeuf*, vol. I, p. 500, and Dalin, *Grakkh Babef*, p. 265. On 14 August 1790 a police raid on Beuvin, a bookseller in the Palais Royal, picked up four copies of this tract. Tuetey, A., *Répertoire général des sources manuscrits pour servir à l'histoire de Paris pendant la Révolution française* (Imprimerie Nouvelle, Paris 1892), vol. II, p. 199, no. 1884.

11. Pellet, M., "Gracchus Baboeuf et Marie Antoinette," *Variétés révolutionnaires* (2ᵉ série, 1887), pp. 183-8.

Dalin, *Grakkh Babef*, p. 263n.

12. Dalin, *Grakkh Babef*, pp. 273-4.

Saitta, A., "Il prospetto del Correspondant Picard di Gracco Babeuf," *Critica Storica* (anno V, 31 May 1966, no. 3), p. 443.

Catalogue de l'histoire de la Révolution française (Bibliothèque Nationale, Paris 1943), vol. V, p. 165. A copy of the prospectus is described in Hatin, E., *Bibliographie historique et critique de la presse périodique française* (Firmin Didot, Paris 1966), p. 247, as *Le Correspondant Picard et le Rédacteur des Cahiers de la seconde Législature, journal dédié aux habitants des cantons, villes, bourgs, villages, hameaux et municipalités des départements de la Somme, de l'Aisne et de l'Oise, par F.-N. Babeuf, auteur de la Pétition sur les aides et gabelles, du Cadastre perpétuel, et de plusieurs autres ouvrages patriotiques* (1790, 8 pp. in 8°).

13. A.D. Somme F129/115, copy of undated letter of F.-N. Babeuf to Marie-Anne Babeuf.

Coët, *Histoire de Roye*, vol. II, p. 122.

14. A.D. Somme F129/54, copy of letter of F.-N. Babeuf to Marie-Anne Babeuf (14 August 1790); printed in *Revue des Curiosités Révolutionnaires* (vol. I, 1910-11), pp. 205-6.

Advielle, *Gracchus Babeuf*, vol. I, pp. 61-3.

Dalin, *Grakkh Babef*, p. 400n.

15. Advielle, *Gracchus Babeuf*, vol. I, p. 74.

Dommanget, *Pages choisies*, pp. 98-103.

Dalin, *Grakkh Babef*, pp. 288-92.

16. A.D. Somme F129/57, copy of letter of Babeuf to Devin (15 September 1790).

Dalin, *Grakkh Babef*, pp. 276-7, 290-3.

Le Scrutateur des Décrets, et le Rédacteur des Cahiers de la Seconde Législature, par continuation du journal intitulé Le Correspondant Picard, dédié primitivement aux Départements de la Somme, de l'Aisne, et de l'Oise, et offert aujourd'hui aux 83 Départements de la domination du peuple français par F.-N.-C. Babeuf (reprint, Editions d'Histoire Sociale, Paris 1966).

17. Saitta, "Il prospetto del Correspondant Picard," p. 442.

Hatin, *Bibliographie historique de la presse*, p. 248.

Dalin, *Grakkh Babef*, pp. 279-80.

18. Dommanget, *Pages choisies*, pp. 98-103.

Dalin, *Grakkh Babef*, pp. 250, 288.

"Défense préparatoire de G. Babeuf contre un jugement du Tribunal de Montdidier, Paris, 3 frimaire l'an II: Gracchus Babeuf à Dumont," f. 3.

Saitta, "Il prospetto del Correspondant Picard," p. 444.

19. "Défense préparatoire de G. Babeuf . . . ," f. 1.

20. Dalin, *Grakkh Babef*, pp. 369, 376-8; *Pétition sur les droits de voierie et de plantation, de cens et de champart. Par les commune et municipalité de Montigny, canton de Saint-Just-en-Chaussée, district de Clermont, département de l'Oise*, printed with prospectus of *Le Scrutateur des Décrets*.

21. Dalin, *Grakkh Babef*, pp. 384-5. Advielle, *Gracchus Babeuf*, vol. I, p. 503, describes this work as *Pétition (à l'Assemblée Nationale) sur les fiefs, seigneuries, cens et champarts, par les commune et municipalité de Méry, canton de Leglantier, district de Clermont, département de l'Oise, le 6 février 1791* (15 pp. 8°).

22. "Bientôt je fus soupçonner, accusé d'en vouloir aux propriétés. Des frères souffrantes et laborieux ne virent en moi qu'un ami compatissant et un protecteur; pour les riches égoistes je ne fus qu'un dangereux apôtre des lois agraires." Babeuf to Sylvain Maréchal, 6 germinal An II, quoted in Espinas, *La Philosophie Sociale*, p. 212. This letter contains a summary of Babeuf's argument in the Méry petition.

23. Dalin, *Grakkh Babef*, p. 399.

24. "Annexe à la séance de l'Assemblée Nationale du 30 juin 1790," *Arch. Parl.,* vol. XVI, p. 583.

Ramon, *La Révolution à Péronne,* 2ᵉ série, pp. 71-4.

A.D. Somme L374, Lambert to Directory of Somme Département, 6 October 1790.

A.N. BB¹⁶858, "Extrait du registre aux délibérations du directoire du département de la Somme en la séance du 14 avril 1791" (copy); "Détail des faits que nous Félix Jean Baptiste Longuecamp, maire de la ville de Roye, et Louis Lefebvre, procureur de la commune de la dite ville . . . dénonçons à MM. les administrateurs formant le directoire du département de la Somme . . . 13 avril 1791" (copy).

Advielle, *Gracchus Babeuf,* vol. I, pp. 487-500.

25. A.D. Somme L374: Longuecamp to the administrators of the District of Montdidier, 4 November 1790; the administrators of the Somme Département to those of the District of Montdidier, 9 November 1790. Ibid., L2073, f. 51, "Registre des délibérations du District de Montdidier," 12 November 1790.

A.D. Somme L374. Delessart to the Directory and the Procureur-Général of the Somme Département, 25 December 1790.

A.N. BB¹⁶858, "Extrait du registre . . . du directoire . . . de la Somme . . . 14 avril 1791": "Babeuf est le principal moteur de la résistance opinionâtre que les habitants de Roye, d'Albert, de Péronne et des campagnes voisines ont opposée au rétablissement provisoire des impôts"; cf. Durand and Estienne, *Inventaire Sommaire des Archives Départementales de la Somme, 1790 - An IV,* vol. I (sér. L), pp. 25-36.

26. *Babeuf, ex-administrateur du département de la Somme et successivement du district de Montdidier, aux Comités de salut public, de sûreté générale et de législation de la Convention nationale et à Gohier, ministre de la Justice* (Imp. de Prault, Paris 1794), pp. 35-7.

Advielle, *Gracchus Babeuf,* vol. I, p. 88.

Dalin, *Grakkh Babef,* pp. 305-8.

27. Coët, *Histoire de Roye,* vol. I, p. 438; A.D. Somme L374, the municipal officers of Roye to the administrators of the Somme Département, 18 January 1791.

Dalin, *Grakkh Babef,* p. 309.

28. A.D. Somme L374: the Directory of the District of Montdidier to the Directory of the Somme Département, 12 January 1791; the administrators of the Somme Département to the municipal officers of Roye, 20 January 1791; Longuecamp, mayor of Roye, to the administrators of the Somme Département, 26 January 1791; the municipal officers and notables of Roye to the administrators of the Somme Département, 11 February 1791.

29. Coët, *Histoire de Roye,* vol. I, p. 441.

A.D. Somme L374: "Extrait du registre des délibérations de la municipalité de la ville de Roye du 14 février 1791"; Longuecamp to the

Directory of the Somme Département, 15 February 1791; the administrators of the Somme Département to the municipal officers of Roye, 17 February 1791 (minute).

30. *Babeuf* . . . *aux Comités de salut public, de sûreté générale et de législation de la Convention nationale*, p. 44.

Chapter 7

1. *Babeuf*. . . *aux Comités de salut public, de sûreté générale et de législation de la Convention nationale*, p. 38.

Grégoire d'Essigny, *Histoire de Roye*, p. 10.

A.N. BB[16]858: "Extrait du registre des délibérations de la municipalité de Roye du 5 avril 1791."

2. Dalin, *Grakkh Babef*, p. 456.

A.N. BB[16]858: "Extrait du registre des délibérations de la municipalité de Roye du 5 avril 1791"; "Détail des faits que nous . . . Longuecamp . . . et Lefebvre dénonçons à MM. les administrateurs du département de la Somme . . . 13 avril 1791."

Legrand, R., "Babeuf en Picardie, 1790-1792," *A.H.R.F.* (no. 162, 1960), p. 470.

3. A.N. BB[16]858: "Extrait du registre des délibérations de la municipalité de Roye du 5 avril 1791." "Extrait du registre des délibérations de la municipalité de la ville de Roye du 12 avril 1791." "Extrait du registre des délibérations de la municipalité de la ville de Roye du 15 avril 1791." "Détail des faits que nous . . . Longuecamp . . . et Lefebvre dénonçons. . . ." "Extrait du registre aux délibérations du directoire du département de la Somme en la séance du 14 avril 1791."

4. Coët, *Histoire de Roye*, vol. I, p. 446; vol. II, p. 137.

A.N. BB[16]858: "Extrait du registre des délibérations de la municipalité de Roye du 5 avril 1791."

Dommanget, *Pages choisies*, p. 148.

A.D. Somme L88, f. 178: "Registre des délibérations des administrateurs du directoire du département de la Somme."

5. *Dénonciation* . . . *d'un libelle infâme intitulé Affaire de la Commune de Davenescourt* . . . , *passim*. Dalin attributes this work to the Abbé P.-F. Tournier, chaplain to the countess de la Myre. But Babeuf apparently believed the author was the countess's son, Gouy de la Myre: *Babeuf . . . aux Comités de salut public, de sûreté générale et de législation* . . . , p. 42.

Mercure de France (samedi, 19 mars 1791, no. 12), pp. 225-6. Babeuf, *Opprimés et oppresseurs: mémoire des habitants de Davenécourt* [sic] *aux représentants de la Nation* (Imprimerie du *Journal de Montdidier*, 1888), reprint of *Affaire de la commune de Davenécourt, district de Montdidier, département de la Somme, contre Philippine de Cardevac,*

*veuve de Gabriel Lamire et ci-devant dame de Davenécourt . . . Dans l'ex-
posé de laquelle on démontre combien sont encore formidables les restes de
la puissance féodale* (Devin, Noyon 1791).

6. Deville, "Notes inédites de Babeuf," p. 42.

Babeuf, *Opprimés et oppresseurs*, pp. 82-4.

Affaire de la commune de Davenécourt . . . (see n. 5 above). On 19
August Cousin, the mayor of Montdidier, wrote to the *Feuille du département de la Somme*, to disavow the pamphlet: *Dénonciation . . . d'un libelle
infâme . . .* , p. 14n.

7. *Mercure de France* (19 mars 1791, No. 12), p. 225.

Dénonciation . . . d'un libelle infâme . . . , pp. 48-9; Babeuf, *Opprimés et
oppresseurs*, pp. 75-6.

8. Babeuf, *Opprimés et oppresseurs, passim; Dénonciation . . . d'un
libelle infâme . . . , passim.*

Deville, "Notes inédites de Babeuf," p. 42.

Dalin, *Grakkh Babef*, pp. 398-9.

9. Coët, *Histoire de Roye*, vol. I, p. 439.

Beauvillé, *Histoire de Montdidier*, vol. I, p. 363.

Dalin, *Grakkh Babef*, pp. 402-3.

Deville, "Notes inédites de Babeuf," p. 42.

Dalin, "Robespierre et Danton vus par Babeuf," p. 392.

Mazière, *Noyon de 1789 à 1795*, pp. 46-7.

Ibid., pp. 36-8. In 1792 the Noyon society was described as "nouvelle-
ment établie dans la ville," but the "Patriotes de Noyon" had been meeting
at least since June 1790.

10. Dalin, *Grakkh Babef*, pp. 439-40.

Walter, *Babeuf*, p. 66.

Dommanget, *Pages choisies*, pp. 93, 95.

Espinas, *La philosophie sociale*, pp. 214, 403-12.

In a letter to J.M. Coupé dated 7 October 1791, Babeuf declared that
since the publication of the *Dénonciation . . . d'un libelle infâme . . .*
pamphlet he had been "décrié dans la classe opprimée," and that he
had been deprived through the loss of the public's confidence of any
honest means of making a living. Draft (?) letter, Babeuf to J.M. Coupé,
7 October 1791, in International Institute for Social History, Amsterdam.

11. Dommanget, *Pages choisies*, pp. 95, 103-121.

Espinas cites an MS manifesto by Babeuf dated 8 September 1791 and
entitled "Qui faut-il choisir?": *La philosophie sociale*, p. 214. H. Baumont
records that an address from the Société des Amis de la Constitution de
Noyon was read out by the president of the electoral assembly on 31 August
on the same subject: "Le département de l'Oise pendant la Révolution,"
Bulletin de la société d'études historiques et scientifiques de l'Oise, vol. III
(no. i, 1907), p. 50. Babeuf was still closely connected with the club as late as

21 August: Dalin, Saitta, Soboul, *Inventaire des manuscrits et imprimés de Babeuf* (Bibliothèque Nationale, Paris 1966), no. 182, p. 68.

12. Espinas, *La philosophie sociale*, pp. 403-412.

Babeuf to Coupé, 7 October 1791, letter in International Institute for Social History, Amsterdam.

Dalin, *Grakkh Babef*, pp. 437-41.

13. Dalin, *Grakkh Babef*, pp. 326-63.

14. Lichtenberger, *Le socialisme et la Révolution française*, pp. 70-71. For a fuller account of the origins of the Confédération des Amis de la Verité see Rose, R.B., "Socialism and the French Revolution: the Cercle Social and the Enragés," *Bulletin of the John Rylands Library* (vol. 41, no. 1, September 1958), pp. 141-9.

15. *La Bouche de Fer*, sér. i, no. 22; no. 20, 3e année (19 février 1791); no. 29, 2e année (December 1790): "Il est impossible de faire une vraie constitution sociale, sans assurer le domaine réel d'existence à tous les membres de la société."

Dalin, *Grakkh Babef*, pp. 319, 321.

16. Dalin, *Grakkh Babef*, pp. 424-8.

Lichtenberger, *Le socialisme et la Révolution française*, pp. 88-9. The articles in the *Révolutions de Paris* have been attributed to Sylvain Maréchal.

17. Espinas, *La philosophie sociale*, pp. 404-407.

Dommanget, *Pages choisies*, p. 96. Dalin, *Grakkh Babef*, p. 430.

18. Dommanget, *Pages choisies*, pp. 107, 107n. Dalin, *Grakkh Babef*, pp. 434-5.

19. Dommanget, *Pages choisies*, p. 110. Espinas, *La philosophie sociale*, pp. 406, 409-10.

20. Espinas, *La philosophie sociale*, pp. 404, 409.

21. Dommanget, *Pages choisies*, pp. 110-119.

22. Espinas, *La philosophie sociale*, p. 407.

Girardin, Marquis de, *L'arrestation du dernier ami de J.J. Rousseau en 1793* (Henri Leclerc, Paris 1919), *passim*.

Girardin, René de, *Discours sur la nécessité de la ratification de la loi par la volonté générale* (Imprimerie du Creuset, Paris 1791).

Baumont, H., "Le département de l'Oise pendant la Révolution," *Bulletin de la société d'études historiques et scientifiques de l'Oise,* vol. III (no. i), p. 39.

23. Talmon, J.L., *The Origins of Totalitarian Democracy* (Mercury Books, London 1966), pp. 203-8, and *passim*.

Chapter 8

1. Dommanget, *Pages choisies*, p. 110.

2. Dalin, *Grakkh Babef*, pp. 378-9, 449-60, 464n.

3. Mathiez, A., *La vie chère et le mouvement social sous la Terreur* (Payot, Paris 1927), pp. 50-66.

Mazière, *Noyon de 1789 à 1795*, pp. 50-69.

Dalin, *Grakkh Babef*, p. 448.

4. Coët, *Histoire de Roye*, vol. I, pp. 453-4.

Dalin, *Grakkh Babef*, pp. 470-1. Carra, the editor, did not print Babeuf's letter.

Beauvillé, *Histoire de Montdidier*, vol. I, pp. 365-6.

5. Coët, *Histoire de Roye*, vol. I, pp. 454-5.

Darsy, *Amiens . . . pendant la Révolution*, pp. 67-8, 154.

Dautry, J., "Où la cagnotte paroissiale servait à défendre les propriétés," *A.H.R.F.* (no. 138, 1955), pp. 71-2.

6. Deville, "Notes inédites de Babeuf," p. 42.

Babeuf . . . aux Comités de Salut public, de sûreté générale et de législation, pp. 23-5; cf. "Défense préparatoire de G. Babeuf contre un jugement du Tribunal de Montdidier," f. 1: "Pourquoi s'étonnerait-on que Gracchus Babeuf, le Marat de ce Département depuis le commencement de la révolution, y eut couru sans cesse les risques d'être immolé?"

7. Legrand, *Babeuf en Picardie*, pp. 21-2.

8. Estienne, J., *Archives départementales de la Somme, Inventaire Sommaire de la série L* (Imprimerie Moderne, Fontenay-le-Comte 1938), vol. I, p. 510.

Dalin, *Grakkh Babef*, pp. 478-82.

Estienne, *Archives départementales de la Somme, Inventaire Sommaire*, vol. II (Registre des Districts: Montdidier), p. 367.

Lefebvre, G., *Etudes sur la Révolution française*, pp. 298-304; Cobb, R., "Babeuf et les électeurs d'Abbeville," *A.H.R.F.* (no. 165, 1961), pp. 392-3.

9. Bergmann, *Babeuf*, p. 96.

Dalin, *Grakkh Babef*, pp. 483-5.

Estienne, *Archives départementales de la Somme, Inventaire Sommaire de la série L*, vol. I, pp. 510-511.

10. A.D. Somme L320, "Assemblée électorale d'Abbeville, 2-18 septembre 1792," ff. 37-9.

Estienne, *Archives départementales de la Somme, Inventaire Sommaire de la série L*, vol. I, pp. 510-512.

Bourgin, G., "Quelques inédits de Babeuf," *A.H.R.F.* (no. 156, 1959), p. 153: "ce n'est que par une sorte de prodige que moi . . . suis sorti du milieu de ces choix."

11. Bourgin, "Quelques inédits de Babeuf," pp. 152-3.

A.D. Somme L74, Registre du conseil-général du département de la Somme, ff. 1-4, 8-10.

12. *Babeuf . . . aux Comités de salut public, de sûreté générale et de législation*, pp. 6-7, 45-7. A.D. Somme L74, f. 14.

13. Estienne, *Archives départementales de la Somme, Inventaire Sommaire*, vol. II (Registre des Districts: Péronne), pp. 392-3.

A.D. Somme L74, f. 14.

Ramon, *La Révolution à Peronne*, 4ᵉ série, pp. 74-8.

14. A.D. Somme L74, ff. 21 verso, 22 verso, 23.

Babeuf . . . aux Comités de salut public, de sûreté générale et de législation, pp. 45-6.

15. A.D. Somme F129/63, copy of letter, Babeuf to his children, 13 Oct. 1792; A.D. Somme L74, ff. 20, 28 verso.

Legrand, *Babeuf en Picardie*, p. 30n.

A.D. Somme L83, Registre du directoire du Département de la Somme, 1ⁱᵉʳ Bureau, ff. 5 verso - 6.

16. Beauvillé, *Histoire de Montdidier*, vol. II, p. 470; Patoux, *Le faux de Gracchus Babeuf*, p. 188. Was the sabre his father's?

17. G—, "Documents historiques tirés d'anciennes affiches du Département de la Somme," *La Picardie* (no. 16, 1870), pp. 344-6.

Dommanget, *Pages choisies*, pp. 134-5.

Babeuf saw things from a different angle than the Directory: "Le gangrené Directoire du Département m'accabla lui-même en soutenant les comédiens corrupteurs"; *Babeuf . . . aux Comités de salut public, de sûreté générale et de législation*, p. 46

18. A.D. Somme L74, ff. 33-4, 34 verso, 41.

Deville, "Notes inédites de Babeuf," p. 42.

Legrand, *Babeuf en Picardie*, pp. 28-9.

19. A.N. BB¹⁶858-9 (Dossier Somme), Procès-verbal de l'assemblée électorale de Péronne, 11-14 novembre 1792.

Babeuf . . . aux Comités de salut public, de sûreté générale et de législation, pp. 46-7.

20. Estienne, *Archives départementales de la Somme, Inventaire Sommaire*, vol. II (Registre des Districts: Montdidier), pp. 365-6; A.D. Somme F129/65, copy of Procès-verbal de l'assemblée électoral du district de Montdidier, 18-19 novembre 1792.

Dommanget, *Pages choisies*, p. 132n.

A.D. Somme L2073, Registre des délibérations du district de Montdidier, f. 183 verso.

21. Estienne, *Archives départementales de la Somme, Inventaire Sommaire*, vol. II (Registre des Districts: Montdidier), p. 360.

A.D. Somme L2073, ff. 182 - 183 verso.

22. A.D. Somme L2073, ff. 186 verso - 187 verso.

Estienne, *Archives départementales de la Somme, Inventaire Sommaire*, vol. II (Registre des Districts: Montdidier), columns 10-12, p. 360.

Dommanget, *Pages choisies*, p. 132.

23. Dalin, *Grakkh Babef*, pp. 497-9.

Babeuf . . . aux Comités de salut public, de sûreté générale et de législation, pp. 8, 48; "Défense préparatoire de G. Babeuf contre un jugement du tribunal de Montdidier," f. 7.

Legrand, R., *Un plaidoyer de Babeuf* (Lafosse, Abbeville 1963), *passim*; A.D. Somme L2134, affaires communales diverses.

24. Beauvillé, *Histoire de Montdidier*, vol. II, p. 469. The date is given in the second edition: Beauvillé, *Histoire de Montdidier* (Claye, Paris 1875), vol. II, p. 473.

Babeuf . . . aux Comités de salut public, de sûreté générale et de législation, p. 8; Deville, "Notes inédites de Babeuf," p. 43.

25. Mannier, E., *Ordre de Malte. Les commanderies du grand prieuré de France d'après les documents inédits conservés aux archives nationales à Paris* (Aubry, Paris 1872), p. 602.

Patoux, *Le faux de Gracchus Babeuf*, pp. 147-73.

26. Mazauric, *Babeuf*, p. 78.

Dalin, *Grakkh Babef*, pp. 501-2.

27. Patoux, *Le faux de Gracchus Babeuf*, pp. 169-86.

"Defense préparatoire de G. Babeuf contre un jugement du Tribunal de Montdidier," f. 7, where Babeuf claims that he went to Paris to appeal to the minister (of the interior) against the Somme Département Directory's confirmation of his suspension.

Chapter 9

1. Caron, P., "Les Défenseurs de la République," *La Révolution française* (no. LXXXVI, 1933), p. 208.

2. Dalin, *Grakkh Babef*, p. 506.

Aulard, F.-A., *Mémoires secrets de Fournier l'Américain* (Société de l'Histoire de la Révolution française, Paris 1890), *passim;* A.N. F⁷6504 (Dossier Fournier).

A.N. AF II 2868.

A.D. Somme F129/72, copy of letter, Babeuf to Marie-Anne Babeuf (18 March 1793).

3. "Défense préparatoire de G. Babeuf . . . ," f. 10.

Procès-verbal de la Convention nationale (Imprimerie Nationale, Paris 1793), vol. VI, p. 274. For Babeuf's claim to have composed and presented the petition see Advielle, *Gracchus Babeuf*, vol. I, p. 98.

For the activities of the "Défenseurs de la République" from January to March 1793 see Caron, "Les Défenseurs de la République," *La Révolution française* (no. LXXXVI, 1933), pp. 193-235; Calvet, H., "Les origines du Comité de l'Evêché," *A.H.R.F.* (no. 7, 1930), pp. 12-23.

Fournier is identified as a leader of the Defenders in two police reports at the beginning of March 1793: Tuetey, A., *Répertoire général des sources manuscrits pour servir à l'histoire de Paris pendant la Révolution française*, vol. IX, pp. 96-7, nos. 459, 462.

4. Mortimer-Ternaux, L., *Histoire de la Terreur, 1792-1794* (Lévy, Paris 1881, 3ᵉ édition), vol. VI, pp. 184-5, 473-5.

Mercure français (no. 68, 9 March 1793), pp. 67-8.

5. Tuetey, *Répertoire*, vol. IX, p. 96, no. 459.

A general account of this incident not mentioning Fournier by name appears in Brissot's *Patriote français* (no. 1306, 10 March 1793). Fournier was accused of inciting the crowd to murder Pétion, in what appears to be the same incident, by Bourdon de l'Oise in the Convention on 12 March: *Journal du soir* (no. 172, 12 March 1793); *Journal de Paris* (no. 72, 13 March 1793). While denying this accusation Fournier admitted being present on the Terrasse: *Journal du soir* (no. 174, 14 March 1793, account of the Convention session, 13 March).

6. *Patriote française* (no. 1306, 10 March 1793). Cf. Buchez, P.J.B. et Roux, P.C., *Histoire parlementaire de la Révolution française* (Paulin, Paris, 1834-8), vol. XXV, pp. 32-3, where the statement that "Fournier dirigeait sa bande sur la maison de Gorsas et sur l'imprimerie de Fiévée" seems, however, to be based on a misinterpretation of Vergniaud's remarks in the Convention on 13 March, in which he accused Lazowsky, a known close associate of Fournier, but not Fournier, of commanding the attacks. Buchez et Roux, *Histoire parlementaire*, vol. XXV, p. 92.

7. *Journal des débats et de la correspondance de la Société des Jacobins* (no. 372, 14 March 1793); Aulard, F.-A., *La Société des Jacobins*, vol. V, p. 85.

Dautry, J., "Sébastien Lacroix," *A.H.R.F.* (no. 10, 1933), p. 517, citing a copy of the address endorsed "l'original entre les mains de Varlet." Cf. *Journal de Paris* (no. 76, 17 March 1793) for an account of Varlet at the Quatre-Nations Section.

Buchez et Roux, *Histoire parlementaire*, vol. XXV, p. 94.

8. Aulard, *La Société des Jacobins*, vol. VI, p. 45. (Arthur's account of 10 March, recalled on 16 germinal, an II.)

Journal des débats . . . des Jacobins (no. 370, 12 March 1793, account of Jacobins' session of 10 March; and no. 372, 14 March 1793, Varlet's account of the events of 10 March).

Buchez et Roux, *Histoire parlementaire*, vol. XXV, pp. 63, 128. (Report by Garat, minister of the interior, to the Convention.)

Aulard, *La Société des Jacobins*, vol. VI, p. 65.

Journal du soir (no. 171, 11 March 1793, extract of the register of the conseil général de la commune for 10 March).

9. *Journal du soir* (no. 174, 14 March 1793, Fournier's account of his activities presented to the Convention on 13 March).

According to the Civil Committee of the Poissonière Section, some time before 11 p.m. on 10 March the general assembly of the section sent a deputation to the Cordeliers Club "prendre les ordres des conjurés." Sée, Adrien, *Le procès Pache* (Société de l'Histoire de la Révolution française, Paris 1911), pp. 102-3.

According to Fournier his address to the Tuileries Section engaged "toutes les personnes qui s'y trouvait de se rendre à leurs sections; c'est là, leur ai-je dit, ou se trouvent des bons citoyens. Je me suis rendu dans la mienne et de là chez moi": *Journal du soir* (no. 174, 14 March 1793).

10. Mortimer-Ternaux, *Histoire de la Terreur*, vol. VI, pp. 230-4; *Journal du soir* (no. 173, 13 March 1793).

Journal des débats . . . des Jacobins (no. 372, 14 March 1793).
Le Publiciste de la Révolution française (no. 145, 15 March 1793), p. 4.
11. Mathiez, *La vie chère,* pp. 141-57.
Journal du soir (no. 174, 14 March 1793).
C. *Fournier (Américain) à Marat* (Imprimerie de Mayer et Cᶦᵉ, Paris 1793). For the attribution of this work to Babeuf see Advielle, *Gracchus Babeuf,* vol. I, pp. 505-6; Dalin, *Grakkh Babef,* p. 510.
12. Aulard, *La Société des Jacobins,* vol. VI, p. 174.
Le Publiciste de la Révolution française (no. 190, 9 May 1793), pp. 4-6.
Babeuf, F.-N. (F.-N.-C., G.), *C. Fournier à Marat, journaliste* (Imprimerie de Lottin, Paris 1793, placard); idem, 7 pp. (pamphlet).
Dalin, *Grakkh Babef,* p. 510.
13. Cf. Dalin, "Babeuf et Marat en 1789-90," p. 16, where the critical attitudes of Mathiez and Dommanget are discussed.
14. Cf. Thomson, *The Babeuf Plot,* p. 15, where the entire relationship is described in the following manner: "[Babeuf] fled to Paris, where he undertook certain literary work for an adventurer named Fournier." Walter, *Babeuf,* pp. 82-3, is scarcely more enlightening.
15. Babeuf, F.-N. (F.-N.-C., G.), *Où en sommes nous? Question par C. Fournier, Américain, à tous les sans-culottes, ses frères* (Imprimerie de Mayer et Cᶦᵉ, Paris 1793), p. 8. Internal evidence suggests that this work was composed in April or May 1793, soon after Dumouriez's defection, to which it refers, had taken place. Dalin has shown that Babeuf was certainly "ghosting" for Fournier as late as 17 April, and probably for a much longer period: *Grakkh Babef,* p. 510. Dalin's view is that "in all probability" Babeuf was the author of *Où en sommes nous?* (p. 509n). A comparison of the text with that of Babeuf's letter to Chaumette on 7 May reveals considerable similarities of style and language. Cf. "la race dévorante des accapareurs est protegée pour pomper jusqu'au dernier denier qui nous reste," "la grande masse nationale, c'est-à-dire l'innombrable phalange des indigents" *(Où en sommes nous?),* and "accapareurs! . . . vous tous qui êtes en possession de pomper à qui mieux les sources vitales de la grande masse du peuple . . . ," "l'innombrable classe des malheureux" (Babeuf to Chaumette, 7 May).
16. Babeuf explicitly states this in a letter to Marie-Anne on 17 April: Dalin, *Grakkh Babef,* p. 510n. Cf. A.N. F⁷6504 (Dossier Fournier): *IVᵉ pétition à la Convention nationale par C. Fournier, Américain, pour la formation d'une Armée Révolutionnaire* (Imprimerie de Lottin, Paris 1793), p. 5, where, in August 1793, Fournier appeals to the Convention to "give our soldiers the assurance of possessing after the war a piece of land of their own where they may peacefully enjoy the fruits of liberty." P. 4 of this work makes it clear that *Où en sommes nous?* was the first version of the petition. This implies that it was substantially the same as that presented by Babeuf on 17 February.
17. Dalin, *Grakkh Babef,* p. 526, cites a note of 10 May: "Caius

Gracchus, who this morning saw the *procureur* of the Paris Commune. . . ."
A.D. Somme F129/72, copy of letter, Babeuf to Marie-Anne Babeuf (18 March 1793).
"Défense préparatoire de G. Babeuf. . .," ff. 9-10.
Letter, Babeuf to Marie-Anne Babeuf (3 March 1793), printed in *Revue des curiosités Révolutionnaires* (vol. I, 1910-11), p. 200.
18. Advielle, *Gracchus Babeuf*, vol. I, p. 99, lists the debts as: "Caté, aubergiste, 49¹¹5ˢ, pour nourriture; Clavieu, traiteur, pour nourriture, 26¹¹4ˢ; Danger, boulanger, 33¹¹, pour pain livré." It is unlikely that Marie-Anne and the children would have run up such bills at an inn or a restaurant.
"Défense préparatoire de G. Babeuf . . .," f. 11.
Advielle, *Gracchus Babeuf*, vol. I, p. 99.
19. Legrand, *Babeuf; ses idées, sa vie en Picardie,* p. 30.
Dalin, *Grakkh Babef*, pp. 464n, 465n, 498.
A.D. Somme F129/73, copy, letter of Babeuf to S. Maréchal, 28 March 1793.
20. Dalin, *Grakkh Babef*, pp. 516-7; "Défense préparatoire de G. Babeuf . . .," f. 10. Dalin consistently has "Makerstrot," in error.
A.D. Somme F129/75, copy, letter of Babeuf to N. Makketros (25 March 1793).
"Defense préparatoire de G. Babeuf . . .," f. 9.

Chapter 10

1. Dalin, *Grakkh Babef*, pp. 517-8.
"G. Babeuf à Anaxagoras Chaumet, Procureur de la Commune de Paris, sur la nécessité et l'obligation pour le magistrat de provoquer la conservation du plus précieux et du plus important des Droits de l'Homme, Paris, 7 mai, l'an II," in Dommanget, *Pages choisies*, pp. 142-6.
Mathiez, *La vie chère*, pp. 178-187.
2. *Oeuvres de Maximilien Robespierre*, vol. IX (ed. M. Bouloiseau, G. Lefebvre, J. Dautry, A. Soboul, Presses Universitaires de France, Paris 1958), pp. 455-6, 459.
Harmand, J.-B., *Quelques idées sur les premiers éléments du nouveau contrat social des français* (Imprimerie Nationale, Paris 1793), p. 6.
In *Tribun du peuple* (no. 35, 30 November 1795), Babeuf paid tribute to "Armand's" speech for demanding "l'égalité de fait et la révolution dans les choses et non plus seulement dans les esprits." His source appears to have been Audouin's *Journal universel*, 26 April 1793: Dommanget, *Pages choisies*, p. 256n.
3. Dommanget, *Pages choisies*, p. 146.
Dalin, *Grakkh Babef*, pp. 507, 526, 529.
A.D. Somme F129/77, letter of Babeuf to Marie-Anne Babeuf, 2 June 1793.
4. Cf. Rose, R.B., *The Enragés: Socialists of the French Revolution?* (Sydney University Press, 1968), pp. 23-6.

5. Soboul, A., "Une lettre de Babeuf du 28 mai 1793," *A.H.R.F.* (no. 171, 1963), p. 75.

A.D. Somme F129/77, Babeuf to Marie-Anne Babeuf (2 June 1793).

6. Letter, Babeuf to André Dumont, 7 frimaire an II (27 November 1793), printed in *Les lettres françaises* (no. 309, 26 April 1950).

"Défense préparatoire de Gracchus Babeuf . . . ," ff. 11-12.

7. Dommanget, *Pages choisies*, p. 157.

Advielle, *Gracchus Babeuf*, vol. I, p. 345.

Cahen, L., "La question du pain à Paris à la fin du XVIIIe siècle," *Cahiers de la Révolution française* (no. I, Paris 1934); Cobb, R., *Terreur et subsistances, 1793-95* (Librairie Clavreuil, Paris 1965), pp. 211-7.

8. Mathiez, *La vie chère*, pp. 259-60.

C. Fournier à Marat, Journaliste (Imprimerie de Lottin, Paris 1793), 7 pp. Babeuf's edition is affirmed by Dalin, *Grakkh Babef*, p. 510.

A.N. F⁷6504 (Dossier Fournier) contains a letter from Garin to Fournier (dated 29 July 1793) complaining about his arrest by the Committee of Public Safety.

[Garin, E.-F.], *Garin, Administrateur des Subsistances, aux 48 Sections de Paris* (Imprimerie de Lottin, Paris 1793), 4 pp.

[Defavanne, G.-J.], *Favanne, Administrateur Adjoint des Subsistances, aux 48 Sections, prenant le fait et cause de Garin . . . attaqué dans un second libelle de deux ex-commis . . .* (Imprimerie de Lottin, Paris 1793), 27 pp.

9. Caron, P., *Paris pendant la Terreur*, vol. I (Picard, Paris 1910), pp. 6-11 (report by police agent Perrière summarizing the sections' case against Garin). Cf. Garin, E.-F., *Réponse à la dénonciation faite à la Section des Sans-culottes par Marchant, citoyen de cette Section, contre Garin, Administrateur des Subsistances* (Imprimerie de la veuve Delaguette, Paris 1793), 20 pp., for Garin's rebuttal.

Soboul, A., *Les sans-culottes parisiens en l'an II. Mouvement populaire et gouvernement révolutionnaire, 2 juin 1793 - 9 thermidor an II* (Librairie Clavreuil, Paris 1958), p. 124.

10. Garin, E.-F., and Defavanne, G.-J., *Suite de Paris sauvé par l'Administration des Subsistances* (Imprimerie patriotique et républicaine, rue S. Honoré, no. 355, Paris 1793), pp. 31-3.

Dauban, C.A., *La démagogie en 1793 à Paris* (Plon, Paris 1868), pp. 246-9.

[Defavanne], *Favanne . . . prenant fait et cause de Garin*, pp. 22-3.

Garin, E.-F., and de Favanne, G.-J. (sic), *Paris sauvé par l'Administration des Subsistances* (Imprimerie patriotique et républicaine, Paris 1793), 32 pp.; published as an *Affiche de la Commune* on 26 and 27 July: Soboul, *Les sans-culottes parisiens*, p. 125n.

11. Mathiez, *La vie chère*, pp. 259-285; Soboul, *Les sans-culottes parisiens*, pp. 124-136.

Caron, *Paris pendant la Terreur*, vol. I, pp. 4-5.

12. Babeuf, F.-N. (F.-N.-C., G.), *Du système de dépopulation, ou la vie et les crimes de Carrier* . . . (Imprimerie de Franklin, Paris 1795), pp. 103n-107n.

Dalin, *Grakkh Babef,* p. 547. Advielle, *Gracchus Babeuf,* vol. I, p. 504.

13. *Babeuf* . . . *aux Comités de salut public, de sûreté générale* . . . *et de législation de la Convention nationale,* pp. 14-16. Dalin, *Grakkh Babef,* p. 551.

Caron, P., *La Commission des Subsistances de l'an II* (Leroux, Paris 1925), pp. ix-xii, 32.

Advielle, *Gracchus Babeuf,* vol. I, p. 99.

14. Deville, "Notes inédites de Babeuf," p. 39.

Dalin, *Grakkh Babef,* p. 554.

Bourgin, G., "Quelques inédits sur Babeuf et ses amis," *A.H.R.F.* (no. 157, 1595), p. 253n.

Chapter 11

1. "Défense préparatoire de G. Babeuf contre un jugement du Tribunal de Montdidier," ff. 1-3.

2. Dalin, *Grakkh Babef,* p. 561.

A.N. BB^{16}858. For Thibaudeau see Tuetey, *Répertoire général,* vol. XI, p. 89, no. 151, and for Daube, Caron, *La Commission des Subsistances,* p. 361.

Deville, "Notes inédites de Babeuf," p. 40.

3. Advielle, *Gracchus Babeuf,* vol. I, p. 99.

"Défense préparatoire de G. Babeuf, contre un jugement du Tribunal de Montdidier" (Subtitled Paris, 3 frimaire l'an II, Gracchus Babeuf à Dumont).

Letter to A. Dumont, 7 frimaire, an II (published in *Les lettres françaises,* no. 309, 26 avril 1950).

Dalin, *Grakkh Babef,* p. 561.

4. A.N. BB^{16}858, Letter of Marie-Anne Babeuf to Herman (18 floréal an II).

Bourgin, G., "Quelques inédits sur Babeuf et ses amis," *A.H.R.F.* (no. 157, 1959), p. 254n.

5. A.D. Somme F129/13, Letter, Marie-Anne Babeuf to G. Babeuf (12 floréal an II); F129/113, copy undated letter, Marie-Anne Babeuf to G. Babeuf.

A.N. BB^{16}858.

A.D. Somme F129/71, copy, letter, G. Babeuf to S. Maréchal (10 ventôse an II).

6. A.N. BB^{16}858, letter, Thibaudeau to S. Maréchal (8 ventôse an II).

Bergmann, *Babeuf,* p. 149.

Babeuf . . . *aux Comités de salut public, de sûreté générale et de législation de la Convention nationale* . . .

7. Dalin, *Grakkh Babef*, pp. 580-1.

A.D. Somme F129/138, copy, letter, Emile Babeuf to G. Babeuf (23 ventôse [an II]).

A.D. Somme F129/142, copy, letter, Emile Babeuf to G. Babeuf (10 germinal [an II]).

Soboul, "L'écrou de Gracchus Babeuf à Saint-Pélagie," p. 175.

Deville, "Notes inédites de Babeuf," pp. 37-44.

Dalin, *Grakkh Babef*, p. 581, identifies four of the deputies as Garnier, Piquet, Gertoux and Desrues.

8. A.N. B¹⁶858.

Dalin, *Grakkh Babef*, pp. 583-5.

A.D. Somme F129/131, copy, letter, Marie-Anne Babeuf to G. Babeuf (14 prairial [an II]).

A.D. Somme F129/133, copy, letter, Marie-Anne Babeuf to G. Babeuf (17 prairial [an II]).

9. Patoux, *Le faux de G. Babeuf*, p. 197; A.D. Somme F129/78, copy, letter, Marie-Anne Babeuf to G. Babeuf (21 prairial an II).

Dalin, *Grakkh Babef*, pp. 586-7.

Soboul, "L'écrou de Gracchus Babeuf," p. 175.

Michelet, J., *Ma Jeunesse* (Calmann Lévy, Paris 1884), p. 10.

G. Babeuf, tribun du peuple, à ses concitoyens, p. 4. Dalin states that the Paris police were ordered to transport Babeuf to Laon by carriage.

10. Melleville, M., *Histoire de la ville de Laon* (Dumoulin, Paris 1846), vol. II, p. 345.

Patoux, *Le faux de G. Babeuf*, pp. 198-206.

Desmasures, A., *Histoire de la Révolution dans le Département de l'Aisne* (Flem, Vervins 1869), p. 221; Melleville, *Histoire de Laon*, vol. II, pp. 355-7.

Tribun du peuple (no. 29, 1-19 nivôse an III), p. 286.

11. Combier, A.E., *Justice criminelle à Laon*, vol. II, pp. 90-97.

Michelet, *Ma Jeunesse*, pp. 10-11.

Tribun du peuple (no. 38), pp. 157-8.

Patoux, *Le faux de G. Babeuf*, p. 207.

12. *Tribun du peuple*, no. 27 (22 vendémiaire an III), p. 228; no. 29 (1-19 nivôse an III), p. 286.

13. Dommanget, *Pages choisies*, pp. 157-160; Dalin, "Robespierre et Danton vus par Babeuf," pp. 398-9.

14. Arnaud, R., *Journaliste, sans-culotte et Thermidorien. Le fils de Fréron, 1754-1802* (Perrin, Paris 1909).

Aulard, A., "Babeuf et son imprimeur Guffroy," *La Révolution française*, vol. LXXXII (1929), pp. 5-21.

Felhemési (J.-C.-H. Méhée de la Touche), *La Queue de Robespierre, ou les dangers de la liberté de la presse* (Imprimerie de Rougyff), 7pp.; *Défends ta Queue, par l'auteur de la Queue de Robespierre* (Imprimerie de Guffroy,

Paris 1794), 8 pp. Cf. Saintomer, J.-C., *Jugement du Peuple Souverain, qui condamne à mort la Queue infernale de Robespierre* (Imprimerie de Guffroy, Paris 1794), 16 pp.

15. *Journal de la liberté de la presse,* no. 1 (17 fructidor an II, Imprimerie de Rougyff, rue Honoré no. 35). No. 2 (19 fructidor an II) contains the advice "On distribue ce journal, qui parôit tous les jours, à l'imprimerie de Guffroy."

Tribun du peuple, no. 27 (22 vendémiaire an III), pp. 229-30.

16. Mathiez, A., *La réaction thermidorienne* (Armand Colin, Paris 1929), p. 96.

Mazauric, *Babeuf et la Conspiration pour l'Egalité,* pp. 19-20.

Tønnesson, K.D., *La défaite des sans-culottes. Mouvement populaire et réaction bourgeoise en l'an III* (Presses Universitaires de France, Paris 1959), p. 62.

Dalin, "Robespierre et Danton vus par Babeuf," p. 402.

17. *Journal de la liberté de la presse,* no. 2 (19 fructidor an II), p. 2. No. 8 (29 fructidor, an II), pp. 2-4.

Tribun du peuple, no. 31 (9 pluviôse an III), p. 313.

Journal de la liberté de la presse, no. 19 (8 vendémiaire, an III), p.5.

Tribun du peuple, no. 31 (9 pluviôse an III), p. 313.

18. *Journal de la liberté de la presse,* no. 19 (8 vendémiaire, an III), p.4.

No. 5 (26 fructidor an II), pp. 1-2; cf. *Tribun du peuple,* no. 26 (19 vendémiaire an III), pp. 7-8, "La liberté est de tous les temps, sous la guerre comme sous la paix."

19. Guffroy, A.-B.-J., *Soufflet à l'imposture par la presse libre* (Imprimerie de Guffroy, Paris [1794]), pp. 2-3.

"G. Babeuf, Tribun du Peuple, Défenseur des Droits de l'Homme, de la liberté de la presse, et de toutes les libertés, à la société populaire des Défenseurs des mêmes Droits, séante au Muséum, et ci-devant à la Salle Electorale. De mon Autre, le 2 brumaire, l'an 3 de la République" (International Institute for Social History, Amsterdam), ff. 4-5. Cf. *Tribun du peuple,* no. 35, p. 60.

20. *Tribun du peuple,* no. 25 (17 vendémiaire an III), p. 223.

21. Mathiez, A., "La campagne contre le Gouvernement révolutionnaire à la veille du 9 thermidor: L'affaire Legray," *A.H.R.F.* (vol. IV), pp. 305-319. Caron, P., "Sur l'opposition de gauche à la veille du 9 thermidor," *A.H.R.F.* (vol. XIX, 1947), pp. 322-5.

Discours prononcé le décadi 30 thermidor dans l'assemblée générale de la section du Muséum qui en a arrêté l'insertion dans son procès-verbal, par le citoyen Penet, un de ses membres (no publisher, place, date). Tønnesson, *La Défaite des Sans-culottes,* pp. 56-66.

Journal de la liberté de la presse, no. 3 (22 fructidor an II), pp. 5-6. Here Babeuf dates the Club Electoral petition 20 thermidor an II (7 August 1794); in no. 13 (1 vendémiaire an III), p. 5, 30 thermidor (17

August 1794); and in no. 10 (1 sans-culottides an II), p. 4, 20 fructidor (6 September 1794). Other sources make it clear that the petition was presented to the Convention on 20 fructidor (6 September 1794). Cf. *Procès-verbal de la Convention nationale*, vol. XLV, p. 121.

22. *Journal de la liberté de la presse*, no. 7 (28 fructidor an II), pp. 3-6.
No. 18 (6 vendémiaire an III), p. 7.
No. 13 (1 vendémiaire an III), pp. 2-3.
Procès-verbal de la Convention nationale, vol. XLV, p. 121.

23. A.N. F⁷4775⁴⁰: Dossier Varlet.
Journal de la liberté de la presse, no. 7 (28 fructidor an II), p. 6.
Moniteur (3 sans-culottides an II; 7 vendémiaire an III).
Journal de la liberté de la presse, no. 22 (10 vendémiaire an III), pp. 1-8.
Adresse de la Société populaire séante à la salle électorale à la Convention Nationale, arrêtée le 7 vendémiaire an III (Imprimerie de Guffroy, Paris, 1794), 8 pp.; also published by the Imprimerie de la Veuve Marat, 7 pp.

24. *Journal de la liberté de la presse*, no. 21 (10 vendémiaire an III), pp. 4, 6.
No. 23 (14 vendémiaire an III), pp. 6-8. Babeuf—or the printer—again confuses dates, substituting 10 thermidor (28 July) for 10 vendémiaire (1 October).
Annales Patriotiques et Littéraires, no. DCXXXX (12 vendémiaire an III), pp. 3086-7. *Procès-verbal de la Convention nationale*, vol. XLVI, pp. 228-9.
Tønnesson, *La défaite des Sans-culottes*, p. 81.
Mathiez, "L'affaire Legray," p. 317.
A.N. F⁷4278: Dossier Babeuf.

25. *Orateur du peuple*, no. x (9 vendémiaire an III), pp. 75, 77-8.
No. xiii (16 vendémiaire an III), pp. 98-100.
Journal de la liberté de la presse, no. 20 (9 vendémiaire an III), pp. 3-5.
Tribun du peuple, no. 26 (19 vendémiaire an III), pp. 6-8.
No. 25 (17 vendémiaire an III), p. 7.
No. 27 (22 vendémiaire an III), p. 230; Guffroy, *Soufflet à l'imposture par la presse libre*, *passim*.

26. *Tribun du peuple*, no. 27 (22 vendémiaire an III), *passim*.
A.N. F⁷4278: Dossier Babeuf.
Aulard, F.-A., *Paris pendant la réaction thermidorienne* (Cerf et Noblet, Paris 1898-1902, 5 vols.), vol. I, p. 203.

27. Babeuf, G., *Les Battus payent l'amende, ou les Jacobins jeannots* (Imprimerie de Franklin, Paris [1794]), 24 pp. Babeuf, G., *Voyage des Jacobins dans les quatre parties du monde. Avec la Constitution mise à l'ordre du jour, par Audouin et Barrère* (Imprimerie de Franklin, Paris 1794), 16 pp.
Journal de la liberté de la presse, no. 16 (4 vendémiaire an III), p. 7.

"G. Babeuf, Tribun du Peuple . . . à la société populaire . . . séante au Muséum . . . 2 brumaire an III," f. 2n.

28. *Journal de la liberté de la presse*, no. 3 (22 fructidor an II), p. 6
No. 7 (28 fructidor an II), p. 6.
No. 13 (1 vendémiaire an III), p. 1.
No. 18 (6 vendémiaire an III), p. 1.
29. *Journal de la liberté de la presse*, no. 6 (27 fructidor an II), p.6.
A.D. Somme F129/79, copy of letter, A.-B.-J. Guffroy to G. Babeuf, 21 vendémiaire an III.
Journal de la liberté de la presse, no. 21 (10 vendémiaire an III), pp. 1-2.
30. Lecocq, *Manifeste*, pp. 18-19.
Cf. Tønnesson, *La défaite des Sans-culottes*, pp. 78 sqq.
"G. Babeuf, Tribun du Peuple . . . à la société populaire . . . séante au Muséum . . . 2 brumaire an III," f. 1. On 1 October the *Journal de la liberté de la presse* writes of "les milliers d'habitués" of the "tribunes" of the club: no. 22 (10 vendémiaire an III), p. 1.
Tribun du peuple, no. 23 (14 vendémiaire an III), p. 7.
31. *Journal de la liberté de la presse*, no. 7 (28 fructidor an II), p. 2.
No. 18 (6 vendémiaire an III), pp. 1-2.
No. 7 (28 fructidor an II), p. 3.
32. *Journal de la liberté de la presse,* no. 22 (10 vendémiaire an III), p. 23; *Annales patriotiques et littéraires*, no. DCXXXIX (11 vendémiaire an III), pp. 3081-2.
Adresse de la société populaire séante à la salle électorale . . . le 7 vendémiaire an III, p. 8.
"G. Babeuf, Tribun du Peuple . . . à la société populaire . . . séante au Muséum . . . 2 brumaire an III." Lecocq, *Manifest* ("Opinion attendu par la société et les tribunes du club ci-devant électoral le 12 brumaire an III").
33. Lecocq, *Manifeste*, pp. 40-41.
Tribun du peuple, no. 27 (22 vendémiaire an III), p. 215. A second edition of the Club Electoral petition of 28 September was published by the "Imprimerie de la Veuve Marat." Marat's "widow," Constance Evrard, and Albertine Marat were living in the same household in 1794.
Lecocq, *Manifeste*, pp. 40-41.
34. Tønnesson, *La défaite des Sans-culottes*, pp. 94-5.

Chapter 12

1. *Journal de la liberté de la presse*, no. 22 (10 vendémiaire an III), pp. 4-7.
Lecocq, *Manifeste*, p. 39.
Tribun du peuple, no. 27 (22 vendémiaire an III), p. 215.
Les Battus payent l'amende; *Voyage des Jacobins dans les quatres parties du monde*; *On veut sauver Carrier. On veut faire le procès au Tribunal révolutionnaire. Peuple, prends garde à toi* (Imprimerie de Franklin, Paris, 1794). *On veut sauver Carrier* was published on or before 7 November:

Aulard, *Paris pendant la réaction thermidorienne*, vol. I, p. 226. Under interrogation in January 1795 Carin, proprietor of the Imprimerie de Franklin and the publisher of the other two pamphlets, admitted also printing *On veut sauver Carrier*: A.N. F⁷4276.

2. Rudé, G., *The Crowd in the French Revolution* (Oxford 1959), p. 145.
Tribun du peuple, no. 29 (1-19 nivôse an III), pp. 263-4.

3. *Tribun du peuple*, no. 28 (28 frimaire an III), pp. 249-50.
No. 29 (1-19 nivôse an III), p. 271.
No. 30 (4 pluviôse an III), p. 301.
No. 31 (9 pluviôse an III), p. 319.

4. *Du système de dépopulation, ou la vie et les crimes de Carrier.*

5. *Les Battus payent l'amende*, pp. 2-3.
Tribun du peuple, no. 28 (28 frimaire an III), p. 234.

6. *Système de dépopulation . . .*, pp. 15-17, 22, 25-29, 31n-36n.

7. *Tribun du peuple*, no. 29 (1-19 nivôse an III), pp. 263, 265-7, 272-3.

8. Walter, *Babeuf*, pp. 110-111.
Tribun du peuple, no. 32 (13 pluviôse an III), pp. 335-7.
Aulard, *Paris pendant la réaction thermidorienne*, vol. I, p. 431.
Dommanget, *Pages choisies*, pp. 57-8, 242-3.
A.D. Somme F129/80, copy, letter, G. Babeuf to J. Fouché (Arras, 19 germinal an III).

9. Tønnesson, *La défaite des Sans-culottes*, pp. 141 sqq.

10. *Tribun du peuple*, no. 29 (1-19 nivôse an III).
No. 30 (4 pluviôse an III), pp. 290-1, 305.
No. 29 (1-19 nivôse an III), pp. 269-279. Bentabole indignantly put up a placard protesting that it was only 3,000 livres.

11. Tønnesson, *La défaite des Sans-culottes*, p. 141.
Tribun de peuple, no. 31 (9 pluviôse an III), p. 315.
No. 32 (13 pluviôse an III), pp. 332-3.

12. Tǿnnesson, *La défaite des Sans-culottes*, pp. 143 sqq.
Tribun du peuple, no. 30 (4 pluviôse an III), p. 295.
No. 31 (9 pluviôse an III), pp. 315, 317-321.
No. 32 (13 pluviôse an III), p. 332.

13. Cobb, R., "L'Arrestation de Babeuf à Paris, le 20 pluviôse an III," *A.H.R.F.* (no. 165, 1961), pp. 393-4.
A.N. F⁷4276, Dossier Babeuf.

14. *Tribun du peuple*, no. 38, p. 154.
Combier, *Justice Criminelle à Laon*, vol. I, pp. 63-4, vol. II, p. 95. Babeuf's hapless guarantors at Laon were ordered to produce him for trial, but, by a stroke of luck, not until they had learned that he was in the hands of the Committee of General Security in Paris. The 2,000 livres bail was not therefore forfeit.

15. Aulard, F.-A., *Recueil des Actes du Comité de Salut Public*, vol. XX, p. 23.
A.N. F⁷4726.

A.D. Somme F129/80.

"Autographes et Documents," *La Révolution française*, vol. VIII (1885), p. 733.

Aulard, *Paris pendant la réaction thermidorienne*, vol. I, p. 468.

16. Tønnesson, *La défaite des Sans-culottes*, pp. 126, 147 sqq.

17. Tønnesson, *La défaite des Sans-culottes*, p. 365.

Cobb, R., *Terreur et subsistances, 1793-5* (Clavreuil, Paris 1965), p. 189.

Tønnesson, "L'an III dans la formation du Babouvisme," *A.H.R.F.* (no. 162, 1966), pp. 423-4, quoting Magnier, B., *L'opinion du Démocrite sur l'insurrection à opérer pour sauver la patrie*.

18. Rudé, G., *The Crowd in the French Revolution*, pp. 142-159.

Chapter 13

1. A.N. F⁷4276.

A.N. F⁷4277: "Lettre de Gracchus Babeuf au Comité de Sûreté Général sur la prétendue conspiration des faubourgs Antoine et Marceau; autre lettre de Babeuf à Bentabole sur son retour à la bonne cause." This is apparently a draft for publication.

G. Babeuf, tribun du peuple, à ses concitoyens. Lebois' *Ami du peuple*, 24 pluviôse an III (12 February 1795), mentions the appearance of this publication: Aulard, F.-A., *Paris pendant la réaction thermidorienne*, vol. I, p. 475.

2. A.N. F⁷4276.

For Lebois' arrest see *Débats du procès instruit par la Haute-Cour de Justice contre Drouet, Baboeuf et autres, recueillis par des sténographes* (Baudoin, Paris 1797), vol. III, p. 172.

3. Charavay, N., *Catalogue des autographes et des documents historiques composant la collection de M. Etienne Charavay* (Charavay, Paris 1900), no. 273, p. 96.

A.D. Somme F129/80, copy, letter, G. Babeuf to Fouché (19 germinal an III).

Soboul, A., "Autour de Babeuf," *A.H.R.F.* (no 194, 1968), p. 546.

Cobb, R., *Terreur et subsistances*, p. 89.

4. Fleischmann, H., "La comédie à Arras," *Annales révolutionnaires*, vol. III (1910), pp. 526-7.

Durry, M.-J., *Autographes de Mariemont* (Musée de Mariemont, Paris 1955), vol. II, pp. 797-802.

Soboul, "Autour de Babeuf," p. 545.

5. A.D. Somme F129/80, copy, letter, G. Babeuf to J. Fouché, Arras, 19 germinal an III.

"Autographes et Documents," *La Révolution française*, vol. VIII (1885), pp. 735-6.

6. Bergmann, *Babeuf*, pp. 212-3.

Advielle, *Gracchus Babeuf*, vol. I, pp. 132-3, 149, 153, 277.

7. Jacob, L., "Correspondance avec Babeuf, emprisonné à Arras," *A.H.R.F.* (vol. XI, 1934), pp. 253-6.

Advielle, *Gracchus Babeuf*, vol. II, p. 86.

Jacob, L., *Joseph Le Bon, 1765-1795* (Paris 1934), vol. II, p. 303, gives the date of the order for Henri Le Bon's arrest as 20 thermidor (7 August 1795).

8. *Débats du procès*, vol. IV, pp. 163-5, 174-5.

Advielle, *Gracchus Babeuf*, vol. I, pp. 132-3, 135.

Dommanget, M., *Sur Babeuf et la conjuration des égaux* (Maspero, Paris 1970), pp. 303 sqq.

9. Dommanget, *Sur Babeuf...*, pp. 309, 313, 318.

10. Dommanget, *Pages choisies*, pp. 207-221.

Dommanget, *Sur Babeuf*, p. 311.

11. Dommanget, *Sur Babeuf*, p. 317.

Ibid., p. 312: "Anéantirons-nous l'industrie en l'organisant, en l'administrant, en assignant à chacun sa tache ... , en proportionnant constamment les products à la consommation ...?"

12. Dommanget, *Pages choisies*, pp. 210-15, 220. Dommanget, *Sur Babeuf*, pp. 314-7.

13. Dommanget, *Pages choisies*, pp. 216-7. No explanation was offered as to how a "surplus" could arise in an economy based on an absolutely equal distribution of commodities.

14. Dommanget, *Pages choisies*, pp. 210-21.

15. Dommanget, *Sur Babeuf*, pp. 312-313.

Dommanget, *Pages choisies*, pp. 205-6, 217-20.

16. Dommanget, *Pages choisies*, pp. 211, 214n.

Coë, R.N.C., "La théorie morellienne et la pratique babouviste," *A.H.R.F.* (no. 150, 1958), pp. 38-64.

Scott, *The Defense of Gracchus Babeuf*, pp. 67-9, 72-8.

17. In *Tribun du peuple*, no. 35 (9 frimaire an IV, 30 Nov. 1795), from which he appears to have drawn some of the material in his general defense before the Vendôme court, Babeuf cites the Morelly passages, but not those from Mably. For Mably cf. *Journal de la liberté de la presse*, no. 19 (8 vendémiaire an III), p. 5.

18. *Tribun du peuple*, no. 29 (1-19 nivôse an III), p. 279.

No. 35 (9 frimaire an IV), p. 105.

Dalin, V.M., "Marc-Antoine Jullien après le 9 thermidor," *A.H.R.F.* (no. 180, 1965), p. 194.

19. Dommanget, *Sur Babeuf*, p. 315.

A.N. F⁷4728, copy of letter, Charles Germain to Guilhem, 4 thermidor an III.

Advielle, *Gracchus Babeuf*, vol. I, pp. 150, 152.

Jacob, "Correspondance avec Babeuf," pp. 257-8.

20. *Débats du procès*, vol. III, p. 67.

A.N. W³561, liasse 15, pièce 15, "Gracchus Babeuf au plébéien Simon, 25 nivôse, l'an 4."

A.N. W³561, liasse 15, pièce 51, "Les égaux d'Arras à leur tribun. Arras, 23 pluviôse an IV." "Notre bon père" seems more likely to have been intended than "notre bon pair." Is this a Freudian lapse into religious terminology, or a deliberate pun?

21. Advielle, *Gracchus Babeuf,* vol. I, pp. 153-66.

Lecesne, E., *Arras sous la Révolution* (Sueur-Charruey, Arras 1882-3), vol. III, pp. 141-2.

A.D. Somme F129/83, MS of "Le Tribun du Peuple à l'Armée infernale."

22. Advielle, *Gracchus Babeuf*, vol. I, pp. 167-70. Dommanget, *Pages choisies*, pp. 221-2.

23. Soboul, "Autour de Babeuf," *A.H.R.F.* (no. 194, 1968), pp. 546-7.

Granier de Cassagnac, A., *Histoire du Directoire* (Plon, Paris 1863), vol. II, p. 461n.

Letters of Charles Germain to Babeuf, 17 and 21 messidor an III (5 and 9 July 1795), Advielle, *Gracchus Babeuf*, vol. I, pp. 137, 139.

Lefebvre, G., *The Thermidorians* (trs. Robert Baldick, Routledge & Kegan Paul, London 1965), p. 162.

24. A.D. Somme F129/82, copy, letter of Marie-Anne Babeuf to Babeuf, 21 thermidor an III (8 August 1795).

Advielle, *Gracchus Babeuf*, vol. II, p. 69.

25. *Débats du Procès,* vol. III, p. 205 (Buonarroti's estimate of the prison population).

Buonarroti, *Conspiration*, vol. I, pp. 59, 61.

Cobb, *Terreur et subsistances*, pp. 189-90.

26. *Débats du procès*, vol. III, p. 204.

Buonarroti, *Conspiration*, vol. I, pp. 59, 69.

27. *Débats du procès*, vol. III, p. 207.

Dalin, "Marc-Antoine Jullien après le 9 thermidor," *A.H.R.F.*, no. 176 (1964), pp. 169-173; no. 180 (1965), p. 188. For Pierre Philip's association with the Club Electoral, see Philippe, *Le grand rappel à l'ordre de Fréron, par un ami de la liberté, membre du Club Electoral* [1794] (John Rylands Library, French Historical Tracts).

Chapter 14

1. Dalin, V.M., "Marc-Antoine Jullien après le 9 thermidor," *A.H.R.F.* (no. 176, 1964), pp. 187-9.

2. Schmidt, W.A., *Tableaux de la Révolution française* (Veit, Leipzig 1867-70), vol. II, p. 452.

Picquenard, C., "La Société du Panthéon," *La Révolution française*, vol. 33 (1897), pp. 322-3, 326-8, 334, 336-7.

3. Dalin, "Marc-Antoine Jullien après le 9 thermidor," *A.H.R.F.* (no. 176, 1964), pp. 189-97.

Buonarroti, *Conspiration*, vol. I, pp. 72-5.

Woloch, I.T., *Jacobin Legacy. The Democratic Movement under the Directory* (Princeton 1970), p. 24n.

4. *Tribun du peuple,* no. 35 (9 frimaire an IV), pp. 57-62.

No. 36 (20 frimaire an IV), p. 127.

5. *Tribun du peuple,* no. 34 (15 brumaire an IV), pp. 4-9, 11-14, 52.

6. *Tribun du peuple,* no. 35 (9 frimaire an IV), pp. 88-107.

7. Ibid., p. 92. On 30 April 1796 Babeuf would tell Rossignol that "la loi agraire n'était nullement dans son système," "qu'il n'était pas possible de faire de la France une espèce d'échiquier" and that his system tended, on the contrary, to "dépropriairiser généralement toute la France": Dommanget, *Pages choisies*, p. 255n.

8. *Tribun du peuple,* no. 35, pp. 102-6.

9. Aulard, *Paris pendant la réaction thermidorienne*, vol. II, p. 459.

Schmidt, *Tableaux de la Révolution . . . ,* vol. II, p. 530.

10. *Tribun du peuple,* no. 34 (15 brumaire an IV), p. 15.

No. 40 (5 ventôse an IV), pp. 238-40.

11. Dommanget, *Pages choisies*, pp. 284-7.

Dalin, "Robespierre et Danton vus par Babeuf," *A.H.R.F.* (no. 162, 1960), pp. 402-3.

Advielle, *Gracchus Babeuf*, vol. I, pp. 133-138.

Tribun du peuple, no. 35 (9 frimaire an IV), pp. 66-7.

12. *Tribun du peuple,* no. 35, p. 84. No. 34, pp. 44-5.

13. *Prospectus du Tribun du peuple*, pp. 6-7. The prospectus was composed *after* no. 34 had appeared on 6 November.

Tribun du peuple, no. 37 (30 frimaire an IV), p. 157.

No. 39 (1 pluviôse an IV), p. 186.

Lefebvre, G., *The Directory* (trs. Baldick; Routledge & Kegan Paul, London 1955), p. 32.

Copie des pièces saisies dans le local que Baboeuf occupoit lors de son arrestation (Imprimerie Nationale, Paris, frimaire-nivôse an V [1796]), pp. 138-9.

14. Mazauric, *Babeuf,* p. 131.

A copy of a subscription list seized by Pernet on 6 December 1795 runs from no. 472 to no. 507: A.N. F⁷3056/119: Police générale, affaires particulières, A-L, 1790-1825.

15. Aulard, *Paris pendant la réaction thermidorienne*, vol. II, p. 459 (3 Dec. 1795), pp. 508-9 (14 Dec.), p. 593 (30 Dec.).

Soboul, A., "Personnel sectionnaire et personnel babouviste," *A.H.R.F.* (no. 162, 1960), pp. 438-44.

Woloch, *Jacobin Legacy*, pp. 39, 45-6.

A.N. F⁷4278, copy, letter of Cormier to Gracchus Babeuf, Autun, 8 nivôse an IV.

16. Combier, *Justice criminelle à Laon*, vol. II, p. 96.

A.N. W³564: Ordonnance de Prise de Corps de Gracchus Babeuf, dated

13 frimaire an IV, and citing a denunciation by the Tribunal Criminel du
département de la Seine, 11 frimaire an IV.

A.N. F⁷3056/118: Rapport fait au ministre de l'intérieur par
Lamaignière, juge de paix à la Section des Champs-Elysées.

Tribun du peuple, no. 36 (20 frimaire an IV), p. 124.

Ministre de police générale de la République, *Extrait des registres des
délibérations du Directoire exécutif, Paris, le 23 floréal* (Morard-Colas,
Vendôme an IV), pp. 58-9 (testimony of Charles-Jean Thiebaut, porter of
the Maison de la ci-devant Conception). For personal notes on Didier:
Lenôtre, G., *Le Tribunal Révolutionnaire, 1793-5* (Paris 1908), pp. 243-4,
326.

17. A.N. W³562: "Registre des expenditures compté avec la C ⁿⁿᵃ Didier
le 27 germinal."

*Acte d'accusation dressé par le jury d'accusation du département de la
Seine, contre Gracchus Baboeuf et les 59 prévenus de la conspiration du 22
floréal* (Baudoin, Paris, fructidor an IV), p. 47.

18. A.N. F⁷3056/118: Rapport . . . par Lamaignière.

Debidour, A., *Recueil des actes du Directoire exécutif* (Ministère de
l'instruction publique, Paris 1910-1917), vol. I, pp. 229-30.

Patoux, *Le faux de Babeuf,* p. 207.

Bourgin, G., "Quelques inédits de Babeuf," *A.H.R.F.* (no. 157, 1959), p.
261.

19. Debidour, *Actes du Dir. exéc.,* vol. I, p. 317.

A.N. BB¹⁸743, dr. 2450 d.

A.N. AF III 42, dr. 152, 13 pluviôse an IV.

Charavay, E., "L'arrestation de la femme de Babeuf," *La Révolution
française,* vol. I (1881), pp. 214-219.

20. A.N. F⁷7160.

Ibid., report by Lamaignière, 23 pluviôse an IV. Bourgin, "Quelques inédits de Babeuf," *A.H.R.F.* (no. 157, 1959), p. 260.

Picquenard, "La Société du Panthéon," pp. 344-5. *Tribun du peuple,* no.
40 (5 ventôse an IV), p. 263.

Advielle, *Gracchus Babeuf,* vol. II, p. 82.

*L'Eclaireur du peuple, ou le défenseur de 24 millions d'opprimé*s (no. 2,
published at the beginning of March 1796), p. 14: "Tel est l'attentat qui
vient de tracer une ligne profonde de démarcation entre le Directoire et tous
les Patriotes et le prive du seul appui qui sembloit lui rester."

21. Picquenard, "La Société du Panthéon," p. 333. *Tribun du peuple,* no.
38 (*c.* 9 January 1796). Buonarroti, *Conspiration,* vol. I, p. 88.

22. Picquenard, "La Société du Panthéon," pp. 336, 340-43.

23. *Tribun du peuple,* no. 36, pp. 119-20.

No. 37, pp. 134, 138, 141.

No. 38, p. 162.

No. 39, pp. 195n, 206n-208n.

24. Woloch, *Jacobin Legacy*, pp. 31-2.
Tribun du peuple, no. 40, pp. 243-262.
Picquenard, "La Société du Panthéon," pp. 345-8.

Chapter 15

1. Buonarroti, *Conspiration*, vol. I, pp. 78-86.
Tribun du peuple, no. 38, p. 175: "Tout ce qu'il y a de pur, d'honnête et de bon travaille dans le secret . . ."
2. Haute-Cour de Justice, *Copie de l'instruction personelle au représentant du peuple Drouet* (Imprimerie Nationale, Paris frimaire an V, B.M. F1124/24).
Police report (16 prairial an IV), in A.N. F⁷4276.
Débats du procès, vol. II, p. 100.
Buonarroti, *Conspiration,* vol. I, p. 86.
For Sergent, A.N. F⁷4775¹⁸, dossier I.
3. Mathiez, A., "Le complot des Egaux," *Revue des cours et conférences* (série II, année XXX, 1929, no. 14), p. 555.
Buonarroti, *Conspiration*, vol. I, pp. 86, 98.
Débats du procès, vol. II, p. 408.
Suite de la copie des pièces, p. 81: Babeuf's notes refer to the distributor as "Did—."
4. Buonarroti, *Conspiration*, vol. I, p. 107.
Acte d'accusation, p. 63.
Débats du procès, vol. II, pp. 365-6.
A.N. W³561.
5. *L'Eclaireur du peuple ou le défenseur de 24 millions d'opprimés*, no. 1, p. 6, no. 2, pp. 13-18.
6. A.N. W³561: Letter of G. Babeuf to an unnamed correspondent (15 ventôse an IV).
Débats du procès, vol. III, pp. 65-8.
Suite de la copie des pièces, pp. 60-64.
7. *Débats du procès*, vol. III, pp. 160, 241.
Saitta, A., "Autour de la Conjuration de Babeuf. Discussion sur le communisme en 1796," *A.H.R.F.* (no. 162, 1962), p. 430.
A tous les Français sur la clôture, par arrêté des réunions de citoyens [Paris, 1796], in A.N. W³563. Attributed to P.A. Antonelle in Dalin, Saitta and Soboul, *Inventaire des manuscrits et imprimés de Babeuf*, p. 98.
8. Buonarroti, *Conspiration*, vol. I, pp. 98-9, 104-5.
According to Grisel, he learned on 30 April that Le Peletier "delivrât des fonds pour les dépenses": Ministre de la police générale, *Extrait . . . des délibérations du Directoire exécutif, le 23 floréal*, p. 24.
Charles-Nicolas Pillé admitted that he had been hired by Le Peletier as secretary and copyist for the committee: Conseil des Cinq-cents, *Messages du Directoire exécutif* (Imprimerie Nationale, Paris floréal an IV, B.M. F1125/10), pp. 40-44. *Acte d'Accusation*, pp. 31-2.

9. Buonarroti, *Conspiration*, vol. I, pp. 99-100, 107. The *Analyse* is reprinted in vol. II, pp. 99-107, but with extensive "preuves" which did not appear in the original.

Débats du procès, vol. II, p. 360.

10. Dalin, Saitta, Soboul, *Inventaire*, p. 99.

M.V. à Gracchus Babeuf, reprinted in Buonarroti, *Conspiration*, vol. II, pp. 143-4.

Réponse à une lettre signée M.V., publiée et adressée le 30 pluviôse dernier à Gracchus Babeuf, Tribun du Peuple, reprinted in Buonarroti, *Conspiration*, vol. II, pp. 145-54.

11. "Fragment d'un projet de décret économique," in Buonarroti, *Conspiration*, vol. II, pp. 204-214.

". . . il est certain que les fonctions publiques eussent été très multipliées et les magistrats fort nombreux"; Buonarroti, *Conspiration*, vol. I, p. 199.

12. Buonarroti, *Conspiration*, vol. I, pp. 158, 168-75, 184-5, 202-8.

13. "Manifeste des Egaux," reprinted in Buonarroti, *Conspiration*, vol. II, pp. 94-8.

Copie des pièces, pp. 58, 138-9, 150-1, 242.

Buonarroti, *Conspiration*, vol. I, p. 149; vol. II, p. 189.

Le Comité Insurrecteur de Salut Public au Peuple. Acte d'Insurrection. Egalité, Liberté, Bonheur Commun ([Paris i796] B.M. F1124/15), reprinted in Buonarroti, *Conspiration*, vol. II, pp. 164-170, 188, but not listed as a separate publication in Dalin, Saitta, Soboul, *Inventaire*.

14. *Le Comité Insurrecteur . . . au Peuple*, p. 4.

Buonarroti, *Conspiration*, vol. II, pp. 106-7 (*Analyse de la Doctrine de Babeuf*), pp. 124-9 (*Doit-on obéissance à la Constitution de 1795?*); vol. I, pp. 192-4, 198.

15. *Le Comité Insurrecteur . . . au Peuple*, p. 8. Buonarroti, *Conspiration*, vol. II, pp. 84, 170.

16. *Débats du procès*, vol. II, pp. 241-4.

Copie des pièces, pp. 72, 130-1, 139-48.

Buonarroti, *Conspiration*, vol. I, pp. 113, 153; vol. II, p. 170.

17. See below, pp. 260-2.

18. *Le Comité Insurrecteur . . . au Peuple*, p. 8.

Copie des pièces, pp. 138-9.

Buonarroti, *Conspiration*, vol. I, pp. 126, 216; vol. II, p. 180.

19. Buonarroti, *Conspiration*, vol. I, pp. 110-196, 200-201.

20. Buonarroti, *Conspiration*, vol. I, p. 152; vol. II, p. 190.

Acte d'accusation, p. 102.

Copie des Pièces, pp. 67, 87, 238-42.

Haute Cour de Justice, *Copie de l'instruction personelle au représentant du peuple Drouet*, p. 167.

21. Buonarroti, *Conspiration*, vol. I, pp. 217-9; vol. II, pp. 190, 201-203.

22. *Tribun du peuple*, no. 35 (9 frimaire an IV), p. 107.

Buonarroti, *Conspiration,* vol. I, pp. 216-7, 221-2; vol. II, pp. 204-5.

23. *Suite de la copie des pièces,* pp. 232-3. The date of Pâris' letter is printed as 19 ventôse (9 March), but this must be in error for 19 germinal.

Suite de la copie des pièces, p. 176.

Bergmann, *Babeuf,* p. 514.

Advielle, *Gracchus Babeuf,* vol. I, pp. 286-7.

Chapter 16

1. Ministre de la police générale de la république, *Extrait des registres des délibérations du Directoire exécutif, le 23 floréal,* p. 85.

Cobb, R., *Les Armées Révolutionnaires* (Mouton, Paris 1966), p. 880.

Débats du procès, vol. III, pp. 292, 322.

2. *Suite de la copie des pièces,* pp. 228, 232-3, 274.

Min. de la pol. gén. de la rép., *Extr. des dél. du Dir. exéc.,* pp. 87, 108; A.N. F⁷4276 (police report dated 5 prairial, an IV).

Soboul, A., "Autour de Babeuf," *A.H.R.F.* (no. 194, 1968), pp. 546-7.

Copie des pièces, p. 333.

3. *Copie des pièces,* pp. 294-8.

Buonarroti, *Conspiration,* vol. I, p. 104.

Suite de la copie des pièces, pp. 52, 239.

4. *Suite de la copie des pièces,* pp. 162-3.

Min. de la pol. gén. de la rép., *Extr. des dél. du Dir. exéc.,* p. 21.

Copie des pièces, pp. 172-81. Buonarroti, *Conspiration,* vol. II, pp. 84-93.

5. *Copie des pièces,* pp. 153-5, 205-6.

Cobb, R., *Terreur et Subsistances,* p. 181.

Two francs was the "journée d'ouvrier" received by Moroy: *Débats du procès,* vol. III, p. 298.

6. Soboul, A., "Personnel sectionnaire et personnel babouviste," *A.H.R.F.* (no. 162, 1960), pp. 446-50, 456.

7. *Débats du procès,* vol. III, p. 268.

Cobb, *Terreur et Subsistances,* p. 204.

Débats du procès, vol. III, p. 293.

Copie des pièces, p. 284: "cet arrondissement n'est composé que de la classe ouvrière, la plus précieuse de la société, ce qui donne un champ libre aux ennemis de la patrie d'en égarer la majeure partie. . . ."

8. *Copie des pièces,* pp. 253, 255-6, 268, 271, 278-9, 285.

9. A.N. W³559: undated interrogation of "Anne Martin fame tissot" (*sic*), in which she stated that Babeuf moved to her apartment "a fortnight or three weeks" before his arrest on 10 May.

10. *Copie des pièces,* p. 54; cf. Buonarroti, *Conspiration,* vol. I, pp. 107-8.

Opinion sur nos deux Constitutions soumise au jugement de ceux qui décrétèrent, présentèrent à la France et jurèrent l'une et l'autre (Paris 1796), 12 pp.

Grisel, G., *Lettre de Franc-Libre, soldat de l'armée circo-parisienne, à son ami La Terreur, soldat de l'armée du Rhin* (Paris 1796); reprinted in Buonarroti, *Conspiration*, vol. II, pp. 108-111.

Doit-on obéissance à la Constitution de 1795? (Paris 1796) 12 pp; reprinted in Buonarroti, *Conspiration,* vol. II, pp. 124-9.

Soldat, arrête encore (Paris 1796), 4pp.

Babeuf, G., *L'adress du Tribun du Peuple à l'armée de l'intérieur* (Imprimerie du *Tribun du peuple*, Paris 1796), 12 pp. Reprinted in Buonarroti, *Conspiration*, vol. II, pp. 130-42.

Le cri du peuple français contre ses oppresseurs (Paris 1796), 8 pp.

11. *Acte d'accusation*, pp. 61-3.

Min. de la pol. gén. de la rép., *Extr. des dél. du Dir. exéc.*, pp. 78, 109.

12. *Débats du procès,* vol. III, p. 297.

13. *Copie des pièces*, pp. 220-221, 282-3.

Schmidt, *Tableaux de la Révolution française*, vol. III. p. 149.

14. *Débats du procès*, vol. III, p. 290.

Copie des pièces, pp. 224, 294.

Suite de la copie des pièces, pp. 103, 148.

Schmidt, *Tableaux de la Révolution*, vol. III, p. 153; Aulard, *Paris pendant la réaction thermidorienne*, vol. III, p. 111.

15. Aulard, *Paris pendant la réaction thermidorienne*, vol. III, p. 111.

Copie des pièces, p. 276.

Débats du procès, vol. II, p. 73.

Schmidt, *Tableaux de la Révolution,* vol. II, pp. 159-61.

Suite de la copie des pièces, p. 219.

16. *Copie des pièces*, pp. 194-8.

Débats du procès, vol. II, pp. 70-71, 73. For Marie Sophie Lapierre see Min. de la pol. gén. de la rép., *Extr. des dél. du Dir. exéc.*, p. 113.

Schmidt, *Tableaux de la Révolution*, vol. III, p. 156. For the text of Maréchal's "Chanson nouvelle à l'usage des Faubourgs" see Buonarroti, *Conspiration*, vol. II, p. 155.

Débats du procès, vol. III, p. 562.

17. Buonarroti, *Conspiration*, vol. I, pp. 105, 128.

18. *Débats du procès*, vol. II, pp. 66-71, 73, 129-32.

Granier de Cassagnac, *Histoire du Directoire*, vol. II, p. 455.

19. Buonarroti, *Conspiration*, vol. II, pp. 112-123.

20. *Tribun du peuple,* no. 41 (10 germinal an IV), pp. 270-81.

Babeuf, *Adresse du Tribun du peuple à l'Armée de l'intérieur.*

L'Eclaireur du peuple, no. 3, pp. 6-7. (Undated, but probably published towards the end of March 1796.)

[Le Peletier, F.], *Soldat, arrête et lis* (Paris 1796), p. 4; cf. Buonarroti, *Conspiration*, vol. II, p. 79.

21. Buonarroti, *Conspiration*, vol. II, pp. 182-5.

22. *Débats du procès*, vol. II, p. 72.

Buonarroti, *Conspiration*, vol. II, pp. 108-111.

Copie des pièces, p. 242.

23. Debidour, *Actes du Dir. exéc.,* vol. I, p. 24n. Tulard, J., "Le recrute-ment de la Légion de police de Paris sous la Convention thermidorienne et le Directoire," *A.H.R.F.* (no. 175, 1954), pp. 38-55.

Debidour, *Actes du Dir. Exéc.,* vol. II, p. 202. For the initiative of Cochon and Carnot see Boucher, P., *Charles Cochon de Lapparent* (Picard, Paris 1970), p. 148.

24. Min. de la pol. gén. de la rép., *Extr. des dél. du Dir. exéc.,* pp. 57, 60-65.

Suite de la copie des pièces, pp. 96-7.

Copie des pièces, pp. 36-7.

25. Min. de la pol. gén. de la rép., *Extr. des dél. du Dir. exéc.,* p. 63.

Copie des pièces, pp. 32-3, 40, 168, 183-4, 255.

Suite de la copie des pièces, p. 217.

Tulard, "La Légion de Police," pp. 57-61.

26. Tulard, "La Légion de Police," pp. 60-62.

Chapter 17

1. Grisel, for one, was convinced that Drouet was mad. At Fribourg Drouet had written a paper attributing France's problems to overpopula-tion. His solution was the migration of a horde of "Gaulish" colonists across the French borders, escaping from the oppression of the "aristocratic Frankish yoke" and establishing settlements (at the expense of France's neighbors) in which "Liberty, Equality and Fraternity" would be firmly enshrined. At a meeting on 8 May Drouet's proposal to change the name of France to Gaul produced an impatient response from Babeuf. Haute-Cour de Justice, *Copie de l'instruction personelle au représentant du peuple Drouet,* pp. 191-203, 168-9.

2. *Le Directoire exécutif à la commission du Conseil des Cinq-cents chargée de l'examen de l'affaire du représentant Drouet,* pp. 5 sqq.

Copie des pièces, p. 223.

Haute-Cour de Justice, *Copie de l'instruction personelle au représentant du peuple Drouet,* pp. 19-20.

3. Boucher, *Cochon de Lapparent,* pp. 144-5, 166.

Copie des pièces, pp. 201, 208-11, 296.

Tribun du peuple, no. 41 (10 germinal an IV), p. 284.

4. *Copie des pièces,* pp. 192-3, 203.

Ministre de la police générale de la république, *Extrait des registres des délibérations du Directoire exécutif, Paris le 23 floréal,* p. 26; *Débats du Procès,* vol. II, pp. 75-80.

5. Buonarroti, *Conspiration,* vol. I, pp. 131-7.

Min. de la pol. gén. de la rép., *Extr. des dél. du Dir. exéc.,* pp. 26-7.

Buonarroti, *Conspiration,* vol. II, p. 188.

6. Buonarroti, *Conspiration,* vol. I, pp. 129, 137, 141, 148.

Copie des pièces, p. 22.

7. Buonarroti, *Conspiration*, vol. I, p. 148.

Copie des pièces, pp. 17-29, 55-9, 238-9.

Buonarroti, *Conspiration*, vol. II, pp. 167, 192-5.

8. Min. de la pol. gén. de la rép., *Extr. des dél. du Dir. exéc.*, p. 22.

Copie des pièces, pp. 17, 58.

Suite de la copie des pièces, p. 189.

Buonarroti, *Conspiration*, vol. I, pp. 143, 145n.

9. *Copie des pièces*, pp. 90, 247, 288-9, 294.

10. Buonarroti, *Conspiration*, vol. I, pp. 143-4; Min. de la pol. gén. de la rép., *Extr. des dél. du Dir. exéc.*, p. 22.

11. Schmidt, *Tableaux de la Révolution*, vol. III, p. 186.

Débats du procès, vol. II, p. 92; cf. undated letters from "Armand" in A.N. W³565.

Haute-Cour de Justice, *Copie de l'instruction personelle au rep. du peuple Drouet*, p. 152.

Débats du procès, vol. II, pp. 71-3. Legrand, R., "Une lettre de Grisel à ses compatriotes d'Abbeville," *A.H.R.F.* (no. 171, 1963), pp. 75-8.

Debidour, *Actes du Dir. exéc.*, vol. II, p. 490n.

Granier de Cassagnac, *Hist. du Directoire*, vol. II, p. 455.

12. *Débats du procès*, vol. II, p. 92.

Legrand, "Une lettre de Grisel," p. 77.

13. Min. de la pol. gén. de la rép., *Extr. des dél. du Dir. exéc.*, pp. 17-19.

A.N. F⁷4278, dr. 4: Declaration of Georges Grisel to Carnot, President of the Directory (15 floréal an IV).

Legrand, "Une lettre de Grisel," p. 76.

A.N. AF III 42, dr. 153/147: Procès verbal by Marcel Regnier (27 floréal an IV).

On 5 germinal an V (25 March 1797) Viellart, prosecutor at the trial of the conspirators, wrote to Carnot to ask for Grisel's commission. Carnot replied that it could not be found and that it was "useless to look." The prosecution dossiers nevertheless contained a copy of the commission: A.N. W³565.

14. A.N. F⁷4278, dr. 4: Declaration of Georges Grisel, 15 floréal; Min. de la pol. gén. de la rép., *Extr. des dél. du Dir. exéc.*, pp. 19-20; *Débats du procès*, vol. II, pp. 79-80.

Débats du procès, vol. II, p. 92; Min. de la pol. gén. de la rép., *Extr. des dél. du Dir. exéc.*, p. 21.

15. *Débats du procès,* vol. II, p. 94; vol. III, pp. 393-5.

Boucher, *Cochon de Lapparent*, p. 167.

Debidour, *Actes du Dir. exéc.*, vol. II, p. 640n.

16. Haute-cour de Justice, *Copie de l'instruction personelle au rep. du peuple Drouet*, pp. 149-50.

Débats du procès, vol. II, p. 112.

On 4 May Grisel told Carnot that the 30 April meeting had been held at no. 27 rue de la Grande Truanderie: A.N. F⁷4278 dr. 4. In a later report he suggested that the police concentrate on no. 30: Haute-Cour de Justice, *Copie de l'instruction personelle au rep. du peuple Drouet*, p. 152.

17. Boucher, *Cochon de Lapparent*, p. 163.

Debidour, *Actes du Dir. exéc.*, vol. II, p. 339.

Copie des pièces, p. 246.

18. Haute-Cour de Justice, *Copie de l'instruction personelle au rep. du peuple Drouet*, p. 150; Min. de la pol. gén de la rép., *Extr. des dél. du Dir. exéc.*, p. 27; Buonarroti, *Conspiration*, vol. I, p. 139.

Débats du procès, vol. II, pp. 105-8.

19. Cobb, *Les Armées révolutionnaires*, p. 881.

Débats du procès, vol. III, p. 558.

Haute-Cour de Justice, *Copie de l'instruction personelle au rep. du peuple Drouet*, pp. 20-21.

20. *Débats du procès*, vol. II, pp. 112-115, 126; Min. de la pol. gén. de la rép., *Extr. des dél. du Dir. exéc.*, p. 23.

Debidour, *Actes du Dir. exéc.*, vol. II, p. 640n.

21. *Débats du procès*, vol. III, pp. 398-9; Buonarroti, *Conspiration*, vol. I, p. 225, *Acte d'accusation*, pp. 46, 52-3.

22. A.N. F⁷4278: Report on Babeuf's arrest. Robiquet, P., "L'arrestation de Babeuf," *La Révolution française*, vol. XXVII (1895), pp. 307-310.

Chapter 18

1. A.N. F⁷4278: Concierge's report for 22 floréal an IV.

Debidour, *Actes du Dir. exéc.*, vol. II, p. 355.

A.N. W³559.

A.N. AF III 42, dr. 153, pièce 4.

2. A.N. F⁷4278.

A.N. F⁷4276.

Dommanget, *Pages choisies*, pp. 298-302.

3. Thomson, *The Babeuf Plot*, pp. 39-40.

A.N. W³563: "Je ne vous ai point cru barbare citoyen ministre. Je vous ai fait une demande avant hier, l'humanité exigeait que vous y répondiez . . ."

4. A.N. F⁷4278. Debidour, *Actes du Dir. exéc.*, vol. II, pp. 368, 373, 592. Min. de la pol. gén. de la rép., *Extr. des dél. du Dir. exéc.*, pp. 1 sqq.

The net was spread so wide that it included Guffroy.

5. A.N. BB³22; Reports of concierge of Temple prison.

A.N. W³559.

Acte d'accusation, p. 8, listing the disposition of prisoners on 11 July.

6. Rémusat, P.-Fr. de, *Mémoire sur ma détention au Temple, 1797-99* (Picard et fils, Paris 1903), pp. 23-4.

A.N. BB³22.

Débats du procès, vol. III, p. 256. *Protestation motivée des citoyens ac-*

cusés d'avoir pris part à la prétendue conspiration du 21 floréal, par laquelle ils récusent et déclinent la Haute-Cour de Justice comme incompétente pour procéder dans cette affaire (R. Vatar, Paris 1796), p. 80.

7. *Débats du procès*, vol. II, p. 487. *Suite de la copie des pièces*, pp. 283-6.

A.N. F^74276. A.N. W^3563: copy, report of concierge of Temple prison (13 prairial an IV).

Débats du procès, vol. III, p. 161.

8. A.N. BB^322: Letter, Etienne Lasne to Directory, 3 thermidor an IV; Lasne's report as concierge (4 fructidor an IV).

A.N. W^3563: Lasne's report (11 thermidor an IV).

Aulard, *Paris pendant la réaction thermidorienne*, vol. III, p. 284.

9. Bouis, R., "Une lettre de Babeuf à Hésine," *A.H.R.F.* (no. 171, 1963), pp. 79-82.

A.N. F^74276: report by police agent Pierre Mazot (27 floréal an IV).

Acte d'accusation, pp. 81-5. *Min. de la pol. gén. de la rép., Extr. des dél. du Dir. exéc.*, pp. 36-45, 70-74. *Débats du procès*, vol. II, pp. 375-83.

10. A.N. F^74276.

11. Aulard, *Paris pendant la réaction thermidorienne*, vol. III, pp. 199-211, 235.

Débats du procès, vol. III, pp. 406-411. *Acte d'accusation*, p. 72.

12. A.N. F^74276.

Aulard, *Paris pendant la réaction thermidorienne*, vol. III, p. 297.

13. Douarche, A., *Les tribunaux civils de Paris pendant la Révolution* (L. Cerf, Paris 1905-7), vol. I, pp. 9, 426; vol. II, p. 248, 897. Charavay, E., *L'assemblée électorale de Paris* (L. Cerf, Paris 1894), vol. I, pp. 41, 257.

A.N. AF III 42, dr. 153, pièce 82. Debidour, *Actes du Dir. exéc.*, vol. III, p. 67.

A.N. BB^322. The arrangements for the transfer of the prisoners to Vendôme at the end of August included a "voiture" for the papers of the trial.

14. *Le Directoire exécutif à la commission du Conseil des Cinq-cents chargée de l'examen de l'affaire du représentant Drouet* (Imprimerie Nationale, Paris prairial an IV), pp. 32-40.

Acte d'accusation, p. 35.

15. *Acte d'accusation*, pp. 38-77.

16. Legrand, R., "Une lettre de Grisel."

A.N. AF III 42, dr. 153, pièce 73.

17. *Min. de la pol. gén de la rép., Extr. des dél. du Dir. exéc.*, pp. 84-5, 89.

A.N. W^3559.

18. *Min. de la pol. gén. de la rép., Extr. des dél. du Dir. exéc.*, pp. 89, 93.

Jugement de la Haute-Cour de justice qui statue sur la validité de la procédure instruite contre G. Babeuf et cinquante-trois de ses co-accusés (Morard, Vendôme 1797), pp. 3-5, 9.

Acte d'accusation, p. 91.

19. Boucher, *Cochon*, p. 166.

20. For a police report of 23 June commenting on frequent desertions and low morale at Grenelle: Schmidt, *Tableaux de la Révolution*, vol. III, p. 252.

Boucher, *Cochon*, p. 168. *Débats du procès*, vol. II, pp. 412, 441-2, 461, 476.

A.N. AF III 42, dr. 153: Grisel to Carnot (27 messidor an IV).

Aulard, *Paris pendant la réaction thermidorienne*, vol. III, p. 340.

21. Aulard, *Paris pendant la réaction thermidorienne*, vol. III, pp. 337-40, 342, 429-30.

22. A.N. F⁷4276; A.N. BB³22: concierge's report of 22 thermidor an IV.

Cochon de Lapparent, C., *Rapport au Directoire exécutif, le 12 fructidor, an IV* (Imprimerie du Directoire exécutif, Paris 1796). *Proclamation du Directoire exécutif sur les évènements qui se sont passés dans la nuit du 11 au 12 du mois de fructidor* (Imprimerie du Directoire exécutif, Paris 1796). Boucher, *Cochon*, pp. 171-2.

23. Javogues, G., "L'affaire du Camp de Grenelle," *A.H.R.F.* (1925), vol. II, pp. 23-32. Cochon de Lapparent, *Rapport au Directoire exécutif du 24 fructidor, an quatrième de la république française une et indivisible* (Imprimerie du Directoire exécutif, Paris 1796). Min. de la pol. gén. de la rép., *Au quartier général à Issy, le 24 fructidor, an quatrième, 6 heures du matin* (Imprimerie du Directoire exécutif, Paris 1796). *Liste officielle des cent trente-deux prisonniers fait au Camp de Grenelle* (de l'Imprimerie de l'Ami de la Patrie, rue Nicaise no. 330, Paris 1796).

Aulard, *Paris pendant la réaction thermidorienne*, vol. III, p. 441.

24. Espinas, *La philosophie sociale*, p. 369. Bourgin, "Babeuf et le babouvism," *Cahiers de la Révolution française* (1934, no. 1), p. 100. Javogues, "L'Affaire de Grenelle," p. 26. Mazauric, *Babeuf*, p. 211.

Boucher, *Cochon*, pp. 176-7.

Granier de Cassagnac, *Histoire du Directoire*, vol. II, pp. 119 sqq.

25. Javogues, "L'Affaire de Grenelle," p. 32. The sergeants were Antione Vaslé and Pierre Rapin: *Liste officielle des prisonniers*.

Chapter 19

1. *Protestation motivée*, pp. 80-81.

Fouquet, R., "A propos du procès de Babeuf. Comment les accusés furent amenés de Paris à Vendôme," *Bulletin de la société archéologique, scientifique et littéraire du Vendômois*, 1954, p. 46.

A.N. BB³20 (concierge's report dated 15 fructidor an IV).

Fouquet, "A propos du procès de Babeuf," *Bulletin de la société archéologique, scientifique et littéraire du Vendômois*, 1954, pp. 46-8; 1955, pp. 13-15.

2. Coach timetable in A.N. BB³22.

Dufort de Cheverny, J.-N., *Mémoires sur les règnes de Louis XV et Louis XVI et sur la Révolution* (publiés avec une introduction par Robert de Crèvecoeur, Plon, Nourrit, Paris 1886, 2 vols.), vol. II, p. 355.

Fouquet, "A propos du procès de Babeuf," 1955, pp. 17-24.

Bonhoure, G., "Notes inédites d'après les registres municipaux de 1796-1797 sur le procès des Babouvistes devant la Haute-Cour de Vendôme," *Bulletin de la société archéologique, scientifique et littéraire du Vendômois* (vol. XLVIII, 1908), p. 36. *Journal de la Haute-Cour de Justice établie à Vendôme ... Soudry, éditeur propriétaire*, ed. Rouzet, no. 1 (1 vendémiaire an V), p. 3.

3. Debidour, *Actes du Dir. exéc.*, vol. III, pp. 370-2, 496.

Bonhoure, "Notes inédites sur le procès des Babouvistes," pp. 32-40.

Vallon, P.G.A., "Conspiration de Babeuf," *Mémoires de la société des sciences et des lettres de la ville de Blois* (1852), vol. IV, p. 324.

Journal de la Haute-Cour de Justice (Hésine), no. 13 (1 nivôse an V), p. 3.

Journal de la Haute-Cour de Justice (Rouzet), no. 34 (3 vendémiaire an V), p. 12.

4. *Journal de la Haute-Cour de Justice* (Rouzet), no. 5 (5 vendémiaire an V), p. 19.

Bouis, R., "P.-N. Hésine, rédacteur du Journal de la Haute-Cour ou l'Echo des Hommes vrais et sensibles," *A.H.R.F.* (no. 162, 1960), pp. 471-2.

Vendôme pendant la Révolution (Huet, Vendôme 1892-3, 2 vols.), vol. II, pp. 99-110.

5. Dommanget, *Pages choisies*, pp. 304-5.

Journal de la Haute-Cour de Justice (Rouzet), no. 9 (9 vendémiaire an V), p. 35; no. 3 (3 vendémiaire an V), pp. 6n, 10; no. 15 (18 vendémiaire an V), p. 65.

Bouis, "P.-N. Hésine," pp. 473-7, 481.

Dufort de Cheverny, *Mémoires*, vol. II, p. 317.

Journal de la Haute-Cour de Justice, ou l'écho des hommes libres, vrais et sensibles (ed. P.-N. Hésine), 13 fructidor an IV to 7 prairial an V.

6. Dufort de Cheverny, *Mémoires,* vol. II, p. 309.

7. *Journal de la Haute-Cour de Justice* (Hésine), no. 3 (9 brumaire an V), p. 2; no. 12 (19 frimaire an V), p. 2.

Journal des séances du Tribunal de la Haute-Cour de Justice établi à Vendôme (deuxième envoy, deuxième partie), p. 7.

Dufort de Cheverny, *Mémoires*, vol. II, p. 311.

8. *Journal des séances du Tribunal* (deuxième envoy, deuxième partie), pp. 6-7.

Journal de la Haute-Cour de Justice (Rouzet), no. 26 (22 frimaire an V), p. 208. A.N. BB³20 (concierge's report dated 29 fructidor an IV; concierge's report dated 5 frimaire an V).

Journal de la Haute-Cour de Justice (Rouzet), no. 6 (6 vendémiaire an V), p. 23.

Dufort de Cheverny, *Mémoires,* vol. II, p. 311.

Journal de la Haute-Cour de Justice (Hésine), no. 22 (4 pluviôse an V), p. 1.

9. *Journal de la Haute-Cour de Justice* (Rouzet), no. 6 (6 vendémiaire an V), p. 23.

Dufort de Cheverny, *Mémoires,* vol. II, p. 309.

Journal de la Haute-Cour de Justice (Hésine), no. 27 (20 pluviôse an V), p. 4. A.D. Somme F129/7: copy, letter, G. Babeuf to Emile Babeuf (12 floréal an V). Other letters show that Babeuf was also able to send out eggs, butter, lentils and haricots: A.D. Somme F129/156-167.

10. Buonarroti, *Conspiration,* vol. II, p. 20. A.N. BB³20 (concierge's report dated 3 jour complémentaire an V; concierge's report dated 1 vendémiaire an V).

Journal de la Haute-Cour de Justice (Hésine), no. 5 (18 brumaire an V), p. 2.

Journal de la Haute-Cour de Justice (Rouzet), no. 4 (4 vendémiaire an V), p. 15; no. 6 (6 vendémiaire an V), p. 22.

11. A.N. BB³20 (procès-verbal dated 11 nivôse an V; concierge's reports dated 13 nivôse an V, 13 frimaire an V, 1 pluviôse an V, 23 and 25 pluviôse an V). Dufort de Cheverny, *Mémoires,* pp. 310-311.

12. A.N. BB³20 (concierge's reports dated 4 pluviôse an V; 12 pluviôse an V; 22 fructidor an IV; 25 fructidor an IV).

A.D. Somme F129/95 (copy, letter, G. Babeuf to Marie-Anne Babeuf, dated 12 vendémiaire an V).

13. A.D. Somme F129/92 (copy, letter, G. Babeuf to Marie-Anne Babeuf, dated 8 vendémiaire an V). "Lettres inédites de Babeuf," *Franzuskii Yezhegodnik* (French Annual) (1960), pp. 268-272.

A.D. Somme F129/98 (copy, letter, G. Babeuf to Marie-Anne Babeuf, dated 23 vendémiaire an V).

Advielle, *Gracchus Babeuf,* vol. I, p. 229.

Journal de la Haute-Cour de Justice (Rouzet), no. 18 (22 vendémiaire an V, p. 92). A.N. BB³20 (concierge's reports dated 24 vendémiaire, 22 frimaire an V, 1 floréal an V).

14. Boucher, *Cochon,* pp. 154-5.

A.N. BB³20 (concierge's reports dated 1 jour complémentaire, an IV; 1 messidor an V; 30 nivôse an V).

Bibliothèque Nationale MS, Nouvelle acquisitions fr. 21589, f. 123: facsimile of letter, G. Babeuf to Marie-Anne Babeuf, dated 4 pluviôse an V.

A.N. BB³20 (concierge's reports dated 3 ventôse an V; 26 brumaire an V).

15. Dufort de Cheverny, *Mémoires,* vol. II, p. 314.

16. Woloch, *Jacobin Legacy,* p. 54. Bigard, L., *Le Comte Réal, ancien Jacobin* (Mercier, Versailles 1937), p. 95.

A.N. BB³20 (concierge's report dated 7 frimaire an V; 17 pluviôse an V).

Soboul, "Une lettre de Babeuf à Hésine," *A.H.R.F.* (no. 171, 1963), pp. 79-83.

17. A.N. BB³20 (concierge's reports dated 22 brumaire an V; 12 nivôse an V; 14 nivôse an V).

Boucher, *Cochon*, p. 155.

18. *Journal de la Haute-Cour de Justice* (Rouzet), no. 13 (15 vendémiaire an V). *Journal des séances du Tribunal* (cinquième envoy, deuxième partie).

Protestation motivée des citoyens accusés d'avoir pris part à la prétendue conspiration du 21 floréal, par laquelle ils récusent et déclinent la Haute-Cour de Justice comme incompétente pour procéder dans cette affaire (Imprimerie de R. Vatar, Paris 1796), 107 pp.

A.N. BB³20 (concierge's report dated 26 fructidor an IV).

Journal de la Haute-Cour de Justice (Rouzet), no. 3 (3 vendémiaire an V), pp. 15-16.

19. Jamin, G., *Des Hautes-Cours de Justice sous la Révolution* (Thèse, Paris 1907), p. 104.

Levot, P., *Biographie Bretonne* (Cauderon, Vannes 1852), vol. I, pp. 762 sqq.

Arnault, A.V., etc., *Biographie Nouvelle des Contemporains* (Librairie Historique, Paris 1820-1825).

20. *Réquisition des Accusateurs Nationaux près la Haute-Cour de Justice sur les Déclinatoires de plusieurs accusés des 13, 15, 17, et 24 fructidor an 4. Jugement de la Haute-Cour du 19 vendémiaire an 5 qui rejette les Déclinatoires, ordonne qu'il sera passé outre à l'instruction du procès* (à Vendôme, de l'imprimerie de la Haute-Cour, chez Morard, an V), pp. 25 + 5. *Journal de la Haute-Cour de Justice* (Rouzet), no. 15 (18 vendémiaire an V), p. 66; no. 17 (19 vendémiaire an V), p. 88.

Journal de la Haute-Cour de Justice (Hésine), no. 6 (21 brumaire an V), p. 2.

21. *Journal de la Haute-Cour de Justice* (Rouzet), no. 19 (2 brumaire an V), p. 100.

A.N. BB³20 (concierge's reports dated 5, 6, 7, 10, 14 and 17 brumaire an V; 19 fructidor; 7 nivôse and 17 nivôse an V).

22. Rabbe, A., *Biographie universelle et portative des contemporains* (Levrault, Paris 1834).

Jugement de la Haute-Cour de Justice qui statue sur la validité de la procédure instruite contre G. Babeuf et cinquante-trois de ses co-accusés (Morard, Vendôme 1796).

Jugement de la Haute-Cour de Justice qui sans avoir égard aux moyens de nullité proposés par huit accusés, ordonne que l'instruction sera suivie. Séance du 29 brumaire, 4 pp.

23. *Journal de la Haute-Cour de Justice* (Rouzet), no. 23 (6 frimaire an V), p. 130.

Jugement de la Haute-Cour de Justice qui rejette la demande de Babeuf, afin d'audition de 4 témoins par lui indiqués. Séance du 27 brumaire

(Soudry, Vendôme 1796), 20 pp.

24. Corps législatif. Conseil des Cinq-Cents. *Rapport et projet de résolution présentés au Conseil des Cinq-Cents par Soulignac, Représentant du Peuple, sur la composition du Haut-Juré et la Haute-Cour de Justice, 1 thermidor an IV* (Imprimerie Nationale, Paris 1796), 14 pp.

Rapport sur les excuses proposées par plusieurs Hauts-Jurés fait à l'audience du 27 brumaire an V (Soudry, Vendôme 1796); *Jugement de la Haute-Cour de Justice qui prononce sur les excuses proposées par les Hauts-Jurés. Séance du 27 brumaire an V* (Soudry, Vendôme 1796), 7 pp. *Jugement rendu par la Haute-Cour de Justice le premier pluviôse l'an 5* (Baudoin, Paris 1797), 10 pp.

Haute-Cour de Justice, *Procès-verbal de la formation du tableau du Haut-Jury 29 brumaire de l'an V* (Imprimerie de la Haute-Cour, Morard-Colas, Vendôme 1796), pp. 1-9.

A.N. BB³20 (concierge's reports dated 2, 3 and 5 frimaire an V). *Journal de la Haute-Cour de Justice* (Rouzet), No. 26 (22 frimaire an V), p. 209; No. 27 (24 frimaire an V), p. 232.

25. Haute-Cour de Justice, *Procès-verbal de la formation du Tableau du Haut-Jury*, pp. 10-16, 27, 49n-52n, 54.

26. *Jugement de la Haute-Cour de Justice qui ordonne un remplacement de cinq Hauts-Jurés* (Imprimerie de la Haute-Cour, Morard-Colas, Vendôme 1796), 14 pp.

Haute-Cour de Justice, *Jugement du 20 nivôse an Vᵉ* (Morard-Colas, Vendôme 1797), 14 pp.

Jugement rendu . . . le premier pluviôse, pp. 4-8.

27. *Journal des séances du Tribunal* (neuvième envoy, deuxième partie), p. 57.

Advielle, *Gracchus Babeuf*, vol. I, p. 232; *Copie des pièces; Suite de la copie des pièces*.

Copie des pièces, p. 259.

28. *Journal des séances du Tribunal* (neuvième envoy, deuxième partie), p. 58. Germain, C.-A.-G., *Discours prononcé par Charles Germain devant la Haute-Cour de Justice* (Imprimerie de l'Ami du peuple, Paris 1797), 15 pp., p. 10.

Débats du procès, vol. I, pp. 15-18.

29. *Journal de la Haute-Cour de Justice* (Hésine), no. 28 (26 pluviôse an V), pp. 1-3.

A.N. BB³20 (concierge's reports dated 27, 29, 30 pluviôse an V).

Chapter 20

1. *Journal de la Haute-Cour de Justice* (Hésine), no. 21 (2 pluviôse an V), pp. 3-4. Dufort de Cheverny, *Mémoires*, vol. II, pp. 312-5.

Débats du procès, vol. I, pp. 7-14.

2. *Journal des séances du Tribunal* (dixième envoy, seconde partie), p. 63.
Débats du procès, vol. I, pp. 19-25.
3. *Débats du procès*, vol. I, pp. 25-64. *Journal des séances du Tribunal* (dixième envoy, seconde partie), pp. 66-70.
4. *Débats du procès*, vol. I, pp. 66-122.
Journal des séances du Tribunal (douzième envoy, seconde partie), p. 73.
Bigard, L., *Le Comte Réal, passim.*
A.N. BB³20 (concierge's report dated 7 ventôse an V).
5. *Débats du procès*, vol. I, pp. 234-45, 278-9, 340.
6. Mège, F., *Gaultier de Biauzat, député du Tiers État aux États-Généraux de 1789, sa vie et sa correspondance* (Bellet, Clermont-Ferrand 1890), pp. 307-8.
7. Advielle, *Gracchus Babeuf*, vol. I, pp. 259-60.
Débats du procès, vol. I, pp. 340-414; vol. II, pp. 7-16.
8. *Débats du procès*, vol. I, pp. 279-84; vol. II, p. 371.
9. Advielle, *Gracchus Babeuf*, vol. I, p. 266.
Débats du procès, vol. II, pp. 245-7, 271-9; vol. III, pp. 83-90, 222-43, 268, 299.
10. *Débats du procès*, vol. I, pp. 125-227.
11. Advielle, *Gracchus Babeuf*, vol. I, p. 261.
Débats du procès, vol. II, pp. 65, 83-116, 118, 120, 132-53, 157-90.
Journal de la Haute-Cour de Justice (Hésine), no. 43 (27 ventôse an V), p. 1; no. 44 (28 ventôse an V), p. 4; no. 45 (30 ventôse an V), p. 1.
12. *Débats du procès*, vol. II, pp. 374-467.
13. *Débats du procès*, vol. II, pp. 491-506; vol. III, pp. 173-202.
14. See, in particular, the session of 14 April, *Débats du procès*, vol. III, pp. 521-3.
15. *Débats du procès*, vol. I, pp. 262-3; vol. II, pp. 244-60, 280-308, 311-17.
A.N. BB³20 (concierge's report dated 30 ventôse an V).
16. Advielle, *Gracchus Babeuf*, vol. I, p. 265.
Débats du procès, vol. II, pp. 198-202, 247-70, 311-17, 347-71; vol. III, pp. 530-8, 621-8.
17. *Débats du procès,* vol. IV, pp. 3-158.
18. Advielle, *Gracchus Babeuf*, vol. I, pp. 296-312.
19. Babeuf, G., *Défense générale devant la Haute-Cour de Vendome*, in Advielle, *Gracchus Babeuf*, vol. II, pp. 1-322. *The Defense of Gracchus Babeuf before the High Court of Vendôme* (edited and translated by John Anthony Scott. With an essay by Herbert Marcuse, and illustrations by Thomas Cornell, University of Massachusetts Press, Amherst 1967).
A.N. BB³20 (concierge's reports dated 16 and 18 floréal an V).
20. Advielle, *Gracchus Babeuf*, vol. II, pp. 28-59, 320-1.
21. *Débats du procès*, vol. IV, pp. 159-233, 241-362.

Advielle, *Gracchus Babeuf*, vol. I, pp. 315-27. Bigard, *Le Comte Réal*, pp. 101-2.

22. Bigard, *Le Comte Réal*, pp. 99-102.

23. *Débats du procès*, vol. V, pp. 1-67.

Advielle, *Gracchus Babeuf*, vol. I, p. 328.

24. *Débats du procès*, vol. V, pp. 67-114.

Journal de la Haute-Cour de Justice (Hésine), no. 73 (7 prairial an V), p. 2.

Débats du procès, vol. I, p. 64.

25. Dufort de Cheverny, *Mémoires*, vol. II, pp. 334-6.

Bergmann, *Babeuf*, p. 477.

Advielle, *Gracchus Babeuf*, vol. I, pp. 250-1.

Journal de la Haute-Cour de Justice (Hésine), no. 20 (29 nivôse an V), p. 3.

26. Bigard, *Le Comte Réal*, p. 102. A.N. BB³20 (concierge's report dated 7 prairial an V).

Journal de la Haute-Cour de Justice (Hésine), no. 73 (7 prairial an V), pp. 2-3.

27. Buonarroti, *Conspiration*, vol. II, pp. 215-17.

Dommanget, *Pages choisies*, pp. 309-18.

28. *Journal de la Haute-Cour de Justice* (Hésine), no. 73 (7 prairial an V), pp. 3-4. *Débats du procès*, vol. V, pp. 118-32. Nodier, C., *Souvenirs de la Révolution et de l'Empire* (7ᵉ édition, Charpentier, Paris 1864), vol. II, p. 295.

29. Bonhoure, "Notes inédites sur le procès des Babouvistes," pp. 50-52. Advielle, *Gracchus Babeuf*, vol. I, pp. 332-7.

A.N. BB³20 (concierge's report dated 9 prairial an V).

Dommanget, *Pages choisies*, p. 318n.

30. Woloch, *Jacobin Legacy, passim*; Robiquet, P., *Buonarroti et la Secte des Egaux, d'après des documents inédits* (Hachette, Paris 1910), pp. 97-106n; A.D. Somme F129/103, copy of letter of Marie-Anne Babeuf to Emile Babeuf, 2 pluviôse an IX; *Dictionnaire biographique du Mouvement ouvrier français*, ed. Jean Maitron (Editions ouvrières, Paris 1964-   ), under Babeuf, Marie-Anne-Victoire; Cobb, R., *The Police and the People: French Popular Protest, 1789-1820* (O.U.P., London 1970), p. 357 and *passim*.

Conclusion

1. Hulshoff, Maria Aletta, *Peace Republican's Manual or the French constitution of 1793 and the Declaration of the rights of man and of citizens ... To which is added debates on this constitution in the national Convention ... translated extracts from pieces seized in Baboeuf's rooms ...* (J. Thiebout, New York 1817), pp. iv, 85n, 91n.

2. Taine, H.A., *The Origins of Contemporary France* (translated by J.

Durand, New York 1876-94), "The Revolution," vol. III, p. 224. Cf. Fleury, E., *Biographie de Babeuf. Etudes révolutionnaires* (Imprimerie d'Ed. Fleury et Ad. Chevergny, Laon 1849); two Paris editions were published in 1850 and 1851. Granier de Cassagnac, A., *Histoire du Directoire* (Plon, Paris 1851-1855), 2 vols.

3. Mathiez, A., *Revue des cours et conférences* (série II, année XXX), pp. 450-467, 609-620.

4. Coë, R.N.C., "La théorie morellienne et la pratique babouviste" (with a discussion on Morelly by correspondence between Jean Dautry, Armando Saitta and R. Coë), *A.H.R.F.* (no. 150, 1958), pp. 38-64. Cf. Saitta, A., "Autour de la Conjuration de Babeuf. Discussion sur le communisme en 1796," *A.H.R.F.* (no. 162, 1960), pp. 426-435.

5. Advielle, *Gracchus Babeuf*, vol. II, p. 51.

6. Spitzer, A.B., *The Revolutionary Theories of Louis Auguste Blanqui* (Columbia University Press, New York 1957), pp. 6, 101.

7. For a summary of views on this subject see Rose, R.B., "Babeuf, Dictatorship and Democracy," *Historical Studies* (vol. 15, no. 58, April 1972), pp. 225-6.

8. *Journal de la Haute-Cour de Justice* (Hésine), no. 9 (9 frimaire an V), p. 4.

9. Palmer, R.R., *The Age of the Democratic Revolution* (Princeton University Press, 1959-1964), vol. I, p. 242.

Bibliography

ARCHIVAL SOURCES

Archives Nationales

Secretairerie d'Etat
  Convention nationale, AF II 2868
  Directoire exécutif, AF III 42
Versements du Ministère de la Justice
  Affaires criminelles, BB^{3}20, BB^{3}22
  Correspondance générale de la Division civile, BB^{16}858-9
  Correspondance générale de la Division criminelle, BB^{18}743
Comités des Assemblées
  Comité des rapports, DXXIX 68
  Comité des recherches, DXXIX 68 bis
Administration générale de la France
  Police générale, F^{7}3056, F^{7}4276-8, F^{7}4775, F^{7}6504, F^{7}7160
Tribunaux révolutionnaires, W^{3}559, W^{3}561-5

Archives du Département de la Somme

E100/ Fonds de la famille Biaudos de Castéja
  14
F129   Dossier Babeuf
L74   Registre du Conseil-Général du Département de la Somme
L84   Registre du Directoire du Département de la Somme, 1^{ier} Bureau
L88   Registre des délibérations du Directoire du Département de la
       Somme
L320   Assemblée électorale d'Abbeville, 2-18 septembre 1792
L374   Evènements de police dans les communes (Troubles religieux, at-
       troupements, pillages de grains, excès des militaires)

L2073   Registre des délibérations du District de Montdidier
L2105   Mémoires et requêtes présentés au District de Montdidier
L2134   Affaires communales diverses

International Institute for Social History, Amsterdam

Copy of letter, C. Babeuf to J.M.L. Coupé de l'Oise, Roye, le 7 octobre 1791.

G. Babeuf, Tribun du Peuple, Défenseur des Droits de l'Homme, de la liberté de la presse, et de toutes les libertés, à la société populaire des Défenseurs des mêmes Droits, séante au Muséum, et ci-devant à la Salle Electorale. De Mon Antre, le 2 brumaire, l'an 3 de la République.

Défense préparatoire de G. Babeuf contre un jugement du Tribunal de Montdidier, Paris, 3 frimaire l'an II: Gracchus Babeuf à Dumont.

Bibliothèque Nationale

Nouvelles acquisitions fr. 21589, f. 123: facsimile of letter, G. Babeuf to Marie-Anne Babeuf, 4 pluviôse an V.

PRINTED WORKS
Contemporary Tracts

Acte d'accusation dressé par le jury d'accusation du département de la Seine contre Gracchus Babeuf et les 59 prévenus de la conspiration du 22 floréal, suivi de l'Acte du Corps legislatif portant accusation contre le représentant Drouet (Baudoin, Paris fructidor an IV).

Adresse de la société populaire séante à la salle électorale à la Convention Nationale, arrêtée le 7 vendémiaire an III (Imprimerie de Guffroy, Paris 1794. Imprimerie de la Veuve Marat, Paris 1794).

A tous les Français sur la clôture, par arrêté des réunions de citoyens ([Paris 1796] A.N. W³563). Attributed to P.A. Antonelle in Dalin, Saitta and Soboul, *Inventaire des manuscrits et imprimés de Babeuf,* p. 98.

Babeuf, F.-N. (F.-N.-C., G.), *L'adresse du Tribun du peuple à l'armée de l'intérieur* (Imprimerie du Tribun du peuple, Paris 1796).

Babeuf, F.-N. (F.-N.-C., G.), *A messieurs du Comité des Recherches de l'Assemblée Nationale, Roye, le 10 mai 1790* (1790).

Babeuf, F.-N. (F.-N.-C., G.), *Babeuf, ex-administrateur du département de la Somme et successivement du district de Montdidier, aux Comités de salut public, de sûreté générale et de législation de la Convention Nationale, et à Gohier, ministre de la Justice* (Imp. de Prault, Paris 1794).

Babeuf, F.-N. (F.-N.-C., G.), *C. Fournier à Marat, journaliste* (Imprimerie de Lottin, Paris 1793).

Babeuf, F.-N. (F.-N.-C., G.), *C. Fournier (Américain) à Marat* (Imprimerie de Mayer et Compagnie, Paris 1793).

Babeuf, F.-N. (F.-N.-C., G.), *Cadastre perpétuel* (chez les auteurs, Paris 1789).

Babeuf, F.-N. (F.-N.-C., G.), *Du système de dépopulation, ou la vie et les crimes de Carrier* . . . (Imprimerie de Franklin, Paris an III [1795]).

Babeuf, F.-N. (F.-N.-C., G.), *G. Babeuf, tribun du peuple, à ses concitoyens* (Imprimerie de Franklin, Paris 1795).

Babeuf, F.-N. (F.-N.-C., G.), *Les Battus payent l'amende, ou les Jacobins jeannots* (Imprimerie de Franklin, Paris [1794]).

Babeuf, F.-N. (F.-N.-C., G.), *Lettre d'un député de Picardie* (1790).

Babeuf, F.-N. (F.-N.-C., G.), *On veut sauver Carrier. On veut faire le procès au Tribunal révolutionnaire. Peuple, prends garde à toi!* (Imprimerie de Franklin, Paris 1794).

Babeuf, F.-N. (F.-N.-C., G.), *Opprimés et oppresseurs: mémoire des habitants de Davenécourt* [sic] *aux représentants de la Nation* (Imprimerie du Journal de Montdidier, 1888); reprint of *Affaire de la commune de Davenécourt, district de Montdidier, département de la Somme, contre Philippine de Cardevac, veuve de Gabriel Lamire et ci-devant dame de Davenécourt* . . . , *Dans l'exposé de laquelle on démontre combien sont encore formidables les restes de la puissance féodale* (Devin, Noyon 1791). Attributed to Babeuf in Dalin, Saitta, Soboul, *Inventaire des manuscrits et imprimés de Babeuf*, p. 95. The reprint only survives at B.N. 4° LK⁷26158.

Babeuf, F.-N. (F.-N.-C., G.), *Où en sommes nous? Question par C. Fournier, Américain, à tous les sans-culottes, ses frères* (Imprimerie de Mayer et Cⁱᵉ, Paris 1793).

Babeuf, F.-N. (F.-N.-C., G.), *Pétition sur les impôts adressée par les habitants de* [Villiers-les-Roye] *en* [Picardie] *à l'Assemblée nationale* (1790. B.N. LK⁷10437).

Babeuf, F.-N. (F.-N.-C., G.), *Voyage des Jacobins dans les quatre parties du monde. Avec la Constitution mise à l'ordre du jour, par Audouin et Barrère* (Imprimerie de Franklin, Paris 1794).

Boissel, F., *Le Catéchisme du genre humain* (Paris 1789).

Cahier des Ordres Réunis de la Noblesse et Tiers Etat du Gouvernement de Péronne, Montdidier et Roye, rassemblés à Péronne (Paris 1789. B.M. FR 32/22).

Cochon de Lapparent, C., *Rapport au Directoire exécutif du 24 fructidor, an quatrième de la république française une et indivisible* (Imprimerie du Directoire exécutif, Paris 1796. B.M. F1124/19).

Cochon de Lapparent, C., *Rapport au Directoire exécutif, le 12 fructidor, an IV* (Imprimerie du Directoire exécutif, Paris 1796. B.M. F1123/3).

Le Comité Insurrecteur de Salut Public au Peuple. Acte d'Insurrection. Egalité, Liberté, Bonheur Commun ([Paris 1796] B.M. F1124/15).

Complot horrible, tramé par la Cour des Aides de Paris pour faire périr sur l'échafaud tous les auteurs de la Révolution (de l'imprimerie patriotique, Maison du Café Liégeois, Porte Saint-Michel, Paris 1790. John Rylands Library, French Historical Tracts).

Condorcet, J.-A.-N. de Caritat de, *Essai sur la constitution et les fonctions des assemblées provinciales* (1788, 2 vols.).

Conseil des Cinq-cents, *Messages du Directoire exécutif* (Imprimerie Nationale, Paris floréal an IV. B.M. F1125/10).

Copie des pièces saisies dans le local que Baboeuf occupait lors de son arrestation (Imprimerie Nationale, Paris, frimaire-nivôse an V, 1796).

Corps législatif. Conseil des Cinq-Cents, *Rapport et projet de résolution presentés au conseil des Cinq-Cents par Soulignac, Représentant du Peuple, sur la composition du Haut-Juré et la Haute-Cour de Justice, 1 thermidor an IV* (Imprimerie Nationale, Paris 1796. B.M. R166/12).

Le cri du peuple français contre ses oppresseurs (Paris 1796. A.N. W³563).

Débats du procès instruit par la Haute-Cour de Justice, contre Drouet, Baboeuf et autres; recueillis par des sténographes (Baudoin, Paris 1797, 5 vols.).

[Defavanne, G.-J.], *Favanne, Administrateur Adjoint des Subsistances, aux 48 Sections, prenant le fait et cause de Garin . . . attaqué dans un second libelle de deux ex-commis . . .* (Imprimerie de Lottin, Paris 1793).

Delegorgue, *Mémoire sur cette question, est-il utile en Artois de diviser les fermes et exploitations des terres; et dans le cas de l'affirmative, quelles bornes doit-on garder dans cette division?* (1786).

Dénonciation à M. l'accusateur public du tribunal de Montdidier et réfutation d'un libelle infâme intitulé Affaire de la Commune de Davenescourt contre Philippine Cardevac, veuve de Gabriel La Myre et ci-devant Dame de Davenescourt [1791].

Le Directoire exécutif à la commission du Conseil des Cinq-cents chargée de l'examen de l'affaire du représentant Drouet (Imprimerie Nationale, Paris prairial an IV. B.M. R166/7).

Doit-on obéissance à la Constitution de 1795? (Paris 1796. A.N. W³563).

Felhemési (J.-C.-H. Méhée de la Touche), *Defends la Queue, par l'auteur de la Queue de Robespierre* (Imprimerie de Guffroy, Paris 1794).

Felhemési (J.-C.-H. Méhée de la Touche), *La Queue de Robespierre, ou les dangers de la liberté de la presse* (Imprimerie de Rougyff, Paris 1794).

Fournier l'Héritier, C., *IVᵉ pétition à la Convention nationale par C. Fournier, Américain, pour la formation d'une Armée Révolutionnaire* (Imprimerie de Lottin, Paris 1793).

[Garin, E.-F.], *Garin, Administrateur des Subsistances, aux 48 Sections de Paris* (Imprimerie de Lottin, Paris 1793).

Garin, E.-F., *Réponse à la dénonciation faite à la Section des Sans-culottes par Marchant, citoyen de cette Section, contre Garin, Administrateur des Subsistances* (Imprimerie de la veuve Delaguette, Paris 1793).

Garin, E.-F., and de Favanne, G.-J. (sic), *Paris sauvé par l'Administration des Subsistances* (Imprimerie partriotique et républicaine, Paris 1793).

Garin, E.-F., and Defavanne, G.-J., *Suite de Paris sauvé par l'Administration des Subsistances* (Imprimerie patriotique et républicaine, rue S. Honoré, no. 355, Paris 1793).

Germain, C.-A.-G., *Discours prononcé par Charles Germain devant la Haute-Cour de Justice* (De l'imprimerie de l'Ami du peuple, Paris 1797. B.M. F1125/4).

Girardin, R. de, *Discours sur la nécessité de la ratification de la loi par la volonté générale* (Imprimerie du Creuset, Paris 1791).

Guffroy, A.-B.-J., *Soufflet à l'imposture par la presse libre* (Imprimerie de Guffroy, Paris 1794).

Harmand, J.-B., *Quelques idées sur les premiers éléments du nouveau contrat social des français* (Imprimerie Nationale, Paris 1793).

Haute-Cour de Justice, *Copie de l'instruction personelle au représentant du peuple Drouet* (Imprimerie Nationale, Paris frimaire an V. B.M. F1124/24).

Haute-Cour de Justice, *Jugement du 20 nivôse an V* (Morard-Colas, Vendôme 1797. B.M. R167/19).

Haute-Cour de Justice, *Procès-Verbal de la formation du Tableau du Haute-Jury. 29 brumaire an V* (Imprimerie de la Haute-Cour, Morard-Colas, Vendôme 1796. B.M. R167/15).

Hésine, P.-N., *Plaidoyer du citoyen Hézine, ex-commissaire du Directoire exécutif à Vendôme* (Soudry, Vendôme 1796).

Ireland, S., *A picturesque tour through Holland, Brabant and part of France, made in the Autumn of 1789* (J. Egerton, London 1790, 2 vols.).

Jugement de la Haute-Cour de Justice qui ordonne un remplacement de cinq Hauts-Jurés (Imprimerie de la Haute-Cour, Morard-Colas, Vendôme 1796. B.M. R167/18).

Jugement de la Haute-Cour de Justice qui prononce sur les excuses proposées par les Hauts-Jurés. Séance du 27 brumaire an V (Soudry, Vendôme 1796. B.M. R167/10).

Jugement de la Haute-Cour de Justice qui rejette la demande de Babeuf afin d'audition de 4 témoins par lui indiqués. Séance du 27 brumaire (Soudry, Vendôme 1796. B.M. R167/13).

Jugement de la Haute-Cour de Justice qui, sans avoir égard aux moyens de nullité proposés par huit accusés, ordonne que l'instruction sera suivie. Séance du 29 brumaire (B.M. R167/14).

Jugement de la Haute-Cour de Justice qui statue sur la validité de la procédure instruite contre G. Babeuf et cinquante-trois de ses co-accusés (Morard, Vendôme 1796. B.M. R167/7).

Jugement rendu par la Haute-Cour de Justice, le premier pluviôse l'an 5 (Baudoin, Paris 1797. B.M. FR377).

[Le Peletier de Saint-Fargeau, F.], *Soldat, arrête et lis* (Paris 1796. B.M. F1124/5).

Liste officielle des cent trente-deux prisonniers fait au Camp de Grenelle (de l'imprimerie de l'Ami de la Patrie, rue Nicaise no. 330, Paris 1796. B.M. F1124/12).

Ministre de la police générale de la République, *Au quartier général à Issy, le 24 fructidor, an quatrième, 6 heures du matin* (Imprimerie du Directoire exécutif, Paris 1796. B.M. R166/16).

Ministre de la police générale de la République, *Extrait des registres des délibérations du Directoire exécutif, Paris, le 23 floréal* (Morard-Colas, Vendôme an IV. B.M. R166/3).

Oeuvres de Maximilien Robespierre, vol. IX (ed. M. Bouloiseau, G. Lefebvre, J. Dautry, A. Soboul, Presses Universitaires de France, Paris 1958).

Opinion sur nos deux Constitutions soumise au jugement de ceux qui décrétèrent, présentèrent à la France et jurèrent l'une et l'autre (Paris 1796. B.N. Lb^{42}1003).

Penet, *Discours prononcé le décadi 30 thermidor dans l'assemblée générale de la section du Muséum qui en a arrêté l'insertion dans son procès-verbal, par le citoyen Penet, un de ses membres.*

Philippe (Philip, P.), *Le grand rappel à l'ordre de Fréron, par un ami de la liberté, membre du Club Electoral* (1794, John Rylands Library, French Historical Tracts).

Procès-verbal de la Convention Nationale (Imprimerie Nationale, Paris 1793-5).

Procès-verbal de l'Assemblée de l'Ordre de la Noblesse du Gouvernement de Péronne, Montdidier et Roye, tenue le 31 Mars 1789 et jours suivans (Paris 1789. B.M. FR32/21).

Proclamation du Directoire exécutif sur les évènements qui se sont passés dans la nuit du 11 au 12 du mois de fructidor (Imprimerie du Directoire exécutif, Paris 1796. B.M. F1126/6).

Protestation motivée des citoyens accusés d'avoir pris part à la prétendue conspiration du 21 floréal, par laquelle ils récusent et déclinent la Haute-Cour de Justice comme incompétente pour procéder dans cette affaire (R. Vatar, Paris 1796. B.M. R166/14).

Rapport sur les excuses proposées par plusieurs Hauts-Jurés fait à l'audience du 27 brumaire an V (Soudry, Vendôme 1796. B.M. R167/10).

Réquisition des Accusateurs Nationaux près la Haute-Cour de Justice sur les Déclinatoires de plusieurs accusés des 13, 15, 17, et 24 fructidor an 4. Jugement de la Haute-Cour du 19 vendémiaire an 5 qui rejette les Déclinatoires, ordonne qu'il sera passé outre à l'instruction du procès (à Vendôme, de l'imprimerie de la Haute-Cour, chez Morard, an V. B.M. R167/2).

Rutledge, J.J., *Eloge de Montesquieu* (J. de Boffe, London 1786).

Saintomer, J.-C., *Jugement du Peuple Souverain, qui condamne à mort la Queue infernale de Robespierre* (Imprimerie de Guffroy, Paris 1794).

Société Civique d'Amiens, *Mémoire à l'Assemblée Nationale pour la Société Civique d'Amiens* (Couret, Amiens 1791. B.M. FR260/12).

Soldat, arrête encore (Paris, 1796. B.N. Lb⁴²322).

Suite de la copie des pièces saisies dans le local que Baboeuf occupait lors de son arrestation (Imprimerie Nationale, Paris 1796).

Contemporary Journals

Actes des apôtres

L'Ami du peuple (Marat)

Annales patriotiques et littéraires

La Bouche de fer

L'Eclaireur du peuple, ou le défenseur de 24 millions d'opprimés

Journal de la confédération

Journal de la Haute-Cour de Justice établie à Vendôme . . . Soudry, éditeur propriétaire, edited by Abbé Rouzet

Journal de la Haute-Cour de Justice ou l'écho des hommes libres, vrais e sensibles, edited by P.-N. Hésine

Journal de la liberté de la presse

Journal de Paris

Journal des débats et de la correspondance de la société des Jacobins

Journal des séances du Tribunal de la Haute-Cour de Justice établi à Vendôme

Journal du soir

Orateur du peuple

Patriote français

Le Publiciste de la Révolution française

Le Scrutateur des Décrets, et le Rédacteur des Cahiers de la seconde Législature, par continuation du journal intitulé le Correspondant Picard, dédié primitivement aux Départements de la Somme, de l'Aisne, et de l'Oise, et offert aujourd'hui aux 83 Départements de la domination du peuple français par F.-N.-C. Babeuf (reprint, Editions d'Histoire Sociale, Paris, 1966)

Le Tribun du peuple

Articles in Periodicals

Advielle, V., "Une brochure de Mirabeau restituée à Babeuf," *La Révolution française* (vol. VIII, 1885), pp. 889-891.

Aulard, F.-A., "Babeuf et son imprimeur Guffroy," *La Révolution française* (vol. LXXXII, 1929), pp. 5-21.

"Autographes et Documents," *La Révolution française* (vol. VIII, 1885), pp. 733-6.

Babeuf, F.-N. (F.-N.-C., G.), Letter to André Dumont, 7 frimaire an II, in *Les Lettres françaises* (no. 309, 26 April 1950).

Bonhoure, G., "Notes inédites d'après les registres municipaux de 1796-1797 sur le procès des Babouvistes devant la Haute-Cour de Vendôme,"

Bulletin de la société archéologique, scientifique et littéraire du Vendômois (vol. XLVIII, 1908), pp. 29-53.

Bouis, R., "Une lettre de Babeuf à Hésine," *A.H.R.F.* (no. 171, 1963), pp. 79-82.

Bouis, R., "P.-N. Hésine, rédacteur du Journal de la Haute Cour ou l'Echo des Hommes vrais et sensibles," *A.H.R.F.* (no. 162, 1960), pp. 471-487.

Bourgin, G., "Babeuf et le Babouvisme," *Cahiers de la Révolution française* (no. I, 1934), pp. 77-106.

Bourgin, G., "Note sur Robert Babeuf, fils de Gracchus et journaliste," *Cahiers de la Presse* (1938), pp. 223-9, 386-95.

Bourgin, G., "Quelques inédits de Babeuf," *A.H.R.F.* (no. 156, 1959), pp. 146-153.

Bourgin, G., "Quelques inédits sur Babeuf et ses amis," *A.H.R.F.* (no. 157, 1959), pp. 252-269.

Calvet, M., "Les origines du Comité de l'Evêché," *A.H.R.F.* (no. 7, 1930), pp. 12-23.

Caron, P., "Les Défenseurs de la République," *La Révolution française* (vol. LXXXVI, 1933), pp. 193-235.

Caron, P., "Sur l'opposition de gauche à la veille du 9 thermidor," *A.H.R.F.* (vol. XIX, 1947), pp. 322-5.

Charavay, E., "L'arrestation de la femme de Babeuf," *La Révolution française* (vol. I, 1881), pp. 214-219.

Cobb, R., "Babeuf et les électeurs d'Abbeville," *A.H.R.F.* (no. 165, 1961), pp. 392-3.

Cobb, R., "L'arrestation de Babeuf à Paris, le 20 pluviôse an III," *A.H.R.F.* (no. 165, 1961), pp. 393-4.

Coë, R.N.C., "La théorie morellienne et la pratique babouviste," *A.H.R.F.* (no. 150, 1958), pp. 38-64.

Dalin, V.M., "Babeuf et Marat en 1789-90," *A.H.R.F.* (no. 150, 1958), pp. 16-37.

Dalin, V.M., "L'historiographie de Babeuf," trans. A. Pelletier, *La Pensée* (N.S. no. 128, 1966), pp. 68-191.

Dalin, V.M., "Marc-Antoine Jullien après le 9 thermidor," *A.H.R.F.*, no. 176 (1964), pp. 159-173; no. 180 (1965), pp. 187-203; and no. 185 (1966), pp. 390-412.

Dalin, V.M., "Napoleone e i Babuvisti," *Studi Storici* (vol. X, no. 3, 1969), pp. 469-79.

Dalin, V.M., "Rivarol et Babeuf," *A.H.R.F.* (no. 171, 1963), pp. 70-72.

Dalin, V.M., "Robespierre et Danton vus par Babeuf," *A.H.R.F.* (no. 162, 1960), pp. 388-410.

Dalin, V.M., "Un inédit de Babeuf: sa Correspondance de Londres, 1-8 octobre 1789," *A.H.R.F.* (no. 151, 1958), pp. 31-59.

Dautry, J., "Ou la cagnotte paroissiale servait à défendre les propriétés," *A.H.R.F.* (no. 138, 1955), pp. 71-2.

Dautry, J., "Sébastien Lacroix," *A.H.R.F.* (no. 10, 1933), pp. 49-60, 516-33.

Dautry, J., "Une lettre de Camille Babeuf," *A.H.R.F.* (no. 128, 1952), pp. 421-2.

Deville, G., "Notes inédites de Babeuf sur lui-meme," *La Révolution française* (vol. XLIX, juillet 1905), pp. 37-44.

Deyon, P., "Quelques remarques dur l'évolution du régime Seigneuriale en Picardie (XVIᵉ-XVIIIᵉ siècles)," *Revue d'histoire moderne et contemporaine* (N.S. vol. VIII, 1961), pp. 271-281.

Dommanget, M., "Babeuf à Flixécourt," *A.H.R.F.* (no. 194, 1968), pp. 534-9.

Dommanget, M., "Babeuf et l'éducation," *A.H.R.F.,* no. 162 (1960), pp. 488-506; no. 163 (1961), pp. 35-46.

Fleischmann, H., "La comédie à Arras," *Annales révolutionnaires* (vol. III, 1919), pp. 522-41.

Foubert, L., "L'idée autonomiste dans les districts de Paris en 1789 et en 1790," *La Révolution française* (vol. XXVIII, 1895), pp. 141-61.

Fouquet, R., "A propos du procès de Babeuf. Comment les accusés furent amenés de Paris à Vendôme," *Bulletin de la société archéologique, scientifique et littéraire du Vendômois,* 1954, pp. 42-48; 1955, pp. 13-29.

G——, "Documents historiques tirés d'anciennes affiches du Département de la Somme," *La Picardie* (no. 16, 1870), pp. 344-7.

Godechot, J., "Les travaux récents sur Babeuf et le babouvisme," *A.H.R.F.* (no. 162, 1960), pp. 369-388.

Goubert, P., "Les techniques agricoles dans les pays picards aux XVIIᵉet XVIIIᵉ siècles," *Revue d'histoire économique et sociale* (vol. XXXV, no. 1, 1957), pp. 24-40.

Jacob, L., "Correspondance avec Babeuf, emprisonné à Arras," *A.H.R.F.* (vol. XI, 1934), pp. 253-9.

Javogues, G., "L'affaire du Camp de Grenelle," *A.H.R.F.* (vol. II, 1925), pp. 23-32.

Lecocq, G., "La Garde Nationale de Ham à Saint-Quentin," *La Révolution française* (vol. V, 1883), pp. 332-5.

Legrand, R., "Babeuf en Picardie, 1790-1792," *A.H.R.F.* (no. 162, 1960), pp. 458-70.

Legrand, R., "Une lettre de Grisel à ses compatriotes d'Abbeville," *A.H.R.F.* (no. 171, 1963), pp. 75-8.

Lemaire, E., "Une émeute populaire à Saint-Quentin en 1790," Société Académique de Saint-Quentin, *Mémoires* (vol. IX, 1889), pp. 345-7.

Letter, Babeuf to Marie-Anne Babeuf, 3 March 1793, in *Revue des Curiosités Révolutionnaires* (vol. I, 1910-11), p. 200.

"Une lettre inédite de Graccus Babeuf," *Revue des Curiosités Révolutionnaires* (vol. I, 1910-11), pp. 205-6.

"Lettres inédites de Babeuf," *Franzuskii Yezhegodnik* (French Annual) (1960), pp. 255-274.

Ludd, E.C., "Helvétius and d'Holbach," *Journal of the History of Ideas* (vol. XXIII, no. 2, 1962), pp. 221-38.

Marion, M., "Le recouvrement des impôts en 1790," *Revue Historique* (vol. CXXI, 1916), pp. 1-47.

Mathiez, A., "La campagne contre le Gouvernement révolutionnaire à la veille du 9 thermidor: L'affaire Legray," *A.H.R.F.* (vol. IV), pp. 305-319.

Mathiez, A., "Le complot des Egaux," *Revue des cours et conférences* (série II, année XXX, 1929, nos. 14 and 15), pp. 554-63 and 609-20.

Mazauric, C., "Le Rousseauisme de Babeuf," *A.H.R.F.* (no. 170, 1962), pp. 439-464.

Pellet, M., "Gracchus Baboeuf et Marie Antoinette," *Variétés révolutionnaires* (2ᵉ série, 1887), pp. 183-8.

Pelletier, A., "Babeuf feudiste," *A.H.R.F.* (no. 179, 1965), pp. 29-65.

Picquenard, C., "La Société du Panthéon," *La Révolution française* (vol. 33, 1897), pp. 318-348.

Robiquet, P., "L'arrestation de Babeuf," *La Révolution française* (vol. XXVIII, 1895), pp. 290-514.

Rose, R.B., "Babeuf, Dictatorship and Democracy," *Historical Studies* (vol. 15, no. 58, April 1972), pp. 223-236.

Rose, R.B., "Socialism and the French Revolution: the Cercle Social and the Enragés," *Bulletin of the John Rylands Library* (vol. 41, no. 1, September 1958), pp. 141-9.

Rudé, G., "La taxation populaire de mai 1775 en Picardie, en Normandie et dans le Beauvaisis," *A.H.R.F.* (no. 165, 1961), pp. 305-26.

Saitta, A., "Autour de la Conjuration de Babeuf. Discussion sur le communisme en 1796," *A.H.R.F.* (no. 162, 1960), pp. 426-435.

Saitta, A., "Il prospetto del Correspondant Picard di Gracco Babeuf," *Critica Storica* (anno V, 31 May 1966, no. 3), pp. 439-45.

Soboul, A., "Autour de Babeuf," *A.H.R.F.* (no. 194, 1968), pp. 534-547.

Soboul, A., "L'écrou de Gracchus Babeuf à Saint-Pélagie en l'an II," *A.H.R.F.* (no. 135, 1954), p. 175.

Soboul, A., "Une lettre de Babeuf du 28 mai 1793," *A.H.R.F.* (no. 171, 1963), p. 75.

Soboul, A., "Personnel sectionnaire et personnel babouviste," *A.H.R.F.* (no. 162, 1960), pp. 436-457.

Thomas, A., "La pensée socialiste de Babeuf avant la conspiration des Egaux," *La Revue Socialiste,* XL (1904), pp. 226-36, 513-528, 696-712; XLI (1905), pp. 58-77, 179-202.

Tønnesson, K.D., "L'an III dans la formation du Babouvisme," *A.H.R.F.* (no. 162, 1966), pp. 411-25.

Tønnesson, K.D., "The Babouvists from Utopian to Practical Socialism," *Past and Present* (no. 22, 1962), pp. 60-76.

Tulard, J., "Le recrutement de la Légion de police de Paris sous la Convention thermidorienne et le Directoire," *A.H.R.F.* (no. 175, 1964), pp. 38-64.

Vallon, P.G.A., "Conspiration de Babeuf," *Mémoires de la société des sciences et des lettres de la ville de Blois* (vol. IV, 1852), pp. 304-325.

Other Printed Works

Advielle, V., *Histoire de Gracchus Babeuf et du babouvisme, d'après de nombreux documents inédits* (chez l'auteur, Paris 1884, 2 vols.).

Archives Parlementaires de 1787 à 1860 (Paris, 1867-1914, 82 vols.).

Arnaud, R., *Journaliste, sans-culotte et Thermidorien. Le fils de Fréron, 1754-1802* (Perrin, Paris 1909).

Arnault, A.V., etc., *Biographie Nouvelle des Contemporains* (Librairie Historique, Paris 1820-1825, 20 vols.).

Aulard, F.-A., *Mémoires secrets de Fournier l'Américain* (Société de l'Histoire de la Révolution française, Paris 1890).

Aulard, F.-A., *Paris pendant la réaction thermidorienne et sous le Directoire. Recueil de documents pour l'histoire de l'esprit public à Paris* (Cerf et Noblet, Paris 1898-1902, 5 vols.).

Aulard, F.-A., *Recueil des Actes du Comité de Salut Public* (Imprimerie Nationale, Paris 1889).

Aulard, F.-A., *La Société des Jacobins: Recueil de documents pour l'histoire du Club des Jacobins de Paris* (Jouaust, Paris 1889-1896, 6 vols.).

Babeuf, F.-N. (F.-N.-C., G.), *The Defense of Gracchus Babeuf before the High Court of Vendôme* (edited and translated by John Anthony Scott. With an essay by Herbert Marcuse and illustrations by Thomas Cornell, University of Massachusetts Press, Amherst 1967).

Bax, E.B., *The Last Episode of the French Revolution, Being a History of Gracchus Babeuf and the Conspiracy of the Equals* (Grant Richards, London 1911).

Beauvillé, V. de, *Histoire de Montdidier* (Firmin Didot fils, Paris 1857, 3 vols.).

Beauvillé, V. de, *Histoire de Montdidier* (2e édition, Claye, Paris 1875, 3 vols.).

Bergmann, K.H., *Babeuf, Gleich und Ungleich* (Westdeutscher Verlag Köln und Opladen, Cologne 1965).

Bigard, L., *Le Comte Réal, Ancien Jacobin* (Mercier, Versailles 1937).

Biollay, L., *Les prix en 1790* (Guillaumin, Paris 1886).

Bloch, C., and Tuetey, A., *Procès-verbaux et rapports du Comité de Mendicité de la Constituante, 1790-1791* (Imprimerie Nationale, Paris 1911).

Boucher, P., *Charles Cochon de Lapparent* (Picard, Paris 1970).

Brinton, Crane, *The Anatomy of Revolution* (Vintage Books, New York 1957).

Buchez, P.J.B., and Roux, P.C., *Histoire parlementaire de la Révolution française* (Paulin, Paris, 1834-8, 40 vols.).

Buonarroti's History of Babeuf's Conspiracy for Equality; with the author's reflections on the ... French Revolution ... also his views of democratic government ... and ... equality (Translated from the French and illustrated with original notes by Bronterre O'Brien; Hetherington, London 1836).

Buonarroti, F., *Conspiration pour l'égalité, dite de Babeuf* (Edition R. Brécy, A. Soboul, Editions sociales, Paris 1957, 2 vols. First published by Librairie romantique, Brussels 1828).

Les Cahiers de Doléances des paroisses rurales du Bailliage de Noyon (Comité Archéologique et Historique de Noyon, *Mémoires,* vols. XIV-XV, Noyon 1898).

Caron, P., *La Commission des Subsistances de l'an II* (Leroux, Paris 1925).

Catalogue de l'histoire de la Révolution française (Bibliothèque Nationale, Paris 1936-1943, 5 vols.).

Charavay, E., *L'Assemblée électorale de Paris* (L. Cerf, Paris 1894, 3 vols.).

Charavay, N., *Catalogue des autographes et des documents historiques composant la collection de M. Etienne Charavay* (Charavay, Paris 1900).

Chinard, G., *L'Amérique et le rêve exotique dans la littérature française au XVIIe et au XVIIIe siècle* (Paris 1934).

Cobb, R., *Les Armées Révolutionnaires* (Mouton, Paris 1966).

Cobb, R., *The Police and the People: French Popular Protest, 1789-1820* (O.U.P., London 1970).

Cobb, R., *Terreur et subsistances, 1793-95* (Librairie Clavreuil, Paris 1965).

Coët, E., *Histoire de la ville de Roye* (Champion, Paris 1880, 2 vols.).

Colloque international de Stockholm, *Babeuf et les problèmes du babouvisme* (Editions sociales, Paris 1963).

Combier, A.E., *La justice criminelle à Laon pendant la Révolution* (H. Champion, Paris 1882, 2 vols.).

The Communist International, 1919-1943 (Documents selected and edited by Jane Degras, O.U.P., London 1956, 3 vols.).

Dalin, V.M., *Grakkh Babef; nakanune i vo vremia Velikoi Frantsuzskoi revoliutsii, 1785-1794* (Izdatel'stvo Akademii nauk S.S.S.R., Moscow, 1963).

Dalin, V.M., Saitta, A., Soboul, A., *Inventaire des manuscrits et imprimés de Babeuf* (Ministère de l'Education Nationale, Commission d'Histoire Economique et Sociale de la Révolution française, Paris 1966).

Darsy, F.-I., *Amiens et le Département de la Somme pendant la Révolution* (Doullet, Amiens 1878, 2 vols.).

Dauban, C.A., *La démogogie en 1793 à Paris* (Plon, Paris 1868).

Debidour, A., ed., *Recueil des actes du Directoire exécutif* (Imprimerie Nationale, Paris 1910-1917, 4 vols.).

Département de la Somme, *Inventaire sommaire des Archives Départementales antérieures à 1796,* ed. Durand, vol. II (Archives Civiles, Kuypers, Amiens 1888).

Département de la Somme. Ville d'Amiens, *Inventaire sommaire des archives communales antérieures à 1790,* vol. I, série AA (Piteux, Amiens 1891).

Desmasures, A., *Histoire de la Révolution dans le Département de l'Aisne* (Flem, Vervins 1869).

Dictionnaire biographique du Mouvement ouvrier français, ed. Jean Maitron (Editions ouvrières, Paris 1964-).

Dommanget, M., *Pages choisies de Babeuf, recueillies, commentées, annotées avec une Introduction et une Bibliographie critique* . . . (Colin, Paris 1935).

Dommanget, M., *Sur Babeuf et la conjuration des égaux* (François Maspero, Paris 1970).

Douarche, A., *Les tribunaux civils de Paris pendant la Révolution, 1791-1800* (L. Cerf, Paris 1905-7, 3 vols.).

Dufort de Cheverny, J.-N., *Mémoires sur les règnes de Louis XV et Louis XVI et sur la Révolution* (publiés avec une introduction par Robert de Crèvecoeur, Plon, Nourrit, Paris 1886, 2 vols.).

[Durand, G.], *Documents pour servir à l'histoire de la Révolution française dans le Département de la Somme* (4 vols. Jeunet, Amiens 1888-1904).

Durand, G., and Estienne, J., *Inventaire sommaire des Archives Départementales de la Somme, 1790 - An IV,* vol. I, série L (Imp. du Progrès de la Somme, Amiens 1925).

Durry, M.-J., *Autographes de Mariemont* (Musée de Mariemont, Paris 1955).

Encyclopédie méthodique (Panckouke, Paris 1782-1832, $166\frac{1}{2}$ vols.).

Engels, F., and Marx, K., *Die Heilige Familie* (Literarische Anstalt, Frankfurt-am-Main 1845).

Espinas, A., *La philosophie sociale du XVIIIe siècle et de la Révolution* (Alcan, Paris 1898).

Estienne, J., *Archives départementales de la Somme, Inventaire Sommaire de la série L* (Imprimerie Moderne, Fontenay-le-Comte 1938, 2 vols.).

Festy, O., *L'agriculture pendant la Révolution française* (Gallimard, Paris 1947).

Fleury, E., *Biographie de Babeuf. Etudes révolutionnaires* (Imprimerie d'Ed. Fleury et Ad. Chevergny, Laon 1849).

Fouquier-Cholet, *St. Quentin, ancien et moderne* (Tilloy, St. Quentin 1822).

Garrigues, G., *Les Districts de Paris pendant la Révolution française* (Editions Spes, Paris 1932).

Girardin, Marquis de, *L'arrestation du dernier ami de J.J. Rousseau en 1793* (Librairie Henri Leclerc, Paris 1919).

Goubert, P., *Beauvais et le Beauvaisis de 1600 à 1730. Contribution à l'histoire sociale de la France du XVIIᵉ siècle* (Service d'Edition et de Vente des Publications de l'Education Nationale, Paris 1960).

Granier de Cassagnac, A., *Histoire du Directoire* (H. Plon, Paris 1863, 3 vols. First published by Plon Frères, 1851-1855).

Grégoire d'Essigny, L.-A.-J., *Histoire de la ville de Roye* (Devin, Noyon 1818).

Hatin, E., *Bibliographie historique et critique de la presse périodique française* (Firmin Didot, Paris 1866).

Hulshoff, Maria Aletta, *Peace Republican's Manual or the French constitution of 1793 and the Declaration of the rights of man and of citizens . . . To which is added debates on this constitution in the national Convention . . . translated extracts from pieces seized in Baboeuf's rooms* (J. Thiebout, New York 1817).

Jacob, L., *Joseph Le Bon, 1765-1795* (Mellottée, Paris 1932, 2 vols.).

Jamin, G., *Des Hautes-Cours de Justice sous la Révolution* (Thèse, Paris 1907).

Las Vergnas, R., *Le chevalier Rutledge, "gentilhomme anglais," 1742-1794* (Paris 1932. Bibliothèque de la Revue de littérature comparée, vol. 81).

Lecesne, E., *Arras sous la Révolution* (Sueur-Charruey, Arras 1882-3, 3 vols.).

Lecocq, G., *Un manifeste de Gracchus Babeuf* (Librairie des Bibliophiles, Paris 1885).

Lefebvre, G., *Le Directoire* (2ᵉ édition, Armand Colin, Paris 1950).

Lefebvre, G., *The Directory* (trs. R. Baldick, Routledge and Kegan Paul, London 1965).

Lefebvre, G., *Etudes sur la Révolution française* (Presses Universitaires de France, Paris 1954).

Lefebvre, G., *La Grande Peur de 1789* (Armand Colin, Paris 1932).

Lefebvre, G., *Les Paysans du Nord pendant la Révolution française* (Rieder, Paris 1924).

Lefebvre, G., *Questions agraires au temps de la Terreur* (Collection de Documents inédits sur l'Histoire economique de la Révolution française publiés par le Ministère de l'Instruction publique, 2ᵉ édition, Henri Potier, La-Roche-Sur-Yon 1955).

Lefebvre, G., *The Thermidorians* (trs. Robert Baldick, Routledge and Kegan Paul, London 1965).

Legrand, R., *Babeuf, ses idées, sa vie en Picardie* (Lafosse, Abbeville 1961).

Legrand, R., *Un plaidoyer de Babeuf* (Lafosse, Abbeville 1963).

Lenôtre, G., *Le Tribunal Révolutionnaire (1793-1795), Mémoires et souvenirs sur la Révolution et l'Empire, publiés avec des documents inédits, par G. Lenôtre* (Perrin, Paris 1907-1912, 5 vols.).

Levot, P., *Biographie Bretonne* (Cauderan, Vannes 1852-7, 2 vols.).

Lichtenberger, A., *Le Socialisme et la Révolution française* (E. Alcan, Paris 1899).

Mannier, E., *Ordre de Malte. Les commanderies du grand prieuré de France d'après les documents inédits conservés aux archives nationales à Paris* (Aubry, Paris 1872).

Mathiez, A., *La réaction thermidorienne* (Armand Colin, Paris 1929).

Mathiez, A., *La vie chère et le mouvement social sous la Terreur* (Payot, Paris 1927).

Matthews, G.T., *Royal General Farms in Eighteenth-Century France* (Columbia University Press, New York 1958).

Mazauric, C., *Babeuf et la Conspiration pour l'Egalité* (Editions sociales, Paris 1962).

Mazière, L., *Annales Noyonnaises: Noyon de 1789 à 1795* (Comité Archéologique et Historique de Noyon, *Mémoires,* vol. XV, 1899).

Mège, F., *Gaultier de Biauzat, député du Tiers Etat aux Etats-Généraux de 1789, sa vie et sa correspondance* (Bellet, Clermont-Ferrand 1890, 2 vols.).

Melleville, M., *Histoire de la ville de Laon* (Dumoulin, Paris 1846, 2 vols.).

Michelet, J., *Ma Jeunesse* (Calmann Lévy, Paris 1884).

Mortimer-Ternaux, L., *Histoire de la Terreur, 1792-1794* (3ᵉ édition, Levy, Paris 1881, 8 vols.).

Nodier, C., *Souvenirs de la Révolution et de l'Empire* (7ᵉédition, Charpentier, Paris 1864, 2 vols.).

Normand, C., *Saint-Quentin et la Royauté* (H. Champion, Paris 1881).

Palmer, R.R., *The Age of the Democratic Revolution* (Princeton 1959-1964, 2 vols.).

Pasternak, B., *Doctor Zhivago* (trs. Max Hayward and Manya Harari, Fontana Books, London 1961).

Patoux, A., *Le faux de Gracchus Babeuf* (Imprimerie du Guetteur, Saint-Quentin 1913. Off-print of *Mémoires de la Société académique de Saint-Quentin*, 4ᵉ série, XIV, 1913, 1ⁱᵉʳᵉ partie, pp. 140-209).

Pottet, E., *Histoire de la Conciergerie* (3ᵉ édition, May et Motteraz, Paris 1895).

Rabbe, A., *Biographie universelle et portative des contemporains* (F.-J. Levrault, Paris 1834, 5 vols.).

Ramon, G., *La Révolution à Péronne* (Quentin, Péronne 1898, 6 séries).

Reinhard, M., *Correspondance de Babeuf avec l'Académie d'Arras (1785-1788)* (P.U.F., Paris 1961).

Remusat, P.-Fr. de, *Mémoire sur ma détention au Temple, 1797-99* (Picard et fils, Paris 1961).

Robiquet, P., *Buonarroti et la Secte des Egaux, d'après des documents inédits* (Hachette, Paris 1910).

Rudé, G., *The Crowd in the French Revolution* (O.U.P., Oxford 1959).

Saitta, A. (ed.), *Le Tribun du peuple (1794-1796) par Gracchus Babeuf, textes choisis et présentés* (Union Générale d'Editions, Paris 1969).

Schmidt, W.A., *Tableaux de la Révolution française* (Veit, Leipzig 1867-1870, 3 vols.).

Sée, A., *Le procès Pache* (Société de l'Histoire de la Révolution française, Paris 1911).

Sée, H., *Histoire économique de la France* (2ᵉ édition, Colin, Paris 1948-51, 2 vols.).

Seligman, E., *La justice en France pendant la Révolution* (Plon, Nourrit, Paris 1901).

Soboul, A., *Les sans-culottes parisiens en l'an II. Mouvement populaire et gouvernement révolutionnaire, 2 juin 1793 - 9 thermidor an II* (Librairie Clavreuil, Paris 1958).

Spitzer, A., *The Revolutionary Theories of Louis Auguste Blanqui* (Columbia University Press, New York 1957).

Taine, H.A., *The Origins of Contemporary France* (translated by J. Durand, H. Holt, New York 1876-94, 6 vols.).

Talmon, J.L., *The Origins of Totalitarian Democracy* (Mercury Books, London 1966).

Thibout, G., *La Doctrine Babouviste*. Thèse pour le doctorat de droit (Librairie nouvelle de droit et de jurisprudence, Paris 1903).

Thomson, D., *The Babeuf Plot: The Making of a Republican Legend* (Kegan Paul, London 1947).

Tønnesson, K.D., *La défaite des sans-culottes. Mouvement populaire et réaction bourgeoise en l'an III* (Presses Universitaires de France, Paris 1959).

Tuetey, A., *Répertoire général des sources manuscrits pour servir à l'histoire de Paris pendant la Révolution française* (Imprimerie Nouvelle, Paris 1870-1914, 11 vols.).

Van Drival, E., *Histoire de l'Académie d'Arras* (Académie des Sciences, Lettres et Arts d'Arras, Arras 1872).

Vendôme pendant la Révolution (Huet, Vendôme 1892-3, 2 vols.).

Walter, G., *Histoire des paysans de France* (Flammarion, Paris 1963).

Walter, G., *Babeuf (1760-1797) et la conjuration des égaux* (Payot, Paris 1937).

Warmé, A.J., *Histoire de la ville de Doullens* (Grousilliat, Doullens 1863).

Woloch, I.T., *Jacobin Legacy. The Democratic Movement under the Directory* (Princeton 1970).

Index

Tonnelier, Louis, 72
Tønnesson, K.D., 158, 183
Toulotte, Eustache-Louis-Joseph, 308
Tournier, Pierre, 94
Trappes, 289
Tribun du peuple, 229, 321; created from
Journal de la liberté de la presse, 165; attacks Committee of General Security, 165-69; on women in politics, 169-70; supports worker-artisan and militant alliance, 172-86 *passim,* 199; advocates Constitution of 1793, 180-81, 216-18; revived during Directory, 208-11; defense of Terror, 214-15; subscribers to, 219-20; government prosecution of, 220-25; advocates communist revolution, 241, 254-56; and Babeuf-Germain correspondence, 331, 335ff, 338f; discusses class consciousness, 340-41
Trotsky, Leon, 1
Tuileries, 111
Turgot, Anne-Robert-Jacques, 41, 98
Turreau de Garambouville, Louis-Marie, 219, 327

unemployment, 55f, 198
universal suffrage, 200
Ursulines, 116

Vadier, Marc-Guillaume-Alexis, 156, 231-32, 261, 280, 291
Vadier, Citoyenne, 290
Valory, adjutant-general, 269

Van der Noot, anti-Austrian leader, 63
Vanheck, Jean-Baptiste, 253
Varennes, 96
Varin, Pierre, 149, 151
Varlet, Jean-François, 133, 140, 162f
Vasseur, Pierre, 67
Vatar, René-François-Charles, 299, 327
Vendée, 135, 291
Vendémiaire, 203, 222
Vendôme, 289-90, 291, 327
Ventôse laws, 85, 153, 176, 223
Veret, *curé,* 67
Vergniaud, Pierre, 133
Vérité, dye-works owner, 249
Victinghoff, General, 110
Viellart, René-Luis-Marie, 291, 298, 300, 303, 309, 312, 322f, 324-25
Vignalet, juror, 308
Villiers-les-Roye, 67
Vincennes, garrison of, 253, 257
voirie, 83, 94
Voltaire, François Marie Arouet de, ‹
Volunteers of the Aisne, 110
Voulland, Jean-Henri, 156

wages, 171. *See also* inflation
"war of the trees," 83-84, 91
Wealth of Nations, 98
Woloch, Isser, 326

Young, Arthur, 56

Zurich, 219